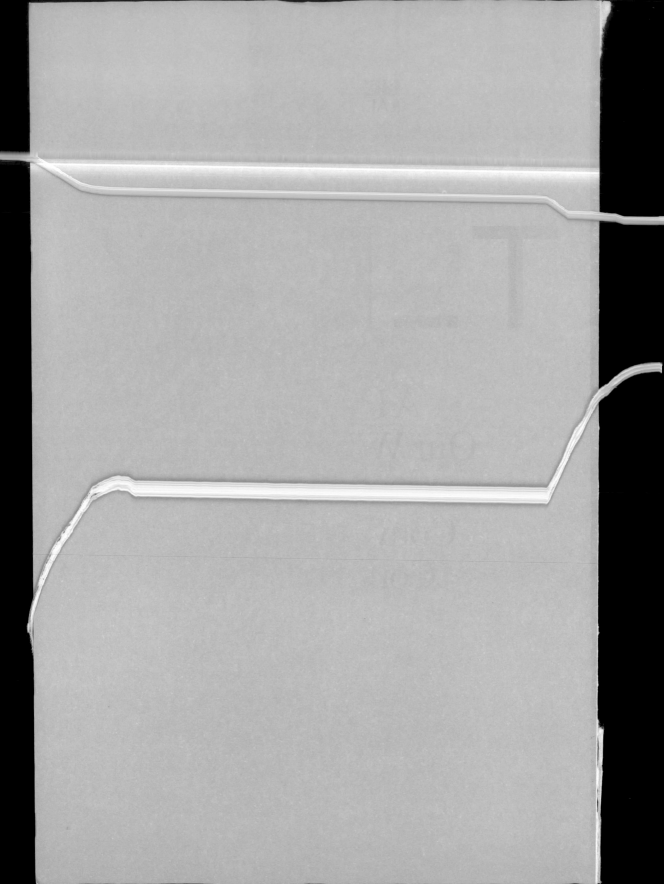

A History of
Our World through
60 Years of
Conversations &
Controversies

An Hachette UK Company

www.hachette.co.uk

First published in Great Britain in 2019 by Cassell,

an imprint of Octopus Publishing Group Ltd

Carmelite House

50 Victoria Embankment

London EC4Y 0DZ

www.octopusbooks.co.uk

ISBN: 978 1 78840 037 4

A CIP catalogue record for this book is available from the
British Library.

Printed and bound in UK

10 9 8 7 6 5 4 3 2 1

Publisher's Note

The text is the work of Mark Hawkins-Dady – an historian with
no BBC ties – and the archive research has been undertaken by
two senior *Today* producers, Laura Cooper, the programme's
planning editor, and John Neal, who is now the editor of
The Andrew Marr Show, and the former BBC current affairs
producer Sarah Harrison. All events featured within this book
were up-to-date when it went to print in June 2019.

T_ODAY

A History of Our World through 60 Years of Conversations & Controversies

EDITED BY
Edward Stourton

FOREWORDS BY
Nick Robinson & Martha Kearney

Original text: Mark Hawkins-Dady & Philippe Barbour

CONTENTS

CHAPTER 4: ART, CULTURE AND SPORT

CHAPTER 5: SOCIAL CHANGE

CHAPTER 6: THE NATURAL WORLD, SCIENCE AND TECHNOLOGY

FOREWORD BY

NICK ROBINSON

The *Today* programme has been part of the soundtrack of my life for decades, just as it has been for millions of other people. Indeed, it's no exaggeration to say that *Today* is the programme of national record – the place to which you come to hear princes, prime ministers and presidents; authors, artists and performers; the people, whatever their titles or jobs or backgrounds, who shape our national life.

This is quite something, especially given the change in the media landscape since *Today* – or what was almost called 'Morning Miscellany' – was first dreamt up as two 20-minute segments of features after the seven and eight o'clock news bulletins. This book would almost certainly not have been written if either of the other names considered for the programme had been chosen. 'Listen Whilst You Dress' or the unselfconsciously sexist 'Background to Shaving' surely wouldn't have matched *Today*'s staying power.

The death or long-term decline of *Today* was first confidently forecast when the bright lights, the bright sofas and the even brighter smiles of breakfast television were imported from America in the 1980s. Each new media innovation – 24-hour news channels, the internet, social media and now podcasts and live music streaming – has been accompanied by stern and steely-eyed forecasts that *Today* cannot preserve its place in our or in the nation's life. Nothing survives forever – but I am delighted to say that, so far, talk of the programme's demise has proved premature.

My relationship with *Today* began as a child. I can still recall the sound of my father cranking up the volume on his radio each morning to ensure that Redhead, Timpson, Hobday and MacGregor could be heard over the sound of his bath running, the kettle boiling or the cacophony of breakfast as his three children prepared to go to school.

What makes my connection with the programme special – unique, even – is that one of the voices I listened to regularly was that of my best friend's dad, Brian. Brian Redhead combined authority, knowledge and an apparently limitless spirit of enquiry with a personality which was warm, witty and engaging. It was and is the recipe for the perfect *Today* presenter – someone you must both trust and be prepared to share your morning with, whether you're in the shower or on the loo, eating your breakfast or driving the car, alone or with those you love or, at least, share your living space with.

When Brian's 18-year-old son Will died in a car crash on a post-A-levels trip around Europe with friends, listeners flooded Broadcasting House with letters of sympathy. They listened anxiously as Brian returned to work, still overwhelmed by grief. I was the only survivor of that crash. It is the reason why joining *Today* was so much more than achieving a career ambition. The first time I presented the programme, I took a deep breath and thought about Brian and Will and how lucky I've been.

Presenting the programme is a privilege because you get the chance to meet and to talk to the men and women who lead the nation's conversation and fashion its culture. As a minister leaves the studio, an archbishop may walk in. A rugby player may brush shoulders with a theatre director. Each loves the idea of meeting the other, if not always, perhaps, of sharing a tasteless cup of BBC canteen coffee. We presenters get the chance to ask the questions we hope you would want to ask if you had the chance to do so and, yes, to give a little of our own take on the state of the world.

When Brian Redhead – who was, famously, not the most modest of men – was asked about the arrival on the nation's screens of breakfast TV's 'Famous Five' – Frost, Parky, Rippon, Ford and Kee – he remarked waspishly that 'if you want to drop a word in the nation's ear' you come on *Today*, whereas if you wanted to 'whistle in the wind' you'd take a seat on the sofa. These days we are, of course, much more respectful of our colleagues or, at least, much more diplomatic.

Now there are, of course, downsides to waking up the nation. Not least those early starts. The alarm – or, rather, alarms (for safety) – have to be set for 3.30am. That, one doctor told me candidly if not reassuringly, is the peak time for death. The body's natural rhythms dip alarmingly, I was told, at the very moment you're waking. A freakishly early bedtime – 8.30pm in my case – is the way most of us handle that challenge. When I joined the team I was regaled with other advice, ranging from the use of soothing whale noises, sleep masks and earplugs to get to sleep, to the best time to take a daytime doze or power nap. One colleague even made the suggestion that I build a soundproofed bedroom in a shed in the garden.

So, is it all worth it, not just for us sleep-deprived presenters but also for you occasionally world-weary listeners, who might just be tempted to start your day with soothing music and reassuring chatter and to escape from the sound and fury of public debate? My answer – and the answer of well over seven million people a week – is a resounding 'Yes!'

Today is the way we connect with the wider world, rather than hide from it. It is the way we listen and engage and try to understand people who think differently from ourselves. It is an opportunity to stretch our minds and to be stimulated, inspired and moved. For all there are, inevitably, presenters who annoy us and guests who irritate, it is – quite simply – a civilising force.

When the BBC celebrated its 60th birthday in 1983, a listener sent a card to the programme adorned with primroses and butterflies. It read:

> **BBC is 60.**
> **Today is 25.**
> **When Today is 60,**
> **Here's hoping it's still live.**

I am happy to report that it/we are very much alive, and looking forward to many more years, perhaps even decades, of starting your day.

Nick Robinson
Presenter, *Today*, 2019

FOREWORD BY

MARTHA KEARNEY

I was given a T-shirt not long after I started work on the *Today* programme which read: 'I really don't mind waking up at 3.30am', while on the back there was the message, 'Thanks for asking'. I could honestly still wear that T-shirt every day, as I get asked so many times about the hours.

I now set three alarms, since I overslept one morning – there is nothing quite like that to wake you up in earnest. There is just time to grab a quick shower and then head out to the waiting car at 3.40am. The driver brings a pile of newspapers, and sometimes a brief for an interview to be recorded as soon as we arrive. They can be relatively straightforward, for example a 'two-way' with Jon Sopel, our North America Editor, because of the time difference – or more complicated; one 4am interview was with the UN secretary general Antonio Guterres about Rohingya refugees in Bangladesh.

The most tricky 'pre-recs' happen while we are live on air during the programme. Listeners may hear the studio door going during the business slot, which is the sound of one of us going into the studio next door to record an interview, praying that the guest isn't too longwinded and that we will get back in time to introduce the sport.

The hours between 4 and 6am are when we write our scripts and prepare for the interviews, reading the research briefs and writing questions. Ideally these are supposed to be finished by the time we get on air at 6am, usually arriving in our seats just a couple of minutes before the pips in time to say good morning to the audience.

The biggest change for me has been working alongside another presenter after 11 years on my own on *The World at One*, and it has surprised me how much I have enjoyed this. Of course, there is competition – we are all journalists, after all – but there is also a spirit of camaraderie. You get to know people's idiosyncrasies, which chairs they prefer in the studio, their favourite breakfast foods, their foibles and passions. I have been saved from beginner's gaffes many times on air by my fellow presenters.

What we call 'the furniture' of the programme is complex, almost like an elaborate 18th-century quadrille. We switch backwards and forwards from the weather, to a trail, to a programme menu, to the headlines. If one partner skips a beat, chaos ensues. If you dare to crash the pips, the Four Horsemen of the Apocalypse come thundering into the studio (or so I have been warned).

I have been listening to *Today* for all of my adult life and can't imagine my early mornings without it. Back in the 1980s I remember listening, while brushing my teeth, when the then chancellor Nigel Lawson accused Brian Redhead of being a Labour supporter. The tension over the airwaves was palpable when Redhead snapped back, arguing that there should be a minute's silence for Lawson to apologise for daring to suggest 'that you know how I vote, and secondly for the death of monetarism which you have now discarded?'

Back then, Margaret Thatcher would have been one of the few female political guests on *Today*, but women have been immensely influential on the *Today* team over the years. In fact, it was a female producer, Isa Benzie, who came up with the title *Today* rather than 'Morning Miscellany', and she became the programme's first 'organiser'. *Today* was also launched by a senior figure in the Talks department, Janet Quigley.

Over the years, behind the scenes impressive ranks of women have been producers of the programme, though there have only been two female editors: Jenny Abramsky and now Sarah Sands. While men have dominated the studio, there have been some formidable women at the microphone, most notably Libby Purves who began presenting *Today* in her twenties; Sue MacGregor, who was poached from *Woman's Hour;* and Sarah Montague, who braved the early mornings for 18 years. Nowadays it is regarded as completely normal for me and Mishal Husain to present together; in my early career in local radio, having two women on air together was regarded as a rota emergency.

There's something about a breakfast show which creates a strong sense of intimacy. Many a listener has said to me with a twinkle in their eye, 'I do enjoy waking up with you, Martha.'

The sense of *Today* being at the heart of the day's news has remained constant over the decades. Despite far greater competition, our interviews regularly set the news agenda for the rest of the day and are quoted widely in the next day's newspapers. But it is certainly a tougher environment for presenters than when I started on Radio 4. An irate letter back then would tend to be about grammar. One furious listener berated me for saying 'at each other's throats' instead of 'at each other's throat'. Nowadays a nation polarised by the Brexit debate is far angrier and inclined to blame the messenger. People who use Twitter give a running commentary on every interview. I think it is lazy journalism to say that if you are getting flak from both sides then you can be sure that you are impartial, but once in a while exactly the same interview will provoke accusations of bias from opposing sides.

Another huge change has come as a result of the revolution in technology. Our equipment has moved on from days of tape and razor blades for editing, much to my relief, as when I was starting out several of my taped reports would arrive in the studio with the odd smear of blood from cack-handed cutting.

New technology has also meant the programme can be much more immediate – we can broadcast live from practically anywhere. I have presented live from an army base in Kabul surrounded by Foxhound armoured cars. When we broadcast live from a prison in South London, our main studio was in the visitors' centre, but, thanks to new technology, we were able to go right into the heart of the jail for the moment when lockup ends and prisoners are let out from their cells, with a clamour echoing down the corridors. I have also presented live from a balcony in Jerusalem with a view over the Old City and calls to prayer echoing in the background, as well as including reports from Gaza. In such a divisive political culture it was much easier to chair discussions face-to-face than down the line. Thanks to our amazing studio managers, we were also able to report live from Svalbard in the Arctic Circle. I am now fully qualified to ride a skidoo, but they decided not to give me rifle training in case of an attack by a polar bear. Never arm a presenter.

The programme may have moved on from its softer, feature-driven start, and we certainly pride ourselves on still setting the news agenda for the day, but there is still space for human stories and the eccentric. John Humphrys kept his cool while interviewing a completely naked woman in the studio (she was protesting about Brexit) and I do hope that a modern producer would still find time for a star of the early days – the man who could play 'Rule Britannia' by hitting himself on the head with a nine-inch spanner. Or maybe some listeners would like to apply the spanner to the presenters.

Martha Kearney
Presenter, *Today*, 2019

THE BIRTH OF THE *TODAY* PROGRAMME BY

SARAH SANDS

The *Today* programme is described as 'the nation's conversation', so a reflection on the past six decades is a shaft of social history.

It was in July 1955 that a young BBC producer called Robin Day came up with the idea of an early morning 'topical talks' programme initially called 'Morning Review'. On 28 October 1957 the first *Today* programme went out on air. It went on to become Britain's most influential news and current affairs programme.

The CEO of a major institution explained his perspective: 'I told my board: if we can't defend our policies on the *Today* programme, we should change our policies.' *Today* is where power is held to account, conventions challenged, ideas debated, stories broken.

For our 60th anniversary, we contacted the first sea lord to check the veracity of a *Today* programme myth. It is that the signal for the nuclear submarines to open the sealed orders of the prime minister is if the *Today* programme has not been on air for three days. Let us say it is not wholly untrue.

What is certain is that the *Today* programme is as near as we can get to a first draft of history. Each day we try to give listeners as much information as we can possibly pack into three hours about the world we inhabit, and other worlds too. The *Today* programme has always been strong on science and, like Stephen Hawking, we have tried to keep an open mind about what we do not know as well as what we do.

Looking back at the *Today* years, we can see a period of extraordinary change. You do not notice this so much as it happens, especially when working on a daily news programme. Wars and elections may happen overnight. Social change seems incremental. Yet when we came to reflect on the years since the programme first went on air, the changes in attitudes to gender, class, faith, diet, and, yes, holidays stood out. Audio archives showed how dramatically the accent of John Humphrys had changed over the years (although not as much as the Queen's).

The *Today* programme has broadcast through interesting times. By reviewing the archives of this daily news and current affairs flagship, we start to see the patterns of history, and we have divided this book into six different aspects of that history.

The first chapter covers rebellion, revolution and protest – change in its most direct form.

In chapter two we turn to Britain's political landscape, from the 1970s and Britain's entry into the EEC right up to the Brexit referendum.

In chapter three we look at war, conflict and security: conflict is a story as old as time, but new battle lines are always being drawn.

Culture casts light on our national identity, a subject with which we have been wrestling on the programme throughout our years on the air. Chapter four includes a rich array of cultural reflections, which tell us stories of ourselves, then and now.

Speaking of stories, perhaps the most revealing of all are contained in chapter five, which showcases the enormous social changes that have taken place since *Today* was first broadcast. Finally, in chapter six, there is scientific progress which alters not just identity, but humanity.

As Anna Ford, a former presenter of the *Today* programme, said, 'I think it is a wonderful way of summarising everything that is happening; you feel bang up to date if you listen to the *Today* programme. One of the things about radio for me is that I remember what I hear on the radio far more than I remember what I see on television.' This book is about six decades of memory – a potted history of ourselves, our country and the world.

PROGRAMMING THE PROGRAMME

The world we cover on the *Today* programme may often seem volatile and unpredictable, but we have always launched the day on the drama of news. What we can offer the listener is to be as well informed as possible, if not always well prepared. The running order is revised throughout the night and indeed throughout the programme.

This is how it works.

The programme starts the day with the stories of the day. We always begin with news bulletins, which run like a spine through the three hours of the show. The running order seeks to find a balance of interests and rhythms. Business rises early, so our City slots are at 6.15am and 7.15am – with more breaking news throughout the programme.

The first hour of *Today* is a constant news drip, with correspondents phoning in from round the world to set the scene. It is also where we run 'Yesterday in Parliament' and a hardcore maths puzzle for our business audience and, as it turns out, the new generation of coders.

By 7am the intention is that audiences are significantly better informed than they were at 6am. The next hour is where you get more of the big set pieces.

The news-making story or interview comes at 7.10am. At 7.30am, you can have an extended piece of reporting, and a change of texture – leading up to 'Thought for the Day'. This interlude – usually a little less than three minutes – has been the subject of years of intense debate. Humanists have asked for the right to a hearing. But the programme is steeped in the history and traditions of the country, as well as challenging them. Listeners mind about change.

The 8.10am interview – during which power is often held to account – is so celebrated that a song has been written about it, called 'The 8.10'.

The last half an hour of the programme becomes more conversational. If people are eating breakfast, it will be more leisurely; if they are walking, cycling or driving – commuting to work – they are ready for some discussion.

This is the time when John Humphrys might mourn the state of his garden magnolia – which will be a page lead in the next morning's newspapers. Radio is intimate and listeners have strong relationships with the presenters.

The trick is to bring everything together in time for the 9am pips. It doesn't always quite come off as one might wish. I remember, for instance, the artists Gilbert and George discussing objections by Presbyterians to their art show in Belfast: the word 'evil' came just a second before the pips.

What can be moving is to play the programme out with a choir or a musician. We did this, for example, on 22 May 2018, the anniversary of the Manchester terror attack. However we have chosen to conclude the programme, the presenters have to master the final seconds, including a thankful mention of the day and night output editors.

As a guest presenter once put it gloomily: 'The *Today* programme is basically a series of time checks, isn't it? Woe betide a presenter who fluffs the time – the nation depends on it.'

Sarah Sands
Editor, *Today*, 2019

THE *TODAY* STORY BY

EDWARD STOURTON

'In the realm of ideas, radio operates with uncluttered lucidity,' declared Tony Whitby, Radio 4's controller, appointed not long after the network replaced the wartime Home Service, 'in the realm of the imagination, it soars where other media limp.' The *Today* archive which has been mined for this book illustrates how triumphantly the programme has demonstrated the truth of that creed. *Today: A history of our world through 60 years of conversations & controversies* reflects the way history has been broadcast on *Today*; it is not intended to be a history of the programme, but a brief account of the way *Today* has developed over the last six decades may help the reader to appreciate the broadcasting moments we have curated.

When *Today* was born, radio was, for the first time in the BBC's history, facing real competition. The BBC began broadcasting a television service in the 1930s, but transmissions from Alexandra Palace were unceremoniously shut down two days before Britain declared war with Germany – it was feared the Luftwaffe might use the transmitters to navigate by – and during the war years, radio reigned unchallenged. But BBC television returned to the air in June 1946, and ITV was launched a little less than a decade later.

Public attitudes had evolved too; a 1957 internal BBC report on 'The Future of Sound Broadcasting in the Domestic Services' noted that there had been 'a profound change of mood in the country, particularly among its younger members, which made the paternalistic flavour of 1945 progressively less acceptable'. The audience for the ultra-brainy Third Programme (which eventually became Radio Three) was so small that the report concluded its 'effort to improve public taste' had in fact 'given indigestion' to listeners, who had 'turned away'. Asa Briggs, the BBC's first official historian, observed that 'In no longer referring... to the Spoken Word in capital letters the Report stripped away what had once been a BBC aura.'

The one area where radio's champions saw a continuing competitive advantage was morning broadcasting. 'The Future of Sound Broadcasting' report argued that television would never challenge radio in the hours between 7 and 9am, 'even if the hours of television were to be extended ultimately so as to cover this time of day'. And it considered a suggestion that one of the existing radio networks should offer the morning audience 'news and information, weather, market reports, food news, press reviews, medical talks, household hints, etc'.

Robin Day's remarkable 1955 memos (noted by Sarah Sands in her Introduction) suggest those ideas were very much in the ether; Day wrote that 'As Television advances Sound Radio will find more and more that early morning programmes command its biggest audiences', and he suggested a show called *Morning Review,* 'a *daily* programme (Monday to Friday)... because its principal feature will be its up-to-date quality – overnight comment on things which people may not have yet read about in their morning papers'. But Day succumbed to the lure of the competition and left to join Independent Television News when the new service went on the air. He never presented the morning programme he so prophetically imagined, although his interviewing style had a lasting impact on many of those who have done so.

The first real hero of the *Today* story is a woman with roots deep in radio and the Reithian BBC. Born in 1902, Isa Benzie joined the BBC in the late 1920s, just as the original British Broadcasting Company was granted its royal charter and became a corporation. She had read German at Lady Margaret Hall, Oxford, but, like almost all ambitious BBC women then, she came in as a secretary. By 1933 she had worked her way up to a senior management role, but four years later she married a fellow BBC staffer and, in accordance with BBC policy, she resigned. According to one account of her life, John Reith himself attended her leaving lunch, and she returned as a radio producer in 1943; the wartime demands on the BBC had by then forced the corporation to relax its rules.

Benzie was a true believer in the Spoken Word. In May 1957 she wrote a note to the chief assistant in the Talks department, Janet Quigley – who was her friend and contemporary, and a fellow alumna of Lady Margaret Hall – proposing herself as the 'organiser' of the new programme. *Morning Miscellany* (the working title at the time) was, she suggested, 'an opportunity to be seized by those who don't believe – and never have – that there is something second-best or second rate about things taken in by ear...' The note included a perceptive comment on the limitations of television: 'Pictures – I do not mean pictorial art – necessarily leave out discussion of what is abstract, illumination of what is abstract. Words do not do this; they can do it as well heard as read.'

Benzie's husband was a television producer, but it seems the household owned no television set. As preparations for the new morning radio programme gathered pace, she fired off a memo listing her requirements: 'I need,' she wrote, 'a suitable television staff set. It is, I know, NOT good sense – in fact, it makes no sense at all to be responsible for a topical programme if not adequately informed about the greatest domestic innovation of our times. BBC and ITV programmes – topical and documentary programmes particularly – I must become reasonably familiar with.' Watching telly, however, was clearly a penance: 'This must be done in the evenings,' the memo continued, 'reluctant homework. I prefer to think that I shall ask you to take away the set after, say, three months (one will have a firm idea of the artists of the time and a sound existing knowledge is not difficult to keep bright and shining) but in the meantime may I ask you to cause a set to come.'

Benzie gave the programme the name it still flies under and wrote its first billing: 'Today, whoever you are, wherever you are in the United Kingdom, face your own day more buoyant and stimulated for having heard *Today*, with something for you, wherever you work, and time checks! *Today!*' As a mission statement it has stood the tests of time and changing broadcasting styles remarkably well.

And the Benzie–Quigley partnership was marked by that quirky curiosity which remains characteristic of the very best radio producers. On 16 October 1957, less than two weeks before the show went on the air, Quigley raised a new idea in a memo to her friend: 'From time to time I am struck by the fact that, as a nation, we are so very bad about fish,' she wrote. 'We are ignorant about choosing it, unimaginative about cooking it, apathetic about eating it.' *Today,* she suggested, offered a 'golden opportunity' for addressing this great issue: 'Some good ideas might occur if we thought about it hard. Meantime, what about devoting a regular item, however short, to it on Friday mornings? I mean just a flash – "The Fish of the Week".'

The first *Today* went out on 28 October 1957. Anthony Thwaite, the poet, academic and literary critic, was working at the BBC at the time and congratulated Isa Benzie in an internal report; 'I listened to both editions,' he wrote, 'and under fairly typical conditions (i.e. the two children of the house were shrieking round the room and the coffee boiled over). I thought the general effect was good.' His reference to 'two editions' reflects the fact that in its earliest incarnation *Today* was broadcast in two 20-minute segments at 7.15 and 8.15. The news – at 7am and 8am – still dominated early-morning broadcasting, and the two segments were also separated by the very Reithian religious strand *Lift up Your Hearts*, which, in a shorter form, later became *Thought for the Day*. That first edition included some Verdi, items on 'Briefing a pilot at Heathrow airport' and 'Sotheby's sale of Napoleana', Eamonn Andrews on boxing and a recording of Petula Clark's singing. Thwaite's generally enthusiastic review included the judgement that 'Petula Clark, in particular, was a terror: my listening-companion was unprintable about this.'

You will find very little archive material from those early days reproduced in this book – that is partly because of the patchy condition of the BBC archives covering this period, but also because the programme's agenda was much lighter. At first the News department seem to have resented their contribution to *Today*. A sniffy 1957 memo from the news editor (written in a tone which suggests a degree of inter-departmental tension between News and Talks) insisted that 'any material we make available to Miss Benzie will be broadcast in the form it leaves here, subject only to such alterations as may be necessary, in consultation with the duty editor, in the light of subsequent developments.' Early News offerings included an interview with Spike Milligan and 'a candle-light auction of a five-acre field of cress in Chard, Somerset'.

Today's real engagement with history did not begin until the 1960s. In 1963 the programme was incorporated into a department called Current Affairs Sound, and a current affairs broadcaster called Stephen Bonarjee took over as its head. He had a brief to give the programme a harder edge and more of a focus on news. He wanted a 'lively, polished product' which offered 'broad extrovert human interests but should not be afraid to be serious when necessary. The programme, he said, 'will need rather more "roughage" in the shape of sharper, harder material'.

Bonarjee's ambitions towards the kind of *Today* we know now faced a formidable obstacle in the form of his main presenter. The first *Today* 'compere' – as he was known at the time – was a now largely forgotten home service announcer called Alan Skempton. He left after less than a year, a victim, the BBC's files suggest, to one of those momentary lapses which so often get live presenters into trouble; we do not know what he said, but in a 1958 memo Isa Benzie remarks that 'It is not really possible to ward off in advance all the little remarks of an unscripted compere which are or are thought to be unfortunate.' That background makes it all the odder that the BBC recruited Jack de Manio to replace Skempton; de Manio was already notorious for one of the most 'unfortunate' mistakes in the BBC's history, by introducing a programme called 'The Land of the Niger' as 'The Land of the Nigger' (the Queen was on an official visit to Nigeria at the time). He was to enjoy 13 years in the presenter's chair.

When Stephen Bonarjee took the programme's helm in 1963 he generously remarked that 'The very strong personal association between Mr de Manio and *Today* has been in the nature of a happy miracle', but it was difficult to turn out a 'polished' programme with a presenter who could scarcely tell the time, and was famously chaotic about those 'time checks'. On one occasion de Manio missed the beginning of the show altogether, and when he did turn up to the studio he cheerfully announced that he had been in the loo.

Jack de Manio lived in a flat in Chelsea, drove a Bentley and drank heroically (he told *Desert Island Discs* that during his days as an announcer he would 'go straight across to the Feathers' whenever a recorded programme was being played out), and he had the prejudices to match his clubman's lifestyle. In July 1968, after some 10,000 people demonstrated against the Vietnam War in Trafalgar Square and marched on to the American embassy in Grosvenor Square, he greeted the nation with the words, 'Good morning – and let's start the morning by raising our hats to the London policemen, who once again have their weekends mucked up by a lot of silly hooligans.'

In answering a complaint about the comments, Bonarjee noted that 'Jack does quite frequently improvise, and within reasonable limits this is regarded as part of the programme's spontaneity.'

De Manio's greatest scoop for *Today* was probably his 1969 interview with Prince Charles – the first broadcast interview from the heir to the throne. The prince was an undergraduate at Trinity College, Cambridge, at the time. Their encounter took place at Buckingham Palace and it began like this:

de Manio: Sir, what was it that you said to me when I arrived here at Buckingham Palace?

Prince Charles: Well, I just said I hoped you found this place all right.

de Manio: Well, I had a great deal of difficulty.

Prince Charles: Did you?

de Manio: Not really. But, er, the papers this week have had some wonderful photographs of you sitting in a dustbin and some very flattering comments about your performance in the show *The Revolution* at Cambridge. Could you tell me a little bit about the show?

Prince Charles: Well it's the most awful, you know, sort of, *Beyond the Fringe* type of revue; we have about 40 skits and I take part in about 16 of them, I think, and most of the jokes are the most awful, sort of groan jokes and everyone goes arghh (groan) and there's one complete one which is called the 'all in groan' and we just walk across making idiotic jokes, 'I say I say jokes' and that sort of thing. It is the greatest possible fun to do, particularly before one even began doing it – you know, discussing what you were going to do – 'cause then one rolled around on the floor in helpless hysterics, you know.

de Manio: But 'the dustman' was inspired by your own experience with a dustman who woke you up one day?

Prince Charles: It was rather, yes.

de Manio: How do you play the dustman?

Prince Charles: I sit in a dustbin, you see, and I'm a great fan of the Goons anyway, and so I thought it was a marvellous opportunity to use one of their voices, I just come on and I say, 'Allo allo allo, I empty dustbins by taking the lid off and emptying them in the dustcart', you know that sort of thing and I wear a cap and a sort of pair of jeans, and, er, it's just a take-off of a dustman.

BBC memos were once an art form, and, writing the following year, Gerard Mansell, the Radio Four controller (and later deputy director general) despatched one which displayed his mastery of the medium. 'I don't want to seem to be overreacting,' he wrote, 'but I think Jack de Manio's reference to "Yoko Hama, or whatever her name is" in this morning's second edition, and his comment to the effect that he didn't care whether or not she and John Lennon went to bed together, went further than we ought to allow Jack to go. Making fun of foreign names is a time-honoured pasttime, but not one that is generally regarded as being in good taste, and dismissive remarks about the sex life of Mr and Mrs Lennon, though no doubt they will evoke wide agreement among listeners, ought not really to have a place in our broadcasting.'

It is not clear which chapter of the John Lennon/Yoko Ono story had prompted de Manio's sally, but Mansell's memo is dated in early April, and at the beginning of the month the duo had, by way of an April Fool, announced that they were both having sex-change operations. Mansell's 1970s memo ended on a chilly note: 'I think,' the controller wrote, 'we should be careful not to allow him [de Manio] to go quite so far in revealing his prejudices.'

It is perhaps unsurprising that when we delved into the *Today* archives for material on that year's general election we found that the big post-election interview with the outgoing prime minister, Harold Wilson, was conducted not by *Today*'s main presenter (as you might expect today), but by David Dimbleby of the BBC election team. De Manio was finally eased off the programme the following year.

For a brief period the programme was presented by John Timpson, who joined in de Manio's final months, and Robert Robinson, who is now probably best remembered as the host of *Call My Bluff*. But the modern, double-headed presentation of *Today* really became established with the John Timpson and Brian Redhead partnership which began in 1973. You will find plenty from both men within this book.

They were very different, but that was why the partnership worked so well. Paul Donovan notes in his history *All Our Todays*, 'It was not simply that, to a nation with a ready ear for the nuances of class and district, they represented north and south, tenor and baritone, town and country; though they certainly played on those differences in their ping-pong verbal exchanges. It was more fundamental than that: they had different senses of humour, different senses of what was important on and off the programme, different approaches to life.' The broadcaster Libby Purves, who spent three years as a third presenter working alongside them, told Donovan that 'There was a phase early on when they were real rivals and wanted to make sure that neither had more lives [live interviews – the most exciting ingredient for presenters] than the other. Both of them reacted exactly the same way with me. If there were five lives, they wanted to be very certain that they had three and I had two.' She described Timpson as 'from the lawn-mowing classes, an old BBC chap, apolitical, who had a rather old-fashioned sort of humour', while Redhead was 'a chippy Geordie, up from the people and, God didn't he know it, ex-newspaper editor. He used to go around saying he was the only real journalist here. He was verbally extremely acute, and mannered, and bumptious.'

Brian Redhead's habit of myth-making about himself was notorious, and almost everyone he worked with has a story of his Walter Mitty-ish carry on. In 1992 I found myself next to him on a plane back from the Earth Summit in Rio de Janeiro, which I had been covering for ITN, and I settled into my club-class seat looking forward to a long journey in the company of a broadcasting legend. Somewhere over the mid-Atlantic, after several hours of self-aggrandising soliloquy from my neighbour, I pleaded a nicotine craving and slipped back to hide in the sin bin in economy; the tipping point came with Brian's claim, expounded at some length, that Douglas Hurd, then foreign secretary, had secured his Cambridge first by copying Brian's exam papers. But Brian Redhead's passion for politics and his journalistic rigour marked the *Today* programme forever. All the subsequent presenters you will meet in the following pages have aspired to the standards he set before his early death in January 1994, and *Today* has been seen as the place where policies and politicians are tested ever since his time in the *Today* chair.

In 1983, more than a quarter of a century after that internal BBC report on 'The Future of Sound Broadcasting in the Domestic Services', the 'hours of Television' were at last extended to the early mornings. TV-am, Britain's first national operator of a commercial breakfast television franchise, went on the air with *Daybreak* in February, fronted by the so-called famous five (David Frost, Michael Parkinson, Angela Rippon, Anna Ford and Robert Kee). The BBC managed to scramble its rival *Breakfast Time* on to the air two weeks earlier. But *Today*'s position was by then unassailable; as the radio enthusiasts of the mid-1950s had predicted, the Spoken Word retained its dominance of the morning hours when the audience was on the move. The *Daily Express* illustrated their story on the morning ratings war between radio and television with a picture of Timpson and Redhead: 'The Odd Couple who outshine the Famous Five' read the caption. 'Their programme, presented entirely without flamboyance and sensation, has captured a daily audience of more than 4 million. That's twice the viewing figure of both TV-am and BBC's *Breakfast Time* combined, with none of the publicity or hype.'

The programme's standing as the place where the national conversation was conducted was confirmed in a 1979 memo from Douglas Muggeridge, nephew of Malcolm Muggeridge and a big figure in BBC radio management. 'I had lunch recently with Henry James, the prime minister's chief press officer,' he recorded. 'He told me that Margaret Thatcher begins the day at 6am by listening to the World Service. She always switches to *Today* at approx. 6.30am and listens through to 8.40am every day. She never listens to LBC. Henry James said her whole approach to the day was "conditioned by what she heard on the *Today* programme".'

In 1988 Mrs Thatcher demonstrated that this was not simply flattery from a Downing Street press officer. When she heard on the programme that Russia's President Gorbachev had cancelled his trip to Britain because of a devastating earthquake in Armenia she telephoned the programme spontaneously. John Humphrys was given 35-seconds notice that he would be talking to the prime minister. 'I heard it [the news about Gorbachev] on your programme,' she told him. 'It was the first indication we had. Then I heard later that you didn't know if I knew, so I thought I had better phone…'

But Phil Harding, who was the programme's editor in the late 1980s, suggests a slightly less cosy relationship between Downing Street and *Today*. 'I was told that, actually, what really used to happen was that Denis [Thatcher, the prime minister's husband] used to listen and then Denis would come down stairs after the programme and say to Margaret, "You've no idea what those pinkos have been doing on that *Today* programme. It's absolutely scandalous." And she would get all her knowledge about the programme filtered through Denis.'

The programme's prominence has inevitably made it a target, and the extracts from the archive in this book are a reminder that its relationship with government and politicians more generally has sometimes been extremely tense. On occasion it has had to cover rows involving the BBC, and sometimes even itself. Controversy is as much part of the *Today* tradition as conversation.

The programme has frequently been attacked – often by its own staff – over the way it deals with women. This is perhaps surprising in view of its history; the first senior producer after the Quigley–Benzie era was, like them, a successful professional woman (Elizabeth Rowley) and one of *Today*'s most influential editors was Jenny Abramsky, who went on to be the BBC's director of radio. But women in front of the microphone have, down the decades, found cause to call out *Today* as a sexist institution.

Libby Purves was appointed as a third presenter when she was very young, but a memo from her editor to the Radio Four controller sent just before her appointment suggests what today we would certainly call tokenism. 'I have been pleased with the way Brian Redhead has responded to the two girls we have had in Nigel's [Nigel Rees, who presented the programme for two years in the late 1970s] absence,' he wrote. 'I am attracted to the idea of making the junior partner in the *Today* presenting team a woman.' Libby Purves has cited an incident that evokes the climate of the time: 'When Thatcher got in, there was a reception we were all invited to, to meet the new lot,' she recalls. 'I was in my duffle-coat as usual, and when we arrived an impatient door guy pointed gentlemen John and Brian and the producer through, but said to me, "Jobless

Youth delegation, that's down the passage the other way.'" After three years she left the BBC, returning in 1984 for her long-running role as the presenter of *Midweek*.

As part of the research for this book we have tried to contact *Today* presenters past and present to ask for nominations of their most memorable interviews, and where possible we have worked them into the themes covered in this book. Sue MacGregor's response was revealing: 'This is indicative of something, I guess, which other women presenters of *Today* might recognise; I can't think of a single really dramatic interview – as they were usually in the field of politics, and the chap on with me, whoever it was... got the 8.10am interview slot [the main interview each morning] unless it was about some terrible global disaster which women could cope with.' Sue began presenting *Today* in 1984, and worked on the programme until 2002, but throughout those 18 years there was real resistance to the idea of two women presenting together. 'I think the very first pair of women to present was Jennie Bond (then royal correspondent) with me,' she writes. 'It was so extraordinary that the *Daily Express* came in to take a picture... and it didn't happen again for ages.'

The more recent women members of the presenting team – Mishal Husain and Martha Kearney – often appear together, and the programme now has a woman editor. But as recently as 2017 *Today* found itself in the firing line over its record in the field of sex equality when Sarah Montague discovered that she was being paid significantly less than her male colleagues. 'I had long suspected that I was paid much less than my colleagues, but until the pay disclosures I had no idea of the scale of that difference,' she wrote, adding that she was 'incandescent with rage' when she found out the truth. The row coincided with her planned departure for *The World at One*, which she now presents.

The programme has also found itself in the line of fire over some of the special features which editors have seen fit to introduce. In 1982 Julian Holland launched *Today*'s Man and Woman of the Year Award. It was a less eccentric idea than Janet Quigley's 'Fish of the Week', but it caused no end of trouble. Tim Luckhurst, himself a former *Today* producer, notes in his book *This is Today* that 'Holland should have listened to advice from professional opinion pollsters. They exposed the faults in his plan: no poll in which participants are entirely self-selecting and voting is not supervised can ever be entirely fair.' The competition had to be abandoned in 1990 after the Man of the Year title was won by L K Advani, one of the founders of the Hindu nationalist party the BJP; the party was not nearly as famous as it is now (India's current prime minister, Narendra Modi, is a member) and it is likely that a large proportion of *Today*'s audience had never heard of Mr Advani. It was found that many of his messages of support 'were identically worded and had been posted from a small number of post offices in the Birmingham area'.

A few years later the idea was revived in a gender-neutral form, but the process of choosing a *Today* Personality of the Year proved equally vulnerable to vote-rigging. In 1996, the BBC was forced to suspend the ballot, issuing a statement that 'Early this morning the BBC discovered that an organised attempt had been made to distort the annual vote for the *Today* programme Personality of the Year in favour of Tony Blair. We deeply deprecate any attempt to interfere with what is intended to be a spontaneous opportunity for the programme's listeners to express their point of view.' A letter from a Labour Party body, called the 'Audience Participation Unit', emerged, which encouraged Labour members to send in votes for the party leader ('though preferably NOT on fax machines which identify the sender as the Labour Party'). Tony Blair had to apologise, and John Major, the prime minister of the day, won the competition. But even that was not the end of the mess; when Sue MacGregor announced the result on Boxing Day she also had to make public that 4,000 ballots for Mr Major had been disqualified because of evidence of 'multiple voting'.

The more recent editorial innovation of asking guest editors to drive the direction of programmes over the Christmas and New Year break has proved less controversial. The idea was the brainchild of Peter Hanington, a *Today* veteran, and since it was launched in 2003 he has scooped an eclectic and high-profile collection of public figures into his net. Norman Tebbit, a fierce critic of the BBC in his ministerial days, was among the first year's guest editors, and other political guests have included the former Labour home secretary David Blunkett and the Liberal Democrat peer Shirley Williams. But it has been the editors drawn from beyond politics – which are so much a part of the programme's daily diet – who have made this seasonal experiment stand out.

They have included a philosopher (Onora O'Neill, 2004); a dancer (Tamara Rojo, artistic director of the English National Ballet, 2017); a radio critic (the former *Today* presenter Gillian Reynolds, 2003); a queen (Queen Noor of Jordan, 2004), and an AI robot (2017). Sport has been well represented (Clive Woodward, 2006, and Bradley Wiggins, 2015), as has science (Stephen Hawking, 2003) and business and finance (Mervyn King, the former Bank of England governor, 2014). In 2007 the Dyfed-Powys police won a competition to offer ordinary listeners the chance to guest-edit. Yoko Ono even took over the show 36 years after she was so notoriously insulted by Jack de Manio; *Today* had certainly changed in the intervening decades, but she, it seems, had not, declaring, 'I am still a radical, I think,' and she told James Naughtie, 'There's only two industries in the world – one is the war industry and the other is the peace industry, and anybody who's participating in the peace industry should be celebrated.'

Some guest editors take the opportunity to ride a hobby horse – often very elegantly. David Hockney, in 2009, took the presenter Evan Davis on a tour of trees around his local Bridlington, Yorkshire, to where he'd migrated after many years living in Los

Angeles. Trees were his latest artistic passion – he called them 'the largest manifestation of a life-force'. Three years later Tracey Emin (a regular Humphrys sparring partner, *see* page 272) re-immersed herself in the Margate of her youth, in the year that the Turner Contemporary gallery opened in the Kent resort. Rarely can one of Britain's economically depressed seaside towns have been celebrated in such ringing terms:

> I say two things about Margate. One, it has one of the most beautiful sunsets in the world... Look at Turner's paintings. Every painting of a sunset comes from Margate... And I always say to people, if you want to have a dirty weekend, don't go to Brighton, go to Margate, and that's what Turner came down here for. Margate has a kind of sexiness, it has this sort of grittiness that's really, really provocative, and that's what Turner also picked up on, the fecundity of everything, and you feel it in the air, something really sensual and good.

The actor Colin Firth designed his programme in 2010, on the basis of the kind of open curiosity which makes for good journalism – even if few journalists would put it as modestly as he did.

> This struck me as an opportunity to explore things which compel me; areas to which I'm constantly drawn, but about which I'm not perhaps sufficiently informed. Now that doesn't stop me having strong opinions – this is part of my problem: I'm perfectly happy to volunteer a view, which gets me into all sorts of trouble, but you know I'm not clever enough to really support it. And what I thought I'd do here was, rather than bang on about things I've got half-baked ideas about, would be to just hand it over to the experts – basically share my curiosity – expose, perhaps, some of my prejudices or areas of bias, and then allow them to be cross-examined, but in the words of people who are cleverer than I am.

The result was an illuminating mix including poetry, inquiries into history teaching, an exploration of the unintended consequences of providing aid in the developing world and a John Humphrys encounter with Barry Humphries' alter ego Dame Edna Everage.

Guest editors can open doors usually closed to journalists: when the late Cardinal Cormac Murphy O'Connor edited the programme in 2008 I had the treat of several days recording with him in Rome, and he slipped us into the Sistine Chapel after closing time to describe what it is like to take part in a papal conclave.

A big-name editor can often deliver big-name guests. In 2017 Prince Harry brought in his father to discuss their shared concerns about climate change – a very different kind of interview from Prince Charles' encounter with Jack de Manio nearly half a century earlier. But the high point of the show was an even bigger coup: Harry also secured the first interview President Obama had given, anywhere, since leaving office in January 2017. Treading carefully around the recent election of President Trump, the focus was on post-presidential life, and on what Obama's new charitable foundation would be attempting to achieve. There was humour at the end with a quick-fire round of 'either/or' questions, in which the prince's cheek ('boxers or briefs?') was matched by the president's wit:

> Harry: Harry or William?
>
> Obama: William, right now!
>
> Harry: White House or Buckingham Palace?
>
> Obama: White House, just because Buckingham Palace looks like it would take a really long time to mow.

Today can call on the services of the BBC's very experienced range of reporters and correspondents – you will be introduced to many of them in this book, and sometimes you will find that the same individuals pop up in different places in different roles – but the programme likes to exploit the unusually intimate relationship between its audience and its presenters. Regular listeners will be familiar with another *Today* tradition, which features frequently in the archive material collected here: the co-presentation, or, in programme argot, 'co-pres', when part of the programme is presented from an outside location.

The bar for these exercises was set memorably high by a three-way presentation back in 1979. Libby Purves opened the show from Peking (as it was then transliterated). 'Here,' she announced, 'to mark the 30th anniversary of the founding of the People's Republic of China, and today, and on Monday, Philip Short [the BBC's China correspondent] and I will be reporting on the changing face of life in the country that holds one fifth of the world's population.' Robert Fox (a BBC correspondent at the time) then picked up with 'Good morning from... Dublin, where we're expecting, in just over 24 hours from now, the arrival of a pope in the land of St. Patrick for the first time in history.' John Timpson was back in the studio, 'And this is John Timpson in London marvelling at all this technological wizardry, and bringing all our usual features and the latest news from Britain and around the world. First this morning's headlines. Labour have won the by-election in Manchester...'

All *Today*'s presenters since the Timpson–Redhead era have had news-reporting backgrounds, and most have relished the chance to get back on the road for 'co-pres' programmes, even though some assignments can be very challenging. Mishal Husain included a trip to Pakistan in December 2014 in her list of her most memorable *Today* moments. While she was there the Taliban killed 130 children at a school in Peshawar, and the following morning she broadcast from the school grounds:

It's just a few moments ago that the army opened the black gate, behind in which the school grounds sit, and let us in. I was the first journalist to be allowed into the school grounds. And as you can probably imagine it is a very eerie atmosphere. These are premises which should be alive at a time of day like this to the sound of hundreds of children who studied here, and to whom the school day began as normal yesterday. But it is desolate. Today the army has been working through the night to clear the premises of explosives. And I walked into the grounds, there's a long path leading towards the main school building. It's lined with explosives, experts and soldiers. And I'm standing now at the bottom of the steps that lead up to the auditorium, white stone steps, and there are bloodstains running right down the steps and towards the auditorium itself. There's a child's shoe that I can see on one of the steps I'm walking past now, and the auditorium is one of the places within the school grounds that the militants first targeted; this is where children were taking their exams. They were sitting in the big hall that I'm looking into now. And the militants burst in and it was one of the first signs that an assault was underway. So as I peer in now it's a scene of total... you know... the chairs that the children must have been sitting on upturned, the place has been turned upside down. And again, I can see the bloodstains on the floor right around me. The army is shortly going to give us a tour where we'll be able to start seeing some of the classrooms. These are just the very first impressions that I have.

Justin Webb's list of memorable moments included an interview which was also conducted when he was out and about, but it was of a very different kind. He chose it to illustrate how some of the programme's best moments come from interviews which are, as he put it, 'typically seat-of-the-pants, madly conducted'. In September 2014 an American businessman and reality-TV presenter called Donald Trump was visiting his newly acquired golf course at Turnberry on the west coast of Scotland. 'Trump's people rang and said he could do a business interview about golf,' Justin explained, 'but the business folks were not around, so it was decided to pre-record with me as I had once been to America [he was based in Washington for eight years from 2001] so might know who he was, but I was on a train waiting to leave Doncaster station where I had been at the UKIP conference. So we just did it from there. I knew almost nothing about him (reality TV was not my thing), except that he had once run for president.'

The interview covered golf, the recent Scottish independence referendum and wind farms (or, as Trump called them, 'these ugly windmills, destroying this beautiful land of Scotland') before getting to the meat of the matter:

Webb: What about your own personal, political career, finally, Mr Trump. You stood for the presidency, didn't you? Are you going to do that again?

Trump: Well, they all want me to and a lot of polls want me to. The thing is, I love what I'm doing. I love Turnberry and we're going to make that something that Scotland and everybody can be so proud of. I love doing that, but polls indicate that I should. And another thing is that our country's not doing well and a lot of mistakes are made by people who are very incompetent.

Webb: There's a real possibility that you will seek the Republican nomination next time round?

Trump: Well, there is always a possibility and there is a real possibility. Absolutely, if I don't see the right person running, because a change has to be made, and if I don't see the right person that's running and if the country continues to do poorly, there is certainly a very real possibility.

Webb: Donald Trump, thanks a lot for talking to us.

Trump: Thank you very much – a great honour.

It seems unlikely that the greater hater of 'mainstream media' would give an interview to *Today* now.

You need a good head for heights to work on *Today*. For a presenter, the programme's hallowed 'furniture' – Isa Benzie's time checks, the pips, the way you back-announce the speaker at the end of Thought for the Day, the weather before the headlines on the half-hour, the racing tips and so on – can at first seem daunting. But once you have learnt not to bump into the programme furniture, it becomes something to hang on to, and *Today* is a surprisingly easy programme to present competently. It is a very difficult programme to present well; you need to be willing to take risks, and many of the moments included in this book were 'seat-of-the-pants, madly conducted'.

Today can be a hostile environment – even for the home team. While I have been canvasing opinion about great *Today* interviews, several people have mentioned John Humphrys's devastating 2012 interview with the BBC's director general, George Entwhistle, after the BBC's *Newsnight* wrongly accused a senior Tory figure of sex abuse; Entwhistle resigned that evening, becoming the shortest-serving director general in the BBC's history.

The air is thin at the top of this broadcasting pinnacle, and a fall can be painful. Jack de Manio's career never recovered after he left the programme; Paul Donovan reports in *All Our Todays* that he was eventually reduced to 'emptying slot machines in pubs to earn a few pounds a week' and had to surrender his BBC pension to settle his debts.

Peter Hobday resented the way he was removed from the presenter rota in 1996, after 14 years in the job. 'I have had no letter of thanks from anyone in authority, no farewell lunch or dinner, nothing', he recorded. 'I walked out of Broadcasting House on the Saturday morning after the programme. It was the end of 25 years with BBC News and Current Affairs and there was nothing left to mark it.' My own departure from the presenter line-up – after ten years on the programme – was involuntary and difficult. Some editors have been badly burnt too, and the Hutton saga (*see* page 301) had an impact on several BBC careers.

But *Today* has – to a remarkable degree – always been able to count on the loyalty of those who work for it. Mike Chaney, who was appointed the programme's editor in 1976, fought a valiant and bitter battle about the length of the programme with the Radio Four controller, Ian McIntyre, aka Mac the Knife. McIntyre took *Today* back to something very close to the two-edition format of its founding years, and introduced a new programme called *Up to the Hour* between the slots. Chaney judged *Up to the Hour* to be 'absolute crap, the floor sweepings', and in a sometimes intemperate memo exchange, preserved in the BBC archives, he addressed the impact of the changes on his staff: 'It is clear,' he wrote, 'that a man who has spent years on nights or other anti-social shifts would welcome the chance to turn his hand to documentaries – and spend his nights at home for a change. But it does not follow that he would trade these new delights for the dismemberment of what he has spent the last six years trying to achieve – morning magazine broadcasting. That is what most of us signed up for. We know we could have a more comfortable life elsewhere. But *Today* seemed uniquely worth the sacrifice.'

Chaney was one of those editors whose time on the programme came to a messy end (he was eased out and ended his BBC career managing Radio Norfolk), but he was on the right side of history, and *Today* eventually got its airtime back.

Edward Stourton
Former presenter, *Today*, 2019

CHAPTER I

REBELLION, REVOLUTION AND PROTEST

Apartheid and its international opponents

'Playing to multiracial audiences is hardly the point'
MICHAEL SHEVELEW, 28 APRIL 1985

'Nothing I do or say will give encouragement to apartheid or racial discrimination,' declared the Archbishop of Canterbury, Dr Michael Ramsey, on *Today* on 13 November 1969. Ramsey had long been a vocal critic of the white-minority rule enacted by South Africa's National Party, but he was about to step into the lion's den with a visit to the country's Dutch Reformed Church, where, the BBC's Church Affairs correspondent Douglas Brown asserted, 'I know for sure apartheid is practised.'

Brown had some blunt questions for Ramsey: 'Will you speak out against racial discrimination, against apartheid, in your sermons and your public utterances, in the same way as you have been doing for years in this country?' and 'Will you refuse to attend any function in which segregation is practised, be it a church service or a social function?' The archbishop defended his visit as evidence-gathering – 'It's very important that comment should be based on first-hand knowledge and experience of the country' – and tried to reassure Brown and *Today* listeners that he would 'be very careful not to do and say things that mean any acquiescence in apartheid as a system'.

Ramsey's dilemma was, at root, the one that governments, companies and individuals in whole fields of endeavour – from trade to sport to the performing arts – struggled with during the apartheid era: how best to change South Africa? Were engagement, dialogue and the spreading of soft power the way to influence the regime? Or should South Africa be shunned in all its shapes and forms, hung out to dry? The issue was complicated by the bigger context of the Cold War. For South Africa's white rulers, the choice of allegiance was never in doubt, since its own internal opposition came, in part, from the banned Communist Party. Could the West afford to isolate such a Cold War ally?

The questions were particularly acute for Britain, the former colonial power. The Union of South Africa was established as a self-governing dominion of the British Empire in 1910, but in 1948 the National Party began to introduce the system of racial segregation known as apartheid, and the dominance of an English-speaking white minority was replaced by one of an Afrikaans-speaking white minority. In 1961

South Africa left the Commonwealth and became a republic. Nevertheless, to many South Africans, Britain remained a sort of motherland, a cultural touchstone, and was regarded as having a duty of post-imperial care. At the same time, British investment in South Africa remained significant. How far could a British government and large corporations go in sacrificing that history and those ties?

Several hundred anti-apartheid representatives gathered at London's Holborn Hall on 26 June 1959. A boycott movement was born, its purpose encapsulated in the words of its chief proponent that day, the future Tanzanian president Julius Nyerere: 'We are not asking you, the British people, for anything special. We are just asking you to withdraw your support from apartheid by not buying South African goods.' Attitudes hardened in 1960 when South African police shot and killed 69 protesters in the township of Sharpeville.

Thereafter, the boycott campaign began to mushroom into a much wider anti-apartheid movement, which sought to lobby governments and influence policy, but also to spread its message into as many spheres of activity as possible: that South Africa should be shunned from normal interactions in the global community of nations. There were, of course, plenty who disagreed with this approach.

Those contending perspectives on South Africa were regularly reflected in reports, discussions and interviews on *Today* over the decades that followed, and the debates ranged through every field from politics and business to the arts.

International sport was a particularly high-profile arena: South Africa wanted to showcase its excellence in rugby and cricket, while anti-apartheid campaigners wanted the all-white South African teams banned from competitions. In the year of Archbishop Ramsey's *Today* interview – 1969 – an extensive tour of Britain and Ireland by the South African Springbok rugby team was disrupted by a campaign of protests and pitch invasions coordinated by the young South African émigré and future Labour cabinet minister Peter Hain.

With South African sport already therefore a potent issue, the announcement of an impending British tour by the South African cricket team in 1970 acted as a red rag to a bull. In mid-May 1970 the matter was debated in Parliament, and the tour looked likely to proceed when Kent cricketer and leading England batsman Colin Cowdrey was invited onto *Today* to discuss it. He was not for banning the tour, as he explained to Douglas Cameron (who was then working on *Today*, but is better known for his subsequent career as an LBC presenter) on 16 May 1970:

> I've always thought, and always will think that... to continue our relations with South Africa, albeit white South Africa for the moment, is right, is healthy, is the best way of breaking down their internal problem and then, one day, we

all hope and pray for, the integration of... [We hope that we will one day have] multiracial cricket over there.

What he resented was both the intrusion of politics into sport and the three-sided nature of the debate, in which (as he called them) the 'coloured' cricketing nations of the world were putting their own pressure on the English cricket authorities not to play:

> These various countries did take a line, two or three months ago, that it was not their business: it was the business between England and South Africa what took place. Now, they've all been pressured into putting the pressure on us, [so] they've come out and made threats they would drop out of test matches with us and so forth. One doesn't like this form of blackmail, but the fact is that these pressures are mounting throughout the cricket world. And one is reaching a situation where one's got to [decide], in the interests of the game of cricket, after all – this is what our job is, administering cricket – is it in the best interest of cricket?

When quizzed by Cameron as to whether the 'thought of playing under pressure' concerned him, Cowdrey just hoped 'it won't be quite as difficult as everyone, as we all, anticipate'. In the end, Cowdrey need not have worried – the tour never transpired. A week later, on 22 May 1970, England's Cricket Council received a 'formal request from Her Majesty's Government to withdraw the invitation to the South African touring team'; a request they felt they could not refuse. For his efforts in stymying South African sporting aspirations, Peter Hain earned the attentions of MI5 and Special Branch.

In contrast to the continuing racial segregation in South African sport, the theatre was a realm struggling to break free. Those actors, directors and writers who gave a voice to South African issues were welcomed internationally. At the forefront was the highly respected playwright Athol Fugard, an anti-apartheid Afrikaner, who spoke to Helen Palmer, reporting for *Today* on 10 July 1980.

Fugard referred to the situation just a few years previously, when, he said, 'You were both breaking the law if you were playing to a mixed audience or had a mixed cast onstage, which then forced you to go underground with your theatre.' But he felt that recent concessions were 'window-dressing, a cosmetic job'. He described to *Today* listeners how apartheid poisoned the lives of *all* South Africans:

> I haven't the slightest hesitation in describing the system in my country, the so-called apartheid system, as a totally dehumanising and brutalising experience in terms of the way black people experience it. What is not often realised... and certainly not by a great many white South Africans, is that they are also the victims of that system, of course. It takes away a living space from them as well, to the extent that it dictates who your friends can be, where you've got to live, etc., etc. They're, they're victims as well...

When asked by Palmer, 'Do you feel this is true in your own case?' Fugard was emphatic:

> Oh yes, enormously so. Just taking, for example, the situation in my hometown, which is Port Elizabeth, simply because of the laws that operate, the fact that [when] we [whites] enter the black ghetto area, [we] need a permit… I will never be given that permit. Half of my own town is not available to me.

Many of Fugard's plays premiered with the Market Theatre Company, who were always warmly embraced when they were able to perform internationally. In contrast, when British performers took their services to apartheid-era South Africa, the response from their peers could be distinctly frosty, as actor Derek Bond discovered. For *Today*'s broadcast of 28 April 1985, reporter Phil Longman set the scene:

> The Royalty Theatre in London… rang to impassioned speeches from leading members of the acting profession, like Vanessa Redgrave and Frances de la Tour. Almost all the speakers denounced Derek Bond for going to South Africa, where he played the title role in a touring production of J B Priestley's play *An Inspector Calls*. At the end of the rather one-sided debate, there was an overwhelming vote for him to quit.

For Derek Bond was not only an actor, he was president of the actors' union Equity. His line of defence regarding 'the right of individual members to hold and express their personal, political and other beliefs, both in their private and professional capacities' did little to sway those calling for his resignation. Particularly unimpressed was a white South African actor, Michael Shevelew, who, as Longman explained, 'rejected arguments that British actors going there to play to mixed black-and-white audiences helped to change the system':

> Those things are basically meaningless within the context of South African society. Building bridges between what and what? Playing to multiracial audiences is hardly the point. It's where the audiences have to go once they leave the theatre, which is to racially segregated areas. Those are the issues that should be foremost in people's minds, but they tend to get pushed to the background; largely, I think, because of ignorance.

Bond felt aggrieved at his treatment. He told Longman:

> All over the whole country I opposed apartheid and attacked it. And what people didn't say is that the white actors and the black actors in South Africa have, actually, achieved a marvellous thing with the support of the management, believe it or not. They have imposed a multiracial theatre on both sides of the

footlights over the last few years and they've done it with courage and guts, fighting against the nationalist government.

However, another actor, Brian Croucher, 'voiced the feelings of the many', as Longman put it, when he said, 'He, as a president, should take the lead and show, he should show the rest of the union an example... He's made a mockery of our union. He should go.' Equity went on to adopt a ban on performing in South Africa, and Bond resigned.

The 1980s were a time of varying fortunes for the anti-apartheid movement. It renewed its commercial boycott campaign, achieving some success with individual companies which cancelled South African contracts, and continued to campaign against sporting fixtures, as well as on many other fronts. Supranational bodies – the United Nations General Assembly and the Commonwealth – imposed sanctions on South Africa, but Margaret Thatcher's government refused to go down that road. Heightened Cold War tensions also restrained the United States, as the perception of South Africa as a regional bulwark against Communism made America reluctant to intervene.

Throughout the 1970s and 1980s, *Today* provided its listeners with snapshots of the complex story – both dramatic high points and notorious low points, such as the death in custody in 1977 of the anti-apartheid activist and leader of the black consciousness movement Steve Biko (whose biography later became the basis of the film *Cry Freedom*). *Today* broadcast an interview with the high-profile solicitor Sir David Napley, who had been an independent observer at the inquest into Biko's death. He told Graeme McLagan, a reporter who specialised in police investigations, why he questioned the magistrate's verdict that Biko had been injured in a scuffle.

> **Napley: The reasons I say that are numerous; I can only pick out one or two of them. In the first case, it was manifest to me that the police were not telling the truth in the witness box. Nor have they been telling the truth earlier on, they had tried to pretend to the doctors that this man was shamming, if they had told the doctors otherwise, different considerations would have followed and I cannot see why they could have gone on with that story and failed to tell the doctors that they suspected he'd had a blow on the head – which the principal police witness said was in his mind – unless they clearly had something to hide and if they had something to hide, then it seems to me it must have been discreditable.**
>
> **In the second place the medical evidence was overwhelming, that with three lesions of the brain of this sort, Mr Biko must have had a period of unconsciousness. Now I believe that is fairly well established but they've never mentioned it and if, of course, he was unconscious they must have known the exact point at which the injury was sustained. There was no meaningful enquiry by the police, as I've said, which seemed to me a reluctance to uncover the truth**

and it seemed to me, moreover, that the whole pattern of the way in which Mr Biko was treated was consistent with the recognised form of conditioning a man for interrogation, and it doesn't seem to me that one can wholly exclude against the total background the possibility that part of the conditioning was to cause him some hurt, and unfortunately this hurt, I believe, went too far and resulted in his death.

McLagan: You also believe that if Mr Biko, after being injured, had been handed over to doctors or to a hospital, that he might still be alive today.

Napley: Up to a point, the medical evidence was very clear on that. The medical showed that it was possible to have done something for him if the real condition had been diagnosed and treated within the first six hours, which the head of the security police refused to permit. After that the complications which developed according to the medical evidence were irreversible.

Today's coverage also highlighted how South Africa was changing. On 18 May 1987, the BBC's Southern Africa correspondent Graham Leach reported from the Johannesburg area of Hillbrow, 'a previously whites-only zone where thousands of non-whites have crept in' – something they did in defiance of the country's Group Areas Act. 'There is quite a lot of harmony in Hillbrow,' one Indian businessman told Leach. But when Leach visited what he described as one of the area's remaining 'bastions of white resistance to desegregation', he found that the old ways were dying hard. Here, a different logic prevailed, summed up by one resident:

Soweto, the black township, doesn't have a white problem; I don't see why we should have a black problem. You will find that where the integration is at its greatest, OK, your racial tensions will be at [their] highest, and where segregation... I like to call it apartheid... where that's at its strongest you'll find that the race relations will be at [their] best. And this is because separation of the races, in fact, is a natural thing, it's not an immoral or unnatural thing, it's a perfectly natural thing.

Leach had gone to Hillbrow to report on the government's decision to reconsider the Group Areas Act, which dictated separate living areas for whites, blacks and 'coloureds'. As the local MP for Hillbrow, Alf Widman, from the opposition Progressive Federal Party, told him on 18 May 1987: 'There is an element of people... they haven't really gone through the race barrier, which I think they must go through, because the whole country is going through an evolutionary period of change.'

Nothing, however, could be taken for granted. For one thing, the National Party stormed back into power in the 1987 election; Widman, for one, lost his seat (to a candidate later jailed for electoral fraud).

Two years later the regular *Today* presenter Brian Redhead interviewed Con Botha, South Africa's information minister. It was the morning after Margaret Thatcher had made a speech in Zimbabwe about the future of South Africa. He reported, '"In South Africa, the world must be ready to respond to genuine change," said Mrs Thatcher, speaking in Zimbabwe last night, but is South Africa itself ready to respond? On the line from Pretoria is Con Botha, who is the chief director of the information service of the ruling National Party. Mr Botha, thank you for joining us. Would you be ready, or would South Africa be ready, to talk about dismantling apartheid?'

> **Botha: Yes, I think South Africa has been ready to talk about dismantling apartheid for some time. You know, in the, in the last decade no few... fewer than about a hundred apartheid laws have been abolished, have been amended or abolished.**

> **Redhead: Now, to whom would you now be prepared to talk? The ANC [African National Congress], the frontline states, Mrs Thatcher?**

> **Botha: We have, we have been trying for the last few years to, to arrange a conference, mainly of black internal leaders and recently there have been quite encouraging signs. The first is the fact that quite a number of the national states leaders are now prepared to come to the conference table, I'm referring in particular to Chief Buthelezi's recent discussions with government leaders [the Zulu leader Ngosi Buthelzi was the president of the Inkatha Freedom Party], secondly there is also the newly elected, quite a large number of local authorities, city councillors in the black towns and townships, and thirdly there is also the very recent pressure brought to bear upon the ANC from the Russian side to encourage them to lay down their arms and to come to the conference table. The South African government has been open about this that it will speak to the ANC, but only once it's renounced its violence. But anyhow...**

> **Redhead: Renounce or just suspend its violence?**

> **Botha: No, no, ah, we believe that you can only be a partner to a negotiating conference if you renounce violence.**

> **Redhead: Would you also wish to release Nelson Mandela as part of the conditions for talks?**

Botha: I do not think you can separate the question of ANC's renunciation of violence and Mr Mandela's position. One must remember that Mr. Mandela is the leader, he is one of the life leaders of the ANC, he is consequently bound by their violence option and, eh, if they should renounce violence I think the same should hold true for him and that is the only precondition this government has set for the release of Mr Mandela.

Nelson Mandela was finally released on 2 February 1990. Four years later South Africa held its first ever election based on a universal franchise. *Today*'s Sue MacGregor, who had grown up in South Africa, broadcast a week of special reports in the run-up to the campaign, and for one of them she returned to her old school in the Cape Town suburb of Claremont. 'Miss Wilkinson's history class is quite unrecognisable from the ones I used to sit in,' she reported. 'For a start South African history no longer begins with the arrival of the white man... And what's more the white girls are now learning to speak Xhosa, the language of Nelson Mandela and most of the black people of the Cape.'

Herschel Girls School was founded as an Anglican private school in the 1920s, and when Sue MacGregor had been a pupil it was whites-only; now it was multiracial. Her report continued: 'Karina and Christine came to the school from Afrikaans-speaking backgrounds – from the culture of the oppressor.'

Karina: Since I came to Herschel, here I've actually realised, I've often felt embarrassed to be Afrikaans. I actually just wanted to hide it. I was so embarrassed I didn't... I was scared my friends would look at me and say... All of you know it's all your fault.

Christine: It was so interesting to hear their point of view because they've been suffering through the years. And I felt so bad as a white Afrikaner.

John Humphrys, who served as a correspondent in South Africa in the 1970s, returned as a *Today* presenter for the elections themselves. 'Here in South Africa,' he announced on 27 April 1994, 'Nelson Mandela, the man who more than any other in the history of this country made it possible, has cast his vote.' Then, turning to Fergal Keane, the BBC's Southern Africa correspondent at the time, who was 'on the line now from Soweto', Humphrys asked: 'What's it like?'

Keane: Absolutely unbelievable, John. Yesterday morning at this time, you and I were looking at a few hundred people, old people, sick people, at a church near where I'm standing now in Soweto. Well, I can tell you, this morning there are thousands of people. The queue stretches for well over a mile, on into the distance under the bright morning sun here. You can hear in the background the sound of some drums. There are Buddhist monks who've come here to pray for peace

and reconciliation in South Africa. All in all, a very jolly atmosphere in Orlando West. Of course, it's significant, I've just been listening to Nelson Mandela there. This, of course, is his home area in Orlando West, the place where he spent much of his life before he was sent to prison, because of his activities in the ANC.

Humphrys: He talked about South Africa moving from an era of pessimism into a new era of hope and reconciliation, and certainly, looking around yesterday and today and looking at people it doesn't seem that he's overstating things. Obviously, one knows the enormous problems that face this country, but there is that sense of new hope, isn't there?

Keane: There is. I mean, it's a question of… of looking at two things. Yes, there are problems, yes, violence is endemic in many areas, yes, there are people who want to disrupt this process, but the overwhelming majority of South Africans, black and white, want to move forward. They want to get away from the tainting and from the guilt of the apartheid era, and I think they're doing that today. As I'm talking to you now, crowds of people are moving, quite slowly, through the gates here of the Holy Cross Anglican Church and with their steps, with every step every single person here takes, it's one step further away from apartheid.

Segregation and civil rights in the American South

'I hope that nothing happens to her personal safety'
GEORGE WALLACE, 13 JUNE 1963

On 11 June 1963, Governor George Wallace of Alabama stood in the doorway of the University of Alabama's Foster Auditorium. He had no interest in entering the building. His objective, rather, was to keep people out – people who, in his eyes, would undermine the right of his state's institutions to determine their own policies and decide their own actions. Two days later *Today* broadcast a revealing interview, recorded for the Canadian national broadcaster CBC, in which he tried to explain himself.

Wallace knew on 11 June that he had no hope of success, but that was not the point. It was an act of theatre, a gesture of grand symbolism. In one sense, the situation from which his actions arose was parochial – a disagreement over university enrolment in Tuscaloosa. But in truth those events marked another milestone in the long journey of African-Americans to achieve their civil rights after slavery – and to enjoy those rights that, in theory at least, they had already won.

Nor was it solely a significant day in terms of race relations: it was, simultaneously, another chapter in the equally long struggle over who governed the United States itself – a battle between those who stressed 'state's rights' and those who emphasised the role of Washington, D.C., the federal government and the US president. So, on that June day, a century on from the American Civil War, the eyes of America were firmly focused on Tuscaloosa.

At the heart of the issue was the segregation of white and black, or, in the terminology of the time, between white and Negro. After a landmark 1954 decision by the US Supreme Court in *Brown v. Board of Education Topeka*, institutions across the United States were required to stop discriminating on the basis of race and colour, but the practice remained deeply embedded. Nevertheless, the tide was turning. The first eruption of popular black protest in Alabama came in December 1955, following the now-famous refusal of Rosa Parks to leave a whites-only section of a bus in Montgomery. Her subsequent imprisonment not only prompted a year-long boycott of Montgomery's buses by the local African-American community, but also infused the civil rights movement with new life and urgency – and brought to prominence the charismatic preacher Martin Luther King, Jr, as its leading light.

Seven years later, in 1962, George Wallace was elected as Alabama's governor in an election that arrived, as his interviewer put it, '30 minutes or 30 seconds before midnight and this has come to mean something in a symbolic sense in Alabama'. In trying to explain the meaning of that expression, Wallace said in the interview broadcast on *Today*:

> **I reckon they meant... that I will stand on the principles that have been enunciated, and many people do feel that it is getting late, in so far as individual liberties and freedoms are concerned in this country.**

Put another way, Wallace had been voted in to stop the desegregation 'rot', as he saw it. As he had been elected governor by campaigning under the slogan 'Segregation now! Segregation tomorrow! Segregation forever!', he now felt he had a mandate to deliver on that promise.

Wallace was a Democratic Party politician (this was an era in which the Republican Party was anathema to many Southerners, identified as it was at that time with the legacy of Lincoln, the humiliation of defeat during the Civil War at the hands of Yankees, and the subsequent dominance of an urban, industrial North). Even though the Democrats held the White House, the president was Wallace's nemesis: a fellow Democrat but one of a very different hue. President John F Kennedy's New England urbanity, liberal social attitudes and Roman Catholicism represented a very different America – one from which Wallace recoiled. The battle lines between the two politicians had been drawn from the start, but the catalyst for their very public clash became the determination of two African-Americans to enrol in the University of Alabama, an institution that had always found ways of excluding African-Americans before.

But, on 11 June 1963, these two African-American students, Vivian Malone Jones and James Hood, who had been emboldened by orders issued by a federal district judge to end segregation, turned up at the university to register for classes. In so doing, they hoped, almost literally, to force open the doors to desegregation. Yet as they attempted to make history, making his 'stand in the schoolhouse door', as history recorded it, was Wallace, to 'denounce and forbid' not only their entry, but also the federal government's actions in granting them the right to enter.

Facing him off to demand entry for the students was no less a figure than the US deputy attorney general, Nicholas Katzenbach, who was on the scene to convey judicial and presidential authority. There was the potential for confrontation between Alabama's defenders and the federal enforcers, but Kennedy neatly sidestepped this by issuing a Presidential Executive Order, which authorised his secretary of defense to 'take all appropriate steps to remove obstructions of justice in the State of Alabama'. Cleverly, this measure passed control of the Alabama National Guard from the governor to the federal authorities, with the result that it was the reluctant National Guard commander, General Henry Graham, who eventually had to tell Wallace, 'Sir, it is my sad duty to ask you to step aside.' Wallace did, having made his speech. The two students were able to complete their enrolment, while Wallace could satisfy himself and his supporters that he had made a very public stand.

In Wallace's subsequent interview, broadcast on *Today* on 13 June, he framed the whole episode as yet another example of the president's and the federal courts' assault on freedom. Looking ahead to 'next year's re-election', i.e. the 1964 presidential election, he conjured a dystopian picture of a looming police state:

> I cannot tell you what President Kennedy [or] the Justice Department will do, I cannot tell you whether they are laying the predicate [groundwork] for the purpose of trying to jail people who oppose them in next year's re-election or not. That's a question that they will have to answer.

As for Vivian Malone Jones, Wallace regarded her actions as an unnecessary provocation, believing her to be:

> ...a pawn in this movement, that she herself is not coming to the University of Alabama for the purpose of acquiring an education, because she could get just as good an education in many schools that are exclusively for her race, but she is a pawn in the hand of the NAACP [National Association for the Advancement of Colored People] and the group of people who want to create a condition that might not be inducive to order.

He denied that he had any 'malice toward her', yet he immediately raised the question of her security while at the university, hoping 'that nothing happens to her personal safety, because I don't think that would be good and I don't think the people of this state want anything to happen to her personal safety'. It might have been a warning for Malone Jones, or a warning-off to the more eager of his own supporters – or both.

More generally in the interview, Wallace flew the flag for Southern segregation:

> I feel that, when the federal courts tell people that you cannot have a swimming pool in this city of Montgomery unless the two races swim together, which they're doing, that they are curtailing my freedoms, because I feel that swimming pools should be segregated and that white children should swim in white pools and vice versa...They're now telling you who you can serve in your business. Private businesses ought to have the right to serve who they want to serve.

In his view, the real enemy of freedom was the civil rights movement, which was working to remove the choices of individuals to deal, if they wished to, only with their own race.

In order to understand the man in his time, one must appreciate the strange equation of segregation and freedom in the history of the Southern states. This in itself was a legacy of the philosophical acrobatics of the Founding Fathers, who had simultaneously espoused liberty and condoned slavery.

The next year, Wallace had even more reason to decry the times, as US legislators enacted the Civil Rights Act to make segregation and racial discrimination illegal. In 1965 his vision of America received another blow when, in part prompted by race-related violence and protest in his own state of Alabama, Congress approved the Voting Rights Act. In this piece of legislation, which President Lyndon B Johnson signed into law on 6 August 1965, Congress sought to demolish the array of qualifications and tests (such as literacy tests) that Southern states were using to disenfranchise African-Americans, who were generally poorer and less well educated than their white neighbours.

The story was covered for *Today* by the BBC's Washington correspondent, Charles Wheeler, who had already made his name reporting from Berlin during the early 1950s and was one of the BBC's greatest foreign correspondents. A few days after the Voting Rights Act was signed, Wheeler was in deepest Mississippi, in Madison County, to find out what registering to vote for the first time meant to African-Americans.

He found it an 'unspectacular and strangely gratifying' scene of calmness – neither cheering crowds of new voters nor counter-demonstrations by opponents, but rather a scene of people quietly yet determinedly exercising their new rights. They were, in his view, 'confounding the sceptics' who believed that inertia would win the day and that the typical African-American was 'too intimidated to use his rights when he finally gets them'.

'The striking thing about this first day of unfettered voting rights,' Wheeler explained to *Today*'s listeners on 11 August 1965:

> ... has been the type of Negro at the front of the queue to register as an elector. Everybody expected to see the young, the militant; [for] the marchers and the picketers to lead the way. But in Mississippi, at least, the pace is being set by the old, the very poor, the illiterate; by the 'oh-so-law-abiding', easily trampled upon, older generation that has been the despair of the activist in the Negro cause.

The first man to register to vote was an illiterate 76-year-old cotton-picker and First World War veteran, whose previous attempts had been rebuffed by the local county officials until he became too afraid to try again. But now the registration offices were no longer under state control, Wheeler described how:

> Today he had no reason to be scared. Being illiterate was suddenly no longer a barrier, neither was the colour of his skin. He couldn't write, so the federal man

filled out the form for him. 'You don't need to sign your name if you can't,' the official said. 'Just make a mark here.'

Charles Wheeler concluded his report with some striking statistics:

> By closing time, nearly 300 more had been registered. This was in Madison County, where, 24 hours ago, 218 Negroes had the vote out of an adult Negro population of 10,366: 2 per cent.

Though it was a watershed moment, African-Americans faced plenty of challenges in the decades that followed. Many would argue that large numbers of African-Americans still represent an underclass, over-represented in the prison system, welfare system and army ranks, and under-represented in the universities, middle-class professions and well-to-do suburbs. But in 2008, voters, including enfranchised African-Americans in their millions, elected Barack Obama as US president – a sign that dark skin was not an impediment even to the highest office.

From his Alabama powerbase in earlier decades, George Wallace, too, had tried to project his influence nationally and run for president, both as an independent and in the Democratic primaries. But his hopes – slim though they were – were ended by an assassination attempt in 1972, which left him wheelchair-bound. In the 1980s, he was again elected governor of Alabama, but the times were changing – and so were Wallace's attitudes on race. By the end of his life, in 1998, he had come to regard his adherence to segregation as a mistake.

Of the two African-American students who had registered at the University of Alabama on that oppressively hot day in June 1963, James Hood did not stay long. Finding the stresses of his situation intolerable, he left the university after only a few months and headed north to study in Detroit. Vivian Malone Jones, however, became the University of Alabama's first African-American graduate, taking a degree in business administration. She went on to work for federal government departments and agencies. In 1995, the ageing George Wallace presented the Lurleen B Wallace Award for Courage (an accolade named after his wife) to this woman, whose journey he had, more than 30 years before, tried to stop.

And he told her that he had been wrong.

Diplomacy in tatters during the Iranian Revolution

'A couple of chaps armed with rifles, breaking their way in'

ARTHUR WYATT, 6 NOVEMBER 1979

It is an accepted principle in international relations that a nation's embassy in a foreign land is sacrosanct. It is a little piece of the home country implanted abroad, and to step into it is to step onto that home country's soil. The principle was codified in the 1961 Vienna Convention on Diplomatic Relations, and it extends to the inviolability of the men and women who work in embassies across the world.

But it is fragile – as the United States was reminded in 1975, when television pictures of frantic helicopter evacuations from the roof of its embassy in Saigon signalled to the world who had really won and who had lost the Vietnam War.

Three years later, in another part of the world, diplomatic crises erupted again, and this time affecting not just the United States. The location on this occasion was Iran, where the repressive regime of its shah, Mohammad Reza Pahlavi, was in the process of imploding in the face of revolutionary protest from across the political spectrum, from Communists to Islamists. By November 1978, opposition parties under the banner of the Iranian National Front were issuing a joint statement with the exiled dissident cleric Ayatollah Khomeini – who was then living in Paris – demanding the shah's deposition or abdication.

A particular demand from the revolutionaries was, as *Today*'s Hugh Sykes was told, 'freedom and independence from foreign dominance'. Interviewing Mr Taqizadeh, the London spokesman for the Iranian National Front, on 5 November 1978, Sykes explored what that really meant.

Sykes: You mentioned foreign dominance and the shah in the same sentence – do you connect the two?

Taqizadeh: Yes, the two are very much related. The shah, in our opinion, is the symbol of foreign dominance. He is there to protect the interest of foreign powers: America, Britain and Russia... We would like to see a government who is against foreign influence. We would like a government who values our Islamic

culture and a government who is for freedom and independence from foreign influence.

At issue was not just the shah's Westernising agenda and international backers, but Iranian resentment of what they saw as quasi-colonial control: an acquiescent ruler who safeguarded foreign-owned interests, notably the country's oil and petroleum assets. Indeed, a quarter of a century before, Britain and the United States, in the shape of the CIA, had both restored the shah to the throne, from which he had been temporarily toppled, and overthrown his disruptive prime minister, who had nationalised the oil industry. Since then, real control of the Iranian oil industry continued to remain beyond the government's hands. Come 1978, getting rid of the shah seemed, to many Iranians, indistinguishable from a fight against British and particularly American commercial and political interests.

In Iran, events moved rapidly. Unable to quell rebellion, the ailing shah and his family fled to the United States in January 1979, while, in February, Khomeini returned to a country that was transforming itself into a revolutionary theocracy. It helped to galvanise the evolving regime's credentials to foster popular hostility against the United States and Britain. And it was at this moment that diplomatic niceties fell by the wayside.

On 6 November 1979, Douglas Hurd, then a minister of state at the Foreign Office, had to tell the House of Commons:

> **At about ten minutes to six yesterday evening, Tehran time, armed intruders broke into the British embassy compound and shortly thereafter took over the whole of our embassy building. The staff in the area at the time were taken, together with those wives and children who live in the embassy compound, to the house of the chargé d'affaires [the head of the British diplomatic mission in Iran, in the absence of the ambassador], Mr Wyatt. They were not ill-treated, but were held under armed guard. The identity of the intruders and the motives for their attack on the embassy are still not wholly clear. Contacts between embassy officials and the intruders took place over a period of about five hours, after which they withdrew from the premises.**

That same morning, *Today* was in direct contact with the chargé d'affaires himself. Arthur Wyatt spoke to Mike Donkin, a newly appointed *Today* reporter, and gave him a vivid account of what had occurred:

> **There was a sudden chanting outside. We looked out of the windows and saw people climbing over the walls of the compound. Those who were present in the embassy stationed themselves on the top floor and within a very short time we heard sounds of breaking glass. We subsequently discovered that this was a couple of chaps armed with rifles, breaking their way in on the first floor.**

Donkin asked him, 'Had you taken any precautions after the attack on the American embassy? Did you try and resist at all?' He was referring to the forcible occupation of the US embassy on 4 November. Wyatt replied:

> **We certainly gave no physical resistance; this is not our policy. We had taken considerable precautions earlier in the day in the light of the occupation of the US embassy and of various public statements that have been made here. We had, in fact, also received a couple of telephone calls on the previous evening, following the occupation of the American embassy, saying that we were next on the list.**

In the House of Commons, Hurd continued, 'If there be a government, calling themselves a government, in Tehran, one of their clear duties under international law is to protect the diplomats accredited to them', prompting Labour MP Tam Dalyell to wonder, 'Given the increasing vulnerability of embassies of all countries throughout the world, is there not a case for international discussion of the updating of the Vienna Convention?' Hurd agreed, but found there was an inescapable conclusion:

> **Our embassies and those of other countries are increasingly at risk. Two of our ambassadors have been murdered in the past few years. But however hard one considers the matter one is driven back to the conclusion that, although we can secure embassies against an individual intruder, there is no escaping the fact that when an armed mob appears the responsibility for protecting an embassy must rest on the host government. However we look at the problem, that is the answer that we are forced back to.**

In fact, Britain, which came to be pilloried by Iranian protesters as 'Little Satan', in contrast with the 'Great Satan' of the United States, had come off relatively unscathed on this occasion. By contrast, the violation of the US embassy in Tehran, to which both *Today*'s Mike Donkin and the chargé d'affaires had alluded, was much more grievous. Revolutionary supporters, whom the media tended to call 'students', had invaded the embassy, taken hostages, and clearly had no intention of leaving.

The BBC's Middle East correspondent Tim Llewellyn reported for *Today* from the US embassy in Tehran during the siege. He sent this despatch on its twelfth day:

> **Just inside the iron gates, padlocked, covered with posters celebrating Ayatollah Khomeini, condemning the American government and condemning Jimmy Carter, but not – as the posters point out – condemning the American nation, inside those gates, [are] armed guards and, bizarrely, a young girl dressed in the full Islamic costume, a chador, a veil over her face, talking on a two-way radio to headquarters, wherever that may be. Outside the gates, [there are]**

armed revolutionary guards in their combat fatigues, unloading and reloading their M16 American-made rifles. [There are] crowds of curious onlookers and, meanwhile, piles and piles of sandbags being made ready just in case. It's going to be a very, very long siege indeed, by all indications. The students inside are determined to hang on and only Ayatollah Khomeini can give the word to release those hostages. Meanwhile, outside in the long avenue which runs alongside the American embassy, there are constant marches, constant movement, hundreds of people, some workers, some students, some just ordinary people many of them dressed in ordinary office clothes, marching up and down and chanting their slogans, continually all day.

[Shouts of Allahu Akbar (God is Great)]

A revolutionary leader stands on the wall of the embassy, addressing the crowd and the chants come back. I don't think there's any element of 'rent-a-crowd' in this. There's nothing they like in the Middle East better than a good demonstration. But there's nothing the Iranians like better than a demonstration to show their solidarity and against the Americans. These people are convinced that they have the Americans on the run now, that they are in charge, it's they who are twisting the American tail and not the other way round. There's a great feeling of relaxation here, there's no worries about any reprisals from the Americans, there's no worries about what the Americans do. The Iranians feel genuinely that they have the reins in their hands.

Two weeks later, though, on 19 November 1979, *Today* was able to inform its listeners of the first releases. Hugh Sykes, who had joined the programme the previous year, had spent time in Tehran as a child and was fascinated by the story; he did so much phone-bashing to the Iranian capital that he can still recite the city code from memory (009821). That morning he was doing a presenting shift alongside Libby Purves.

Sykes: The three hostages freed so far were put on an SAS plane in Tehran at about quarter past ten this morning, local time (quarter to seven here in Britain). The blacks are marines, the girl, a 22-year-old secretary, Kathy Gross, who's been in Iran for only a month. Last night, still a prisoner at the embassy, she took part in a press conference.

Gross: Our conditions here have been very good. We haven't had any problems, we've been fed more than fairly, we've slept nights, we haven't had any problems physically. Maybe, people have been mentally upset, but other than that we haven't had any problems.

> Sykes: In spite of the fact that she'd had to sit 16 hours every day with her hands tied, but all the same she was looking animated and cheerful, holding a microphone rather like a speaker at a rally in Hyde Park. This morning, at Tehran airport, she was just as happy.

> Gross: I'm glad to get out of here [laughs]. I really didn't expect to leave the country, it was sort of a surprise to me, but I'm glad to be out of the whole situation.

Kathy Gross told an American reporter that she thought she'd 'be living in that house forever. Not dying necessarily, but living there forever, because they gave us no signs of any hope of being released at all until yesterday afternoon'.

But *Today* also reported more ominous news: Ayatollah Khomeini's stark warnings at a press conference that, unless the shah was sent back to Iran, the remaining hostages could be tried for espionage and subjected to the 'verdict of the court'.

'Which could be death?' a reporter asked. The response was mumbled, prompting Sykes to remark, 'Hard to hear, but that reply, I think, was, "That cannot be prophesied."'

On 3 December 1979, Sykes was bringing *Today* listeners up to date on the situation. Jerry Plotkin, a businessman from New York who had 'happened to be in the embassy when it was occupied', had been allowed to send out a recorded message. It was partly to reassure his family that he was well and that his captors were considerate, but it also carried a clear message from those captors. As Sykes explained:

> He said that, in spite of the language barrier, they'd managed to establish some rapport with their captors, that he was most impressed by their determination and dedication to see this matter through, that they believed in their cause, wanted the shah returned and would settle for nothing less. Part of his message was addressed to the American people as a whole. In it Jerry Plotkin said that the shah had brutally murdered and tortured tens of thousands of his people. He concluded with this direct appeal to President Carter: 'In the name of God, return the shah and free the hostages. Let the world know that no tyrant or dictator can ever find safe harbour in the United States.'

The United States international prestige was especially badly damaged by a catastrophic rescue attempt by US special forces in April 1980. The mission was aborted in the Iranian desert, and in the ensuing chaos a helicopter hit a transport plane, killing eight servicemen. The news broke in the early hours in Washington – so just after the *Today* programme went on the air in London on the morning of 25 April 1980. Brian Redhead was presenting, and he went straight to an interview with the BBC's Washington correspondent, Clive Small, who been woken after midnight by a call from the White House.

Redhead: The time now is eighteen minutes past seven. We hear there are new and dramatic developments in the Iranian crisis and Clive Small, I think, is on the line now from Washington. Clive, good morning.

Small: Good morning.

Redhead: Now what has happened?

Small: I've just had a phone call from the White House and they've read me a statement that they've just issued. It reads as follows – I won't go right through it – but what it amounts to is this, that the United States has attempted a rescue mission to get its hostages out of Iran. That mission has failed. The reasons given are these: that the first part of the mission was an attempt to prepare for the rescue. The mission was terminated, as the White House puts it, because of the equipment failure. During the subsequent withdrawal of American personnel on this mission, there was a collision between two aircraft on the ground at a remote desert location in Iran. There were no military hostilities – that's the word from the White House – but the president deeply regrets that eight American crew members of the mission, of the two aircraft involved that is, were killed and two others were injured in the accident.

The crisis dogged Jimmy Carter's presidency and divided his administration. In addition, according to the US State Department's official historian, 'The Soviet Union took advantage of America's weakness to win strategic advantage for itself'; this was, after all, the Cold War. Fifty-two US embassy hostages remained in captivity for well over a year, until 20 January 1981, when they were released after a deal was brokered by Algeria. It was the day of Ronald Reagan's inauguration as president; Carter's hopes of re-election in 1980 had been fatally undermined.

And in an unexpected twist to the Iranian saga, violence visited London's diplomatic quarter just a week after the calamitous US rescue attempt. On 30 April 1980, regional separatists backing an Arab insurgency in Iran's Khuzestan province took control of the Iranian embassy in the British capital. They demanded a prisoner-release in Iran and, in London, free passage for themselves, a request refused by Margaret Thatcher's government. On 5 May Abbas Lavasani, the embassy's press officer, was killed and his body was dumped out of the front door. Shortly before 7.30pm, in extraordinary scenes relayed on live television by the assembled news cameras, SAS servicemen stormed the building, killing all but one of the hostage-takers and rescuing most of the hostages unharmed.

One ex-hostage, who had been released earlier on medical grounds, was in fact a BBC producer. Chris Cramer (who rose to be the head of the BBC's news-gathering operation and later ran CNN International) had been in the Iranian embassy trying to get a visa when the hostage-takers struck. During the evening of 5 May 1980, he spoke to John Timpson at some length for a *Today* special. Cramer described how it had all begun:

> There was a massive commotion at the door; the policeman on the door was struggling with a man who had a gun. I beat it into the waiting room. There were several shots fired, a smashing of glass. I tried to get out of the window, but the window was one of those up-and-down ones and wouldn't move. There were two or three other people in the waiting room and I suggested we should all stick our hands up, which is what we did.

Asked by Timpson to describe the other hostages, Cramer recounted his conversation with the policeman who had been stationed on the door, Trevor Lock, who was a member of the diplomatic protection squad and now a captive of the hostage-takers too:

> Well, I was sitting next to the policeman, who had blood running down his face, and the gunmen allowed me to get a tissue and some water and I tried to bathe his face. And I said to him, 'Tough luck they got your gun,' and he said, 'They haven't got my gun, I've still got it.' I said, 'Well, I'm sorry but I just don't believe that,' and he said, 'It's under my coat, why'd you think I'm sat here with my arms crossed?' I said, 'Look, I don't want to appear morbid, but if something happens I want to know how to use it,' and he said, 'Right, it's in a holster, it's under my jumper, you pull it out, it's got no safety catch on it, and you fire it. What I'm telling you is, you can't possibly take out more than one or two and there's no way we're going to try it for a while.'

Trevor Lock was awarded the George Cross for his cool head and his valour.

Cramer also described how, accidentally, the captives had at one point facilitated a brief conversation between him and Scotland Yard, and then John Timpson asked him for clarification on an important issue: 'Just to clear up the point that you raised about the number of the gunmen, how many actually were there? Is five the correct figure?' Cramer's response was: '...I saw five and their faces will remain with me for a long time.' In fact, five hostage-takers were killed and one was captured and sentenced to life imprisonment. The British government could claim to have upheld the Vienna Convention, discharging its duties as a host nation in protecting the integrity of a foreign embassy.

As for the British presence in Tehran, by September 1980 the embassy was closed, the number of Britons in Iran had dwindled to an estimated 90, and the sole remaining British diplomat, the stoic Edmond Barrett, was in effect renting space in the Swedish embassy, as he described to *Today*'s Paul Burden on 11 September 1980:

Barrett: It's now part of the Swedish embassy, it's [housed in] the British Interest Section of the Swedish embassy. We now have the Swedish flag flying from the building, and we have a plaque on the gate to the effect, showing that this is now the Royal Swedish Embassy British Interest Section.

Burden: If you're working in the British Interest Section of the Swedish embassy, what does that make you?

Barrett: Well, it still makes me a British subject and I'm working under the direction, and to, the Swedish ambassador…

Burden: … Did you feel any apprehension, at all, about taking up this job?

Barrett: Well, I think inevitably one… one does speculate on what might happen if things went wrong, but it's all the same if one, you know, speculated about being knocked down crossing [the road] in a mass of traffic.

The British embassy in Tehran did not reopen until 1988 – though that was not to be the end of anti-British protests outside, and sometimes within, its grounds.

In 2012, as Ben Affleck's film *Argo* reignited interest in the US diplomats' plight in 1979, the reflections of Arthur Wyatt, the former British chargé d'affaires, were widely quoted in the media. When brute force confronted protocol, there could really only be one winner:

The revolutionary regime ignored all the rules of diplomatic protection and the Vienna Convention. When they overran our embassy too, I said to one of them, 'You can't do this; we're diplomats.' He just waved his machine pistol around and replied, '*This* is what matters.'

The miners' strike, 1984–5

'One of the political events that had defined the era'
JAMES NAUGHTIE, 5 MARCH 2009

In a small town in North Yorkshire, on 18 December 2015, part of Britain's long industrial revolution finally burnt out.

On this day, men worked the last-ever shift at the country's last deep coal mine, at Kellingley, and when it was over so was a 200-year-old mining tradition. The moment brought grief at the finality of it all, but no surprise. For more than a decade, the UK had imported more – and cheaper – coal than it had produced; in addition, polluting fossil fuels were now on the wrong side of both history and the battle against carbon-dioxide emissions.

With Kellingley's demise, the membership of the once-mighty National Union of Mineworkers (NUM) shrank to little more than a hundred people. This was the same trade union whose membership, three decades earlier, had numbered some 170,000. With that strength in numbers, in 1984–5 the NUM had staged a titanic year-long struggle to prevent a programme of pit closures, at a time when coal mining was still a nationalised industry and there were around 170 pits across the country.

As the *Today* archives make clear, this epic battle was never going to be just another industrial dispute, for there was too much at stake. Its historical importance was recognised even in its own time. It was variously regarded as a clash of cultures, a fight between past and present (and future), a confrontation between an ideological left and an ideological right, a battle over who really ruled the country, a struggle to preserve communities and an act of political vengeance by a political party whose previous government had been undermined by unions.

To complicate matters, there were more than two sides in the dispute. When the NUM leader, Arthur Scargill, refused to ballot members on strike action, the miners themselves split, between NUM strikers in regional strongholds such as Derbyshire, Yorkshire, Kent and South Wales, and the breakaway miners who rejected strike action and, in Nottinghamshire, went on to form their own Union of Democratic Mineworkers. Opposing the strikers were their employer, the National Coal Board (NCB), and its ultimate master, the Conservative government of Margaret Thatcher. On the frontlines, there were pickets and 'flying pickets' – the mobile strikers who spread the action to other, working pits, coking plants and steelworks – and many thousands of police. Caught in between the pickets and police were miners who broke the picket lines to return to work, and who became pariah 'scabs' to those on strike. Friendships and families were shattered, some irrevocably.

It began on 6 March 1984 with the announcement by the National Coal Board's recently appointed chairman, Ian MacGregor, that 20 pits would close and 20,000 jobs would go. Miners at the first one on the list, Cortonwood in South Yorkshire, immediately stopped work, feeling that promises to them had been broken. Scargill would consistently claim, as he did to *Today*'s presenter Brian Redhead on 15 June 1984, that the NCB's real agenda was much larger.

Ian MacGregor had appeared on the programme the previous day, and had told Brian Redhead that the closure of pits was a matter for regional negotiation.

> **Redhead:** ... you've been saying things like 70, he says 20, everyone knows that some eventually have to go 'cause pits have always got to be closed when they become unworkable. How are you going to get output to the level of the amount of coal you can sell unless you negotiate some kind of restructure of the industry?

> **Scargill:** Well, let me make three points: first of all the 70 pit closures that I have quoted is a direct quote from the previous chairman of the National Coal Board, Sir Norman Siddall, who made that statement in a meeting on the fourteenth of June and it's contained within official Coal Board minutes, when he says that they're going to take out of the industry 25 million tonnes of capacity and if you work that out on the basis of the number of pits involved it's about 70 pits with about 70,000 jobs on the line. Secondly, what we've said is that we want to see the plan for coal, which is an agreement signed between the government, the Coal Board and the unions, continue to operate and that agreement was re-emphasised only, ah, two-and-a-half years ago by the present administration. Now, that agreement provides for any assistance necessary to offset short-term market fluctuations and, I would have thought, producing the cheapest deep-mine coal in the world, that British miners were entitled to have the same sort of protection as other coal-producing nations who produce more expensive coal. And thirdly, and, I think, probably most important of all, it is not fair and it's totally unreasonable to say to people who've invested their very lives in this industry, such as people at Cortonwood colliery and Polmaise colliery, that one week they can be told they've got about 25 or 30 years, or, in the case of Cortonwood, five or ten years life, and, in fact, at Cortonwood to transfer some people from a closing pit to that pit, and one week later tell them that it's going to be closed – that is not the way that you deal with human beings.

Scargill's interview momentum was almost unstoppable once he got into his stride – even by experienced professionals like Redhead. His claims were widely dismissed as scaremongering, but Cabinet papers made public in 2014 confirmed that in private meetings at No. 10 Downing Street in 1983, MacGregor 'had it in mind' to close 75 pits over three years, with the loss of 64,000 jobs, but to reveal the closures piecemeal.

Another consistent claim by Scargill was that the government was always pulling the strings, and that the NCB was unable truly to negotiate independently from government directives. Here's how Scargill explained the failure of recent talks in the same interview:

> ...the fact of life is that Mr MacGregor sits down and appears to be a very, er, amiable person at one meeting and then suddenly blows his top at the next meeting. It may surprise you to know that on two occasions during our meetings, once in Edinburgh, once in North Yorkshire, the National Coal Board intimated to us that they were willing to withdraw the pit closure programme and that was on the basis of working out an arrangement in line with the plan for coal that they would ensure that there was a proper and reasonable development programme [which would] take place within the industry. Now, we went away and we produced a document towards that end, which we thought was a basis for negotiation. Astonishingly, Mr MacGregor, showing the same belligerence that he did towards you on the programme yesterday, came back, didn't want to talk and it was apparent to me and to my colleagues that he'd had his card marked by Mrs Thatcher.

At one point the parties seemed close to agreement, until it collapsed over an adjective: the NUM was content with the 'beneficial' management of pits, but rejected 'economic' management as code for pit closures.

Almost exactly a year after that first stoppage at Cortonwood, it was all over. Scargill had to tell the press, in front of stricken NUM members, that 'we have decided to go back to work for a whole range of reasons', having faced 'not an employer but a government aided and abetted by the judiciary, the police and you people in the media, and at the end of this time our people are suffering tremendous hardship'. Added to the bitterness was a sense that the suffering of diehard strikers had been for nothing.

In an illuminating 2009 retrospective for *Today*, James Naughtie, who was working for the *Guardian* at the time of the strike and joined the *Today* presenting team ten years later, reflected on what he described as 'one of the political events that had defined the era of Margaret Thatcher' and 'a struggle that divided communities, tested government, split the Labour Party [and] eventually emasculated the National Union of Mineworkers, which had once been the pride of the trade union movement'. He interviewed Norman Tebbit, who had been a central figure as employment secretary. From Tebbit's vantage point, the NUM was holed beneath the waterline by one of its early decisions:

He [Scargill] couldn't get a majority for a strike in his own union; he knew that, which is why he didn't have a ballot. And, of course, that was a fatal thing for his union. Also, partly because of that and partly because of the changes in the law which were coming into effect in employment law, he could not persuade any other union to take sympathetic action for him. And from that moment on, without a national ballot, without the full support of the miners... the strike was doomed to fail.

Failure to hold a ballot lost Scargill support, including from the Labour Party under its leader Neil Kinnock (the son of a miner), and gave his opponents a stick with which they could beat him. It is true that the NUM found itself largely alone. On that day of capitulation on 3 March 1985, Scargill saved a few stinging words for his 'fellow' trade unions: 'We have decided to go back to work for a whole range of reasons. One of the reasons is that the trade union movement of Britain, with a few notable exceptions, has left this union isolated.' Unlike in 1978–9, when a Labour government was beset from strikers on all sides during the Winter of Discontent (*see* page 124), the Conservative government of 1984 knew the shape of its antagonist. It had been able to prepare, too, gathering stockpiles of coal against the possibility of disruption in supply.

When Naughtie asked Lord Tebbit (who became a peer in 1992) if appointing MacGregor had been 'a mistake', on account of his being a 'famously abrasive figure who talked in black and white about the future of the industry' and whose appointment was a 'red rag to a bull', Tebbit would not be drawn, wondering instead, 'Who else would have been the alternative candidate?' By contrast, however, Tebbit repeated what had been a common refrain in 1984–5: that 'Scargill was perfectly unwilling to negotiate.'

Media coverage of the time dwelt on law and order. The strike prompted a massive and proactive national police operation, which mobilised thousands of officers away from other duties. Early on, a chief objective was to interrupt the controversial 'flying picketing' against power stations: after a court injunction in March 1984 declared the practice illegal, groups of miners on the move were intercepted by police. A bigger objective was enabling the still-working miners to get to and from pits. On 19 March 1984, the BBC's labour correspondent, Nicholas Jones, who followed the strike closely, picked up the theme on *Today*:

The biggest police operation was in Nottinghamshire, the scene of most of the violence last week. There were some clashes this morning and there were scuffles at the Hucknall pit, but the Nottinghamshire miners got to work without difficulty. Pickets had travelled to the Midlands from Yorkshire, South Wales and Kent, where the miners are on strike, but many of them were stopped on the way. In Lancashire there was considerable police activity, with officers turning back cars and coaches carrying pickets from Yorkshire. Some pickets from Kent were turned back at the Dartford Tunnel. The police operation was coordinated during the night from a special operations room at Scotland Yard.

President of the Association of Chief Police Officers David Hall, the man described by the BBC's Home Affairs correspondent Chris Underwood as 'masterminding the whole operation', chose the politic answer when asked if he had overseen a 'victory': 'I wouldn't use the word victory; we've maintained the law and order and that's our job.'

Unsurprisingly, Home Secretary Leon Brittan viewed the strike as a confrontation between striking miners and the police, and supported the latter absolutely, as he told the *Today* presenter Peter Hobday on 11 May 1984:

> There's absolutely no justification for any kind of violence at the pits or elsewhere and I am fully behind the police in clamping down on it, 'cause you see the sort of incidents that have occurred have been very nasty ones, indeed... What happened a couple of nights ago was that the police took into their possession a three-foot piece of wood with barbed wire attached, a metal pipe and other pieces of wood. That kind of thing has got to be taken seriously and the police have my full support for doing so.

When challenged by Hobday on whether the scale of the police operation was itself 'fairly provocative', Brittan rejected the idea as 'absurd' and declared:

> I think that very many people, who might otherwise be sympathetic to miners, are disgusted at events of this kind and the escalation of violence. You see, there was a time in the first part of the strike when injuries to the police were running at some 15 a week. They're now running [at] 25 a week – and that's just injuries to the police. Quite apart from acts of intimidation, such as marking with paint the homes of miners who've gone to work and damaging cars... there was a case, not so long ago, in which a loaded coal lorry was in an accident and it turned out that what [had] happened was that the wheel came off and all the wheel nuts had been loosened... This kind of very dangerous behaviour is something that has *got* to be taken seriously.
>
> ...
>
> When hundreds of people come to the picket line it is not to communicate or to persuade, it is to blockade, to obstruct and physically to prevent people going to work who want to do so. And I don't think anyone in this country is going to listen with any sympathy to somebody who says, 'Because I can't stop my fellow worker going to work, because the police [are] there to protect him, I'm now going to intimidate his family, I'm going to exert acts of violence, I'm going to

throw things.' And those are simple breaches of the criminal law, which would be breaches of the criminal law wherever they're committed.

The intimidation of the families of miners who worked through the strike – 'scabs', as they were known – left a legacy that endured. In April 1985, a month after the strike had ended, the BBC correspondent Stephen Cape reported for *Today* from the Hatfield Main colliery near Doncaster.

> **Cape: A short drive… to the town takes you past a bridge where the word 'scab' has been painted alongside the name of a working miner. To protect himself the man bought a shotgun. Others have been less resilient. One couple have decided to move because of intimidation.**
>
> **Anonymous wife: I've just been threatened in streets. 'Part from having his windows broken, my little boy, two-year-old, been spit on. Can't sleep on a night and I'm not eatin' properly. I'm on sleeping pills. I'm just terrified to go shopping. I don't take my little boy to nursery, 'cause I'm too frightened. I'm just frightened to go out, that's it.**
>
> **Cape: And there are the stories of violence and vandalism, but those working miners who want to stay in the community hope life will improve over the next few months. They may have misjudged the feelings against them. Miners' Union treasurer, Jim Moores.**
>
> **Moores: Treat like lepers, scabs, that's all they are.**

Over time, interpretations change, and that has certainly been the case with regard to the single most notorious confrontation between police and miners: what became known as the Battle of Orgreave on 18 June 1984. It involved mounted police and several thousand strikers in and around the South Yorkshire village of Orgreave and its coking works, and Scargill himself was injured. But what, at the time, was accepted as a straightforward narrative of a justifiable police reaction to a stone-throwing rabble soon began to unravel. The subsequent trials of miners charged with 'riot' started collapsing as counter-narratives emerged. Out-of-court settlements followed, and investigations discovered a series of concocted police witness statements.

Thirty-two years later, the home secretary, Amber Rudd, controversially decided against a public inquiry into what had really happened at Orgreave – not because the South Yorkshire police had behaved well, but because, in her words, 'I cannot see that that would be in the public interest, given the substantial policing changes that have taken place since 1984.'

Whatever the injustices at Orgreave, images of truculent miners spread across TV screens and newspapers and did nothing for the NUM's image. Journalists, including members of the *Today* team, were sometimes treated aggressively. The minutes of an internal BBC News meeting on the lessons of the strike noted that 'Radio staff are less conspicuous than those from television, and, therefore, physical attacks on radio reporters were less of a problem. But at one point Hugh Sykes, a *Today* reporter, was hung upside down over a bridge on the Leeds and Liverpool canal, near Wigan, and threatened with a dowsing.'

The nadir was an incident in December 1984, when two young South Wales strikers dropped a heavy piece of concrete from a road bridge in an attempt to stop escorted miners getting to work: a taxi driver was killed, and the two perpetrators were jailed for manslaughter. That same month, the Coal Board offered inducements for miners to return to work, and thousands did, many of them by now in dire straits financially. As 1984 rolled into 1985, the strike seemed more and more like a miners' civil war, between those desperate not to lose their jobs and those desperate not to become destitute from striking.

The question of policing led to the deeper question, much argued over, about whether the Conservative government 'brought on' the strike in order to defeat it visibly. Norman Tebbit was clear that there was an elemental struggle of sorts being played out, as he told James Naughtie for his 2009 retrospective. He recalled 'how high the stakes were in that strike':

> Ted Heath had been brought down, his Conservative government, by industrial action, by strikes; Jim Callaghan had been brought down by strikes as a Labour prime minister; and it was quite clear that Scargill was aiming to veto the actions of a Conservative government, if not to bring it down. And had that been allowed to happen, no prime minister, whether Labour or Conservative, would have been able to govern in the interests of the whole country.

Naughtie pressed Tebbit on whether the entire strike had in fact been manufactured for the government's own ends:

> It's often said on the union's side that you came into office in '79... and there had been a plan drawn up by your old colleague, the late Nicholas Ridley, to fight and win a strike because it was thought that at some point there would be a great test. And it is asserted, as a result of that, that there had always been a plan to do this, to goad someone into a strike which could then be won and effectively would smash the most powerful unions. How much truth is there in that?

Naughtie was alluding to a memo by Nicholas Ridley, who, among other points, had observed that a strike over pay had the potential to unite miners, whereas one over pit closures would sow division. Lord Tebbit sidestepped neatly:

I don't think anybody had to goad Mr Scargill into a strike; he was a self-goading strike machine. We did have to have a plan to withstand a strike if one should arise. It would have been irresponsible not to have done… not to have been prepared to deal with that sort of eventuality would have been stupid and irresponsible, and, as you will well recollect, Margaret Thatcher was neither stupid nor irresponsible.

According to Margaret Thatcher's official biographer, Charles Moore, the prime minister had, in 1979, declared to her first home secretary, William Whitelaw, her intention to 'have another' miners' strike, one that we'll win'.

Right at the beginning of the strike, the Reverend Nicholas Jowett, the vicar in the mining village of Brampton Bierlow, had told *Today* that the decision to close the nearby Cortonwood colliery was 'an act of violence to our community. A decision at five weeks' notice to end the thing that's given this community its life.'

The Women's Peace Camp at Greenham Common

'We will protest with our bodies'

LIZ FORDER, 9 NOVEMBER 1983

Historic England, the body once part of English Heritage, is concerned with the care and protection of many of the most ancient and revered sites in England – such as Stonehenge and Avebury, to name but two. And yet, in 2003, a cluster of very un-ancient and utilitarian buildings in West Berkshire, along with their perimeter fence, entered its roster of historic monuments.

The site in question was the Cruise Missile Shelter Complex at the former Greenham Common airbase, and while the official reasons for designation spoke of the strategic, historic and political significance of this missile technology, Historic England concluded their statement on a rather different note: 'The site has wider cultural significance in the late 20th century as the focus of mass protest against the nuclear arms race.' Long after the missiles themselves have disappeared, 'Greenham Common' continues to be synonymous with a particular phase in the decades-old Campaign for Nuclear Disarmament (CND); it became, specifically, a women's protest – and probably not since the heyday of the suffragettes had a collective women's protest movement been so assertive in Britain.

The background was the ramping up of the nuclear arms race and the increasingly bellicose atmosphere in US–Soviet relations. After 1979, both superpowers were locked in an indirect war in Afghanistan following the Soviet invasion, while, in March that year, fears of potential catastrophe from civilian nuclear power were stoked by an accident at the American facility at Three Mile Island.

Among those alarmed by the multifaceted nuclear threat were a small group in the Cardiff area who called themselves 'Women for Life on Earth'. They decided to shape their own form of protest. And so, in late summer 1981, they (and a handful of men) walked across into England to occupy some common land surrounding the Greenham Common airbase, near Newbury. In September, in a gesture which was to become a signature of their protest, 36 women chained themselves to the base fence.

The site was chosen because it was the principal UK site intended to accommodate new US nuclear weapons called 'ground-launched cruise missiles' (GLCMs). Their deployment, along with Pershing ground-based missiles in other European countries, was the US and NATO response to Soviet deployment of its own SS20 missile system. The prospect was of a Europe awash with nuclear weapons – and therefore the possibility of a Europe obliterated by those weapons in any future superpower confrontation. The new missiles would not be 'dual control' – so the United Kingdom had no veto over their use and it was theoretically possible that the United States could unilaterally launch them from British soil.

At Greenham, to the annoyance of both the Newbury District Council and the Ministry of Defence, the 40-odd original protesters grew and grew in number. In February 1982, they took a defining decision: this would be a women's peace camp – men would be able to visit by day, but not stay overnight, and some areas were exclusively for women. Notwithstanding filthy conditions, spartan facilities, inclement weather and official hostility, the camp burgeoned. But, as Jean Stead put it in the *Guardian*, 'Life was hard: no lavatories, no washing facilities, no shops, no proper shelter.' The protesters began by chaining themselves to fences, then began mounting blockades in May 1982 (prompting arrests), and two months later Newbury District Council managed to get an eviction order enforced. But protesters simply relocated to another area of the common land; as the camp spread, its various sectors were given colour names – Yellow Gate, Green Gate, Turquoise Gate and so on.

By now, Britain was distracted by the Falklands War, as were the news media, but the Women's Peace Camp was beginning to get wider attention from supporters and opponents alike. In October 1982, Defence Secretary John Nott was telling Prime Minister Margaret Thatcher that: 'There is particular concern over the basing of US weapons – much more cruise missiles (GLCMs) than US aircraft – in this country, which I'm sure will become an issue of much higher political importance over the next year or so as the time for the deployment of GLCMs approaches.'

At the same time, the protesters were learning their trade. The *Today* programme caught up with campaigners on a role-playing day. David Stevenson reported for the programme on 21 March 1983:

> Unlike the Sixties, when non-violent direct action split the CND movement, the emphasis now is on cooperation and the careful planning of all demonstrations. In the stark upstairs at the co-op hall the discussion ranged from the theory of non-violent action, to how to deal with the media, to individual fears about dealing with the police on a blockade... The training session ranged from knowing your legal rights to making friends with the police and avoiding violence, but the crucial aspect lies in the role-playing, which tries to prepare the activists for what may happen on the blockade. The group of eleven women

and five men divided into two: one group became demonstrators, the other the police.

One woman participant observed that if the police 'appear to be the traditional British bobby, fairly jovial and just doing a job, it's very different from if there is a fairly clear hostility', while another felt:

> I don't think I'm actually frightened of being arrested, because it's an unknown. I might have a totally different attitude to it once I have been arrested, and what I am frightened of is any aggression and what I'm going to feel like if I'm grabbed by the hair or whatever and dragged away.

As Stevenson described:

> There then followed the sort of scenes we've all seen on television: as fast as the 'police' removed one demonstrator, another took his place. As a result, everyone learned how irritating demonstrators can be to the police, and the demonstrators learned to wear thick clothes to avoid injury while being dragged along the ground...

The reality of the non-violent yet utterly determined protest, as it unfolded at Greenham, posed unusual challenges for the law enforcers. What, exactly, do you do when women dressed in furry animal costumes climb the fence and have a picnic on the site? What tactic do you use against women who trespass in order to dance on top of weapons silos? Although much of the British press was hostile to the Greenham Common women, by 1983 these women had an international audience, and any heavy-handed treatment caught on camera could risk backfiring badly.

As *Today* broadcasts over the period show, the anti-nuclear campaign diversified too. From spring 1983, the Greenham Common base was being prepared to receive the new missiles at the end of the year. On 1 April, around 70,000 CND supporters linked hands in a 14-mile human chain that connected Greenham with nearby nuclear-related sites. On 22 October, CND held what the BBC described as its 'biggest ever' protest, as an estimated 200,000 people marched through London to Hyde Park.

On 9 November 1983, as deployment of the cruise weapons was imminent, some Greenham protesters were outside a federal court in New York. Their spokeswoman, Liz Forder, told *Today* why:

> We can't sue our government, because we have no constitution and they're protected by parliamentary privilege, and so we've come to this country to sue the Reagan administration to seek an injunction against the deployment of cruise missiles. We don't know what else to do.

The attempt was unsuccessful, but the determination remained, as Forder described:

> We will take our protest wherever it is going to be most directly felt – if it's on the base, if it's on the street where the transporter erector trucks are being driven, we will take our bodies, we will protest with our bodies. We are trying the legal process. We feel it is very important that justice should be done. However, we will not disperse, we will not stop, and we will take up the challenge.

A week later, 300 women breached the 19th-century prohibition about protesting within a mile of Parliament. In a report for *Today* on 16 November 1983, the BBC's Julian Marshall asked the redoubtable Conservative backbencher Anthony Beaumont-Dark whether the protest was 'any indication of the strength of feeling against the siting of cruise missiles in this country', a question that brought scorn:

> No, of course it's not. I mean these people are a rent-a-mob, really. I mean there's now, like there used to be a rent-a-mob against changes in trade union laws, there's rent-a-mobs against cruise missiles or anything you care to name. Some of them are very sincere, but the most important thing is that this country's defences can't be left to the likes of this lot who, as I say, are sitting on their brains at the present time.

Inside Parliament the defence secretary, Michael Heseltine, raised the temperature of the debate. On 1 November 1983, a Labour MP, Roland Boyes, a member of CND, posed this question:

> It was reported recently that if any of the demonstrators – the ladies from Greenham Common – arrived near the bunkers where the nuclear warheads were held, there was a possibility that they would be shot. Will the Right Honourable Gentleman assure us that he will instruct the people responsible for Greenham Common cruise missile base that under no circumstances will shots be fired at the peace protesters?

Heseltine replied:

> I shall categorically give no such assurance. It has been the absolute duty of all governments to defend the nuclear weapons in this country, as well as all the military bases of this country's defence forces.

Today picked up the debate the following morning, 2 November 1983. Boyes was invited onto the programme along with the Conservative MP Michael NcNair-Wilson, who had come to Heseltine's defence by claiming that:

Anybody who gets into that area is getting into an area where there are missiles and possibly nuclear warheads, and therefore they might themselves be going to perpetrate the most appalling crime that any of us could possibly imagine, namely in some way creating a nuclear explosion.

Boyes' response was blunt:

I think it's absolutely ridiculous to suspect that an army, [that] trained army personnel, can't deal with women protesters at Greenham Common without resorting to shooting them. I find it incredible and unbelievable.

John Timpson was managing the discussion, and he suggested 'that the women may be used as a cover by people with much more sinister motives, who may be really there to cause trouble?'. Boyes was having none of it.

Boyes: Do you think a terrorist is going to get into this internal high-security system, pick up a cruise missile and lob it over a fence and start blowing us all up, is that what you're suggesting to the people of Britain? That that's the kind of nightmare society we're living in at the moment? That somebody can walk in, put it under his arm, take it away and fire it? I mean, really, Mr McNair-Wilson and Michael Heseltine must think we're all daft to believe that kind of nonsense...

Timpson: So, do you think he should have given a categorical assurance that shots would not be fired at anybody in these circumstances, and that the final line of protection would not exist?

Boyes: No, I'm saying that under normal circumstances, soldiers, and surely there's not going to be one young early recruit guarding these missiles, soldiers ought to be able to deal with an intruder without shooting. And if we take the logic to its conclusion, then the minister can continuously redefine which areas are a high security risk. And it might get to a stage that anybody climbing up the fence at Greenham Common is becoming a high security risk and get shot. I hope we're not suggesting in that in Britain demonstrators for peace, unarmed people, are likely to be shot? I mean this really is...

Timpson: I don't think they were suggesting that, obviously, we can't...

Boyes: Of course they are, none of these people protesting at Greenham Common are armed.

Timpson: Ah, but they're not the ones that we apparently were worried about, but we've been over that point several times. Now you had your answer from Mr Heseltine, what do you plan to do now?

Boyes: Well, let me just say I think that not only the Labour side, but I think a number of people in the House of Commons, were shaken by his reply and I don't think we can leave it at that. We've got to bring pressures, as many pressures as possible, on the government to get what Mr Heseltine said reversed. First of all, I'm going to talk to Helen John, one of the founders of the Greenham Common air base protest group, to see what the political implications are for their women. Now nobody wants to see innocent and unarmed women shot. But secondly, I'm travelling immediately to Brussels to investigate it at an international level whether or not pressure can be brought on the government to get this attitude changed.

The debate certainly gave Greenham protesters an additional factor to consider. In New York, during that injunction hearing a week later, Liz Forder was telling *Today* listeners: 'If we have to be shot, this is something we've been faced with, something a lot of us are spending sleepless nights considering. We can't stop.'

In the end, no shooting took place. Protests continued, however: after word went out in chain letters, more than 30,000 women, including some celebrities, assembled at Greenham in December to ring the entire perimeter in their 'embrace the base' event, pinning all sorts of mementos, baby clothes and soft toys to the fence. Some of the perimeter fence was torn down, and it was followed by many arrests.

That same month, the Conservative peer Lord Beloff referred dismissively to the Greenham women's 'ululations', which, in his view, reflected 'an induced mass hysteria impervious to argument'. In a memo, Beloff wrote that he wanted to 'abandon the kid-gloves approach and seek publicly to discredit the Greenham Common women', demanding that the intelligence services conduct 'proper investigation of the background and characters of the Greenham Common women... we need to know more about their political and personal backgrounds so that the aura of martyrdom can be stripped from them'.

But then the proliferation of nuclear warheads in Europe that was so feared went into reverse, as, well away from Greenham Common, another dynamic got underway involving politicians, not protesters. Ronald Reagan and his Soviet counterpart Mikhail Gorbachev agreed the Intermediate-Range Nuclear Forces Treaty in 1987. By 1991, the last cruise missile had left Greenham Common.

But some protesters stayed on and, as James Naughtie put it on *Today,* they 'decided to turn their attentions to nuclear weapons in general and they stuck it out' until September 2000 – 19 years after it had all begun.

When the last of them left, they did so to make way for a memorial to their protest. By then much of the site, restored as common land, had already been given back to cattle, while much of the airbase itself had become a business park. As the veteran protester

Sarah Hipperson explained to *Today*'s reporter Tom Feilden on 9 May 2000, they had stayed so long because 'just as cruise missiles were going away, there was Trident coming along... and we turned around and looked at Aldermaston and we took that on within our scope of work.'

No one was ever killed by the weapons that, it was feared, might vaporise millions. But one protester died at Greenham Common, ironically just days after the first of the cruise missiles was withdrawn. On 6 August 1989, 22-year-old Helen Thomas, from Wales, was killed in a road accident involving a police vehicle. She is the only individual whose name is memorialised in the Greenham Peace Garden, where a spiral sculpture proclaims, 'You can't kill the spirit.'

The fall of the Berlin Wall

'I made it, I've made it!'

MAN CROSSING THE BERLIN WALL, QUOTED BY THE BBC'S
EUROPE CORRESPONDENT GRAHAM LEACH, 9 NOVEMBER 1989

In November 1989, Graham Leach, the BBC's Europe correspondent, who was based in Brussels, managed to reach Berlin in time to report one of the biggest stories of the late 20th century. He gave *Today's* listeners this flavour of the evening of 9 November, when the Berlin Wall was breached.

> **Truly remarkable scenes taking place here tonight on the Eastern side of the Berlin Wall at Checkpoint Charlie. Hundreds of people have gathered here in the hope of getting across, in the light of the new concessions which have been announced, allowing East Germans to cross to West Germany, through the Berlin Wall and across the Iron Curtain frontier between the two Germanys. In the distance, on the other side of Checkpoint Charlie, I can see numerous flashlights going, the cameramen from the newspapers and ordinary people who [have] turned out in their hundreds just to be here on this historic evening. People on the other side are chanting, urging East Germans on this side to come across.**

The wall was thrown up almost overnight in August 1961 – and in its early days it was little more than barbed wire and fencing. Berlin was still formally under the control of the four victorious powers of the Second World War – Britain, France, the United States and the Soviet Union – but it had become a Cold War front line.

The Soviet sector served as the capital of the Communist East German state, the GDR or German Democratic Republic, while the free-world values embraced in West Germany flourished in the rest of the city. The East Germans reinforced what they called the Anti-Fascist Protection Rampart as a permanent structure, and the wall became the single most powerful symbol of the Cold War's ideological divisions. The idea that it might come down had seemed unimaginable, and when it did everyone understood that the moment marked the end of an era. That background explains the sense of excitement captured in the *Today* broadcasts over those heady November days.

The fall of the Berlin Wall would have been unimaginable without the transformational figure of the Soviet leader Mikhail Gorbachev, who refused to force

Moscow's satellite countries into line with tanks, in the way the Soviet leadership had done in Hungary in 1956 and Czechoslovakia in 1968.

The 1989 crisis began when, in June, Hungary removed its own Iron Curtain along the border with Austria. East Germans, who were allowed access to Warsaw Pact-ally Hungary, now found a back door to the West: if they could make their way to West Germany via Austria, they could claim citizenship.

Erich Honecker, the old-school hard-line East German general secretary, tried to stem the flow by closing the country's borders, but he faced a growing protest movement and in mid-October he was forced out of office by a younger leader, Egon Krenz. Krenz, under constant pressure from pro-democracy rallies, reopened the GDR's border with Czechoslovakia, and television news bulletins were again full of young East German couples heading for the West in their Trabant cars or 'Trabis', with their two-stroke engines and plastic bodies.

But the final fall of the wall occurred almost by accident. When Egon Krenz decided to ease travel restrictions, the Party boss in Berlin was given the task of announcing the changes, but no one told him that the new regime was due to come into force a day later. At a press conference on 9 November he announced that, with immediate effect, anyone wishing to visit the West would receive a temporary visa. Crowds of East Berliners gathered at the wall's checkpoints, swamping bewildered officials and border guards, and the guards, confused about their instructions, began to abandon the habits of a lifetime.

Graham Leach's *Today* report captured the chaos as well as the euphoria.

> **Around me there are heated arguments taking place between East Germans trying to get over and the police. Apparently, there are still some obstacles, some difficulties with the papers; some people don't have the right documents, they're being told to come back tomorrow.**

One interviewee was being stopped from crossing because 'the major said "no"', but, as Leach told *Today* listeners, the bureaucratic niceties started to evaporate:

> **The police commander on duty here at Checkpoint Charlie has suddenly announced that they can go over even though they may not have the right documents, and they're simply charging now through the small gate in the fence where they're queuing up to get across to the western side of the Berlin Wall.**

Struggling to make himself heard above the cheering and whistling crowds, Leach shouted:

> **I've now reached the western side of Checkpoint Charlie and there's a huge number of people here waiting to greet the first of the East German arrivals.**

A bottle of champagne has been uncorked. The first East German has come across now, he's been raised aloft, he's holding up his, uh... identity pass, his East German identity pass, to show the crowds of West Berliners who've gathered here tonight. I'm being showered with champagne by somebody above me, who's literally sitting on one of the border fences. One man, who has just come through, [has] raised his arms in the air and has declared, 'I made it, I've made it!'

For decades East Germans who tried to cross the wall had risked death; now that these wide-eyed East Germans could be here legally, just by walking across, they could hardly believe it.

Leach: So, why have you come? Just want to visit?

East Berliner 1: Yes, I go back, of course.

Leach [to another man]: What will you do when you're in West Berlin?

East Berliner 2: I will look, only looking.

Neither East German interviewee was in any doubt that this was anything other than 'wonderful' and a 'very, very important day'.

One of *Today*'s presenters that morning, Peter Hobday, interviewed the German Social Democrat politician Egon Bahr, who, in the 1970s, had been one the leading architects of *Ostpolitik,* the West German policy of engagement with East Germany. Hobday asked whether West Germany could cope with 'the sort of numbers that some people are suggesting? Up to a million-and-a-quarter immigrants seeking a better life in the West?' Bahr reasoned that the new visas would be 'a first step to stop the flow [of] refugees, because the people know by now it's possible to leave, it's possible to go back. This morning a lot of people will go back to the GDR after they have had their beer in West Berlin.'

And he reflected on the bigger picture:

Undoubtedly, we will have a lot of difficulties, but undoubtedly these are the difficulties we've hoped for, we expected, we demanded, so we cannot quarrel if things are going in our direction...We have coped with 13 million people at the end of the war when we were really a poor society. I think we will handle it.'

In his mind, the political transformations actually held the prospect of defraying the potential costs to the West German state, because 'we can stop a lot of things which we have planned in the military field'.

Within 24 hours of those first cross-border day-trippers, something even more fundamental had begun: the dismantling of the wall itself. Graham Leach reported the scene for *Today* on 11 November:

Around me scores of people have arrived, being held back by the police, to watch this first incision into the Berlin Wall since it was put up on the night of 12 August 1961. City engineers are gathered alongside the wall. One man is just pointing to the very spot where they will make the first breach. He's produced a felt-tip pen, he's drawing a square!... Here we go now!... A huge cheer's going up. This huge digger is angling itself alongside the Berlin Wall. They're swinging it round. And here we go! The digger has gone onto the top of the Berlin Wall and literally munched off the top of it. The first row of bricks in the Berlin Wall has come away and the chants around me from the crowd rise and rise... The city engineers are now distributing bricks as souvenirs to the crowd gathered here tonight. They're holding them up, brandishing them. Souvenirs of what will always be a rather ugly monument to the post-war era. And a young lady has come forward with a bunch of flowers for the man who's been driving the digger that's been taking apart this section of the Berlin Wall.

In the days, weeks and years that followed, thousands of tourists would leave the city having purchased their own small portions of the wall, as this Berlin icon became a truly global property.

By the time the programme went on the air on 11 November Peter Hobday had arrived himself, and was presenting from Berlin where, he told the listeners, 'It's been impossible to stay indoors. Even though the television stations are carrying special reports at length, you have to go out on the streets.' By now, the wall was almost inaccessible, besieged as it was by crowds and media, so Hobday sought out something quieter in the Gedächtniskirche, 'the memorial church bombed out during the Second World War'.

'What's fascinating,' he observed, 'is that everyone feels that they want to come here and sit quietly and just think about the events of the last 24 hours. Both East and West Germans are sitting here murmuring quietly.'

Heading out into the Kurfürstendamm, 'that wide, elegant boulevard with all the big shops, restaurants, bars and food stalls', he found families reunited: 'I just met two sisters... Fascinating story: one lives in the East, one lives in the West. Talking to the one in the East, she... she just rejoices that she can actually come over here now and see her sister... It's the normality, suddenly, after all these years.'

Two days later, Hobday and Graham Leach were together at the Brandenburg Gate. Hobday described Leach as now 'my guide, philosopher and friend' (an extravagant introduction by the programme's usually sober stylistic standards) and Leach told him:

You can see three cranes just beyond the wall. They're there for the benefit of the American television networks, as are the searchlights there. It's become a film set over there with West German television carrying live broadcasts throughout

the weekend. It's a sign of the more relaxed times that we're [even] talking here now. At this particular spot a month ago I was arrested. Nevertheless, for East and West Berliners this city will never truly be reunited again until that part of the wall goes there behind the Brandenburg Gate.

Neither broadcaster could quite believe the freedoms they were enjoying. As Leach said, 'The fact that we are here is a sign of the changing times, isn't it, too? With the guards all around us, watching us, while we actually record this conversation!'

Four months later the *Today* programme was back in Berlin, as John Humphrys covered the first-ever free, multi-party elections in East German history. The poll returned a Christian Democrat-led coalition, which would govern an independent East German democracy for a few brief months until, at the end of 1990, Germany was reunited. On 19 March 1990, Humphrys was to be found at the wall, short of breath as he chipped away for his own bit of Cold War history:

I borrowed the equipment to do this from a couple of Americans who say that in Manhattan they're selling these bits of the wall for $25 a time. I reckon it's probably worth it considering the effort that's involved in getting a decent chunk, because when they built the wall, they knew [what they] were doing. It's as hard as you'd imagine... reinforced with steel rods and concrete that is absolutely rock hard!

Mission completed, Humphrys's broadcast continued, with him now standing on top of the wall itself, 'in the centre of what must be the most popular tourist attraction in Europe today'. He painted the picture for *Today*'s listeners:

Behind me the Brandenburg Gate, in front of me the Reichstag and everywhere thousands, upon thousands, upon thousands, of tourists. Some of them taking photographs of each other standing on the Wall, leaning against the Wall; some of them buying souvenirs from the hundreds upon hundreds of souvenir stands. Every other stand, it seems, [is] selling little bits of the Wall stuck into little plaques with numbers to prove [laughs] that they're genuine bits, [with] signed certificates to say this is a genuine bit of the Berlin Wall.

Nothing could compare, though, with those first few days of discovery, of testing the water; experienced less by foreign tourists and more by Berliners themselves. Peter Hobday summed up his impressions like this:

What we have discovered is that the East Germans have come here, not to spend, not to get drunk, but just to look. And most of them we met have not come to stay; they all say, 'Well, we've got jobs back there, we've got homes, we want to go home. We just want to come and have a look.' The few people we found really celebrating, those who have been drinking quite a bit of beer, tend to be the West Berliners. But again that drives home the point: they're the ones who can afford to buy the beer here on the Ku'damm; it's not the East Germans. No, most of them will be back in the East tomorrow. Back at work, back to their normal lives, but with one difference: they know that this time they can come back here any time they want to. That's the difference.

It has been estimated that during the first three days after the Berlin Wall was breached, half the population of East Germany visited West Berlin.

China's brief experiment with democratic protest

'Long live freedom, long live democracy, down with corruption'

CHINESE PROTESTERS, 18 MAY 1989

For seven weeks from late April to early June 1989, the world looked on mesmerised as China appeared to stand at a crossroads. To the protesters who gathered in Tiananmen Square, in the heart of Beijing (and it is estimated that at the height of their protest they numbered as many as a million), this was the flowering of a Chinese Spring.

The demonstrations were inspired by the death of the former Communist Party general secretary Hu Yaobang on 15 April. Hu, a reformist and a protégé of China's paramount leader Deng Xiaoping, had been forced out of office two years earlier for failing to contain earlier student demonstrations. That made him a hero for the pro-democracy movement.

Ignoring warnings from the authorities, and angered by an attempt to quell discontent via a *People's Daily* editorial on 'The Necessity for a Clear Stand Against Turmoil' (which may have been drafted by Deng himself), protesters mounted what the BBC described as 'the biggest pro-democracy demonstrations of their kind since the Communists came to power' across several cities. And by the time the Soviet leader Mikhail Gorbachev made a state visit to China in mid-May, the students in Tiananmen Square were on hunger strike, demanding negotiations with the government. A regime sensitive to slights found itself embarrassed on two counts – its people were appealing to Gorbachev as a liberalising Communist, and Tiananmen Square, the setting for so much Chinese political ritual, was becoming out of bounds to its political masters.

The shackles of censorship and self-censorship were being thrown off. James Miles was the BBC's Beijing correspondent at the time, and for *Today* on 18 May 1989, against a backdrop of singing, chanting and cheering, he described these scenes:

> **A column of workers are marching past, singing the Communist anthem 'The Internationale' as they march towards Tiananmen Square in support of the student demonstration. It seems the whole city is now coming out in support: millions of people, young and old, in an unprecedented outburst of defiance against the government.**

The Chinese regime could not dismiss the disaffection as merely the wild rhetoric of pampered students. Here, too, was the workforce. As Miles explained:

> **Workers' discontent has been building up in China in recent years. Inflation is now running at 30 per cent a year – its highest level since the Communists came to power. For many urban residents, living standards have actually been dropping in recent months.**

Deng Xiaoping's economic reforms were about a decade old, and they had already brought about huge change, from private enterprise in agriculture to the mushrooming of 'special economic zones' and an open-door policy to foreign investment. But they had also brought deep corruption and, by 1988, rampant inflation and runs on the banks. When the authorities responded by re-exerting some state control and cancelling capital projects, many manual workers found themselves unemployed. Their anger reinforced the disaffected mood of the students, as Miles discovered:

> **'Long live freedom, long live democracy, down with corruption!' the workers are shouting. 'The workers are marching!' they're saying: an ironic reference to the old marching slogan. These people believe that the powers that they have officially had enshrined in the Communist constitution are completely meaningless. The banners displayed by the workers have questioned whether the workers are really masters or whether they're in fact slaves of the Communist government.**

Miles wondered, 'Is this a revolution?' At least one protester thought so:

> **In my opinion, this is a very deep-going revolution. You know, it seems to me that all people in China have been mobilised. Not only the students. This is not only the students' hunger strike. It has been spreading. Even the professors are involved, even the workers are supporting them.**

Miles explained:

> **Many workers complain that they live on low state salaries while officials are able to line their pockets through profiteering and bribes. But here outside the Great Hall of the People overlooking the square, a large group of workers is not just demanding the end to corruption, they also want political change.**

As the chanting continued, he described acts of disrespect unthinkable in an earlier era:

> **They're calling on the prime minister, Li Peng, to come out. They're calling on China's senior leader, Deng Xiaoping, to come out. A banner held up by one of them says, 'Stick out your head' and there's a picture of a turtle with its head**

withdrawn under its shell. What they want is a dialogue with the top leadership and what many of these people want more than anything else is for China's senior leader Deng Xiaoping to step down... There's a man in front of the crowd who's got his head roped through an imitation cloth. There are slogans painted on it saying, 'Dictatorship and despotism', indicating that people are being shackled by Communist leadership.

The day after Miles's broadcast, Li Peng announced the imposition of martial law. Li and his hardline faction had prevailed over the inner circle's principal advocate of dialogue and reform, General Secretary Zhao Ziyang, who was forced to surrender his party role for years of subsequent house arrest. The split within the party that had thus far stayed the hand of the authorities therefore disappeared, and with it an ominous momentum began.

At first, though, it was halting. As troops moved through Beijing towards the centre, they had to make their way through blockades and barricades, but their orders were not to open fire. In the last week of May and the first two days of June, the occupiers of Tiananmen Square remained in a heightened sense of tension and excitement. In their midst they created their own symbol, the 'Goddess of Democracy', reminiscent of the Statue of Liberty – an astonishing sight in the People's Republic of China. An almost carnival atmosphere pervaded the square, as Beijing seemed caught in suspension between a festival of democracy and the threat of martial law.

In a broadcast of 2 June 1989, which intercut reportage from the streets with reflective summary, James Miles was able to capture some of that atmosphere for *Today* listeners:

> Even down to the drums sounding the alarm, Tiananmen Square, with its rows of army-style tents, each with their own flags and banners, resembled a military camp under siege. A few thousand ragtag students still occupying the square had been expecting the call for days, aware that they were no longer protected on the outskirts of the city by waiting crowds of workers and barricades. But, somehow, huge groups of demonstrators materialised from the darkness, and they chanted as defiantly as ever, in contempt of the prime minister, as the troops approached.

Rather than the demonstrators being overawed by the military, it seemed to be the other way around:

> The young foot-soldiers appeared to be unarmed, unprepared and in no mood for an actual fight. There was a brief confrontation, a few scuffles and the soldiers began to pull back in disarray. Many just huddled at the side of the road as they were taunted and then educated by the demonstrators.

Miles acknowledged, 'Language was a problem even among the Chinese, many of the soldiers having been sent from distant provinces – possibly to make them less susceptible to just this sort of persuasion.' Yet this did not stop the evangelistic students:

> Soldiers now, many of them in their vests, knapsacks on their backs, sitting in the bushes at the side of the road looking quite bewildered as the students come to talk to them… A big crowd of workers and students now surrounded one soldier who, they say, has changed sides. He decided to take off his army uniform and join the democracy movement.

'As it became clear that the soldiers' advance had been halted on all sides,' Miles concluded, 'groups of students, workers and other citizens began parading in triumph around the vast square, China's symbolic seat of power, singing the socialist anthem they've also made their own, "The Internationale".'

In reality, the stalemate was almost over. Whatever the pro-democracy activists may have thought, in the minds of those who dominated the two pillars of state – the party and the army – China stood not at a crossroads but on the edge of an abyss.

The decisive moment came overnight on 3–4 June, with the violent crushing of dissent around Tiananmen Square and in other parts of Beijing, as the army's new orders to use force were implemented. The night developed into a battle between civilians and the troops trying to converge on the square, as ambulances, rickshaws and human hands ferried the thousands of injured to the city's overwhelmed hospitals. In the small hours of 4 June, the massed protesters in the square – under an army ultimatum – agreed to leave, but violence continued throughout the day around the square.

Vivid broadcasts from the midst of the mayhem, notably by the BBC's chief news correspondent Kate Adie and World Affairs editor John Simpson, left an indelible impression. But perhaps the single most powerful image to catch the world's imagination was that of a young, unidentified man with a carrier bag who, the following day, stood alone in front of a column of tanks to impede their progress. The David and Goliath moment encapsulated, for much of the outside world, a confrontation of right versus might.

Four days later, Deng Xiaoping – invisible during the protests – congratulated senior army figures on suppressing the 'counter-revolutionary riots', thereby also ensuring that responsibility for the events was well shared out. The battle thereafter was over the truth of Tiananmen Square. Had 241 died (as the government claimed), or was it nearer 10,000, as a source in the ruling state council told the British ambassador to China? When Li Lu, one of the student leaders who had managed to escape, spoke to *Today* presenter John Humphrys on 28 May 1990, his figures, spoken in somewhat broken English, seemed nearer to the ambassador's:

At four o'clock in the morning we tried to send a delegation to negotiate with the army, who had surrounded [us] at Tiananmen Square; and it's quite possible that at that time the final 5,000 people would have died. And the delegation came back to us and said that the army promised we could leave Tiananmen Square at the south-east entrance by 7pm, and by voice voting we decided to leave. And just ten minutes after we decided to leave, the students began to form in order to leave the square. And the lights were suddenly all shut off. And I don't know how many hundreds of soldiers moved in and began to shoot in the north side of the square; dozens of tanks began to move in to crush the Goddess of Democracy...

The British ambassador to China, Sir Alan Donald, described how 'students understood they were given one hour to leave the square, but after five minutes APCs attacked', before summarising a horrific massacre that then took place.

Li Lu, whom Humphrys described as 'on the list of the 21 most wanted men and women' in China, would have had reason to stress the regime's brutality. Yet, 20 years after the event, the numbers were still under debate. James Miles, by this time *The Economist*'s Beijing correspondent, suggested in 2009 that 'few, if any' deaths occurred in the square. 'There was no Tiananmen Square massacre,' he concluded, 'but there was a Beijing massacre.' Miles supported the conclusions of the *New York Times* journalist Nicholas Kristof, who had estimated up to 800 civilians had died.

'I believe that, eventually, as part of a process of political change in China, the government will revise its official account of what happened,' Miles wrote in an article for the BBC on 2 June 2009. Perhaps so. He suggested that the 'first draft of history can be crude'. In mid-May 1989, in the heat of the people's protest, he had once told *Today* listeners that, 'It seems the leadership is running out of time.'

Civil disobedience and the poll tax

'Scenes... we have never seen before in Weston-super-Mare'

JOHN DAWS, 7 MARCH 1990

It was meant to be the 'community charge', but hardly anyone remembers that. Instead, it rapidly became known as the 'poll tax', a term freighted with connotations of civil strife stretching back to the 14th century.

Britain's Thatcherite revolution in the 1980s had many elements, and one was reform of local government and local government finances. For years, local taxation was based on property values – how much business premises and people's homes were theoretically worth. It was hardly a flawless system, since it took no account, for example, of how many people occupied a property, and the Conservative government believed that it encouraged local-council overspending. As the environment secretary, Kenneth Baker, told the House of Commons on 28 January 1986:

> **At present in England, around 35 million adults are eligible to vote in local elections. Only 18 million are directly liable as ratepayers. Of these, 3 million have their bill met in full by housing benefit. In many authorities, well over 50 per cent of the voters pay no local rates and therefore have little interest in restraining spending by the local authority; indeed, they have a clear interest that it should spend more.**

These arguments about fairness and representation were coloured by party politics, since the perception was that a more naturally Conservative-voting demographic of property owners was having to subsidise a Labour-voting demographic of those not liable (or less liable) for rates.

The 'solution', worked up in a 1986 green paper, was to tear up the property tax and instead introduce the community charge – a flat rate, set by the local council, chargeable to *every* adult living in the borough, in whatever sort of property they lived. As the minister said, 'Each local authority would set its own charge and there would have to be registers of all adults. The registers would be entirely separate from the electoral register.' The theory was that with everyone having to pay something, council accountability to its residents would be transformed. After the Conservatives were re-elected in 1987, the bill passed into law, and in 1989 Scotland became the test-bed for the policy's implementation.

The problems with such a radical measure were immediately apparent. The rates system may have been unfair to single homeowners, who had to pay the same as the family of four next door, but in a system that now took no account of the *nature* of the property and very little account of income, the owner of a luxury mansion could pay the same as the occupant of a bedsit. There was meant to be a system of rebates for students and other categories, but these were worked out on a notional standard poll-tax charge, rather than on the (often much higher) actual charges levied by councils. In a familiar remark of the time, 'It came across as if the duke and the dustman were paying exactly the same.' The poll tax was a windfall for landlords, too, who were relieved of having to pay rates on their properties, while their renters incurred the new tax on top of their rents. In all these ways, people felt that the poll tax seemed to transgress the natural laws of justice.

The rollout of the poll tax in Scotland was met with a mood of civil disobedience. In droves, people refused to pay and took themselves off the radar – they changed accommodation, even moved cities, and removed themselves from the electoral roll, which was regarded as a key source for the authorities trying to enforce payment. Councils, already faced with the turmoil of introducing a new system that many of them opposed, were then also hit by falling income, causing them to increase poll-tax levels for those who were complying, which encouraged even more refuseniks.

The poll tax was a gift to Mrs Thatcher's opponents. It was easy to portray the new charge as a smash-and-grab raid on the poor. The Labour Party opposed the measure but could not officially condone non-compliance. That left the field wide open for other activists, and the poll tax quickly became an issue around which those opposed to the government ideologically could join with those opposed specifically to the measure. Across the country, anti-poll-tax unions sprang up, and the tide of protest rose in advance of the planned introduction of the tax in England and Wales, which was scheduled for April 1990.

On the evening of 6 March 1990, protests erupted across England, as the BBC's Steve McCormack reported on *Today* the next morning:

> The most violent scenes were in Bristol, where at one stage police drew batons and moved in on parts of the crowd. Missiles were thrown, barricades were knocked over and scuffling went on well into the night. Four police officers were injured and about 20 people were arrested. Order was eventually restored after the crowds dispersed peacefully. Other trouble spots included Bradford, Birmingham, Reading, Worcester, Runcorn, Gillingham and Dover, featuring varying degrees of violence and damage and a number of police injuries. At

Norwich the council meeting was abandoned after disruption in the public gallery, and proceedings were suspended temporarily amid similar scenes at Maidenhead and Weston-super-Mare, where the Conservative council chairman is John Daws.

Mr Daws, speaking on *Today* on 7 March 1990, described himself as being 'absolutely disgusted':

> This is a council meeting to discuss the poll charge, the community charge, and we have had more violence during tonight and seen scenes here which we have never seen before in Weston-super-Mare. It's been absolutely disgusting.

In the view of Alan Eastwood, chairman of the Police Federation, also interviewed by Steve McCormack, 'Peaceful demonstrations have been a way of our life for years, but the people that are orchestrating the violence are not from the local communities.'

Today presenter Sue MacGregor then interviewed Steve Nally, the secretary of the National Anti-Poll Tax Federation, an umbrella group. She quizzed him on his political allegiance to the Militant Tendency, the Trotskyist group which was working to infiltrate the Labour Party, asking him whether Militant had, in her words, 'been helping to organise these anti-poll-tax riots'. And she challenged him with Mr Eastwood's claim:

> MacGregor: Now, what do you say to Mr Eastwood's allegation, the chair of the Police Federation... who calls your lot 'rent-a-mob' [and says] you're *not* from local communities, [that] you just go around taking part in these demonstrations wherever they happen to be...

> Nally: I would say that 99.9 per cent of people on these local demonstrations are from the local area from my own experience.

> MacGregor: And what about the violence?

> Nally: Well, as I said just a second ago, the National Federation does not condone the violence, but again, let's put in the context, it's been many peaceful protests and what we are arguing now is that the stuff in the press [and] on the TV is really a media smokescreen to avoid the real issues – that in Scotland there [are] one million non-payers of the poll tax... and this government is now split in an absolute crisis on this issue.

> MacGregor: But it's not little old ladies who are kicking and punching policemen, is it?

Nally: But the National Federation is set up precisely to defend those people in the community, through legal advice and other measures, like little old ladies, like people who are disabled, and [like] low-paid workers who are in no position to pay the poll tax, and unless we mount a serious campaign, you know, we'll be intimidated and harassed by local authorities.

Nally declared his intention 'to build ten million non-payers in England and Wales and Scotland' and added, 'We intend to defeat the government on this issue.'

Two days later, on the evening of 8 March, the BBC's reporter Peter Hunt was in the thick of protests after 'as many as 5,000 people, some holding *Socialist Worker* and Militant placards, had gathered outside Hackney Town Hall from early evening':

A number of people are now being dragged off. A woman in front of me is being dragged by two policemen... and taken away. There's another surge now. As police try to arrest individuals, people are falling down, placards [are] being thrown, people are being pushed over in the crush. A bottle was just thrown and broke in front of me, and hit a policewoman on the head. Another stick has been thrown. This really has deteriorated.

On 9 March 1990 Police Commander John Pernell reflected on the events in the area:

It must be said that there were a lot of local people here, who clearly feel strongly about the subject of the poll tax. There was also a large element of Socialist Workers and Militants and I think it must be said that they were the element which caused most of the violence.

Another reason for the crowd's ire on that particular evening was apparent too. As Hunt told *Today*'s listeners, 'Away from the violent protests, Hackney councillors set their poll tax at £499 – £202 above the government estimate.'

Most seriously for the government's political calculations, unhappiness with the poll tax was building in interest groups that the Conservative Party wished *not* to disturb, and even among those that the measure was meant to benefit. Steve Nally's 'little old ladies' might indeed now be paying more than they had done under the rates system. Hard-working people and pensioners of modest means, in modest homes, were finding themselves adversely affected too.

One retired couple from the village of Great Snoring, faced with paying double what they had paid under the old rates, wrote to the prime minister, accusing her of taking 'advantage of your position to impose your will upon us to the point where you are now virtually a dictator riding roughshod over anyone who opposes you'. And voices from the shires could not be easily dismissed. As the veteran left-wing Labour MP and former

Cabinet minister Tony Benn told *Today's* John Humphrys on 9 March 1990, 'You can't say that Colonel Gaddafi is financing the West Oxfordshire councillors.'

The extent of the government's miscalculation was reflected in acute disquiet among government ministers and Conservative MPs, many of whom faced real anger in their constituencies. On 23 March the *Today* reporter Allan Little broadcast a piece from Stockport, which was then a Conservative marginal. The deputy chairman of the local Conservative Party, Dorothy Meredith, told him that 'There are an awful lot of people – as we've gone around knocking on doors and around the terraced properties – who are very angry about it.' Meredith herself supported the poll tax and criticised her local council, a Liberal Democrat and Labour coalition, for setting too high a rate, but she conceded that 'it's unpopular and the government is being blamed for it and I don't think it makes a scrap of difference what we say to them. That is how they feel and nothing will convince them differently.'

The deputy prime minister, Sir Geoffrey Howe, came onto the programme that morning to defend the government in an interview with John Humphrys.

> **Howe: Well, first of all, one has got to recognise that there was a very strong case for making fundamental change in the rating system and most of the people who have been complaining now would have been arguing exactly that case a year or so ago. Any change in the tax system is bound to produce consequences that are unforeseen one way or another. This particular change, which was designed to spread the responsibility of paying tax more widely to people who have previously not been paying local taxes at all and enjoying the services, was bound to lead to a number of people being hit for the first time. So one's not surprised by that.**

> **Humphrys: You said unforeseen, did you not foresee the consequences?**

> **Howe: Oh, the general shape of the consequences, of course. The idea of spreading the load more widely was precisely foreseen. The next point, as was pointed out by the lady who spoke just before we came on air, is that the local authority itself actually sets the level of the community charge. And far too often, we have found that councils controlled by the Labour party or a Lib-Lab alliance have set charges far too high.**

Three days later 40 Conservative MPs rebelled against the government in a vote on the poll tax. By the spring of 1990 even Margaret Thatcher was pondering ways to soften its impact by beefing up council funds from increases in indirect taxes.

Popular protest peaked on 31 March 1990 in a huge demonstration in Central London, which, around Whitehall and Trafalgar Square, descended into fully fledged rioting as tempers flared on all sides. Shops and businesses were looted – there was even an attempt to burn down the South African embassy. Around 113 people were injured

– 45 of them police officers – and there were some 340 arrests. The most telling symbols of the day, though, were the burnt-out high-end cars – in the wrong place at the wrong time – to be found smouldering in St Martin's Lane and elsewhere. The following week the Conservative leader of Westminster Council, Lady (Shirley) Porter, suggested on *Today* that the Home Office should consider banning demonstrations in London. They could, she said, take place 'in the Salisbury Plain, anywhere, and the media can follow them there. But what they shouldn't, I think, be allowed to do any longer is to disrupt ordinary people's lives.'

It was no coincidence that 1990 was the year Margaret Thatcher left Downing Street. Michael Heseltine, who challenged her in the leadership election which led to her resignation, had been a vocal critic of the poll tax, making the point that a tax must not only *be* fair, it had to be *seen* to be fair. Heseltine did not win the leadership, but his consolation prize was to become environment secretary in John Major's new government – a portfolio which carried responsibility for killing off the poll tax.

In 1993, the poll tax was officially replaced by the council tax – a property-based local tax, but one that classified properties in bands and that offered various discounts, for example to people living alone. It was, in other words, a variation on the rates.

It is estimated that the changeover to another new system, combined with the chaos of uncollected and uncollectable arrears from the poll-tax episode, cost the country at least £6 billion.

Student protests and controversy over student fees

'Two battles, really: one on the streets and one in Parliament'

JUSTIN WEBB, 10 DECEMBER 2010

In late 2010, students were on the streets and at the top of the political agenda, dominating headlines and *Today* coverage, in what became a stiff test of the newly formed coalition government.

The issue was student finance. A generation earlier, in 1980, to be a student was to be among just 13 per cent of the age group, in a sector divided largely between universities (academic) and polytechnics (vocational). The number of university places was limited by government budgets, but for the successful student, the choice to study was a cost-free one: tuition was funded by general taxation, and there were means-tested maintenance grants for students' living costs. It was entirely possible to graduate without incurring debt.

To many 21st-century students, that will seem like a dream. But it was a system under pressure. Some argued that the rest of society subsidised the offspring of a largely white, middle-class elite, thus undermining social mobility and perpetuating class divisions. At the same time, with comprehensive schools also preparing students for higher education, student numbers were rising, and government budgets were struggling to cope. The need for up-to-date facilities for science, medicine and engineering, and the requirements of the computer age, put university funding under additional stresses.

There was a political consensus behind the idea of increasing access to a university education, and in 1992, under a Conservative government, polytechnics were rebranded as universities – which immediately increased the proportion of young people attending a university. Tony Blair's Labour government then introduced 'top-up' tuition fees, first of £1,000 (1999) and then £3,000 (2004), for which students could obtain a government-backed loan. The state still contributed the major chunk of universities' teaching budgets, but a cultural change had begun, as part of the cost of university education was transferred directly to the consumer of that education (or his/her family).

In 2010, following the general election that delivered a hung parliament and then a coalition government, came a radical government proposal, formulated in the wake of a report by Lord Browne. It would affect only England, as education policies in Scotland, Northern Ireland and Wales had been devolved. The proposal was to triple the maximum fees to £9,000 per year, to make up for what Exeter University's vice-chancellor, Steve Smith, described on *Today* on 25 November 2010 as a '£3 billion reduction in the teaching funding for universities'. In other words, the new fees would no longer be 'top-ups'; they would largely replace the government's teaching grant. The transformation of student into consumer would be complete and, with each student becoming self-financing, in theory universities could grow according to demand for their courses.

Despite the arguments that the new system was progressive – that the loans were unlike ordinary loans in that repayment was only activated once future salaries reached a certain threshold, and that after a few decades any remaining amount would be written off – it was the dramatic figure of £9,000 per year that made headlines.

To varying extents the plan, justified as a necessary measure after the 2008 financial crisis, was a reversal of *both* coalition parties' earlier positions. The Conservatives had opposed Labour's £3,000 fees rise in 2004. More significantly the Liberal Democrats had, in the run-up to the 2010 election, proposed getting rid of student fees altogether, and all the party's MPs had signed a National Union of Students pledge promising that they would 'vote against any increase in fees in the next Parliament'.

By 10 November 2010, students were at the barricades to vent their feelings. A protest march in London attracted 50,000 people, a minority of whom generated some ugly scenes at 30 Millbank – the office building that houses the Conservative Party's headquarters on the Thames, where windows were smashed and the building invaded.

It was not, though, purely a howl of anger from the young. Vice-chancellors themselves were split, exposing a division between the traditional universities and the ex-polytechnics, with the latter fearing their sorts of students would now be deterred from higher education. On 25 November, a day after further student demonstrations, two vice-chancellors debated the fees rise on *Today*. Baroness Blackstone, the vice-chancellor of Greenwich University and a former Labour education minister, favoured a graduate tax, while Steve Smith, president of Universities UK (UUK) and vice-chancellor of Exeter University, backed the fees rise. The presenter was Justin Webb.

> **Webb:** Er…Professor Smith, it's not the students is it, it's your own people… you've had a revolution in the ranks, haven't you, some people writing to the *Guardian* and saying that actually they… they don't want this system to go through. There's some *chaos* it seems among your ranks.

> **Smith:** No, I don't think so. I think no one, er… I think no vice-chancellor likes the thought of a 76 per cent reduction in the funding of teaching at universities and we've spoken out against that repeatedly. The problem we have is that we

think that there's no alternative plan, no plan B, if you will, to the government's proposal. So...

Webb: Some of your vice-chancellors think there is an alternative and the alternative is for a bigger contribution from taxes.

Smith: Yes, and I think *all* of us as individuals will have our views that, maybe, taxation *is* the way to pay for higher education, but let's be clear, the UUK board, the body that makes policy, UUK, has discussed this on many occasions and without dissent has taken the view that we need to get the government's policy through. Obviously, in an organisation of our size there are going to be vice-chancellors, naturally, who have different views, but the overwhelming majority of members think that unless there is an alternative, a plan B, we can't see an alternative to accepting the government's proposals.

Webb: Lady Blackstone, no plan B?

Blackstone: I think it's perfectly possible to push the government to think again about this. It isn't quite true what Steve Smith has just said, that there's never been any dissent about supporting a... a huge increase in fees, there has been. I've, all along, said that this was a bad idea and that if we went down this road we would end up with a huge reduction in grants and that's exactly what's happened.

Webb: What is your plan B, Lady Blackstone?

Blackstone: Um, my plan B would be to work up proposals for a graduate tax which would be more efficient and much more progressive and, actually, in the end bring more money into higher education. I would also accept that a small increase in fees is... is... is... a... the right thing to do, but to *treble* fees, this is going to have the most appalling effect on access to universities. Many young people coming from families that are not used to taking on huge debts of this kind and are quite debt adverse are going to decide that they don't want to go into higher education.

By 28 November, the BBC was reporting at least 12 student occupations and sit-ins around the country. And then, on 9 December 2010, the day of reckoning arrived – a five-hour parliamentary debate followed by a vote on whether to increase tuition fees to £9,000. Justin Webb was again on shift for what he described as a day of:

... enormous political significance, you could argue, for the coalition and its long-term viability, but for the millions of people with children who are going to go to college in England, and indeed for those who are already there, this day

will have significant practical effects, both on what they pay and, in the longer term, on the kind of education they receive.

For the morning's broadcast, *Today*'s reporter Nicola Stanbridge had been at the University of East London, one of the former polytechnics, getting views from some current students while also hearing from Dale Bassett of the right-of-centre think tank Reform. 'While we were there,' Stanbridge told listeners, 'students stepped up their protest, trying to occupy the vice-chancellor's office despite his support for their cause.'

While Bassett advanced the arguments about the old system being a burden on non-university-educated taxpayers, he thought that 'fees will introduce an element of competition into the system and what this will do, particularly at a time when funding is under great pressure, is actually to drive up standards'. The new fees regime would be, he thought, 'a small price to pay for three years of really high-quality education'. His student audience was not won over. One student interviewed, 'Michael', argued that a university education was a social good and a social necessity: 'We aren't the only people who benefit from our education. Imagine if Britain didn't have any doctors, or nurses, or teachers. I think it's a ridiculous idea!'

The Liberal Democrat MP Greg Mulholland, who opposed the fees rise, was also interviewed on the programme – by Justin Webb. He deplored the lack of what he felt was a proper amount of time to debate the issue in Parliament and admitted:

This policy has done a huge amount of damage to the Liberal Democrats already. That's evident from the polls and from the comments that are being made. And my view is that we should never [have been] put into the situation. Being asked to support a policy of trebling tuition fees, from the position that we used to have, is something that we should never have been asked to do. We should have found a compromise and this, most certainly, is not a compromise.

That said, Mulholland rejected Webb's suggestion that the fees vote might be 'sealing your fate at the next election'.

While MPs debated inside Parliament, outside the crowds of protesting students surged and the mood began to darken. One student told *Today*'s reporter Nicola Stanbridge:

The first two hours of the protest were absolutely delightful, lots of bands, lots of music and really in very good spirits. What you'll notice, now that the riot police have turned up, is that the people that are congregating here are what we call 'black bloc'... I can almost guarantee that if you're in the middle of that kettle, which is a large space, you probably wouldn't even know you were being kettled, whereas if you were on the edge near police the chances are you're in a much more dangerous position.

On the frontline, nerves were fraying:

> Stanbridge: Placard sticks are being broken off and hurled at the police. A couple of students have been injured and are sitting down catching their breath. (Speaking to one of the protesters) You've come out of the crowds in a pretty bad state: you've got a head wound, blood streaming down your face onto your trousers. What happened?

> Student: Well, we were on the frontline, we were keeping the line, we weren't pushing forward at that point. Police decided they were going to make a move, so we couldn't get back any further. A big policeman just whacked his truncheon straight down the middle of my head. Totally unprovoked.

In the Commons, once MPs had debated the issue, the government won by a comfortable margin of 323 to 302 votes. But the Liberal Democrats were split on the issue, as 28 'ayes' were slightly outnumbered by the combination of 21 'noes' (including Mulholland) and eight abstentions. Tristram Hunt, Labour's shadow education spokesman, described to Stanbridge the day's strange juxtaposition of parliamentary process and civil disorder:

> This place is... a bubble... and here we are sitting surrounded by Pugin and Minton tiles and all the rest of it, and outside there are flares going off, and police being injured, and real visceral anger about the nature of politics, and promises, and pledges, and the consequences of the vote here today.

The passing of the bill did unleash fury outside, which erupted during the evening and night of 9 December 2010. As Justin Webb announced on the following morning's *Today*, it was 'Quite a day in central London yesterday. Two battles, really: one on the streets and one in Parliament.'

The BBC reporter Rowan Bridge was in Parliament Square, and reported on the aftermath for *Today*:

> Well, you can probably hear they're using high-pressure hoses to try and clear up some of the damage from yesterday. They started about four o'clock this morning. I'm standing next to the Treasury building, and they've been blasting it with water hoses to try and clear off the anti-cuts graffiti, and then also, of course, there is the physical damage to the buildings themselves – the bent and buckled windows of the Supreme Court, which got smashed yesterday. There are three red telephone boxes on Parliament Square which have not got a single piece of glass left in them. The receivers have been ripped off the ends of the phone... There were 43 protesters taken to hospital and 12 police officers were injured. Six of those needed hospital treatment; one of them, you may have seen,

was an officer who suffered neck injuries when he came off his horse when he was attacked by rioters yesterday.

The moment that really caught the headlines was the unexpected entry of the Prince of Wales and Camilla, Duchess of Cornwall, into the proceedings. The royal car, on its way to a Royal Variety Performance at the London Palladium, was surrounded by a group of protesters. *Today* broadcast recordings of urgent calls to 'put the window up' as shouts of 'Tory scum! Tory scum!' rang out. BBC reporter Rowan Bridge recounted how:

> ... about 20 demonstrators were able to get to the car and attack them with fists and boots and bottles, and they were chanting, 'Off with their heads!' and 'Tory scum!' Now, I have to say there were pictures that I suspect will be in the papers this morning, of shock on the royal couple's face when they were attacked, but afterwards the Duchess of Cornwall tried to laugh it all off. She said, 'There's a first time for everything.'

Today presenter Sarah Montague commented:

> Yesterday's violence will be summed up by one image: the photo of Camilla, Duchess of Cornwall, in the back of a car with Prince Charles, mouth open in shock, arms outstretched, as paint was thrown at one of the car's windows and one of the car's windows was smashed. It was an extraordinary and a very difficult day for London.

Very quickly, questions were asked about how the royal security team and the police could have allowed it to happen. Sarah Montague interviewed the mayor of London, Boris Johnson, on the morning of 10 December 2010, at ten past eight, the time which has traditionally been reserved for the most important interview of the day; he defended the police and blamed the 'large number of agitators who were determined to cause the maximum possible trouble and provocation'. Sir Paul Stephenson, the Metropolitan Police commissioner, reminded listeners how high the stakes actually were:

> I do think that the officers who were protecting their Royal Highnesses showed a very real restraint. Some of those officers were armed. Their priority was to get that car to a point of safety, which was a venue, and that was achieved, but it was a hugely shocking incident and there will be a full criminal investigation into it.

When pressed by Montague as to whether he was 'suggesting that the security officers showed restraint by *not* shooting those people who were attacking them', the commissioner replied, 'I think you and, you know, your listeners can draw their own conclusions', and continued to emphasise 'restraint' in the face of 'thugs'.

'Let's turn to the politics of it all,' Justin Webb said as he introduced Vince Cable, the Liberal Democrat secretary of state for education, later in the programme: 'You were split as a party, top to toe,' Webb suggested, as Cable attempted to defend the fees policy and the vote, frequently resorting to the word 'difficult'. When Justin Webb put to him that most of the key Liberal Democrats must have known their pre-election promise to remove fees was untenable, Cable maintained it had been a collective decision, which had failed to stand the test of the reality of coalition politics and the true state of the national finances. For Cable, the ordeal of the fees vote had at least proved something about the durability of the coalition and his party:

> It was a very difficult day yesterday. We knew this was coming and we had to face it. And I think, actually, we're stronger as a result of having been through this experience.

Despite a temporary dip, student numbers rose over the next few years and university courses expanded – it appeared that fees were not putting off prospective students. But the thriving market in fees – forecast by Dale Bassett of the think tank Reform and others – did not emerge, as almost all universities, from the most ancient and hallowed to the newest and untried, adopted the maximum £9,000 fee. Few universities wanted to lose the chance of that income level, and neither did they want to make a public admission, through a lower fee, that their degrees or standards were in any way inferior to those of other institutions, despite great differences in the entrance qualifications required.

At the same time, interest rates on student loans increased and the remaining levels of maintenance grants were abolished in favour of even more loans, which further increased the debt burden for individual students. By 2017, student applications were dropping again. There was also a ticking time bomb for taxpayers in the increasingly high proportion of debt that, it was forecast, would eventually default to the public purse. And universities were facing accusations of greed, not least because of the 2017 row over the six-figure salaries paid to some vice-chancellors.

In the view of Lord (Andrew) Adonis, one of Labour's chief architects of the earlier top-up loans, the system had become a 'Frankenstein's monster'. And in 2018 Prime Minister Theresa May announced a review of post-18 education and funding, to be led by the former banker Philip Augur, admitting that there was no real market, that England possessed 'one of the most expensive systems of university tuition in the world' and that the fees charged did 'not relate to the cost or quality of the course'.

The Liberal Democrats paid a heavy political price. On *Today* on 10 December 2010, the morning after the fees vote and the disorder in Whitehall, the BBC's assistant political editor Norman Smith compared the potential reputational damage of the fees issue on the Liberal Democrat leader Nick Clegg to that of the Iraq War on former

Labour leader Tony Blair: 'Once you've lost the trust of a significant part of the electorate, they close their ears to you…' he said. At the 2015 general election the Liberal Democrats' seats in Parliament fell from 57 to 8. Nick Clegg resigned as leader.

Egypt's Eighteen Days and the Arab Spring

'We want freedom; we want the end of this oppression'

EGYPTIAN PROTESTER TO JAMES NAUGHTIE, 29 JANUARY 2011

It all started, most commentators agree, in Tunisia with one man, Mohamed Bouazizi, who tried to make a living selling vegetables. He was so humiliated by the way he was treated by the police and government officials that, on 17 December 2010, he set fire to himself. It was the catalyst for a revolt against the authoritarian rule of Tunisia's President Zine al-Abidine Ben Ali, and within a month Ben Ali was gone – fleeing the country he had ruled for 23 years. It was also the beginning of what became known as the Arab Spring, and demonstrations against governments spread right across North Africa and the Arab world.

On 18 January 2011 the foreign secretary William Hague came onto *Today* to discuss developments. 'Yesterday', said the presenter Sarah Montague, 'an Egyptian man set himself on fire in Cairo to protest against the government there. And at least five Algerians have set themselves on fire over the past few days.' From Cairo, correspondent John Leyne reported that things were quiet and no protests were planned until 25 January, while from Algeria, the BBC's Chloe Arnold reported that, after the self-immolations and 'riots here over New Year over the price of sugar and cooking oil', there was an 'uneasy calm' on the streets.

When Montague asked the foreign secretary whether he welcomed the recent changes in Tunisia he replied that, 'On the whole they are certainly welcome, although it is not for us to judge the membership of the government.' She pressed him on whether revolution was catching in the region and whether the British government, fearful of Islamic radicalism, had been too restrained about the authoritarian regimes being challenged. Hague trod a careful line:

> **Hague: I am not calling for a violent revolution anywhere, but...what is important in many countries in the Middle East is sound economic development, which in turn requires rule of law, independent judiciary and [the] confidence that comes from those things, and, yes, political development and more open and flexible societies in their own way, each in their own way, but that's not a new**

thing, and it's not for British governments to argue for that. I think that recent events in Tunisia do reinforce that case...

Montague: So I'll ask again, would you like to see peaceful revolution in Arab countries?

Hague: I'm not calling for revolution in the Middle East.

Montague: But you are calling for change, and given what you're saying, you must be calling for quite dramatic change, which leads one to suggest revolution.

Hague: Britain will always be in favour of the steady extension of democracy, of human rights, of believing that for both political and economic reasons the key attributes of free and open press, of an independent judiciary, of the rule of law without arbitrary government – these are good things, good things for the world and they are good things in the development of any society. But that doesn't lead us, and I stress that again, to say to individual countries you must adopt exactly this form of government.

Things did not stay quiet in Cairo for long. On 25 January 2011, huge crowds gathered in the city's Tahrir Square to demonstrate against the rule of the country's strongman, Hosni Mubarak. For decades, despite a veneer of democracy, Egypt had operated under a state of emergency, which gave the authorities and security apparatus arbitrary powers. The justification was framed as threats to the state, most notably from the Muslim Brotherhood, Egypt's long-standing Islamist movement. But that justification was no longer keeping the people in their place. Instead, fuelled by the internet and social media, protests and clashes with police spread across Egypt. By Friday 28 January, the army was on the streets and a curfew was imposed in Cairo, but it made no difference. That evening, thousands concentrated their protests on key state assets, and the governing party's HQ.

The BBC correspondent John Sudworth, described what happened on *Today:*

With methodical, purposeful calm, the offices of Egypt's ruling National Democratic Party are torn apart. Well, this is a remarkable scene in downtown Cairo. This is a government building now engulfed in flame, and standing outside of it hundreds, possibly a few thousand, people watching it burn, and the bangs and the crackles you can hear [are] the sound[s] of furniture being smashed on the street in front of them here. It's clear that the police have totally lost control of this area of Cairo tonight; there is no authority here. A little way further up the road, though, there is an evidence of state control, preventing Egypt's state television building from suffering a similar fate.

Under pressure, Mubarak began a series of governmental changes to try and soak up public anger, first dismissing his Cabinet, then naming a vice-president. He acknowledged the legitimacy of Egyptians' aspirations. But who, exactly, were the protesters? On 29 January 2011, the British ambassador in Cairo, Dominic Asquith, was telling *Today*'s John Humphrys:

> I have been struck by the variety of age, class and indeed gender. It is across the board, you can see it, people can see it [on] TV screens, can see the variety of people there. It's not, from my perception, religiously driven – it's not the Muslim Brotherhood pushing it. These are people who have been, over the past two or three years, making clear what their aspirations, their desires, are and what kind of Egypt they want to live in.

The following week, on Saturday 5 February, *Today*'s James Naughtie presented a special edition of the programme from the Egyptian capital, as protesters milled uneasily around the parked tanks and beneath the circling helicopters. He found Dr Mamdouh Hamza, 'one of the leading figures in the anti-government movement', ferrying banners to protesters which carried slogans such as 'The martyr – we will take revenge when Mubarak falls'. By this time, around 80 people had died during the unrest. But Naughtie also confirmed the ambassador's view of the diversity of the opposition to Mubarak. He was told by one woman:

> You find today a lot of workers who were demonstrating before, but nobody paid attention to their demands; you find people from the American university; you find people who went to Egyptian universities and didn't find jobs for years and years. This man is an entrepreneur and founder of a mobile-phone company... and he is one of the best rowers over the Nile; we used to row together.

In another exchange, Naughtie heard how people had found their voice:

> Egyptian woman: I am here because I am standing with the people. I have to tell you that the youth are the people and they were the ones who made the revolution and we didn't help them at the beginning...
>
> Naughtie: You already call it a 'revolution'...
>
> Egyptian woman: Yes, of course, this is people power at its best and I want to tell you that we, the older generation, were scared at first after years and years, scores of years of oppression, and now is the time to stand with them and stand for our rights. We want democracy. We want freedom; we want the end of this oppression.

Naughtie gauged the mood of the protesters and told his listeners: 'Looking at this crowd, they are not scared.' Another woman interjected:

> Why should they be scared? We don't aim for any destroying of our country; we love our country as any other. We need the world. We need freedom.

James Naughtie was joined live in Cairo by Dr Ibrahim Kamel, a member of the general secretariat of President Murabak's ruling National Democratic Party. When Dr Kamel told him that 'all the people in Tahrir Square represent a minority and not the majority of the Egyptian people', Naughtie responded:

> What struck me, very forcibly, yesterday particularly, was that when you get Mr Suleiman, the vice-president, saying these people should go home, these people's parents should tell them to go home... for goodness' sake, I was talking to doctors, businessmen, to one of the most important commercial lawyers in Cairo, who was going to Tahrir Square. These weren't kids on a day out. The kids who were rough in the streets were the people who were supporting the president, who I personally saw wielding chains, knives and swords on the street, unmolested by the police, unmolested by the army, and there to attack those who wanted to protest peacefully. That is the problem. Does the president realise it?

Dr Kamel said it was wrong to suggest that the demands of the protesters had been fully rejected, but Naughtie was sceptical:

> I was in the square on the night before last. There was shooting from high buildings, there were attacks, there was an armed camel charge, which you are well aware of, there was stone-throwing. I didn't see among the protesters – and I was there for several hours – a *single* weapon. They were fired on and they were attacked. *Why*, if they were making what you have described as peaceful protest, for changes which might be acceptable, why were they attacked?

Naughtie concluded by asking Dr Kamel, 'We are agreed on one thing: that you accept that as a consequence of this there will be a change in Egypt. Will it be change under the president or not?' Dr Kamel replied, 'Hopefully the change will take place under President Mubarak, until the end of his term. I also hope that Egypt will become a better place for all Egyptians.'

The first hope, at least, was not to be. Amid burgeoning protests, and despite ever more concessions and the promises of elections, Mubarak's position grew weaker by the day. Running battles involving gangs of Mubarak loyalists did not help his cause, and, in an important move, the army declared that it would not use force to suppress the 'legitimate rights of the people'. On the evening of 11 February 2011, the vice-president announced Mubarak's resignation, with immediate effect. Between 25 January and 11 February a revolution had occurred, one soon to be dubbed the Eighteen Days.

A year and a half later, William Hague was back in the *Today* studio to talk about Egypt. The intervening time had been a rollercoaster for the Egyptian people. When free elections finally came, in May 2012, they produced a slim majority for the Muslim Brotherhood under the new president Mohammed Morsi, but the diversity that had been such a strength during the anti-Mubarak protests now exposed the fractures in Egyptian society, as Morsi's rule increasingly alienated secular Egyptians, Coptic Christians and – crucially – the army. The end came on 4 July 2013. For *Today* listeners, John Humphrys summed up the story that morning.:

> Democracy was born in Egypt on May 23rd last year, when the country voted in the first free elections in its history. It died at one o'clock this morning, when the army arrested the very man who had been elected president; and the very people who had brought about the overthrow of the previous regime, with their mass protest against the old military dictatorship, were back on the streets last night, cheering the very military who are now once again in power.

Having set the scene, Humphrys turned to the foreign secretary in the studio.

> Humphrys: So, do we now, having recognised the former president, do we now say he is gone and do we now recognise a new military government in Egypt?

> Hague: Well, we don't support military intervention as a way to resolve disputes in a democratic system as I made clear in my statement overnight. There is, of course, a dangerous precedent to do that, and if one president can be deposed by the military than another can be in the future, so that is a dangerous thing. However, we have to recognise now the situation will move on and the important thing is for political leaders and others in Egypt to work together in a way they haven't done over the last year to bring in the checks and balances that should be there in a constitution respected by all, to make sure that elections are respected by all, and to make urgent improvements to the Egyptian economy. I think that is the practical agenda whatever the rights and wrongs and whatever our feelings are about operating in this way.

> Humphrys: So that answer to my question, is yes, we do recognise this new military regime?

> Hague: Well, we want to see a civilian-led…

Humphrys: Indeed, I know what we want to see, but I am asking our present position is, as of this morning, the British government accepts there is a new government in Egypt?

Hague: We recognise states not governments and we recognise the state of Egypt. Therefore we recognise the state of Egypt, and we have to work with whoever is in authority in Egypt and we have to do that for the safety of British nationals, we have to do that because there are so many British companies there, so there isn't really a question of not recognising a particular government, we work, of course, with the authorities in Egypt, we make our views clear as I have just been doing, this is a military intervention in a democratic system – we have to understand it is a popular intervention, there is no doubt about that, in the current state of opinion in Egypt – so while warning the precedent that it sets for the future of course we have to work with the Egyptians and the majority will in Egypt and that is what we will do.

Humphrys: Do you condemn it?

Hague: I always condemn a military intervention in a democratic system.

Humphrys: Yes, but specifically in this particular case do we condemn what the military has done? After all, we supported the elections, we supported the notion of democracy in Egypt and we recognised the new president who emerged from those elections. So therefore, are we now in all conscience saying that what the military have done is plain wrong?

Hague: Yes, I think I have made that clear already, we don't support military interventions in a democratic system but that is an impractical question. In practice this will now move on very quickly. We have to recognise the enormous dissatisfaction in Egypt with what the president had done with the conduct of the government over the last year. And that is not for us to decide about that, so we will always be clear, as we were in the statement we have issued, we don't support military interventions, but we will work with the people in authority in Egypt: that is the practical reality of foreign policy.

When challenged by Humphrys as to whether Western-style democracy actually was a universally exportable system, Hague claimed people wanted 'the freedom to express their views, to choose their governments; they certainly want economic progress'. He concluded that, in the end, 'Autocracy cannot be the way of the future, in the 21st century, and it doesn't bring stability for British interests.' But, Hague asserted, in the Middle East, where religion and politics were so closely aligned, countries had to find their own way:

We do have to understand, however, that the root to those [democratic] institutions and the broad acceptance of them can be a complex one. There is a major debate taking place in many Islamic countries... about the role of religion in the state. New political parties are being formed. What is happening in the Arab Spring may well take a generation and there will be upheavals, there will be great turbulence from time to time in each of the countries. So I think we have to have the strategic patience, if you like, to live with that, and to work with that, and to respect the fact that people are having [the] debates we had in Europe for hundreds of years about the role of religion in the state.

The British riots of 2011

'I'm gonna cause some more damage!'
HACKNEY RIOTER, 9 AUGUST 2011

It's usually the Silly Season: the summer months of parliamentary recess when politicians make a getaway to warmer climes, when serious decisions are put on hold and when desperate news outlets, starved of the normal political diet, start picking through the leftovers for something to broadcast. But not in 2011. On Tuesday 9 August that year, John Humphrys announced to *Today* listeners: 'The prime minister has cut short his holiday and he'll be chairing a meeting of the COBRA emergency committee this morning.' It was not just the prime minister's break that was interrupted; Parliament was recalled two days later.

The previous morning, on 8 August, Humphrys had summed up the story so far for the *Today* audience:

> **Not for many years has London seen anything like it. On Thursday [4 August] a 29-year-old man, Mark Duggan, was shot and killed during a police operation to arrest him. By Saturday night, the area where he lived, Tottenham, was in flames. The riots had begun with a small, peaceful protest – a group of Mark Duggan's family and friends had marched to the police station to demand some answers. They wanted to know why he had been shot. Had there been an exchange of fire with the police? Did he have a gun, and did he use it? For five hours they waited and they say no one spoke to them. Soon after, the riots broke out. Shops were looted and set on fire, a bus and two police cars were burnt out, police officers were injured. It all evoked memories of the early Eighties and the Broadwater Farm riots. And it didn't stop there – there was trouble again last night.**

At first that trouble was focused on places which had seen past explosions of anger against police actions involving London's Afro-Caribbean population. Humphrys's mention of the Broadwater Farm housing estate in Tottenham brought back memories of the violence there, including the death of a suspect's mother during a police search and the brutal murder of a local policeman. But the character of the new disorder very quickly started to change and became something different from those 1980s street battles between youths and the police. As the BBC reported, branches of the opticians Vision Express, as well as Boots, Argos and JD Sports – businesses not generally thought of as symbols of police authority or the oppressive state – were attacked and looted. A bus was set on fire.

The geography of rioting was broadening too. By midnight on Sunday, shops a few miles north of Tottenham in Enfield Town and a few miles south on Oxford Street were damaged, and the fire brigade had attended scores of fires. In the early morning of Monday 8 August, the Foot Locker store in Brixton, South London, was set ablaze, while shops in Walthamstow were also targeted. There was trouble in Hackney and in Waltham Forest, and the police were talking of 'small and mobile' groups of looters roaming the capital's streets. As for Tottenham, its MP, David Lammy, was mourning a locality that had had its 'heart ripped out' by what he called 'mindless, mindless people… intent on causing violence', many of them, he judged, from outside his constituency.

On Monday morning, *Today* heard from Nicola Stanbridge, reporting from the scene of the disturbances in North London:

> **We've just moved away from Enfield's town centre and the surrounding residential roads, one blocked with wheelie bins, and hundreds of young people are running along by our car, wheel jack in the hand of one, bricks in the hands of others. Residents are out protecting their property. We took temporary refuge in the home of an off-duty policeman.**

Stanbridge's host told *Today* listeners: 'Neighbours are being attacked for defending their property… neighbours are in fear of their own lives.' The local Conservative MP for Enfield North, Nick de Bois, deplored the 'cowardly' hoodies:

> **…these people who you've just seen running up and down this road, passing their threats, cowardly, covered up with their hoodies and their face masks – they've got their mobile phones, they're organised, they're playing around on social media – there's no cause here, there is just sheer criminal behaviour.**

A bystander who had witnessed the pillaging of the Tottenham Hale retail park described what he had seen:

> **I saw people pushing trolleys into the windows, chucking bricks into them, chucking planks of wood – just to get inside, you know. Some English family, they were… you'd think they were out shopping or something. They would just come with their trolley – the wife, she was with the trolley just filling [it up] with stuff… like TVs, clothes, trainers, whatever they wanted, laptops, *everything*, and she'd pass it to her husband who's waiting round the corner. He'd take the trolley, then she'd walk back again and start filling up the trolley and keep giving it to her husband. It just kept happening. Police were not there – some turned up, but they came and just went.**

Another man told Nicola Stanbridge that these were 'unemployed people doing it for fun':

> If they're homeless, they don't have no job, they'll do anything… One guy just came out of JD Sports and he showed me, what, a T-shirt with an alarm on. They don't have nothing to do apart from looking for jobs, but they can't get jobs, so this is the kind of behaviour they get. The anger in this community.

Following Nicola Stanbridge's report from the scene, John Humphrys interviewed the Metropolitan Police assistant commissioner, Steve Kavanagh, who offered this explanation for what had happened:

> Well, part of this is the frustration of the family and the community and not getting the information they needed on the Saturday night, but also the disorder we saw later on the Saturday and on the Sunday was about greed and criminality.

Humphrys challenged the assistant commissioner over the widespread view that the police had been overwhelmed:

> Humphrys: …the impression we've all got, having looked at the pictures this morning and seeing the television pictures on Saturday and Sunday, is that things were completely out of control, there were whole areas that were effectively lawless.

> Kavanagh: On Saturday night, I agree, the levels of violence and the scenes of fire were not anything that we would have expected, but I can tell you that the number of officers that were deployed last night was three times higher, and the Metropolitan Police is actively committed to working closely with local businesses and local communities to make sure that we deal with these individuals.

> Humphrys: Yes, but I mean, we saw what was going on and it was pretty scary, and what was perhaps terribly worrying to an awful lot of people was the casual nature of a lot of it, I mean, people were going into looted shops and trying on shoes, there was a woman pushing a shopping trolley clearly out to do a bit of looting. People were taking their time about it, people were tweeting each other to say, let's meet up so and so, because there's going to be a spot of bother, let's go and do that shop. I mean, these things were *allowed to happen* and the police never seemed quite [corrects himself] – not never, that's an exaggeration – but often were not in the right place at the right time to stop it happening. It seems as if you were a bit flat-footed.

Kavanagh: On the Saturday, we weren't flat-footed on either occasion, what we were doing was protecting fire crews who were trying to put out these fires of local businesses. Clearly when there were less officers on the Saturday night decisions were made to, er, decide how we protected those fire crews...

Humphrys: Right, so there were too few people, you accept there were too few officers on Saturday night?

Kavanagh: I would accept that priorities had to be determined, and the resources were put where the greatest risks were. And we're going to be having meetings this morning with businesses, both in Tottenham and more broadly, to identify how we can try and support, consistently across London, all those businesses who are trying to make a living.

Humphrys: Well, but it's not just businesses, is it? It's buses – a bus was destroyed, a police car was set on fire. It's the impression that the mob was able, and a relatively small number of people at that, were able to take over the streets of London.

Kavanagh: The Metropolitan Police did not let people take over the streets of London. We experienced a very rapid increase in levels of violence and we got as many officers into the Haringey area as quickly as possible. Last night we had three times as many officers out. We had command and control to try and make sure the whole of London was covered. But we've got to recognise social media and other methods had been used to organise these levels of greed and criminality, and we need to adapt and learn from what we're experiencing.

As the day wore on, police and youths fought in Hackney, and fires and looting were spreading to the South London suburbs of Peckham and Croydon. At 11am, Boris Johnson, mayor of London, who was on holiday in Canada, expressed his 'complete confidence' in the police, and rejected calls for him to return home. By 6pm, when it became apparent that the situation was not improving, his spokesman announced he was on his way back to London. By around 9.30pm, Prime Minister David Cameron made the decision to abandon his own break in Italy. And by the time the leader of the opposition, Ed Miliband, announced the suspension of his holiday in Devon, two hours later, the rioting, fires and looting had spread to Woolwich and Ealing, and disturbances were reported in the West Midlands and Nottingham too.

Whatever 'it' was, it appeared to be going national. That impression was confirmed in the small hours of Tuesday morning by reports of cars aflame in Liverpool, and a police station on fire in Handsworth, Birmingham. At the same time, in London, more cars were burning in Hackney, a Panasonic retailer in Ealing was being emptied, and the Metropolitan Police reported more than a hundred people looting a Bethnal Green Tesco. Shortly before 10am on Tuesday 9 August, the London Fire Brigade declared the night to have been the busiest in its modern history, the result of more than 2,000 emergency calls. Among the bigger fires were an office block and shopping centre in Woolwich and an enormous Sony warehouse in Enfield, which destroyed thousands of music CDs.

For the Tuesday morning's *Today*, reporter Andrew Hosken caught up with the newly appointed Bishop of Stepney, Rt Reverend Adrian Newman, just two days after moving into his East London diocese:

> **Hosken: You're here on Clarence Road looking at this devastation – burnt-out cars, looted shops, masked men walking around. What do you make of it all?**
>
> **Newman: Well, I think most people here would recognise this as an apocalyptic scene, in which the rule of law seems to have faded into the background.**

And the bishop described the dilemma he saw facing the police:

> **When they're here, they are the butt of violence and people attack them, and that seems to set off further violence. When they withdraw, people set cars on fire and loot shops and they get attacked for not being here.**

'We're obviously in the presence of looters and rioters,' Hosken explained to *Today* listeners. He then tried to extract a rationale for their behaviour from the looters themselves. He didn't get very far, eliciting only: 'In Hackney, I wanna hear my voice on [the] BBC! If I don't, I'm gonna cause some more damage!'

That same morning, presenter Sarah Montague interviewed a furniture retailer, Trevor Reeve. Of all the fires that had been burning in London, the one that most caught the media eye was Mr Reeve's premises in Croydon: an imposing Victorian corner building, now engulfed in flame. When the first fire engines had arrived on the scene, they had been forced to leave, because the fire was too intense to fight.

'I understand this building's been in your family for, what, generations?' Montague asked.

'Yes, five generations – 1867 is when the company started,' Reeve replied.

The destruction of a local family firm of this kind seemed to call into question at least one interpretation – that the riots were an explosion of anarchist revenge against corporate giants.

But John Humphrys, presenting alongside Sarah Montague that morning, observed that 'You can't open a newspaper this morning without seeing the word "anarchy" splashed everywhere.' The big-name interviewee of the day was the home secretary,

Theresa May (also back from holiday). She was eager to emphasise the 'sheer criminality' the police faced, commending them for doing their job. Humphrys picked her up:

> That's my point, Home Secretary; that is exactly the point. We're seeing all of this happening *even though* the police are trying to do their jobs. I come back to that same question, we have lost control [of the streets, haven't we?] – if the police are doing the very best they can in the face of this criminality, and they are not prevailing, the conclusion must be that we have lost control of our streets... Should we be thinking about saying to the military that there's a job for you to do as well?

Theresa May would not be drawn on that, preferring to insist that the police would, in this instance, get the resources they needed.

Other voices in the course of that morning's programme included Councillor Paul Brant, the Labour deputy leader of Liverpool Council, who echoed May by talking about 'nothing short of pure criminality'. Jerry Blackett, the chief executive of Birmingham's Chamber of Commerce, saw it as 'opportunistic looting... some kind of mass kickback against the system'. David Cameron's decision to recall Parliament was announced mid-morning, and the prime minister also ordered a surge of police numbers in affected areas, before visiting badly hit Croydon. As night fell, however, further trouble was brewing in Manchester, Salford and Nottingham, including attacks on police stations, thefts and vandalism.

That evening, the Independent Police Complaints Commission confirmed that the gun allegedly owned by Mark Duggan had not been fired.

By the time *Today* was on air on Wednesday morning, 10 August, Bristol too had seen rioting, while in Birmingham three men had been killed in a hit-and-run incident associated with the disorder. London, however, had been 'relatively quiet'. John Humphrys told listeners, 'The tactics of flooding the streets with so many police officers – 16,000 altogether were available – seems to have worked and the looters went to ground.'

In Manchester the previous night, reporter Nick Ravenscroft spoke to some of those out on the streets.

> Ravenscroft: So, why have you been stealing this stuff? Can you not afford to buy it yourself?
>
> Youth 1: Why are you going to miss the opportunity to get free stuff that's worth, like, loads of money?
>
> Ravenscroft: So, you're saying that you could probably afford some of this stuff?
>
> Youth 1: Yeah, obviously, but it's not about that.

Ravenscroft: What is it about?

Youth 1: The government, obviously… More kids don't go [to] college no more 'cause they don't get paid, innit?

Ravenscroft: So, the fact that you're nicking shoes that you could probably afford to buy, that's about the government, is it? I don't understand.

Youth 1: It's not about that, it's about that the government aren't in control.

Ravenscroft: So, because the government can't stop you doing it, that's why you're doing it?

Youth 2: Yeah, why, what can the government do? They tried, they failed… How many people have they arrested, really, though? Like, ten? I'm not bothered. I'm going to keep doing this every day until I get caught.

Another young looter reasoned that if he were caught, he'd only get an ASBO and he'd 'live with that'.

Ravenscroft: What about if you got home tonight [and] your home had been broken into and someone had nicked all your stuff, all your parents' stuff? Nothing in the house?

Youth 2: I'd be really annoyed…

Ravenscroft: You'd be outraged.

Youth 2: Exactly.

London mayor Boris Johnson, interviewed by John Humphrys, found these youths' testimony 'chilling… absolutely chilling', before bemoaning the 'absence of respect' and offering his own solution as 'some sort of National Citizen Service, something like that to give these kids boundaries… This is about gang culture, apart from everything else. Certainly in London. Those gangs are giving kids boundaries, excitement, all those things that we need to replicate in better ways.'

The prime minister revealed his own analysis during the day, which was of a kind of meltdown in society. It was all the fault of…

… a lack of proper parenting, a lack of proper upbringing, a lack of proper ethics, a lack of proper morals – that is what we need to change. There is no one trigger that can change these things. It's about parenting, it's about discipline in schools, it's about making sure we have a welfare system that doesn't reward idleness – it is all of those things.

By the early evening, the number of arrests for riot and looting offences had exceeded 1,100, and magistrates' courts adopted 24-hour operations to process them.

When *Today* aired on Thursday 11 August, James Naughtie pressed David Cameron's coalition partner Nick Clegg, the deputy prime minister, on whether he shared the prime minister's analysis. 'David Cameron's talked about a sickness. Do you think there is a sickness in our society?' Clegg deplored the lawlessness, pointing to the very different behaviours from people of similar circumstances, but signalled a subtle difference of opinion with the prime minister, reminding listeners not to forget about other 'healthy expressions of a strong society'. He also commented that when it came to 'acquisitive crime', the generally working-class looters were by no means acting in isolation in society. After all, 'MPs break the rules on MPs' expenses.'

And then, as suddenly as it had erupted, it was over; with the streets of Britain's cities awash with police, the first quiet evening in nearly a week passed off. And whatever that week revealed, it turned out to be a violent spasm rather than a terminal shock. Within a year, London and Britain staged a notably successful Olympic Games.

Thought for the day: Tina Beattie

16 November 2017

Good morning. The fate of Zimbabwe hangs in the balance, as that beautiful and troubled country struggles to break free of tyranny.

In December 1980, we went to live in Bulawayo with our young children. Zimbabwe had become independent that year, marking the end of white minority rule. Shortly after we arrived, in February 1981, forces loyal to Joshua Nkomo's opposition party ZAPU attempted a military coup. We were warned to stay indoors, as tanks rolled into the outskirts of Bulawayo.

The uprising was quickly put down. It was a brief interruption in an otherwise happy and peaceful time in my life. Many years later, it was reported that Mugabe's government had launched a vicious purge after the coup attempt, and thousands of Ndebele people had been massacred. That story haunts me. It's a reminder of how fragile and illusory peace can be, when it's built on the silenced stories of the victims.

It's also a reminder of the importance of an independent media, with journalists who have integrity and courage in their pursuit of the facts, especially in these days of alternative news and cyber lies. Yet while facts and evidence are crucial, they're not in themselves sufficient to constitute truth. To discern truth within the raw facts of history is to be caught up in what philosopher Paul Ricoeur calls the conflict of interpretations.

I remember visiting a museum in Bulawayo where the captions on the exhibits were being changed. Terrorists were being renamed as freedom fighters, and history was being rewritten before our eyes. The factual evidence – the photos and artefacts – remained the same, but the interpretation was changing. It's a reminder of the saying that history is written by the victors.

Meanwhile, the trauma of Zimbabwean people continues, as the political battles rage on. It's too early to know who the winners will be – who will write the definitive history of these turbulent times. Yet behind every official history, there lurk the hidden victims, the bodies of those whose stories disturb our illusory peace.

When Pontius Pilate asked Jesus, 'What is truth?', Jesus did not respond. For me, that silence is an eloquent affirmation that testifying to truth isn't about abstract propositions and beliefs, nor about factual evidence alone – important though that is. It's about what we stand for, whom we stand with, and whose stories we seek to tell, in the face of tyranny and despotism.

CHAPTER 2

BRITAIN'S POLITICAL LANDSCAPE

The electoral upset of 1970

'Signs of a very big vote'
HAROLD WILSON, 19 JUNE 1970

Election results were still coming in when *Today* went on the air on the morning of 19 June 1970. The programme broadcast an interview given by the prime minister, Harold Wilson, to David Dimbleby during the election-night coverage on BBC television. Mr Wilson was trying to put a brave face on things, hoping that northern and Scottish constituencies would prove to be the cavalry coming to his rescue:

> Well, of course I'm disappointed by the results that we've been having, but it could turn out to be a very close-run thing. Your computer, which, may I say, in 1964 and '66 exaggerated the Labour majority... has been sliding from a Conservative majority, at one time of a hundred down to the forties, and of course... a lot of the major industrial seats, including Scotland, [are] still to be declared.
>
> ...
>
> Dimbleby: Prime Minister, what do you think went wrong with what seemed to be a very popular and successful campaign?
>
> Wilson: Umm... I think it is very hard to say...

Wilson found himself in an unexpectedly uncomfortable position; he had begun the campaign with the polls looking good, and a recent by-election win in the bag. Economic prospects seemed to be improving, and a somewhat stiff and uncommunicative leader of the opposition, Edward Heath, was getting poor ratings with the public. Wilson's decision to call a snap election had looked like a low-risk gamble.

The Conservatives had left office after 13 years in 1964, shortly after the Beatles found themselves spearheading a cultural revolution. The 'Swinging Sixties' – culturally, 1963–70 – were then almost entirely Labour years, during which time legislation to modernise, to liberalise, to de-imperialise and to 'comprehensivise' the schools paralleled the unfolding freedoms in personal and social behaviour. But the government struggled with a persistent trade deficit, and in 1967 Wilson was forced to devalue the pound.

Labour lost 16 seats in 27 by-elections over those years, but in March 1970 they had a satisfying win in the South Ayrshire by-election, and that was followed by healthy local election results in May. Britain's 18-year-olds had finally got the vote the year before, in May 1969, and the Labour Party hoped that women voters would reward it for the Equal Pay Act, which became law in the same month. There was enough encouraging news, from the economy to the polls, to convince Harold Wilson that 18 June 1970 would be the time to go to the country. An experienced prime minister with an easy-going common-man touch, he seemed likely to outshine his Conservative rival, Ted Heath, in the upcoming election campaign.

The government's economic policy had by now generated impressive surpluses and a healthy growth in GDP and, in April 1970, there was a widespread expectation that the chancellor, Roy Jenkins, would present an election budget including substantial tax cuts. But Jenkins stuck to his plans for consolidating the economy's recovery instead. The following month the run of good economic figures was rudely interrupted by a trade deficit, and Heath took the opportunity to remind voters of the bad old economic days of 1967, suggesting that a Labour victory risked more troubles for sterling. And less than a week before polling day England was knocked out of the World Cup quarter-finals in an extra-time defeat by West Germany. Wilson could hardly be blamed for that, but it spoiled the mood nonetheless.

For all that, and the narrowing polls, a Labour victory still seemed assured on election morning. But by midnight the results were showing swings to the Conservatives, mostly of around 4–6 per cent. In his interview with Dimbleby, Wilson cried foul about what he called Heath's 'unscrupulous exploitation of one month's trade figures', and when reminded that he had 'accused Mr Heath of lack of patriotism in bringing up this question of the strength of sterling', Wilson again suggested shabby behaviour: 'I think it's very irresponsible for any statesman of any party to start playing politics with sterling.' In Wilson's view, Heath may have been winning, but he wasn't playing fair. And he then tried to rally the troops: 'Much too early to start to analyse the situation. We've had tremendous enthusiasm and signs of a very big vote.'

The Liberal Party was suffering too. Its eventual 7.5 per cent of the national vote did not translate into a proportionate number of seats – the typical fate of a third party in the British electoral system – and it lost a third of its MPs, which returned it to the dismal plateau of six seats, on which it had slumped for most of the 1950s and 1960s. In another interview broadcast on *Today* that morning Robin Day, back at the BBC after his time at ITN and now part of the corporation's election team, asked the Liberal leader Jeremy Thorpe:

> If there is a Conservative government, and the contrary hasn't yet been predicted, your forecasts, and your strategy, in the election has [sic] been totally wrong, hasn't it? Because you've been saying Labour's going to get in, therefore put in the Liberals as a sensible kind of opposition.

Even this political leader, so often described as 'charismatic' and whose self-confident swagger and *élan* had enlivened the House of Commons, could offer only subdued rhetoric, resorting to, 'I think it's too early to say.' But Thorpe correctly observed that 'there has obviously been polarisation' and 'there has been a swing to the right'.

That was a reference to one of the salient features of the campaign: the prominence of the Tory MP Enoch Powell and the issue of immigration he had done so much to raise. Powell, a compelling orator and vocal about his patriotism, had become both famous and notorious following his so-called 'rivers of blood' speech two years earlier. In an address to the West Midlands Area Conservative Political Centre on Labour's Race Relations Bill, he said, in a reference to the Latin poet Virgil (Powell had taught classics before serving in the army during the Second World War), that if Commonwealth immigration from the Caribbean and Indian subcontinent was allowed to continue 'like the Roman, I seem to see "the River Tiber foaming with much blood"'. By the following evening Heath had sacked him from the Shadow Cabinet for a speech 'liable to exacerbate racial tensions'.

Opprobrium poured on Powell from many quarters, but so did support from like-minded politicians and some sections of the public; 'Powellism' grew as a force of its own: a thorn in the side of Heath's mainstream Conservatism. Dimbleby picked up the theme in his election night interview with Harold Wilson:

> **Dimbleby: What part do you think that Mr Powell's speeches on race and on 'the enemy within' may have had in swinging votes to the Tories?**
>
> **Wilson: Well, I always thought that there would be an adverse swing to us in the constituencies round about his own... particularly those fought by Powellite candidates, which, as I warned, Mr Heath has got to cope with... And where Mr Powell has spoken for his candidates, he's put us in a very difficult situation, but, of course, there will be a serious reckoning for that. But I'm very, very glad that we held Smethwick, where we had an anti-racialist candidate, who fought with great courage and held.**

Today listeners in 1970 would have known the significance of Wilson's reference to the Birmingham Smethwick seat, which, in 1964, had witnessed what the *Guardian* later described as 'Britain's most racist election'. It was won by a Conservative candidate said to have used the slogan, 'If you want a nigger for a neighbour, vote Labour.'

In the 1970 election, Powell retained his Wolverhampton South-West seat with a swing towards him of 8.7 per cent. He had become such a prominent figure on the political landscape that when Robin Day interviewed him for the election-night coverage he asked him whether his election message had really been more about his own party's leadership:

Mr Powell, a lot of commentators were saying that you had judged the Tories were going to lose, and therefore you made, by the character of your speeches, in effect, a bid for the Tory leadership if the Tories were out of office. Did you mistime your activities?

It looked very much as if Edward Heath would be prime minister by this stage, and Powell responded, 'In the last few days the consensus has been that I have done a great deal more to help my party than to hinder it, if indeed anything to hinder it.' When Day pressed him outright on whether 'the Tory Party needs new leadership', Powell gave Heath a qualified vote of confidence:

> I understand that it has leadership at present, and indeed we've had the advantage of reading, week by week, that that leadership itself shows itself renewed, in new forms, in new facets. I can't see this point about asking for a new leadership.

When asked, 'Do you pay tribute to Mr Heath's leadership in this campaign?' Powell could not quite reply in the affirmative, preferring the formulation, 'If he has won it, which I take it you are assuming he has, that is the best tribute, to win.' So Robin Day continued to press Powell on his relations with Heath:

> Day: Mr Powell, the implications of some of Mr Heath's remarks were that some of your speeches were a divisive force in the community. Are you going to moderate this after the election?
>
> Powell: I would hate to bandy words, above all adjectives, with my leader.
>
> Day: What do you mean you would hate to? You love it.
>
> Powell: What, bandying words with my leader? Certainly not! Certainly not! Only on one occasion and in the mildest terms have I uttered any personal criticism whatsoever of Mr Heath...
>
> Day: You did the other night. You complained that he had referred to you as 'un-Christian' and so on and 'inhuman'.
>
> Powell: Yes, those are *his* words about *me*, not my words about him!

The BBC routinely calls in reporters from all over its news and current affairs operations for election night, and Michael Charlton, a reporter on the BBC's *Panorama* programme, was at the count in Ted Heath's Bexley constituency. He asked the Conservative leader, 'How do you explain yourself this dramatic reversal of everything the polls have been saying up till now?' Despite a few words of caution, for the sake of decorum, Heath – with some accuracy – stressed turnout: 'A complete determination by our supporters to go to the poll; and this convinced me, in fact, that we were going to get the results we wanted.' But quickly the issue of the Powellites reared its head, as Charlton asked:

> In your own constituency here, you had a candidate standing against you on the issues of immigration and the Common Market, both of which, of course, you've taken strong positions on yourself. How much do you think this present result tonight has been helped by Mr Enoch Powell?

Charlton raised the difficult paradox that, despite the Conservative manifesto's rejection of Powellite views, the presence of Powell and his supporters in the party seemed to have helped give it an electoral boost; indeed, possibly given it a decisive edge. Heath was dismissive of its influence in his own constituency, but admitted that the nature of the pro-Conservative swing differed around the country:

> Charlton: It's a problem you think you'll be able to handle, Mr Powell?
>
> Heath: We have a very clear policy on immigration, and that's a policy we shall put into effect when we become the government.

Could Heath, though, now afford to marginalise the Powellites if they had been influential in his victory? Heath stuck to his line: 'As far as I'm concerned, I have no personal animosity towards Mr Powell. The policies which we're going to pursue are those we've placed before the electorate.'

When Charlton asked him, 'But the support for both of you, does it mean that you will have to repair the breach with him?' Heath was dogged in his response: 'It is a question of policy.'

The Conservatives did, of course, win, with 46 per cent of the vote and an overall majority of 30 seats. Enoch Powell remained on the Conservative backbenches, until Heath's commitment to joining the European Economic Community drove him from the party altogether.

Four years after snatching victory from the jaws of defeat, Heath – by then administering a country rocked by energy shortages and industrial strife but leading a party ahead in the polls – called his own snap election. He won the popular vote – just – but Labour emerged with more MPs. After four days of struggling to put together a coalition with Jeremy Thorpe's Liberals, Heath threw in the towel. The man who replaced him was Harold Wilson. Heath lost another election in the autumn of that year; in 1975 he resigned as party leader, and Margaret Thatcher replaced him.

It was Enoch Powell who once said, 'All political lives, unless they are cut off in midstream at a happy juncture, end in failure, because that is the nature of politics and of human affairs.'

Britain joins the Common Market, 1 January 1973

'The main celebrations were in Brussels'

COLIN DORAN, *TODAY* 1 JANUARY 1973

On 1 January 1973 *Today* opened with the French national anthem, the 'Marseillaise'. As the programme's headlines reported in its first broadcast of the new year, 'Britain is now officially in the Common Market. The main celebrations were in Brussels, the community's administrative centre... Here in Britain, the historic occasion passed with little special celebration, either public or private.'

Douglas Cameron, presenting from the studio, called it an 'historic and significant morning', but followed this up with the news that 'Common Market or not, we've still got some good old-fashioned British fog' and 'black ice, I am afraid, in Dorset'. He then introduced one of those *Today* rituals that could not be interrupted, even by such a momentous development: Eileen Fowler, the programme's regular fitness instructor, talked the listeners through her exercise for the day, promising them they would 'feel much better and more alive if you pep up the circulation' and exhorting, 'Let's swing into 1973 with a warm-up.'

The news bulletin did offer the listeners some good cheer –'The first effect of membership will be more duty-free allowances for travellers' – and the programme reminded its audience that 'The new Common Market, with a population of more than 250 million people, is the world's largest trading group'. The New Year's Day programme always included items on the latest honours: 'Several people who helped to get us into Europe are honoured in the New Year's list,' the bulletin announced.

It was the culmination of a long and sometimes difficult journey. In the immediate aftermath of the Second World War, Europe's nations had been forced to look inward rather than outward; Germany had been defeated, Britain and France had both been terribly drained by the conflict. The dawning of the Cold War saw the emergence of two superpowers, the United States and the Soviet Union, and Europe found itself caught between them. Much of Western Europe owed its security to the new (1949) US-dominated North Atlantic Treaty Organization (NATO).

But in 1951 six countries (France, West Germany, Italy, Belgium, the Netherlands and Luxembourg) formed the European Coal and Steel Community (ECSC). Robert

Schuman, the French foreign minister who proposed the project, stated explicitly that his ambition went beyond economics; he wanted, he declared, to 'make war not only unthinkable but materially impossible' by creating a common market in the two commodities most essential to munitions production. With the signing of the Treaty of Rome in 1957 the ECSC became the broader European Economic Community, or EEC.

Britain refused to join the ECSC – partly because Clement Attlee's post-war Labour government had nationalised much of the coal and steel industries. And there were of course deeper political, diplomatic and cultural reasons for British reticence about the project; the so-called 'special relationship' with the United States (a very prominent factor in the aftermath of the Second World War), historic ties to empire and the Commonwealth, scepticism about supranational institutions, and the folk memory of Britain's lonely – for a while – resistance to Hitler all played a part.

Harold Macmillan, who became the Conservative prime minister in 1957 in the aftermath of the Suez crisis, concluded that, to maintain its prosperity and influence, Britain must join the EEC after all. But the British application for membership was twice (in 1963 and 1967) vetoed by the French leader Charles de Gaulle. 'The entry of Britain would completely alter the entire set of arrangements, understandings, compensations, rules that have been agreed between the Six,' de Gaulle declared, adding, for good measure, his suspicion that Britain would prove a Trojan Horse for American influence, so that the EEC 'would take on the appearance of a colossal Atlantic community under American dependence and direction'.

It was not until de Gaulle had been replaced by Georges Pompidou and Edward Heath was in Downing Street that negotiations really took off. Heath, who, as an artillery officer during the Second World War, had seen what nationalism could do, was a passionate believer in the European ideal.

That background helps to explain the ambiguous tone of some of *Today's* coverage on the morning of Britain's accession.

Robert Robinson presented part of the programme from Paris – *Today* was to be co-presented from different European cities throughout the week – where he found the early morning 'faintly more aromatic, an immemorial compound of lavatories, stockpots and tobacco', and played cheerfully with national stereotypes in a way no broadcaster could possibly do today. Now that what had 'for so long been promised or threatened, depending which way you look at it, has come to pass', would British fears that their country might be overrun by 'foreigners with their funny ways' from day one of membership be realised?

Would the British streets be full of Frenchmen forcing butter at 30 bob a pound on innocent passers-by? Italians selling striped day-glow ice cream to

Englishmen, whose religion, of course, forbids them all save vanilla? Germans with two-acre faces... pressing eight-foot sausage rings through the letterboxes of Anglos and Saxons, who only bangers knew?

'No,' he declared, 'not really, not a dachshund barked... Bacon and eggs and not Dutch cheese, as I am sure Douglas [Cameron] will know, is being served for breakfast as usual...'

As the American magazine *Newsweek* comically put it, 'The British were sleepwalking into the Common Market.' Bit of a let-down, if truth be told. You can't help feeling the occasion might have been marked with some sort of public ceremony: free issue of black berets, say, or a dinner of *Spargel* [asparagus] and *Petersilienkartoffeln* [parsley potatoes] with the diplomat of your choice – but, no, it seems that going into the Common Market was little more than a state of mind.

Heath's government did, in fact, earmark £350,000 for celebrations in the weeks following accession to the EEC, but that was something the then leader of the opposition, Harold Wilson, railed against; the British economy was in a parlous state. In addition, the Northern Ireland Troubles were causing mayhem; another *Today* headline of 1 January 1973 stated, 'In Belfast, the New Year was marked by several shooting incidents...'

Edward Heath himself was on an official visit to Canada that morning, but before leaving he had given an interview to the BBC which was broadcast on *Today*. He summarised what he saw as the potential long-term benefits to Britain joining the EEC, and downplayed the idea that there would be big changes in everyday life for 'ordinary' British people:

It's going to be a gradual development. Obviously, everything isn't going to happen overnight. They won't find things entirely different the next day. They'll see changes in a wide variety of ways. If you take businessmen, they'll find that, more and more, they're working more closely in Europe with firms... firms coming together, developing markets, sales organisations... They'll be going to Europe; Europeans will be coming here from the [European Economic] Community, and so on... I think we will see that with the increase in business and trade, we shall have more jobs for people, which is what really matters... We shall find that there's a great cross-fertilisation of knowledge and information, not only in business, but in every other sphere.

Later in the programme, Robert Robinson, interviewing a French Gaullist MP, Michel Boscher, reflected some of the common British concerns about the EEC and its ambitions:

> Robinson: We have the impression that all members of the Common Market are equal, but that some are more equal than others, and there is some feeling that France considers herself to be the major force in the community. Is this true or is it simple mythology?

> Boscher: I think, you know, the community after all did spring up from an idea which was primarily a French one... I think France was and remained for a long time the major power, not so much economically speaking, but by the willpower she showed in this matter. And at the beginning, actually, France and Germany were the major powers, obviously. Now Britain's coming in, there will be three major powers, there will be three larger powers, economically speaking and politically speaking. I wouldn't say that France is wishing to play, or willing to play, a predominant role, but probably one of the major roles, which we will share, obviously, with both Britain and Germany.

Robinson next tackled the European Parliament, because, in his words, 'There's some impression that it's a kind of mime, or charade, and it has no real power. Do you foresee,' he asked Boscher, 'a time when it will have real power?' The French MP admitted that:

> ...a parliament can hardly wield power if it hasn't any government, responsible government, in front of it to criticise or to overthrow, as the case may be. As there is, for obvious reasons, no possibility in the very near future of a European government of a traditional style to come into existence, the European Parliament is of course curtailed in its powers, but, nevertheless, morally speaking, it is doing a very good job.

'Well now,' continued Robinson, 'this sort of brings us on to something that is very central to anyone in Britain who has given thought to the Economic Community here, something that worries them.' He was referring to 'the possibility of a loss of national identity as a consequence of membership, a fear that our own political institutions may ultimately become subservient to some kind of supranational body staffed by faceless European bureaucrats'. 'Has that,' Robinson wondered, 'in any way been France's experience?' Boscher was adamant:

> No, no. We've always taken that very same stand which you've just mentioned, that is to say, we are dead against the 'Eurocratisation' of our country. And the way the market and... the EEC has been working has always preserved our

national identity which we desire to maintain most strongly. And I don't think that we can expect or hope for some type of united Europe which would do away with national identity. I think national identities are part of the heritage of Europe and they must remain so.

Two other big issues – agriculture and the scale of Britain's contribution to the budget – were raised on *Today* by the BBC's agricultural correspondent, Archie McPhee:

Farmers are certainly confident that they can meet the challenge of the new policy, which, offering as it does the prospect of better prices, is not always seen to be fair, especially to countries providing the major share of the community's budget. Our net contribution in 1973 is estimated to be £100 million, or about 8.5 per cent of the total budget, rising to £200 million, or 19 per cent, by 1977. Guaranteed prices for farmers will also be raised gradually during the transitional period of five years.

Today asked one of Britain's first European commissioners, George Thomson, to answer specific questions from listeners' letters. In response to one, he covered the right to free movement of labour:

The ordinary worker is in a relatively privileged position compared to professional people because, immediately, ordinary workers will be able to go where they want within the community to find the jobs they want, but with the professional people, there are still barriers, because of the different qualifications and diplomas... The real work on this very vital aspect of freedom of movement will in fact be done with Britain in from the beginning... and we won't be faced, as we have [been] faced so often in the Common Market, with a *fait accompli*.

But that edition of the programme also included an interview which foreshadowed the now widespread perception that freedom of movement threatens jobs and pay at home. Today that concern is felt most keenly by workers in manual trades such as plumbing – in January 1973 it was expressed on *Today* by Peter Plouvier, the general secretary of the actors' union Equity. He was talking to the *Today* reporter Malcolm Billings.

Plouvier: Entry into the Common Market of itself isn't such a grim prospect. What we've got is an extremely grim situation of underpayment and underemployment in this country amongst British performers, so that any additions to the competition, any swelling of the workforce available for the very few jobs that are there, is obviously very detrimental to us.

Billings: But would you expect many actors, many entertainers coming from Common Market countries taking jobs from British entertainers?

Plouvier: Well, I think that quite a few will, and quite a few already have.

Billings: For example, what sort of things?

Plouvier: Immediately, of course, the people who perform without having to use the language, the singers, the dancers, singers in opera, dancers in ballet, chorus dancers, variety artists, speciality acts in particular.

Billings: What about actors?

Plouvier: Indeed, there will be some competition, and due to our lamentable education system in this country... I think they are better equipped to compete with us than we with them when it comes to language.

The BBC's correspondent in Brussels that morning was Ian McDougall, and he interviewed Walter Farr, Brussels correspondent for the *Daily Telegraph* (a position later held by the future Conservative foreign secretary Boris Johnson). McDougall describe political union as 'the Community's ultimate aim', and asked Farr about the chances that it would be achieved by the end of the decade. Farr replied:

I think they are very, very considerable. It isn't certain. Any country, particularly one of the bigger countries, can slow things down, but it can't prevent what Mr Heath and the other heads of government were committed [to] at the October summit in Paris: to first of all preparing a report, an outline plan on European union, by 1975. This looks to the establishing of a European Union by 1980. I think there's a very good chance of that coming about.

That prediction proved premature; the Maastricht Treaty which created today's European Union was not agreed until 1992. But even in January 1973 there was plenty of debate about what a real union might mean. On 2 January *Today* broadcast an interview with the German foreign minister Walter Scheel; it was conducted by the Berlin-based correspondent Norman Crossland.

Scheel: I'm delighted that Britain has finally joined our European club. I think your people will find that it is not a bad club. Britain's sense of statesmanship and traditional spirit of enterprise will be of inestimable value to this European Community. Mark you, we must be clear in our minds about what sort of a Europe we want. Certainly, its economic potential will be remarkable. But we should not regard it as just another economic lobby or as a sort of giant limited stock company. The Europe we want must speak with one voice politically. And become a solid pillar of world peace. Otherwise we cannot expect the rest of the world to listen to us. The last European summit in Paris has mapped out our long-run goal. Union by nineteen hundred and eighty. Until then a lot of hard work is required from all of us.

Crossland: Herr Minister, how do you think the political organs of the community can be strengthened?

Scheel: The political cooperation is the life and soul of our European partnership. It means a continuous process of consultation, coordination, harmonisation of national attitudes towards the manifold political problems confronting the community.

In February 1974, just over a year after Britain joined the EEC, Edward Heath lost a general election to Labour, who offered the British people a referendum on whether to stay in. On 5 June 1975, in the only nationwide British referendum of the 20th century, 67 per cent of voters who participated chose for Britain to remain in the EEC. That referendum secured Britain's membership in the club, but Britain remained a sometimes awkward partner, criticised by its European neighbours as 'semi-detached'. The 1975 vote certainly did not settle the European debate in Britain, and the 2016 EU referendum was to provoke perhaps Britain's most intense political debate since the Second World War.

In 1973, however, all that was to come. On that New Year's Day, as Ian McDougall, the BBC's man in Brussels, reported, it was simply time to raise a glass:

A main centre of celebrations was an English-style pub of the type that have recently sprung up all over Belgium, and a fair proportion of the 12,000 or so British inhabitants of Brussels seem to have managed to squeeze into it... In a radio station belonging to the [European] Commission, toasts were drunk in champagne by senior officials and their guests, while a piper, dressed in the full Royal Stewart regalia, played the bagpipes. In private life, he's a sergeant in the Belgian army, but he told me he spent many of his holidays studying the bagpipes at classes in Glasgow.

Belgian bagpipers?
Back then it seemed a fitting emblem of the new European era.

The Winter of Discontent

'You're really helping to bring down a Labour government'

TONY WILKINSON, 22 JANUARY 1979

The prominence of trade unions in the national discourse in 1978 and 1979 seems, by comparison with today, astonishing. Although they remain important players in some traditional industries – such as the railways – their role in what is, in many ways, a post-industrial economy is much diminished. But for politicians of both the Conservative and Labour parties in the 1970s, reaching an accommodation with union leaders was a necessary condition for the smooth running of the country; it was all part of post-war consensus politics, whereby – when it worked – all interested groups and classes exercised restraint for the sake of stability, social cohesion and the gradual economic improvement of the country as a whole.

It was a consensus, though, that was breaking down. Since 1974 the Labour administration had struggled with high inflation, high unemployment and falling sterling values, which had forced Chancellor Denis Healey, in late 1975, into the humiliation of asking the International Monetary Fund for a loan – a bailout. The IMF in turn demanded extra public-spending cuts, which enraged many Labour politicians and their supporters.

The government did, however, have some success in achieving restraint in pay demands, the result of a 'social contract' with leading unions. In May 1976, the Trades Union Congress (TUC) agreed to the second stage of the government's incomes policy, limiting weekly pay rises to no more than £4.

By 1978, with inflation down to less than 10 per cent, the economy was in a considerably better shape, and the country expected Labour, by then governing without a Commons majority, to call a general election and capitalise on the improved position. But the prime minister, Jim Callaghan, delayed, anticipating an even more strengthened position in the coming year. It turned out to be a fatal error; he faced wholesale rebellion against his government's policies by large numbers of working people, who were fed up with their wages falling behind.

The first sign of trouble for the government had come back in February 1977, when a few thousand toolroom workers at the nationalised car-making giant British Leyland unofficially withdrew their labour, complaining of narrowing differentials in pay; in so doing, they caused much larger lay-offs elsewhere in the company. This totemic company was receiving considerable government investment to keep it afloat, but only on the condition that it generated a defined proportion of profit; at the same time, it was plagued with industrial disputes and lost production, and now one sub-section of its workers had had enough of pay policy.

On 3 March *Today* broadcast an interview with Gerald Kaufman, minister of state for industry. The BBC reporter Tony Wilkinson asked him bluntly, 'Do you think, in fact, that this is the end of British Leyland? Do you think it could possibly survive now?' Kaufman hedged his bets: 'I'm neither optimistic nor pessimistic and I never am. I just hope that good sense will prevail.' The company staggered on, although so did its travails.

For a while, consensus held, and in July 1977 the government introduced the third stage of its incomes policy, limiting pay rises to 10 per cent maximum. The straw that broke the camel's back was Healey's move, a year later, to cut that limit to 5 per cent. This time, the government received a chorus of disapproval, from within the Labour Party and from the TUC.

The first major rebellion against the incomes regime was at Ford, where workers put in for a 30 per cent pay rise, backed by the Transport and General Workers Union (TGWU). The credibility of the government's pay policy was at stake, and on 25 September 1978 *Today* revealed just how polarised the unions and government were becoming. First of all, the BBC's David Mellor (a journalist not to be confused with the Conservative politician of the same name) summed up the dilemma for Ford:

> What's happening this morning is that at mass meetings throughout the country, the Ford workers are being asked to back the committee which has been negotiating on their behalf and to recommend an indefinite stoppage. The guess is that they will, overwhelmingly, and that the company will be shut down probably by the middle of this week. For the Ford management it's a terrible dilemma. If they give in to the unions, they might well have sanctions taken against them by the government, costing more than £100 million. On the other hand, a strike closing all the factories could run up a bill of around £10 million a day.

David Mellor's reporter package included interviews with Ron Todd of the TGWU and Joel Barnett, chief secretary to the Treasury. Todd said that Ford workers would consider a productivity deal but only if they got a decent share of Ford profits. He had a message for Ford and the government:

> The company have got to determine whether they're going to acquiesce to the government's threat of sanctions or whether they are going to make an offer to their workforce in line with their profitability. If they choose to allow the

government criteria to influence their judgement, that's their business. It's getting so in this country today, that to talk in terms of free collective bargaining is to sound revolutionary.

Joel Barnett warned Ford workers that, 'It would not help them and it certainly wouldn't help the country if they were to have an all-out strike, whether they win or lose,' adding that 'As far as the government is concerned, we are determined… that we shouldn't get back to the kinds of price inflation that we had all too recently.' Though Ron Todd rejected the arguments that wage claims would make Ford cars more expensive, Barnett was having none of Todd's logic:

> What I find surprising about trade union leaders in particular, many of the trade union leaders, who are using this argument of having a bigger share of the profits that were made in one year, is [that] the same trade union leaders, all too frequently, wouldn't be prepared to accept a cut in salaries were they working for a firm that was losing money. And, you know, over the country as a whole, if everybody were to settle at the same kind of levels of claims we're getting, then the money wouldn't be worth the paper on which it's printed.

As Mellor explained, 'Many of the union men feel that Ford are [being] singled out unfairly, that their pay talks are held up as a norm, by which later settlements with other groups will be judged.' At the end of the package Barnett told Mellor: 'I can assure you, the Ford workers and everybody else, [there's] no question about it: the government intend to stand firm because we believe it's right.'

After a five-week strike, Ford workers settled for a 17 per cent pay rise, more than three times the government's limit. Many other companies, less in the spotlight, were breaching the 5 per cent ceiling too. Government threats to punish the transgressor companies were rebuffed when, in December 1978, proposed legislation to impose sanctions was diluted in the House of Commons.

A Pandora's Box had been opened. Ironically, it was Jim Callaghan, a one-time union official who had opposed union reform in the previous Labour government, who now felt its effects, as unions tested what was possible. Under existing laws, unions did not need to conduct ballots of members to declare strike action; they could pursue secondary picketing at unconnected sites and premises that were still working; and there was no requirement to accede to arbitration. As chilly December 1978 turned to a consistently sub-zero January 1979, the ripple effect of strikes spread out.

Following an overtime ban by fuel-tanker drivers, hauliers in the TGWU stopped working in many parts of the country on 3 January 1979. A *Today* report from that day included this exchange between Radio Solent's Nigel Farrell and Albert Simpson of the Road Haulage Association:

Farrell: What kind of goods are we talking about? Indeed, what kind of trade are we talking about?

Simpson: We're talking about pretty well everything that you and I use in our daily lives. Everything that you use from the time you get up in the morning until the time you go to bed has got to you by a lorry.

The reporter, *Today*'s Mike Wooldridge, summed up what a strike could mean for ordinary people:

The impact of the strike will be reduced, initially anyway, by the fact that the present weather conditions would probably have kept quite a number of lorries off the road anyway. But, whatever the outcome of the strike, one thing is certain, say the employers: any wage increase will mean higher haulage charges, and that ultimately means higher prices in the shops.

Petrol stations, devoid of supplies, closed, and secondary picketing spread to ports and refineries. Since lorries provided useful mobile barricades, roads were blocked: the city of Hull acquired the nickname 'Siege City' in the media and was virtually cut off. Behind the scenes, the government made contingency plans to call troops in to take over fuel deliveries. There were stories of still-working drivers leaking their destinations to strikers, so that secondary sites would then be picketed. In the end, after about four weeks of striking, the drivers settled for a 13 per cent rise.

Government PR efforts were not helped by the fact that Callaghan, after attending an international conference on arms reduction in Guadeloupe, had stayed in the Caribbean for a winter-sun getaway. At the Heathrow press conference on his return on 10 January, his tone-deaf rejection of a picture of 'mounting chaos' at home was mercilessly translated by the *Sun* into the headline 'Crisis? What crisis?' The phrase stuck.

The prime minister returned home in time to see an epidemic of strikes now spread to the very men and women whom the government employed directly – public service workers – who now wanted their own, often very low, pay to catch up. Railwaymen went on strike, as did ambulance drivers and nurses. Schools could not stay open. Monday 22 January marked a 'Day of Action', including mass rallies and demonstrations. It was now that the members of the National Union of Public Employees (NUPE) flexed its muscle to negotiate a 14 per cent pay rise, as water and sewage workers withdrew their labour too.

On the *Today* programme on 22 January 1979, Tony Wilkinson made this case to NUPE's general secretary Alan Fisher:

> It could be argued that by having a day of strikes, like you are today, that you're putting yet another nail in the coffin of the social contract and that you're really helping to bring down a Labour government which you're meant to support.

Fisher rejected that view, reminding Wilkinson and *Today*'s listeners of the delicate relationship between the government and unionised labour:

> Of course, looking at it the other way round, the government itself must be very sensitive about the possibility of having a confrontation with such a large group of low-paid workers who they themselves employ. They are the employers and I think they must realise the situation, just as we realise it, and for that reason I think that we shall be able to reach an agreement with the government about the way in which we should tackle this particular problem.

The most lurid episodes of what, borrowing from Shakespeare, history remembers as this 'Winter of Discontent' were provided courtesy of striking refuse collectors and grave-diggers. In Liverpool, bodies had to be stacked up in temporary storage facilities, awaiting burial. In London, Westminster Council designated Soho's Leicester Square as a dumping ground for uncollected rubbish. 'Fester Square', as it was nicknamed, was a short way from the *Today* offices in Portland Place, and in early February 1979 Hugh Sykes was reporting from the scene:

> Well, back to Leicester Square, where at half past 12 this morning people were still bringing their own office rubbish to dump it at this emergency refuse site. Even though the site is not a particular fire risk because it is carefully supervised, the council are keeping an eye in another particular respect. There are signs – red-lettered signs – all round the piles of rubbish here, which read 'poison baits are being used here to eradicate rodents.'

At the end of January, *Today* broadcast an interview with Edward Heath in which the former prime minister offered his own view of the national situation. Any temptation to exult in Labour's woes was tempered by the memory of his own bruising treatment at the hands of the miners' union five years previously, though he felt that Callaghan had a bigger problem because he was being 'challenged almost across the board'. Instead, Heath tried to apply a statesmanlike long view. He told the BBC's Ray Gowdridge:

> In the House of Commons, we've all got to accept a number of things. The first is that we are all confronted with common problems: there is no point really in going on any longer in saying that these things occur with one side or the other side, but not with us. The whole country knows that in fact they occur with

BEHIND THE SCENES

Today programme production team listening back to the programme, 1959.
Left to right: Paul Stephenson, Jocelyn Ferguson and Elizabeth Brewer.

The presenter's view from the studio looking into the production cubicle, 1959.
Left to right: producer Robert Craddock, John Sykes and studio manager Maureen Milton-Dinnis.

Josee Robinson and Muriel Timpson, wives of *Today* presenters Robert Robinson and John Timpson, are photographed with their husbands in the studio behind them, 1971.

Brian Redhead, who presented the *Today* programme from Manchester for nearly three years, reads the morning papers before going on air, 1976.

John Humphrys in the production office, 1988.

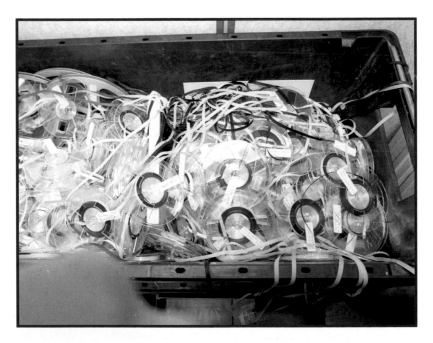

Before the development of digital technology, *Today* producers and reporters painstakingly edited their radio recordings on reels of tape. This photograph from 1994 shows a box full of taped recordings for the *Today* programme, destined either to be archived or wiped and re-used.

Members of staff in the *Today*
production office, 1994.

John Humphrys in the *Today* production office
in Broadcasting House on the last day before its
move to BBC Television Centre, 1998.

Presenter Sarah Montague reads the newspapers and briefing notes to prepare
for the *Today* programme, 2003.

John Humphrys takes a picture of newsreader Corrie Corfield and sports presenter
Garry Richardson during the first broadcast of the *Today* programme
in its new home in studio S33, New Broadcasting House, 2012.

John Humphrys and Evan Davis presenting a broadcast of the
Today programme from New Broadcasting House, December 2012.

Left to right: sports presenter Alison Mitchell, newsreader Corrie Corfield, and presenters Mishal Husain and Sarah Montague, 2013.

Presenters Justin Webb and Sarah Montague in the studio in New Broadcasting House, 2016.

'On Air' and 'Mic Live' signs outside the *Today* programme radio studio in BBC Television Centre.

John Humphrys and Martha Kearney in the *Today* studio, 2018.

John Humphrys and Justin Webb, 2018.

ON LOCATION

Brian Hanrahan on HMS *Hermes*, reporting during the Falkland Islands conflict in 1982.

Producer Tamzen Audas and Edward Stourton in Helmand province, Afghanistan.

Presenter James Naughtie in the city of Karbala in Iraq in 2003.

John Humphrys broadcasting from the Basra Palace British military base in Iraq, 2006.

Producer Terry O'Neill and presenter Evan Davis broadcast live from a rooftop in Liberia, 2012.

Today programme kit on a military aircraft.

John Humphrys preparing to broadcast for a special edition of the *Today* programme
from Basra in Iraq, 2008.

Evan Davis reports from Liberia, for the *Today* programme in 2012.

Mishal Husain broadcasts live from a Syrian refugee settlement in Lebanon's Bekaa Valley, 2014. Beside her is Ninette Kelly, UNHCR's representative in Lebanon.

Mishal Husain talks to Syrian women living in a refugee camp near the Lebanese border during the Syrian conflict, 2014.

Justin Webb broadcasts live from Bournemouth Hospital, 2018, for a special programme to mark the 70th anniversary of the NHS. With him is Tony Spotswood, the then chief executive of the Royal Bournemouth and Christchurch Hospital NHS Foundation Trust.

Martha Kearney reports from Israel and the Occupied Palestinian Territories, 2018.

Martha Kearney broadcasts live from Jerusalem, 2018.

POLITICAL FIGURES

Sir John Eden, minister of post and telecommunications, pictured in the centre, with *Today* presenters Robert Robinson and John Timpson, 1972.

Today presenter Peter Hobday interviewing Alan Beith MP at the Liberal Democrat Party Conference, Bournemouth, 1991.

Prime Minister John Major being interviewed by James Naughtie, 1995.

Former prime minister Baroness
Thatcher being interviewed, 1992.

William Hague as Conservative leader,
in the *Today* studio, 2001.

Prime Minister Tony Blair being interviewed by James Naughtie on the *Today* programme,
in Bournemouth at the Labour Party Conference, 2003.

James Naughtie with Prime Minister Gordon Brown at the *Today* studio at the
Labour Party Conference, Manchester, 2008.

Labour leader Jeremy Corbyn being
interviewed on the *Today* programme, 2017.

Prime Minister Theresa May being interviewed on the *Today* programme by Nick Robinson
(far right, next to Justin Webb) in 2017. The BBC's political editor Laura Kuenssberg
is behind the prime minister.

Environment secretary Michael Gove, himself a former *Today* producer,
being interviewed, 2018.

governments of both kinds, both Conservative and Labour, but they occur in every Parliament and they've been going on, really, for the last 30 years.

Heath advocated discussions and a bipartisan search for common ground. Gowdridge wondered, 'You're not, though, speaking of a coalition government of any kind, are you? Or government of national unity?' Heath wouldn't be drawn on that:

> How you go about that, whether it's best to do it in public or whether it's best to do it first of all behind the scenes and reach agreement about it, this is a matter which the leaders of both major parties must decide.

For this Conservative politician, the real enemy was a kind of a mob mentality that had got the better of workers' common sense:

> There is something really very deep and rather strange going on in our society today. What we're really seeing is that groups of people are feeling they've got to assert themselves, in a way which really contradicts what they know is right for the community as a whole. If you ask them, they'll say, 'Of course we've got to deal with inflation,' but when they feel as a group, then their emotions overcome their reason. This is really the basic struggle which is facing us today and this is why I feel that we can only deal with it if in Parliament we show that we are united on a common ground... Then people in the country will also feel that they ought to achieve a unity and they will recognise what is [in] the national interest.

It was the classic voice of a politician of the war generation, prioritising national cohesion and unity rather than tribalism. And as with other politicians of that era, the war defined his sense of proportion – no amount of union militancy could compare to the dislocations of that seismic global event.

In due course over the spring of 1979, union leaders, knowing that wage settlements at such levels could not continue without deleterious effects on employment and inflation – and alarmed by the more strident members of their own rank and file – came to a compromise agreement for a more gradual slide towards a future 5 per cent pay limit. But for the Labour Party, and in many ways for the unions themselves, it was too late. For it was not just strikers who had been discontented that winter. Large swathes of the country were transferring their political allegiance to the opposition, appalled at the disruption, the power of the unions and the inefficacy of Callaghan's government in ensuring basic services.

On 22 January 1979 in their *Today* interview, Tony Wilkinson had asked NUPE's Alan Fisher whether the risk of strike action was that 'you bring down the Labour government at the same time'. Fisher remained sanguine:

No, I don't think that it will bring down the Labour government... I don't think if we had a general election, either today or whenever that general election comes, that what is happening now will be the major issue that will be in front of the public when they come to the ballot box.

He was wrong.

The Winter of Discontent had, in many ways, fixed a view of both the Labour government and the striking unions in voters' minds. When a general election arrived, in May 1979, the unions and Jim Callaghan found themselves facing not the consensus-minded Mr Heath, but the woman who had toppled him from the Conservative leadership back in 1975: Margaret Thatcher. She had very different ideas to her predecessor and would change Britain, and its unions, forever.

The rise and fall of Margaret Thatcher

'Make me thoughtful but not moody, helpful but not bossy'

'THE OLD NUN'S PRAYER', 17TH CENTURY, QUOTED ON *TODAY*, 28 OCTOBER 1982

Margaret Thatcher was a regular *Today* listener, even if not always a fan of the programme; after a round of campaign interviews during the 1987 election she records in her autobiography, 'Over the weekend I had several more big interviews. The *Today* programme on Saturday was characteristically hostile.' She appeared as a guest many times during her long political career, and the *Today* archive reflects a politician who went through a more complex evolution than her reputation for uncompromising ideology suggests.

As a new education secretary in the Conservative government of Edward Heath – following his unexpected victory in the snap general election of 1970 – she quickly reversed her Labour predecessor's drive to force local authorities to abandon the 11-plus examination, saving the remaining state and 'voluntary-aided' grammar schools (some permanently and some for a few more years). But she also found that the general move towards a national system of comprehensive schools carried its own momentum, and she was, in fact, responsible for ushering many such schools into existence.

In July 1970 she gave an interview to the BBC's education correspondent David Smeeton – which was broadcast on *Today* – about her decision to give local authorities the freedom to decide what kind of schools they would fund.

> **Thatcher: Let's look at the position from two different standpoints. Before today's policy decision, what was happening was that the then government was saying, 'Whitehall knows best about the sort of secondary schools you shall have locally.' It further went on to say, 'You shall not have new schools until you provide the sort of schools we say now.' Since today's policy decision we are saying that local education authorities and parents and electors have some right to a say in the sort of schools they shall have locally and that we're not having any sanctions on their decisions by holding up schools from being built. Indeed,**

as you know we have today released some 3 million pounds' worth of school building programmes to go full steam ahead.

Smeeton: I think it's very firmly in people's minds that this decision is also designed to preserve the grammar schools and possibly slow up the drive towards comprehensive schooling.

Thatcher: Well, the difference between then and now is that compulsion is gone. And now if people want to go comprehensive and this has full support – and a number of Conservative authorities have already gone comprehensive – they're free to do so. We really have increased the amount of freedom to local authorities either to go further comprehensive, or if they think they've got a very good system of education as it is now, then they can continue with it.

The Margaret Thatcher Foundation (a website offering historical documents relating to the Thatcher period) describes this period as 'a rough ride' for her, one during which 'the opposition press vilified her'. Her decision to end the provision of free milk in the nation's primary schools earned her the soubriquet 'Thatcher, Thatcher, milk-snatcher'. But when Edward Heath lost office in 1974 his loss became her opportunity. In 1975 this relative outsider made an audacious bid for the party leadership – and won.

In opposition, her party had to make a decision about Europe: would the Conservatives back renegotiated terms of Britain's membership of the European Economic Community? In an interview broadcast on *Today* on 17 April 1975, just two months into her leadership, Robert Fox asked her, 'Do you think that this issue overrides your responsibilities as a parliamentary opposition? Should you in fact be seen to be helping a Labour prime minister out, against the majority of his party?' Her answer revealed both a warmth towards the concept of Europe and a belief that principle should trump party politics:

I feel very strongly indeed that as a political party, the Conservative Party, my party, must make up its mind on the big issues of the day. Having made up its mind, it must pursue the line which it has decided upon, regardless of the party political consequences. We've always been a party that has recognised that Britain has a future in Europe. Britain can represent the Commonwealth in Europe. It would be absolutely wrong for us to play politics with that and turn round and say, well, because we could topple the present government we're going to be non-European. That would be, oh, fundamentally wrong, and I couldn't possibly do it.

Following the collapse of Jim Callaghan's authority in the Winter of Discontent, she won the general election held in May 1979, but during her first years in power she presided over a divided government; she was opposed by the so-called Wets, one-nation Conservative traditionalists who emphasised social cohesion. Margaret Thatcher was, however, helped by the fact that the opposition was also divided; in 1981 four senior Labour figures – Roy Jenkins, David Owen, Bill Rodgers and Shirley Williams – left the party to form the new centrist Social Democratic Party, or SDP.

During Thatcher's first term in office unemployment soared to 3 million, the sales tax (VAT) almost doubled to 15 per cent, controversial reform of the unions began, public spending was cut, the privatisation of state-owned companies and industries commenced, and there were full-blown race riots in London, Liverpool, Bristol and elsewhere, while the IRA attacked Central London. But her electoral prospects were greatly improved by the huge personal boost from an unlooked-for war in the South Atlantic. Her bold decision to sanction the risky venture to recover the Falkland Islands from Argentinian invaders was rewarded by success.

In October 1982, still enjoying the post-Falklands euphoria, she gave an interview to *Today*'s John Timpson about a prayer which she had chosen for a charity anthology. 'The Old Nun's Prayer' is a 17th-century text which is still much quoted as a source of down-to-earth wisdom.

> **Timpson: There are various points in this prayer which are difficult enough for ordinary people to follow. It must be even more difficult for prime ministers to follow, if I could quote one or two – the first one that says, 'Keep me from getting talkative and particularly from the fatal habit of thinking I must say something on every occasion.' Presumably, part of a prime minister's job *is* to say something?**

> **Thatcher: Oh no, no! Prime ministers have to do a tremendous amount of listening. Listening to other ministers, listening to foreign statesmen when they come. A tremendous amount of listening. And you really can't say something on every single occasion...**

> **Timpson: Well, it goes on to say, 'Release me from the craving to try to straighten out everybody's affairs.' Now, surely that must be part of your duties?**

> **Thatcher: No, no, no! People must try to straighten out their own affairs. That's very much in keeping with everything I believe. Governments have to do certain things and then people, but it's far better, you know, for people to straighten out their own affairs than governments.**

'I love it! I love it!' she breathlessly proclaimed, warming to the exchange; 'Come on, let's go on to the next one. There's so many, phrase after phrase; they're wonderful!'

'"Make me thoughtful but not moody, helpful but not bossy." How do you feel about that?' ventured Timpson. She replied:

> Well, I can't stand people who are moody. I think it's one of the worst things in life. You know: a great heavy pall comes over the whole atmosphere if one person is moody and you're having to smooth and calm them down the whole time, being tactful and, oh… it's not at all nice.

The interview was regularly interspersed with Timpson's chuckles.

But there was no jollity two years later when, on 12 October 1984, Timpson found himself an early-morning witness to the gravest personal threat to Margaret Thatcher during her premiership: the IRA attempt on her life.

> Good morning, from John Timpson in Brighton. Where, at ten to three this morning, an explosion extensively damaged the Grand Hotel, in which the prime minister and a number of her Cabinet were staying. They escaped unhurt, but it's reported that two people have died and about 24 are injured. Reports are still coming in. The prime minister's suite was badly damaged, the windows were blown in, and it's thought that the policemen on duty in the corridor or outside were among the injured. The foreign secretary's suite next door was also damaged; the sitting room was wrecked. But he too escaped injury, and so did the home secretary, Mr Leon Brittan, who was in the adjoining suite. I was in my room in the Metropole Hotel next door when the explosion woke me.

The broadcast then switched to a noticeably emotional Margaret Thatcher speaking to the BBC's political editor John Cole half an hour earlier, at Brighton Central police station:

> Thatcher: Geoffrey Howe [the then foreign secretary who had escaped unhurt] is here with us and Leon is here with us, the home secretary. We are all very, very fortunate people, very fortunate indeed.

> Cole: Were you asleep at the time, Prime Minister?

> Thatcher: No, I was up working. The bomb went off somewhere between quarter to three and three. I know that because I looked up when I'd finished something at quarter to three and I just turned to do one final paper. And then, it went off. My husband was in bed, and all the windows went, and the bathroom was extremely badly damaged…

> Cole: Have you any message for people at breakfast time about the atrocity?

> Thatcher: I can only say, as usual, the police were there very quickly, almost immediately, on the scene there. We are very worried about the policemen who were on duty outside. The firemen came extremely quickly. We were very, very,

very fortunate and anxiously awaiting news of other people. You hear about these atrocities, these bombs: you don't expect them to happen to you... But you must go on as usual.

Cole: The conference will go on?

Thatcher: The conference will go on *as usual*.

The conference opened on time, at 9.30am, and her annual conference speech, which she delivered that afternoon, became an address to the nation. Last-minute tweaks took out party-political point-scoring ('This was not a time for Labour-bashing,' as she later recorded in her memoirs). She knew that her very presence at the conference spoke volumes, as she told the delegates and the world:

> The fact that we are gathered here now, shocked but composed and determined, is a sign not only that this attack has failed, but that all attempts to destroy democracy by terrorism will fail.

Five people were killed and more than 30 were injured by the bombing at the Grand Hotel. But it had failed in its chief aim – the assassination of the prime minister. The Brighton bombing's political legacy was, instead, to make Margaret Thatcher an even more dominant presence over the British political landscape.

At the end of the following year, however, she faced the first really serious challenge to her leadership over what became known as the Westland Affair. The cause of the crisis – which very nearly brought her down – now seems oddly inconsequential; Westland, Britain's last helicopter manufacturer, was in trouble and needed to be rescued. The defence secretary, Michael Heseltine, favoured a takeover by a European consortium including British Aerospace, while Mrs Thatcher and her trade and industry secretary, Leon Brittan, wanted a merger with the American company Sikorski. On 9 January 1986 Heseltine resigned and delivered a broadside against the Thatcher leadership style.

The following morning the government fielded the foreign secretary, Sir Geoffrey Howe, to face Sue MacGregor on *Today*.

MacGregor: What has emerged from Mr Heseltine's press conference yesterday is a picture of a Cabinet gagged and muzzled by a very autocratic leader. Is that how you see it?

Howe: No, I don't. I think that it's a wholly exaggerated and misleading picture that he's presented. I think that that's his view. And one cannot quite understand why he puts it in that fashion. But if you compare what one reads about previous Cabinets with what is being said by the press about this Cabinet, for heaven's sake, Churchill was said to be a dominant prime minister with whom people had to stand up to him to make their point of view heard. Attlee was said to be a silent strong dominant character up to whom you had to stand to get your point across, and people fully appreciate that the prime minister is the prime minister, the leader who takes a party to success and takes the party to office. And if the Cabinet has to work together there has to be a ready, robust and vigorous exchange of views. I didn't think it should end as this has ended with resignation, that's what makes me so sad.

McGregor: But neither of the two prime ministers that you mention, Sir Geoffrey, really had the reputation, certainly when they were prime ministers, of being quite as autocratic as Mrs Thatcher does.

Howe: Well, I happen to have spent quite some time during the Christmas holidays reading some memoirs of previous Cabinets. And if you look back in history in that way, you'll find many examples of prime ministers exercising the role of leadership, organising the Cabinet agenda, steering the general path of government and having their colleagues challenging them quite firmly from time to time. And in this government of course one has occasions when ministers speak out very plainly to the prime minister and vice versa. That's true of life in almost every form...

The saga still had another chapter to run: later that month Leon Brittan resigned from his job as the trade and industry secretary in a row over the leaking of a legal letter which criticised Michael Heseltine. On 28 January the home secretary, Douglas Hurd, told *Today* she 'must not run the government as a one-woman band'.

The prime minister rang *Today* after the programme broadcast news that the Soviet leader Mikhail Gorbachev had cancelled his visit to Britain because of a catastrophic earthquake in Armenia. Mrs Thatcher had earned her reputation as the 'Iron Lady' because of her credentials as a Cold Warrior, but after Gorbachev's rise in the Kremlin in the mid-1980s she developed an unusually close relationship with him.

It began with Gorbachev's visit to Chequers in December 1984 and reached a climax with her visit to Moscow in the spring of 1987. The Thatchers (her husband Denis accompanied her on the trip) were taken to watch the Bolshoi Ballet by the Soviet leader and his wife Raisa, and, in addition to the usual grand diplomatic banquet, the Gorbachevs entertained their British visitors at a small, informal dinner in a Foreign Ministry guest house. But there was also a long day of talks between the two leaders in the Kremlin which her foreign policy adviser Charles Powell described as 'frank, with no quarter taken or given'. Speaking from Moscow, she was interviewed by John Humphrys on *Today:*

Humphrys: How did you get on with Mr Gorbachev? On a personal level? One of his spokesmen talked about a personal chemistry between you.

Thatcher: I think that's probably right because we have always got on well together because we're both direct, we neither talk in jargon, and we prefer to talk directly. I always say when I'm talking to heads of government: Look, I know nothing about diplomatic niceties. I've never learned them. I got on quite well without them. And please I'd rather talk in very direct terms. But I hope that you will always think that they're friendly terms because they're designed to get at the truth so that we can decide which way to go.

Humphrys: So, now that you have had these meetings, do you trust him?

Thatcher: If he gave me his word on something I would trust him...

Humphrys: I think people might be intrigued to know how you set about these sort of one-on-one talks. Do you sit in easy chairs and chat or do you sit around a table and deliver set-piece speeches to each other?

Thatcher: I'm not a set-piece speaker and neither is Mr Gorbachev. No, because if you do that immediately it becomes stilted. Of course, you exchange a few pleasantries. You always do. Just to get on easy terms and just to break the ice. And there's always a little bit of nervousness particularly, when you know, as I knew at the beginning of this visit, what a very important visit it was. But then we decide the subjects we wish to discuss and the order in which we want to take them and we get down to discussing them.

Humphrys: And it's a chat? It's a discussion?

Thatcher: Oh yes, it's a genuine discussion. Oh yes, oh yes.

Humphrys: Argument?

Thatcher: Oh yes, yes, you have to have arguments.

Humphrys: Voices raised?

Thatcher: Not very often.

Humphrys: But sometimes?

Thatcher: Well, passionate arguments. I suppose when you're feeling very strongly about things you naturally raise your voice and put more passion into your tone. So yes, some passionate arguments.

Humphrys: And we're told he enjoys arguing?

Thatcher: We both do.

Gorbachev reported to the Politburo that 'she is an audacious woman' who 'acted as if she were in her own Parliament. You could not see this in a theatre.'

In 1989 Nigel Lawson resigned as chancellor after a long battle with Downing Street over the European Exchange Rate Mechanism. Just over a year later Sir Geoffrey Howe, by now deputy prime minister, also left the Cabinet; in his resignation speech, with Lawson sitting on the backbenches beside him, he famously told the Commons that her stand on Europe made negotiating there 'rather like sending your opening batsmen to the crease, only for them to find, as the first balls are being bowled, that their bats have been broken before the game by the team captain'. Howe's resignation prompted a political crisis and a leadership challenge, which culminated in Thatcher's departure from Downing Street on 28 November 1990.

On 11 January 2017, to mark the 30th anniversary of joining *Today,* John Humphrys reflected on his interviews with prime ministers: 'Mrs Thatcher was,' he said, 'insofar as any politician has ever been, unspun.' 'Imagine,' he added, 'getting into a discussion with a modern party leader a few days before a general election and talking theology.' He then replayed the interview in which she had told him that 'the fundamental reason for being on this earth is so to improve your character that you are fit for the next world'. Margaret Thatcher died on 8 April 2013.

New Labour's road to power

'It is time to break out of the past'

TONY BLAIR, LABOUR PARTY CONFERENCE, 4 OCTOBER 1994

In October 1994, three months after his election to the Labour leadership, Tony Blair gave his first leader's address to the Labour Party Conference. In a speech that promised devolution, a minimum wage, a Freedom of Information Act and a commitment to full employment, he planted solid signposts for the reshaping of his party: 'To middle- and lower-income [families]... Labour is on your side: your aspirations are our aspirations.' He acknowledged 'self-interest' as a motivating force, but added that it 'demands that we work together to achieve what we cannot do on our own.' He proclaimed, 'It is time to break out of the past and break through with a clear, radical and modern vision for Britain.' To achieve it involved a 'strong and stable economy', which 'will not be done by state control, but it will not be done either by market dogma. It can only be done by a dynamic market economy based on partnership.'

He told delegates:

I believe it is time that we had an up-to-date statement of the objects and objectives of our party. John Prescott [Labour's deputy leader] and I... will propose such a statement to the NEC [National Executive Committee]... If that statement is accepted, then let it become the objects of our party for the next election and let it take its place in our constitution for the next century.

And he rebranded his party: 'Our party – New Labour; our mission – new Britain. New Labour, new Britain.'

The next morning, 5 October 1994, James Naughtie, co-presenting *Today* from the conference in Blackpool, declared that Blair had earned 'this morning an extraordinary harvest of headlines such as no Labour leader has known in recent years, so he can be happy'.

His speech also produced, Naughtie reported, 'late into the night here in Blackpool, a bitter chorus from parts of the left, crying, "Betrayal!"'

The conference was an important milestone on Labour's long road back to power. Events during the 1980s had proved that Labour had no electoral answer to Margaret Thatcher's Conservatives; the decade became a battle for the soul of a fragmenting Labour Party, and for the left and centre-left in British politics. After managing less than 28 per cent of the votes in the 1983 general election under Michael Foot, the party elected a new leader, Neil Kinnock, who tried to drag its policies and its image towards the centre ground that had been redefined by Thatcher's success. In 1985, Kinnock appointed Peter Mandelson, a television producer (and grandson of the 1940s Labour grandee Herbert Morrison) as his communications director; Mandelson began a makeover that abandoned Labour's Red Flag symbol, so resonant of socialist struggle, in favour of a red rose. He also cultivated two new MPs from the 1983 election, Tony Blair and Gordon Brown, who shared an office – and a modernising agenda.

The task Labour faced involved recognising the lessons of Margaret Thatcher's electoral success. Voters did not trust Labour on the economy or defence. They objected to impediments to aspiration, whether in the form of excessive regulation or block-voting unions. They were also, increasingly, home-owners, including of former council houses, so no longer dependent on the state or the local council to put a roof over their heads, and, many of them, owners of shares in privatised state utilities and companies. They were also concerned about the amount of their income a government might take from them in tax.

Neil Kinnock lost to Margaret Thatcher in 1987 but he went into the election campaign of 1992 with most polls predicting a Labour victory. After his surprise defeat by John Major he stood down, and John Smith continued with the task of modernising the party until his sudden death in 1994. By that time, Blair and Brown were shadow home secretary and chancellor respectively, and both had seats on the party's ruling National Executive Committee. Blair's cheeky adoption of the slogan 'tough on crime, tough on the causes of crime' typified his desire to park Labour's tanks on the Conservative lawn. Tony Blair stood for the leadership after some kind of agreement between the two rising stars – it was widely known as the Granita Pact after the Islington restaurant where it was said to have been concluded, but there has been much debate about where their conversation – possibly conversations – took place, and what was actually agreed.

In his interview with James Naughtie at the Blackpool party conference on the morning of 5 October 1994, Blair was unapologetic about his ambitions for giving the party a new direction:

> **So, of course, there will be those that disagree, I mean you never [have] change and have unanimity, but I think that not just in the Labour Party but outside amongst Labour supporters, people know that we've got to reach out, they know that we've got to build a new coalition of support amongst the British people: the sensible modern change.**

He was anxious to dispel accusations that it was all tactical, all about electoral leverage:

What is sacred are the principles. And the reason why I said we had to start with a clear, positive statement of where the Labour Party stands is precisely to give the party identity.

Yet in revisiting the party's constitution, was there not a risk, Naughtie wondered, of Blair getting into 'some awful and tangled argument about whether "public ownership" in any form is in or out of the final statement?' But Blair promised 'words that will be clear' and offered a succinct summary of his economic vision for New Labour:

As for public ownership, I think any sensible person wants to see public services in public ownership and know that it is entirely right to do that at the same time as having a competitive market economy in which private industry is thriving. And, you know, we've really got to put behind us some of these battles from the past – there is so much change in the world, technological change, change in the way that whole markets are opening up in different parts of the world. This country has got to modernise – it's not just the Labour Party that's got to modernise, the country has to.

Tony Blair's main target in his first months as leader was Clause IV of Labour's 1918 constitution, which committed the party 'To secure for the workers by hand or by brain the full fruits of their industry and the most equitable distribution thereof that may be possible upon the basis of the common ownership of the means of production, distribution and exchange, and the best obtainable system of popular administration and control of each industry or service.' That had come to be identified with the policy of nationalisation, and was widely seen as an obstacle to restoring the trust of the electorate. It was also a powerful symbol for the left, and Blair had to fight hard to jettison it, but at a special conference in the spring of 1995, Blair secured a new version of the Clause IV commitment, 'The Labour Party is a democratic socialist party.' It reads, 'It believes that by the strength of our common endeavour we achieve more than we achieve alone, so as to create for each of us the means to realise our true potential and for all of us a community in which power, wealth and opportunity are in the hands of the many, not the few, where the rights we enjoy reflect the duties we owe, and where we live together, freely, in a spirit of solidarity, tolerance and respect.'

At that autumn's party conference, a year after laying out his ambitions to James Naughtie on *Today,* Blair began his speech with these words:

New Labour, new Britain. I know that, for some of you, New Labour has been painful and there is no greater pain to be endured in politics than the birth of a new idea, but I believe in it and I want to tell you why. Socialism for me was never about nationalisation or the power of the state, not just about economics or even politics. It is a moral purpose to life, a set of values, a belief in society, in cooperation, in achieving together what we cannot achieve alone.

As Blair joked about himself, the politician once referred to as 'Bambi' was now being described as 'Stalin' for his single-mindedness. Along with the modernising policy agenda he introduced a new discipline and control over Labour's image and its press operation. On 6 October, at the end of that 1995 conference week, John Humphrys introduced Peter Mandelson, by now an MP, with these words:

> And there are still some in the party [who] are not happy with Mr Blair and his leadership, his style of leadership – too dictatorial, they say. He has a small group of close colleagues who push through their own policies and ignore everyone else. And it's impossible for those stories to appear anywhere without the name of Peter Mandelson cropping up somewhere. He occupies a modest position in the party hierarchy – a humble junior whip – but popular legend has it that in reality he's the puppet master jerking the leader's strings, the 'evil genius' they say: 'Prince of Darkness'.

'Are you enjoying yourself, John, with that introduction?' asked the urbane Mandelson.

> Humphrys: [laughs] Well, you can't argue with what they are saying about you. We shall discuss whether it's true or not, but that's what they say about you and you know that that is the case.

> Mandelson: Yes, but one thing I've learned, John, is that you must never ever believe everything you read in the newspapers. Now that's the advice I give you for free.

> Humphrys: Thank you very much. I accept it. Now in fact there's a story in that on the front page of the *Daily Express* this morning.

> Mandelson: Yes.

> Humphrys: 'Prescott's fury at new snub.' The suggestion is that you're appearing on this prestigious programme for this 'major end-of-conference interview' – as it's described – instead of John Prescott, and he's very cross about it.

> Mandelson: Well, it's a laughable story from a newspaper which has become a comic, but I can tell you that John Prescott neither feels snubbed and nor is he furious. He was invited to come onto the programme if he chose to, later on in your programme, not now. He is instead writing his speech and I'm here as a poor and lowly substitute.

Humphrys: Poor and lonely substitute. What – lowly, not lonely. Lowly. How do you see your position in the party, quite seriously? I mean, you, you're a whip, but how do you see your influence in the party?

Mandelson: I see it in very simple terms. When I was director of campaigns and communications of the party from 1985 to 1990, and now, since becoming member of parliament for Hartlepool, I have one aim and one idea, and that is to do all I can to secure the election of a Labour government, to bring about that strong and decent society and that strong economy that we want in our country and I will devote every inch, every acre, every moment, every waking hour of my life to bringing that about.

Mandelson put the popular 'stories' about his influence, down to the fact that 'one or two people in the party, in the absence of anything else to grumble about or complain about in Tony Blair's leadership, pick instead on the one or two people around him who they think are sort of lightning conductors of their party'. His leader, he said, 'calls upon my advice, just as he calls on other people's advice' – to which a sceptical Humphrys ventured, 'Rather more than most other people, wouldn't you say?' Mandelson stuck to his air of humility and argued:

…if Tony Blair were simply centralising authority, and imposing changes on the party, as some claim, then he would never have been able to get the changes through that he's done this week in Brighton. He hasn't sort of strong-armed people. He hasn't stage-managed all these votes in order to get backing for modernisation. Delegates have been persuaded.

Equally important to the New Labour image was Blair's press secretary, Alastair Campbell. Campbell had been a close adviser to Neil Kinnock and was working as the political editor of the now defunct *Today* newspaper at the time of John Smith's death, so he was already a well-known figure in Labour circles when Blair recruited him. His robust approach to managing New Labour's media relations – particularly with the BBC – is the stuff of legend.

The Blair Years, extracts from Alastair Campbell's diaries published in 2007, is full of insights into New Labour's sophisticated media strategy. One of the party's big election promises in the 1997 campaign was not to increase the basic or top rates in income tax. Gordon Brown, the shadow chancellor, was to announce the policy in a speech on 2 January, but he trailed it in an interview on *Today*. Campbell recorded in his diary: 'GB had an enormous hit on the *Today* programme. The overnight briefing was headlining the news and then, bang in the middle of his interview with Jim Naughtie, he dropped it in. He did it very effectively. It was a big hit, one of those moments that you knew mattered.'

Labour's manifesto in the 1997 campaign promised to adopt the Conservative government's spending limits for two years. And it included phrases to tempt Conservatives – 'zero tolerance of underperformance' in schools, promoting 'personal prosperity for all', helping 'to create successful and profitable business'. The concluding pledges it made (such as 'cut class sizes to 30 or under for five-, six- and seven-year-olds by using money from the assisted places scheme') were limited, and by promising not to revolutionise, New Labour looked serious. Blair won a landslide; Labour secured 418 seats, the highest number the party has ever achieved. It heralded 13 years of New Labour in power.

After a Blair interview with John Humphrys (on the broadcaster's *On the Record* television programme rather than *Today*), Campbell noted in his diary, 'Humphrys was full of himself and I was probably a bit too rude to him, but he was so up himself it was hard not to be.' The strain of government quickly told on the relationship between New Labour and the *Today* team. During his 2017 reminiscences about 30 years on *Today*, John Humphrys recollected how an interview with New Labour's Harriet Harman 'produced a response from Downing Street the like of which this programme had never generated before: a letter threatening to withdraw cooperation from *Today* unless something was done about what they called the "John Humphrys problem".'

The 2001 election produced one of the most memorable Blair–Humphrys confrontations. In 2000, Keith Vaz, a junior minister at the Foreign Office, was accused of failing to declare money he had received from a firm of solicitors and was investigated by the Parliamentary Standards Commissioner Elizabeth Filkin. Humphrys chose that as the starting point for the interview on 14 May 2001.

> **Humphrys: Nine minutes past eight. When Tony Blair invited us to make him prime minister four years ago he was a relatively unknown quantity. He'd been in politics for a long time but he never served a day in government. He told us at his victory party that a new dawn had broken, his would be a different kind of government. Well, has it been? Mr Blair is in our radio car in his constituency for the first of our leader interviews this week. Good morning, Prime Minister.**
>
> **Blair: Good morning, John.**
>
> **Humphrys: You said that your government would be purer than pure. Has it been?**
>
> **Blair: I think where we haven't been, where people have fallen down, then action has been taken against them. But I think on the overall record of the government**

in terms of economic stability, investment in public services, the measures we've taken to make this country fairer and stronger, then I think that even though there is a very great deal more to do we can be proud of what we've done.

Humphrys: Purer than pure is a very high standard though, isn't it? And if you have in your government still a minister about whom very serious questions have been raised then you have to wonder whether that very high standard has been met, don't you?

Blair: I think you've got to ask is, if there are questions raised, what are the answers to those questions? And you actually want the answers not the questions.

Humphrys: Well, difficult in the case of Keith Vaz to know what the answers were if he failed to deal with allegations against him from the Parliamentary Standards Commissioner Miss Filkin eight times, he did that, did you not say to him, 'Look you should have done this?'

After a couple of minutes of quickfire exchanges over Mr Vaz, the prime minister went onto the offensive:

Blair: I have to tell you I find it absolutely extraordinary. You've got one of the two people here who could be prime minister of this country on June the 8th, and you've got issues to do with the economy and schools and hospitals and crime and Europe and issues of fundamental importance to the country. What you're raising are a set of allegations that were made, which are a stream of allegations that have been made, against this particular minister. All of them were looked into, in respect of the vast majority of them there was found to be no case to answer, in respect of one aspect that was found to be a case to answer, but the Commons committee recommended no disciplinary action should be taken. Can I just – hang on, John – in those circumstances to say that the man should be dismissed I think is a little harsh.

Humphrys: Can I tell you what I am trying to do? It was your ambition to restore trust in politics in this country, to clean it up. What I'm saying to you is that nothing is more important than that. It happens that after four years – and I'm not suggesting this is your direct fault – the fact is trust in politics in this country is, according to all the measures that we have, lower than it has ever been. You said you wanted to be purer than pure, on that basis all these questions should have been addressed...

A little later Tony Blair tried again:

We've been now, about, almost ten minutes into the interview, you've not asked me a single question on the economy or schools, or crime or welfare or Europe or any of the things that I would have thought your listeners would like to hear about.

Towards the end Humphrys raised the question – which was already filling plenty of column inches in the newspapers – of what exactly Tony Blair and Gordon Brown had agreed at that seminal New Labour moment alleged to have taken place at the Granita restaurant:

Humphrys: Can I just finally clear up one thing that puzzles many people still? Notwithstanding the interview you gave to the *Evening Standard* last week about Gordon Brown and any agreement you may or may not have had. You said you didn't have a written agreement with Gordon Brown to, as it were, hand over the leadership of the Labour Party to him at some point in the next four or five years, or whatever it may be; if not a written agreement did you have an unofficial agreement? Did you talk to him about it? Did you say, 'Well, look Gordon, I'm sorry you didn't get it this time around, but, you know, next time.' Something like that?

Blair: Well, I think I've answered this question.

Humphrys: Well, I'm not sure that that you have in those terms.

Blair: No, there is no agreement at all.

Humphrys: At all? Did you talk about it to him?

Blair: I stand for the full Parliament, and that's what I do, and whereas he's concentrating on being chancellor of the exchequer, I'm concentrating on being prime minister. All I would say about him is that I think he is probably one of the most successful post-war chancellors this country's seen, he is someone that we can be very proud of, and I think the country is very lucky to have him.

Humphrys: Did you talk about it to him?

Blair: I'm not going into what I talk and what I don't talk about with people. And this is back to the old personality and process rather the policies...

Humphrys: Personalities matter in politics, don't they?

Blair: Of course they do, John, of course they do. But this is not a discussion that we have. What we discuss is how we try and do the jobs that we've got.

Tony Blair's role as the moving spirit behind New Labour was, for many of the party's supporters, tarnished forever by the Iraq War. And a *Today* programme in the aftermath of that war led to one of the most serious confrontations between the BBC and the government in the corporation's history.

But since leaving office in 2007 Blair has returned from time to time to the *Today* studio, often to talk about the Middle East because of his role as a special envoy to Israel and the Palestinians (a position he held until 2015). On 10 April 2018 he faced John Humphrys again. After discussion of Syria's war and problems in the Middle East, the conversation turned to domestic politics. 'Do we need in this country a new centre party?' asked John Humphrys. Blair replied:

> If you have a Conservative Party that becomes increasingly defined by Brexit and... engages in a sort of narrow-minded nationalism on the one side, and then you have on the other side a Labour Party that is increasingly in the grip of the far left, and moving further and further to the left in its politics... you leave that vast uncultivated centre ground... At some point, someone's going to come along and cultivate it... Ultimately they've got to understand that there is a constituency in this country which is socially liberal, in favour of strong methods of social justice, but also believes in a well-run, properly run economy.

'You're not talking about New Labour, by any chance, are you?' mused Humphrys, 'because I do read that the Tony Blair Institute for Global Change is putting together the infrastructure for a new political party.' No, protested Blair, it was merely a 'policy platform'. But listeners who could remember 1994 might have been forgiven for detecting just a little of the old zeal to shake things up.

The death of Diana, Princess of Wales, 31 August 1997

'Her natural sympathy with the victims of today's world just shone through'

JONATHAN SACKS, 31 AUGUST 1997

The car crash which killed Diana, Princess of Wales, Dodi Al-Fayed and their driver, Henri Paul, took place at 12.23am, French time, on 31 August 1997, near the Pont d'Alma in Paris. Since it was a Saturday night the *Today* office was unmanned – the programme is not broadcast on Sunday – but some time after midnight London time the *Today* editor, Jon Barton, telephoned James Naughtie, one of his presenters, at his South London home. Barton told Naughtie that Dodi Al-Fayed was dead, but he reported that Diana had merely been injured. Nevertheless, he asked Naughtie to come into the office to stand by for a possible special programme.

There is a well-rehearsed BBC protocol for dealing with what are known as Category One deaths: the radio networks come together for a special rolling programme. If a member of the Royal Family has died, it is customary to wait for confirmation from Buckingham Palace before announcing the death on the air.

On 31 August Naughtie and Peter Allen, a senior presenter on Radio 5 Live, broadcast a rolling programme across Radio 2, Radio 3, Radio 4 and Radio 5 Live from the *Today* studio at Television Centre in London's Wood Lane.

Naughtie recalls that confirmation of Diana's death reached the team in an unusual way. The foreign secretary, Robin Cook, was, he says, on a trip to the Far East and had a group of journalists with him on his plane. He was summoned into the cockpit to be given the news and emerged in tears – he had come to know the princess because of her work on landmines – and told the press corps what had happened. When Naughtie and Allen went on the air at 5am the palace still had not officially confirmed the deaths; the programme began with an announcement by a newsreader, Andrew Crawford:

> This is BBC Radio in London. According to the French news agency, a French government minister has said within the past few minutes that Diana, Princess of Wales, has died. He said she was killed in a car crash in central Paris. I'll repeat that; Diana, Princess of Wales, has been killed in a car crash in the centre of Paris. Her companion, Dodi Al-Fayed, also died in the accident late last night in a road

tunnel near the River Seine. The driver of the Mercedes they were travelling in was also killed and a bodyguard was injured. Police say they were being followed by press photographers when their car apparently overturned. The princess was taken to a hospital in the city. The Prince of Wales was woken at Balmoral where he is spending his summer break with the Princes William and Harry to be told of the crash. The prime minister was also informed.

This is James Naughtie with Peter Allen bringing you the news from Paris in a special programme. We go straight to Paris now....

Confirmation of the deaths from the palace finally came at 5.20am. The special programme continued for five hours, until Naughtie and Allen gave up their seats in the studio at 10am. Naughtie remembers the strain of having to remain constantly aware that on a Sunday morning many people would be turning on their radios late, perhaps expecting some Radio 2 music to cheer up their breakfast.

BBC correspondents on the programme reflected on two factors which had made Diana stand out: the drama of her marriage to and divorce from the heir to the throne, and her quite extraordinary celebrity. The marriage had begun with the spectacularly successful royal wedding of 1981, but as the BBC's royal correspondent, Paul Reynolds, put it on the morning of 31 August, 'It was a tragedy right from the start... The wedding set such a happy tone, but it soon went wrong.' But Diana evolved into a phenomenon, and became, if anything, more famous when she and Prince Charles were divorced. The BBC's media correspondent, Torin Douglas, put it like this, 'It's a worldwide market. She sold magazines. They were worth hundreds of thousands of pounds, certain pictures... It was said that the photographer who took the first pictures of her and Dodi Al-Fayed could have made £3 million from them worldwide.'

The sense that she was different from the rest of the Royal Family and had found a new way of connecting with the public was a recurring theme of the condolences and tributes on the BBC's special programme. The prime minister, Tony Blair, described her as a 'wonderfully warm and compassionate person who people, not just in Britain, but around the world, loved'; for himself, 'She would be mourned as a friend.' Later, famously, Blair would describe Diana as 'the people's princess'. The leader of the opposition William Hague declared, 'The princess had real star quality. I think the whole nation will be in shock, and much of it in tears.'

From his Asian tour the foreign secretary, Robin Cook, said, 'I was fortunate to have the opportunity of working with the princess on her international charity work. I believe what has happened is a tragic loss at a young age of someone who'd shown great courage and commitment in drawing attention to serious issues.' Lord (David) Steel, the former Liberal leader, focused on the way Diana was able to use the power of royal celebrity to raise awareness about landmines:

> **Some of us had been campaigning on this issue, fruitlessly, for two or three years, and then suddenly she takes the issue up and it becomes a talking point and governments start to change their policies on landmines. She did that single-handedly, when all the rest of us had failed... She could get the messages home when others couldn't.**

The Archbishop of Canterbury, George Carey, was on a walking holiday in the Lake District and proved difficult to contact, but Britain's Chief Rabbi, Jonathan Sacks, a familiar voice on *Today* because of his regular contributions to Thought for the Day, declared:

> **A dazzling light has gone out of public life... I think her natural sympathy with the victims of today's world just shone through. There was something very direct and unaffected about the way she spoke to people who were ill or hungry or homeless and I think that's what made so many people warm to her and identify with her.**

One of Diana's most notable contributions to public life was her willingness to engage with those suffering from HIV/AIDS – at a time when many people still kept their distance due to a combination of prejudice and fear. Ben McKnight, of the HIV/AIDS charity London Lighthouse, came onto the special programme to speak about her work in the field, 'She's been a great supporter over many, many years. She has always been very, very sympathetic, helpful and generous. It's a huge loss for her family, obviously, but I think also for people around the world who live with HIV and AIDS.'

5Live's Peter Allen asked him, 'And when you heard the critics, and there were many, what did you think?' McKnight replied, 'I thought that they weren't really registering what she was doing, to help people in lots of different areas of deprivation and sorrow and distress.'

There had indeed, as Peter Allen suggested, been many Diana critics. In 1992, she secretly collaborated with the writer Andrew Morton on the book *Diana, Her True Story*, which made sensational, but factual, revelations about her life. The former *Sunday Times* editor Andrew Neil, interviewed on the BBC Radio special programme, described the book as 'an enormous kiss-and-tell on the House of Windsor... It brought the monarchy to a new low in public opinion.' Equally sensational was her appearance on BBC's *Panorama* in 1995, excerpts from which were repeated on BBC Radio on the day of her death: 'I'd like to be a queen of people's hearts... but I don't see myself being queen of this country. I don't think many people would want me to be queen. Actually, when I say "many people", I mean this establishment that I'm married into.' Andrew Neil noted that Diana was becoming a thorn in the monarchy's side: 'There was always going to be a problem of Diana as something of a loose cannon in the years to come. Even the fact that she was having an affair with Dodi Fayed, from a very obviously controversial family, impinged on the Royal Family.'

'It was,' declared Peter Allen in the hours after her death, 'almost a classical tragedy, the whole story.' It was suggested, time and time again during the special programme on 31 August 1997, that the press had effectively killed the Princess of Wales by obsessively pursuing her. Listeners were reminded that seven members of the paparazzi who had chased her in Paris the previous night were now being questioned by French police, who had opened a criminal investigation. Peter Allen hazarded, 'It finally seemed to be the media that drew her to her death, almost.' Robin Cook noted, 'In the longer term, serious questions will need to be asked as to whether aggressive intrusion into her privacy contributed to this tragedy.' The father of Dodi Al-Fayed, controversial Egyptian businessman Mohammed Al-Fayed, who owned the famous London store Harrods, was in 'no doubt', his spokesman Michael Cole declared on the air, that 'this tragedy would not have occurred but for the press photographers who have dogged and pursued Dodi and Princess Diana for weeks now.' Diana's brother Charles, Earl Spencer, would later go further, speaking of the paparazzi as having 'blood on their hands'.

The British press, heavily criticised already for intruding into the private lives of celebrities, was certainly scrutinised that morning; but Alun Michael, a Home Office minister, argued that there had been improvements in Britain – though he acknowledged that there still needed to be limits on excesses. Nonetheless, he added that it should be left to the British press to regulate itself. He passed the buck across the Channel: 'France has the reputation for very strict privacy laws, but the way in which the press and photographers pursue people [there] is beyond what we expect nowadays in this country.'

Mark Saunders, a photographer who, for ten years, had made a living from photographing royals, explained, 'Like a lot of people, I specialised in the Royal Family and about 70 per cent of that was Princess Diana.' He had spoken to her many times, he said, revealing that:

> **The final conversation I had with the Princess of Wales was when she said she couldn't take any more – the constant press harassment – and she was trying to get away from it… It was about six months ago… She actually followed us that day… She wanted to talk to us about the problems that she was facing with the media. And I was with my partner, Glenn Harvey. And after that conversation, you know, we decided to knock it on the head, the job. Because I felt she had a point. Maybe it was too much and that we just didn't need to do it… And then**

I saw the money that was being made by the photographers that came up behind us and I often wondered if we were right...

Saunders warned against being too fast to blame the media: 'I hate this idea of immediately blaming the press, because we don't know yet.'

The BBC broadcaster Jonathan Dimbleby, who was close to Prince Charles, suggested that rather than blaming journalists and photographers, who were acting on orders from above, attention should instead be turned to the newspaper proprietors and editors who had given those orders. Dimbleby felt they should take full responsibility for their actions. But the historian Ben Pimlott pointed to the hypocrisy of the British public blaming the paparazzi; he evoked the 'ghastly way in which we're all responsible', referring to the insatiable appetite the British public had for stories about the princess.

When *Today* was back on the air on Monday 1 September, Diana's death still dominated the news agenda. In the lead 8.10am slot James Naughtie picked up the theme of press harassment:

Naughtie: Ten past eight is the time. 'If I were a paparazzo photographer I would be keeping my head low today,' Simon Jenkins writes in *The Times* this morning. These are going to be difficult times for the press. Earl Spencer said that editors who encouraged the pursuit of the famous had 'blood on their hands'. There are some calls for privacy legislation – not, apparently, from the government. The defenders of press freedom have to acknowledge that there are excesses which make their own case a little more difficult to argue. Now in some ways, it's a very familiar debate with familiar characters arguing their cases. But there are some new questions. Will the enormity of this event, all its poignancy and tragedy, affect the way that editors make their judgements, and, just as much to the point, what readers decide to buy? Or after a decent period will nothing much have changed? I asked one former tabloid editor Richard Stott, who once edited the *Mirror* and the *Today* newspaper.

Stott: I think it probably is an event that will change things. I think that newspapers will now be much more wary about what they run, particularly on members of the Royal Family. Earl Spencer, what he said is quite understandable. I don't really think that it's a justified attack. I think that what happened in France was something that was inexcusable, in terms of a 100-mile-an-hour chase, but I don't really believe that this is something that newspapers themselves – particularly in this country – were responsible for.

Naughtie: Do you believe that, although there are obviously examples that everyone could think of which crossed a line, there are limits beyond which people generally don't go?

Stott: Oh yes, I'm absolutely certain that that's true in this country. These paparazzi are people who operate very much on the fringe of journalism. They – particularly the French ones – are ruthless aggressive thugs.

Naughtie: Do you think that habits are going to change? Because that's what we're talking about, isn't it, the habit of editors to be tickled by some picture and the habit of readers to want to buy publications that have those pictures in them.

Stott: Well, it will change because there was only one Diana. She was absolutely a one-off. She was the most famous woman in the world. She could single-handedly – and did single-handedly – put on circulations. I can't think of anybody else in the world who is in that position.

By this time more of Diana's friends were talking to the media. The BBC correspondent Gary O'Donoghue had interviewed Sarah Lindsay, the widow of Major Hugh Lindsay, who was killed in an avalanche during a skiing trip with the Prince and Princess of Wales in 1988.

Lindsay: I knew her a little bit before I got married because my husband was a friend of hers and he was the equerry to the Queen and got to know her through his job. And then when he was killed, skiing out with the Prince and Princess of Wales in Klosters, she was a tower of strength for five years, really. She looked after me and supported me and encouraged me. She was amazing.

O'Donoghue: When your husband was killed, she was there at the time?

Lindsay: I think she was out skiing. I was seven months pregnant so I was in London. But she was out in Klosters and she, yes, she came back with him.

O'Donoghue: What sort of comfort did she bring you at the time?

Lindsay: She was marvellous. I went and stayed several weekends at Highgrove. She would ring me every, I mean to begin with many times a week and then for two or three years, every Sunday evening, which she knew... She would ring me. In the summer holidays, she was fantastic. She invited me for my daughter's first birthday and had a cake for her which we shared with Prince William and Harry. She took Alice when she was one and a half to see Father Christmas with her boys. She was endlessly, she was just thoughtful and kind and knew the bad moments really. It's just beyond belief what has happened.

The sequence continued with a live Sue MacGregor interview with 'two people who knew the princess well professionally, and became her friends too', Vivienne Parry, former national organiser of the charity Birthright, and Judy Wade of *Hello* magazine.

Parry: Well, when she was a very new princess, I recall the very first event I ever ran with her. And she was shaking and trembling and sweating and kept on turning around to me and saying, 'Vivienne, was that all right, was that all right?'. And yet by the end of the time I knew her, when she was working still as patron of the charity, she was tackling huge roomfuls of people, she was confident. I was immensely proud of her, immensely proud of her.

MacGregor: But behind that confidence there was often a private crisis which she managed to mask pretty well?

Parry: Oh yes, I mean, I recall actually running an event that she attended which was the day before the Andrew Morton book was released and she must have been in the most dreadful state. Or, in fact, indeed, an event with lots of small children just before Hugh Lindsay's funeral, which must have been a terrible time for her, but she hid it all and was wonderful with everybody.

MacGregor: Were you aware of the bulimia and those problems that she had?

Parry: I was certainly aware of crises in her life and I was aware of the way in which I think people were immeasurably unjust to her.

MacGregor: Judy Wade, were people unjust to her? There has been a lot of understandable fury at what the paparazzi appear to have done, generally at the pursuing of the princess. You worked for *Hello* magazine and I imagine you have rather mixed views on this?

Wade: Well, I certainly do, Sue, because, I mean, I think it's understandable that some people are feeling very emotional and they make rash statements, but I do think there's a bit of a rush to judgement going on, especially perhaps by Earl Spencer, the princess's brother, because I think the jury's still out. We don't know what caused the accident. It could have been that Dodi and Diana asked the chauffeur to drive too fast or it could be a mechanical failure in the car. I mean, I've seen the French paparazzi in action, they're notorious and they are dreadful pests, but we can't be certain that they're responsible for the accident. And if the princess and Dodi had just stopped for a second outside the Ritz and posed for a photograph, perhaps this dreadful car chase wouldn't have happened, because there was no secret that they were having a romance.

A startling degree of media and public anger was also turned on the Royal Family itself. They were perceived by many as coldly aloof, as choosing to stay in their Scottish summer retreat of Balmoral rather than returning to London, where the princess's body had been flown. The display of public mourning, much of it focused on the princess' London home at Kensington Palace, was unprecedented, and in the immediate aftermath of Diana's death it seemed that the Royal Family had failed to grasp the national mood.

The Royal Family of course had its defenders, too. On the morning of 6 September 1997, the day of Diana's funeral, John Humphrys interviewed the Duke of Norfolk. The 82-year-old Major General Miles Fitzalan-Howard was introduced by Humphrys as 'a personal friend of the Royal Family, Britain's most senior duke and, as Earl Marshall of England, the man responsible for organising official state funerals, the last of which was for Churchill'. Diana's funeral, although it took place in Westminster Abbey, was not a full state funeral, but Humphrys asked what the duke thought of the public's response to Diana's death, and he noted the sheer 'extent of it'. 'I mean,' the duke commented, 'when Winston died, there was a great sort of national thing, and of course when George VI died too, and so on, but this, it really beats them, tops them.' Humphrys asked him whether he thought the Royal Family had misjudged the national mood:

> Duke of Norfolk: I myself... This all happened and I said, 'My golly', you know, and we saw on television this awful accident had taken place. And it never occurred to me that the Royal Family should come down from Balmoral, they should... I mean I thought obviously the Prince of Wales would come down and go to Paris. But then after they brought the coffin back to England, I'd already thought he'd go back to Balmoral, which is a sort of family holiday home for this time of year, the Royal Family holiday home. And I thought well that's fine and the poor young princes and poor Prince Charles are being comforted and the Queen Mother would be helping and so on. And it never dawned upon me that they should come down. But then, looking back on it, perhaps they ought to have come down.

> Humphrys: Do you believe that any lasting damage has been done to the monarchy as a result of this?

> Duke of Norfolk: Oh no, no, no, no. I'm sure the monarchy is totally firm here. There is always one or two people who say we ought to have changes but basically the monarchy is immensely popular. And just look at the way in the Common Market, six of the countries are monarchy and the other six republican – poor devils.

> Humphrys: But, things do change?

Duke of Norfolk: Things do change. But I'm absolutely certain that our monarchy is installed for another thousand years. You know we're all being modernised all the time, aren't we? And I think the Queen's got it very, very right, you know. And she goes forward steadily and she knows what she's doing. Obviously, the Queen Mother is consulted and the Duke of Edinburgh is consulted. And I think it goes jolly well. Now, I… You mustn't become too…. you know… familiarity can breed contempt, as they say. And she must remain royal, the Queen, you know.

At the funeral later that day the Princess of Wales's brother, Earl Spencer, caused a gasp by admonishing the Royal Family in the most public manner possible: during the eulogy itself. There was a distinct sense of the Royal Family being beleaguered, at the very least.

The cause of Diana's death still had to be addressed, and ultimately inquiries would be held in France and Britain regarding the fatal car accident. The conclusion in France was that the chauffeur Henri Paul, who had been drinking, was wholly culpable. In Britain, it was only in 2008 that a final inquiry officially brought the matter to a close, apportioning some blame to the paparazzi, although a grief-stricken Mohammed Al-Fayed remained convinced his son had been murdered at the Royal Family's instigation.

Battered banks and the financial crisis, 2007–8

'Who'd have thought it? Nationalisation is back!'
JOHN HUMPHRYS, 18 FEBRUARY 2008

On 14 September 2007 it was revealed that the massive British mortgage lender Northern Rock had been forced to go cap in hand to Britain's 'lender of last resort', the Bank of England, for money to save it from collapse. It was the moment the scale of the danger to the British financial system really struck home. Robert Peston, then business editor at the BBC, broke the story, and on that morning's *Today*, he put Northern Rock's volatile position in the wider perspective:

> We've been experiencing really appalling conditions in the financial markets over the past few weeks, conditions almost without precedent, in which really very big and important financial institutions have found it very difficult to raise money... The origin of the market turmoil was... losses on loans to borrowers in America with sort of dodgy credit histories. It's called sub-prime loans, but it's basically mortgage lending... Now, thousands of miles away in the UK, Northern Rock is the biggest UK specialist mortgage provider. It's broadly all it does... It's got a hundred billion plus of assets and most of what it does is provide loans to home-buyers. Now, traditionally, this bank has funded itself by essentially selling its loans to other investors. But in the current climate, global investors, global banks, don't wish to buy such debt. They don't wish to lend to such institutions [as] Northern Rock, so Northern Rock has had a problem over the last few weeks. It's only been able to raise money for very short periods... So it approached the Bank of England, the Treasury and the Financial Services Authority for, frankly, access to greater funds... If the chancellor hadn't stepped in, Northern Rock might well have collapsed and that would have caused not only enormous damage to its depositors, but also to the wider economy.

Asked by John Humphrys whether there might be other British financial institutions in difficulty around the corner, Peston reported that 'the market doesn't believe there's an immediate danger of another bank running into difficulties.' But the market hadn't seen that financial storms had been brewing for some time in the United States, where a colossal housing bubble had been forming since the start of the new millennium.

Banks and mortgage companies there had lent recklessly to countless uncreditworthy clients; when interest rates rose sharply in the mid-2000s, many of these borrowers were unable to fulfil repayments. Importantly, these risky 'sub-prime' loans had been, to use the market jargon, 'sliced and diced', sold on in larger, diversified packages of investments to other financial institutions, in order to spread the risk. It meant that when things started to go wrong no one had a clear view of how wide and deep the risk was.

The first signs of deep failings in financial companies appeared in the United States from early 2007. New Century Financial, a mortgage company, went bankrupt in April. By the summer, the reputable US investment bank Bear Stearns was in trouble with certain funds. In Europe, in early August 2007, the bank BNP Paribas suspended investment funds with significant exposure to the US sub-prime mortgage market. Stock markets plummeted and the banks were now very reluctant to lend to one another – it was the start of the credit crunch.

The European Central Bank acted swiftly, injecting €94 billion of liquidity into European banks to try and stop the continent's banking system seizing up. The central banks in the United States and Japan followed suit. But these first interventions did not put a halt to the turmoil. Through the rest of 2007 and throughout 2008, far more major players in the financial game would be brought to the brink of disaster.

On 14 September 2007, the day that Northern Rock's vulnerability became apparent, Professor Charles Goodhart, an economist who had served on the Bank of England's Monetary Policy Committee, appeared on *Today* to discuss the significance of what was happening. He explained how the capitalist financial system had suddenly ground to a halt: 'Well, it's a remarkable example of a relatively small problem in the United States feeding through the financial system in a weird and wonderful way, and causing all kinds of markets to seize up. And it's because markets seized up that Northern Rock couldn't maintain its business model.'

He continued:

> **With the markets seizing up, a lot of market activity on capital markets that would normally be financed otherwise is coming back in to the banks... So the banks see a huge amount of additional calls on them for loans and they don't quite know where they're going to get the money from, so they're not lending to each other... Banks are going to be much more cautious about taking new borrowers on.**

Goodhart seemed to regard the situation almost as a potentially useful correction to a bloated system, and not as a major threat to the global capitalist economy:

There was so much money, so much liquidity, in the system in the last few years it just wasn't true…In some respects, what has been happening has been a reversion to the much more sensible attitude to risk that we had in the past.

Northern Rock's chief executive, Adam Applegarth, also appeared on *Today* that morning and he was interviewed by Edward Stourton:

Stourton: So, is it true, are we right in understanding this morning, that if you hadn't got this overdraft from the Bank of England, this facility for it, you would have gone under or you might have gone under?

Applegarth: That's a really theoretical question…

Stourton: Well, not entirely, is it? I mean presumably that's exactly the question you confronted when you asked for the money or the facility to borrow this money?

Applegarth: I think it was the uncertainty behind your question that made us approach the Bank of England for this facility because we can't tell when the global freeze is going to unwind. You heard yesterday the United States secretary for finance say that he thinks it will last for some time. The governor has said the same thing. On that basis it made sense to go and get this facility now as opposed to wait.

Stourton: Let me be clear about this: I think I understand you to be saying that there was a real question mark about the viability of a huge financial institution – which you are – a real question mark over whether you could survive without this facility?

Applegarth: Without interbank lending. There's a question behind the financial system and that's why the appropriate thing to do to ensure that our customers were looked after was to approach the Bank of England earlier, which is what we did.

Applegarth ended the interview with reassurance for Northern Rocks' depositors: 'If I was a depositor, and I am,' he said, 'my funds are with Northern Rock, and given the fact it's backed by the Bank of England it's probably one of the safest places to be.' But from 14 September onwards, shares in the company dived and savers queued at branches to get their money out. In a single day, spooked investors withdrew £1 billion in savings. It was the first run on a big British bank in over a century; and this happened despite the Bank of England giving the company an emergency loan of £25 billion, and Chancellor

Alistair Darling promising that the government would guarantee all deposits held by Northern Rock.

By 19 September 2007, the Bank of England decided it had to pump £10 billion into the money markets to stimulate interbank lending. Mervyn King, its governor, had, not so long before, been celebrating, alongside Gordon Brown (previously chancellor, before he took over from Tony Blair as prime minister), how they had stabilised the British economy, stopping Britain's boom-and-bust cycle – notably through Brown granting the Bank of England independence from the government at the start of New Labour's tenure in 1997. Now, King was accused of being caught asleep at the wheel, while the Financial Services Authority, also created in 1997, confessed it had failed in its regulatory role over the banks.

On 11 November 2007 the chancellor, Alistair Darling, appeared on *Today*. John Humphrys asked him the question on everyone's mind.

> Humphrys: Are you worried?
>
> Darling: I think there's a lot of concern about the extent of the exposure that... American banks have, but I think two things are important to bear in mind. First the banks and many banks in this country have very strong balance sheets after years of making very good profits. Secondly the prospects for growth in the American economy, certainly our own economy and the wider world economy, are good, although as I said a few weeks ago, we expect the rate of growth to slow down, the point is that growth will continue. So, I do think you need to keep this in perspective. But in relation to the big banks it rather reinforces what I've been saying for some weeks now – we need to get to a far better situation where there is a great deal more transparency and more openness so that people understand the risks to which these banks become exposed and they could avoid being so exposed in the future. So, I do think we need to get into perspective but without doubt some of these big banks will see a reduction in their profits as you've seen today.
>
> Humphrys: Well, it's not just the reduction in profits. Now you make the point, sure, about it being a reduction in profits for the bank, but that isn't the main point, apart from the shareholders of the bank, of course, that isn't the main point for most, which is that if the banks stop lending money the economy has to slow down and perhaps can come to a halt, that's the problem, isn't it?
>
> Darling: I think that there are two things here; I think banks will be more cautious about their lending, and indeed, when it comes to revisiting some of the more foolish lending in the US sub-prime market that's no bad thing; as I

said before, people should be cautious about lending money if they can't be sure they would get that money back. Now, because of what has happened there is bound to be more caution in relation to lending, that's why I revised downwards my estimate of what I think will happen to the British economy in the next year, but the fundamental point is – the British economy is strong.

But there was much worse to come. From that autumn, some of the giants of the banking world, notably UBS, Citigroup and Merrill Lynch, gradually revealed how deeply exposed they were to sub-prime bad debt. Six months on, for example, Citigroup had written off $40 billion on account of its exposure.

Back in Britain, on *Today* on 18 February 2008, John Humphrys announced:

> Well, who'd have thought it? Nationalisation is back! For decades, governments, Conservative and Labour, have been selling off every state institution they could lay their hands on, and now this government's gone into reverse and bought a bank, a retail bank, of all things. What makes it even more extraordinary, as far as many observers are concerned, is that it has taken so long to do it – if it had to happen, they say, it should have happened earlier. Instead, we have had months of damaging dithering and delay and indecision.

The bank was, of course, Northern Rock. Up for interview with Humphrys was Vince Cable, the Liberal Democrats' treasury spokesman and deputy leader. Cable outlined unnecessary costs the government had incurred by initially trying to sell Northern Rock to private bidders. He then emphasised what he saw as further consequences of government indecision since September 2007:

> There's also been a cost to all the uncertainty: some of the deposits have drained away; the bank has continued to mismanage its affairs; it's been making ridiculous loans, more than the value of people's property, and that kind of thing has got to stop... So there is a tangible cost over the last few months, but we're talking here about millions, whereas the key issue is to protect the vast public investment, the £50 billion of loans and guarantees that have already been made.

Northern Rock would eventually be stabilised, but it was far from the only Western financial institution to have recklessly overextended itself. Almost exactly a year after Britain had witnessed the run on that bank, the world watched amazed as the US government stepped in to rescue America's two biggest mortgage lenders, Fannie May and Freddie Mac, from collapse. John Humphrys explained the magnitude of these companies: 'They account for nearly half of mortgages in America, that's nearly £3 trillion worth, which is why the American government has taken the extraordinary step of guaranteeing all their loans, effectively nationalising them.' On *Today,*

Jim O'Neill of Goldman Sachs described the vast bailout as a 'very, very bold and necessary move' which, he reckoned, saved the US economy from a fall of 2–3 per cent of its GDP. Asked by Humphrys why governments should interfere in the workings of capitalism like this, O'Neill replied:

> Because, at the end of the day, the government's job – and that's what they're elected for – is to look after the broader interests of its population, its people. You can't afford to have the kind of degree of mortgage-lending decline that's going on in the US and in the UK without having severe consequences for everybody.

Shockwaves still went around the financial world one week on, when the US government refused to prop up one of the most prestigious of all financial institutions, Lehman Brothers. On 15 September 2008, it earned the unfortunate honour of becoming the biggest ever company to file for bankruptcy in US history.

Today's Sarah Montague flew to New York to co-present the programme from the city's financial district on the morning of 16 September 2008. The time difference between London and the Eastern Seaboard meant that *Today* went on the air at 1am New York time, but Montague had been recording at the scene of the crime, and she introduced her pre-recorded material:

> Montague: No one here in New York can remember times like this. One of Wall Street's oldest institutions forced into bankruptcy. Another forced into a sale. Stock markets knocked for six. But, despite all that, it's what comes next that people here are really worried about. AIG was once the world's biggest insurance company. It has a trillion-dollar balance sheet and employs more than 100,000 people all around the world. But many here fear its problems are now so great that it cannot survive, and they say that could affect us all. The test will come when Wall Street opens today. The speed of this contagion is phenomenal. It was only at the weekend that Lehman Brothers was hoping to survive. It's a very different picture today, as I've been finding out. Come to Lehman Brothers here in New York and you see what it's become. A tourist attraction. People on the pavement outside and taking photos on their mobile phones – a souvenir of the moment that one of Wall Street's big names went under. It's the subject of every conversation in every bar here: Lehman's, Merrill's and the fear of what could be to come.

> Man 1: Jobs are disappearing and, as far as Lehman Brothers and Bear Stearns unravelling, it seemed like a big deal locally; AIG unravelling is a much bigger deal.

Man 2: I've been more nervous than I've been for quite some time. We're in a kind of tough downward spiral with asset price deflation, the banks trying to assure balance sheets and, you know, the end game for consumers and us and anyone else is going to be negative.

Man 3: There's been a fantastic amount of wealth destroyed.

Montague: Is it just some guys who made a lot of money in the last few years losing a bit of money?

Man 3: No, it's some guys who've made a lot of money losing all of the money. Lehman Brothers has 25,000 employees, most of them are highly paid. That's if you take a town like New York, and you look at all the people that work at Lehman and all the people that work at Bear who no longer have a job and have had all their wealth decimated, you know it's a macro event.

Among Sarah Montague's guests was Matthew Bishop, correspondent in America for *The Economist* magazine. The worries about American AIG, were ominous; there was real concern of a massive domino effect striking Western financial, investment and insurance institutions – and beyond.

Montague: When do you think was the last time we saw conditions like this?

Bishop: At the moment, we're like in the late 1920s, when you had the '29 Wall Street Crash. And the question is: are we going to get a bad government policy response, as you saw in the 1930s, that created the Great Depression? We're not in the Great Depression yet, but if the governments of the world get it wrong, this time it could become the Great Depression.

It seemed as though the overconfident masters of capitalism could indeed bring everyone else down with them. National governments had increasingly realised, throughout 2007, that they would have to step in, on an unprecedented scale, to stop the vast interconnected Western capitalist system from imploding. Sarah Montague pressed Matthew Bishop:

Montague: What is it that governments should be doing now?

Bishop: Governments face a really difficult challenge between imposing what you call 'moral hazard' – which is making sure that people who take bad risks bear the consequences of those risks – and maintaining the confidence in the system so that people who are good credits can borrow money. And it's a very thin line to walk, and I think governments have to walk that line so that people feel that they can take a risk and get rewarded, but equally that they don't get bailed out automatically if the system fails. And at the moment I think governments are out of their depth. I mean no one quite knows what the right thing to do is.

In the end, reluctantly, Western governments decided that there were some institutions that were simply 'too big to fail'. If these disintegrated, they risked causing whole sections of the overall system to collapse, with catastrophic effects for the world economy.

In Britain, on 8 October 2008, a little more than a year after Northern Rock had gone cap in hand for funds, it was decided that other, much bigger banks would need to be propped up, and on a much greater scale: to the tune of £500 billion. Britain's financial sector had been so proud of the power of its big banks, growing ever larger in recent decades to become global players, that it was flabbergasting to see the trio of HBOS, Lloyds TSB and RBS having to be rescued. The story of RBS was the most telling. Its chief executive, Sir Fred Goodwin, who had once been lauded for his aggressively expansionist ambitions, was wrestling with Barclays over the Dutch giant ABM Amro even as the credit crunch was kicking in.

New financial regulations would soon be put in place, potentially useful for the future, but in this crisis it was rather a case of locking the stable door after the horse had bolted. On *Today* on 17 June 2009, Alistair Darling argued that regulation by itself would never be enough:

> At the end of the day, a lot of this comes down to judgement and I'm going to make the point very forcibly that the first line of defence is in the bank boardrooms themselves, because it's quite obvious that if you look at what's happened over the last few years, as more and more products become more sophisticated, more complex, quite simply too many people just didn't understand what was happening and they didn't understand the risks to which they were becoming exposed.

Many Western central banks would embark on years of quantitative easing – pumping vast sums of money into their financial systems to help keep their economies afloat. Shareholders, including those of the big institutions investing people's pensions, lost huge sums. As for the taxpayers and the public at large, who were footing some of the vast bills for supporting these failed financial institutions, they saw a sharp economic recession kick in, with job losses and, in many places, house-price falls. Low interest rates virtually wiped out returns on some forms of savings. In Britain in 2010, the new coalition government of the Conservatives and Liberal Democrats ushered in 'austerity' as a central policy – for both government spending and the public sector. It meant, notably, large cuts to public spending and the freezing, over many years, of public-sector pay. These were just some of the long-term consequences of the financial crisis.

Large parts of Northern Rock, including its branches, would be acquired by Virgin Group in 2012, becoming Virgin Money, but the higher-risk assets were only sold by the government in 2016. While eventually the government's stakes in HBOS and Lloyds TSB were sold off, a decade after its rescue by the public purse RBS remained in taxpayers' hands.

What happened to the bankers?

A number lost their jobs. Some lost their reputations. A very few of the smaller fry in America were prosecuted. As to RBS's Goodwin, in a very British manner, he was stripped of his knighthood by way of punishment – what is formally known as a 'debasement'. Other knights who have suffered this indignity include Sir Roger Casement, found guilty of high treason during the First World War, and Sir Anthony Blunt, who was unmasked as a Soviet spy in 1979.

On 13 September 2018 Simon Jack, the BBC's business editor, broadcast a *Today* sequence to mark the tenth anniversary of the collapse of Lehman Brothers. He had recorded an interview with Bob Diamond, the former boss of Barclays, which had survived the financial crisis without resorting to a government bailout by securing a £12 billion loan from the state of Qatar, a move that, as the years went by, proved to be increasingly controversial, ending up in the courts. Jack introduced him as:

> ... the poster boy, if you like, for buccaneering highly paid risk-taking bankers. He turned Barclays from a pretty sleepy retail UK bank into this investment banking powerhouse, and ten years on he is still very defiant. He defends the culture that existed at Barclays despite it being involved in a number of scandals along with other banks. And he says the public should be cross with RBS because they got a 45-billion-pound bailout, but they shouldn't be cross with Barclays because they didn't. Here he is...

Diamond went on to explain:

> We were able to raise capital privately. So, I think that was very, very important for the United Kingdom and for Barclays that Barclays did not have to go to the government for funding. I think people should be angry in the way that RBS failed. We're ten-years on from the financial crisis and the shareholders have still not had the money back. And I think separating those institutions that put themselves at risk and failed and cost the taxpayers money from those institutions that were able to continue to operate. I'd like to see more balance in it.

Justin Webb, presenting the programme that morning, followed up by asking Jack, 'Is he [Bob Diamond] suggesting in the future, then, lighter touch regulation? And if he is, does he not address the kind of systemic issue that banks and all financial institutions didn't grasp the nature of the various risks that they faced and are forced to now?' Jack said:

> I asked him, was there no point in the run up to 2007/8 did you ever think, 'Gosh, you know what, we're taking too much risk, this could actually be really big trouble for us and others?' and he said, actually, in 2007 his investors came to him and said, 'Can't you take more risk? Can't you deliver higher returns?' and said he was under no regulatory pressure at all, and if you haven't got a regulator – an effective one – then you know the Darwinism of the city: you'll fill your boots with as much money as he can. And what he says now is that the reforms have been put in after they have swung too far the other way. We're trying to totally de-risk banks and he's saying without risk you don't lend to companies that need the money. Without risk you don't create economic jobs, economic growth and jobs...

In his *Today* sequence Jack followed the Bob Diamond interview with one he had conducted with Gordon Brown for BBC Television. The message from the former Labour chancellor and prime minister could not have been more different:

> I feel we're sleepwalking into the next crisis. I feel that this is a leaderless world and I think when the next crisis comes – and there will be a future crisis – we'll find that we neither have the fiscal and monetary room for manoeuvre that we had in 2008/9, or the willingness to take that action. But, perhaps most worrying of all, we will not have the international cooperation that was necessary to get us out of this worldwide crisis. So, in 2008 and 2009 we could get all the countries together – they recognised there was a common cause. They didn't start to shift the blame between each other, they just got down to the task with the G20 [Group of 20 wealthy nations] leading the job of getting the problem sorted out, but now with the trade wars, with the disagreements on climate change, with the nuclear deals that are falling through, there is no spirit of cooperation. There is division and there is protectionism, and I fear that if a new crisis came it would be an exercise for countries in shifting the blame to each other rather than acting together to solve the crisis.

The parliamentary expenses scandal, 2009

'Every receipt, from every claim, by every MP for four years'

NICK ROBINSON, 8 MAY 2009

On 8 May 2009, Harriet Harman, the leader of the House of Commons, appeared on *Today*. A voice from the government was sorely needed, to respond to the morning's newspaper revelations about the way MPs were using their parliamentary expenses. 'In our system,' Harman offered, 'we do not have the level of corruption that occurs in many other countries.'

Telling *Today* listeners that their country's elected representatives were not *quite* as awful as the hopeless cases abroad did not sound like a ringing endorsement of parliamentary probity. Perhaps she would not even have ventured it, had she had a full appreciation of the humiliation that would wash over the British political class over the next few days and weeks – a result of an old-fashioned journalistic scoop.

In 2005 the dogged writer and campaigner Heather Brooke and two national newspaper journalists spearheaded a campaign under the new Freedom of Information (FoI) legislation to have records of MPs' itemised allowances made public. It soon became clear that Parliament would only be brought kicking and screaming to a disclosure of this information, and over subsequent years it became a battle of wits between the FoI campaigners and the House of Commons, adjudicated by the information commissioner and the courts.

By June 2007, it was clear that various *categories* of MPs' subsidised expenditure would have to be made public, and the battle progressed to the question of detail – the identification of particular amounts spent on particular items or services, and the identification of addresses, too. The latter would reveal the second homes that MPs maintained as a way of running dual lives in their constituencies and at Parliament, and which incurred many of their expenses.

One MP was suspended from the House in 2008 for paying his student son £1,000 a month for unspecified 'work', of which there appeared to be no records. The employment of family members by MPs was not uncommon, but this example smacked of flagrant abuse. ('Absolutely fiddling the system' was Harriet Harman's verdict on the

Conservative MP.) Then, in March 2008, both the public and MPs got to see a document called the 'Additional Costs Claim Guide'; it was given instant celebrity in the media as the 'John Lewis List'.

It was the Parliamentary Fees Office's internal *aide memoire* for MPs' claims, and the media pored over it with glee. So now everyone knew that among the £23,000 of claims MPs were entitled to annually, the informal limit for, say, a coffee table was £250, for a TV £750 and – moving up the scale – for a new bathroom £10,000. The Fees Office appeared to dislike garden furniture (not covered), but it did allow for mortgage-interest payments on the second homes. As for receipts, until quite recently they were only required for items over £250, until the threshold was reduced to one-tenth of that. And receipts were not required for food, for which an MP could be recompensed for around £400 per month.

A few brave voices tried to argue that the allowances system was behind-the-scenes compensation for the fact that since the 1970s MPs' salaries had been kept artificially low to set a good example while governments tried to impose income policies; but it was a difficult argument to make without falling between a rock and a hard place. Would not a transparent higher salary actually be more publicly acceptable in a modern, open democracy?

By the beginning of 2009, the receipts of a handful of MPs had trickled out as a result of a test case, but more importantly, Parliament had accepted that the release of a further 1.2 million receipts would be unstoppable. But still MPs haggled over reform, scrutiny and disclosure, with proposal and counter-proposal. Party politics reared its head again. When, in January 2009, Harriet Harman tried unsuccessfully to lead a government rearguard action to exempt future receipts from FoI legislation – on the assumption that a properly audited system would be in place to stop abuses – the Conservatives refused to back it. By the end of March 2009, Sir Christopher Kelly, chairman of the Committee on Standards in Public Life, had launched an independent inquiry into the whole business of MPs' expenses.

On 8 May 2009 the *Daily Telegraph* began to publish leaked details of individual MPs' receipts. It was the beginning of an almost daily round of torture that would turn the screws on each political party in turn. On that morning's *Today*, Nick Robinson, the BBC's political editor (he only joined the programme's presenting team in 2015), explained what was to come:

> Every receipt [is to be published and scrutinised], from every claim, by every MP, for four years, made under a system which, all parties now agree, was not only open to abuse, but all too often encouraged it. The Commons had been bracing itself for this ever since losing a battle in the courts to prevent publication under Freedom of Information laws that they themselves passed. What MPs

were not ready for was a leak of every detail to a newspaper, probably in return for a very large sum of money. What ministers call 'inadvertent mistakes', others will describe much less charitably. What they say was 'within the rules', others will call plain 'greedy'.

The honour of being the subject of 'the first instalment of the gory details', in the words of *Today*'s presenter Evan Davis, went to the governing party, Labour, and Harriet Harman had the awkward task that morning of adopting a repentant tone while also trying to defend the Commons' reputation. Before introducing her, Evan Davis told listeners:

> You might be, when you read about it, surprised to see the tricks of the trade laid bare. Sequencing different properties through the designation of second home, for example, thus ensuring the taxpayer finances the bills for more than one home. You might be more shocked by the trivial. The MPs who claimed small amounts – 67p for ginger crinkle biscuits, in one case.

Within days, 'sequencing' became better known as 'flipping' – the dubious practice of swapping the 'second home' designation between an MP's two (sometimes even three) homes, and so permitting the allowances to be spent on whichever property the MP wished. And the reason the public found out about the practice was the revelation of the actual addresses linked to the expenses: a level of detail Parliament had fought hard to keep under wraps, claiming potential security risks for MPs.

'Are you proud of the Commons, of which you're leader, today?' was Evan Davis's first question to Harman. Clearly, a 'Yes' would have been inappropriate, so Harman opted for: 'Well, I know that people are angry and I know it looks bad,' before getting to the 'but', which was to emphasise that 'MPs believe in the cause of public service'. Harman tried to portray her fellow MPs as enlightened reformers who 'recognise the system has got to change' but who had slipped up because 'the rules were not sufficiently clear, they were not sufficiently robust'. Davis came back with 'Hang on... the rules are very clear' – before going on to cite a few of them.

The issue, he suggested, was not clarity, but the fact that the system depended on a level of trust that was plainly abused: 'These claims are not remotely... in touch with or in the spirit of these rules.' Harman acknowledged the 'need to restore the reputation' of the Commons, and the need to 'win back the respect of the public', but Davis picked up the belated nature of the government's reformist fervour, harking back to Harman's attempts in January to, as he put it, 'exempt details of MPs' expenses from the Freedom of Information Act':

> Now, it appears that you weren't interested in reforming the system very significantly until it became obvious you couldn't prevent publication of this

information. It looks suspiciously like you were covering it up, and your interest in reforming this system, rather late in the day, came just before we were all going to find out what the MPs were up to.

'What I don't want to see is for people to feel that all MPs are corrupt, and the system is rotten,' concluded Harman. It was certainly not the case that all MPs were corrupt – the expenses data also revealed that many acted perfectly reasonably, some even abstemiously.

But during the weekend that followed, more details emerged about Labour politicians. Luton MP Margaret Moran inexplicably had a taxpayer-subsidised second home not in London, but in Southampton, where her partner lived. The following Monday, *Today* replayed her justification that 'any MP has to have a proper family life', but the second-home system was meant to provide MPs with proximity to the House of Commons. That morning, 11 May 2009, Tony Wright, Labour MP and chairman of the House of Commons Commission, was on air to propose that MPs' expenses be externally vetted. Wright made no effort to defend the indefensible when he spoke to James Naughtie:

> **Wright: What we've been seeing is a kind of masterclass in ingenuity in how to exploit an over-generous and insufficiently scrutinised expenses system. I mean, if people haven't got the message now, they will never get it. People talk as though somehow they're the victims of this system, rather than the people who have been exploiting it.**

> **Naughtie: So, you mean the argument which we're hearing from all sides, 'It was within the rules so it's OK'… is not one that impresses you?**

> **Wright: I think if the Great British public hear that trotted out one more time, they will reach for their collective sick bag. I mean, it is the most extraordinary thing. I think we haven't had anybody yet, despite all these disclosures, who's simply said, 'Look, yes, I behaved badly,' owned up, 'I did wrong.'**

However, Labour then had a chance to breathe, for that morning's *Daily Telegraph* revelations were all about the Conservatives, such as Shadow Cabinet members Michael Gove and Andrew Lansley, both accused of flipping. Naughtie was speaking to Liam Fox, the 'frontbench spokesman that the party has made available this morning'. Fox acknowledged that 'The rules themselves were drawn in much too lax a fashion, and need to be changed, and changed in a way which is quick, which is thorough, which is independent and which is transparent.' Fox would not, though, be drawn on individuals such as the fellow Conservative who, as Naughtie put it, spent '£2,000 for some plumbing underneath a tennis court'. Or another who claimed for a wreath laid at a remembrance service. 'That's for individual MPs to defend themselves,' Fox asserted.

This day's revelations included a striking statistic about a senior Conservative MP. 'David Willetts had 25 lightbulbs changed at the cost of £100 plus VAT,' Naughtie noted, producing what the BBC's Nick Robinson referred to as 'the inevitable joke about how many members of the Shadow Cabinet are needed to change a lightbulb'. The BBC's political editor also added an unusually personal piece of commentary: 'I have grown up my entire life believing in the notion of Honourable Members. It's that that's died.'

By the end of the day the speaker of the House of Commons himself was at the centre of controversy. A peeved Michael Martin unwisely picked this moment to have the police try and trace the leak to the *Telegraph*. For horrified MPs, he was undermining all their attempts to eat humble pie and spoiling their new-found dedication to 'transparency', instead solidifying the impression that the House had something to hide. On the morning of 12 May, James Naughtie announced, 'These are torrid days and nights in the Palace of Westminster.' It was not an exaggeration. Nick Robinson followed him to confirm an atmosphere of:

> ... misery, of being misunderstood, of being misrepresented, for this simple reason, Jim. People feel that the rules of the game have changed halfway. That they do have the cost of second homes, which they need money to pay for. That they had a system of allowances, not of expenses – in other words, they were allowed a lot of money in order to contribute to their cost[s]. That they made claims under the rules, and in confidence, and that now they're being told that the rules were absurd, everything is public, and some small example is being held up to public ridicule. That is the atmosphere, like it or loathe it as an attitude, and Speaker Martin is, in many ways, speaking up for that. Why he is being criticised, is [that] there are people who say you should not merely act as a shop steward representing the House of Commons's anger, you should speak to them on behalf of the country, and on behalf of the Commons to the country, in finding a resolution to it, and yesterday he proved completely incapable of doing that.

By 13 May, expenses details for Labour, Conservative and Liberal Democrat MPs had been leaked, and party leaders were falling over themselves to offer their own reform ideas and exert discipline on their more aberrant members. There was a new spirit of all-party thinking, too. As Nick Robinson observed, 'Nothing like public outrage, is there, or the fear of looking flat-footed compared with your rivals, to produce agreement where none previously existed.' For Conservative MP Ann Widdecombe, interviewed that morning on *Today*, the result so far was not clarity but cacophony:

> The first thing to point out, which has almost been lost sight of, is that we have an independent inquiry going on under Sir Christopher Kelly, which is supposed to make recommendations, independently, to the House of Commons as to how we sort the system out so that it's both transparent and fair, but also does enable people of modest means still to be able to come into Parliament... The parties all want to come up with their own solutions, and it's becoming a competition of 'my shirt is hairier than yours', and the problem is that we will have about 25 preferred solutions of increasing hairiness before Sir Christopher Kelly is even to report.

Such calls for calm tended to be in the minority as the shockwaves of the scandal spread. Commentators predicted public vengeance against the mainstream parties at the upcoming European elections, while on 19 May, on *Today*, Conservative Party leader David Cameron argued the case for a general election, without which, in his view, 'None of this is any good: paying back money, saying sorry, trying to make amends.' Cameron had been more sure-footed than Brown in his responses when the details were leaked and saw potential electoral advantage. Yet, at the same time, on 13 May Evan Davis commented on the fact that because big amounts of money paid for mortgage interest were getting less attention than some of the more trivial claims, 'David Cameron charges the max on mortgage interest, [and] is lucky to get away with it, really, compared with some of his colleagues who have frippery on their expenses.' 'That is certainly the view of many, many Labour MPs,' noted Nick Robinson, as well as 'some on David Cameron's own side'.

The fleeter-footed among the offending MPs were quick to start repaying taxpayers' money voluntarily. Michael Gove speedily apologised, paid back £7,000 he spent on furniture after 'flipping', and lived to see his star shine brighter. Slower and more uncertain movers did less well. Labour minister Hazel Blears, who had wobbled in semi-denial, underwent the ritual humiliation of a televised handing-over of a cheque for £13,332 to compensate for the unpaid capital gains tax she'd kept on the sale of her second home: it was the beginning of her political eclipse. Speaker Martin stood down, several MPs announced they would not seek re-election, and many more were assessed for varying levels of repayment – some of them going on to fight their corners. And, eventually, the old system of allowances was swept away. Gone were the first-class travel and the flippable second homes, to be replaced by travelling with the general public and a monthly rental allowance for a single-bedroom flat.

On 25 September, the assistant editor of the *Daily Telegraph*, Andrew Pierce, explained to John Humphrys that the leak had originated in the Stationery Office at the House of Commons where civil servants were busy redacting MP's expenses before complying with a court order to publish them.

Humphrys: Taking out the stuff...

Pierce: The contentious stuff, the stuff that MPs didn't want us to read. And this was being done in a room, at the Stationery Office, which was in charge, a government agency. They employed 20 security staff, 20, to protect this operation because, clearly, they realised the stakes, how sensitive this was, the security staff included serving soldiers who'd been to Afghanistan and as civil servants were redacting or censoring or covering up or tipp-exing out the difficult details. They were exclaiming out loud to each other – just as we did in the *Telegraph* when we had the file – 'Oh my God. Can you see what they've claimed for?' And these were soldiers, some of whom were there to earn a little bit of extra money to pay for their kids' Christmas presents.

Humphrys: They were on leave or something?

Pierce: Yeah, but others were there to pay for essential body armour, gloves, boots to serve in Afghanistan...They became increasingly upset and a few of the trigger points were when they heard the civil servants saying, 'My God these Tory MPs have claimed for maintenance of their swimming pools...'

Humphrys: Final quick thought. Did money change hands between the *Telegraph* and...

Pierce: It did... We paid £110,000 to the source. And let me just say so far the taxpayer has been reimbursed by MPs £500,000 and there'll be more. We've got a much better Commons as a result of it.

The scandal did not settle down without leaving a couple of enduring details that the public and media alike seized on as symbols for the whole affair. The first was the £2,200 that Douglas Hogg MP had claimed for moat-clearance on his estate. The second was the £1,645 claimed by the no-longer-obscure Conservative backbencher Sir Peter Viggers, for what the BBC could only describe as a 'floating duck island'.

The Scottish referendum, 2014

'The genie is out of the bottle'
ANGUS ROBERTSON, 9 SEPTEMBER 2014

The genie is out of the bottle. What is on the ballot paper, what is on offer, is that Scotland can become an independent country, with all the powers that independence offers: we will always elect our Parliament; we will always elect our government; we won't be governed by a Tory government with one seat in Scotland. All of that nonsense will end. What the three UK parties are proposing does not give us control over all corporation tax, all income tax, over oil taxation, over all our job powers... to stop our troops being sent into illegal war. This is what is on the ballot paper.

So spoke Angus Robertson, one of the strongest voices for independence in the Scottish National Party (SNP), on *Today* on 9 September 2014, just nine days before Scotland's electors would decide whether their nation would detach itself from the United Kingdom. He was responding to a last-minute promise from the UK's three main political parties to devolve more powers to Scotland if the country voted 'no' to independence.

The relationship at stake was more than 400 years old. The crowns of Scotland and England were united in 1603, when James VI of Scotland became James I of England, succeeding the childless Queen Elizabeth I. The Act of Union strengthened ties from 1707, and the Scottish Parliament was dissolved. Labour's Alistair Darling, who led the 'Better Together' campaign in the Scottish referendum of 2014, summarised his view of Scottish history since union on *Today* on 8 September 2014:

If you look at what Scotland has contributed to the UK not just recently, but over the last 300 years, we have all built the UK together and we've all benefited from that strength that comes from acting together, pooling and sharing resources, in good times and in bad times, and I think that it would be a tragedy if that relationship were broken.

Since the Second World War, though, Scotland had voted predominantly Labour (until the surge for the SNP after the millennium), while Conservative governments often ruled from Westminster. Scotland had long retained control of its own legal and educational systems, yet on matters such as taxation and social policies, the UK government remained in command.

But in the 1970s things began to change. Labour won the 1974 general election by only a hair's breadth, and by 1976 had lost its parliamentary majority: so, it made a pact with the SNP and the Welsh nationalist party Plaid Cymru – in exchange for support in the Commons, it would instigate legislation to devolve some political powers to Scotland and Wales. A Scottish referendum was held in 1979, gauging if there was enough support among the Scots for a Scottish Assembly; although Yes won narrowly, the low turnout (around one-third of the electorate) rendered the result void.

Tensions were heightened when Margaret Thatcher came to power in 1979. It was widely felt in Scotland during the 1980s that the British government was siphoning off tax monies from the Scottish oil fields while using the Scottish people as guinea pigs for such measures as the poll tax. Analysis of the so-called 'Barnett Formula', the Treasury's basis for allocating public spending in the nations of the UK, consistently showed that the Scots benefited more per head, on average, than the English, but nevertheless bitter feelings of mistreatment of Scots often surfaced.

The state of the union soon became a major issue, with New Labour promising devolution, subject to referendums, to Scotland, Wales and Northern Ireland if it won the UK general election in 1997. Consequently, John Major's Conservatives mounted a last-ditch campaign during that election, declaring there were 'only 72 hours to save the union'. Major, during the Scottish referendum campaign of 2014, would remind *Today*'s listeners on 14 September of how he had highlighted the potentially irreversible splits that devolution could lead to: 'I said it 20 years ago, when I first warned that devolution would be a high road to separation.'

With New Labour victorious in 1997, it moved rapidly to create devolved Parliaments. Asked their view at the time of that landslide victory, 74.3 per cent of those Scots who voted supported the devolution plans. Elections to the Scottish Parliament followed in 1999. Labour, led by Donald Dewar, emerged as the largest party, but with 56 seats in the new Parliament it was short of an overall majority, and the Scottish National Party, led by Alex Salmond, won 35 seats. It meant Labour going into coalition with the Liberal Democrats, and raised the possibility of different Labour policies north and south of the border, especially on university tuition fees. On 7 May James Naughtie reported the election results for *Today* with the help of the BBC's chief political correspondent, John Sergeant.

> **Sergeant: Well, this very serious problem about tuition fees. It's the kind of issue which if anyone is asked, 'Are you in favour of tuition fees?' they will say no...**

> **Naughtie: Big issue in the campaign, it's worth reminding people?**

Sergeant: Big issue in the campaign – the Parliament have absolute power in this area, over education. It has knock on effects for England; it's almost a nightmare issue for the government... There's probably a majority in this new Parliament – almost certainly – against the government's policy on tuition fees. What does Donald Dewar do with a new Labour majority on this?

Naughtie: It's the kind of issue that points the way forward for this Parliament, isn't it?

Sergeant: Well, I think he's got to attempt to get a compromise with the Liberal Democrats. I suspect what will happen is they will fight very hard behind the scenes, and we'll have to see whether Donald Dewar can pull it off.

Labour's Donald Dewar did indeed become, with Liberal Democrat support, Scotland's inaugural first minister, presiding over the first session of a Scottish Parliament since the last one was adjourned in 1707. With its new powers, limited though they were, the Scottish Parliament was able to run public services differently from England; the clearest distinctions were in the lack of university fees for Scottish students and the care packages offered to the elderly in Scotland.

A taste of power left many Scots wanting more. A turning point came in May 2007, when the SNP became the biggest party by just one seat in the Scottish parliamentary elections – enough for Salmond to become first minister and form a minority government. He launched a national conversation white paper to consider Scotland's constitutional future, and in the next Scottish parliamentary elections of May 2011, the SNP trounced the opposition, winning 69 seats, while Labour achieved just 37. The SNP, with an overall majority of four MSPs, was now confident enough to press for a referendum on independence.

Through 2012, legal procedures to ensure a fair referendum were negotiated between the SNP and the UK government, leading to the signing of the Edinburgh Agreement on 15 October 2012. The referendum was announced for autumn 2014 – the question on the ballot paper would read: 'Should Scotland be an independent country?' As early as May 2012, the 'Yes Scotland' campaign for Scottish independence had been launched, followed by the 'Better Together', or No campaign, the following month. The No campaign's leader, Alistair Darling, memorably said at the launch of 'Better Together' that voting Yes to independence 'is like asking us to buy a one-way ticket to send our children to a deeply uncertain destination'.

In the early stages, the No campaign was far out in front: by some 20 percentage points in many polls. As the referendum approached, however, the gap appeared to close considerably. The main questions debated included the Scottish economy, a currency union, taxation and social services, defence and nuclear issues, foreign policy, participation in the EU and immigration, plus the impact of possible Scottish independence on the rest of the UK.

As the European Parliament elections fell on 20 May 2014, it was appropriate for Evan Davis to ask Alex Salmond about Scotland's EU membership on *Today* that morning: 'Do you worry about the membership of an independent Scotland of the EU?' he enquired. Salmond replied confidently:

> **No, because the balance of opinion, in Scotland, is that we should be an independent member of the European Union and we don't have the same agonised debate as is taking place in England... We should look to further Scotland's interests within the European context, so it's not really a worry.**

He outlined Scotland's importance to the rest of the EU:

> **Scotland has an enormous amount to contribute: 60 per cent of the oil reserves, 25 per cent of the offshore marine renewables, 20 per cent of the fish stocks... but also the democracy – where Scotland wants to be a member of the European Union, then of course, it would be very difficult in terms of the fundamental principles of the rest of Europe to try and deny that aspect.**

Davis then asked Salmond about the SNP's prospective policy on immigration. He replied:

> **We'd have our own immigration policy, the same way that Ireland has its own... We've put forward a points-based system, which indicates how people can qualify to be allowed to live and stay and work in Scotland... We think it's madness at the present moment, that we take a huge number of international students into Scotland, people that we spend years raising their human capital, who want to be in Scotland and then who want to work in the Scottish economy, contribute to Scottish society... and the policy of the current United Kingdom government is to refuse them the ability to do so... One of the advantages we'll have, from having control of these matters, is being able to allow these people who want to contribute to Scottish society to do exactly that, and make Scotland a wealthier and a better society.**

A thorny question was the SNP's position on NATO and British nuclear arms, should independence be achieved. Salmond asserted on *Today* on 11 April 2014:

> **Well, you would act exactly in the same way as the other 25...28 current non-nuclear members of NATO do, like Norway and Canada. You would act in compliance with the obligations of NATO membership, but you wouldn't have nuclear weapons stationed in Scotland, as we have at the present moment.**

> It can't be an unreasonable position, if it's the position of the vast majority of NATO members at the present moment. And the sort of apocalyptic nonsense that Lord George Robertson [a senior figure in the Scottish Labour Party and former NATO general secretary] was spouting in Washington over the last few days is an indication that the pressure seems to be getting to the No campaign as the Yes vote steadily increases month by month.

The campaigning became more fraught as the referendum approached. Alex Salmond, though, on *Today*, described the build-up as 'probably one of the most exhilarating campaigns in Western Europe'. Alistair Darling pointed out on the programme how even journalists had been intimidated by certain militant Yes campaigners: 'Frankly, to have people demonstrating outside the BBC, thousands of people holding up placards of journalists they disapprove of, you don't expect to see that in this country.' He also rejected Salmond's claim to represent his country: 'He is not Team Scotland.'

Many British, pro-Union newspapers and the three main parties in Westminster seemed to be panicking in the final fortnight. British papers ran the headlines 'Ten Days to Save the Union!' on 8 September 2014. On *Today* that morning, John Humphrys explained, 'Given the YouGov opinion poll published by *The Sunday Times* yesterday, you can see why [the No campaign is panicking] – [it is] the first poll published since the campaign began that has put the Yes campaign in the lead.'

James Naughtie, in Scotland, talked to people in Edinburgh about the No campaign: 'You do hear a common refrain: "Totally negative."' But it was pointed out that the leaders of the three main Westminster parties had responded by putting on a united front, reiterating that firm promise of much-increased devolution for Scotland should the Scots vote No – not entirely new ideas, but trying to make them sound like new concessions. Naughtie commented:

> The extra powers aren't exactly chickenfeed. They do go much further, in terms of the devolution of taxation, for example, than David Cameron was prepared to contemplate only 18 months ago. But the problem for the No side is that the facts about extra powers, which amount pretty well to the 'devo-max' that's long been favoured by a majority of voters here, are taking second place to the appearance of a campaign that's had its confidence shaken.

By 'devo-max' he was referring to the proposal for full fiscal autonomy, i.e. collecting all the tax for Scotland, then paying a contribution to Westminster for union functions such as defence and foreign policy. However, Alistair Darling told *Today*:

> I am confident that we will win because we do have a very strong, positive vision of what Scotland can be, both in terms of the opportunities and the security that

come from being part of the UK, a strengthened Scottish Parliament with more powers, which is what people want and you can do that without having to break up the country to do it, with all the risks that come with that.

The former Conservative prime minister John Major made perhaps the most emotional case for the 'No' campaign. Since leaving office Major has, for the most part, avoided public debate; he has only intervened on issues he felt especially strongly about, and has often chosen to speak on *Today* when he does want to make a point. On 10 September 2014 he spoke to John Humphrys:

> I am desperately concerned at what is happening. We would be immensely weaker as a nation in every respect – morally, politically, in every material aspect – were Scotland and the rest of the United Kingdom to part company. It seems to me almost incredible... Suddenly, Scots who work next to us, live next to us, are our friends, our neighbours, our workmates, would suddenly become foreigners. Is that not an extraordinary proposition for a nation that has marched together? I mean, this year is the 100th anniversary of the First World War. As we honour the people who fought together then, would it not be extraordinary if the SNP broke up the most successful union and partnership in all history, in any part of the world?

Earlier in the programme, Major had gone through his key concerns one by one. Defence was top of his list:

> If Scotland voted to leave it would be disastrous for the whole of the UK. Firstly, because Trident [nuclear programme] is in Scotland and so are the submarine pens and much else. Our defence would be imminently weakened. There are a lot of Scots in the British army. We would lose Trident, which has been our protection for a long time and if we lost Trident not to an enemy, but to the actions of a neighbour, that would be just extraordinary. Our role in NATO would be reduced; our relations consequently with the United States would be damaged.

On international cooperation, Major warned, 'The United Kingdom would be weaker in every international body it attends. It would certainly be weaker in the European Union in the forthcoming negotiations. We would lose our seat at the top table in the United Nations.' On a Scotland going it alone and trying to get into the EU, he sowed doubt:

> There is the easy assumption that Scotland will be waved into the European Union. Well, maybe... but it's not certain. Spain, for example, wouldn't welcome

a separatist nation… What are Scotland proposing? To leave the most successful union in history in order to join a European Union, perhaps in some years, that is facing difficulties.

He said of the Scots:

They have in the United Kingdom representation in the UK government always, representation among UK ministers. They have a large number of seats in the House of Commons. They'd have none of that in the European Union. They'd be 5 million people amongst 500 million people, and in a much weaker position to influence the interests of Scotland than they are now.

As to the uncertainty over which currency the Scots might have after the referendum if the Yes side won, Major was scathing:

They assume they can join a currency union. I think by now they should realise that they can't… Really, what currency are they going to use, John?… It's one week away from the vote and the people of Scotland do not know what currency they would have. I've never known such incompetence, for someone to propose something as big as independence and not have the faintest idea what currency they're going to use.

Discussion of currency union engendered the bitterest debate to the end. Chancellor George Osborne and the No campaign firmly rejected the idea put forward by the Yes campaign that an independent, sovereign Scotland could still use sterling. But Salmond and his finance secretary, Jim Swinney, saw the British government as engaging in fear-mongering brinkmanship. Swinney was sure the Tories would relent if Yes won:

The minute the UK political establishment believes there is a possibility of us being successful, they'll rush to come to some agreement… So if we get a Yes vote a week today, then what we will have is an emphatic mandate to ensure that Scotland secures that currency union on behalf of the people of Scotland… I'm very confident.

The turnout, of 84.64 per cent of the electorate, was the highest recorded in the UK for any election in the era of universal suffrage. In the end, despite the SNP's confidence, the No campaign won by roughly 55 per cent per cent to 45 per cent. In the wake of the Yes campaign's loss, Alex Salmond moved over to be replaced by Nicola Sturgeon as leader of the SNP and Scotland's first minister.

The Scottish referendum was meant to settle the question of whether or not the Scots wanted independence for a generation. However, in politics, times can quickly change. With David Cameron's surprise general election victory in 2015, a referendum on whether Britain should remain in the EU suddenly loomed, with far-reaching implications for Scotland. And when a clear majority of Scots voted in favour of continued EU membership in 2016, but the majority in England voted to leave, it raised the possibility of a new referendum on Scottish independence.

The Brexit referendum, 2016

'You can't have your cake and eat it'
GEORGE OSBORNE, 18 APRIL 2016

It was on Saturday 20 February 2016 that the prime minister David Cameron declared the date of the Brexit referendum and the form it would take: a simple in/out poll to decide whether Britain should remain a member of the EU.

Cameron had included the pledge to grant the British people a referendum in his party's manifesto for the 2015 general election. It seemed unlikely he would win, but with Labour and the Liberal Democrats polling poorly, the Conservatives secured a surprise majority. The Eurosceptic UK Independence Party (UKIP) gained 13 per cent of the vote but succeeded in getting only one MP elected. Even the party's leader Nigel Farage failed in the constituency in which he was standing (though he already had a seat in the European Parliament).

But political pressure from UKIP's rise was one of the factors behind Cameron's referendum pledge. Another was the hope that it would unite the Conservatives, who had been divided over Europe for decades. Back in the 1990s John Major's premiership had been haunted by rows over the Maastricht Treaty (which formally created the 'European Union'), despite his success in negotiating an opt-out for Britain from the single currency. Divisions over Europe were not, of course, an exclusively Conservative Party phenomenon. Although the Liberal Democrats were consistently pro-European, the Labour Party had also always had its pro- and anti-European voices. The referendum campaign – and its aftermath – would reveal deep divisions across the United Kingdom and between the UK's constituent parts – not to mention divisions with other places likely to feel the impact of the decision, such as Gibraltar and the Republic of Ireland. And this whole exercise came only two years after the divisive referendum on Scottish independence.

The Brexit referendum date was set for 23 June 2016. David Cameron had, just before announcing that date, tried to get all the other EU countries to agree to special new concessions for Britain to strengthen his case for remaining. The agreement he secured included a British opt-out from further moves towards political union, a so-called 'emergency brake' to limit the access of newly arrived EU workers to in-work benefits, and a guarantee that countries outside the Eurozone, such as Britain, would not be required to fund euro bailouts. On *Today* on 20 February the BBC's assistant political editor, Norman Smith, reported on the reaction to the deal:

> Smith: Downing Street are resigned to around six Cabinet ministers opposing the prime minister's deal. Most wounding will be Michael Gove's decision to side with the Leave campaign, a close personal friend of the prime minister. He brings legitimacy and credibility to the Leave side and will further crank up the pressure on Boris Johnson to join him. After Cabinet Mr Cameron will make a statement in Downing Street to announce the date of the referendum expected to be June the 23rd and to set out the case for his deal – a package described by the former Conservative attorney general Dominic Grieve as a remarkable achievement.

> Grieve: It is the single, without doubt, it is the biggest change in our relationship with the EU that we have ever had. And it's interesting that in the context of this debate on the referendum coming up this point seems by the detractors, the people who want Brexit and want to leave, to be completely ignored.

> Smith: Mr Cameron has also guaranteed with a few exceptions the support of the Labour Party. The shadow foreign secretary Hilary Benn.

> Benn: The vast majority of Labour MPs, the Labour movement, the Labour Party conference, the trade union movement supports our continued membership. Why? Because being in the EU has given us jobs, investment, growth, it gives us security and it gives us influence in the world. And why would we want to exchange all of that for a leap into the unknown?

> Smith: Critics insist the deal secured by Mr Cameron has failed to match his pledge to fundamentally change the UK's relationship with the EU. The Conservative MEP Daniel Hannan who supports the Vote Leave group said Britain banged the table and aggressively demanded the status quo. And at a rally last night the UKIP leader Nigel Farage was scathing about the agreement.

> Farage: It does not address the issue that our Parliament is not able to overhaul bad EU law. It does not address the issue that we should not be paying £55 million pounds a day to a club whose accounts have not been signed off for nearly 20 years, and it does not address the fundamentalist view that we have a total open door to over five hundred million people.

> Smith: Many Tory MPs will now wait to see Mr Cameron's plans for bolstering parliamentary sovereignty, likely to be outlined tomorrow. Among them the mayor of London, he is understood to be waiting to see the final details before

declaring what he will do. A decision which could yet radically transform the course of this referendum.

Boris Johnson entered the ring the following day, declaring that 'having been veering all over the place like a shopping trolley', he had decided not to support the prime minister, but to side with the Brexiteers. His declaration for Vote Leave was a terrible blow to Cameron, and a turning point in the campaign overall.

From the first, Conservative divisions were a focus of *Today*'s coverage. On 22 February John Humphrys interviewed the defence secretary, Sir Michael Fallon:

Humphrys: History tells us this, doesn't it: it's going to be very difficult for David Cameron to hold the government together after this referendum almost whichever way it goes, to see him arguing perhaps on a stage against people like Michael Gove and Boris Johnson and then to have to sit in the Cabinet and say, 'Right, we're all mates together now, even though the vote went this way or that way.' Difficult, isn't it?

Fallon: At the cabinet meeting on Saturday... even those who want to leave made it absolutely clear that we're going to come together again after 23 June and continue the programme, and indeed up until the referendum itself there is work to be done. George Osborne will be delivering his budget. We'll be continuing our programme of economic and social reform working together as colleagues. And when you talk about history, if you look back at the 1975 referendum – and I fear I'm old enough to remember it – the then Wilson government came together after the referendum, the prime minister was strengthened, if you recall.

Humphrys: But the party didn't stay together, did it? There was a severe split, and a lot of people think that was part of it. We ended up with the SDP.

Fallon: Well, the party stayed together right through that Parliament, I think there were other fault lines in the party between left and right. Look, we've made it clear that there are going to be disagreements. The prime minister, I think to his credit, is allowing members of the Cabinet to dissent, he's allowing Tory MPs to take a different view. He's allowing that, but at the end when it's all over and the votes have been counted, you can be sure that the government will come together again and continue the programme that we got elected on last year.

The chancellor, George Osborne, was Cameron's loyal second-in-command. On *Today* on 18 April 2016, he used new Treasury analysis to argue that each British household would, by 2030, be worse off by £4,300 outside the EU. The BBC's economics editor Kamal Ahmed thought, '2030 is an awfully long forecast period.' And as Nick Robinson put it to Osborne, 'Surely, Germany, France and the like would still want to sell their cars, cheese and more to us in the most advantageous manner, even with Britain out of the EU?' Osborne quoted trading statistics in reply: 'Forty-four per cent of our exports go to the European Union; eight per cent of their exports come to Britain... We shouldn't assume that they need us come what may.' Robinson interjected: 'In cash terms, we buy more from them than they buy from us.' Osborne retorted:

> **It depends whether you include services, where of course they are massive consumers of British services and that's not just banking and financial services... if you want to have tariff-free, quota-free access to the single market, if you want, crucially, to have the common standards that mean you can get off the plane in Madrid or Munich if you're an architect or an engineer, or if you're working in a car plant in the north-east of England, your car is automatically accepted into the EU market without extra checks for safety and the like... if you want all these things, then you have to bear some of the obligations of EU membership. You can't have your cake and eat it. These people who go round saying Britain would have all the benefits of the EU without any of the obligations – that is economically illiterate.**

One of Osborne's predecessors, Nigel Lawson – chancellor of the exchequer under Margaret Thatcher and by now chairman of Vote Leave – was tasked that day with outlining the Leave side's economic view on *Today*: 'We are the fifth largest economy in the world. They [the other 27 EU members] desperately need our market. They sell us £300 billion a year, far more than we sell them.' Lawson continued, 'Our exports to the EU are slightly less than 15 per cent. Of course, we have to abide by EU regulations for those 15 per cent... What we don't need to do is have this morass of EU regulations for the other 85 per cent.' He dismissed talk that it had taken Canada seven years to secure a free-trade deal with the EU.

When Nick Robinson introduced Michael Gove on the *Today* programme the following morning, he began by quoting Gove's own words on the Remain campaign. Robinson said, '"They're treating the public like children capable of being frightened into obedience by conjuring up new bogeymen every night," so says Justice Secretary Michael Gove, who's head of the Vote Leave campaign, about his friends and colleagues who are leading the campaign urging us to remain in the EU.' Gove responded by comparing Britain to a kidnap victim: 'If we vote to stay, we're not settling for a secure status quo,' he declared. 'We're voting to be hostages, locked in the back of the car, driven headlong towards deeper EU integration.'

And the justice secretary turned to one of the recurring themes of the campaign, the idea of 'taking back control':

> We can take back control of our borders: inside the EU we have to accept that anyone with an EU passport – even if they have a criminal record – can breeze into Britain. That freedom will be extended to people from countries in the pipeline to join the EU – Albania, Macedonia, Montenegro, Serbia and Turkey.

Robinson questioned Gove's tone:

> You talked about hostages, you talked about the danger of criminals and immigrants and asylum seekers – far from being a positive vision, this was you conjuring your bogeymen about staying in the EU, wasn't it?

Undeterred, Gove hammered home some of the best-loved assertions of the Leave campaign:

> If we were to leave we can take back control. We can take back the £350 million that we give to the EU every week. We can then spend more on our priorities, like the NHS.

Robinson challenged Gove on the much-disputed figure, notably because it didn't take into account the annual British rebate from the EU's budget that Prime Minister Margaret Thatcher had negotiated in 1984. Gove parried: 'You mention the rebate, Nick; the rebate isn't in any of the treaties... There is a real risk that our rebate could be whittled away.'

Boris Johnson appeared on *Today* on 11 May 2016, launching the so-called 'Brexit battle bus' in Cornwall. John Humphrys asked whether he would advocate leaving the single market. Johnson replied from beside the bus (which, he was keen to explain, was 'not funded by the taxpayer, I stress to say; unlike the government's £9 million they're infamously spending on leaflets.'). He eventually replied, 'The answer is yes, we should get out of the empire of EU law-making and what we should have instead is access to the single market.' Johnson was often accused of being the principal advocate of the 'have-your-cake-and-eat-it' vision of Britain's future.

UKIP's campaigning techniques attracted controversy when Nigel Farage appeared in front of an outsized poster featuring a long line of migrants (the photograph had been taken at the Croatia–Slovenia border) and the words 'Breaking Point'. Farage appeared on *Today* on 20 June just after the appearance of those controversial posters – and the shocking murder of the Labour MP Jo Cox by a nationalist extremist. Farage explained that the posters had been quickly withdrawn on news of the tragic murder. He stuck, instead, to his main lines of attack: 'Why would we want to be part of this failing club?' he asked, repeatedly claiming that the northern EU countries were being crippled by the refugee crisis which had begun the previous year, while southern EU countries would soon be hit by another euro crisis. He wanted to see immigration 'back down to post-war levels of 30,000 to 50,000 a year'. He argued that tariff-free trade with the EU would be possible outside the organisation, and that no deal was better than a bad deal. In conclusion, he reckoned, it was all a matter of confidence: 'Do we believe we're good enough to run our own country?'

Certain successful British entrepreneurs and economists, like James Dyson, Anthony Bamford (of JCB), Tim Martin (of Wetherspoon) and Gerard Lyons, spoke on radio of British prospects outside the EU. A much larger group of big-hitters in business and finance supported Remain. As Osborne pointed out one morning on *Today*: 'Where is a single ally, trading organisation... that says it's a good idea for Britain to leave the EU?' Among seasoned politicians, the passionate radio contributions of two former prime ministers, Tony Blair and John Major, stood out for Remain, but they were voices from the past, and Blair particularly came with baggage (Iraq, and the hostility of new party leader Jeremy Corbyn's Labour to New Labour). Even US president Barack Obama stepped into the general debate, to complaints by Brexiteers. He warned that Britain outside the EU risked going to the back of the queue on future trade negotiations with the United States.

In a speech outside Downing Street on 21 June 2016, Cameron stuck to the mantra of the Remain side: 'We're stronger, safer and better off in the EU.' He said it again when he appeared on *Today* the following day – on the eve of the vote. John Humphrys pointed repeatedly to the way Cameron was trying to link his final round of EU negotiations in February with opt-outs which had been agreed long ago, for example keeping Britain out of the euro and the Schengen Zone of countries where EU citizens could freely cross internal borders without passports. Humphrys cited criticism of the one clearly defined new concession – that EU migrants to the UK would have to pay in to the social security system for four years before acquiring full benefits – concluding 'it doesn't add up to a row of beans'.

Cameron clung on, deflecting blows on immigration with counter-thrusts on business:

> I've also been frank about the warnings to our economy, because I genuinely believe them. Today, with over 1,000 businesses, including over half the FTSE 100 companies, representing 1.75 million people in work, warning that we'll have more jobs and more growth if we stay and less if we come out, it really is worth listening to.

He added, with reference to a major televised Brexit special of the previous evening:

> What I think we learnt from that debate last night is that we don't solve our immigration challenge by leaving the European Union, but we do create a massive problem for our economy if we leave the EU... As I said, there are good

ways of controlling immigration – welfare changes are a good way – [but] there are [also] bad things to do – leaving this market of 500 million, hitting our businesses, giving us a decade of uncertainty. In the debate last night, the Leave campaign admitted it could take ten years to negotiate a trade deal with Europe.

At the beginning of *Today* on the morning of Friday 24 June, Nigel Farage could be heard in jubilant mood: 'Let June 23 go down in our history as our Independence Day!' But it wasn't a landslide result. Voters had been almost split down the middle: 52 per cent to leave the EU, 48 per cent to remain. Scotland, along with London and many of the big cities and university towns – the powerhouses of the British economy – had voted clearly for remain, while in Northern Ireland, too, Remainers had won. The result did not, of course, settle the issue of what sort of relationship the United Kingdom should have with the EU after leaving.

One thing became clear almost immediately. For David Cameron personally, the result was a catastrophic rebuff. Within hours, he announced his resignation as prime minister.

Thought for the day: Rabbi Lord Sacks

10 November 2017

Coming in to Broadcasting House this morning I saw for the first time the statue unveiled this week, of George Orwell, with its inscription on the wall behind, 'If liberty means anything at all, it means the right to tell people what they do not want to hear.' How badly we need that truth today.

I've been deeply troubled by what seems to me to be the assault on free speech taking place in British universities in the name of 'safe space', 'trigger warnings', and 'micro-aggressions', meaning any remark that someone might find offensive even if no offence is meant. So far has this gone, that a month ago students at an Oxford college banned the presence of a representative of the Christian Union on the grounds that some might find their presence alienating and offensive. Luckily the protest that followed led to the ban being swiftly overturned. But still…

I'm sure this entire movement has been undertaken for the highest of motives, to protect the feelings of the vulnerable, which I applaud, but you don't achieve that by silencing dissenting views. A safe space is the exact opposite: a place where you give a respectful hearing to views opposed to your own, knowing that your views too will be listened to respectfully. That's academic freedom and it's essential to a free society.

And it's what I learned at university. My doctoral supervisor, the late Sir Bernard Williams, was an atheist. I was a passionate religious believer. But he always listened respectfully to my views, which gave me the confidence to face those who disagree with everything I stand for. That's safety in an unsafe world.

And it's at the very heart of my faith, because Judaism is a tradition all of whose canonical texts are anthologies of arguments. In the Bible, Abraham, Moses, Jeremiah and Job argue with God. The rabbinic literature is an almost endless series of Rabbi X says this and Rabbi Y says that, and when one rabbi had the chance of asking God who was right, God replied, they're both right. 'How can they both be right?' asked the rabbi, to which God's apocryphal reply was, 'You're also right.' The rabbis called this 'argument for the sake of heaven'.

Why does it matter? Because truth emerges from disagreement and debate. Because tolerance means making space for difference. Because justice involves *Audi alteram partem*, listening to the other side. And because, in Orwell's words, liberty means 'the right to tell people what they do not want to hear'.

CHAPTER 3

WAR, CONFLICT AND SECURITY

Bobby Sands, hunger strikes and Northern Ireland's Troubles

'There can be no giving way to their demand for political status'

HUMPHREY ATKINS, 19 DECEMBER 1980

Bobby Sands's 60-odd days as MP for Fermanagh and South Tyrone, brief though they were, marked a new phase in the longest-running and most deadly conflict to have afflicted the United Kingdom since the Second World War: the Troubles. The circumstances in which Sands died were, as one Belfast man told *Today* in May 1981, 'a symptom of the deeper sickness which is the Northern Ireland problem'.

The start of the Troubles is generally dated to the late 1960s and the civil rights campaign. Catholics were aggrieved at the discrimination they believed they faced in housing, in employment, in policing and in electoral rights, which stemmed from years of rule by a Protestant-dominated executive at Northern Ireland's seat of government, Stormont. However, many among the Protestant majority of Northern Ireland feared that the civil rights campaign masked a resurgence of the IRA and a renewed effort to unify Ireland.

In August 1969 British army forces were sent into Northern Ireland in reaction to the growing sectarian rioting and violence. They were initially welcomed by Catholics as protection against what were widely seen as Unionist security forces, but the Catholic population soon turned against them. In August 1971 the British government, acting in response to a request from the Unionist administration at Stormont, introduced internment without trial; on 9–10 August nearly 350 people were rounded up, suspected of involvement with the IRA.

In the sectarian violence that followed, several thousand Roman Catholics left their homes for the Irish Republic, fleeing from Loyalist paramilitaries. Here is John Timpson on *Today,* broadcasting from Belfast on 12 August 1971.

> **Timpson:** The estimate is that between three and four thousand people have, so far, headed south for the Republic. There have been a lot of extra trains laid on by

the Catholic voluntary relief organisations. There are more due to leave today. BBC reporter Joanna Hixon watched one of them leave last night.

Hixon: The last of the refugee trains out of Great Victoria Street station here in Belfast picks up speed as it pulls away from the platform. It's packed full with about 200 refugees, mostly children and their mothers. They've got prams, cardboard boxes packed with belongings and carrier bags but really very little to take with them. They're headed for Dundalk about 20 miles over the border. Apparently their trip to the station wasn't without incident. Some of them told me their buses were stopped and stoned as they passed through some areas of the city, and here on the station a few rocks have been flying from a bridge which passes over the station from Sandy Road, and some rocks were thrown from there onto the platform as these people waited for their train. Before they boarded the train, I talked to some of them.

Girl: I live in Esdale Gardens, right, and at the top of the street every night there is shooting. All them kids are terrified, so they are, and that's why we're moving. Why should we have to leave our homes that we've worked for, our parents worked for and lived for, lived all our lives there? And we have to run? That's what I want to know, why do we have to run? One of my aunties was burnt out, they run down after her with a machine gun, and wouldn't let her out of the entry. One of my aunties is expecting a baby and they done the same with her, give her ten minutes to get out...

Second voice: ... they just opened fire, so they did, they didn't care who they killed or anything else.

Hixon: Were you very frightened?

Second voice: Yeah, I was frightened for my babies.

Hixon: How do you feel? Do you know what you're going to find at the other end?

Second voice: I don't care, we'll be a lot safer, I think.

The way the British army carried out Operation Demetrius, as the internment round-up was called, led to widespread allegations of brutality. A large number of those arrested were released within 48 hours, and many of the internees were kept aboard HMS *Maidstone*, a prison ship moored in Belfast. On 25 August Bob Friend, *Today*'s Northern Ireland correspondent, interviewed one of them.

Internee: Well, first thing I heard was me mother telling the soldiers that I wasn't at home, that I was away to work. And then they rushed upstairs and they told me to get up. They said, 'You're being arrested under the Special Powers Act, and you have only five minutes to get ready'. And, after he finished saying all this he said, 'Now you have only two and a half.' So when I was getting my clothes on he said, 'If you try to escape you'll be shot.' And they took me downstairs and put me in the back of a Land Rover, and then they took me about two minutes from my home and they made me get out and tied my hands behind my back with a rope which cut right into your arms, and left a track for about a day after it. And the driver of the lorry behind said, 'If you get those ropes off you should be doing me the biggest favour you've ever done in your life'... and if I by any chance decide to jump out of the Land Rover that he would be coming straight behind me in the lorry. And if I got in his way he wouldn't stop.

Friend: What about the treatment on the ship? There've been all sorts of allegations about brutality. None of them proved yet, of course, what about you?

Internee: The only brutality I received was having my hands tied behind my back and threats, and the police were rattling the huts when we were trying to get to sleep. After myself and another man complained about the rattling huts to a sergeant or one of the detectives, I was removed by the policeman we'd made the complaint against into another hut, and whilst they were outside the huts they kept passing remarks, 'Hut number 13 is all the toughs, all the hards are in there.'

Friend: What about the conditions on the ship: what were they like?

Internee: Overcrowding in the living quarters. And the food was... well wasn't terrible; it was eatable, but there was very little of it, and it kept getting worse every day. And this played a big part in the decision that we would go on a fast rather than any other form of protest.

Friend: How many of the detainees on board are now on a fast, in fact?

Internee: They are all on a fast except for about five who have stomach trouble or other ailments.

The 'fasting' aboard HMS *Maidstone* was probably the first instance of hunger striking in the Troubles, although the practice has a long pedigree in Republicanism; Terence MacSwiney, the Irish author and Sinn Féin Lord mayor of Cork, starved himself to death in Brixton prison after being arrested for sedition in 1920.

In the spring of 1972 Edward Heath's government in London suspended Stormont and introduced direct rule of Northern Ireland; William Whitelaw was appointed the first Northern Ireland secretary. In May that year Whitelaw faced a hunger strike led by Billy McKee, a Belfast IRA leader who had been arrested by the army for possessing a weapon and was serving his sentence in Crumlin Road gaol. The hunger strikers wanted IRA prisoners to be given the status of political prisoners; when McKee was close to death Whitelaw granted them what was called 'special category status', which allowed them to mix freely with one another, to avoid prison work and prison uniforms, and to receive food parcels and extra visiting rights.

At the disused Long Kesh RAF base, now known as the Maze prison, where many Republican and Loyalist paramilitary men were housed, the special status allowed prisoners from both sides to set up their own organisations within the prison walls. In 1976 Harold Wilson's Labour government responded by abolishing special category status for new prisoners; they now had to do prison jobs, wear uniforms, and their ability to intermingle was limited. The change sparked an escalating series of protests,

First came the blanket protests: forbidden their own clothes, Republican prisoners consented only to the wearing of blankets rather than putting on prison uniforms. In 1978, this refusal to accept the prison regime was extended to what became known as the dirty protest: prisoners refused to leave their cells and smeared the walls with excrement. Finally, on 27 October 1980, seven prisoners resorted to a hunger strike, demanding the restoration of five special-status rights.

The 1980 hunger strike ended after 53 days amid claim and counter-claim. On 19 December Richard McAuley, the spokesman for the IRA's political wing Sinn Féin, explained on *Today* the IRA's understanding of what had happened: the prisoners had, he said, been given assurances by Margaret Thatcher's first Northern Ireland secretary, Humphrey Atkins:

> They have said they received a copy of the Humphrey Atkins statement, which he is to give to the House of Commons at 11 o'clock this morning, and they also received a new document, which is entitled 'Regimes in Northern Ireland Prisons: Prisoners' Day-to-Day Life, with Special Emphasis on Maze and Armagh', which is a totally new document and, in their words, contains a new elaboration on their five demands. That was enough in their view for them to end the hunger strike.

Clearly, the prisoners seemed to believe they had won some concessions. But when the BBC Northern Ireland correspondent Brian Hanrahan spoke to Atkins himself, the Northern Ireland secretary put matters rather differently:

> Atkins: I imagine that those who have called it off have now finally got the message, which the government has been trying to get over to them, ever since they started 53 ago, that there can be no giving way to their demand for political status.
>
> Hanrahan: There hasn't been a deal struck behind the scenes?

Atkins: No, not at all. The government's position was made absolutely clear on the 23rd of October and we haven't moved since then.

Hanrahan: You wouldn't expect, therefore, to be willing to make further concessions on the present regime generally in Northern Ireland?

Atkins: We are seeking to find improvements in the prison regime for all prisoners, not just strikers and protesters, and we have done this over the time that I've been the secretary of state for Northern Ireland, and I hope we can make further progress.

In the same edition of *Today*, Edward Daly, the Catholic bishop of Derry (which Protestants and Unionists call Londonderry), told listeners that he thought a telegram from the Catholic primate of All Ireland had had a considerable impact on the men. 'It was a very heartfelt plea to them to end their hunger strike', he said. Gerry Fitt, the founder and former leader of the Nationalist Social Democratic and Labour Party (SDLP), who had become increasingly vocal in his condemnation of the IRA, had a different perspective:

I didn't think that the hunger strike had any hope of success. It was too closely identified with the activities of the IRA, and the Catholic population in Northern Ireland have never given any support to the dreadful campaign of violence and murder by the IRA and indeed by the Protestant paramilitary organisations, who have indiscriminately murdered Catholics.

In his view, the main reason the strike had ended was that the Catholic population didn't come out and give this any support, and that was what they were depending on.
'Do you think,' Brian Redhead asked Fitt, 'good can come out of it?' Fitt replied:

I would like to sit here this morning and to say that I hope that the hunger strike as a weapon in the armoury of Irish nationalism would have finally been stopped by this strike, because a hunger strike is a very cruel thing.

His hopes were in vain. As the weeks went by, and no significant concessions emerged, angry IRA prisoners decided to resort to a new and more determined hunger-strike campaign, to begin on the fifth anniversary of the removal of their special status, 1 March 1981. The strategy was opposed by the Provisional IRA outside the prison, but to no avail. This time, at the forefront was Bobby Sands, popular among his incarcerated peers and by now commander of the Republican inmates. Sands, who had joined the IRA in 1972 and was serving a 14-year sentence for possession of a weapon, volunteered himself as the first striker – the intention being that one new prisoner would start striking each week.

It was four days into this renewed strike that the MP for Fermanagh and South Tyrone, an Independent Nationalist, happened to die. Sinn Féin decided to nominate Sands for the seat as the 'Anti-H-Block' candidate. Extraordinary though it may seem, there was at that time no law preventing a serving prisoner from standing for Parliament. Posters appeared calling on electors to support the 'blanket men' and the 'women of Armagh' – for women in Armagh prison were conducting their own 'no wash' protest. Sands's victory on 9 April 1981 by about 1,500 votes over the Ulster Unionists was considerably helped by the decision of the SDLP not to split the Republican and Nationalist vote by putting up a candidate. The publicity generated by Sands's candidacy helped attract worldwide attention to the hunger strike, to the Republican cause and to Sands personally. Despite the increased pressure, the Conservative government in London stood firm and made no concessions to the strikers. On 5 May 1981, Sands breathed his last.

The reaction was immediate. For *Today* that morning, reporter John Spicer was out on the streets of Belfast:

> Everybody – his mother, the H-block committee – have all appealed for quiet calm, at least... until the funeral, but there's certainly violence out there now already, and it's only, what, four o'clock in the morning.

One Republican interviewee rejected the claim that Sands's death was a propaganda coup:

> Republicans have all the martyrs they need in Irish history – we don't need any more martyrs. We didn't want Bobby Sands to die. We made that very clear from the beginning. The only people who seem intent upon using that as a propaganda stick are the British.

In his view, many Republicans on the streets now were not 'fighting' nor 'rioting', but 'praying' for Bobby Sands: an impression quite different to that of John Spicer. He told John Timpson:

> As I speak to you, the situation really is serious. The army say a full-scale alert has been called in the province: 30,000 security forces are involved, 11,000 of them troops. In those Republican areas in West and North Belfast, vehicles were hijacked earlier on [and] burned, [and] barricades have been erected, petrol bombs, acid bombs are being thrown at the troops, and one small army camp called New Barnsley in the Ballymurphy area has been virtually besieged by youths throwing petrol bombs, and I understand a grenade was thrown... violence has erupted, and it really is in every part of the Republican areas of this city.

> I've now moved to the Springfield Road, just up from the Falls Road. There's a
> group of army vehicles across the road. The place is strewn with glass everywhere...
> And a few petrol bombs are being thrown at the other side of barricade. I can hear
> soldiers firing what they call baton rounds and we call plastic bullets.

Some opponents of the IRA expressed little remorse over Sands. The hardline Unionist
MP and leader of the Democratic Unionist Party Ian Paisley told *Today* that morning,
'Many hundreds of people have been done to death by the Irish Republican Army and
they had absolutely no choice whatsoever – but Bobby Sands made a choice to die...'

In the same broadcast, Sands's mother told *Today*, 'It will not end with Bobby's
death.' Humphrey Atkins, however, was very much hoping it would; the following day,
Today broadcast the Northern Ireland secretary's comments to an American TV station:

> Their strike – their hunger strike – is pointless, because it isn't going to get what
> they say they want – namely political status – and I hope very much they'll call it
> off, because any death diminishes us all, and there've been too many deaths here.

However, more were to come. The strategy of staggered strikes held, and within two
weeks another three men had starved to death. How long would this go on? The answer
was another three months, by which time ten striking prisoners were dead, despite
frantic efforts by their families, friends and religious leaders who pleaded with them
to stop. At the same time, behind the scenes and through intermediaries, there were
channels of negotiation and signs of government concessions. The hunger strike finally
ended on 3 October 1981. By that time there was a new Northern Ireland secretary,
James Prior. He told *Today* on 5 October:

> The government have always said that once the hunger strike was out of the way,
> there were certain reforms that could be introduced and those were set down by
> my predecessor in office, and we will try to see what all we can do about those...

The day after Prior spoke, prisoners in the Maze were permitted to wear their own
clothes again, and in due course other attributes of the special status were restored.

War reporting and the Falklands conflict, 1982

'All we could do was just sit and watch'

BRIAN HANRAHAN, 6 JUNE 1982

The Falklands, like the Second World War, was very much a radio war – a war experienced by the British public first through voices and sounds. The conflict was fought 8,000 miles from Britain's shores, and it was judged that the bandwidth required to send television pictures back from warships might interfere with their reception of defence data, so for much of the war no television pictures reached the home audience.

When, on 2 April 1982, troops of Argentinian General Galtieri's military junta overwhelmed the Falkland Islands' small defending force, the British governor, Sir Rex Hunt, surrendered quickly. The United Nations Security Council voted to condemn the action on 4 April, and diplomatic efforts to negotiate a resolution began. But at the same time, British service chiefs set to work planning the liberation of the islands, and once they assured Margaret Thatcher that it could be done she authorised a task force. A mixture of warships and hastily converted merchant vessels began to embark on 5 April – the first elements of what would become the largest British naval force gathered since the days of the Suez Crisis in 1956.

In Argentina there was widespread support for the invasion; Buenos Aires had long claimed sovereignty over what were known as the Malvinas islands. On *Today* on 27 April the BBC foreign correspondent Paul Reynolds reported on a demonstration in the Argentinian capital, and found people undaunted by the threat of British military action:

> Reynolds: Many of the demonstrators were young and poor. They jumped up and down and chanted like an English football crowd. But Argentinian people generally are in favour of resisting any British incursion into the Falkland Islands. I spoke to one man, a car worker who'd lived in the United States for a time, and so spoke quite good English.
>
> Man: Argentine people don't want to fight but if England guns are coming, Argentine people will fight to recover what is ours.
>
> Reynolds: Are you worried, though, about a possible war with Britain?

Man: Of course, the war is not convenient, not for Argentina, not for British; these are young people, 18 years... the war is not convenient for anybody.

Reynolds: Not all Argentines agree with loud and angry demonstrations, but all agree that the Falkland Islands, the Malvinas, should be Argentine. If Britain should invade them the anger of this demonstration will seem quite restrained.

Hitching a ride aboard the ships of the task force were 30-odd members of the British press corps, including the BBC's Brian Hanrahan (who had moved on from his job as Northern Ireland correspondent) and Robert Fox. Without any independent means of getting near the Falklands, they had no alternative but to 'embed' themselves with the British forces. They relied completely on their military hosts for transport, daily necessities and, crucially, communication. Correspondents had to be flown over to Royal Fleet Auxiliary ships to file their reports, as broadcasting from Royal Navy ships was forbidden. 'The sheer physical circumstances,' recorded Fox later, 'made our band of fractious brothers more constrained than any accredited reporter of a campaign in living memory.'

On 2 May, the British submarine HMS *Conqueror* sank the Second World War vintage Argentinian cruiser *General Belgrano*, with a loss of more than 300 lives. The ship was just outside the 200-mile exclusion zone Britain had declared around the Falklands; whether the vessel posed a real threat to British forces was controversial and continued to be a matter of sometimes heated debate. This is how the story was reported on *Today*'s news bulletin on 2 May; the newsreader was Colin Doran:

Doran: The Ministry of Defence would not give the precise location of the attack but said it took place just outside the 200-mile total exclusion zone around the Falkland Islands. The *General Belgrano* is the only cruiser in the Argentine navy and its second largest fighting ship. With an assessment of the action, here's our defence correspondent Christopher Lee.

Lee: This was a comprehensive attack, not a warning shot. The Defence Ministry statement talks about torpedoes in the plural. The ministry won't say which submarine launched the attack, but it is possible that one of the Royal Navy's nuclear-powered Swiftshores is in the area. That carries Tigerfish torpedoes that can hit targets from about 20 miles range. The cruiser may not have been inside the original 200 nautical mile maritime exclusion zone, but that only had academic interest some time ago. The task force commander is indicating that he is willing to exercise the right to attack anything that he believes could pose a threat to his forces, and is indicating that he has the political backing as well as the military determination to carry out that policy. On paper the cruiser may appear to be old and fitted with elderly armaments, but nevertheless it must have been seen as a threat. As a weapons platform it is impressive in quantity not quality, and the task commander Rear Admiral Sandy Woodward recognises that.

Although British Special Forces and Commandos had already recaptured the archipelago's South Georgia, and although, on 1 May, British bombers had tried to render the Falklands' airport at Port Stanley unusable for the enemy, the sinking of the *General Belgrano* represented action of a different order, and it marked the end of any real prospect that a full-scale war could be avoided.

Thereafter, the Argentinian navy kept to port. While the British task force tried to consolidate its position, degrade Argentinian defences, and prepare to land ground forces, the real danger it faced was from air attack. This was brought home just two days after the *Belgrano* sinking, when an Exocet missile from an Argentinian fighter-bomber penetrated the destroyer HMS *Sheffield*. The loss of 20 dead and around 25 injured was a sobering reminder to the British public of what the conflict might bring.

The *Sheffield* was the first Royal Navy ship to be sunk in hostilities since the end of the Second World War. The third British vessel to suffer a similar fate was the frigate HMS *Antelope*, whose end on 23–4 May was witnessed by the BBC's Brian Hanrahan in a neighbouring vessel. It happened as Commandos clawed their way onto a beachhead off San Carlos Bay, East Falkland. An attempt to defuse a bomb that had hit the ship went wrong, resulting in an inferno. Hanrahan spoke to the BBC correspondent John Spicer, who was back in London, and his despatch was broadcast on *Today* on 25 May. He described the fire and the 'hole quite clearly in the side':

> The metal had bent back. The interior was revealed. It had spread from deck level right down to the waterline, and you could see through binoculars water seeping in and sending up clouds of steam and smoke.

The fire 'intensified':

> It grew white hot in the centre as I watched, and it spread upward, sending great showers of sparks, small explosions – a big explosion at one point, throwing up a horrendous cloud of debris – and then it just glowed on through the night, and then around about 1.30... I think it was in the afternoon, about 2.30 in London time, we saw that suddenly it was breaking its back and then, agonisingly slowly, the bows lifted out of the water, the stern lifted out, the centre sank down, and then the two sections followed it down until, at dark, there was just a tiny part of the bow thrust up.

All the while, as Hanrahan told listeners, rescue helicopters 'were looking to see if there was anybody who'd been forced over the side, away from the intense heat and into the equally intense and equally killing cold of the water'. On the day Hanrahan's report was broadcast, British naval losses continued, with the sinking of HMS *Coventry* and the fatal holing of the SS *Atlantic Conveyor*, which sank along with its cargo of helicopters.

Hanrahan was also able to report an early aerial encounter in which a single Harrier jump-jet pilot had downed two enemy Mirage aircraft simultaneously with his two missiles:

> **Hanrahan: Two Harriers came across three Mirage fighters, some time on Monday afternoon, over Pebble Island, which is the place where the Commando raid took place – good heavens, was it just about a week ago now? – and as they came by, the two Harriers, which are slower and not supposed on paper to be a match for the Mirages, took on the three Mirages, and they shot all three of them down. One pilot fired two missiles and took two planes down, and the wingman – the man who was with him – took down the third Mirage.**

> **Spicer: As far as you're aware, is that the first time a Harrier pilot – a single Harrier pilot – has shot down two aircraft?**

> **Hanrahan: I believe that is the case. You can imagine that it's not very often that two planes present themselves in the right formation for two missiles to be able to be fired simultaneously and to take down the two of them, so I suppose for that pilot, it would have to be said this was something notable. I don't suppose he'll be glorying in it – the pilots, while they take pride in their own skills, do not take enormous pride in shooting down other airmen. On this occasion, two parachutes – two ejections rather, which I hope means parachutes – were seen, so it is possible that, of the three planes that went down, two of the pilots did survive.**

The BBC and Independent Television News (ITN) had agreed to 'pool' their coverage, and on 26 May, ITN reporter Michael Nicholson, using the 'shared line from the Falklands', spoke to *Today*'s Hugh Sykes. 'This new picture we have of ships not only loaded with extremely sophisticated 20th-century missile systems, but guns lashed on the deck, that seems rather like a Second World War picture,' said Sykes. Nicholson explained how, especially on the normally unarmed supply vessels, the Commandos had 'lashed their guns to the side of these ships'. He was astonished when he 'found out the kind of firepower these guys can put up'. Nicholson elaborated:

> **I remember on one ship, they had 18 of these guns, some time ago... and apparently, they fire at such an enormous rate that they could chuck up in one**

minute 24,000 rounds. That's 24,000 bullets in a blanket in the air from 18 of these guns. Now, you know, they may be small little bullets, but that's an awful lot of lead in the air, and you can imagine what it's like for a very thin-skinned high-performance jet flying through it. Now, you know, today I interviewed one of the lieutenants of the Marines who was behind one of these guns and he had the Mirage in his sight as it came across San Carlos Bay, and he gave the order to fire and… he saw the belly of the Mirage being ripped open as it went through this wall of lead and it went into the hill all a good mile and a half beyond us.

'To a novice like me,' said Nicholson (who had in fact been covering wars since Biafra in the 1960s), 'for a machine gun to be hitting down Mirages seems to be exceptional.' Sykes asked, 'Do you get a sense that when a Mirage or the Skyhawk is shot down, there is a huge relief because the fear of it killing you has gone, or is there great excitement at having succeeded?'

'I would be wrong to say,' Nicholson replied, 'there wasn't a great cheer when one of these things go down.' Yet he was keen to emphasise the distinction between the machine (the enemy) and the person operating it:

I mean, a great cheer when the plane goes down, and then, you know, because we're men, there was an enormous relief that the guy inside had survived, and no more could have been done than was done to get this man aboard ship as quickly as possible. Landing craft went out, picked him up, hurried back, straight into the sick bay, flying suit…ripped apart as quickly as possible to see what his injuries were.

In this case, the injured Argentinian airman was sent ashore for an emergency operation.

By the end of May, British forces had taken Goose Green on East Falkland, where there was an Argentinian airstrip, after a bitterly contested battle lasting more than 24 hours. In the aftermath, there was an alarming discovery made among the abandoned Argentinian supplies, as Brian Redhead told *Today* listeners on 6 June:

I suppose there's no such thing as a nice weapon, but a napalm bomb is a particularly nasty weapon. Dropped from an aeroplane, napalm bombs explode into flames on impact and anybody caught in the blast is burnt to death. You may remember they were used in Vietnam. Well, napalm bombs have been found in Goose Green on the Falkland Islands and Argentine troops appear to have been preparing to use their weapons before they were forced to surrender. British commanders now say they fear that the Argentine forces at Port Stanley might turn to napalm in desperation.

Reporting on the napalm, Brian Hanrahan described how 'a lot of tanks – 50 on the airfield – had been filled already', carrying instructions in Spanish 'telling you how to clip the bombs onto either the Skyhawk or the Pucará [both attack aircraft]'. Hanrahan did not know whether the Argentinians had tried to use the weapon, yet, but he could confirm that the reaction of the British military authorities was 'one of horror, because napalm is a dreadful thing; one of surprise, because they said they assumed that no one would attempt to use it'.

A week later, on 12 June, Hanrahan reported what happened when two support ships, the *Sir Galahad* and the *Sir Tristram*, were hit by Argentinian bombs as they brought in units of the Scots and Welsh Guards to Port Pleasant near Bluff Cove on East Falkland. 'All we could do was just sit and watch,' he said, with 'everybody desperately anxious to help but totally unable to do so'. Hanrahan was speaking to the BBC reporter Neil Bennett in London.

> **Hanrahan: As ever, the people whose heroism has got to be unmatched were the helicopter pilots, who dropped everything they were doing, went across to the ship [*Sir Galahad*], which was well alight by this time – the stern of it was covered in black smoke, flames beginning to come out, ammunition exploding all the time, constantly a crackle of the small arms going off, and every now and then a huge explosion as probably an artillery shell or a mortar or a whole batch of them went up together. And, despite all this, the helicopter pilots went into the clouds, they pulled people off the bows of the ship where we could see them, little dots clustered on the front, trying to get off. They went searching round the back of the ship in through the cloud – how they saw in a thick black smoke, greasy smoke, I have no idea – but in they went and they hovered around and we could see bits of the helicopter drifting in and out of the smoke, the lines hanging down, the winchman desperately trying to fish people out of the water. I mean, it really was like that – he was dropping his rope and putting it in front of people and giving them a chance and then pulling them up and moving them on. And it was those helicopter pilots – risking their own lives all the time 'cause that ship must have been in imminent danger of exploding in a tremendous way – that saved as many people as were saved.**

> Bennett: Were the men able to get off into life rafts?

> Hanrahan: There were life rafts around the place. There was a little cluster of them along the front of the ship, when I got there by the bows and men going down over the side into them. There were also the ship's boats – they managed to get a fair number of those away. And *Sir Tristram*, which at that stage didn't appear to be badly damaged, was sending its boats along to help too. And so

we got this little armada of boats scattered all round the bay. They were rowing about, trying to get the engine starting, trying to fish people out of the water where they saw them, and the whole expanse between us and the shore was just covered with little boats all trying to row into us and finding it very hard to – because a very strong wind blowing, which was blowing out from the shore, so these men – very dazed I would have thought, they had to pull themselves ashore in that freezing cold wind, to be met by the medical orderlies, who were waiting for them.

Bennett: It must be extremely distressing, witnessing all this and yet being powerless to do anything about it.

Hanrahan: There really was nothing that one could do. The teams that were there to do the aid were there. The helicopters were whirring backwards and forwards. The casualties were being rushed off, the doctors and the medical orderlies, they were rushing in to give first-aid treatment immediately. Bottles of plasma were being put up and put into the men who had burned. The explosion had been – or the attack had been so swift, there'd been no time for men to get their anti-flash masks on – these are the gloves and the hood that people wear when there's a danger of attack, which protects almost all the exposed skin – and you could see that the most of the damage was – was burns to exposed skin. You can understand that in the confusion which occurs after this, the first priority is to get everybody who can be reached onto land, into the hands of the medical men, and away back to a rear field station where the maximum can be done for them. And they scatter all over the place, they just – the helicopters just take them where they can and nobody bothers to count. Sounds dreadful, but counting the dead comes after saving the living.

(When reporting events like this the correspondents were all too aware that relatives of those involved were likely to be listening.) Hanrahan continued:

I don't think I should give the impression that there are a dreadfully large number of casualties. I mean there are some severe casualties, there are a lot of dazed men and there are undoubtedly some people missing. But while you see this drama played in front of you, it – it's so vivid, I don't want to suggest that the whole ship's company and the troops on board had somehow been caught up in a roaring fire. They weren't. It's a remarkable thing, looking at just how severe these flames are, how fast they spread, how much there is to explode on board a ship, it's astonishing every time to see how many people manage to get off alive.

In every case so far, it's undoubtedly been the bulk of the ship's company and in this case I think it's certainly the majority of them and – and considerably more.

In this attack, there were around 200 casualties, a quarter of whom died.

While real war raged in this corner of the South Atlantic, back in Britain a war of words broke out between the Conservative government and the BBC. The former clearly thought the BBC should put patriotism before editorial impartiality. Particularly loathed by Mrs Thatcher was the BBC's refusal to speak of 'our' troops and 'our' ships, instead referring to the 'British' forces. It was, she later wrote, a 'chilling use of the third person'. But she had many other criticisms, including that the BBC (though not only the BBC) was giving away information potentially useful to the enemy.

The BBC's perspective was entirely the opposite: an expeditionary force despatched to reclaim an overseas territory did not constitute the kind of threat to the realm that should redefine the BBC's function. Director General Sir Ian Trethowan insisted that 'telling the truth' remained the corporation's task, even if it was tempered by the need to take account of the 'emotional sensibilities of the public'.

Argentinian forces surrendered on 14 June 1982. Over the previous two weeks, British troops had laboriously made their way across the boggy land eastwards to capture the strategic ground around Port Stanley. The enemy they had overcome was significantly superior in numbers – and 11,000 of them surrendered – but, as reporters discovered, many of the Argentinian conscripts were frightened and their morale was low. On 15 June, *Today* listeners heard how Max Hastings, at that time reporting for the London *Evening Standard*, had made his own way into Port Stanley on ceasefire day:

I was looking up the road ahead and there seemed to be no movement. I thought, I'm a civilian, so why shouldn't I go and see what's going on? Because there didn't seem to be much resistance up ahead. So I stripped off all my combat clothes, and I began to walk up the road, with my hands in the air, my handkerchief in my hand...

Almost casually, he found himself chatting to 'the senior Argentinian colonel' on the steps of his HQ. He also got to see 'hundreds, maybe thousands, of Argentinian troops milling around, marching in columns through the streets, some of them clutching very badly wounded men, and looking completely an army in defeat, blankets wrapped round themselves'. By contrast, an exuberant Mr King, owner of the 'famous Falklands hotel, the Upland Goose', had 'never doubted for a moment that the British would turn up'.

With the fighting over, Hastings could risk some criticism aimed at his own side: 'I think intelligence has not been one of our strong points throughout the campaign.' The 'thousands of rounds of ammunition, masses of weapons and plenty of food' that Hastings discovered suggested that the war could have been a much closer-run thing.

Even Port Stanley's airfield had still been receiving Argentinian transport planes, its runway strangely unmarked by the British bombing.

Robert Fox, one of the first reporters into Port Stanley, described to *Today* listeners on 16 June how, during a warehouse fire, he and the local fire-brigade members found themselves herding Argentinians to safety, and was amazed 'that the officers felt no responsibility, in that particular unit, for their men. They felt no responsibility for each other's safety. Now, this is the contrast with the British forces, where officers, men, NCOs, they care about each other and they work for each other.' Indeed, according to Fox, 'discipline had just broken down' and the situation was becoming mutinous, for ordinary conscripts 'were evidently frightening the officers'. 'Usually,' Fox remarked, 'it was the other way round. There is also evidence that in the trenches the officers may even have resorted to shooting their men in the legs to prevent them running away.'

The casualty count for the war, including the injured, exceeded the size of the Falkland Islands' population; at least 649 Argentinians died, along with 255 members of the British armed forces and three islanders. Twenty years after the war the novelist Julian Barnes described it in the *Guardian* as the 'worst-reported war since the Crimean'. Marking the 30th anniversary ten years later, the BBC's defence correspondent, Caroline Wyatt, echoed that historical comparison, writing in her BBC blog on 1 April 2012 that the military authorities 'noted (with quiet approval) that reports from the Falklands at times took longer to reach London than some despatches from the Crimean War in the 1850s'. She quoted the judgement of Brian Hanrahan that being embedded is 'a pact with the devil': 'Inside the military machine you get much greater access, but in return you give them the opportunity to limit what you can report.' But Hanrahan had also defended what he and his fellow correspondents achieved: 'In theory, the military had absolute power, but in practice it wasn't enforced very strongly at all.'

Brian Hanrahan died of cancer in 2010. He was the author of what was probably the most quoted piece of reporting of the conflict: after watching a group of Harriers returning safely from a mission, he said, 'I'm not allowed to say how many planes joined the raid, but I counted them all out, and I counted them all back' – it told the audience at home everything they needed to know, without revealing any information that might be useful to the enemy.

Saddam's 'guests' and the Gulf War

'It is really very, very strange'

HAROLD WALKER, 14 AUGUST 1990

Iraq invaded Kuwait at 2am local time on 2 August 1990. Relations between the two countries had been fractious since the end of the Iran–Iraq war two years earlier – Iraq was heavily in debt to its rich neighbour – and they had a long-standing border dispute. Iraqi leader Saddam Hussein had also argued the historic case that Kuwait was part of Iraq, and that the separation of the two was a British invention. But the invasion still came as a shock to the region and the world's big powers.

Iraq's armed forces were well equipped with French- and Soviet-supplied hardware; tens of thousands of troops and hundreds of tanks poured across the border, while the Iraqi air force hit the capital, Kuwait City. Within hours, Kuwait was overwhelmed and its Emir was in exile. Kuwaiti citizens were not the only ones suddenly to find themselves under occupation; thousands of foreign nationals were also caught by the invasion. They included the unlucky passengers on a British Airways flight bound for India, which had stopped to refuel at Kuwait City's airport. Many of them would become, in a phrase that became all too familiar during the crisis, 'human shields'.

By the time *Today* was on air that morning, much of the fighting was already over. The *Today* reporter Dominic Arkwright had been able to speak by phone to an American journalist in the city – her name was withheld – who gave listeners a glimpse of the confusion there as people woke up. The BBC's 'initial reports' at this stage suggested 200 people had been killed in the brief invasion:

> Journalist: I was driving down what they call the fifth ring road, and I saw trucks full of soldiers going towards the Bayan Palace, which is one of the emir's residences, and then they stopped the whole freeway and made everybody get off. We heard gunfire and, I've never heard explosions before so I don't know what kind they were, but I heard some explosions – they didn't sound very big – and then we came to the newspaper, and then left again and tried to go to the centre of the city. They've blocked off all roads to the centre of the city. There was more gunfire, soldiers in the roads making people turn around. And there's another palace among the emir's residences, which is near the sea. We were on what is

called the Arabian Gulf Road and they blocked that road, and, I think that the heaviest fighting is there, near his house that's closer to the sea. There was more gunfire there, shells on the sidewalk. We were detained by Iraqi soldiers, and they are detaining many citizens, on this green area, behind that palace, and not letting anyone go anywhere. They've shut off the gas. You can't get gas in your car. They've taken the radio also – at least the FM. Iraqi radio has come through saying they support the revolution in Kuwait. They're calling it a revolution of the younger generation of Kuwait and Iraq... Iraqi radio said that soldiers will stay here until the government is set in and operating. They said it might be a few days, they said it might be a few weeks.

Arkwright: Has there been resistance from the Kuwaiti army?

Journalist: ... yes, they're trying. Word is that they [the Iraqis] came through the border and they just rolled right over the army. That's what I've heard, and over the medium-wave radio they've called for citizens of Kuwait to try and help fight the invasion.

Arkwright: What are they saying to you, though, when they arrest or talk to you and stop you?

Journalist: They said everything's fine. They said not to worry and everything is fine. So... the Iraqi soldiers were saying that.

Arkwright: But how do you feel? Do you feel satisfied by that or do you feel scared or what?

Journalist: Absolutely not satisfied. There seemed to be some confusion as to what they were going to do with us when they detained us. They detained me and a Kuwaiti – a fellow Kuwaiti reporter, and one soldier said that I could leave and that they would take my Kuwaiti friend, and then another soldier said no, keep her – and him. And then the commander – we walked over to the commander, and the commander said we both could go. So it seems like there was some confusion as to what to do with people.

The United Nations Security Council was quick to condemn Iraq's action, and called for an 'immediate and unconditional' withdrawal. Control of Kuwait would give Saddam power over one-fifth of the world's oil production, and there were concerns about how far his ambitions extended: Saudi Arabia's main oil reserves are along the Gulf, not far from the border with Kuwait.

On the day of the UN Security Council resolution *Today* broadcast an interview with Victor Mallet, the *Financial Times* correspondent in Kuwait City. Dominic Arkwright asked him how Kuwaitis were reacting to what had happened.

> **Mallet: The initial mood was one of stunned surprise – that the Iraqis should have got as far as they did in actually invading the country. That's now given way, perhaps not to the sort of active resistance which the government in exile is calling for, but, certainly, a good deal of resentment.**

> **Arkwright: Do they feel scared?**

> **Mallet: I'm surprised, in a way, by the extent to which people have been very calm and relaxed throughout the whole thing, despite a great deal of shooting and artillery fire. Most people, as far as one can tell, have been extraordinarily calm.**

> **Arkwright: What kind of an Iraqi presence is it possible to actually see in the city?**

> **Mallet: Well it's extremely patchy in some parts of the city, particularly in the centre and around the strategic points, like the media centre and so on, there are very large numbers of Iraqi troops with vehicles, in some cases tanks, standing guard – but in some of the more suburban residential areas of Kuwait City and in fact where I am at this moment, there's no sign of Iraqi troops whatsoever.**

As *Today* listeners learned, Kuwaitis still had access to what the correspondent called 'clandestine radio and television broadcasts on the old frequencies', including 'patriotic songs' and appeals from the Crown Prince for his people 'to stand firm'.

Internationally, events moved fast. Sanctions were imposed on Iraq; Britain and the United States began to blockade the country, and George Bush started to build an international coalition to enforce the UN's resolutions. Saudi Arabia, caught between its role as guardian of Islam's holy sites and the reality of the Iraqi threat, broke with tradition and allowed hundreds of thousands of US and coalition troops into the area near the Kuwaiti border as part of what the Americans named Operation Desert Shield.

In Kuwait, around 115 US nationals were detained and distributed to sites that might become targets for any future American airstrikes. Many more foreign nationals, including an estimated 2,000 Americans, lay low in Kuwait, and a few tried to make a run for it. Such an attempt was to end tragically for one Briton, Douglas Croskery. He had been working in Kuwait for just a few weeks when Iraq invaded. Days afterwards, he opted to travel with a small convoy of Kuwaitis trying to escape across the desert to the Saudi border. They were intercepted, and Mr Croskery was reported as shot and killed.

The Foreign Office minister William Waldegrave advised Britons in Iraq and Kuwait to 'keep their heads down and stay where they are'.

On 14 August 1990, *Today* obtained the first interview with the British ambassador in Baghdad, Harold Walker. 'British citizens in Iraq,' presenter Sue MacGregor told listeners, 'are having to make the best of an extraordinary situation. They live in a country not officially at war, yet which puts heavy restrictions on their freedom.' The ambassador estimated there were about 500 of the normal Baghdad population of British expatriates still in the city, but by this time there were also 'over 120 British subjects [who] have come up from Kuwait', who were 'in a hotel called Mansour Melia'. Trying to find the right words, he concluded that the latter were 'detainees, um, interned, imprisoned... it's a fact they can't move'. 'It is really very, very strange,' he added, 'perhaps a unique state of affairs.'

The oddity was that the other Britons in Iraq were still able to move around freely, and in fact they 'did a whip-round and collected a lot of money' for their compatriots from Kuwait, some of whom had arrived 'without adequate changes of underclothing or nappies'. In Walker's estimation, there was confusion within the Iraqi bureaucracy. It was true that, as he put it, no 'Western foreign individuals are allowed out of the country at the moment'. On the other hand, they could move 'freely from Kuwait to Baghdad, because in Iraqi eyes Kuwait is just part of Iraq'.

'The murder of Mr Croskery,' Sue MacGregor asked, 'must have sent a shockwave through the community?'

Yes, Ambassador Walker confirmed, but he asserted that morale remained high, and that he had 'yet to come across here in Baghdad a single incident of personal hostility' against the city's British population.

A few days later, Iraq announced its compulsory 'guest' policy in Kuwait for the nationals of what it termed 'hostile countries'. Years later, one British 'guest', Wendy Major, told the *Daily Telegraph* how she had been taken to an oil refinery and made to 'work all day on cleaning duties, and given little to eat and drink' before being ferried to Iraq.

Three weeks into the crisis, a suited and smiling Saddam appeared on Iraqi television, welcoming a group of mainly British nationals in what was widely condemned as a PR stunt. 'We hope,' he told them, 'your presence as guests here will not be for too long.' Handshakes and photographs with the nervous attendees followed. Viewers in Britain were especially repelled by the way Saddam ruffled the hair of the young Stuart Lockwood, a seven-year-old boy from the British Airways flight. Foreign Secretary Douglas Hurd was unimpressed: 'I think the manipulation of children in that sort of way is contemptible.'

The British prime minister, Margaret Thatcher, accused Saddam of 'hiding behind the skirts of women'. The following month he authorised the release of most women and children, along with some men in poor health. They left in several planeloads in early September 1990.

By this time, a number of prominent individuals and delegations had appointed themselves as humanitarian ambassadors and were trying to intercede on the remaining foreign nationals' behalf. They ran the risk of breaching international sanctions by having any dialogue with Saddam, and the senior US diplomat at the Baghdad embassy, Joseph Wilson, was critical of their efforts: 'They would be photographed sitting attentively next to him, would make some inane anti-war comments to the camera and, as a reward, Saddam would bestow a few hostages on them.'

But some were more influential than others. Most significant among the Americans was civil rights campaigner Jesse Jackson, while from Britain there came a former prime minister, Edward Heath.

On 19 October 1990, Sue MacGregor told *Today* listeners:

> **Edward Heath sets off on his delayed trip to the Gulf today. He flies to Oman, and then he goes to Baghdad tomorrow, to meet President Saddam Hussein on Sunday. He hopes of course to gain the release of more than 40 British hostages, but his trip's been criticised at home for the signals that it sends to the government of Saddam Hussein.**

In Baghdad, the BBC correspondent Allan Little explained, 'The British community has coined a new word, "guestages" – guests officially, hostages in effect. More than 40 of them are ill, some seriously. It's they who have inspired Mr Heath's humanitarian mission.' The wife of a British man suffering from terminal cancer explained that much of the tension arose from the fickleness of the Iraqi authorities: 'It is a bit like a horse race, and it could happen that you fall at the last fence.'

The tedium of life as a 'guestage' had to be broken as best it could. In the same broadcast, MacGregor told listeners how:

> **A group of British hostages has clubbed together to turn a small single-storey villa into a nightclub. They call it 'The Pit'. It begins to get lively around midnight and many of the hostages, with little else to do, gather here till three, sometimes four in the morning...**

Ambassador Harold Walker wanted to dampen down expectations for Heath's visit:

> **If you look at the numerous missions [that] have been here, German and Japanese, Spanish, etc., some go away with some people – by no means always**

the people they wanted to go away with – and some go away empty-handed. And I think it's very unwise to maybe arouse what could be false hopes.

Sometimes, too, there was a price to pay. Allan Little explained how, in return for the freedom of 15 Spanish 'guests', Saddam had managed to extract from the initiative a 'peace medal' and a statement that read: 'We find President Saddam Hussein wise, and he possesses deep feelings and the real desire for progress. Iraq is the cradle of civilisation.' As Little warned, 'The Iraqis will want a *quid pro quo* from Mr Heath, too. How far he's prepared to go may determine how many hostages he's allowed to take with him.'

'Despite their efforts to be cheerful,' Little concluded, 'there's a distinct atmosphere of sadness and even despair among the British here.' There was, therefore – and contrary to the generally critical press Heath was receiving at home – a welcome for his efforts.

In the early morning of 24 October 1990, a Virgin Atlantic jet touched down at Gatwick Airport carrying Heath, Virgin boss Richard Branson (who had been operating mercy flights to Jordan too) and 30 hostages, 'most of them sick and elderly', as *Today's* Emma Hill reported that same morning. The blinking former hostages were outnumbered three times over by 'more than a hundred members of the press and media'. But in the eyes of one ex-hostage, Heath had 'done a wonderful job'. 'I can assure you,' he added, 'talking to people like President Saddam Hussein and the ministers out there is not a picnic, and I think he's a wonderful man.' Heath, 'looking pale and drawn but smiling', was keen to dampen down expectations that as many as 200 would have been with him. When asked, 'What's the experience been like for you on a personal level?' he replied in characteristically laconic style, 'Very interesting.'

Three weeks later, on 13 November, *Today* listeners gained an insight into what life was truly like for those still trapped in Kuwait. As Sue MacGregor explained:

A British man in hiding in Kuwait has smuggled out a tape to his wife in Britain describing living conditions in the country. In an hour-long recording, he speaks of his hunger, his boredom and the desperation as he tries to avoid the Iraqi patrols, and he accuses on the tape the British government of not doing enough to get them out. He and his fellow hostages are, he says, the forgotten people.

'I've got some carrots left,' listeners heard. 'What I'm doing, I'm eating those raw so I get all the goodness out of them, having one every other day.' Reporter Richard Hannaford confirmed that 'Food shortages are becoming desperate. The lack of fresh vegetables is causing his teeth to become loose and his gums to become sore.' The man described the casual Iraqi looting going on around him – a car park of 80-odd vehicles reduced to four – and the periodic arrests and detainments: 'One day something will happen, and it could be a case of diving to the basement.' His only hope, he felt, was that one day he would 'see the boys roaming around in the desert or waving the Union Jack and, God willing, they'll come and get us.'

In early December 1990 Saddam agreed to the release of 3,000 hostages in Iraq and Kuwait. On 10 December, Edward Heath was able to reap more fully the rewards of his efforts, landing at Heathrow with around a hundred former 'guests' and (as the BBC put it) 'the promise of a further 400 to follow'. 'The Foreign Office expects,' said the BBC, 'all those held since Iraq invaded Kuwait in early August to be home by the weekend.'

The following day, in the House of Commons, Heath earned a government acknowledgement, from Douglas Hurd, the foreign secretary: 'Today is an occasion to step back from immediate events, to look at the crisis as a whole and to consider what is at stake. One immediate event is wholly welcome, and that is the release of hostages which is now underway.' Heath responded by saying that he wanted to make 'just one point about that, drawn from the experience that we have had since a considerable number of hostages returned with me a few weeks ago':

> There is a major problem of adjustment to the conditions of ordinary life. That is, perhaps, true of those who were with me because most were ill, some dying, and others were very old and infirm; but I suspect that it is even more true of those who have been in hiding in Kuwait, as well as those who have been in Iraq, experiencing reasonable conditions but denied their freedom.

Operation Desert Storm began on 17 January 1991, and by the end of the following month Kuwait was liberated and Saddam's Iraq had been forced into surrender. The world stood in awe at the effects of the most advanced precision-guided weapons: the swift war represented, according to some analysts, a 'revolution in military affairs'. At the same time it was a diplomatic revolution of sorts: an extraordinarily broad alliance of nations contributing to the effort; and, for once, the United States and the Soviet Union cooperated to secure the United Nations mandate for action.

That UN mandate did not go as far as toppling Saddam; that would have to wait for another war over a decade later.

NATO's first war – Kosovo, 1999

'A faraway land of which many Americans know nothing'

MARK DEVENPORT, 25 MARCH 1999

Edward Stourton: It's six o'clock on Thursday the 25th of March. This is *Today* with John Humphrys in London and Edward Stourton at the European leaders' summit in Berlin.

John Humphrys: The news headlines this morning: dozens of targets have been hit on the first night of the NATO bombing against Yugoslavia. The authorities in Belgrade have declared a state of war. They claim women and children were killed in the raids.

Thus began, in 1999, what was the first-ever campaign against a sovereign state conducted by the world's most powerful military alliance. It was never imagined it would be this way; NATO had been born as a Cold War institution, and it was developed to defend the West against the Warsaw Pact. But following the collapse of the Soviet Union at the beginning of the 1990s, when the superpower system was replaced by a 'unipolar' world dominated by the United States, its role was redefined. The Kosovo campaign was not fought in defence of a NATO member; the alliance was acting in the role of an international police force, intervening in a sovereign state to protect some of its citizens.

The foreign policy doctrine known as 'liberal interventionism' emerged from the collapse of Yugoslavia, the federation of six republics that had been held together by the Communist war hero Marshal Tito. After Tito's death in 1980, nationalist and religious tensions began to pull Yugoslavia apart, and the federation eventually fragmented in a series of wars. The bloodiest was fought in Bosnia from 1992–5, and international outrage at some of the atrocities committed during that conflict prompted NATO's first intervention. From 1993 NATO airpower was used in support of the UN's operations in Bosnia, and in February 1994 NATO fighters shot down four Serb fighters in the first ever combat operation in the history of the alliance. The Bosnian war ended with the Dayton Accords, agreed at an American airbase in Ohio in November 1995. However, a new flashpoint was already emerging in the province of Kosovo, which Serbia regarded as part of its territory. Under Tito, Kosovo had enjoyed a measure of autonomy, but the nationalist Serbian leader Slobodan Milošević had curtailed that, which stoked an insurgency by ethnic-Albanian separatists. It led to the formation of the Kosovo Liberation Army, fighting on behalf of the province's ethnic-Albanian majority. The more powerful and better equipped regular forces of the Yugoslav army, the JNA, went into action against the KLA, and the counter-insurgency campaign soon evolved into what the Kosovar Albanians regarded as ethnic cleansing.

An agreement in October 1998 was breached by both sides. By March 1999, international talks to broker a settlement had failed, and the JNA and Serb paramilitary police were pressing ahead with their programme of ethnic cleansing. The situation deteriorated so badly that international monitors were withdrawn. US envoy Richard Holbrooke flew to the Serb capital Belgrade to make a last-ditch effort at peace, but also to deliver a final threat. In NATO's words, Milošević 'refused to comply, and on 23 March the order was given to commence airstrikes (Operation Allied Force).'

The next evening, the bombs and missiles hit.

'Serbia is waking up to a new reality,' *Today* listeners heard from correspondent Jeremy Cook, in Belgrade on 25 March. The newsreader that morning was Vaughan Savidge:

> **Around a hundred cruise missiles are believed to have been fired during the raids, which went on until the early hours of this morning. Among the sites reportedly hit were an aircraft factory and a military base near Belgrade, and a barracks near Pristina [the capital of Kosovo]. In Belgrade, the authorities claimed that women and children were killed in the raids. A state of war has been declared.**

Later that day, NATO's General Wesley Clark explained to the press that 'In the operation thus far, almost 400 aircraft and several warships have been involved from most nations in the alliance, of all different types' against around 40 targets. 'What we are targeting here,' he added, 'are military and security forces and the associated facilities.' First on the list – understandably – were Serbia's anti-aircraft systems.

In the same broadcast, John Humphrys spoke to 'our reporter in Belgrade, one of those who managed not to get arrested by the Serb police last night, Mike Williams', who added some colour and texture to the unfolding story, against a background of air-raid sirens:

> **There have been months of ultimatum and bluster. Bluffs were called, threats ignored. The result last night: NATO bombs falling on a European capital. The air-raid sirens howled across Belgrade, columns of smoke rose into the sky lit from within by flames and flashes of secondary explosions. There were traces**

from anti-aircraft artillery and the burning rockets of the cruise missiles. Eventually, though, the fires cooled and faded into the blackness and Belgrade became dark and quiet. Sunrise brought respite from the bombing, and a realisation that this was real. That, last night, people died.

On the streets, Williams spoke to uncomprehending Serbs, full of 'fear and anger and confused disbelief'. For some of them, this was a betrayal of history: 'I remember 1941, when Hitler's aeroplanes bombed Yugoslavia, and then I compare it. This situation, for me, is the same.' And then Williams paraphrased him: '"I am," he said, "very surprised that an old ally of ours, Great Britain, joined with the forces standing against us."'

NATO's member states had acted on their own initiative, without a United Nations mandate; any attempt to get a resolution through the Security Council authorising the use of force would have been blocked by Russia, a permanent member of the council and traditional ally of Serbia. Russia's UN ambassador, Sergey Lavrov (who went on to become Russia's long-serving foreign minister), described the airstrikes as an 'illegal act of unconcealed aggression'; a view supported by China. And as *Today* reported, 'The United Nations secretary general, Kofi Annan, has said he should have been consulted more closely about the airstrikes.' But the BBC's UN correspondent Jane Hughes also told *Today* listeners, 'Other members expressed regret that the airstrikes had gone ahead without United Nations authorisation, but few condemned the action.'

In the United States, President Bill Clinton went on what the BBC's Mark Devenport called 'an all-out PR assault' to convince the American people 'why their forces are engaged over a faraway land of which many Americans know nothing'. In an effort to educate, as Devenport explained to John Humphrys, 'President Clinton, in his address, used maps and actually became something of a geography teacher: recognition on the part of the administration that they've got to really teach the Americans from basics.' Most Americans, Devenport figured, would 'give this operation a fair wind' – unless the Serb air defences actually started taking a toll of American lives.

From Moscow, however, correspondent Paul Anderson described to Humphrys something quite different: 'Tremendous anger, I think. Goes way beyond mere annoyance. We're seeing politician after politician on Russian television screens this morning warning of dire consequences.' Could it really be the start, as some Russians were claiming, of a new Cold War? 'That surely is just rhetoric in the heat of the moment?' exclaimed Humphrys. But perhaps not so. After all, as Anderson explained:

I think this whole issue has forced them to confront their own impotence in the post-Soviet world. They had an opportunity to try and persuade Milošević to back down. They were uniquely placed to do that because of this so-called Slavic brotherhood between Yugoslavia and Russia, and they failed to do that, and now they have to try and pick up the pieces.

Russian opposition was, perhaps surprisingly, echoed by the British Labour Party elder statesman Denis Healey, who told Edward Stourton on that morning's programme:

I think it was a terrible mistake to attack a sovereign state without even consulting the United Nations. I think it will have – indeed has already had – a catastrophic effect on Western relations with Russia and China. For [Boris] Yeltsin [President of Russia] it is a catastrophe because it strengthens his Communist and nationalist opponents... already describing it as a second Vietnam.

Continuing his doom-laden predictions, a somewhat tetchy Healey sounded a warning:

Healey: I think we made a mistake in acting so fast and in committing ourselves to a prolonged campaign in which we've given total power of decision not to NATO's governments, but to the NATO military commanders.

Stourton: How seriously do you think we have to take the threats from Russia?

Healey: There is no threat from Russia in the sense that they're threatening to intervene in the war. I don't think they're capable of doing that.

Stourton: But do you think they might sell weapons to Serbia?

Healey: But there is – would you listen to me? There is a very serious risk that Yeltsin, who is trying very, very hard to maintain good relations with NATO and the West, already upset by the enlargement of NATO to Poland, Hungary and Czechoslovakia – there's as a great risk that he will be overthrown by a coalition of nationalists and militarists, which will face us with problems which could lead to far more suffering than anything that's happening in Kosovo.

Today's round-up of the day's press headlines, read by Vaughan Savidge, also dwelt on the potential ramifications. After all, this was the Balkans – the crucible of the First World War:

The *Express* says the Continent faces its greatest conflict since the Second World War, and few of the papers ignore the danger of violence spreading across the Balkans. The *Independent* says anxieties are high in neighbouring states, such as Macedonia and Albania, but also in Greece and Turkey and in Italy, where air-defence batteries have been set up on the south-east coast.

For President Clinton, however, as he told the American people, fighting *now* was a case of nipping a problem in the bud *before* it became a wider regional conflict. This was also the view of the Western politician who had done more than any other to stiffen his allies' resolve to take action: Britain's prime minister Tony Blair. Blair was in Berlin for a European Union summit when the bombing began, and Edward Stourton was co-presenting the programme from the German capital. As he reported:

> ... it was left to his deputy, John Prescott, to give details last night of the British involvement in the NATO attack on Serbia. From the official opposition spokesman, the support was firm, but backbench opinion on all sides was more mixed.

Parliamentary correspondent Viv Robins took up the story:

> Mr Prescott told the House the NATO attack, the first against a sovereign country in the whole of its 50-year history, was justified to prevent an overwhelming humanitarian catastrophe in Kosovo.

Belgrade's citizens would have been heartened, though, to hear opposition from veteran left-winger Tony Benn, now on Labour's backbenches:

> It was the Serbian resistance to Hitler that gave us the opportunity of the victory which we secured and to demonise Serbia now, when Yugoslavia was deliberately broken up by Western policy-makers, is to mislead the public into a crusade that does not exist.

Deputising for Blair, Prescott responded, 'I think the Right Honourable Member should bear in mind that they were allies and of many years ago; what they are doing today is murdering an awful lot of people in Kosovo.' From the Conservative opposition, there was another dissenting voice from Douglas Hogg, who asked, 'Does he [Prescott] agree that we have gone to war without there being a sufficient national interest, without there being a clear understanding of the strategic and political objectives, without there being a proper exit strategy, and indeed without the authority of this House?'

At the Berlin summit Edward Stourton explored German reaction to the attacks with the German Europe minister, the Social Democrat Dr Günter Verheugen:

> Stourton: Are you convinced there's sufficient support for a *sustained* campaign in Germany?
>
> Verheugen: Yes, I think so. Public opinion in Germany is very clear. There was strong support for the chancellor's [Gerhard Schroeder of the SPD, or

Social Democratic Party] decision. It's the decision of the government in the Parliament. There's a strong national consensus on this.

Stourton: What about the Russian threat?

Verheugen: Well, the Russian threat, of course, is serious but a cool calculation shows that it can't be in Russia's interest to jeopardise Russia's relations – vital relations – with the rest of the world.

Stourton: The trouble with cool calculations is they sometimes get lost in these circumstances.

Verheugen: Yes, we know, we know. And therefore it is very important to use the channels which we have with Moscow and to stay in close contact. That is yesterday what happened, for example Chancellor Schroeder as president of the European Council had a telephone call with Prime Minister Primakov, and my view is that we can avoid a situation where Russia seriously would stand against the West.

John Humphrys was also pondering strategy: 'So what now? Another night of attacks tonight, then another and another until... well, what?' It was a question he put to the foreign secretary, Robin Cook, who affirmed the operation's objective as being to 'curb the capacity of Milošević's army to repress the Kosovar Albanians'. But what, Humphrys wondered, 'if he carries on, if he says, "I'm going to sit tight; I'm going to stick this out"? Then what do we do?' After all, Humphrys had heard former commander-in-chief of the British forces, General Sir Peter de la Billière, say this very morning, 'Airstrikes do not destroy a nation's will and capacity to fight.'

Robin Cook stuck to his line, insisted that there was a thought-through plan, and emphasised the potential consequences of inaction. As for the 'armchair generals' who criticised, he offered them a little advice:

What would be the credibility of NATO if, having made the demands that we have done of President Milošević – if having entered into the agreement that we did with him last October – we were then to stand idly by as he quite flagrantly broke those agreements, ignored what we were demanding? Where would the credibility of NATO be then?

As it turned out, for a while Milošević did 'stick it out' – and even intensified the ethnic cleansing. In that sense, he called NATO's bluff, and in the short term the plight of Kosovar Albanians, many of whom had returned to Kosovo expecting better times, worsened. On 31 March *Today*'s James Naughtie reported from the Kosovo border:

Macedonia, Montenegro and Albania are now havens of sorts for tens of thousands of ethnic Albanian refugees fleeing from Kosovo, fleeing from what they say are atrocities perpetrated by Serbian forces and indeed by civilians. No one knows the details, no one knows the whole truth, but we do know the consequences; they are evident around me here on the border between Macedonia and Kosovo. Far to the north of us there is of course war – there are the bombing raids, there are the orange flashes in the sky. There is none of that here, but there is a human tragedy on a vast scale. Cartloads, tractor loads of refugees, pouring across the border all night, wherever they can, to seek refuge in mosques, in schools, in homes, to make contact with their families. This is a refugee crisis in Europe on a huge scale.

Naughtie interviewed Jo Hegenauer from the office of the United Nations High Commissioner for Refugees (UNHCR) and asked him about the atrocity stories the refugees brought with them. 'Refugees have a history of giving accurate accounts of what they've gone through,' Hegenauer replied, 'and the stories that UNHCR is receiving, from Albania, from Macedonia, from other places – Bosnia – there's some that are consistent. So, we do believe the stories they are telling us. We do believe that the problems they have are tragic, and also UNHCR was present in Kosovo and we saw a lot of this.'

Later in that edition of *Today,* Naughtie broadcast some of the stories he himself had heard. A light-weight satellite broadcasting system – which can be easily operated by a producer – allowed him to introduce his own report live from the border.

Naughtie: Ten minutes past eight. I'm looking down into Kosovo through the valleys of Northern Macedonia, towards a cluster of snowy peaks across a plunging landscape. And this is a place of intense human drama. A simple stone school alongside me on the hillside is full of refugees, ethnic Albanians who fled their Serb enemies across the border from Kosovo. The mosque in the little village beyond the trees there is now a bunkhouse and a place of refuge. All night here, as in the crossing places along this border and along the border with Albania and Montenegro, ethnic Albanians have been pouring across, the river of refugees has flowed and flowed. They've come through the hills any way they can and they're still coming. Through the night, what a sight it was...

Out of the darkness the rattle of an old tractor and on the cart, a load of humanity, families piled on top of one another, their faces are grey, they are cold and they tell terrible stories. And around us on this hillside on the border with Kosovo, the relatives wait to see if the next load carries faces that they will recognise.

This man is carrying a bag of milk cartons for children whom he doesn't know if he'll ever see. As he speaks you can sense rather than see a crowd shuffling away into the dark. Those who wait, and those who after a 15- or 20-hour march have left Kosovo behind.

Kosovan man: I meet today many people from home in the morning, and a man say in my town, many people killed. He walked 15 hours and he say eight children died because it was very cold.

Naughtie: This is the kind of story they all bring across these hills, they say not very far from us here. They've left bloody scenes and death. A man waits beside us, as he will for as long as it takes, knowing that his parents are on the march, not knowing if they'll arrive....

Air and missile strikes against Serbia continued for 77 days and nearly 10,500 combat sorties, the targets expanding beyond purely military ones to include the country's electricity grid and other infrastructure. By June 1999, Milošević had been pressured into agreeing to withdraw all Serb forces from Kosovo and accept an international peacekeeping force in the province. Russia had played a key role in devising the terms for the Serbian climb-down in agreement with NATO.

Kosovo remained under UN administration until 2008, whereupon it declared its independence – recognised by the United States, much of Europe and by international organisations, and rejected by Serbia, Russia and China, and by the Serb minority within Kosovo.

Today, complex agreements allow it to function as a de-facto state.

9/11 and the advent of the new terrorism

'We've heard that the world will never be the same again'

SUE MACGREGOR, 12 SEPTEMBER 2001

James Naughtie: It's six o'clock on Wednesday 12th September. Good morning on the day after the world's worst terrorist attack, the assault that brought fire and death to the heart of the United States. This is *Today* with Sue MacGregor and James Naughtie.

Sue MacGregor: The main news this morning is that President Bush has signalled that America will retaliate for the devastating terrorist attacks on New York and Washington. More than 300 firefighters are among the thousands of dead in the wreckage of the World Trade Center. There's still no clear indication about how many people have died in New York... we'll be devoting the whole of today's programme to the horrific events of yesterday...

Naughtie summarised the story so far:

> The American people are struggling with the aftermath of yesterday's devastating terrorist attacks... The coordinated strikes began, of course, during the morning rush hour when two airliners on internal flights were hijacked and flown deliberately into each of the two towers of the World Trade Center in New York. Both buildings collapsed a short time later. Then, that third hijacked aircraft crashed into the Pentagon in Washington, causing a great deal of damage. Another plane went down in a field near Pittsburgh in Pennsylvania, its intended target apparently the presidential retreat at Camp David. The scale of the atrocity has stunned the United States and the rest of the world.

Plane hijackings had become a favoured terrorist tactic during the 1970s and 1980s, but 9/11 changed all the rules. Here, the killing not just of a few, not just of hundreds, but of thousands *was* the goal. And those thousands included the perpetrators, who sacrificed themselves for their cause. The planes were hijacked not because they contained useful hostages to be bartered, but because aircraft full of fuel can become flying bombs. And where was the hijackers' demand? There wasn't one. The act was the message: mass casualties and the destruction of famous American institutions representing business, finance, defence and – had the fourth plane not ploughed into a field – the presidency itself. Sue MacGregor said: 'Sheer statistics, such as we have them, can't possibly capture the full horror of the terrorist attack on America. Certainly, thousands of people have died.' But how many? Everyone knew that they could only guess the scale of the attack.

'The latest news from the Arlington Fire Brigade, the local fire brigade close to the Pentagon, is that there may be 800 dead in the building,' Naughtie told listeners, and the same figure was reiterated at various points that morning. The real toll turned out to be 125, along with the nearly 60 passengers, crew and hijackers on board the plane that hit the building. As for the Twin Towers, they could accommodate up to 50,000 people, and the assumption in the early days was that a substantial proportion of those had to be among the dead. After all, the impact of the aircraft and the subsequent collapse of the buildings seemed so devastatingly catastrophic. Eventually, however, the deaths of nearly 3,000 people that day would be directly ascribed to the attacks; but Sue MacGregor had been right to say that 'more than 300 firefighters are among the thousands of dead in the wreckage of the World Trade Center'. Ultimately, New York City firefighters comprised more than one-tenth of the day's toll.

The BBC correspondent Robert Pigott was on the road in the United States when the attack took place, 'travelling through what I suppose you might call the real America, away from the great metropolitan centres where people have been trying to absorb the shock', and he spoke to *Today*. Pigott was moving up from Birmingham, Alabama, and 'as we came north there was fresh realisation at each stage of just how bad this disaster has been'. In the past, there was:

> ... violence against American property and people abroad, but not really here... people are equating this with Pearl Harbor back in the Forties, because it is this sense of a complete shock and a sudden awareness of vulnerability that the United States *itself* can be under threat.

From the Pentagon, *Today* listeners heard from a commander on the defence staff who 'asked to remain anonymous'. He and his colleagues had been 'riveted' to the TV, watching the Twin Towers burn, when suddenly they found themselves participants in the same drama. 'All of a sudden we felt the rumble and we heard the boom... it was almost like you were in a movie and you were watching these panic scenes that you see in a movie happening before your eyes.'

While the world struggled to comprehend the 'what' of 9/11, thoughts simultaneously turned to the 'who'. 'Is it inevitable,' Naughtie asked George Joffé, a Cambridge University specialist in Middle East, 'that the finger will point at bin Laden?'

'It's quite likely,' answered Joffé, his response based on first comments from US officials and the airlines involved; but what was bewildering, he said, was the sheer 'complexity of the operation'. When asked if that complexity suggested a 'state-sponsored' element, Joffé was dubious because, 'Any state must know what the response must be.' In the end, Joffé admitted, 'We're still simply searching for evidence of one kind or another to begin to indicate who might be responsible, and we just don't know.'

No one could be certain, but eyes turned instinctively to the Middle East. 'American domestic opinion has no idea at all about the way in which attitudes of the Middle East have hardened and become virulently anti-American in recent months, because of the situation between the Arab world and Israel,' said Joffé. Some Palestinians in the West Bank, East Jerusalem and Lebanon celebrated the attack, Israel went into lockdown as if *it* had been attacked, as the BBC's Middle East correspondent James Reynolds reported from Jerusalem:

> **There is a very uneasy atmosphere across this land. Israelis are on high alert. Security sources believe that Islamic extremists are responsible for yesterday's attacks in the United States. Because of this, the government has closed Israel's airspace to foreign aircraft and shut the country's land border crossings.**

The BBC's Frank Gardner, who was based in Cairo, reported, that although 'Arab leaders are appalled by what's happened. Except for Iraq, almost every Arab country has come out to condemn the attacks', the mood among those leaders' populations was quite different:

> **The Arab world is almost unanimous over these attacks. It says America had it coming. US policy in the Middle East has long been criticised here for its support for Israel and the almost daily bombing of Iraq by Western warplanes. Now the streets of Palestinian refugee camps have been echoing to the sound of celebratory gunfire. In parts of Gaza and in Lebanon there's an almost party atmosphere. The US, the perceived enemy of the Islamic world, has been hit hard. Now, Arabs say, Americans can taste the suffering of the Palestinians.**

However, from Jerusalem James Reynolds was reporting that 'Many Palestinians are also very worried. They fear that Israel may now decide to step up its military action against targets in the West Bank and Gaza.' As the world knew, Israel and the Palestinian Territories were still being rocked by violence meted out by both sides in the aftermath of the al-Aqsa intifada of 2000–2001. Israeli leaders, meanwhile, were calling for what Naughtie described as 'an international war against terrorism'.

'Until it's clear that Osama bin Laden is not a suspect in yesterday's attacks on America, Afghans fear they will be caught up in the crossfire,' reported BBC

Afghanistan correspondent Kate Clark that morning. They were right to worry. Bin Laden had been identified as the man behind the earlier bombing of US embassies in Nairobi and Dar es Salaam, but, as Clark told listeners, 'The Taliban have repeatedly refused to give up Osama bin Laden for trial for those attacks, despite cajoling, threats and United Nations sanctions – they say it would be un-Islamic to hand over a guest to his enemies.'

The view that the Taliban should be held responsible for bin Laden's actions was reinforced by the fact that, just two days before the attacks of 9/11, al-Qaeda had done the Taliban a favour. They had assassinated Ahmad Shah Massoud, the charismatic and internationally regarded leader of the Northern Alliance, which was fighting to overthrow their regime in Kabul.

By the time *Today* was broadcasting on the morning after 9/11, US President George W Bush had already addressed his nation and promised that America's military was 'powerful and prepared'. The British Cabinet was in emergency session trying to determine, as the BBC's political editor Andrew Marr told listeners, 'what can be done at this relatively late stage to make things a little bit safer here; and, as important, what kind of influence can Britain and other European countries bring to bear on the American response to ensure that, you know, they don't make things worse.' For President Bush, as Naughtie commented, 'These are going to be testing days.' Providing his analysis again, Cambridge University's George Joffé explained that time was not on Bush's side:

> He's going to have to make some decisions very quickly if he's going to satisfy domestic opinion. Those decisions must be correct and proportionate if he is not to outrage foreign opinion. And, in the end, whatever he does do will have a lasting effect on the relations of the United States with the wider world.

James Naughtie continued the theme:

> His difficulty, presumably, is that domestic opinion, naturally outraged and inflamed by these events, is bound to be pushing him towards action, which, if it isn't based on accurate information and turns out to be the wrong action in the wrong place on the wrong scale, could have devastating effects itself.

'We've heard that the world will never be the same again,' observed Sue MacGregor, which few would deny. And James Rubin, a former US assistant secretary of state, felt that the deterioration in the Middle East was already a red herring:

> First of all this isn't about Middle East policy. Even at the time when the United States was hopeful and the world was hopeful there would be peace between the Palestinians and the Israelis a couple of years ago, Osama bin Laden was

still at war. So he isn't doing this on behalf of the Palestinians, and that needs to be understood.

Rubin, a New Yorker, was mourning his hometown, but he drew attention to something very important:

> The World Trade Center is home to international commerce, to the intercourse between nations all over the world, and we're going to find Japanese and Asians and Europeans and people from all over the world who were working in that building who were killed.

All airspace over North America was closed in the immediate aftermath of the 9/11 attacks, so non-American news organisations faced additional challenges in covering the story. The BBC and a consortium of British television and newspaper companies chartered a passenger airliner from Stansted, and after some two days of frustration it was allowed to fly to Canada. A *Today* team reached New York in time to co-present the programme from Manhattan on Saturday, 15 September, and again from Washington on Monday 17 September.

By that time – less than a week after the attacks – the scale of the American response was already becoming apparent. *Today* broadcast an impromptu street press conference given by the American defence secretary, Donald Rumsfeld, after his appearance on one of the Sunday television talk shows. After laying out the administration's ambitions he was questioned by *Today*'s Edward Stourton:

> Rumsfeld: The terrorists who were attacking our way of life do not have armies, navies or air forces. They do not have capitals. They do not have high-value targets that the typical weapons of war can go in and attack. Which is why the president has said what he has said; it will take a broad, sustained effort, that will have to use our diplomatic, our political, our economic, our financial strength, as well as our military strength, and unquestionably unconventional techniques, and it will take time. It's not a matter of days or weeks – it's years. It's going to take the support of the American people, and I have every confidence it'll be there. It'll take the support of countries around the world. There are a number of countries that are harbouring terrorists, in some cases facilitating them, in some cases financing them, in other cases just tolerating them. But these people could not be functioning around the globe with the success they are, unless they had that help from countries. And those countries, some of them, do in fact have armies and navies and air forces, and they do have capitals, and they do have high-value targets. And we're going to need them to stop tolerating terrorists.

Stourton: Do you think it's achievable in the light of the difficulties that you've outlined?

Rumsfeld: I do think it's achievable. I think that [terrorism] is particularly something that strikes at free people. Every one of the people listening got up this morning and walked out of the door of their house and they did not have to look to the left and look to the right. They didn't have to wear a flak jacket. They didn't have to get into an armoured car. They didn't have to hide in their basement. Because we have enjoyed all of the privileges and opportunities of free people and it's a wonderful thing. And we cannot allow terrorists to deny that to us. Therefore we must. There is no choice other than to root out terrorists, wherever they are across this globe.

America's outrage in the face of the attacks united Republicans and Democrats. The future Democratic presidential candidate Hilary Clinton, then one of New York's senators, gave an interview to the *Today* reporter Andrew Hosken for the same programme:

Clinton: Well, first I want to thank Prime Minister Blair and the people of Great Britain for the extraordinary support that has already been given to our country. I would have expected no less given our relationship that goes back so many years, but it is very heartening that we are joined in this war against fanaticism. The United States is going to do whatever it takes along with our allies, like Britain, to hunt down those who committed these acts and any who harbored them, and then we will also be engaged in the challenging but necessary task of rebuilding lives and rebuilding buildings. But I have no doubt that America will come back even stronger than ever.

Hosken: It's going to be a very difficult war. It is an effort against terrorists who are very well protected.

Clinton: It will be difficult, but we've met difficult challenges before. You know, I've been thinking a lot over the last few days about the Battle of Britain. It's a great example of courage under fire. Where just ordinary people went about their daily business, refused to be cowed by the incredible barrage that came from the Nazis, and gave an example to everyone as to how to carry on. And that's what we will do.

Today producers face particular difficulties in setting up interviews in the United States; the programme's broadcast time (the small hours of the morning on the Eastern Seaboard of the United States) is anti-social, and American politicians inevitably give priority to the domestic media market. But after 9/11 Washington was talking to the world; the secretary of state, Colin Powell, also answered questions for *Today* that morning and, with al-Qaeda's Afghan base in mind, he focused on the support of a key ally in the region:

> Powell: I have confidence in the words of President Musharraf [of Pakistan], he's been very, very supportive. He indicated support to me directly, and then he spoke to President Bush yesterday. They had a good conversation, and he pledged his support, and I expect in the next several days we'll be sending an interagency team to Pakistan to get into greater details about what our campaign plans might be like, and what kind of support might be needed. But the Pakistanis have been very forthcoming, and I think we should stop saying, 'Can we trust them, can't we trust them?' We will see what they are going to be able to do. And yes, I trust [them]. And they have been very forthcoming, and we should compliment them on that forthcomingness rather than start speculating about their sincerity or support.

> Stourton: What support are you looking for from America's NATO allies? Does it extend to military support?

> Powell: What NATO has done is [invoke] Article 5 of the Washington Treaty, which says if there is an attack from outside the alliance on any member of the alliance the whole alliance will respond, and in the days ahead I'll be having more in-depth discussions with my NATO colleagues as we structure our response, and see how NATO members can participate in that response in one way or the other. Don't always think of it... just in military terms, there are a lot of other things we can do with respect to the pressure that we can put on countries that harbour or provide a haven for terrorists. And so we'll be looking to work with NATO and all of our European, Asian, African, South American allies throughout the world, to deal with a crisis that has been directed against the civilised world. Let me also say that while America is in a state of grief over the losses we suffered, some 40 countries lost people in the World Trade Center, and some of those numbers are not trivial. Hundreds [were] lost from other countries, and so our hearts go out to all of those countries that lost citizens, and that's why this is an international matter, and not just solely an American matter.

Four years later, Britain acquired its own shorthand terrorist atrocity – '7/7' – when suicide bombers attacked London's transport system on 7 July 2005, killing 52 travellers and the four perpetrators. But 9/11 remains not only America's most deadly terrorist attack to date; it is Britain's too, as there were 67 British victims of the 9/11 attacks.

From reconstruction to counter-insurgency in Afghanistan

'Well, our mission is to protect ourselves'

DAVID MILIBAND, 11 JULY 2009

In 2009 Dr John Reid, who had been Labour's defence secretary in 2005–6, protested to the House of Commons:

> I never at any stage expressed the hope, expectation, promise or pledge that we would leave Afghanistan without firing a shot.

He was alluding to a moment three years earlier when he had authorised the deployment of 3,500 additional British troops to Afghanistan's Helmand province. Reid had been widely pilloried for suggesting that the mission could be accomplished 'without a shot being fired'. He had in fact said:

> We would be perfectly happy to leave in three years' time without firing one shot because our mission is to protect the reconstruction.

By the time of that deployment, events in Iraq had sorely tested the public's trust in politicians' reasons for military commitments. Despite all the warnings about Saddam Hussein's weapons of mass destruction in the run-up to the Iraq War, none had been found by the allied forces. The invasion of Iraq had, however, been followed by a violent insurgency.

The British contribution in Helmand was part of the UN-mandated, NATO-led 'International Security Assistance Force' (ISAF), which had gone into Afghanistan after the 2001 invasion to fill, in the United Nations' words, the 'security vacuum' in the country, once the Taliban regime had been toppled. For two years, the sole secure ISAF area (and even that only relatively so) was the capital itself, Kabul. Later, the international effort focused on 'provincial reconstruction teams' in this country of 30 million people, which faced varying levels of danger and produced highly variable results.

British forces had, in small numbers, been involved in the American operation in Afghanistan since it began, and in 2006 it was agreed that the UK would take responsibility for the challenging Helmand province in the south: a large desert and opium-producing area where the Afghan government of Hamid Karzai had only a tenuous influence. Their headquarters were in the provincial capital, Lashkar Gah, and the idea – as it was later expressed by the British government – was that 'provisional reconstruction teams... would establish development zones, which in time would spread outwards across Helmand like ink on a blotting paper'.

'The time, 24 minutes to 9,' began presenter Sarah Montague as she introduced a report on *Today* on 15 December 2006:

> In Afghanistan, the winter has arrived. There appears, though, to be little let-up in the south, with the fighting going on daily, and suicide bombs now a regular occurrence. Another Royal Marine was killed this week. That's 20 who've died in the fighting in Helmand this year, and almost that number again have died in accidents.

From Afghanistan, the BBC's Alastair Leithead described how 'It was an intense summer, and the fighting goes on. Two Royal Marines have died in the last ten days, one in a friendly-fire incident', before a spokesman for the Taliban offered his view of who was winning:

> In Sangin, NATO send us elders to ask us not to fire at them. The British are staying inside the administration building which is just 150 metres square. They ask that we let two Afghan soldiers buy their daily supplies at the bazaar. Now, who is weaker? The rest of the area is under the control of the Taliban.

As troops sought to establish strongpoints in these Helmand centres, civilians and their homes were caught in the crossfire. In Musa Qala, north of Sangin, local elders had brokered a deal with the British and the Taliban for both to pull out, after what Leithead described as 'some of the heaviest fighting in the summer'. Paratroopers had been under fire there for more than 50 days. Leithead spoke to General David Richards, who was the British commander of NATO forces. He defended the British withdrawal from Musa Qala against American criticism:

> They [the Americans] are giving it fair wind, but they probably see it more as some sort of deal with the Taliban. I don't know whether that is right or wrong. As far as I'm concerned, if we can get local people to take responsibility for their own security, we ought to do so, and that's a common international position here. We'll see how it goes into the new year.

As Leithead observed, 'It certainly freed up British forces to be more mobile, but this wasn't supposed to be a war.'

It certainly wasn't. In the three years since the Taliban regime had been so swiftly toppled following 9/11, its adherents had regrouped, grown and evolved – they had looked and learned. Academics speak of the 'neo-Taliban' that emerged in this period; they were increasingly organised, their motivations were more varied and they had noted what had (and hadn't) worked for insurgents in Iraq. In January 2004, the first British soldier to die on a mission in Afghanistan fell prey to a suicide bomber. And soon IEDs – improvised explosive devices, aka roadside bombs – became a persistent threat to British forces.

'It's fair to say,' commented the US commander General Karl Eikenberry, speaking to Sarah Montague that morning of 15 December 2006, 'that the level of fighting in Helmand, and enemy capabilities, are at a higher level than I think any of us anticipated.' The general concurred when Montague invoked the US ambassador in Afghanistan, quoting him as saying, 'I expect next year to be quite bloody. My sense is that the Taliban wants to come back and fight.' Eikenberry also offered what was, for a military man, a sobering recognition of his profession's limitations – the war was technically unwinnable:

> Sarah, what the military can do in a campaign [such] as [the one] we're engaged in [in] Afghanistan, [is that] we can provide a shield behind which the Afghan people, as our partners, can, over time, develop their governance, establish justice systems, develop their security forces and slowly rebuild the middle ground of their civil society, which was decimated through 30 years of very brutal warfare. So, we can help create conditions – but, no, militarily, this is not a campaign that can be won.

By the end of 2006, British troop numbers in Helmand had doubled. Six months later, Alastair Leithead was out with British forces on a night-time operation, his report airing on *Today* on 22 June 2007:

> I'm walking down the main street in Garmsir district centre in Helmand province with a large group of British forces. This road, with its shops all abandoned and empty, has been the frontline for the last six months, with Taliban positions about 500 metres away to our right... and the objective is to try and push the Taliban back, to go into their positions, and to gain ground... Artillery shells have been fired, and they're landing in the areas which are classed as Taliban positions.

The 'main part of this operation', he informed listeners, was to 'put a big bridge in place' across a canal, so as to 'allow big vehicles, armoured vehicles, to cross, and to then push even further into the land that's Taliban-controlled'. With that achieved,

Apache helicopters hovered overhead, 'bringing fire down just ahead of where we are', to cover their escape. Just three Taliban fighters were encountered – two ran away, while the third was surrounded by a pool of blood, 'shot as the British forces came into this compound'. The mission was a success, but it also suggested the constrained ambitions in Helmand, as in so much of Afghanistan. ISAF and US forces were having a hard enough job taking care of their *own* security, putting in place the infrastructure they needed for themselves, let alone reconstructing a liveable environment for an Afghan civilian population battered by decades of war.

In 2008, Lashkar Gah was attacked by several hundred Taliban fighters. They were successfully repulsed, but the fact that the Taliban had the audacity and the numbers to mount an operation like that was telling in itself. By late June 2009, Bob Ainsworth, the new defence secretary, was visiting Sangin, where security had improved. Yet just two weeks later, on 11 July, John Humphrys was telling *Today* listeners that 'Eight people have been killed in Afghanistan in twenty-four hours' – eight British troops. Five of them had been victims of Taliban IEDs. They had been killed while on, as the BBC's defence correspondent Caroline Wyatt explained, 'a normal foot patrol around Sangin'.

'Stating the obvious,' observed Humphrys, this was 'going to increase the pressure on the government to justify what we're doing in Afghanistan.' Wyatt added, 'It has also increased the chorus of voices... saying, "Has the government actually funded the campaign properly? Has it given forces the kind of equipment they need?"'

The foreign secretary, David Miliband, was interviewed by John Humphrys that morning:

> **Humphrys: We've been given a number of reasons for our presence in Afghanistan. We have heard talk about nation-building, building democracy, getting children to go to school, defeating the Taliban, shoring up the government. What *is* the reason?**
>
> **Miliband: The reason is to ensure that Afghanistan cannot again become an incubator for international terrorism, and a launching pad for attacks on us. That applies in Afghanistan, and it applies in Pakistan, and that mission is very, very clear... And while the professionalism and bravery of those we send to Afghanistan is absolutely second to none, and does deserve thanks and admiration, we know that they are engaged in a very, very difficult mission and we have a responsibility to engage the country in understanding that mission and supporting it.**

With lives being lost, Miliband appeared keen to stress British national self-interest in the military commitment, yet the message was still mixed, for he also spoke of 'building up Afghan governance so that their own political leaders, national and local, can provide a framework for their own citizens'.

'So,' Humphrys asked, 'we *are* nation-building?'

Miliband tried to square the circle: 'Well, our mission is to protect ourselves. Our strategy is to build up Afghan capacity to look after themselves.'

Indeed, such was the stress and intensity of operations in Afghanistan that protecting one another had become uppermost in the minds of many a soldier on the ground. Humphrys quoted the words of one serviceman: 'We don't care about the future of Afghanistan. We don't care about democracy, clean water, schools for girls, or the political overview. All we care about now is each other and making sure that our mates get out of this alive.'

Three days later, reporting from Helmand, Sarah Montague provided a glimpse of a ritual that the British public had only witnessed in its final stages back home:

> We saw something here last night you never normally see: the repatriation ceremony for eight of the soldiers killed here in Afghanistan last week. It was a private ceremony in Camp Bastion, and so the brigade asked us not to report everything we saw... In the midst of the usual comings and goings at the airstrip stood a vast C-17 transporter plane: its rear ramp down, the light from its interior illuminating the runway, and two lines of men, in single file, forming a corridor away from the rear of the plane. Two hundred men, silently waiting to say goodbye to their friends. For the next hour, with the sound of the planes' engines as a backdrop, an intensely moving silent vigil took place.

At the other end of this repatriation was the small Wiltshire market town of Wootton Bassett, which is close to RAF Lyneham, the airbase to which the repatriated bodies were flown; the flag-draped coffins were brought through its streets, the townspeople respectfully lining the route, mounting their own vigil.

Present at the Camp Bastion ceremony was Sir Richard Dannatt, chief of the general staff. The next day, he was with Sarah Montague at a lookout tower in Sangin, which, Montague recalled, had been 'the scene of remarkable battles three years ago, when 120 British soldiers were holed up here, 40 at a time we're told, on the roof, controlling only as far as their weapons could fire'. Now she asked Dannatt, 'Do you have the resources that you need to do what you're now being asked to do?'

Dannatt replied, 'We're building our resources up... We've got a plan to increase the amount of campaign equipment we've got. It's probably not moved as fast as I would have liked it to have moved.'

As well as the vulnerability of certain British vehicles to IEDs, the (in)sufficiency of helicopters had become a political football between the New Labour government and the Conservative opposition. So Montague asked, 'The fact that the head of the British army is flying on an American helicopter… does that tell us anything about the shortage of helicopters?' To which Dannatt responded:

> **Sarah, that's an interesting observation, which I think I'd said to you, take it as an object lesson and don't ask me about. Self-evidently, if I move in an American helicopter, it's because we haven't got a British helicopter.**

That year, 2009, turned out to be the bloodiest for British forces in Afghanistan. It was also the year in which the context in which they operated changed. A surge in US forces was accompanied by a new American general, Stanley A McChrystal, who instituted a new counter-insurgency strategy that aimed (among other things) to build up indigenous Afghan forces and to redeploy US forces to where the threat was greatest. Responsibility for northern and southern Helmand passed to US forces, leaving the British to handle Lashkah Gar and central Helmand.

In the autumn of 2009 Major Richard Streatfeild of A Company, 4th Battalion of the Rifles, began providing *Today* with a series of extracts from his diary from the Sangin Valley. The last was broadcast on 24 April 2010. 'It's been gripping stuff,' John Humphrys judged, 'sometimes amusing, sometimes whimsical, sometimes deeply emotional. Always enlightening. Now, he's on his way home. He and his soldiers will be back tomorrow, and this is his last dispatch.' And then Streatfeild spoke:

> **I salute you. Ricky, Ginge, Sonny, Legs, Owens, V, Ed, Smudge, Rolfie, Archie, Cam, Hitch, Eddie, Lips, Monty, Bobby, Sam, and Thorpie…**

The list went on. 'These are the men and women who I have had the privilege to lead. Mothers, brothers, husbands, sons and daughters: I salute you.'

Later, having left the army, Streatfeild would criticise the Ministry of Defence over equipment deficiencies, admitting that, if anything, he had held back on the unvarnished truth for *Today* audiences to save the British army any embarrassment.

In 2011, Britain's coalition government announced a timetable for the end of operations. The British headquarters in Helmand was moved from Lashkar Gah to the desert fortress of Camp Bastion in the summer of 2013, and on 26 October 2014 there was another ceremony at Bastion, this time to mark the handing over of the base to the Afghan army. As the British forces withdrew, David Loyn, the BBC's Afghanistan correspondent, reported on what they left behind. This report was broadcast on *Today* on 27 January 2014:

> **Loyn: At the end of a rather half-hearted patrol, police in western Helmand fire a few rounds over the hill from a large machine gun mounted on top of an armoured vehicle [sound of gun shots]. It is an impotent gesture against an**

elusive enemy. Claims by the Taliban to control much of the countryside of Helmand look increasingly credible. The police commander here knows his limits.

Police commander: With the police we have, we can only secure this side of the canal until we have reinforcements – we will not be able to place police permanently on the other side.

Loyn: And on the other side of the canal the green shoots of this year's poppy crop can be seen spreading across the desert landscape. Most of the world's illegal opium comes from Helmand. Last year was a record harvest. Police head back along roads pockmarked by frequent explosions into the Shaukat base occupied by British soldiers until last year. More than 50 of the 447 British soldiers who've died in Afghanistan died in this part of Helmand. The Afghan forces who've replaced them do not dominate the ground in the same way and their area of control is diminishing daily. The police are seizing vast quantities of bomb-making equipment. The Taliban are planting dozens of bombs every day according to a police bomb-disposal expert.

Police bomb-disposal expert: Every morning I wake up for prayers and then we go out and check bridges for bombs; they lay bombs under bridges and then fire at us from neighbouring houses. After we find them, we defuse bombs; this morning I defused six bombs. Hardly a day goes by when we don't defuse bombs. There were days I defused 50.

Loyn: I visited Helmand frequently since the start of the British involvement in 2006. Places where I walked openly three years ago, even in the main towns, have become more risky. It is not all bad news. This is a football match between Afghan troops and police. They are far better than they were and are unlikely to lose the towns. They are diffusing many bombs. Schools are open for girls and boys, and local government works. But corruption has prevented much progress in justice, an open goal for the Taliban who provide their own courts. Ask anyone which works better and you get the same answer.

Afghan voice: Because of flaws in the judicial system most people take cases to the Taliban courts.

Loyn: The British engagement here is bracketed by two statements that I think will come to haunt the politicians who made them, the defence secretary who sent in British troops, John Reid, who said, 'We'll be happy to leave in three years and without firing a shot,' and David Cameron just before Christmas when he declared, 'Mission accomplished.'

Over 13 years, 454 British service personnel gave their lives in Afghanistan, and around 2,000 were injured. A BBC study in 2017 concluded that 'About 15 million people – half the population – are living in areas that are either controlled by the Taliban or where the Taliban are openly present and regularly mount attacks.'

The Iraq War and the city of Sinbad

'Why is it that the British cannot walk down the streets of Basra?'

JOHN HUMPHRYS, 25 OCTOBER 2006

'There's an awful lot in war, and in these political conflicts, which doesn't come out of the cricket rulebook.' The author of these words was the former British commander in southern Iraq, General Jonathan Shaw; the place that inspired his comment was Basra, Iraq's second city, better known to generations of children as the city of Sinbad. The time was the years spanning 2003 to 2007, following the toppling of President Saddam Hussein and his Ba'ath Party regime.

The British and Basra were old, if uneasy, acquaintances. It was from Basra that British imperial forces began their Mesopotamian campaign in the First World War, securing oil supplies and progressing from the Shatt-al-Arab waterway up the Tigris and Euphrates rivers. After the war, Basra's status as a petroleum-refining centre grew under the British mandate to govern 'Iraq', the new entity glued together from three former Ottoman provinces. Even after formal Iraqi independence in 1932, Britain retained a military presence, and Basra was again important to the Allies in the Second World War.

The city had suffered under Saddam Hussein. It was on the front line during the Iran–Iraq War of 1980–88, and again during the Gulf War just three years later. Much of its largely Shia population joined the rebellion against Saddam in the aftermath of Iraq's defeat in 1991, and Saddam duly punished it when he crushed the Shia uprising. So, during the 2003 campaign – after a relatively hard-fought battle against the Iraqi army around Basra – the British should have been able to expect something of a welcome. And a welcome there was – at first. But within a month of Prime Minister Tony Blair thanking British forces for their 'great courage' in May 2003, six members of the Royal Military Police were killed at a Basra police station. They had been besieged by an armed crowd, angry at earlier Iraqi deaths that occurred amid rising tensions, as British forces tried to disarm the local population. It was a warning of what was to come.

The failure of the United States to prepare adequately for a post-invasion administration in Iraq and its decision to disband Saddam Hussein's Ba'ath Party in the immediate aftermath of victory over Saddam's forces left a power vacuum, and the first phase of the insurgency began almost immediately. Three years later it became a full-blown sectarian civil war. 'Iraq,' announced *Today*'s John Humphrys on 25 October 2006, 'is in ferment.' The violence continued long after most foreign forces had withdrawn from the country. No one knows how many died in the conflict; the Iraq Body Count project has estimated a figure close to 200,000, other sources put the number much higher. The United Nations reported that nearly 35,000 people were killed in 2006 alone.

Humphrys spent a week in Basra in October 2006, reporting for *Today*. At this stage, the question was: would the British stay or leave? BBC defence correspondent Paul Wood explained the official line – 'We will stay the course. We will not cut and run' – before explaining why there were reasons to doubt it. As Wood described to listeners:

> **We're in the Foreign Office compound now. As usual, there was a barrage of mortar fire overnight. Yesterday afternoon the building that we're talking from was showered with shrapnel from a rocket, which landed a very short distance away.**

Wood had been conducting an interview at the time and, as it replayed, *Today* listeners heard him scrabbling for cover amid the confusion of shouts and gunshot. 'A very common sound here in the compound,' Humphrys added.

As with all the conflicts in Iraq, the situation in Basra was never so simple as just two sides in contention, as Wood explained:

> **What you get from middle-class English-speaking Basrawis – the kind of people who are Western-leaning, Western-supporting, and want the coalition here – is a feeling almost of betrayal. A lot of them say to me, well, you know, we've now got the rule of the gun on the street, the rule of militias, we had enough clerics before but now it's the rule of clerics – and they don't like that.**

He gave one graphic example:

> **A couple of days ago the Mahdi army, the Shia militia loyal to the cleric Muqtada al-Sadr, went systematically through the market here assaulting women who were not wearing the *hijab*, the Islamic headscarf. One of our local staff attempted to talk to people about this, and people were too scared to say on tape what they had seen, the eyewitnesses. There are many similar stories to that, and each time when the police are asked, 'Please intervene, please stop this,' the police are either in with the militias or they're too scared to do anything.**

There was, Wood reported, a project to implant 'a human rights champion' in every Basra police station to try and improve a culture that, when it was not ineffective, was often corrupt. For *Today* listeners, it might have been small comfort to be told by Humphrys that it was 'much worse in Baghdad, of course', where the Americans were responsible for security.

Today's press review, read by newsreader Alice Arnold, quoted the *Guardian*'s Simon Jenkins's view that 'two of the most powerful and civilised nations' had turned Iraq into 'the most hellish place on Earth', amounting to the 'stupidest paradox in modern history'. Resolving that paradox by disengaging – and newspapers were reporting that the Americans were considering it too – could never be straightforward, though. As Humphrys explained from Basra:

> It's not only British military here. There are civil servants, diplomats, police and civilian contractors too. They clearly can't stay here without the massive protection they get from the military… There are private protection people, but they cost a fortune to employ and there aren't enough of them anyway to provide the sort of cover the Foreign Office insists on for its staff.

'Once you're in Basra Palace,' as Humphrys knew only too well, 'you're a virtual prisoner.' He continued:

> There are British diplomats here who have never been outside the security compound into the streets of Basra in all the months they've been stationed here. The rules say they must have their own security detail and the soldiers can't be spared unless there's a very good reason.

Nevertheless, during Humphrys's time in Basra he did get out on some escorted visits, including a trip to see what was being done to build up the basic infrastructure of the city. His mode of transport was a heavily armed Warrior vehicle, because, as he put it, 'If you're going to get blown up by a roadside bomb, then it's best to be in one of these.' The price for safety was a ride that was unforgettable for all the wrong reasons: '[It's] absolutely foul… incredibly noisy. It's dark – I can barely see the faces of the other men here – and it is amazingly hot.' One destination was 'the biggest hospital in Basra'. Humphrys took up the story: '… which, they say, has had a lot of money spent on it. It didn't look like that… Everything is covered with dust, and it's just run-down and grubby.' He spoke to 'the most senior consultant in this hospital', who had once worked in Ireland until returning to his home country 18 years previously – in Humphrys's eyes, 'a good man, who gave up a comfortable life'. The doctor spoke of 'old machines' which sometimes didn't work, lack of spare parts, and the fact that no one cared about cleaning and sanitation.

Was this all the fault of the war? Mark Etherington, the head of the Basra Provincial Reconstruction team, thought not. Putting a positive spin on a 'low-level economy' that was 'beginning to gather speed' and which was witnessing a doubling in household appliances and new cars, Etherington wanted to stress that:

> The feeling that we have somehow invented all of these problems is erroneous. Clearly we have inherited a great deal and are now being blamed for them, which of course is entirely understandable. What is needed is massive investment in infrastructure, massive investment in oil infrastructure particularly, in electricity infrastructure, and this can only take place, of course, within a security environment that's slightly more benign than it is now.

Another paradox, as Humphrys told listeners, was that 'Iraq is rich. There's more oil under my feet than anywhere else in the world, except Saudi Arabia and Iran – but the revenue from it is being stolen. At least, a huge chunk of it is.' He was referring to the rampant, and sometimes deadly, corruption stemming from the smuggling of cheap oil and the pay-offs to officials and politicians. One 'influential tribal leader', Sheikh Mansour, told Humphrys of the 'huge amount of money' spent by the British and other donor countries which had vanished, pocketed somewhere en route and leaving, for example, Basra's hospital the way it was.

One major problem was the lack of employment. Humphrys told listeners at the end of his week:

> Every single person I've spoken to in the past six days has told me it's jobs that matter. It's reckoned that as many as two-thirds of the men in Basra are out of work. If they had jobs, they'd be less tempted to do the bidding of the militias and the death squads. If you've no money to feed your children and someone pays you 50 dollars to kill someone – well, there are plenty of people who will do it. So, no jobs means no peace.

And if you couldn't even earn money that way, you lived in poverty, which Humphrys found at a village just 'five miles from the air-conditioned comfort of government offices':

> It's a squalid place, tiny huts made from old concrete blocks, a few emaciated buffaloes and piles of their dried-out dung, which they are used to eating. The children are stick-thin, begging for a bottle of water, and everyone is dirty. It's this that so upsets the head man, who keeps apologising for the state of his dress. Third-world poverty in the midst of such potential wealth. It breaks your heart to see it, and you can't help thinking this is the other tragedy of post-war Iraq.

'Even for someone who's been here for as short a time as I have, it's obvious what this country needs,' reflected Humphrys during his Basra week. 'It needs an enormous amount of money spent on it to make good the awful damage of war and the destruction wreaked by a dictator who raped and pillaged his own country.'

'Operation Iraqi Freedom' had been the name of the US-led invasion. Clearly, there was not yet freedom from want; but what about freedom to speak one's mind? The overthrow of Saddam had brought Iraq the novelty of a sudden explosion of contending voices. From Basra, Humphrys told listeners, 'There are more newspapers of one sort or another being printed these days than you can shake a stick at, and some neighbourhoods even have their own television stations.' But after the first few weeks of this new dawn, there had come a catch: 'Life is not easy for the journalists. If they speak out about the corruption of the death squads and the warring gangs, they literally risk their lives.' In the same broadcast on 25 October, Humphrys interviewed three such local journalists. As one of them explained, in his imperfect yet still powerful English:

> Here in Basra we have gangs, I call them, they are ghosts – the ghosts coming from the moon, commit some assassination, kidnap, theft and disappear. No one catch them. For this reason, we live in fear. We have some article in newspaper, but we didn't mention our names because if we mention our names, this means on the second day we will die.

Perhaps surprisingly, one of the journalists affirmed that, underneath the surface, trust of the British was relatively high, prompting Humphrys to ask, 'If they trust the British, why is it that the British cannot walk down the streets of Basra?' The answer was fear of the militias and fear of the past:

> We still fear of Saddam. Of Saddam we don't speak lightly. So this is a ghost of Saddam upon us. We can't express our feeling, because 30 years, you can't express or you can't say that you are angry... we hate this militia... we'd like to change, to change our lives, but they can't say that in public.

Towards the end of his time in Basra, Humphrys reflected on what he had learnt. He knew its limitations:

> I've been in Iraq for almost a week, no time at all to make judgements about the state of a nation. What you need for that is to live in a place, live with the locals, go everywhere, talk to everyone. But you can't do that in a week, nor could I if I stayed another week or another month. Why? Because you cannot see most things for yourself here. You have to rely on official briefings and second-hand reports mostly. That alone tells you a huge amount about what's going on here, how the country has fared since the end of the war three and a half years ago.

And he added, 'Security is not just a problem; it overwhelms everything.' From Basra, Humphrys was able to challenge International Development Secretary Hilary Benn on the British government's position. ('We had hoped to talk to Mr Blair,' the broadcaster told listeners, 'but he wouldn't do it.')

> Benn: Well, it's grim and there's no good pretending otherwise, particularly in those parts of the country where a lot of violence is taking place, although it does tend to be concentrated in certain parts of Iraq. But I think there are certain things we just have to recognise: one is that no one wishes that Saddam was still there. That those who are responsible for the sectarian violence bear a very, very heavy responsibility for what's going on currently, and Iraq does have now an elected democratic government which we are supporting, which I think everybody, whether they were in favour of the military action, John, or against it, *should* support because it's the only way that Iraq is going to build for itself a better future. At least it has the mechanisms in place to do that, but it's tough, of course it's tough.

> Humphrys: The fact is, of course, it *doesn't* have the mechanisms in place to do that and it *doesn't* have any form of democracy because you cannot have, as you well know, democracy without the rule of law, you cannot have the rule of law in the chaos that operates here.

> Benn: Well, it does have a democracy and a lot of people voted in the elections, including the Sunnis who had boycotted the previous elections in large numbers, and that was a step forward, but you're right, John, of course, the basic foundation of any society is security. And what Prime Minister Maliki is trying to do – with the support of the international forces, including the British troops who are in southern Iraq and who you've been talking to during your time there – what they're trying to do is to work together to build the Iraqis' capacity in the end to provide security for themselves.

Humphrys and Benn returned to the question on everyone's lips: when would the British leave Basra?

'The right course of action is to stay until the job is done,' Benn asserted.

Humphrys, during his Basra sojourn, concluded that:

> **The British on the ground are doing their damnedest. It's hard not to be impressed by the bravery of the soldiers; the integrity and the commitment of the people who run this operation, and easy to understand why so many of them resent having to pick up the pieces of policy decisions taken at the very top levels in Washington and London before the invasion was even launched.**

But in the end they were overwhelmed, and their military reputation was also becoming tarnished by accusations of abuse against Iraqi prisoners.

The British contingent abandoned the beleaguered Basra Palace in September 2007 for an easier-to-protect redoubt around the airport. In December that year, Iraqi authorities formally took over responsibility for security in Basra province. A reduced number of British forces remained at the airport, in a training – and sometimes fighting – role, but in 2008 it was the Iraqi army itself that, with American and British air and artillery support, took on the Mahdi army militias in Basra and forced them to withdraw. By 2009, Basra airport was handed back too. The legendary city of Sinbad was Iraqi once more.

It is difficult to disagree with a prevailing view that the eventual British withdrawal from Basra was anything 'other than a defeat', as a US general put it; when you have to negotiate with your enemies just to get to the airport, you are not exactly triumphing. The British commander General Shaw put it this way: 'You play the cards you get at the time. We knew we had to get out.'

The hubris of Islamic State

'The most notorious extremist group in the world'

SARAH MONTAGUE, 29 FEBRUARY 2016

'The militant group ISIS,' presenter Evan Davis told *Today* listeners on 30 June 2014, 'says it's restoring a caliphate to the areas of Syria and Iraq under its control... If you're not entirely clear as to what exactly that word caliphate means, who better to explain it than Jeremy Bowen, our Middle East correspondent. Jeremy, what is a caliphate? What is the difference between an Islamic state and a caliphate, for example?'

> **Bowen: Well, by using the word caliphate, they're harking back to the days of the Islamic Empire that was set up at the time of Muhammad. Muhammad died in the seventh century. After that there were various caliphs who ruled the large territories that Muslim forces had conquered and had imposed their religion on... so they are trying to hark back to those times and it's also setting up the caliphate, a large religious state, covering all sorts of existing borders and ignoring them. It has been an objective of radical political Islamists of different hues for quite a long time.**

It was the moment the group known as Islamic State in Iraq and Syria, or ISIS, and also as Islamic State in Iraq and the Levant (an old-fashioned term for the lands of the eastern Mediterranean), or ISIL, really caught the public's attention. The group had first flourished in the violent chaos in Iraq that followed the United States-led invasion and moved into Syria after the outbreak of the civil war there. In early June 2014 it captured Mosul, one of Iraq's biggest cities, and the declaration of a caliphate was made in the Syrian city of Raqqa, which became the capital of the movement's self-proclaimed state, at the end of the month. Abu Bakr al-Baghdadi, the movement's leader, was, by declaring himself the 'first caliph', suggesting he had authority over *all* Muslims.

Professor Fawaz A Gerges of the London School of Economics described the declaration in these terms on that morning's *Today* programme:

> **It's really about the unification of the global Muslim community, the *Ummah*, and a centralised Muslim rule [in which] anyone, anywhere in the Muslim world, from Indonesia to Malaysia to Libya, who does not basically give fealty, swear allegiance, to Abu Bakr al-Baghdadi is basically, in Arabic, a *murtad*... [a person who] would be killed... This is about an intra-jihadist struggle for power, in**

particular to challenge the legitimacy and leadership of Ayman al-Zawahiri, the leader of al-Qaeda.

...

What Abu Bakr al-Baghdadi is trying to do is to basically force armed groups in Syria and in Iraq to accept his own leadership... It's about power politics; it's about leadership... In particular, there is a major civil war taking place in Syria between the Islamic State on the one hand and al-Nusra Front, the official arm of al-Qaeda.

The group decided to glorify and consolidate their territorial gains with a new, all-embracing name: they became simply 'Islamic State', or IS.

In early August 2014 President Obama authorised airstrikes against IS forces advancing against the Iraqi city of Erbil. IS responded by murdering an American journalist, James Foley, in Syria. His killer spoke with an English accent, and his words were replayed on *Today* on 20 August 2014.

'What do you make of this?' John Humphrys asked security correspondent Frank Gardner, referring to the act and its recording.

'It's utterly cowardly,' Gardner replied:

It attracts the worst kind of psychopaths. You know, this is not about religion. It's not even about territory. It's attracting a kind of ghoulish psychopath... the sort of people that show off beheading videos on their mobile phones to each other and, yes, I'm afraid it probably will attract some people.

Foley's killer apparently went by the nickname Jihadi John, one of the so-called 'Beatles': a foursome of notably vicious IS operatives hailing from Britain who were associated with several video murders. 'Jihadi John' was later identified as Mohammed Emwazi, who had disappeared from his London home in 2013. In 2015 he was killed by a US drone strike.

In that same broadcast of 20 August 2014, John Humphrys raised the question of why middle-class, well-educated British Muslims could be so radicalised as to be impelled to join IS. Gardner responded:

They are, many of them, vulnerable to a very compelling narrative, one of oppression and of the need for revenge... Remember Islamic State has mostly been in Syria. It's only very recently kind of swept back into Iraq... it's mostly been in Syria, fighting a very unpleasant regime, the Assad regime, that carried out atrocities against its own people, and the idea of going to defend your fellow Muslims is a very compelling one for a lot of people. Unfortunately, what they don't realise is that they are very unlikely to end up fighting the Assad regime. They're not going to get near them. They're going to end up actually fighting other rebels who are Muslim, but not quite or nothing like as extreme as they are, and essentially acting as kind of policemen in places like Raqqa, where they're imposing this very draconian rule.

By 2015 the reach of IS was alarming, and its practices notorious. That year represented the peak of IS conquests in Syria and Iraq, stretching west almost to Aleppo and east beyond Mosul. Abroad, jihadis were swearing allegiance to IS, and new intra-jihadist battles began, such as in Afghanistan between IS adherents and the Taliban. In the Middle East, IS's period of expansion sucked in thousands of foreign fighters and would-be jihadis (and some willing jihadi brides), the greatest number coming from Russia's Caucasian republics (who had their own recent histories of bitter conflict, notably in Chechnya), but with sizeable contingents from Western European nations too, including perhaps 800 from Britain.

Along with IS's lightning advances went its excesses: its attempted genocide of the Yazidi minority in Iraq; its extortion and decapitations; its rape of women and girls and its theft of property; its hatred of difference, whether of ethnicity, religion, gender, sexual orientation or any other marker.

That background made the use of the term Islamic State controversial. On 29 June 2015 the prime minister, David Cameron, challenged the BBC during a *Today* interview with John Humphrys:

> I wish the BBC would stop calling it 'Islamic State' because it's not an Islamic state. What it is, is an appalling, barbarous regime... It is a perversion of the religion of Islam and many Muslims listening to this programme will recoil every time they hear the words 'Islamic State'.

Cameron (who preferred 'ISIL') was supported by more than a hundred MPs from across the political spectrum, who wrote to the BBC. Some, including Scottish Nationalist Alex Salmond, wanted the BBC to adopt the derogative Arabic transliteration 'Daesh', which, the *Guardian* explained, punned on the Arabic to mean 'one who sows discord'. The BBC defended itself: 'We call the group by the name it uses itself, and regularly review our approach. We also use additional descriptions to help make it clear that we are referring to the group as they refer to themselves, such as "so-called Islamic State".'

The air forces of the United States, Britain, France and regional countries were already striking IS positions and IS oil production and distribution facilities – its black market in oil being a chief source of its revenues. The American secretary of state, John Kerry, began the process of building a coalition against IS at a NATO summit in Wales in September 2014. British planes took action against IS in Iraq that same month, and in December 2015 Parliament voted to extend the air campaign to IS targets in Syria.

In February and March 2016 *Today* broadcast a series of diary extracts from a member of the underground group Al Sharqiya 24 in Raqqa, the IS capital. They reflected 'the realities of life under a brutal regime', and as Sarah Montague explained on 29 February: 'For obvious reasons, we've changed some details – details of his story – and got an actor to voice his words.' The instalments ran over several days, and the anonymous diary-writer began:

> It's Friday. This is the day we used to gather in the street after prayers and have long chats, but not anymore. Anyone gathering in public without permission now risks being accused of plotting against Daesh. I'm passing a crowd in a public square – I don't want to join them, because they may have been told to watch a beheading, but thank God, it's only a lashing this time. The offender is one of theirs. His offence, I'm told, was carrying out a homosexual act. Tomorrow I go back to work, a new week, with new hopes of being liberated.

He described the first days of Daesh's control of the city, some weeks after his father had been killed in an airstrike by Assad's warplanes. After witnessing some beheadings for such crimes as working in the media, the diarist's own run-in with the new authorities was uttering a swear word: 'You were cursing out loud! Your punishment is 40 lashes.' When his pregnant sister needed to see her gynaecologist in an emergency, she found his practice closed – IS forbade male doctors from treating women. When a shop owner, who had already paid IS a demand for a 'charity' payment was touched again for another '100,000 Syrian pounds', he protested, 'That's too much money' – before paying up. As the diarist noted, 'The severed heads of others who've crossed Daesh are hung on park fences and lampposts as a brutal warning.' Daily life brought daily brutalities:

> A crowd had gathered around a deep hole. Crouched inside it was a woman. I asked people who she was and what she was doing there. Before I got an answer, a large masked man began reading: 'This woman was adulterous and her punishment is to be stoned to death.'

A panoply of restrictions eroded daily life:

> My boss, who was quietly sipping tea, gave me a weary smile. I noticed he wasn't smoking. That was very unusual. He usually had a cigarette with his tea, but Daesh has banned smoking now. After smelling his cigarette, they'd humiliated him in front of everyone. Then they beat him up, as if he was a criminal.

Some things, like the veil for women, became compulsory; other things, like televisions in shops, were banned. On meeting a friend he had given up for dead following his fourth arrest by IS, the diarist heard how 'The last time he was arrested, it was because his trousers were too long. Daesh insists that they should always be above ankle-length. Anyone found breaking this rule has to undergo a week-long Sharia course.' A revealing detail about life in IS-run Raqqa was the fact that the diarist's failure to bring home much food because of the shortages and high prices was instantly forgiven: 'Like most parents here, my mother was just delighted that I hadn't been arrested or killed, and was safely home again.'

IS's most severe penalties were reserved for 'spies': those passing information to the enemy, for now Raqqa was under frequent aerial attack –attacks that, as the diarist vividly recorded, were often deadly for civilians, particularly the non-surgical strikes carried out by Syrian and Russian warplanes.

The problem with being, as Sarah Montague put it, 'the most notorious extremist group in the world' was that IS was beyond the pale, fighting *everyone*. This was particularly notable in the extraordinarily complex Syrian war, which the BBC's Middle East editor Jeremy Bowen liked to call a 'mini world war'. Each active party had several foes, but all loathed IS. Arrayed against IS were not only Russia, Assad and the West, but all other regional players, and all the other Syrian factions, including, of course, the jihadist competitors of the al-Nusra Front.

Come 17 October 2017, John Humphrys was telling listeners:

> It's not so very long ago that Islamic State seemed on the verge of commanding its own powerful caliphate in the Middle East with its own capital, the Syrian city of Raqqa. But its territory has been shrinking and it's on the point of being thrown out of Raqqa altogether. The battle for the city seems to be over and an official statement from the coalition forces opposing IS... is expected in the next 24 hours.

Raqqa fell to the Kurdish-dominated alliance known as the Syrian Democratic Forces, or SDF. *Today* reporter Emma Vardy, ringing Raqqa from London, managed to speak to 'a British woman from Blackburn, Kimberly Taylor – she's 28, a former student. She joined the Kurdish Women's Militia [the YPJ] to fight against IS.'

Vardy asked, 'Tell us a bit about why you're doing this, why you decided to fight?' The response was eloquent and illuminating:

> I was working in civil society before I joined the YPJ. I saw the impact that the political and social revolution was having on women, especially. So I was really inspired. And people have been under the oppression of Daesh for three years now. Before that it was al-Nusra, before that it was the Syrian Army, before that it

was the regime. We've never had freedom and women have always been opposed, especially.

Taylor had seen 'so many friends killed and injured' but had 'never felt like I've questioned what I'm doing'. They continued:

Vardy: Explain for us: why do you call this a revolution? What do you mean by that?

Taylor: We've made a new system, a new way of democracy that includes every ethnicity, every religion and empowers women at the same time. And this is what we're doing in all the new liberated villages, all the new liberated cities…

Vardy: So it isn't just about fighting against ISIS, but it's about fighting for an ideology that you believe in?

Taylor: This is the biggest part, the liberation of women: this is why I'm here.

In the same programme John Humphrys interviewed Major General Rupert Jones, the deputy commander of the Combined Joint Task Force which had been established by the American-led coalition against IS.

Humphrys: What about the future for IS? I mean what we've seen in the Middle East in the past is that we may destroy a force on the ground militarily, but it'll pop up somewhere else.

Jones: Well, I think the first thing is just to take a take a moment to pause. This has been a long, hard fight since the dark days of 2014. With the liberation of Iraq, when it comes, really that compromises any claim by Daesh, ISIS, to a caliphate…

Humphrys: OK, but that's over. That caliphate is over as far as we can tell, at least it's going to be fairly soon. Is there not the danger that their ideology lives on?

Jones: Well, of course, there is that danger. I mean, I think the first thing I'd say is we shouldn't be naive enough to think that with the liberation of Raqqa, and of course that follows the liberation of Mosul in the summer, that the caliphate is over. There is still hard fighting to be done. They still hold areas down towards the rocky Syrian border and that area will need to be cleared, so there should be no sense of complacency. But you're right, there is more there to do. This is about an idea. But I think importantly the physical military defeat of Daesh to a very significant degree compromises that idea. The narrative is undermined.

> The days of foreign fighters flooding across Europe to come and join the flag have long since died because the narrative has been so compromised.

During her interview with Kimberley Taylor, the British woman fighting with Kurdish forces, Emma Vardy asked her, 'What is left of Raqqa now?' The response was simple: 'There's nothing left of Raqqa. The coalition have bombed everything.'

Russia and Britain –
a poisoned relationship

*'We can't allow London and the Home Counties to
become a kind of killing field for the Russian state'*
DIANE ABBOTT MP, 6 MARCH 2018

The Russian émigré Alexander Litvinenko had 'met a slow, painful and public death in a London hospital' after being poisoned by a cup of tea in a Mayfair hotel – so the BBC's security correspondent Gordon Corera reminded *Today* listeners on 21 January 2016. It was the day a public-inquiry report into the matter was finally due to be published, ten years after the assassination. Corera explained, 'At the time of the Litvinenko killing, a handful of Russian diplomats were expelled… The subsequent years have seen successive [British] governments spend most of their time trying to avoid doing any more, preferring to normalise relations with Russia.' It was only thanks to the persistence of Litvinenko's widow, Marina, that the inquiry had happened.

The brazen nature of Litvinenko's murder shocked Western Europe. It involved an exceptionally potent nuclear isotope, polonium-210, and the finger of blame was rapidly pointed at members of the FSB, Russia's secret service and once Litvinenko's employer. As Corera summarised: 'Police followed a radioactive trail that matched the movements of two Russians, Andrei Lugovoi and Dmitry Kovtun… They both deny any role in his death.' In Britain, the story had echoes of the assassination of Bulgarian dissident Georgi Markov in 1978, who was killed by a ricin-poisoned pellet delivered from the tip of an umbrella.

The edition of *Today* on 21 January 2016 went out in advance of the report's publication. It included the first broadcast interview with Litvinenko's British-raised son Anatoly, and he underlined the case's wider implications: 'If you look at the fact that polonium was used as a murder weapon, a nuclear isotope with the potential to kill an untold number of people, at the end of the day, you want to find who was behind the murder, who planned it, who commissioned it.' And beyond the hitmen lay the question, as Corera put it, of 'whether responsibility can be proved to lie with the Russian state'.

There were, as Gordon Corera explained, plenty of reasons for laying the blame at the Kremlin's door: 'Alexander Litvinenko was a fierce critic of Putin personally. In 1998, he went to Putin to complain about corruption in the Russian security service, which

Putin then ran. Litvinenko fled to Britain, where he wrote books claiming the [Russian] security service had bombed its own citizens to blame it on Chechens and justify a war.' He was referring to the bombing of apartment blocks in Moscow and two other cities in 1999. Chechen separatists had been a thorn in the Russian side at the time, Vladimir Putin – then prime minister – was keen to quash their uprising, and these bombings became a catalyst for war.

While still in Russia in 1998, Litvinenko had been arrested on charges of abusing his office after speaking of an alleged plot to murder Boris Berezovsky, one of the new opportunistic oligarchs to emerge when President Boris Yeltsin opened the former Soviet economy to private enterprise; Berezovsky was powerful, and had even gained control of Russia's main television channel for a time. Litvinenko was acquitted, but in 2000 fled to Britain, the same year Berezovsky sought refuge there after being convicted in Russia, in his absence, of fraud and corruption. The British government refused to have Berezovsky extradited.

Once in Britain, Corera added, Litvinenko 'also, we learnt, began working for MI6, receiving regular payments'. There was more: 'Litvinenko was also investigating the nexus between the Russian state and organised crime, helping the Spanish authorities arrest individuals and writing reports on high-level figures at the heart of the Russian state.' Plus, he was said to have been contacted by campaigning Russian journalist Anna Politkovskaya. She had accused Putin of trying to reinstate Soviet-style dictatorship, before being shot dead in Moscow in 2006. It was Putin's birthday, 7 October.

On *Today* on 21 January 2016 Justin Webb raised the implications of the case for British relations with Russia in an interview with Sir Tony Brenton, who had been Britain's ambassador to Russia between 2004 and 2008, and so was based in Moscow at the time of the Litvinenko assassination:

> **Webb: And all of it comes down now, doesn't it, to what the reaction of the British government is going to be. If, as we expect, the report is pretty hard hitting, and even if it doesn't come up with proof, it comes up with some strands of evidence that seem to go right to the top… what should the Foreign Office, what indeed should David Cameron do now?**
>
> **Brenton: Well, they're going to have to be quite careful, because on the one hand obviously we have to react quite strongly to the murder of a British citizen, which is what Litvinenko was, on a British street by the use of a dangerous nuclear isotope. On the other hand, we have quite important other fish to fry with the Russians. They're very important in carrying the Iran denuclearisation through, they're absolutely crucial in sorting out the mess in Syria. So, I mean there are some obvious things that we can do – like try and tighten the likelihood of**

Lugovoi and Kovtun being brought to justice – but really tearing up relations with Russia is almost certainly not in our national interest.

He repeatedly called for caution and dialogue with the Russian authorities, given that Russia was such a key strategic player on the world stage.

However, Alexander Goldfarb, the head of the Litvinenko Justice Foundation – which had campaigned for the inquiry alongside Litvinenko's widow – emphatically rejected the former ambassador's argument that diplomatic priorities should dictate a measured response:

> Goldfarb: I think people who say so do not know history, they don't know psychology and have no understanding of what's going on in Russia. Mr Putin is driven by hatred towards everything – Western values, the policies, the specific people – which is probably no less rabid than the attitudes of radical Islamists, because it's in him. The West is threatening his power. So appeasing this kind of regime only invites more and more aggression.

> Webb: ... It's interesting you say that about Mr Putin and how he is motivated. There is a view in this country – you look at what people, very senior people, in the Labour Party think – that actually we've got Putin wrong, and that he is responding to threats from outside. What would you say to them, and to all of us, about Mr Putin as a person, and as a person to be trusted and dealt with on Syria and other matters as well?

> Goldfarb: Well, I think he should be judged by his record and he has lied to the face of Western politicians many times, particularly about Ukraine. I think you should read his own statements about the clash of values of so-called new Russian values and the Western European values. He is a homophobic murderous dictator and those who do not recognise it do it at their own peril.

In the same edition of the programme the businessman Bill Browder pointed to what the British government's restraint so far meant:

> If the Russian government sends assassins to the United Kingdom to kill people and there are no consequences, it basically gives them a green light to carry on killing people. And for people like me who are at odds with the Russian Federation, that's a very disturbing concept.

Browder's own Moscow lawyer, Sergei Magnitsky, had died in jail in 2009. It was Browder's lobbying that had helped persuade the US Congress to pass the so-called Magnitsky Act enabling targeted actions and sanctions against Russian individuals violating human rights, which President Barack Obama signed into law in 2012.

When the report was published later that day it was clear that Sir Robert Owen, who chaired the public inquiry, had concluded that the highest Russian authorities could indeed be implicated in Litvinenko's assassination. 'Taking full account of all the evidence and analysis available to me, I find that the FSB operation to kill Litvinenko was probably approved by Mr Patrushev [the director of the FSB at the time of the assassination] and also by President Putin,' Sir Robert wrote.

On *Today* the following morning, 22 January 2016, presenter Nick Robinson reported the reaction of Theresa May, then home secretary. 'The denunciation could scarcely have been stronger,' Robinson said, before quoting May. '"An unparalleled act of state-sponsored terrorism" was how the home secretary described the poisoning.'

Robinson pointed to the indifference of the Russian most clearly implicated in the murder: 'The man identified as the murderer [Lugovoi] said it was "nonsense", before going back to work on a new TV documentary about the fate of those who dare to betray Mother Russia. It is called, chillingly, *Traitors*. The Kremlin said pointedly that this affair could poison relations with London.'

Nick Robinson also picked up on the fact that the murder was by no means the only suspicious death of an influential Russian in Britain. 'The report also suggested that perhaps seven others could be linked directly to the FSB and probably to President Putin,' Robinson stated.

Fast-forward to March 2018, and for all who remembered Litvinenko it seemed like a case of *déjà vu* when Russian double-agent Sergei Skripal, who had been granted British residency in a spy swap with Russia, was found mysteriously poisoned in Salisbury. Alexander Goldfarb, on *Today* again two days after the poisoning on 6 March, spoke out against the weakness of previous British governments: 'The problem, as we learnt in the Litvinenko case, is that there is a major component of appeasement of Putin's regime on the part of the British establishment.' Goldfarb interpreted this latest assassination attempt on British soil as a twisted move to invigorate Putin's campaign for the upcoming presidential elections, to display to electors his ruthless ability to dispense with Russia's opponents, even under the noses of foreign governments.

With Skripal and his daughter – who had also been poisoned – languishing in a critical state in hospital, *Today* focused, that morning too, on the unsettling deaths of other well-connected Russians living in Britain. Andrey Kiyashko of RT, Russian government-supported rolling news, squared up to Heidi Blake from the US news channel BuzzFeed, who had investigated the murky business. Blake explained:

> Our research showed that there were 14 other cases [beyond Litvinenko] where evidence clearly pointed to Russia. In all those cases, the deaths had been treated as non-suspicious by the British police, but we established that US intelligence agencies had passed the British government intelligence connecting all of those

deaths to Russia… We connected nine of those individuals to Boris Berezovsky, who was Russia's public enemy no. 1… there's clearly a pattern here… In one case, the case of Alexander Perepilichny – it's a case quite similar to Sergei Skripal; he was a whistle-blower – he came here and gave evidence to the British government and to the Swiss authorities about Russian money laundering. He dropped dead in Surrey, with traces of a plant poison in his stomach – the police have said that's not a suspicious death.

Kiyashko retorted:

I think that you are indeed seeing patterns – each of these cases, you have the official British police saying that those deaths are not suspicious and then you're jumping in with something that the US intelligence has fed you.

But Blake hit back:

We know that the US intelligence community has handed the US Congress and the UK government an intelligence assessment stating with high confidence that Perepilichny was assassinated on the direct orders of Vladimir Putin.

Blake underlined how compromised she felt the British government had been by Russian influence in key areas of British life, yet she discerned a shift:

There's an unwillingness to jeopardise the flow of money, Russian money, into British banks and properties. And there's a genuine fear about Russia and cyber capabilities. But our information is that there has recently been a step change in response to growing concerns about Russia's interference in democracies in the West.

Diane Abbott, Labour's shadow home secretary, stepped into the *Today* debate too on 6 March 2018, saying, 'I don't like defaulting to a Red Menace analysis, but we can't allow London and the Home Counties to become a kind of killing field for the Russian state and its enemies.'

Britain and the West responded with more resolve than had been shown after the Litvinenko poisoning. Theresa May, now prime minister, successfully called for much tougher, united sanctions on the Russian elites, and there were international expulsions of Russian diplomats. Even US President Trump backed May, despite the ties with Russia that his campaign team was alleged to have forged in the run-up to the 2016 US presidential elections.

Nick Robinson highlighted the angry Russian government's response on *Today* on 3 April:

It may have sounded like a line from a James Bond movie: 'Britain's special services are known for their ability to act with a licence to kill.' But those were actually the words of Russia's foreign minister, Sergei Lavrov, who argued yesterday that Britain had both the means to carry out the Salisbury nerve-agent attack and the motive. It might have been carried out, he hinted, as a distraction from Brexit. Some in Moscow go further still, predicting war if this diplomatic confrontation is mishandled.

Lieutenant General Evgeny Buzhinsky – once a member of the Russian General Staff, but now with security think tank the PIR Centre – appeared on *Today* that morning to defended Putin's innocence of the Skripal poisoning: 'In this crime, Russian President Putin is the last guy to benefit, because [it's] on the eve of the presidential election, on the eve of the soccer world championship.' However, the atmosphere, he asserted, was 'worse than the Cold War, because if the situation will develop in the way it is now, I am afraid it will end up in a very, very bad outcome'. Robinson asked him to clarify, which he did, apocalyptically: 'A real war. Worse than the Cold War is a real war. It will be the last war in the history of mankind.'

'You are saying,' asked Robinson, 'that the fallout from the Salisbury poisoning could lead to a real war?' For Buzhinsky, it was the totality of events that mattered:

Not the Salisbury poisoning, but all the actions you see because the pressure. The United States [is] saying, you are saying, that the pressure will continue. What are you going to achieve? If you [think you] are going to achieve regime change, it's useless; you don't know Russians. The more external pressure [there] is, the more the society is consolidated around the president... Actually, you're cornering Russia and to corner Russia is a very dangerous thing.

The former British ambassador to Russia, Sir Tony Brenton, was back in the studio that morning, and gave this reaction to the general's interview:

The views expressed by General Buzhinsky are very widely shared among the Russian elite and among the Russian people. We keep on telling ourselves in the West that Vladimir Putin is a petty autocrat and when he goes, everything will get better. The fact is that what we have is not a Putin problem, it's a Russia problem.

He continued:

I think there's a real fear in Russia, and again among the Russian elite and among the security elite, that the West is intent upon encircling Russia, humiliating Russia, doing Russia down in every way it can. The West, in Russian eyes, has wandered around the world overthrowing sundry dictators and they fear that our attention may turn to Putin.

Then Brenton came up with another revelation that suggested confusion in the Kremlin:

> Just after the Litvinenko affair, and this is not a widely known story, the Russians launched another attack on Berezovsky. They sent a man over to kill him. We caught him and sent him back and it didn't happen, but I then went into the Russian Foreign Ministry, saying, 'What are you up to?' And they'd never heard of it. They didn't know. So the Russian security agencies, the FSB and others, often operate well out of sight of the rest of the Russian government.

In reiterating his main line of argument, Brenton concluded:

> We have to remain tough in response to the Skripal affair, obviously, and demonstrate to the Russians that the costs of doing this sort of thing are too high, but… you're not going to solve problems like strategic weapons, like control of cyberspace, like Islamic terrorism, without talking to the Russians and we're going to have to get back, sooner or later, to doing exactly that.

On 18 March 2018, two weeks after the Skripal poisoning, Vladimir Putin was re-elected president with 77 percent of the vote. A month later the Organisation for the Prohibition of Chemical Weapons (OPCW) released its report on the Salisbury poisoning, saying Russia was clearly to blame, and lambasting the Russian government for trying to muddy the waters. A month later, Andrew Parker, head of MI5, was publicly warning about Russia's 'aggressive and pernicious' actions and its meddling in elections across the democratic world.

In May 2018, Skripal was well enough to be allowed out of hospital. Putin's response was that his very survival proved the perpetrator could not have been the Russian state, otherwise he would certainly be dead. But just as Russia was freshening up its international image by hosting the football World Cup, the poison intended to kill Sergei Skripal claimed new victims. On 30 June a Wiltshire couple fell ill with suspected Novichok poisoning, and on 8 July 2018, John Humphrys reported on *Today*:

> **Humphrys: The Novichok attack in Salisbury has claimed its first death. Dawn Sturgess, the 44-year-old woman who was poisoned by the nerve agent last weekend, died in hospital last night. Hospital staff said they did all they could to save her. She'd been on life support ever since she fell ill and her partner Charlie Roley who was poisoned with her remains critically ill. Frank Gardner is our security correspondent. Frank, what will this do now that this is a murder investigation? … How will it affect the investigation?**

Gardner: Yes, I think it pushes it up into a different plane really, John. It was already very serious. It already led to the worst possible relations between Britain and Russia. Britain of course, the British government is convinced that the Kremlin was in some way behind this. The Kremlin absolutely denies it. It was serious enough when Sergei Skripal and his daughter were poisoned back in March: they of course had a Russian connection. He was effectively a double agent, a traitor who had been pardoned but still got poisoned, pardoned by Russia. And in this case this is a British couple poisoned on British soil. Accidental victims, it appears, of the same attack. I don't think there are any plans at the moment for any new sanctions on Russia, but I think the NATO summit that's going to be held on Wednesday, a two-day summit which Theresa May is attending, that will add, I think, a new urgency to it. They're already going to be discussing alleged Russian aggression. This I think will be right up at the top of the agenda.

On 5 September 2108 the British police released images of the two men alleged to be responsible for the attempt on Sergei Skripal's life. The prime minister, Theresa May, told the Commons the operation had been planned at a senior level of the Russian state. Yevgeny Buzshinski, the Russian general who had so startlingly predicted 'the last war in the history of mankind' when the diplomatic row over the Skirpals first blew up, was back on *Today*. 'I suggest that after six months of investigation, UK government had to produce something', he told presenter Martha Kearney, 'but what they have produced, well, for me it's absolute nonsense. Sorry about that.'

On 13 September two men who said they were the suspects named by Britain appeared on the Russian television channel RT and claimed they had visited Salisbury as tourists to see its 'famous' cathedral spire. Two weeks later the *Daily Telegraph* revealed that the real identity of one of the men was Colonel Anatoliy Vladimirovich Cepiga of the GRU, Russia's military intelligence, and on 8 October the other man was named as Dr Alexander Mishkin, also of the GRU.

The British Security Service: new threats and a new openness

'They've got to engage the public more with the terrorist threat'

GORDON CORERA, 7 JANUARY 2009

'Could the secret services have prevented the July 7th London bombings in which 52 people were killed? That's the question that has bothered many victims and their families ever since we learnt that the bombers were known to MI5.'

With these words on 19 May 2009, *Today* presenter Sarah Montague began a discussion about an imminent report from the British Parliament's Intelligence and Security Committee (ISC). It was not the first publication on the subject by this body, which was set up to scrutinise all the branches of the British intelligence services, but it was poised to address significant weaknesses in the British Security Service.

The coordinated attack on 7 July 2005 against London's transport system was the worst single atrocity on British soil since the Second World War; it was also the first Islamist suicide mission carried out successfully in Britain, by four British jihadists in total. Earlier attempts in Britain had been thwarted, but inevitably 7/7 became a turning point in British security, as it was a devastating demonstration of the Islamist threat 'within'. BBC security correspondent Gordon Corera looked back at the record in that same broadcast:

> In the immediate aftermath of the attacks in 2005, it was said the bombers were unknown; they were so-called 'clean skins'. Then it slowly emerged that in fact MI5 had come across some of them, particularly the ringleader, Mohammad Sidique Khan, in the context of another counter-terrorist operation, when MI5 was looking into a group of men planning fertiliser bombs. Now, the first ISC report in 2006 said the decision not to investigate Khan further and identify him was understandable, because at the time there was no suggestion he was planning attacks in the UK and so, with limited resources, the secret services had to prioritise other targets.

'But then in 2007,' continued Corera, 'after the trial of the fertiliser-bomb plotters was over, more information came into the public domain and this suggested that Mohammad Sidique Khan hadn't just fleetingly come across the MI5 radar, but had done so on a number of occasions.'

The public debate over whether 7/7 was preventable went on and that in itself was testament to the way the security environment of the 21st century had changed. A new spirit of openness prevailed, in which the role of the intelligence services in national life was more freely discussed.

By the time the 7/7 bombers struck, Britain's intelligence services were close to celebrating their centenary. Dealing specifically with threats within or to the nation, the British Security Service (or MI5 – short for Military Intelligence, Section 5) was founded in 1909. The Secret Intelligence Service (MI6), founded that same year, had as its remit foreign intelligence. These agencies were later augmented by the Government Communications Headquarters (GCHQ) in Cheltenham, which emerged from the Second World War operations at Bletchley Park; it now also deals specifically with cyber security (yet another developing threat), as well as intelligence-gathering generally. All the British intelligence agencies are overseen by the Joint Intelligence Committee (JIC) at the heart of government.

For decades after 1945, the principal threats identified by the men and women of this security apparatus were defined by the Cold War, subversion in Britain's diminishing number of colonies and, much nearer to home, the Troubles in Northern Ireland. Come the millennium, the Cold War was no more, the Troubles had come to an end with the Good Friday Agreement, and the colonies were long-since independent. The emergence of powerful new threats – of Islamist/jihadist terror at home and abroad, which aimed at mass casualties; of cyber warfare; of the unpredictable activities of rogue states – created new challenges and new questions. How should the security services react? Did they have the right people, with the right skills? Were they using the right techniques? Critically, security services across the West found they lacked credible operatives and inside information from the communities where some of the new threats had emerged.

One reaction by the British Security Service in the new millennium was to open up to the public. It embarked on a campaign to foster trust, to encourage the public to submit information, and to attract new recruits, particularly from 'non-traditional' sectors of society. And the number of intelligence workers has increased, considerably, since 2005. The service also embraced transparency as a way of meeting criticism of its far-reaching powers and concerns about the expense and effectiveness of covert operations. As a result, senior intelligence personnel are in the public eye in a way unimaginable even 20 years ago – suddenly they are prepared to appear in the media, including on *Today*.

In 2007, Dame Stella Rimington, director general of MI5 from 1992 to 1996 and the first ever woman to hold that post, went so far as to accept an invitation to be a guest editor of *Today* – at the end of a year in which another woman, Eliza Manningham-Buller, had retired as head of MI5. *Today* presenter Edward Stourton quizzed Rimington, on 26 December 2007, about the changing nature of the British intelligence services over the past few decades:

> **You come from a professional background that is mandarin, in the best sense of the word, in the sense that we had to let you get on and do what you did quietly, because if it wasn't secret, it wouldn't help us very much, and you presumably therefore felt very strongly the burden of responsibility to do that in as thorough and honest a way as you could?**

Rimington replied in the affirmative, of course, but she acknowledged the calls for, and indeed the necessity of, increased openness in the modern day:

> **The media is so important in talking to the public and explaining things to the public that I think that the days when mandarins could get on in a mandarin-like way are actually over and everybody, including the intelligence services, have got to adapt themselves to that. And that's one of the reasons why you see the intelligence services more open in explaining themselves, in talking about themselves, than they ever were in the past... But one has to try and get the best out of the modern situation and not allow the media or the need to explain yourself or political short-termism to set the agenda.**

She had, by now, retired, so she could speak more freely. But to the surprise of many, at the start of 2009 the *serving* head of MI5, Jonathan Evans, gave a ground-breaking newspaper interview to the *Guardian*, which Gordon Corera interpreted on *Today* on 7 January 2009 as another stage in an incremental opening-up. 'I think the decision is part of a gradual shift that's been going on from the Secret Service towards more openness,' he said, 'a recognition that they've got to engage the public more with the terrorist threat and with their role in trying to defeat that. Also, it's their centenary year, so I think they're edging out of the shadows a bit.'

On the scale of the Islamist threat in Britain, Corera noted that, 'He's talked in the past about a figure of a couple of thousand people out there, but also he says that it's impossible for his service to have what he calls "comprehensive coverage".'

The next year, Evans made a well-publicised speech, summed up by *Today*'s Justin Webb on 17 January 2010:

> **The head of MI5 Jonathan Evans does not make many speeches. And when he does speak it is rarely to deliver comforting news. What he told the Worshipful**

Company of Security Professionals last night was that hundreds of his officers were involved in an intense struggle to prevent successful terrorist attacks. Then he raised a number of concerns about radical prisoners being released, about new places of training including in Somalia and Yemen.

This was the starting point for a discussion on that morning's *Today* about yet another pressing security challenge: the radicalisation occurring within prisons. Webb asked James Brandon of the anti-radicalisation Quilliam Foundation, about getting new imams into prisons to counter the extremist message: 'There's been a few piecemeal attempts here and there', said Brandon, 'getting more chaplains working in prisons, Muslim chaplains, for example. But there's been no intelligent, joined-up sophisticated attempt to really roll this ideology back in prison. The attitude has been, "They are in prison, out of harm's way." We need to worry.'

On 17 September 2015, *Today* had a journalistic coup. As presenter Mishal Husain explained, 'The director general of MI5, Andrew Parker, is with me now. It is the first time that a serving head of the organisation has done a live interview in the organisation's 106-year history.' Parker was appearing as the then home secretary, Theresa May, was talking of introducing a new Investigatory Powers Bill, which was intended to give the intelligence services what were described as up-to-date tools to tackle terrorist activities – although critics regularly referred to such new laws as 'snoopers' charters'.

Husain first asked Parker to describe the prevailing terrorist threat from his perspective. He outlined how terrorists, rather than other countries, were perceived as the main menace facing Britain, and then continued:

> **The terrorism threat is the most serious threat that Britain faces in security terms currently and it takes up most of the work of MI5 and our partner agencies. It's set currently at the level of severe, which means that attacks are highly likely… We've seen six attempts at terrorism in this country just in the last 12 months that we and partner agencies, with the police, have had to intervene in to stop. And that is the highest number I can recall in my 32-year career, certainly the highest since 9/11.**

Parker pointed to the shifting nature of the main threats, in terms of both geopolitics and communications:

> **The shape of the threat we face today has changed in some ways – changed because, of course, it's driven from conflict zones and the way people react to that, but [also] because of the internet and the way terrorists use social media, including from Syria, and the way we all live our lives, using the smartphones in our pockets. The terrorists do the same and they're using secure apps and**

internet communications to try to broadcast their message and to incite and direct terrorism amongst people who live here, who are prepared to listen to their message.

Husain noted how the independent reviewer of terrorist legislation, David Anderson QC, had criticised the legal framework in which the British intelligence services had been working in recent years. Anderson had described it as 'undemocratic and in the long run intolerable'. Parker responded:

> I think he's made a strong case which government is taking very seriously, to update the legislation, because if it isn't transparent, what the sorts of capabilities are that agencies use these days – and bear in mind the laws we operate under now were drafted back in the year 2000, before many of the new technologies that are around now were being used... It's important that it's explained to people, because of course this is a free, liberal democracy, and the role that MI5 has is to protect that against those who mean us harm.

Parker was at pains to show how precisely targeted the efforts of his service were, to allay public fears about snooping by his agency: 'I think the important thing to say is that we're focused on the people who mean us harm. We're not about browsing through the private lives of the citizens of this country; we do not have population-scale monitoring...'

Husain encouraged Parker to speak of the potential problems the British intelligence services might face if the new measures weren't written into law, querying the situation in the United States:

> Husain: What is at stake if, for whatever reason, you don't get the new tools, the powers, that you see as adequate for the technological age we live in? Your counterpart in the United States, the director of the FBI, has spoken of the dangers of, in his words, 'going dark'.

> Parker: James Comey has referred a few times publicly to what he calls 'going dark' – by which he means shifts in technology and particularly in internet technology and the use of encryption and so on – creating a situation where law-enforcement agencies and secret agencies can no longer obtain under proper legal warrants the content of communications between people they have reason to believe are terrorists. I think that is a very serious issue.

Parker immediately moved the discussion on to the responsibility of internet social-media giants:

> Parker: It also requires the cooperation of the companies who run and provide services over the internet that we all use and it's in nobody's interests that

terrorists should be able to plot and communicate out of the reach of any authorities with proper legal power.

Husain: And isn't it the case that even if you do get the new framework in UK law that gives you those tools, you will still have a problem with those tech companies, many of them based in the United States and therefore beyond the remit of UK law?

Parker: I think it will be a continuing challenge as technology shifts and we've seen the way that technology's moved so far and so fast in recent years. It will keep doing that and maybe in unpredictable ways. I think it is important into the future that not only is there a framework of clear law in countries like Britain, as there is now (but updated), but also that there is international agreement and arrangements whereby companies have a confident basis on which to cooperate with agencies like mine and with the police in order to protect society and of course their customers from people who might do them harm.

Husain: But an international agreement might mean that they have to cooperate with the Russians and the Chinese and that – surely you can see why – that is the kind of thing that makes people very apprehensive.

Parker could only try to reassure: 'Look, I think you can see that Britain stands for high standards in these things...'

The tragic case of Lee Rigby was then brought up. The young, off-duty soldier had been hacked to death on a South London street by two British Islamist extremists, Michael Adebolajo and Michael Adebowale, on 22 May 2013. After his murder, information was found on social media revealing the potential dangers posed by at least one of his killers before the attack.

Husain: Just to talk about one of those technology companies, Facebook for example: when the Intelligence and Security Committee report into the murder of Lee Rigby was published, it said that there had been a private conversation between one of his killers, Michael Adebowale, on Facebook, with an extremist. Now that drew a lot of attention to the role of tech companies, but would you really expect it, Facebook in this case, to report conversations like that? It would say that a) it's not its job to do that; and b) it might not have the tools to report conversations of that kind.

Parker: I don't think the ISC report named any particular company, but your point is well made and I think it goes to the question of the ethical responsibility of these companies for the communications and data that they hold and that they carry... Some of the social-media companies operate arrangements for their own purposes, under their own codes of practice, which cause them to close accounts, sometimes, because of what's carried. I think there's then a question about why not come forward, if it's something that concerns terrorism, or concerns child sexual exploitation, or some other appalling area of crime.

The wider issues of cyberattacks were brought to the fore on *Today* on 14 February 2017, the day of the Queen's dedication of the new National Cyber Security Centre at GCHQ. In recent years, Russia, China and North Korea have been perceived in the West as being the world leaders in this new arena of potentially massive-scale disruption. *Today* presenter John Humphrys began the discussion by quoting the head of the new centre, Ciaran Martin, whom he was shortly to interview: '"Britain is under attack, cyberattack, by criminals at home and other governments abroad – and the attacks are causing us harm. There have been significant thefts of personal data and threats to our national infrastructure; two a day." And the man who makes these claims is the head of a new agency, set up to stop it happening.' Gordon Corera then went on to paint in the background:

Britain is one of the most digitally advanced economies in the world, but that also makes it one of the most vulnerable: vulnerable to criminals, other states and even teenage hackers. Espionage, warfare, crime – all are now rapidly moving online. Our security and prosperity will depend on whether we're ready to deal with that.

Today's report that morning also cited an even more alarming speech from the British chancellor Philip Hammond, which had been given a few months before, in November 2016:

If we do not have the ability to respond, in cyberspace, to an attack which takes down our power networks, leaving us in darkness, or hits our traffic-control system, grounding our planes, we would be left with the impossible choice of turning the other cheek and ignoring the devastating consequences – or resorting to a military response.

But the head of the new centre, Ciaran Martin, was more reassuring when he spoke to John Humphrys on 14 February 2017:

There's absolutely no need to be defeatist about the risks of cyberattack – and our job at the new Cyber Security Centre is to focus on protecting the services that really matter from cyberattacks, [and] to manage those attacks that do get through so that they cause as little harm as possible. And I think what's really important is that we improve the technology that we use in everyday life and we educate people better in how to use that technology safely, so that we can really reduce both the risk of the attacks happening and the harm that they do.

Reducing risk was, at its heart, the key directive of the security services. As such, and with this target in mind, a premium was also put on 'joined-up approaches': the different agencies should talk to one another and share their discoveries and concerns.

That Britain needed such an approach had been highlighted by the London attacks of 7/7. On *Today*'s broadcast of 19 May 2009 Rachel North, of the 7/7 Inquiry Campaign Group – which was pushing for an inquiry into the bombings that would be independent of the government – gave this powerful response to Sarah Montague's question, quoted at the beginning of this section, about whether the 7/7 bombings could have been prevented:

> The terrible, awful question about 7/7 is: if the police had been informed of MI5's suspicions about Mohammad Sidique Khan in 2005, they could have talked to the neighbours, they could have gone round to his house and they would have found him mixing bombs. And the need for communication... that needing to share a rich picture of intelligence with police, secret services and foreign intelligence agencies – is something that people are always reluctant to do, but it's absolutely crucial now in the 21st century, [especially] with global, fast-mutating networks.

Rachel North herself was a survivor of the 7/7 attacks; she was on the tube train hit by one of the bombs as it pulled out of King's Cross.

Thought for the day: The Right Reverend Jim Thompson

12 September 2001

I was sitting late last night in front of a blank piece of paper, my mind numbed by all we had seen, when a fax came in telling me that a daughter of two friends was missing in New York.

The pictures had seemed for a moment like an apocalypse or a brilliantly devised disaster movie, but now this was not myth or virtual reality but life and death.

On a perfect morning in New York – looking impregnable, the vast Twin Towers reduce to dust, and thousands on thousands of people crushed in the fall. The mayor of New York said the casualties would be more than any one of us can bear.

So many questions: Who did it? How would we all be affected? And rumbling from the ruins the fear. This volcano didn't come from below but above, raining terror on Manhattan; not a natural disaster but man made. What just cause could possibly deserve such an evil and unjust response. Will the appetite for retaliation lead to indiscriminate reprisals? Can ever the good in the human mind cope wisely and effectively in the face of such evil? In this war no attempt was made to avoid civilian targets – indeed, somewhere people planned over a long period this blow precisely against innocent victims. As their bodies are recovered they remind us that buildings can be replaced but lives cannot – they are beloved, and unique to those who love them.

This is man made, but as a believer in God I still ask: what does God make of it? Perhaps the perpetrators believe in God. Some people even said this was a gift of God. Yet this denies everything that God means to me and I know of no sane faith which would justify it.

And I asked God to say something I can say. 'Jesus wept', perhaps, or Christ's own words: 'My heart is ready to break with grief.' How God must grieve at the way we use the freedom He gives us. I know that even now prayer will be incessant in millions of minds – people waiting for news of a loved one, people already fearing reprisals, people so shocked and scared of what might happen – will turn to God, and maybe use old and familiar words to restore their courage and find confidence for the future – 'God is our hope and strength, a very present help in trouble – Therefore will we not fear though the earth be moved.' The earth has moved. Please, God, help us.

CHAPTER 4

ART, CULTURE AND SPORT

The interviewer, the artist and the unmade bed

'Get ready to become outraged'

JOHN HUMPHRYS, 2 DECEMBER 1998

The presenters of *Today* know that their primary function is to be intermediaries between the listening public and the extraordinarily wide-ranging array of people and issues they encounter in their professional capacities. This is not to say that the presenters are not personalities – after all, they have their own distinct styles – but their *Today* roles are principally to chair and guide debate, to play devil's advocate when necessary, to analyse and question, but not to be personally opinionated.

But now and then, there are permissible exceptions to that rule, and here context is everything. A *Today* presenter's opinions suddenly to intrude when covering politics would break all the BBC's guidelines on impartiality, but in the 'softer' realms of arts and culture, occasionally the presenter is allowed to reveal his or her views, and to use their own reactions as one way of engaging the listenership in the discussion. Among long-serving presenters, James Naughtie was able to infuse the programme with his love of books, opera and classical music. And John Humphrys has been allowed to be expansive on his bugbears. One of those has been abuse of the finer points of the English language, against which he sometimes rails; for balance, others are allowed to rail at him for pedantry.

Another Humphrys tradition is his incomprehension of the contemporary art world, which is accompanied by a barely concealed suspicion that it is all a case of the Emperor's New Clothes. This relationship with art, particularly, has made for entertaining, baffling, funny, spiky broadcasts. And it has, quite unexpectedly, thrown up an odd-couple relationship, one that began rockily – indeed, almost disastrously – but which regular listeners have heard mature over the years. That is the John and Tracey show – the periodic encounters between the broadcaster and the doyenne of the 1990s 'Young British Artists' (Brit Art) explosion, Tracey Emin.

'I'm not sure,' Humphrys once told the *Mail on Sunday*, 'I have an artistic bone in my body.' His credentials as sceptic-in-chief were firmly established in the 1990s, though the broadcaster knew that he was also channelling the befuddlement, even scorn, of a broad swathe of the general public. 'Twenty-two minutes past eight,' he announced on 2 December 1998, 'and get ready to become outraged...'

> The Turner Prize for modern art has been awarded again. In the past we've had a house full of concrete, sheep pickled in formaldehyde, and policemen on video standing in a row. Now: elephant dung. There is a problem this time, though – a serious problem. Dung notwithstanding, it looks like a real picture. What are they trying to do to us?

The victorious Chris Ofili was the first *painter* to have won the British art world's most high-profile prize in 13 years. An amused arts correspondent, Rosie Millard, was already feeling a little protective of an artist faced with having 'to meet John Humphrys in the morning'. Ofili's work, though a painting, was nothing so mundane as a landscape in oils. *No Woman, No Cry*, depicting a crying black woman and incorporating visual references to murdered black teenager Stephen Lawrence, was a work redolent of politics and issues of black identity. It was serious, thoughtful work. However, technically, as Millard described, 'Chris Ofili's paintings are very wacky... the surface is all blobs and abstract squiggles... they have a lot of texture on them, sort of collage.' Humphrys was keen to cut to the chase of what that texture actually was: 'We mustn't forget the elephant dung!' It turned out that Ofili would visit London Zoo to collect it in person, whereupon he waited for it to dry out and, in his own words, 'for the meaning to saturate into it'. Humphrys exclaimed, 'Perhaps he's not going to let us down entirely then.' And at least this work did not descend to the level of artistic duo Gilbert and George who, Humphrys reminded listeners, 'used a certain amount of dung in the past, haven't they? Their own... loathsome.'

Come September 1999, Ofili, along with *enfant terrible par excellence* Damien Hirst and others, had been showing work in the Sensation exhibition, which, having been mounted first at London's Royal Academy, was now about to open in New York. There, it was already attracting complaints from a group called People for the Ethical Treatment of Animals (PETA), who were appalled by Hirst's 'pig sliced nose to tail preserved in two tanks of formaldehyde' (Humphrys's description). In addition, the show had earned the scorn of New York City mayor Rudy Giuliani, who had threatened to withdraw subsidy. The mayor was not, it seems, a fan of dung. In a somewhat meandering *Today* interview – which fell well short of Humphrys's standards on grammar – on 24 September 1999, Damien Hirst defended Ofili. He was speaking to the *Today* arts reporter Mark Coles:

> Coles: The mayor – Mayor Giuliani – seems to take a particular offence against the Chris Ofili painting in which elephant dung is used to depict the Virgin Mary. I mean he is a Catholic, after all, isn't he? We shouldn't be surprised he's going to be offended.

Hirst: Well, I'm a Catholic.

Coles: So, you don't think that there's any grounds for opposition or offence?

Hirst: No, I mean, I think you said, '[What's] the point of people throwing elephant dung at the painting?' But it's not [that]. I mean he's used elephant dung to make paintings, you know, I mean, people, you know, dung is – is actually, was actually used to make paints, you know. I mean, you know, there's burnt umbers, you know, we use. In the beginning, you know, people were painting on cave walls using dung before they were doing anything else. I think it's just to revisit that. I mean I don't think – I mean, are you allowed to do paintings with tomatoes stuck on them of the Virgin Mary, or is that like throwing tomatoes at her? But they're all about life. I just think – I don't think he's [Guiliani] taken it [seriously] – I think he's glanced at it and it's election year.

Coles: What about your own work? In the States, they're now being picketed by animal rights groups who don't like the idea of pigs, cows or sheep in formaldehyde. Are you worried by their actions?

Hirst: Now, I mean, the thing is, it's like, you know, as you know people can look at it – I mean I had a conversation with some people from animal rights and I made a big effort to say, 'Look, I'm not pro this, I'm on your side on this.' And they said, 'We don't care if you're on our side or not, we're, you know – this is an opportunity for publicity and we're going to take it.' And you can kind of see their point. It's a bit of a catch 22, but I think, you know, in the, you know, you walk past any butcher and it's full of cows and pigs and sheep and then you suddenly take one out of that context, and it's bought from exactly the same place, and you're making a statement in a way against it, you know, of kind of saying, you know, I mean you're kind of trying to put the personality back into the animals. And then all of a sudden everybody's up in arms, it's like – I mean they should be picketing the local butcher's, I think.

....

Coles: Any particular message for Mayor Giuliani?

Hirst: Grow up.

'There we are.' Humphrys picked up at the end of the interview. 'That was the message from Damien Hirst, the man who says he's putting personality back into animals by pickling them in formaldehyde. There we are.'

The opening in 2000 of Tate Modern ('without the definite article for reasons I don't understand,' grumbled Humphrys) was, in the broadcaster's words, 'going to raise all sorts of interesting questions' about what would fill this new institution dedicated to modern art. Rosie Millard was again on hand to explain to Humphrys in the 11 May broadcast that the gallery's exhibits would run the gamut from the French Impressionists up to 'Damien Hirst, your particular favourite', along with 'a floor for installations – again, one of your favourites'. The latter would include 'old shockers like *Equivalent VIII* by Carl Andre, more familiarly known as "Tate Bricks"'.

'Oh, the bricks, they're still there… ? Good heavens alive. Are they the same bricks or did somebody mix them up?' asked Humphrys cheekily.

In the history of contemporary art 'outrages', Andre's rectangular composition of house bricks held canonical status. Indeed, the controversy over its purchase by the Tate in 1972 almost single-handedly jumpstarted contemporary art furores in Britain generally.

And it was on this morning in 2000, too, that Humphrys finally got to Emin. 'One of the artists,' Humphrys informed listeners, 'Who is going to be in there… is Tracey Emin, a somewhat controversial person herself.'

Indeed, she was. 'Emin's work,' asserts the Royal Academy, 'is uninhibited in the way it absorbs and reflects her personal life' – a statement that is undeniable. In 1998 Emin had attracted fascination and prim tut-tutting with her mattress-in-a-tent installation entitled *Everyone I Have Slept With 1963–1995*. Two years before that, she had confined herself, naked, with some blank canvases in a gallery room, where viewers could spy on her as she struggled with the unavoidable task of having to paint and draw. It was a cross between performance art and a kind of art exorcism.

In her first interview with Humphrys, Emin enthused over the new Tate:

Emin: It's probably one of the most fantastic things to happen to London, and you compare it to something like the Dome, which is just a massive sort of public embarrassment, and then we look at something like Tate Modern that's going to be there for, like, you know, hundreds and hundreds of years… I'm just incredibly proud of it. And it's just fantastic being an artist at the moment, living in London, living in Britain, when something like that is happening.

Humphrys: Couldn't you argue, though, that if modern art is meant to reach out in a different way to people, and modern art is meant to be different from traditional art, then the last thing you should do with it is lock it up in a building that only a very few people out of the entire population will ever go to see?

Emin: That's absolute rubbish what you just said, you're just trying to have an argument with me to make good radio–

Humphrys: It's a perfectly serious point...

Emin: No, if you...

Humphrys: I'm sorry if I disagree with you, it's not because it's rubbish, it's because I have a view.

Indeed, he did. When Humphrys insinuated that she and Damien Hirst might have deliberately sought out 'shock and self-publicity' in order to attain the pre-eminent positions they now occupied, and from which they could command large commissions, Emin emphatically disagreed:

I worked for ten years absolutely without a penny. It's only in the last five years – I'm 37 now and I'm old enough to be successful and be respected for what I do... Damien's publicity comes from the work that he does, first of all, and that's the same with me: it's the work that I make that leads on the publicity, not – not *me*.

After all, as she put it, 'You wanted to interview me this morning. I didn't ring you and ask you about it.'

But then they touched on something more substantive, about the nature of art. Referring to *My Bed* (1998), Emin's most renowned work to date, which consisted of her 'unmade bed' arrayed with the detritus of a life lived (used condoms, soiled sheets, and so on), Humphrys wondered, 'How can that become as famous as it does when somebody else's bed doesn't?'

'Because,' Emin replied:

Their bed isn't in the Tate Gallery demanding the attention that mine was and it's not put into a critical position where they make a judgement over it. I decided to make a judgement over this object in my life... I looked at the bed and I decided that it wasn't just the bed, it was something else: it represented something else in my life.

Emin was offering the essential justification of conceptual art that the Dadaists would have understood: that to take an object out of its ordinary life and context and to place it (almost literally) on a pedestal or in a changed environment – especially in a gallery that positively *invites* the gaze – is to redefine the status of the object. It is what the French artist Marcel Duchamp did with his urinal, redefining it as art object and calling it *Fountain* in 1917. Emin, iconoclast though she was, was yet in a traceable tradition – the 20th-century tradition of such 'ready-mades' or *objets trouvés* (found objects).

'Where does that end, though?' asked a hard-to-convince Humphrys. 'I mean, why couldn't somebody say, you know, "I happen to think that my child's potty is a particular whatever?"' Emin's response was direct and straightforward: 'They could do if they had the conviction to stand by it, but they probably wouldn't.' She might also have said if they had the courage and *chutzpah* and self-knowledge, for all were required; Emin knew that most people had no inclination to open themselves up to the public gaze in the way that being her sort of an artist involved.

On *Today* that May morning, Emin was also keen to dispel any idea that *seeming* randomness should be mistaken for *actual* randomness. Her work and her success were projects of hard graft: 'It didn't just come, you know – I'm not lucky. I work incredibly hard.'

By 2000, she had indeed found enviable success, a status she reflected back through her art in a print depicting her shovelling money into her crotch. In the words of the Saatchi Gallery, it was 'two fingers up to her critics. Emin's triumphed over all, and has money up the wazoo to boot!'

The prickly *Today* interview was in reality longer than the version listeners heard: missing were some unbroadcastable comments Emin apparently made at the end. The next year, on television, interviewer and contemporary artist squared up for a second bout, this time on opposing teams of the satirical BBC news quiz *Have I Got News for You*. Freed from the confines of *Today*'s etiquette, Humphrys's scorn of unmade beds had freer reign, while Emin pronounced the broadcaster 'an incredibly rude, arrogant person', though she denied having previously called him a 'beard-and-sandals tosser'. It was surely the end of an unbeautiful friendship. But time passed...

Roll on a decade and more. On 16 May 2011, *Today* listeners heard Humphrys telling them:

> I've been to her [Emin's] new exhibition, opening this week at the Hayward Gallery in London, called 'Love Is What You Want'. There's an awful lot of it you might not want your ten-year-old to see, as well as some rather lovely, almost classical stuff, but I suggested to her that, in the end, it's all about herself.

'Some rather lovely, classical stuff?' Listeners were unaccustomed to this sort of concession. And while Humphrys was more thoughtful in his responses and less judgemental, his interviewee, for her part, sounded far less defensive and a little more trusting. As regards the autobiographical core to her work, Emin made a distinction:

> It isn't necessarily all about my ego. It's actually about my art practice and how I look at things and how I think about things, but the things always start off personally, to do with me or something which I've experienced.

Acknowledging the gap of time, Humphrys wondered whether it was inevitable that the 'Young British Artists' were now 'part of the Establishment'. 'You voted Conservative last time,' he pointed out (which she conceded she had done, on the basis that she liked their plans for arts funding better). Humphrys wondered: had she achieved contentment? He wasn't sure, because, referring to her self-documented troubles:

> **There was a certain amount of self-loathing, maybe because of your – what happened to you as a young girl, you were raped and all the rest of it – and your apparent obsession with… your past lovers.**

Emin admitted that with time and her success 'people tend to have more regard for you, so even if they don't like what you do, they're more respectful and then… you calm down and the chips fall off your shoulders… and then you walk through the world feeling a lot happier.' Yes, she admitted, she had joined 'the Establishment', and how could she not: 'I'm nearly 50 and I've been doing it for 20 years. I'm a Royal Academician. I've got three honorary PhDs.'

'So,' wondered Humphrys, 'the old Tracey Emin is gone for good – the one who'd get drunk, go on television and do all those outrageous things and say and perform outrageously, that's all gone?'

That was a step too far for the artist, who still hoped her epitaph would be 'Something like, you know, "[Bleep] me while I'm sleeping."' She continued, 'It's like – you know, I never… even when I die, I don't really wanna be asleep. I don't really want to be gone.' As Humphrys explained to listeners, 'The fact that we've had to bleep out the crucial word in that sentence suggests that the old Tracey Emin is still present.' And on this topic, at least, interviewer and interviewee were of one mind. 'Alive and very, very present, yes,' confirmed the artist.

Some commentators were mildly disconcerted by this interview – not because of the bleep or the sentiment it revealed, but because of the amount of laughter punctuating the conversation. Perhaps, remembering that first interview back in 2000, they had been hoping for another combustion. Humphrys and Emin had themselves reminded listeners of those old fireworks, which they agreed had been 'good radio'. In 2011, however, there was mutual respect, even mutual admiration.

Roll on another seven years, and 'Hello, wotcha, hi, John!' was Emin's greeting over the airwaves. It was the morning of 10 April 2018, and she was standing in London's St Pancras station underneath her latest installation – a giant neon sentence that read 'I want my time with you'. It had been erected the previous night (which had involved a partial station closure; 'People will hate you for that,' quipped Humphrys) and she was, she said, 'a bit overwhelmed for my own work', as she had just encountered it for the first time *in situ* and lit up. As Emin explained, 'One of the most romantic things in the world is to be met at a train station by someone you love… it's just a very romantic place, a train station… I want my time with you, nobody else but you.' The installation had another purpose too: in the post-Brexit-referendum era, it was about openness to Europe at this Eurostar terminal – a rejection of isolation.

For a while, the discussion that morning veered into the topic of sexual harassment, a subject on which Emin had lately been quoted in the press, until the artist pulled it back: 'I want my time with you, John. Can we please talk about my work?' And Humphrys was happy to oblige.

> **Humphrys: OK. Do you expect people… I'm, I'm nervous about putting words into your mouth, because I've done that in the past and got into terrible trouble.**
>
> **Emin: No, no, don't worry, you're safe with me now. You're safe with me, I promise.**
>
> **Humphrys: What *is* the message?**
>
> **Emin: The message is about love. The message is about wanting. The message is about warmth…**

'Tracey,' responded a relaxed interviewer as they concluded, 'thank you very much indeed.'

In the end, a train station turned out to be the perfect backdrop to a radio relationship that had travelled on its own winding journey for over 18 years.

The Rushdie Affair, 1988–98

'The condition of the writer is solitude'
SALMAN RUSHDIE, 27 APRIL 1990

On the evening of 12 July 1991 a middle-aged Japanese academic called Hitoshi Igarashi discovered that the humble business of translation could have terrible consequences; he was stabbed to death. Just a week earlier an Italian translator had been luckier, escaping a knife attack with what the *New York Times* called 'superficial wounds'. Although they lived half a world away from each other, what both translators had in common was the prize-winning contemporary novel they had worked on. The title was *The Satanic Verses*, and the author was the British writer Salman Rushdie, a man who was already in hiding and under a death threat.

The offence that *The Satanic Verses* attracted was not instantaneous. Rushdie, a rising literary star, had written a complex and extravagant book, which he once summed up to the *Guardian* as revolving around themes of 'migration, metamorphosis, divided selves, love, death, London and Bombay'. But it included a narrative-within-a-narrative (or scenes within scenes) – it has been described as a dream sequence – that some interpreted as playing mischievously, even satirically, with Islamic tradition. It was published in 1988 and in Britain won the prestigious Whitbread Prize for novel of the year. But then several countries with Muslim populations banned it, including India, the land of Rushdie's birth.

In December 1988, opposition in Britain grew. There were protests against the book in Bolton, and a copy was burned; the latter ritual was repeated in Bradford the following month. The publication of *The Satanic Verses* in the US in February 1989 lifted the furore to an altogether different scale. Already that month some protesters in Pakistan had died during a demonstration against the book, and on St Valentine's Day 1989, Ayatollah Khomeini, the supreme leader of Iran, who wielded spiritual authority over a large Shia community, issued a *fatwā*, or Islamic ruling:

> **I inform the proud Muslim people of the world that the author of *The Satanic Verses* book, which is against Islam, the Prophet and the Qur'an, and all those involved in its publication who are aware of its content, are sentenced to death.**

Rushdie spoke out. 'It is not true,' the author asserted, '[that] this book is a blasphemy against Islam.' He offered his regrets for any offence inadvertently caused. But he might as well have saved his breath, for the momentum against him was already too great. The day after Khomeini's *fatwā* was issued, crowds attacked the British embassy in Tehran with stones, and, to incentivise any would-be assassins, an enterprising cleric offered a bounty of $1 million.

The *fatwā* was condemned in the West, and European ambassadors to Iran were recalled for several weeks in protest (Iran recalled its own diplomats too). In early March 1989 Anglo-Iranian diplomatic relations were formally broken, although the British government seemed to have no great enthusiasm for Rushdie's book: on 2 March the foreign secretary Sir Geoffrey Howe told the BBC World Service that the novel was not only understandably offensive to Muslim sensitivities but, 'offensive in many other ways as well'. A week later the 46-member states of the Islamic Conference Organisation declared Rushdie an 'apostate' and his book blasphemous. Some leading moderate Muslims who urged calm were themselves threatened – a Belgian imam was murdered. In Turkey's capital, Ankara, the British Council offices were attacked.

On the day the *fatwā* was announced, Rushdie himself experienced a sudden rupture in the life he had known. Whisked away to a secret location by Special Branch, he could not know that he was about to begin nine years in hiding under police protection. The authorities acted immediately, lest there were 'death squads' already in the UK, primed to carry out Khomeini's sentence. Rushdie would move around between 30 different places over these years, as his case, and his cause, ebbed and flowed. To help with his subterfuge, he took a new name – 'Joseph Anton', combining the first names of two of his favourite authors (Conrad and Chekhov) – which would later form the title of his memoir of this period.

Staunch in their defence of Rushdie were writers, artists and free-speech campaigners everywhere – an international defence league was formed to campaign for him. His publishers stayed true to him, and *The Satanic Verses* was not withdrawn from print. But a great danger perceived by Rushdie and his campaigners was that his case might wither into obscurity through neglect, possibly leaving him vulnerable and isolated should the machinery of protection be withdrawn. On 18 April 1989, *Today* broadcast a report about two men who were trying to do something about it. Veteran Pakistani-born activist and writer Tariq Ali had teamed up with political playwright Howard Brenton to stage their modestly fictionalised response to the Rushdie Affair, *Iranian Nights*. Tariq Ali made their case in conversation with the *Today* reporter Dominic Arkwright:

> **In Germany, in Scandinavia, in Holland, in North America, people are still feeling as strongly as ever. This seems to be a peculiarly British trait, to hide your head under the sand and hope things will go away. This is the time to speak up before it is too late, because the author's life is still under threat and, without**

taking positions on the content of his book, we are taking a position on his life. We want him to live and we want people to discuss, to debate and not to kill.

'Despite the possibility that this play too might have repercussions,' as Arkwright put it, Brenton was bullish:

If you can't put on a play like this in this country, because people are frightened either to put on such a play or to go and see it, that's a disgrace. I will not have this in my country. I will not have a fellow writer, as a British citizen, threatened by a clerical fascist state for his life, and I will not have people getting scared.

In June 1989, Khomeini died. Unfortunately, the *fatwā*, it was argued, was personal to the individual issuing it – Khomeini's death did not invalidate it; rather, it removed the one person who *could* revoke it. So Rushdie stayed in hiding. But radio allowed him an audience. On 27 April 1990, just over a year after the *fatwā* was announced, he gave an interview to *Today* on the telephone. 'Clearly,' announced John Humphrys, 'I'm not going to ask you where you are.' Indeed, Humphrys had no idea whether Rushdie was even in the country.

The reason for the interview was to enable Rushdie to add his considerable intellectual weight to a campaign to introduce a written British constitution to codify citizens' rights, so that all parties would (in his view) have a much clearer point of reference when legal disputes arose. The parallels with his own case were clear. But soon the conversation migrated to the rhythm of Rushdie's extraordinary life. 'How are you coping at the moment, Mr Rushdie, with the way you're having to live?' asked the presenter.

'Well, it's amazing what people can get used to,' replied the author, now in more subdued tones. 'So, I'm doing my work and I suppose that keeps me going, but I would like to think that this isn't a permanent condition.'

Humphrys responded, 'There are many people who believe the only way that [it] can be ended is by yourself saying what it is that the Iranians want to hear.'

But in Rushdie's eyes the ball was in the Iranians' court:

I'm not sure what it is that the Iranians want to hear, but the fact is that it seems to me, I've written… a book quite legitimately. It was published quite legitimately, and it's not really, you know, for the person who is the object of an attack to solve the problem.

'In the meantime,' Humphrys suggested, 'you're in this – what some might consider to be – impossible position… What's the worst about it?'

Rushdie reflected:

Well, the worst about it is the loss of ordinary life. The worst about it is not being able to do things that everybody else would take for granted, like walking down a street. You know, writers anyway are, I suppose, fortunate in that the condition of the writer is solitude; but normally at the end of a day of work, you can leave the room and go and see other people. Now the problem is when that is withdrawn. Well, there's no doubt it's a very difficult situation…

'I do,' Rushdie added, 'whatever you might do if your life were confined to the interior of a house.'

Would it be possible, Humphrys wondered, for the author to 'start a new life somewhere else'? Here, Rushdie recovered some of his defiance:

You know, I am who I am. I wish to continue to be a writer. I wish to continue to be myself. I mean, the idea of becoming somebody else in Paraguay is completely unattractive. I mean that's, that's for defeated dictators, not for working novelists.

Just before Christmas 1990, and by this time almost two years into his ordeal, Rushdie went as far as he would go in trying to mollify his opponents. Having spoken to Muslim intermediaries, he expressed new commitment to Islam and indicated his willingness to stop the spread of *The Satanic Verses* by prohibiting new translations and paperback editions. His words fell on deaf ears. Immediately, Tehran Radio broadcast the affirmation of Khomeini's successor as Iran's supreme leader, the former President Khamenei, that the *fatwā* 'remains unchanged even if he repents and becomes the most pious man of his time'. Rushdie appeared to have been correct – it was not within his gift to provide the solution.

It seemed to be within Rushdie's gift, however, to irk some Conservative backbenchers, as one of their number, Toby Jessel, demonstrated on *Today* three years later. The immediate issue was a meeting Rushdie had secured with the prime minister, John Major. During a discussion on the *Today* broadcast of 12 April 1993, Jessel explained why he did not think the writer deserved his audience with Major, 'whose time is at a premium':

I think Salman Rushdie's behaviour is highly irresponsible. He's an intelligent man. He's a former Muslim, so he knew how they would be likely to react. He's highly intelligent. He knew perfectly well what he was doing. He's caused deep offence… Now of course Rushdie has become a British subject and there is an honourable tradition to protect the lives of British subjects, but some deserve it more than others.

Jessel's interlocutor, another Conservative MP, David Harris, did not exactly leap enthusiastically to Rushdie's defence: 'I wish he hadn't written the "wretched book", as Ted Heath called it.'

The discussion was moderated by the BBC correspondent Graham Leach, who was doing a presenting shift that day. He wondered whether a consequence of this meeting with the prime minister could be 'that the more militant wing of the Iranian leadership will be strengthened, when Britain is trying to prise moderates away from that hardline stance'. Jessel's objections were more fundamental:

> I don't think Salman Rushdie deserves it. He knew what he was doing. He was playing with fire. He was sailing close to the wind. He was sticking his neck out. He probably hoped to get some publicity which would help to sell his book. He knew perfectly well, as a former Muslim, how they were likely to react, and he has triggered a threat to himself, and he now expects the British taxpayer to pay a six-figure sum every year to provide police protection for him.

He wasn't alone in complaining about the expense of protecting Rushdie. The author had to contend with the accusation that he was 'costing' the nation £11 million per annum, as if the 30 properties he lived in over this period were a lifestyle choice.

One year later, BBC correspondent Lyse Doucet, reporting from Iran on 23 February 1994, was telling *Today* listeners that 'The Iranian government is trying to distance itself, as a government, from this very controversial *fatwā*.' The edict was an unfortunate fact, as was the still vehement hatred of Rushdie in some quarters (and the bounty on Rushdie's head), but five years after Khomeini's death, signs were building that Iran wanted to extricate itself from its pariah status, because, as Doucet put it, 'Political and economic affairs continue to suffer.' But she added, 'Ayatollah Khomeini died shortly after he proclaimed the controversial edict, but his voice still resounds on Iranian media, almost as if he never left. In some ways he hasn't. No Iranian politician can rein in a *fatwā* which is now as much about politics as religion, and neither British not Iranian diplomats have found a way around that'.

Rushdie's life did at least seem to be improving. On 16 March 1995, he gave another interview to *Today*. The Council of Europe had urged its 49 member states to 'refrain from trade and other relations with Iran until these threats are removed'. It was a welcome declaration, but James Naughtie questioned its significance:

> Naughtie: Do you worry sometimes that although you get grand statements, delivered after great deliberations in bodies like the Council of Europe, in fact you've slipped out of the headlines a bit, governments aren't running around saying this is dreadful, we've got to do something about it, and that really, after six years, it doesn't look as if it's going to end quickly?

Rushdie: Well, I'm afraid, I think you're probably right about that, and I think there is a lot of talk and relatively little action. I must say I was rather disappointed recently when there was a meeting between the minister Douglas Hogg [Conservative minister of state at the Foreign Office] and representatives of my defence campaign, and basically what they were told by Mr Hogg was that the Foreign Office policy... on this issue was to wait for a change of government in Iran. That strikes me as being, let's say, not the most dynamic policy one could hope for.

Naughtie: He would say that it was simply a statement of realism.

Rushdie: Well, realism is what you make it, isn't it?... The point that we've been banging on about for years now is that Iran is not a country impervious to pressure. The question is whether people choose to put that pressure on it.

Naughtie: Now, you're out and about a bit more these days, but does it still feel as if you were in prison?

Rushdie: Well, it feels less as if I'm locked up in a room than it used to, but the fact is I'm told by the British security that the threat remains, and that the threat is really from only one source, which is the government of Iran and its acolytes. So that's why one is concentrating on that, and it really must be solved, because whereas I know there are some criticisms – particularly from the right wing of the Tory party – about the cost of this protection and its maintenance; let me tell you that nobody is more fed up with it than me, and I would be the first person who would wish it to end. And that's why I'm encouraging the government to bring about a situation in which it can end.

The breakthrough came in 1998, when Iran publicly stated it would not carry out the 'sentence' against Rushdie. His true re-entry into something resembling normal life could begin. He even did some ironic film acting in the romantic comedy *Bridget Jones's Diary* (2001), playing himself at a glittering book launch – a social event inconceivable in the earlier years of his ordeal. Although the *fatwā* could never be revoked formally, with every passing year memory of it recedes.

As for the book that caused the furore, it remained in print throughout, and well beyond, the nine years of the 'Rushdie Affair', slowly making the argument to be judged on its literary merits rather than on the noise of the *fatwā*.

The press, the politicians and the Australian entrepreneur

'You simply could not argue with the power of the Murdoch empire'
NICK ROBINSON, 8 JULY 2011

On 8 July 2011 the BBC's political editor Nick Robinson told *Today* listeners:

> For 20 years… it has been a view that no one challenged at the top of either of the big parties… either Labour or the Conservatives, that you simply could not argue with the power of the Murdoch empire. You invited them to your parties, they came to your house, you went to their weddings, you did anything, really, that you could do to get in with these people and not really to challenge them.

The foundations of that empire were laid by Rupert Murdoch's father, the Australian newspaperman Sir Keith Murdoch. Murdoch senior was based in London during the First World War. He covered the Gallipoli campaign as a correspondent and formed a friendship with the press baron Lord Northcliffe, the founder of the *Daily Mail*. He returned to Australia as the chief editor of the *Melbourne Herald,* and from the mid-1920s led a campaign to take over other Australian papers – following the Northcliffe playbook so closely that he was nicknamed 'Lord Southcliffe'. Rupert Murdoch inherited his father's News Ltd in 1953 at the age of 22, not long after leaving Oxford, where he had joined the Labour Party.

For 15 years Murdoch worked on building an Australian media empire across that continent, purchasing widely dispersed regional papers and founding one national one. In 1969, he made an audacious move – one of many throughout his career – by launching himself on the UK market, snapping up the top-selling *News of the World,* beating off a rival bid from British publishing tycoon Robert Maxwell in the process. It was a foothold in the British market, and later that year he again beat Maxwell when he acquired the *Sun*, then a left-leaning broadsheet.

Murdoch turned the *Sun* into the brashest tabloid. Its page three girls removed their tops in 1970, and by 1978 it was selling four million copies, overtaking the *Mirror* as the country's top-selling newspaper. The *Sun* soon demonstrated the political clout that came with those circulation figures; its editor, Larry Lamb, turned the phrase

'Winter of Discontent' into a headline to describe the outbreak of industrial action in the winter months of 1978–9, and damned Prime Minister James Callaghan's too-easy unflappability amid strike-ridden Britain in another memorable splash under 'Crisis? What Crisis?' The paper swung solidly behind Margaret Thatcher in the 1979 election. Her Falklands War gave it perhaps its most striking (and controversial) front page: the word 'Gotcha' printed above an image of the sinking Argentinian cruiser *General Belgrano*.

Murdoch had already made inroads into American journalism, buying the *New York Post*. In Britain, although he now owned two popular papers, he had not yet tried his hand in the broadsheet market. But that changed in 1981 with his hugely controversial purchase of the paper once dubbed the 'Thunderer', the most famous newspaper in the world – *The Times* – along with its sister paper, *The Sunday Times*.

It was widely assumed that his bid to own these papers in addition to the *Sun* and *News of the World* would require scrutiny by the Monopolies and Mergers Commission because of the press power that would now become concentrated in Murdoch's hands. But, amid circumstances still contested, including – it was later revealed – a lunch with Prime Minister Margaret Thatcher, this scrutiny did not happen. Murdoch's new acquisition received parliamentary approval on the basis that the papers were on their last legs financially. In the view of Harold Evans, the then editor of *The Sunday Times*, who was trying to put together a management-buyout package for both papers, 'The greatest extension of monopoly power in modern press history was planned and executed with such furtive brilliance.'

The next stage of the Murdoch revolution was to transform the means of production. 'To be in Fleet Street is to be at the heart' of newspapers, Murdoch said in 1969. However, once he had acquired his four national papers, his love for the place turned sour, not least because of its strictly defined roles and closed-shop union practices. The advent of new computer and printing technology, the availability of a small army of replacement workers, and very careful planning allowed him to effect an industry coup. Murdoch's News International consolidated operations for its papers in a purpose-built site at Wapping, sacking thousands of striking print-union workers overnight in January 1986.

The papers' journalists were offered a straightforward bribe-cum-threat: accept a £2,000 bonus (a considerable sum at that time) and come to Wapping, or face the sack. On 3 February 1986 *Today* broadcast interviews with some of the strikers on the picket line, and they were asked about those journalists who had taken the Murdoch shilling:

Although we see them on the television crying that they didn't want to come to Wapping, I suppose when you see £2,000... but I don't think they're happy, and I wonder how many of them are going to be left here at the end of the year, still working for Mr Murdoch.

Another striker, imagining a sweatshop in 'Fort Wapping', as he called it, explained he had 'come out on strike for a great principle: that someone was pinching my job'. In the ensuing year-long dispute, involving pitched battles between thousands of strikers and police outside Wapping's high fences, Murdoch triumphed, and every day his newspapers continued to appear – each edition another hammer-blow on the coffin nails of the old practices. Within a few years, most major papers had followed Murdoch's lead and headed east to the London Docklands developments.

By this time, Murdoch's global, multi-media aspirations were well established, and he was living mainly in New York. He had added to his media empire 20th Century Fox films and was launching the Fox national TV network in the US. In the UK he also had televisual ambitions in the shape of the new satellite broadcaster Sky, which in 1990 merged with competitor BSB – both were losing money at the time.

In 1992, as Nick Robinson reminded *Today*'s audience in his review of Murdoch's political influence, the *Sun* had deployed a devastating election-day headline against Neil Kinnock's Labour Party: 'If Kinnock wins today will the last person to leave Britain please turn out the lights.' Kinnock lost – against the evidence of most polls – and the *Sun*'s follow-up front page claimed, 'It's the *Sun* wot won it!' When Tony Blair became Labour leader he took due note of that history, making time in his diary in the summer of 1995 to fly to Australia for a rendezvous with the press baron. The BBC political correspondent Steve Richards travelled with Blair, and challenged him about whether the trip was justified. The interview was broadcast on *Today* on 15 July 1995.

> Richards: It might be seen as a pretty extreme act to take, to spend in effect 48 hours in an aeroplane to make one speech in front of Rupert Murdoch. Is this not perhaps overestimating the power his newspapers might have in this country?

> Blair: Well, that's a matter of personal inconvenience, but this is a conference of people from the organisation all round the world, so you're reaching much more simply than the British press, and that is important. It's given me an opportunity, obviously to meet the Australian prime minister [Paul Keating] and colleagues in the Australian Labour Party, but it's important also because, you know, there are huge changes that are happening politically, culturally, technologically, that these very large media outlets, operating on a worldwide basis, have a big role in and big part to play in, and I think it's tremendously important that we make sure that at least we understand where each other's coming from.

> Richards: Given that, how important do you see it to get either the endorsement of a newspaper like the *Sun* at the next election, or certainly to avoid the vilification that Neil Kinnock experienced at the last one?

> Blair: I'm not coming here, sort of, looking for endorsements and all the rest or anything of that nature. However, I think what is important is that the Labour Party's obviously changed dramatically since the early Eighties, and even since before the last election when relations were at their nadir, if you like, between the Labour Party and elements in the press – not just the Murdoch press, but elsewhere. And, of course, I am anxious to make sure that if people are criticising us, it's at least for what we are saying not for some misrepresentation.

Power flows both ways in the relationship between politicians and the press – as Murdoch's success when he bought *The Times* had demonstrated. The interview continued:

> Richards: There's been much talk of you wooing the Murdoch press, but, of course, he issued the invitation, and he to some extent will be wooing you. You know what his worries will be: that his current dominance in Britain in newspapers and broadcasting will be threatened by Labour's desire for greater diversity of ownership. Are those threats justified, or will you be offering him reassurances that, largely, his empire would remain unchanged under a Labour government?

> Blair: Well, I'm not offering any changes of policy in what the Labour Party has done, but what we want – because of the way that the whole market has changed – is an open, competitive market that has diversity in it. Because new opportunities are being opened up, and I think that that's very clearly understood, not just within the Labour Party but also outside of it too.

In the event, New Labour *did* win the *Sun*'s approbation – and, despite some choppy waters, retained it in subsequent elections, too, and even beyond Blair's tenure as Labour leader for a while. But on 30 September 2009, *Today*'s James Naughtie, broadcasting from the Labour Party Conference in Brighton, informed his listeners:

> The news that the *Sun* newspaper is throwing its weight behind the Conservatives reached the Labour conference last night just as people were gathering at the evening drinks reception in a reasonably jolly mood after Gordon Brown's speech.

'It was,' Naughtie explained, 'perhaps not an entirely surprising decision in the Rupert Murdoch camp – they haven't liked Mr Brown for quite a while.' BBC political correspondent Iain Watson had managed to interview the *Sun*'s Trevor Kavanagh, formerly the paper's political editor and still an influential figure in the Murdoch empire, at Brighton's Grand Hotel, and wondered how far criticism of the UK's media regulation by James Murdoch, son of Rupert, had influenced the decision. 'I don't think that was a factor at all', Kavanagh loyally asserted. 'I think that it's the readership that we represent, who feel let down by a government which has, in many ways, spent an awful lot of their tax money on projects which they regard as wasteful in some respects, and not for their best benefits and interests.'

Watson had also canvassed opinion among senior Labour figures attending the News International conference drinks party. He found the home secretary, Alan Johnson, more sanguine than some of his colleagues about the *Sun*'s defection: 'It's a free press. The politician that complains about the media is like the sailor who complains about the sea.'

By the end of the first decade of the new millennium, traditional newspapers were themselves experiencing great flux, tossed about in an ocean of new media, and the voice of a single newspaper, even a bestselling one, was not as loud as it used to be. The Murdoch operation was also threatened from within, by the return of old accusations about phone hacking. These would, ultimately, plunge the Murdoch empire into crisis and expose the sometimes cosy networks of press and power that operated at the highest levels. James Naughtie brought *Today* listeners up to date on the twists and turns of the story on 6 July 2011:

> It seems that the floodgates are opening at the *News of the World*: the alleged hacking of Milly Dowler's phone; the warning by Scotland Yard to one of the families of a victim of the 7/7 bombings, and to the families of the murdered Soham schoolgirls, that they may have been targeted; emails found by Rupert Murdoch's News International that indicate that the *News of the World* was making payments to the police while the paper was being edited by Andy Coulson, who of course went on to become [Prime Minister] David Cameron's communications director.

This phone-hacking saga was exposing a lurid, unedifying tale of invasion of privacy, greed, corruption, cover-up and terrible decision-making, drawing in the press, the police and politicians. Four years previously, the *News of the World* royal editor, Clive Goodman, and his private-investigator source, Glenn Mulcaire, had been convicted and imprisoned for conspiring to hack the phones of Royal Family aides, but despite – in James Naughtie's words – 'the efforts of Rupert Murdoch's empire to shut it down', the story had not ended there.

The full ramifications of the scandal began to become apparent in 2011. As the presenter of BBC Radio 4's *The Media Show*, Steve Hewlett, told *Today* listeners on 22 January 2011, 'Not even the judge in the original trial believed that the private investigator Glenn Mulcaire had only dealt with royal editor Clive Goodman.' The police had chosen not to follow other leads contained in Mulcaire's notebooks. But that did not mean the leads did not exist. 'All the evidence,' Hewlett concluded, 'which is now proving so troublesome for News International has been there from the start.' Particularly egregious, in the public's eyes, was the revelation that the phone of murdered schoolgirl Milly Dowler had been hacked when she had first gone missing in 2002, potentially misleading police and her parents into believing she was still alive. And the phone-hacking scandal came just as News International's parent company, News Corporation, was attempting to win official favour as it navigated media-competition rules in order to take full control of BSkyB.

The prime minister, David Cameron, was touched by the scandal in a manner summarised by Nick Robinson on *Today*, on 8 July 2011:

> **I think the Cameron circle know that this is the third great crisis of trust in recent years. We had the banks. We had MPs' expenses. Now we have the press, and he finds himself right at the centre of that, tainted by the past – because of his decision to hire Andy Coulson, and his friendship with Rebekah Brooks and his relationship with the Murdochs – and responsible for the future. Not just the future of press ethics, not just the future of inquiries into the police, but the future of the relationship between British politicians and the most powerful media organisation in Britain.**

Rebekah Brooks (previously known as Rebekah Wade) was now News International's chief executive, but in the 2000s she had been editor of the *News of the World* and later the *Sun*. Andy Coulson had been editor of the *News of the World* from 2003 until 2007, when he resigned over the Goodman and Mulcaire trial, although he insisted he had known nothing about what they were doing. He became the Conservative Party's director of communications that same year, and David Cameron took him to Downing Street in 2010. He was forced to resign less than a year later, in January 2011, amid continued allegations that the scale of phone-hacking at the *News of the World* had been much wider than anyone realised. Coulson would eventually receive an 18-month prison sentence for conspiracy to hack phones.

The Labour Party was able to extract some political advantage from the scandal, not only because their MP Tom Watson had been doggedly pursuing the issue for years and was now being vindicated, but because, as Nick Robinson put it on *Today*, leader Ed Miliband had finally 'found his voice':

> **It's only a few days ago that people were saying that he wasn't up to the job. He has found a cause. He's united a party that for a very long time has been hugely frustrated by being seen to pay homage, if you like, to the Murdoch empire, and**

he's taken a very big bet, of course, because if indeed Rupert Murdoch carries on being a powerful figure, he's no friend of Ed Miliband.

In what was both a *coup de théâtre* and a *coup de grâce*, Murdoch implemented a dramatic decision. For *Today*, on 8 July 2011, presenter Justin Webb described what had happened:

> 'Take action,' cried the critics of News International, and take action they did; but it was, in typical Murdoch style, not the action the people had expected. The closure of the *News of the World* is a bombshell, but for many of its staff and many outsiders, it was the wrong bombshell. The accounts from insiders of the speech made to *News of the World* staff by Rebekah Brooks – chief executive of News International, editor of the *News of the World* when Milly Dowler's phone was hacked – speak of their utter amazement. They assumed she was going to announce her departure. Instead, she announced theirs, and she took no questions.

Today's Tom Bateman had gathered reaction from *News of the World* staff at the Cape pub, 'a favourite', I am told, 'with a lot of the reporters'. He spoke to Jules Stenson, the *News of the World*'s head of features:

> Bateman: How are you feeling after what's happened today?
>
> Stenson: We're devastated, collectively. The paper's been going for 168 years. We won four press awards this year. We were nominated for 11. That was the most nominations we've ever had. We're on a creative high and, you know, the rug's been pulled from our feet. There's collective devastation. There wasn't a lynch-mob mentality, as [it was reported] there was, a kind of pride in the paper and utter shock and bewilderment – but no lynch mob.
>
> Bateman: How were you told?
>
> Stenson: Told by Rebekah Brooks this afternoon. There was no prior warning. She made an announcement, talked about the horrific events of the last week, which we all share her sentiments about how awful it's been, and then she made the announcement about the closure.

'Nobody who works in that newsroom,' complained one stunned journalist, 'had anything to do with any of those things that happened in the past.'

Less than two weeks later, on 19 July 2011, Rupert Murdoch and his son James appeared before a select committee of MPs to answer questions, amid intense media scrutiny. It was, Murdoch said, the 'most humble day of my life'. The press baron reiterated his 'zero-tolerance' policy towards wrongdoing at his newspapers, while also denying that he, his family or other executives could have known the more granular goings-on of their empire. A moment of silent-comedy farce disrupted the decorum when Rupert Murdoch was attacked by an angry onlooker with a foam pie.

If the purpose of closing the *News of the World* was to draw a line under past wrongdoing, it was a tactic that failed. The BSkyB bid had to be abandoned, and new improprieties emerged at the *Sun* – it was always hard to believe that phone-hacking was limited to just one newspaper. The Leveson Inquiry began to investigate the hacking scandal and press freedom. For some time, the very name 'Murdoch' was looking toxic, scaring the other shareholders in the empire, and damage limitation was in order. James Murdoch took a lower profile, and News Corporation split itself into newspapers/publishing and the more profitable TV and film divisions.

On 24 May 2018, Les Hinton, News International's chief executive at the time of the hackings, was reflecting on past events with John Humphrys on *Today*. He described how, when tendering his own resignation from the Murdoch empire at the time of the Milly Dowler revelations, he had found Murdoch 'shattered... slumped in his chair, wringing his old hands, his glasses had fallen down his nose, and he looked at me and said, "This is the worst day of my life."' It was brought about by the very newspaper with which Murdoch had begun his international expansion.

Musicians in interview – an evolution

'You hear my heart and soul screaming in pain or joy'
JOHN LYDON, 19 OCTOBER 2014

'We're in London with one of the most fabulous women in the world today.'

'Oh!'

'She's that delectable exciting firecracker Shirley Bassey!'

'Oh! Flattery will get you everywhere.'

'Shirley, the turbulent, tempestuous, but successful and unhappy Sixties are over. What do the Seventies hold for the new mature Shirley?'

'Oh, lots of lovely things! If this is how I feel at 30, I can't wait to be 40, you know!'

A *Today* devotee tuning in to the programme on 17 April 1971 would have caught this torrent between interviewer Keith Alexander and singer Shirley Bassey. It's fair to say that – as a sampling of *Today* encounters over the years suggests – the art of the musical interview has come a long way since then. In 1971 the fact that Shirley Bassey was a woman, rather than discussing her music, seemed to dictate the interview territory. Her husband was alongside her.

'I was, um, neurotic, and now I'm sort of calm,' Bassey admitted, at which point Alexander leapt in: 'What's brought about the change – your marriage to Sergio Novak?' She was, as she said, enjoying having 'security now, and I have a man that takes care of me'.

Turning his attention to the man in question, Alexander asked, 'Sergio, you have a dual role: husband and also manager. What's she like to manage these days?'

'It is a difficult thing to manage an artist of her size,' Sergio replied, which turned out to mean, as Bassey herself decoded, that she was 'temperamental'.

'Does she change when she goes on stage? Is she a different person?' Alexander asked. There was a vague sense that Bassey wasn't present.

Sergio admitted he found her to be, 'Two different women. One is the artist with, er, its advantages and disadvantages... And the other one is the woman who forgets about the stage and becomes a plain, normal woman.'

Bassey chipped in to confirm that as a 'normal woman' she would, 'come home and put on an apron and go in the kitchen and still have time to fool around with the children.' She added, 'And he's constantly amazed that there are these two characters.' Sergio conceded the point, remarking that 'at the beginning you were not able to leave Shirley Bassey completely on stage and become Shirley Bassey, woman.'

It was a very different era.

The following month the musical guest was the smooth American crooner Perry Como, who was by then nearly 60. He appeared on the programme on 3 May 1971, and was clearly a man not to be ruffled. 'I'm doing as little as I can right now. I do a little television. I do a few records here and there. I do a little golfing, a little fishing.'

'You've been a star now for, well, as long as I can remember,' observed his interviewer, the *Today* presenter Malcolm Billings. Billings enquired whether Como had in mind any new musical avenues, any surprises?

'I've been doing the same thing for, hmm, 35 years, and they've told me in many ways that they don't want the change, you know.'

'People do expect your relaxed style, don't they?' agreed Billings, to which the megastar replied, 'Relaxed or tired or whatever you want to call it... Basically, I think I'm that kind of person.'

Como's life had in fact involved some very hard graft indeed. The seventh of ten children born to first-generation Italian-immigrant parents in Pennsylvania, he began work at ten and by the age of 14 had set up his own barber shop. And he had risen to the very top of the music business, as Billings reminded him:

> **When you were here last, 11 years ago, you were reported as being the most highly paid entertainer in the world. You were – I think you were – getting something like £9 million for a television show.**

Even that figure, very large today, but astonishingly huge in the 1960s, failed to draw out anything like an admission of exertion. 'Money isn't too hard to make in our profession, you know,' Como replied languidly. And, remembering the hit that had made his name, 'Till the End of Time' ('the old Chopin melody'), he knew that his back catalogue would provide an ample pension: 'Those old things always sell.'

Several months later, on 30 October 1971, *Today* listeners heard from a versatile singer-songwriter with a crystal voice, Judy Collins, who had emerged during the 1960s from the US folk-revival scene. She was, like many singers of her generation, deeply involved in the anti-Vietnam War protest movement, and campaigned against the military draft system which was used to send young conscripts off to fight. She may not have reached quite the dizzying financial heights of laid-back Perry Como, but she was successful enough to prompt a question about her money and her left-wing politics from the interviewer, Tony Aspler:

> Aspler: Is a contradiction in your life that you sing protest songs, you try and get people on the move, and yet you make a lot of money out of it?

> Collins: It is a conflict, sure. There's always that conflict. You know... How does one deal with success in a monetary way? And I think we all have our different ways of dealing with [it]. I support a lot of things that I believe in. Um, I give a good percentage of my money to things that are important to me. In this business of the draft, for instance – part of the money from this new record is going to the ACLU [American Civil Liberties Union], which tries to legally change the draft laws.

In many ways, Collins embodied the figure of the Vietnam-era protest singer: simultaneously engaged and otherworldly. She acknowledged how crowded the politicised music scene had become – yet she did not regard this as a threat to her own niche, but instead welcomed the multiplicity of voices:

> The popular music area has, at least in the States, enlarged itself, to include many, many subjects that before weren't touched in popular music: the problems with the ecology, the problems that men have who are faced with the draft, the problems that black people have, Puerto Ricans, Chicanos – popular music today encompasses so much more of that and it's marvellous.

'I don't,' she added, 'sing a song unless I feel it's a good song and I relate to it,' assuring listeners that her musical antennae tested the air first. She would go on to perform and record for several decades, with notable successes as diverse as 'Amazing Grace' and Stephen Sondheim's 'Send in the Clowns'.

Longer even than Collins's career has been that of Cliff Richard. On the *Today* broadcast of 4 August 1972, in an interview with Malcolm Billings, Richard reflected with his usual boyish enthusiasm on his enduring relationship with 1950s rock 'n' roll. Although The Beatles had begun their own musical journey by trying to define themselves as everything that Cliff Richard and the Shadows were *not*, they all shared a common ancestry in the peculiarly British skiffle revival of the period, before encountering the sounds from across the Atlantic:

> No one tried to compete with Elvis, no one ever tried to compete with Bill Haley. They were just sort of phenomena... You just revered from a distance. Bill Haley

was something fantastic, I mean *phenomenal*. I mean, I remember queuing up from about three or four in the morning 'til about ten in the morning just to get tickets. I mean, I know kids sleep out all night, but to me... I've never done that for anybody since or before.

The United States did not repay the compliment to Cliff – his music did not travel that way – but his home turf rewarded him with a monster career and a loyal fan base, even if critical acclaim was in short supply. His espousal of a Christian lifestyle, in contrast to his peers' various forms of counter-cultural rebellion, debarred him from achieving *authentic* rock-star status in the eyes of many. But, in this relaxed interview with Billings, he expressed his love for his musical roots and for that *one* part of the trinity of sex and drugs and rock 'n' roll that appealed to him. He had his place in history, too, having performed 'the first real rock 'n' roll record to be made in England; it was called "Move It" and I'm very proud it was one of the first.'

Much later – 36 years, to be precise, on 27 October 2008 – *Today* presenter Evan Davis encountered another musician who had also made a bid for a place in history, with a possibly unique skill-set. It was immediately clear from Davis's introduction that this was not going to be your run-of-the-mill showbiz interview:

> Unlikely as this may sound, the American rapper 50 Cent has produced a book on how to get ahead in business. He knows a thing or two about it, actually. He made a name for himself with the album *Get Rich or Die Tryin'*. He in fact did get rich – very rich – and he did almost die trying. He was shot nine times in an incident in 2000. The new book, which is more interesting than many other business books, I can assure you, is called *The 50th Law*. It's written with Robert Greene and is based on 50 Cent's early... experiences hustling on the streets of Southside Queens, selling drugs. The book is about getting on in business by overcoming your fears.

What Davis wanted to know was, were there 'parallels between the world he grew up in and modern corporate life?' The rapper (real name Curtis Jackson) suggested that ordering a hit on the opposition as a way for a crime boss to 'expand business' was comparable, if not quite literally, with attempts to kill the competition in 'corporate America'. As for fear, he felt his own had dissipated since his shooting, since he had acquired a sense of perspective:

> The core of my power is me being in business situations and being the person with the least fear at the table. And that's because I weigh these things up against my biggest losses in my life, so, like, the loss of my mom is the biggest thing that I've experienced.

'The book,' Davis ventured, 'does describe some fairly nasty incidents... In the chapter about the Hustler King, you slash the face of a rival's assistant who's out to hurt you...'

> **Davis: Looking back on all of that, how do you .. feel? 'Cause you've just, sort of, moved so far away from that now.**

> **50 Cent: Yeah, I did, but, you know, like, I think the things you go through make you who you are, so I don't regret those things. I don't regret them because I don't think I'd be who I am today if I wasn't exposed to those situations. Those are unfortunate situations that I've had to experience, and if I'd have had a choice, I would have definitely went in a different direction – I might have went to go to school for business instead of having to go through [that] portion of my life.**

Then there was the music and its relationship with aggression; Davis described the world of rap, or hip-hop, as 'bizarre'. 'I have to ask you why you have all these "beefs" with people? You just get into – get into arguments with people all the time, feuds. What's going on?' 50 Cent put it this way:

> **The competitive nature of hip-hop has always been one of the driving forces, one of the elements in the art form that keeps it thriving... I'm in more feuds than the average artist, because I'm more vocal, I generate more interest, and I'm obviously in a space that they'd actually like to be in.**

Unlike Cliff Richard, 50 Cent had no qualms about indulging in many of his profession's outsize rewards, as he readily acknowledged: 'The big house is still there, the nice cars are there, the attractive women are there.' Davis made it through the interview with apparent relief: 'Actually,' he informed *Today* listeners, 'we always have a problem with what you call rap artists. I know Jeremy Paxman interviewed Dizzee Rascal and called him "Mr Rascal"... so I just avoided calling him anything during the interview.'

If the pairing of the BBC's former economics editor with a rap performer who had a reputation as a slasher was an unexpected combination, potentially stranger still was the encounter between *Today*'s John Humphrys and the former Sex Pistols frontman Johnny Rotten (real name John Lydon) on 19 October 2014. Listeners of a certain age would have remembered that the band achieved its instant notoriety by virtue of an earlier, potty-mouthed interview in 1976, which went out before the watershed. 'He shocked the nation. He was denounced as a traitor in the House of Commons. He railed against the Establishment,' continued Humphrys in his introduction. 'But,' he added, 'you can hardly call him an "angry young man" any longer, because of course he's no longer young, he's 58... He's been on reality television. He's advertised butter.' Was Johnny Rotten perhaps, like Perry Como, heading off to play a little golf? Not yet.

Lydon did admit to being 'vastly more experienced' because 'like a fine wine, I've learned to mature with age'. What, Humphrys wondered, was the difference between the Johnny Rotten years and the John Lydon years? Lydon rejected the idea that the Sex Pistols were about trying to shock. Instead, as he put it:

> I felt that that was just me being angry and expressing my anger as honestly as I could, and I was quite amazed by the resentment that that kicked up in a lot of people... I was offering a more honest approach and a much more sensible message; a direct assault, if you want, on mediocrity.

Between then and now, he felt:

> The subject matter is different, it's now personal politics rather than the political slant I used in the Sex Pistols, and I felt I needed to because there was no hope for none of us at that time. There was unemployment, there was trash and rubbish everywhere, and all manner of nonsenses, and it was kinda like apt that I dealt with it in song.

Punctuating their jocular, sparring conversation were snatches of the band's guitar-thrashing hits – the politically provocative (terrifying to some) 'Anarchy in the UK', the ironic, almost post-modern 'Pretty Vacant' and the Cold War- and Berlin-obsessed 'Holiday in the Sun'. Missing from the playlist was 'God Save the Queen', with its rhyming reference to the fascist regime – which was banned by the BBC when it came out in 1977.

When Humphrys suggested that 'what you were doing then was what every young person with a bit of energy and a bit of interest in life is [doing], and that is being anti-Establishment', Lydon demurred strongly: 'I was standing up and being counted... I made my opinions very clear... It was no fun to be discussed in the Houses of Parliament under a traitors' and treasons act... It carried a death sentence.' His last point was an exaggeration, but he swiftly curtailed the suggestion that it was all 'good publicity': 'Let's get serious, right?' he told the presenter.

Above all, Lydon told Humphrys:

> I've got a different angle here, lyric-wise, that's always been my thing. I mean, I love reading, I love writing. The best I can do or offer you is in my songs. You hear my heart and soul screaming in pain or joy or bliss or anger. All of these things, they come from inside me.

Humphrys conceded that Lydon had 'had a lasting influence on music', but, he asserted, 'What you haven't succeeded in doing is changing society.' But this was a burden that Lydon rejected ('You put an awful lot on me, don't you?'). The message of his work was, rather: 'Don't dictate to me that I should toe the line along with the rest of you, because I'm not going to do that.'

And finally they got to butter. A few years earlier, the British viewing public had raised a collective eyebrow when a tweed-clad Johnny Rotten had appeared on their screens extolling the virtues of Country Life butter. For Humphrys, this was proof that Lydon was now 'part of the Establishment'. 'Am I not allowed to eat?!' exclaimed a theatrically indignant Lydon. 'It's a food product, and it's one I like... Look at me, I put the weight on. It's not just beer. It's butter too!'

What concerned Humphrys was that Lydon/Rotten was trying to have it both ways as insider–outsider, but his interviewee was having none of that:

> Don't tell me what to do. Don't tell me nothing. Don't tell me what to wear. Don't tell me what to think. I mean you no harm. I let you trundle on as merrily as you like. I'm indifferent to that, so long as you do not step into my space.

When they got back onto music, Lydon rejected any idea of a 'Sex Pistols: The Musical'. Not only would it be 'a very short musical. The album was, what, 40 minutes at most?', but this man-who-refused-to-be-pigeonholed took a dim view of 'a bunch of strangers contemplating my navel'.

There were, perhaps, two big surprises in that interview: that the worst insult Johnny Rotten came up with was calling John Humphrys a 'silly sausage', and that the musician whom Humphrys described as the 'high priest of punk' found 'the idea of doing *Jesus Christ Superstar*... a thrilling prospect'. Johnny Rotten performing Andrew Lloyd Webber? Stranger things have happened.

Today and the BBC – scrutinising the parent

'What political pressures have been exerted?'

CHRIS MORRIS, 5 JUNE 1980

'Now what is going on *at* the BBC, *with* the BBC, *to* the BBC?' asked *Today*'s Brian Redhead in September 1992. 'The BBC is in a state of crisis!' exclaimed John Humphrys in January 2004. Six years later, on 8 March 2010, the same *Today* presenter was quizzing former BBC governor P D James: 'You are not happy for all sorts of different reasons with the way the BBC has developed over the years. What's wrong with it, as we speak?'

A regular *Today* listener could be forgiven for imagining the BBC to be an organisation prone to perpetual meltdowns. Yet the very fact that listeners were hearing these interrogations of the BBC *on* the BBC's *Today* programme was a reminder of the singular status of the broadcasting organisation, and in a sense a sign of health. The real crisis in the nation's broadcasting would be if a programme such as *Today* was no longer in a position to ask these questions of its parent organisation.

The BBC's public-service remit means that if the organisation itself becomes the subject of news, even if critical or adverse, it is more or less obligatory for the organisation to report it, as it would do any other newsworthy event. More than that, its reputation and credibility *rely* on it not brushing whatever topic it may be under the carpet. Public self-scrutiny, in other words, which is alien to the fixed-smile, good-news-only PR agendas of most commercial companies, is part of the BBC ethos. The BBC must be answerable to the public, to its millions of licence-fee payers who are, in a manner of speaking, shareholders. In day-to-day terms, this means that although the BBC is hierarchical, periodically the movers and shakers of BBC leadership find themselves in the *Today* studio, at the sharp end, to justify themselves before these 'shareholders'.

While this has been a recurring feature of the programme through the decades, much has changed over the years. It was in a much more deferential and easy-going age that Charles Curran rose to become BBC director general and was interviewed on 1 April 1969 by Brian Johnston, later to become famous as 'Johnners' of the *Test Match Special* team, but at this stage of his career making occasional contributions to *Today*. Curran was invited onto the programme to be introduced to the public and welcomed to his new role, rather than to defend this or that policy decision:

> Johnston: Now what about your private life? We can delve into that in a second. What are your sort of hobbies and activities?

> Curran: Well, I put one down in *Who's Who* about a year ago as refereeing coarse rugby. It was a bit of a joke, really. I do listen to an awful lot of music, go to concerts, chamber music and so on – but apart from that, one's work takes up an awful lot of time.

'Are you a sort of comedy man?' Johnston continued, genially. 'Do you think that making people laugh is one of the objects of the BBC?'

'Indeed it is,' replied the new director general, happy to endorse Marty Feldman's comedy vehicle *Marty* and, from an earlier radio era, *The Goon Show*.

'And finally,' Johnston asked, 'when you sit down at the director general's desk, what's going to be the very first thing you do?'

> Curran: Well, I know what'll happen: somebody'll bring me in a great pile of papers and say, 'This is what you've got to deal with today,' and the first thing I've got to do is decide which of them I throw away.

> Johnston: And you believe in throwing away paper, if you can?

> Curran: As much as possible.

Three years later, Curran was again on *Today*, this time facing a tougher grilling – from the public, who have always had strong views on the content of BBC programmes. On the morning of 13 November 1972 he responded to listeners' questions and complaints in a live phone-in. One listener was notably exercised:

> Why does the BBC continue to show the programme *Till Death Us Do Part*, which in its blasphemy and obscenity is really offensive to a very large number of Christians, particularly when there's some wording on the outside wall of the BBC – I think it's over the door – which dedicates the BBC and its work to Almighty God? Can you answer that?

The director general apologised for a particularly 'inappropriate' allusion to the Virgin Mary being 'allegedly or supposedly on the pill', but otherwise came to this TV comedy series' defence. Curran agreed that the show's larger-than-life antihero Alf Garnett was famously 'foul-mouthed and he's bigoted and he's ill-tempered and he's really revolting', but Curran noted that he was therefore a comedy construct, rather than a messenger to be taken literally. Curran could not quite convince his caller, though, that patriotism, belief in God and devotion to the Queen were not being mocked. 'Well, there we are,' said *Today*'s John Timpson, wrapping it up: on this particular occasion, the BBC and the *Today* listener would have to agree to disagree.

For many decades, the director general – the 'CEO' of the BBC – reported in turn to the BBC's governors and their chair. The governors' role was, at a high level, to represent the interests of viewers and listeners and where necessary hold management to account, but they also were the interface between the BBC and Parliament. Sometimes the governors, too, came under the spotlight on *Today*, defending BBC actions or policy. One such occasion was on 5 June 1980, before that year's Moscow Olympic Games. Following the Soviet invasion of Afghanistan the year before, some nations (including the USA) had chosen either to boycott the games completely or send reduced teams of competitors. Great Britain was in the latter category, and British politicians were divided over how much the BBC should cover the event.

Chris Morris, a BBC news presenter and correspondent, was keen to get to the bottom of suggestions that the BBC had been leant on. 'Why,' he asked BBC chairman Sir Michael Swann, 'has the television coverage been so drastically reduced when, after all, the British team is still going?' In particular, he wanted to know 'what political pressures have been exerted' and especially whether 'Mrs Thatcher's [prime minister] request that the television cameras should be reduced' had browbeaten the BBC into submission. Sir Michael was keen to stress that 'a lot of very important countries have pulled out' and that 'It is not the original Olympics. It's nothing like it.' Nevertheless, he acknowledged the games retained 'a considerable amount of interest for British people' and had 'tried to settle it entirely on the basis of its sporting value, which is nothing like what it was but is not nil'. 'I think,' he continued:

> The viewers are just as aware as we are that it's not what it was, and a medal at this Olympics is not like a medal at a real Olympics. I mean, it doesn't have anything like the same value. The medals are tarnished. How much they're tarnished I suppose depends on individual opinions, but I think that viewers will accept that it's the right level of coverage for the very complicated situation with unpleasant political overtones that we find ourselves in, and my guess is that some people may think it's not enough and others will think it's too much. Well, that's a pretty familiar situation in the BBC.

He was correct: built into the fabric of the BBC is a certain inevitability of being 'damned if you do, damned if you don't' when it comes to matters of editorial judgement and taste. The right of the viewing and listening British public to give their opinions and advice is a price the BBC must pay for the public-funding formula of the licence fee.

The beginning of the 1990s saw significant and controversial internal restructuring at the BBC in the run-up to the 1997 renewal of its charter – the document which, in the organisation's own description, 'provides the constitutional basis' for the BBC, framing how it is governed and funded. It was the lead-up to these changes that saw another round of public self-scrutiny, and caused Brian Redhead to wonder just what was going on at the BBC in September 1992. Trying to explain in the *Today* studio was director general Michael Checkland.

Checkland tried to stress that the BBC would continue to do 'everything that we have done well', but perhaps 'not so many quizzes' or 'lower-cost purchase programmes that we've sometimes put into our schedules'. He was adamant that, as the government's recent white paper had put it, the BBC would remain 'the cornerstone of British broadcasting'. Then they got to the crux of the matter. Redhead asked:

> **Right. Now, who will provide all the programmes? I mean the great thing about the BBC in the past is it produced everything. Everything was in-house and indeed that's where people learned how to carry out the business, and then if they wanted to go and work for ITV or something, fine; but it was the great training place, it was also the great doing place. Will it still be that?**

'That role will change,' admitted Checkland, but he went on to stress that the BBC should remain 'the production heart of the British broadcasting industry... We are not going down the road of becoming a publisher contractor.'

'And are you,' Redhead asked Checkland, 'surrounded by a "pseudo-Leninist"?'

He was referring to John Birt, Checkland's deputy, who was soon to become director general himself, and whose management style had been explicitly criticised in these very words by Channel 4's chief executive Michael Grade earlier that year.

Birt's controversial reign as director general ran from 1993 to 2000 and witnessed something of an internal BBC revolution, whose merits and demerits remain the subject of debate. An internal market was introduced whereby producers could choose to 'buy in' services from outside the BBC, cutting costs but also BBC jobs; at the same time, the BBC expanded services as the digital age dawned. The main criticism, as summarised at the end of Birt's tenure by BBC media correspondent Nick Higham, was that Birt was 'a remote figure who cared more about structures and cost-savings than programmes, whose reforms neutered BBC news and current affairs'.

Yet as Higham also noted, Birt was nevertheless seen by some as 'the man who saved the BBC', making the hard decisions that would allow the corporation to survive in a new media age. One of the battles Birt won was to retain the licence fee, in the face of those who preferred out-and-out privatisation of the BBC, and to tie it to the rate of inflation too. In an increasingly diverse media world that largely relied on advertising or the various subscription/pay-per-view models, there were many voices arguing that the licence fee, agreed at the dawn of the BBC in the 1920s, was an anachronism and should cease. Birt himself, in conversation with John Humphrys on *Today* on 5 November 1993, had an interesting long view, which ran against the grain of much of the general commentary.

> **Humphrys: The BBC is seen to be losing the battle for the audience. We have – what is it? – about a 40 per cent share at the moment. At what point do people start saying seriously, 'That share is too small, it doesn't any longer justify a universal licence fee?'**

> **Birt: Not in our lifetimes. At the moment, each household in Britain, which is paying 23p a day through its licence fee for the services it consumes, each week is consuming 50 hours of television and radio on average... I cannot foresee a time when we're not going to be very, very significantly consumed and extraordinary value for money by any terms. I think that the licence fee will become more accepted rather than less accepted, as people get used to the idea of paying for their television.**

John Birt stood down in 2000 and was replaced by Greg Dyke. The two men had been colleagues at London Weekend Television, but Dyke's style was more informal and accessible, and his promise to 'cut the crap' in the way the organisation was run went down well with staff. But his tenure was cut short by one of the most serious confrontations between the BBC and the government in the corporation's history.

On *Today* on 29 May 2003 Andrew Gilligan, a *Today* reporter, broadcast accusations that Tony Blair's government had deliberately embellished ('sexed-up' was the term Gilligan used) the dossier it had published on Saddam Hussein's alleged weapons of mass destruction (WMDs) in the run-up to the invasion of Iraq the previous year. The charge focused particularly on the claim that Iraq could launch a WMD strike within 45 minutes. Similar stories were broadcast by two other journalists on the *Ten O'Clock News* and *Newsnight*. The government denied the stories and attacked the BBC's journalism; the prime minister's communications director, Alastair Campbell, was especially vocal in his denunciations of the corporation. But the BBC insisted there was a reliable source for the reports. The stakes in this confrontation were high; the 'dodgy dossier' – as it became known – had been important in securing parliamentary backing for the war.

On 9 July Dr David Kelly, a biological warfare expert and former UN weapons inspector in Iraq, was named in the press as the BBC's source; just over a week later Dr Kelly committed suicide in the countryside near his home. Lord (James) Hutton, a former Lord Chief Justice of Northern Ireland, was appointed to head an inquiry into the circumstances surrounding Dr Kelly's death.

On *Today* on 29 January 2004, John Humphrys reported the conclusions of the Hutton Inquiry:

> There was a received wisdom about what Lord Hutton would say in his report. It went something like this: the BBC was at fault, but so was the government – blame on all sides. Well, received wisdom was wrong. Hutton found one or two minor faults with the government, but not so as anyone would notice. It was the BBC that got it in the neck. Within a few hours of the verdict, the chairman of the BBC had resigned. The governors are meeting this morning and it is possible that more heads will roll. Has the director general offered his resignation? There are rumours, but we don't know. No one from the BBC wants to be interviewed until after that meeting. The BBC – and for once this is not an abuse or an exaggeration of the word – is in a state of crisis.

In the absence of a BBC representative, Humphrys quizzed a former BBC chairman, Sir Christopher Bland, on the fallout. Hutton had found the BBC's editorial procedure 'defective', so 'Should the person or persons responsible for those defects not carry the can?'

Bland pulled no punches:

> Well, it depends if you think that success should be measured by the number of scalps hanging from Alastair Campbell's belt. I don't think that's the right measure. We've – the BBC – lost an extremely good man in Gavyn Davies. He was a good chairman. It shouldn't lose an extremely good director general, Greg Dyke. It shouldn't lose an extremely good director of news, Richard Sambrook. I notice, John, that you were on Alastair Campbell's lips. Don't you resign! I don't think that's appropriate. Now, there were mistakes made and they should be corrected, but the idea that there's a systemic failure that requires mass execution at the BBC is just wrong.

Director general Greg Dyke was also the BBC's editor-in-chief, responsible for all the BBC's journalism. As Bland spoke, Dyke was on his way out too, having failed to get the backing of the BBC governors. To the delight of the *Today* night-shift team, Dyke telephoned the programme in the early hours of the following morning offering himself for interview, and he was questioned by the presenter Edward Stourton. Admitting mistakes, for example in responding too hastily to Campbell's complaints and not launching an internal inquiry before responding publicly, he nevertheless could not conceal his astonishment at the nature of the inquiry's verdict. He quoted another TV executive's observation about Hutton that 'It's remarkable how he's given the benefit of judgement to virtually everyone in the government and to no one at the BBC.'

Dyke offered a robust defence of certain aspects of his and the BBC's behaviour, but, alluding to the formal role of the director general as also editor-in-chief, he stressed that 'in all honesty... the idea the editor-in-chief of an organisation with 28,000 people should actually – *can* actually – vet what goes on air all the time is just unreal.'

'It does raise the question of whether the director general can actually be editor-in-chief, doesn't it?' suggested Stourton, which, Dyke agreed, was 'an interesting question'.

Dyke also argued that the Hutton verdict had grave implications for all journalism based on 'whistle-blowing':

> **I think it's not only the BBC who should be concerned... I think it's every journalistic organisation, every newspaper, every broadcaster in this country should be concerned. Because what it says is: someone inside, say of government, someone inside the civil service who has very real concerns, as Dr Kelly had, could not be broadcast, unless you could demonstrate that their concerns were true. That's what – that's the reading – that's my judgement of what Lord Hutton says.**

For *Today* listeners, following Dyke's interview, BBC political editor Andrew Marr summed up the uneasy and opaque situation as it stood on 30 January 2004:

> **Well, I think you hear not only a former director general of the BBC who feels that its processes, while imperfect, were unfairly traduced by Lord Hutton. I think behind [that], also... you hear somebody who probably feels that the final arguments about that dossier haven't yet been had – probably can't be had – between the BBC and the government; but you know there's a great big gap... where [the] truth lies here.**

It was another report, the Butler Report, published later in 2004, which analysed and found a series of flaws and over-confident assertions in the dossier, including about the way the 45-minute claim was phrased. In an interview to Channel 4 News on 14 July 2004, Greg Dyke reiterated his view that 'the BBC was perfectly right to report Dr Kelly's allegations and concerns'.

During his interview with Sir Christopher Bland on 29 January 2004, John Humphrys had asked the former BBC chairman, 'What is the danger that the BBC will now be cowed?' 'I think there is a real danger of that,' Bland replied, before adding, 'Now the BBC, I have to say, in my experience, doesn't stay cowed for long.' An interview with another senior BBC figure eight years later demonstrated that the *Today* culture was anything but 'cowed' when it came to scrutinising the parent.

George Entwistle became director general in September 2012. He had joined the BBC in 1989 after a career in magazines, and on his way up the corporation's hierarchy he had held a number of senior jobs in news and factual programmes. The month after he took on the top job, the BBC became embroiled in the Jimmy Savile abuse scandal, and Entwistle was questioned by a parliamentary committee about why a *Newsnight* investigation into Savile had been shelved after the entertainer's death the previous year. The committee accused the director general of displaying an 'amazing lack of curiosity' about the investigation.

Then in early November 2012 *Newsnight* (of which Entwistle had himself once been editor) was again at the centre of a controversy when the programme broadcast a report on allegations of abuse at children's homes in North Wales. It included the claim that a senior Conservative figure had been involved, and although *Newsnight* did not identify anyone, the name of Lord (Alistair) McAlpine, a former party treasurer, soon surfaced on social media. The *Guardian* then reported that it was a case of mistaken identity, Lord McAlpine denied any involvement, and on 9 November *Newsnight*'s source, a former care-home resident, accepted, after seeing a photograph of Lord McAlpine, that he had made a mistake. The BBC was forced to apologise, and later paid Lord McAlpine £185,000 in damages (Lord McAlpine later asked members of the public who had tweeted his name to contribute to the BBC charity Children in Need).

Entwistle faced John Humphrys in the *Today* studio on the morning of 10 November 2012.

> **Humphrys:** When did you know that this film was being broadcast, and when was it drawn to your attention that it was going to make extraordinarily serious allegations about a man whose identity would inevitably be uncovered – wrongly, as we now know?

> **Entwistle:** The film was not drawn to my attention before transmission.

> **Humphrys:** At all? Nobody said anything to you at all?

> **Entwistle:** No, John, but I need to explain that there are an awful lot of pieces of journalism going on around the BBC which do not get referred to the editor-in-chief. Not everything gets to the editor-in-chief. The key is, is it referred sufficiently far up the chain of command, and in this case I think the right referrals were made.

> **Humphrys:** But you must have known what happened; a tweet was put out 24 hours beforehand, 12 hours beforehand, telling the world that something was going to happen on *Newsnight* that night that would reveal extraordinary things about child abuse, and that would involve a senior Tory figure from the Thatcher years. You didn't see that tweet?

Entwistle: I didn't see that tweet, John, I now understand…

Humphrys: You didn't see that tweet? Why not?

Entwistle: I check Twitter at the end of the day sometimes – or I don't.

Humphrys: You have a staff, but you have an enormous staff of people who are reporting into you on all sorts of things – they didn't see this tweet that was going to set the world on fire?

Entwistle: John, this tweet, I'm afraid, was not brought to my attention so I found out about this film after it had gone out.

Humphrys: Can I just be absolutely clear? Nobody said to you, at any time or to anybody on your staff who would then report it to you at any time, 'Look, we've got this *Newsnight* film going out – *Newsnight* should already light a few bulbs with you – but we've got this film going out on *Newsnight* that is going to make massively serious allegations about a senior, a former senior political …' Nobody even mentioned it in the context that we understand, nobody even mentioned it?

Entwistle: No.

Humphrys: Isn't that extraordinary?

Entwistle: In the light of what's happened here, I wish this had been referred to me, but it wasn't. I run the BBC on the basis that the right people are put in the right positions to make the right decisions…

Humphrys: So when did you find out about it?

Entwistle: I found out about it the following day.

Humphrys: The following day? You didn't see it that night when it was broadcast?

Entwistle: No, I was out.

Entwistle's lack of grip on the controversy enveloping the organisation he was supposed to be running became painfully evident as the questioning unfolded:

Humphrys: Did you see the *Guardian* yesterday morning? Did you read the *Guardian*'s front page yesterday morning?

Entwhistle: No, John, I was giving a speech yesterday morning early on…

Humphrys: Aren't some things rather more important than others? I mean do you not have to have a different set of priorities?

Entwhistle: But you have to prepare for speeches you have to make, John.

Humphrys: The *Guardian* yesterday carried a front-page story, which we now know was right, that cast doubt, serious doubt, on the BBC's *Newsnight* programme – a flagship news programme for the BBC. You didn't know that that actually happened?

Entwhistle: No, I'm afraid I didn't.

Humphrys: When people ask questions about, and this is perhaps where we should get to your own future, when people ask questions about the role of the BBC, the director general of the BBC, they point out, as Mr Whittingdale [the Conservative MP John Whittingdale, then chairman of the Commons Culture, Media and Sport Select Committee] just did that he is the editor-in-chief. How do you define the responsibility of the editor-in-chief?

Entwhistle: The editor-in-chief has to take complete responsibility for the BBC's journalistic output, but that does not mean that the editor-in-chief sits and signs off every single piece of it. The organisation is too big, there is too much journalism going on. The way the system works is that things brought to the attention of the editor-in-chief are effectively handed over to him, responsibility is given to him at that moment. If the system is not referring things it should refer to the editor-in-chief, then it's not working properly. This is one of the things I need to look at.

And so it continued – relentlessly – for nearly ten minutes. By the end of the day Entwhistle had gone, after just 54 days in the director general's chair. Speaking truth to power, whether that power be the government in Westminster or the BBC's own great and good, remains at the heart of what the listening public are entitled to expect of the BBC and of *Today*.

Actors' lives and the art of acting

'To look into the heart of ourselves'
FIONA SHAW, 17 FEBRUARY 2014

In the many *Today* interviews with actors over the years, certain motifs recur. Women actors have, since they first trod the professional stage in the 17th century, contended with specific issues. Three eminent female actors to appear on *Today* were Phyllis Calvert (in 1970 and 1972), Dame Flora Robson (1981) and, on the 60th anniversary of her debut in *Hamlet*, Dame Judi Dench (2017). Collectively, they represented about a century of achievement in English acting, though their conversations were all characterised by disarming modesty. Entirely absent from all their conversations was any sense of prima donna-ish entitlement.

Phyllis Calvert (1915–2002), who was described in the *Guardian*'s obituary as the 'bourgeois beauty of the British stage and screen', remembered during her *Today* interview on 2 June 1970 the days of her peak as a genteel 'Gainsborough girl' – acting in the wartime costume dramas produced by Gainsborough Studios. 'You were very English, very English rose, weren't you?... Very upper class and very good,' her interviewer, Peter Robbins suggested, which Calvert readily acknowledged. She provided a glimpse of what that era was like, which allowed an actor such as herself to be both a public and private person:

> I loved making films during the war. There was very little newsprint going at the time. There was very little nightlife. There was very little private life. One's private life wasn't delved into at all; one's publicity was got by working. Then after the war, of course – this is what put me off films – the limelight was switched on and I didn't really enjoy it, and I find that I'd much rather be in the theatre, working in the theatre, because it isn't such a public display. Your private life, I mean.

Two years later Calvert was back being interviewed on *Today,* and she regretted her lack of access to classical roles ('nobody's ever asked me'), freely admitting that those old 'escapist' films had stories that were 'pretty phony', and, that in retrospect, she was horrified at the old acting style: 'I think if they were shown I'd be sick here. It was such a different technique in those days. She explained:

> **If you had a crying scene in those days – and let's face it, when you cry, your face crumples – we weren't allowed to have our face crumpling because it made nasty lines on the face, so if we cried, lumps of glycerine were put at the ends of our eyes and it was hoped it would run down at the very right moment, you see.**

'I think it's so marvellous now,' she continued, 'when you go to a cinema and you see faces in colour and you can actually see the freckles and this sort of skin texture.'

Phyllis Calvert began acting at age 12 and went on until a few years before her death. Flora Robson (1891–1984), who became a great presence on the classical stage as well as playing – as *Today* put it – 'an impressive list of empresses and queens', began even younger. It is part of acting lore that parents have traditionally discouraged their daughters from a life on the stage; not so in Robson's case, as she confessed to *Today* on 17 October 1981:

> **I was five years old. I did a school concert and Father turned round and said, 'You're going to be an actress.' I started then and there a very hard life. Reading my own biography, it really upsets me. I had lessons for elocution and piano and dancing and singing. So when other children went out to play, I was working. It's been like that all my life, and when other people were having fun, I had very little social life. I have never had any chance to *live*.**

Success did not come easily. Abandoning bit-parts in repertory companies, she – probably uniquely among actors – 'went to work in a Shredded Wheat factory', as her interviewer Helen Palmer put it. But it worked wonders. 'You see what that did for me,' Robson explained, 'it taught me about people. I think it made me as an actress. When I came back, I blew the roof off the theatre.'

Unlike Phyllis Calvert, Flora Robson was never a conventional beauty, as she well knew. All stage and screen casting depends, to some extent, on physical appearance, but that has always been a more strictly conditioning factor for women (as is age; the complaint of a dearth of parts for older female actors remains a common one). 'I would love to have played Juliet,' Robson admitted, 'but I never got a chance to play her. I went on getting turned down, because I hadn't got the looks.' Whatever her regrets, whatever her resentments at paternal authority, Robson told *Today* she 'wouldn't have chosen any other profession'. The idea of acting as a vocation, rather than a career you choose, is a subtext of many actors' conversations.

Widely prevalent, too, but difficult to avoid – as both Calvert and Robson hinted – is typecasting. When John Humphrys spoke to 82-year-old 'national treasure' Judi Dench on 11 September 2017, she had just completed her second film performance as Queen Victoria, in *Victoria and Abdul*. This well-known workaholic, never content to rest on her laurels, rejected any thoughts of retirement ('What is that word "retire?"'), but also hoped her next role would be 'nobody like Queen Victoria'. Judi Dench had managed a very varied career, across all media, in comparison with many of her female peers, but now she wanted 'to play a villain':

> **I did a film called *Notes on a Scandal*. I *absolutely* adored it, *adored* it, and the thing is that people see you as something, you know, they've seen you as Queen Victoria... so they then offer you a part that's very like it, and in actual fact, what you want is a part that's most unlike it, really unlike it.**

In the morally complex *Notes on a Scandal* (2006), Dench played a suffocating, repressed, lonely schoolteacher, whose friendship (perhaps love) for a fellow teacher, played by Cate Blanchett, turns hostile on discovering the Blanchett character's affair with a male student. Dench's performance was a *tour de force*, its power enhanced by its unexpectedness; although she had played Lady Macbeth memorably in the late 1970s, on screen she had rarely been given free rein to be malevolent.

For the best actors, there is always something more to strive for. Colin Firth spoke to *Today* on 28 February 2011, just after winning an Oscar for his performance as King George VI in *The King's Speech*.

'What would you choose to be doing next?' asked presenter Sarah Montague.

'I want to do comedy,' replied Firth. 'I think gravitas is usually overrated and I just would like to do something that amuses me now and change the pace, change the tone.'

However, he also displayed a cheerful nonchalance about the TV role in the Jane Austen adaptation *Pride and Prejudice* that had provided the cornerstone of his fame back in 1995. 'Do you think,' Montague asked, 'that one thing that will result from it [the Oscar win] is that you'll no longer be known as Mr Darcy?' 'No,' Firth replied. 'I think Mr Darcy will be alive and well for the rest of my life.' He added:

> **I think Mr Darcy will be put to rest when he is buried at a crossroads at midnight with a stake through his heart. I don't see that happening any time soon. And actually, I'd be rather sad to see him go. I think there's a bit of a misperception that I'm disgruntled about the Darcy thing, and I'm not remotely bothered by it. I would hate to see that tag leave me.**

Actors of the calibre of Judi Dench, or Chiwetel Ejiofor, the Oscar-nominated (and BAFTA-winning) star of *Twelve Years a Slave* (2013), frequently find themselves drawn back to the live stage, whatever riches and celebrity TV and film may bring. In a conversation with *Today*'s James Naughtie, broadcast on 25 September 2015, Ejiofor declared – despite all the razzamatazz surrounding his film success – that the highlight of his recent year 'was actually being at the National Theatre, and doing *Everyman* here in London'. In other words, despite having just starred in the sci-fi Hollywood epic *The Martian*, what he had really relished had been a piece of medieval English drama, albeit in a modern setting. Ejiofor had started out acting with the National Youth Theatre, and when asked by Naughtie, 'Do you still love the stage?' he was unequivocal:

> **Ejiofor: It's an incredibly important part of being an actor, I think. There are some actors now who don't do theatre, you know. For me, it's an unmissable part of the experience. I don't think there's much point in being an actor if you don't do any stage work at all, you know.**

> **Naughtie: So in a sense, without being patronising, I mean, you feel sorry for actors whose entire career has been in film and they just say, 'Well, that's it, I'm a film actor.'**

> **Ejiofor: I do. I do. I feel like it's essentially missing a part of the experience.**

Ejiofor did acknowledge that 'if you had the opportunity to [do] film and chose not to, then I think that would also be a shame'. But one craft is acting for an audience, the other acting to a machine and to a director, and they have very different technical demands. Flora Robson told *Today* in a broadcast on 17 October 1981 that she 'had to learn the difference between theatre and films. They keep on saying to you when you start films, "You must stop acting." What they should say is, "Act less, feel more." It was Charles Laughton who told me the difference.'

Judi Dench, reflecting on her stage debut as Ophelia in *Hamlet*, for the Old Vic's production at Liverpool's Royal Court Theatre in 1957, felt that a sense of economy also came with experience. 'How much has acting changed over that time?' John Humphrys asked. She replied:

> **I could play Juliet much better than I did for Franco Zeffirelli in 1960. I know now, because you have that much more experience, and you understand that wonderful thing that less is more. You know, when I was Ophelia, I tried every single thing to say that she was mad in the mad scene. I know that I needed only to do one thing, now. Well, because you learn to pare down and – and it is right that less is more, if you can learn that and if you can trust it.**

'Less is more' was also a mantra of the influential 20th-century dramatist Samuel Beckett, whose singular, brilliant and profound pared-down plays make ferocious demands on actors. Ideas of realism, dialogue, even 'action' in a conventional sense disappear in his works, which unremittingly – although not without humour – focus on individuals trapped in confusions of their pasts, presents and futures. In an extended interview for *Today* on 12 March 2009, James Naughtie discussed the demands of Beckett with a quartet of eminent actors who were about to take his most renowned play on the road: Ian McKellen, Patrick Stewart, Simon Callow and Ronald Pickup. Naughtie set the scene:

> **Samuel Beckett's play *Waiting for Godot* caused shockwaves when it had its London premiere way back in 1955: a play without a traditional linear plot, pondering the meaning of life through the medium of two tramps waiting for a man who never comes. But Beckett's language, his speech rhythms, his depiction of humanity at its rawest and its most moving, has established *Godot* as a 20th-century masterpiece.**

For these four actors, it was a labour of love and of choice. Clearly, they did not *need* to do it – the blockbuster successes of the *Star Wars*, *X-Men* and *Lord of the Rings* franchises had made McKellen and Stewart particularly into global stars. But as with Ejiofor, they were driven by the importance of returning to roots, of self-challenge and of the encounter with a real, live audience. Simon Callow summed up the rollercoaster they were on:

> **Oh, we're making it in the furnace of art. We really are. Every night changes... I mean, we're not *rewriting* it – naturally – but apart from that, almost anything else can change. Any element of the set. Any element of the performance. And particularly the physical blocking of the play changes a great deal as we begin to understand the story more and more, because that's the element that the audience gives us more than anything else, is the narrative: what it's about.**

Ronald Pickup, who had worked with Beckett in the 1970s, recalled that 'The one thing I caught from him so much was his incredible sense of rhythm. It was like working with a musician.'

'How difficult, Patrick,' Naughtie asked, 'is it to perform?' Patrick Stewart was unabashed to admit that:

> **It's the hardest thing I have ever done... It was hard, initially, to memorise it, to learn it. His repetitions, which are almost repetitions but not quite; the change of rhythms; the non sequiturs; the sudden intrusion of a brand-new subject out of nowhere. These make what actors use to link lines together – you know, the subtext and the continuing thought process that has to underlie everything – quite complex.**

Beckett's work has a paradoxical reputation. It is perceived to be 'difficult', and yet, perhaps because it is so charged with fundamental human frailty, it has the capacity to communicate almost by osmosis, as *Waiting for Godot* has proved when playing to non-traditional audiences such as prison inmates. For Ian McKellen, the experience of performing *Godot* was a revelation:

> I thought this was the most difficult play in the world, not to be involved with, but to understand and to take home as an experience – but now I've done it, after just five weeks I realise this is an absolute masterpiece, and I think the world is divided between those who think that *Waiting for Godot* is absolute rubbish and those who know it to be absolutely vital.

McKellen's belief that this was *necessary* theatre, as Patrick Stewart explained, underpinned their decision that 'we have to take this to the people'.

The social function of theatre also permeated the conversations that James Naughtie had, five years later, with alumni and current students of London's Royal Academy of Dramatic Art (RADA). The most established acting school in Britain was, on the evening of 17 February 2014, about to celebrate at Buckingham Palace the Queen's 60-year patronage. That morning, *Today* listeners heard RADA's director, Ed Kemp, offer up his own justification for the art and purpose of acting:

> Theatre, drama, can transform people's lives. I think telling stories, getting out onto a stage and telling stories that matter to a society, is important. I think having people who have the best possible skills to tell those stories is important to us as a society.

The accomplished and articulate Irish actor and director Fiona Shaw, who remembered her happy RADA years as a time of 'landscapes opening to you of possibility', went eloquently further when speaking with James Naughtie that same morning:

> Naughtie: So RADA, like all the other drama schools, cherishes the English-speaking stage and the great works written for it. Where would we be without it? Fiona Shaw can't imagine it.

> Shaw: You know, what the language does is it releases chaos in an ordered way and therefore allows the world to experience dark feelings, bad feelings, good feelings – I mean I honestly think it's a peacekeeping force because the better a culture, the more robust it can be in describing the darkness of the human soul, [and] the less likely it is that they will act on that darkness. So the English-speaking drama tradition allows us to look into the heart of darkness and to look into the heart of ourselves and hopefully, you know, become or remain more civilised.

English writers exploring Englishness

'In the middle of that, he has a great love of England'
JOHN LE CARRÉ, 14 SEPTEMBER 2011

'How do you regard your reputation,' the interviewer asked, 'because obviously you are, if not the greatest, very nearly the greatest of all living novelists?'

The 75-year-old Graham Greene, author of *Brighton Rock* and much else, opted for evasion: 'Well, I wouldn't know about that.'

The follow-up question could have provoked an authorial rebuke: 'It's said that you actually want to be judged by your books and not by what anyone says about you. Is that how you feel?' The author merely replied, 'Well, naturally, yes.'

The occasion for this interview on 14 March 1980 was rehearsals for what Greene described as his 'sixth play', *For Whom the Bell Chimes*, its title a pun on Ernest Hemingway's Spanish Civil War novel *For Whom the Bell Tolls* (itself taken from the great John Donne poem which includes the same phrase). Greene had always enjoyed being closely involved with productions of his plays, partly because, as he told *Today*, 'It's also an escape from one's proper profession, and escape's always valuable.' The play's production had brought him to London, back from his self-imposed exile in France, which he had made his home. *Today*'s interviewer, Helen Palmer, explored his relationship with the land of his birth.

Palmer: Coming back to England, how does it affect you, because you do live in the South of France?

Greene: I feel more at home really in France now than in England. I've been living permanently in France now for 14 years. I enjoy coming back. I enjoy the English beer and English sausages – those are the two things I miss principally in France.

Palmer: But you don't regard England as in the same way your homeland, now?

Greene: To tell you the truth, I feel more at home in Paris and in Antibes than I do in London.

Palmer: Even though England made you?

Greene: Yes, but even the characters that made me were living in Sweden, I think.

'Even though England made you' was a reference to an early Greene novel, *England Made Me* (1935). It was set in Sweden but peopled largely by what the *Guardian* later called 'a puppet cast of deracinated Englishmen and women'. 'Greeneland', as his imaginative world was dubbed by a critic, is littered with such characters.

The context of the Cold War – an ideological battle for the world's hearts and minds – provided Greene and other English writers with the perfect backdrop against which they could explore themes of identity, allegiance and betrayal. The beginning of the Cold War inspired Greene's screenplay (also a novella) for the celebrated 1949 film *The Third Man*, which was set in a noirish racketeering Vienna, a city on the edge of the new East–West divide. And the long struggle between Communism and Liberal Democracy proved a catalyst for the burgeoning genre of English spy fiction, in which two great enduring – but very different – literary characters emerged.

One was Ian Fleming's James Bond, unleashed on the reading public in *Casino Royale* (1953) and spawning the hugely successful book series and film franchise. Fleming's conceit of a super-suave spy with a 'double-O' licence to kill became part of the nation's sense of its identity, as the opening of the 2012 London Olympics demonstrated. It also had an impact on the real world of the intelligence agencies, at least so one interview on *Today* suggested. On 5 October 2012, Alan Judd, a contemporary spy-novelist who, in the words of the BBC's security correspondent Gordon Corera, 'will only admit to having served in the Foreign Office', explained that:

> There's no doubt that the Bond reputation, which is a global brand, means that anyone in British intelligence can go anywhere in the world and say, 'I'm from British intelligence and I'd like you to help me,' and people, whether or not they agree, they know who you are, they know what you are, and they respond; a little light comes on in their brains saying, 'James Bond.' It's not like, as a former chief of MI6 used to say, going anywhere in the world and saying, 'I'm from Belgian intelligence and I'd like you to help me,' and having to explain.

The other fictional spy, nearer to the complex truth, is almost an anti-Bond. It is that quiet and dogged hero of British intelligence George Smiley, the man at the heart of a series of highly rated books by the pseudonymous 'John le Carré' (real name: David Cornwell). Le Carré spoke to *Today*'s James Naughtie for a broadcast on 14 September 2011. The previous night had seen the premiere of a film version of his 1974 spy novel *Tinker Tailor Soldier Spy*, starring Gary Oldman as Smiley.

Authors do not always appreciate what TV and film do to their works, but le Carré was full of praise for both the classic television incarnation of George Smiley (played by the cerebral actor Alec Guinness) and for Oldman's portrayal. In le Carré's words,

Oldman 'has, quite obviously, a male sexuality which he represses like all these other feelings in this story... Oldman is waiting patiently to explode.'

In analysing what makes Smiley tick, Naughtie put it to the author that:

> Smiley has always struck me as someone who understands the way the world works, it makes him sad, but he understands in meticulous detail what moves people and how they behave, and yet simultaneously he's puzzled by it, and that seems to be one of the secrets of his personality and I think why he's so attractive.

'I think,' replied le Carré, 'he's also puzzled by his own emotions.' He continued:

> Yes, he sees a lot; yes, he knows all the possibilities of the people he's interrogating – he knows his own possibilities. But he has two romantic poles, as you might say: his great enemy and antagonist Karla – the Russian secret-service guy who is responsible for the manipulation of the secret service here – and he has this mysterious love for his wife. So he has a romantic enemy in a sense, somebody whose humanity he believes he can exploit if only he can get to it. And he has a great love that constantly deceives him, but he will not renounce.

'So I think,' le Carré explained, 'Smiley himself is a divided man.'

As le Carré knew well from his own former career with the British intelligence services, the world he depicted was genuinely fraught with contradiction, and deception cut both ways. With good authority he could tell *Today* listeners that 'In my day at least, it was really quite impossible to tell your nearest and dearest who you were or what you were doing. And therefore home, as for George Smiley, became a place of deception.' Instead:

> The real bonding was done within the office. The more you worked together, men and women, the more the sexual undertow expressed itself, if you like. There is a tremendous sense of, if you will, regimental pride within those services still... And the parties, at least in my day, were a kind of mad alcoholic expression of these moments.

Le Carré suggested the prevailing atmosphere of secrecy also led to a psychological desire, even cathartic need, to trust colleagues you might barely know at those moments when hair could be let down. And those circumstances create the conditions of shock when that trust is betrayed, for it is both personal and political betrayal. But le Carré was also adamant that these men and women conceive of themselves, as Smiley does, as defenders of their country:

> I have never met anybody working for any secret service who didn't think he [or she] was a moral man or woman. They collectively believe they share some

mysterious morality, that they also perform a duty: they clean the drains so that we can have the clean water. They do the dirty jobs so that we sleep well at night. And they see themselves collectively as, in a way, the chosen ones.

Bringing the discussion back to Smiley himself, Naughtie reminded listeners that 'Smiley is wrestling with a series of moral dilemmas in every book in which we see him, and in many ways it's a very moral story throughout', giving le Carré the cue to pick up this thread:

I think for me – it sounds very corny to say it – I think for me he represents something like a decent man. He is trying to find the path of decency through the moral maze... I think it's something to do with what happened to me out of the mess of my own childhood, at a certain period I embraced that service, that life, as being a path to some sort of virtuous truth, very simply put, and I think that's always remained with me, and I think it is invested in Smiley. I mean, I did two things with Smiley that were very intimate to me: first was, I tried to answer the question how to be a decent person in a very flawed world, and I came from a very flawed background; and secondly the more general question of, what can you do in the name of democracy and make sure that democracy survives? So these were two very simple moral questions.

'I think you say of Smiley somewhere, don't you,' noted Naughtie, 'that he's a man who would carry his horse uphill?'

'Yes,' agreed le Carré, 'carrying the horse uphill is almost... it's almost a priestly occupation. There is that streak in him of shouldering other people's burdens and being quiet about it and getting on with the job.'

Decency, duty, getting on with the job – traits often claimed as solid English values. No wonder that le Carré felt of his 'divided' character Smiley that 'in the middle of that, he has a great love of England'.

Hilary Mantel's Thomas Cromwell novels are set during the reign of Henry VIII, a period which helped define Englishness, and her hero is, like Smiley, a servant of his country with an intimate understanding of the darker arts of statecraft. One of the factors which make her imaginative achievement so remarkable is that her characters speak in a way that feels authentically Tudor without seeming stilted. On 7 October 2009, the morning after winning the Booker Prize for *Wolf Hall* – the first volume of her Cromwell trilogy – she was interviewed on *Today* by Justin Webb, where she reflected on the way she had written the dialogue:

Mantel: There is the kind of Tudor inflection running through it, sometimes a Tudor rhythm which you pick up from people's letters, actually; letters were so often dictated that that's where you hear the human voice. But what I didn't want to do is a 'zounds' and 'prithee' and 'unhand me' sort of pastiche, because that's just so clunky, and then the book becomes all about language, even if you do it skilfully – I don't think that should really be the point.

Webb: And is there a point at which you can read this book and draw parallels with the modern world other than the obvious ones about power and life generally? I think David Starkey the historian compared Thomas Cromwell to Alastair Campbell [Tony Blair's communications director].

Mantel: Alastair Campbell with an axe!

Webb: Yeah, what about Peter Mandelson? Do you see, you were listening to George Osborne there [Osborne had been interviewed from the Conservative Party Conference in the 8.10am slot], do you listen, do you watch our current political shenanigans and think, 'Oh yes, I had a message about that in the book?'

Mantel: To an extent, but to a limited extent. I think what you have to remember about the 1530s, the stakes were so much higher. If you made a mistake you didn't get to spend more time with your family. You've got your head cut off.'

Alan Bennett has been a relatively frequent literary guest on *Today*, and this 'national treasure' has often explored conflicted ideas of Englishness in his works. Bennett, a contemporary of le Carré, originally emerged in the early 1960s satire boom, but later pursued a varied career as (in James Naughtie's words) 'a diarist, a dramatist, a wit'. On 12 October 2017, he looked back on his life for *Today*.

He and James Naughtie discussed one of Bennett's greatest successes on stage and film, *The History Boys* (2004), which is set in the 1980s and concerns a group of sixth-form (Year 13) boys aspiring to Oxbridge and their inspiring, eccentric teacher Hector, whose wandering hands, in a later era, would doubtless have brought his career to a swift end. *The History Boys* was an international success, which on the face of it Naughtie thought surprising, 'because the subject matter, although the idea is universal, it's terribly English.' Naughtie felt Bennett's Englishness to be deep-rooted: 'And that's something that's fascinated you right throughout your whole writing time. And in a curious way that's one of the things that's still there, whereas 50, 60 years ago you might have thought that that would change.' Bennett admitted:

It is still there, it's partly because I have mixed feelings about England. And it's left hanging in the air whether you're on the side of the traditional England embodied in the headmaster or the, as it were, the new England.

'And that ambiguity,' Naughtie asked, 'is one that you are very conscious of yourself?'

'Yes,' Bennett acknowledged:

In some ways I'm very conservative with a small 'c', and traditional. And because I went to a state school where there was assembly every morning and you sang a hymn and so I knew... without realising it, you absorb all the words from them and words remain with you for the rest of your life. But at the same time, I am uneasy about that, I don't want to be... to push it. It's there. I don't want to be someone who's propagating that somehow.

'And I very often feel ashamed to be English,' Bennett added. 'I mean, at the time of the Iraq War I did. And now with Brexit I wanted to explain to people that we didn't all feel the same way.'

In contrast to the geopolitics which form the backdrop to Greene and le Carré's world, and the court intrigues which drive Hilary Mantel's great historical drama, the backdrop to Bennett's literary work is often the domestic rituals of English social and personal life – the more everyday constraints, pretences, repressions. And as he told James Naughtie in that 2017 interview: '[The] big change, I suppose in a sense, in my life, is that you don't hide the fact that you're gay. And now I never even think about that, I mean, it's so much, so accepted.' (see page 344).

Another writer who used her *Today* appearance to reflect on the changes she had seen during her lifetime was the crime novelist P D James, creator of that most English of detectives, Inspector Dalgliesh. She was interviewed by John Humphrys on her 90th birthday, 3 August 2010. Baroness James had served as a BBC governor, and for much of the interview they discussed the state of the corporation, but towards the end, the interview took a more personal turn:

Humphrys: A final thought: [do] you have any ambitions left?

James: Not I think very much from the point of view of writing; just to keep on writing and writing as well as I can. I think at 90 you turn your attention rather more not to ambition, but what you should do with your life and how you should live it for the little time you may have left. And I think we all try to do that really. We just realise that you cannot alter the past, but if there is unhappiness in it, it's as well to come to terms with that, to understand it, and put it on the side. And that we cannot foresee the moment of our going. Except it can't be very far ahead. And therefore one lives for the day, I think just to rejoice in being alive, which I do, and I know I'm an extremely fortunate woman; I'm grateful for all I've been given. I live in an England, of course, which is so different from the England – and in fact the domestic world – in which I grew up, that sometimes it seems to me as if it's something I've made up – a story, not something I've actually experienced. It is so different.

Lady James died on 27 November 2014 at the age of 94.

Sport – a back-page subject on a front-page programme

'A great way of shutting out the rest of the world...'

ROBIN COOK, 27 DECEMBER 1997

The half-hour after eight o'clock is *Today's* showcase. The news lasts until 8.10am, and is followed by the big political or hard-news item of the day. At around 8.20am there is usually a second, lighter item before the sports slot. But sometimes a really big interview is allowed to run for 20 minutes or more, from the end of the news until sport, and David Cameron's first *Today* appearance as prime minister, on 27 May 2010, qualified for a clear run across this coveted airtime. So Cameron was still sitting in the studio when James Naughtie said, 'And now at 28 minutes past eight, Garry Richardson with the sport.'

> **Richardson: Prime ministers are often blamed for lots of things. What about the racing tips? Do you want to give a racing tip, prime minister?**

> **Cameron: I'll leave those to you.**

> **Richardson: I tell you what, I'll give you the paper and you've got a couple of minutes while we do the cricket. Just have a look. Pick any of them – really, don't worry about it, because we never get them right! And let me talk about cricket while the prime minister's doing that. The first test starts this morning at Lord's. Here's our correspondent Jonathan Agnew...'**

While Agnew reflected on the test prospects of the England fast bowler Steven Finn ('at six-foot eight he certainly has the height, but has he the pace to harry the tail?'), the prime minister gamely engaged with the racing pages; the ability to negotiate your way out of a hijacking during an interview is an essential part of the modern political skill set.

When Agnew signed off, Richardson picked up with a trail ahead to *Test Match Special*: '...Commentary on Radio 4 long wave from *Five Live* sports extra. At the end of that 40-second report, the prime minister will tell us the tips.'

> **Cameron: Well, if you're a fan of the coalition you could go for Daring Dream at the 3.50 at Ayr, and if you're slightly more sceptical about how our arrangements**

are going to work out, you could try Midnight Fantasy in the three o'clock at Wolverhampton.

Richardson: Thank you very much.

The presenter Evan Davis, who had just been grilling the prime minister about weightier matters, was impressed: 'That is very good, that was spontaneous.' Cameron settled on Midnight Fantasy, at odds of 10-1. (In the end, Daring Dream came in second in the 3.50 at Ayr, and Midnight Fantasy finished fifth out of ten runners at Wolverhampton.)

The racing tips have become a familiar part of the *Today* furniture, a moment when the studio team can relax into some licensed fun. They gave John Timpson the opportunity for one of his trademark puns: when the sports presenter Mike Ingham had finished delivering the tips one morning, Timpson picked up with 'A horse, a horse, Mike Ingham for a horse.' And the conceit that they are generally useless as a guide to successful betting must be one of the longest running gags on radio.

The slightly surreal prominence of the tips in the *Today* landscape also reflects the curious place sport occupies in the mix; it is a back-page subject on a programme with relentlessly front-page ambitions. 'It is often very hard to get high-profile sports guests, because unlike politicians, sports stars tend not to be *Today* listeners,' says Richardson, who has been presenting *Today* sport for many years. 'I still have conversations with sports press and PR agents who say, when I ring, "Oh, the *Today* programme... just remind me when that's on?". That never happens in politics.'

David Cameron is not the only politician to have been roped in for the racing tips. On 27 December 1997 Robin Cook, then Labour's foreign secretary, who had a sideline in tipping horses for the *Glasgow Herald*, was introduced by Garry Richardson in the style of a *Mastermind* competitor.

Richardson: Our first contestant. Your name please?

Cook: Robin Cook.

Richardson: Your occupation?

Cook: Tipster, but I have a day job as foreign secretary.

Richardson: Ah, right. I did wonder. Yes, it's a very good morning to the foreign secretary Robin Cook, who is a very big racing fan. How did the interest start?

Cook: We just went riding about 15 years back and then took an interest in various different equestrian sports, and racing was mine. The great thing about racing is that you have to focus for the three hours you are at the meeting. And it's a great way of shutting out the rest of the world, and that's important as a politician, you've got to shut off sometime.

The foreign secretary had made disobliging comments about the record of the *Today* tips, which were included in a book published to mark the programme's 40th anniversary. He had been invited to debate with the man responsible for the tips, Cornelius Lysaght (now the BBC's racing correspondent). Richardson challenged the *Today* tipster by saying, 'Robin Cook says our tips are not very good, Cornelius'

He replied, 'Well, I read the blistering attack. I know what an ambassador visiting from a naughty foreign country feels like now when he gets summoned to the Foreign Office. Sweaty palms, sleepless nights. The therapist says I am getting better though. Unlike the tips.'

David Cameron was ambushed about the tips when he had come on to talk about politics; Robin Cook came on to talk about tips but was ambushed about politics. He gave an impressive display of his grasp of racing form, and Richardson was about to let him go when James Naughtie intervened:

> Naughtie: Foreign Secretary, while you are on the line, we can't ignore the front page of *The Times* – sometimes we'd like to but we can't.

> Cook: I frequently ignore the front page of *The Times*.

> Naughtie: For those who haven't read it, it says that you're considering leaving the Cabinet next summer to run for the post of first minister, to stand for the post of first minister in the Scottish Executive namely, as it no doubt will be known, the Scottish prime minister. Now you can forget all the havering about racing tips, you can be absolutely clear about this, either this story is wrong and it simply isn't going to happen, or you're considering it? Which is it?

> Cook: I think it's very rude of you to break into the racing tips, Jim, but since you have, let me tell you this race has not yet been declared. There'll be plenty of runners, the punters themselves will have a vote on it, and I would advise commentators not to place bets.

> Naughtie: We will digest that, Foreign Secretary, thank you very much.

Although sports airtime on *Today* remains modest, it has come a very long way from the position it occupied when Garry Richardson first broadcast the sports news in March 1981 – Richardson is now the longest-serving member of *Today's* on-air team, having arrived even before John Humphrys, and most of the exchanges in this chapter are from the list of his most memorable moments. 'In the old days the content was just a recorded clip of whoever had been making the sports news the previous day,' he remembers.

'On a Monday morning the interview clips were invariably from interviews that had appeared on Saturday's *Sports Report*, so we were broadcasting interview clips that were 36 hours old.'

A *Today* sports presenter's shift back then began with a late-night round-up of sport for Radio 2, followed by a night in the Langham building opposite Broadcasting House. Now a very chic hotel, the Langham of those days was a BBC office block, and it was reputed to be haunted by a number of ghosts, among them Napoleon III of France and a German aristocrat who is said to have thrown himself out of an upper room. Garry Richardson found it 'an eerie place to sleep'. In the early 1980s *Today* came on air at 6.30am, so there were only two sport slots – at 7.25am and 8.25am. Richardson remembers a more formal *Today* studio: 'In the 1980s we always wore a jacket, shirt and tie,' he remembers, 'often a suit.'

Richardson believes *Today's* producers have learnt to take his area more seriously because 'sport is now a seven-day-a-week industry' and 'finance and sponsorship have also played a key part in giving sport an incredible profile'. Sport has also frequently forced itself onto the mainstream news agenda which represents *Today's* natural territory – and not always in a good way. On 8 February 1988 Richardson found himself reporting a sports event that had gone badly wrong; the world middleweight clash between the United States' Fran Tate and the English boxer Tony Sibson (Sibo, as he was known) at Stafford.

> **Richardson: The trouble started when a CS gas canister was thrown into the crowd. Hundreds of fans and press men were affected by stinging throats and streaming eyes. The BBC radio programme covering the fight went on the air several minutes late because the commentary team, which included Henry Cooper, was affected. It was over the public address system that he appealed for fans to behave.**

> Cooper: We're going to see a great fight now. Sibo's done a lot of work. He doesn't want his night ruined by just a few, and it's not the true fans who throw bloody gas canisters and do things like that. So can I just appeal to you all; let's give Sibo and Tate a great welcome here tonight, and let's give 'em every opportunity to give us a great fight. Thanks, lads, I know I can rely on all of you.

> **Richardson: A dozen people, including a policeman and a boxer on the supporting bill, were treated by St John's Ambulance men for effects of the gas. Among the crowd was sports minister Colin Moynihan.**

> Moynihan: Well, it was sickening… to have police reinforcements to be called in at a major event like this, the drunkenness that was associated with the incident.

And on top of it all the appalling nausea that results from CS gas being thrown, and the effect that had throughout the whole of the stadium. I mean it was sickening in every sense of the word.

Richardson: How were you affected, because you were right amid the trouble weren't you?

Moynihan: Yeah, I've felt a lot better in my life, if you want to put it that way. I mean I still feel pretty sick, but I was fortunately not close enough to get the full effect that a number of people did. And a lot of people are being treated. Obviously it's amongst the ugliest scenes we've seen for a long time in British sport.

Later that year Richardson was sent to South Korea to cover the Olympic Games – abandoning the safety of the *Today* studio for the streets of South Korea's capital.

Richardson: Hot, sticky and incredibly crowded in the city of Seoul. Even the shortest distances can take forever. It's a traffic nightmare, seemingly 24 hours a day, with drivers who are intent on travelling at grand prix speed, literally, all the time. And as I discovered they think nothing of driving the wrong way up a one-way street.

He then introduced an earlier recording:

Richardson: We have been driving up a one-way street. It's a busy one-way street. And we've been stopped by the police. And I'm just going to ask my interpreter what actually happened there?

Interpreter: As you said, we are going the wrong way on a one-way street. However, I told the policeman that we were working for Olympic Games broadcasting and he's letting us go. So on our way with just a warning, but this excited city is ready, and wherever you are in the world it will just about be impossible to miss the Olympic Games.

Richardson made his way to the Olympic Village, where he found members of the British Olympic team – some of them, in the best British tradition, with quirky habits.

Richardson: One of only four defending Olympic champions in the British team is Malcolm Cooper, described as the world's greatest marksman. His wife Sarah will also be shooting in the air rifle competition having started from humble beginnings.

Cooper: I used to stand by the kitchen sink, shoot through the dining room through the lounge, and the pellet catcher was hung up on the back of the front door.

Richardson: So you didn't need to, sort of, keep re-wallpapering or anything like that?

Cooper: Oh no. No, no. The pellet catcher is quite large and you've got to be a terrible shot to miss it.

Richardson: Of almost 14,000 competing athletes, the majority are staying here in the Olympic Village. They're accommodated in 122 high-rise buildings, with banks, post offices, a shopping centre and launderette all on hand. And once you've been through three security checks, including having your belongings x-rayed, it is possible to meet the village people. I spoke to Kate Parker of our ladies' hockey team.

Parker: We came into the rooms and we were a bit mortified that we've only got two beds here. We didn't have a locker. We don't have a bedside table and we had a nice lino floor. So we made our own bedside table. We managed to get a locker after three days of asking. But I mean it's fine, its fine and it's comfortable enough. We're just happy to be here really.

Richardson: You entertain the girls in a certain way, don't you?

Parker: I brought a trumpet along just to try and outplay the Dutch, or try and make a greater noise than they do, because whenever we've played the Dutch they always have drums and trumpets and everything going, so I thought right, this time we'll do that...

The item was duly played out with a blast on the trumpet.

The 1988 Olympics made the mainstream news agenda when the Canadian sprinter Ben Johnson was stripped of his 100-metres gold medal for taking steroids. The incident was followed by an eighth-month investigation into doping in sport by a Canadian judge, Charles Dubin. Charlie Francis, Johnson's coach, told the Dubin inquiry that Johnson took drugs because everyone else was doing so – as the BBC reporter Bob Simpson explained on 2 March 1989:

Simpson: It wasn't until Johnson was already a top-flight sprinter at national level that the question of using anabolic steroids came up. In 1981 Francis, the only coach Johnson ever had, first discussed the matter with him, and the athlete took his time before deciding to use the drug, according to Francis. But in the autumn of 1981 he took the plunge. At the commission hearing, Francis was asked what part Johnson took in making that decision.

Francis: I think he was stuck in the same situation as I would be stuck in: he could decide if either he wanted to participate at the highest levels of sport, or not. So he was stuck with that decision, if he wanted to compete. It's pretty clear that steroids are worth approximately a metre at the highest levels of sport, and he could decide to set up his starting blocks at the same line as all the other competitors in international competition, or set them up a metre behind them all. And obviously that would be an unacceptable situation for a top-level athlete.

When sport escapes its usual home at the back end of *Today*'s half-hours it can, on rare occasions, make the 8.10am lead. On 8 July 2013, the morning after Andy Murray's Wimbledon win, John Humphrys and the BBC's sports editor, David Bond, could be heard competing in a search for superlatives:

Humphrys: It was Britain's greatest sporting moment since… well, what? Maybe the football World Cup in 1966? You can't really make a comparison though, because it was a whole team that beat another team then: yesterday it was one man. And what a victory it was…

Bond picked up the baton:

…the papers' front pages absolutely reflect the enormity of the achievement of Andy Murray yesterday. You know it was a privilege to be sitting on Centre Court watching it. And although comparisons are a bit futile with other big sporting events, big sporting achievements, I'm going to have a go anyway. You mentioned the World Cup in 1966. It has to be up there. I guess the 2003 rugby World Cup, and of course a lot of yesterday felt a bit like last summer's Olympics and Paralympics – that golden glow. You know the atmosphere on Centre Court was more like the Olympic Stadium, and perhaps Wembley, than we're usually used to down here. But yeah, I mean in terms of his achievement he's absolutely guaranteed his place in the history books.

The exchange was interrupted by the arrival of Murray himself.

Humphrys: Hello, Andy. Congratulations from all of us. And you'll be fed up to the back teeth with doing interviews, I'm sure, but nonetheless, has it sunk in, I mean did you wake up this morning thinking, what, am I really Wimbledon champion?

Murray: I think it was a bit different to the US Open last year. I think about 45 minutes or so after the match, I sat down, I was waiting to do the drug testing and it kind of all just hit me. I'd got so, so tired, and it just, just felt like everything kind of started to sink in then. And yesterday was a long day but… best day of my life so far.

There were moments when *Today's* longest-serving interviewer seemed to be straying outside his comfort zone;

Humphrys: Final quick thought about the balls that you play with. It's said that you don't like fluffy ones, you like smooth ones. Is that right?

Murray: Er, no idea where that…?

Humphrys: Ah, he's vanished… Are you still there Andy? I think you were trying to say you had no idea where that came from? I haven't either to be honest, but everyone is asking me about it.

Murray: I don't remember saying that.

Humphrys: I think it was when you're looking for the last ball to serve with, the crucial ball of the game maybe, you're looking for one that's a bit smoother than the others?

Murray: When you're serving for the match, the newer the ball, the faster the ball travels through the air. So when you're serving you prefer the new balls, when you're receiving it's better to receive with the slower balls.

Humphrys: Right. Well, whatever it is, it worked for you yesterday brilliantly. And again, congratulations from all of us. Andy Murray, many thanks.

Most of the sports reporting on *Today* is – like much of the rest of the programme – live, and therefore replete with risk. On 23 September 2004 the sports presenter Steve May introduced 'somebody… who could be the next Wayne Rooney… one of the hottest properties in the game [of football], certainly up north'. Jack Higginson, May told the audience, had attracted the interest of five Premiership clubs, 'after scouts spotted him scoring 37 times last season'. He was, however, only seven years old, and, excusably, unfamiliar with the give-and-take you expect in a national radio interview:

May: Okay, here we go. Hello Jack.

Higginson: Hello.

May: Hi, Jack how are you doing?

Higginson: Good.

May: Excellent. Now, you want to sign for Manchester United, I know, don't you?

Higginson: Yeah.

May: But you can't until April the 4th, and that's when you're eight years of age? Because football regulations mean that you can't sign until eight. But that's really what you want to do isn't it?

Higginson: Yeah.

May: Yeah. You are a big Man U fan then, obviously?

Higginson: Yeah.

May: Right. And your speciality is scoring double hat-tricks isn't it?

Higginson: Yeah

May: Tell us about that…

Higginson: Ummm… what did you say?

When May finally gave up – after an agonisingly long minute-and-a-half between the first and last 'yeah' – Humphrys paid a back-handed compliment to his interviewing technique, 'Well you got direct answers, which is more than we get most of the time. We'd give a lot for a one-word answer occasionally, we would.'

When the England cricket team beat Australia in the Sydney test on 6 January 2003, Garry Richardson was given a phone number for the England captain, Alec Stewart. 'I phoned the number several times,' he recalls, 'but there was no reply. Eventually, just at 8.25am, the producer came through from the [studio] gallery and told me that he'd got Stewart and he was ready to do the interview.' Richardson announced confidently to the audience '…and we can go live to Sydney, and Alec Stewart's waiting on the line, hello, Alec.' The voice that answered had a distinct Australian accent and sounded slurred:

Stewart: How are ya?

Richardson: I'm very well, how are you? It was a good way to finish.

Stewart: Yeah, I was rapt… it was tremendous.

Richardson: What would you have learned from this, you and the England team?

Stewart:… ahh I'd say a bloody good team.

Richardson: Absolutely, and now the World Cup. Are you looking forward to this?

Stewart: Yeah... argh... we think we're in for it now... just having a few cans now...

Richardson: Terrific. Well, Alec, many thanks indeed for coming on the programme to talk to me this morning... [laughing] do you know, I think the Aussies are so annoyed that we've beaten them, I don't think that was Alec Stewart. I think... was that somebody doing an impression?

Naughtie: I had the distinct feeling that that's exactly what it was, but I may be wrong.

Richardson: We had a few problems getting through to him, and I think somebody's picked up his mobile telephone and done a bit of an impression there, I know Alec's voice.

Naughtie: It didn't sound like a Surrey voice to me!

Richardson: No, it didn't sound like a Surrey voice. Anyway, there we are, here is some information that's genuine, no it's not because it's the racing selections...

The producer had dialled the wrong number. The real Alec Stewart appeared on the programme the following day.

The opening ceremony of the London 2012 Olympics

'It was about wonder'

FRANK COTTRELL-BOYCE, 28 JULY 2012

'The International Olympic Committee has the honour of announcing the games of the 30th Olympiad in 2012 are awarded to the City of London.' That announcement, made in Singapore by IOC president Jacques Rogge on 6 July 2005, was greeted with delight in Britain. But it was a shock to this country's neighbour; Paris had been firm favourite to host the games. London beat the French capital by 54 votes to 50 on the committee's fourth ballot. Tony Blair, who had just led his party to a third general election victory, was watching from Gleneagles, where he was waiting to host the G8 Summit; the French president Jacques Chirac, en route to Scotland for the summit, declared himself 'very disappointed'.

But within 24 hours London's celebrations were interrupted in the most violent manner: on 7 July four suicide bombers murdered more than 50 people on the capital's transport system. In Singapore, London mayor Ken Livingstone had to throw away his congratulatory scripts to proclaim instead his city's defiance of the murderers. France graciously joined in too, and its recent humiliation was forgotten as Chirac pledged to Londoners his 'solidarity, the compassion and the friendship of France'.

As London's giddy joy was hijacked, a sense of the sheer challenge began to dawn. Britain was now committed to following what turned out to be the most expensive and grandiose Olympics ever in 2008: an event staged in Beijing, which had trumpeted China's superpower aspirations. A budget approaching £3 billion was set aside for the London games... and then in 2008 came the financial crash, and billions more went into propping up the country's financial infrastructure. As a new coalition government began a programme of austerity from 2010, the costs of transforming the Olympics' East London site from post-industrial decay into glittering venue doubled, and then rose higher still.

It began to seem as though Paris, in losing the bid in 2005, had avoided a poisoned chalice. In the summer of 2011, the eyes of the world were on London again, and for all the wrong reasons, when an eruption of rioting, burning, looting and general lawlessness suggested a city in the grip of crisis. Given these threats from civil disorder and terrorism, was the security for the Olympic Games ever likely to be reliable? The private company, G4S, tasked with providing much of that security, threw in the towel, and the state, in the form of the armed forces, had to come to the rescue. Costs still increased – they would triple, to around £9 billion, in the end. The BBC even aired an uncannily on-the-nose comedy series entitled *Twenty Twelve*: it was a fly-on-the-wall mockumentary about the pretension and ineptness of the London Olympic bureaucracy, which, in a post-modern touch, occasionally featured cameos from the real-life games organiser Sebastian Coe, playing himself. To top it all, there was the weather. In the weeks before the games were due to open, the British 'summer' performed true to form – London was damp, chilly and unpleasant.

However, something began to turn. Amid the controversies and complaints about the cost of the Games, people began to snap up tickets. There were signs of enthusiasm. And then, come the opening day on 27 July 2012, the sun shone, bestowing a welcoming glow over an Olympic site that was a feat of design and engineering. A question mark still hung over the opening ceremony, since each was expected to be grander than the last. How, exactly, would Britain attempt to outmatch the mass choreographic glitz of Beijing? In the end, it did not even try. In the hands of film director Danny Boyle, the event that unfolded confounded everyone's expectations. Whether they liked it or loathed it, most struggled to find words to encapsulate what they had witnessed, and no one could say it was predictable.

'This has been billed,' announced *Today*'s reporter Tim Franks, whose record of proceedings aired the following morning on 28 July, as 'an antidote to the bombastic rhetoric of your average Olympic opening ceremony'. In an initial film montage, a dizzying, swooping camera tracked a route from the source of the Thames to the Olympic Stadium itself, swapping scenes of verdant river valley for the textures and sounds of urban life, set to snatches of the 'Eton Boating Song', the theme tune for soap-opera *East Enders*, and pop music. Then, cyclist Bradley Wiggins, lately triumphant in the Tour de France, sounded the Olympic bell to begin proceedings proper. A child's voice rang out with William Blake's hymn to pre-industrial England, 'Jerusalem'. What followed in the Olympic Stadium was the segment entitled 'Isle of Wonder', in which, as Franks put it, 'an utterly enticing agrarian idyll, bizarrely in the middle of the stadium' provided scenes of rural life – complete with morris dancing, farm workers, a village cricket match, thatched cottages and fields of turf. This gave way to the drumbeat of history (literally so, from prodigy Evelyn Glennie and hundreds of drummers) and to what Franks called 'pandemonium in the shape of the Industrial Revolution'. Factory chimneys miraculously rose from beneath the ground, belching smoke. From a grassy hillock (real turf), evoking Glastonbury's Tor and ancient British forts, a tree lifted to disgorge 'a sea of men and women, their faces blackened by grime', as if coming off shift from the mine, ready to populate this revolution. Presiding approvingly over this transformation was a top-hatted Kenneth Branagh in the guise of Victorian engineering genius Isambard Kingdom Brunel, his legs akimbo, a cigar firmly in hand. 'Be not afeard; the isle is full of noises,' he declaimed (from Shakespeare's *The Tempest*), stirringly backed by Elgar's 'Nimrod', as around him a human machine of workers and capitalists nurtured a land into prosperity. As the 19th century slipped into the 20th, processions representing popular movements streamed across – Jarrow marchers protesting against unemployment and poverty, suffragists fighting for the women's vote, Tommies from the trenches, the post-war Windrush generation of Caribbean immigrants, Chelsea pensioners, Pearly Kings and Queens, and even a Sgt Pepper's Lonely Hearts Club Band. In one of the evening's *coups de théâtre*, molten metal seemed to flow through the stadium to physicalise the metaphor of a nation being forged. The 'metal' formed rings, five of them, which were then raised aloft to become the Olympic emblem.

'And then,' described Franks, 'on the video screens: Bond, James Bond.'

He walked into Buckingham Palace – the real Buckingham Palace – and met the real Queen. The scene ended back in the Olympic Park with two figures dressed in a tux and a salmon dress parachuting out of a chopper over the stadium, just before the Queen, also in a salmon-pink dress, took her seat in the stadium.

The monarch was treated to no less than *two* verses of the national anthem, provided by the KAOS children's choir (which included partially deaf children), before the stadium transformed again into a different kind of sea – of beds, of nurses, of children in pyjamas, dancing to Mike Oldfield's 'Tubular Bells'. Many of these performers were actual patients and staff associated with Great Ormond Street children's hospital, and the purpose of the next two phases was to celebrate both the National Health Service and then – via an introductory reading by *Harry Potter* author J K Rowling – children's culture and literature. Famous characters, from the Child Catcher of *Chitty Chitty Bang Bang* to Voldemort himself, stormed the stage, before a profusion of Mary Poppins figures descended on their umbrellas. Afterwards, conductor Sir Simon Rattle led the London Symphony Orchestra in playing Vangelis's theme to the heroic, Oscar-winning sporting film *Chariots of Fire*, which pricked any pomposity when it evolved into a sketch in which Rowan Atkinson's comedy alter ego Mr Bean imagined himself cheating his way to victory in the film's most famous athletic sequence. A myriad of aural and visual stimuli followed – snatches of pop music, film, television, pop-up appearances by Sir Tim Berners-Lee, inventor of the World Wide Web – all loosely based on the idea of modern suburban life in an interconnected world. 'This, a first,' reflected Franks, 'at least I'm sure it's a first – Her Majesty the Queen watching a stadium full of people rocking out to the Sex Pistols and the Happy Mondays and Dizzie Rascal.' The emphasis was on Britain and London's multicultural dynamism.

Decorum was restored first in the procession of athletes into the stadium, then by the speeches, and ultimately in the revelation of the final mystery: who would carry in the torch and light the Olympic flame? When rower Steve Redgrave ran in, it seemed as if the bookies' predictions were correct – until he handed the torch to a group of seven teenage athletes, each sponsored by a leading sportsperson. Then, as Franks put it, 'They carried their flaming torches around the stadium, before lighting the 204 copper petals carried in by the competing teams. The petals rose and gathered in one tall, blazing blossom.' It was eloquently and elegantly done, and the message was clear: this was all about the future, about potential and about collective endeavour – the whole greater than the individual parts. The evening was rounded off by another kind of royalty, Sir Paul McCartney, who led the crowd in a rendition of 'Hey Jude'.

What, exactly, had the country and a large part of the world witnessed? Boyle's vision was idiosyncratic, reverential and irreverent, patriotic yet self-critical (Her Majesty also got to savour the Sex Pistols' 'God Save the Queen'), exuberant, humorous, solemn at times, emotive, self-absorbed yet brashly exhibitionist. Had it succeeded? And if so, how? On the following morning, *Today* tried to get to grips with it.

In Franks's view, 'Some of this show may have been incomprehensible to the outside world, but to a British audience, where scepticism isn't just healthy, it's practically a national sport, this felt like a winning start.' The BBC's home editor Mark Easton largely agreed, adding that:

> **My absolutely favourite bit of analysis comes from Robert Lloyd in the *LA Times*, who said the ceremony 'had at times the quality of seeming completely random. If there's a through-line to be untangled it might be something like, "Sorry for the unintended consequences, but we did give you steam engines, great pop music and comedy, and the roots of social networking. It was ugly there for a while, but we're all right – and everybody dance now."'**

If Boyle had wanted to eschew anything resembling the massed ranks of Beijing 2008, he certainly seemed to have succeeded – his confection owed something to a vast 1960s-style 'happening' or a contemporary flash mob.

'The adjectives I'm seeing in the international press this morning,' Easton continued, 'are, you know, "thoughtful", "quirky", "baffling". Er, the *Toronto Star*'s correspondent, apparently reporting from a London boozer, said, "I think I've seen the most chaotic but possibly greatest entertainment event of my generation."'

Baffling it certainly must have been to those unfamiliar with a clutch of references that were touchstones of the modern British cultural experience (a brief snatch of

BBC weather forecaster Michael Fish batting away rumours of a 'hurricane' that duly materialised; a landmark lesbian kiss on TV, from soap opera *Brookside*).

'Did we,' asked John Humphrys on *Today* the following morning, 'learn anything about ourselves as a result of it?' For Easton, the primary message seemed to be of a nation confident enough to laugh at itself – 'Even the Queen can be in on the joke.'

Humphrys introduced Frank Cottrell-Boyce, who 'actually wrote the script for the ceremony. But I didn't spot the script.' Humphrys was joking, sort of. But Boyce, illuminatingly, responded:

> **Maybe you shouldn't have been able to kind of interpret it that much, because it was about wonder, you know, and... we had on the wall all the time this great line from G K Chesterton where he said, 'The world is not perishing for lack of wonders; the world is perishing for lack of wonder.' The theme of the show was to take things that we're very familiar with and make them seem again wonderful to us.**

'Maybe it was all right,' he ventured, 'that you're a little bit bewildered.'

After all, Danny Boyle, who had also been the director of the 1996 cult film *Trainspotting* (which got its own three-second reference in the ceremony), often dealt in juxtaposed images, not necessarily in a linear narrative. Cottrell-Boyce emphasised Boyle's credo that 'the more true to yourself you are, the more universal you'll be', so that for Boyle and his chief collaborators 'for something on this scale, it's a very, very personal show'. The ceremony was not a film, but it was nevertheless the production of a filmmaker's vision – the director as *auteur*.

'Did it do that for you, Giles, "repolish the patina of life?"' Humphrys asked journalist Giles Coren, echoing one of Cottrell-Boyce's phrases.

'Absolutely,' replied Coren, who cheerfully admitted to having entirely metamorphosed from cynic to enthusiast, although the readers of his *Times* column would have been confused. As he explained:

> **I'm in this slightly embarrassing position because... depending on where you live in the country you've got a piece by me saying this is a load of inflated nonsense and then a piece by me saying this is the best night of my life.**

In other words, between filing a sceptical response for the newspaper's early editions and then actually experiencing the ceremony before filing for the late edition, he underwent a complete conversion: 'I'm not a patriot, but... it made me feel incredibly proud to be British for reasons that I hadn't really realised,' he explained. Those reasons stemmed in great part from the spectacle's refusal to be trammelled, and from its capacity for irreverence. '[To] hop backwards and forwards between laughter and tears like a great Shakespeare play was, you know, it was stunning,' concluded Coren.

Another convert was the classicist Mary Beard, who reflected to listeners that:

> Government ministers are always telling us that we should be more patriotic and we should stand up for our country and feel that we're British, and they do it in such a terribly finger-wagging way – you know, 'Thou shalt read *Midsummer Night's Dream* or else,' and here was Danny Boyle, and he understood patriotism better than the rest of them, and he'd listened and been alert to the kind of things that really matter to you if you're British.

Writer Lynne Truss, delivering one of her humorous occasional monologues on *Today*, was largely in sympathy with the foregoing commentators. She had dreaded the opening ceremony since 2008, 'at the end of the last Olympics, when a pathetic model of a double-decker London bus drove into the arena at Beijing and a singer completely unknown to me came out of the top of it, weirdly attached to a stick'. It was therefore with relief that in 2012 she witnessed 'a ceremony with style, wit, colour, warmth, intelligence, spectacle and a fantastic soundtrack', though best of all, in her view, was the fact that 'Boris Johnson played no part whatsoever in the proceedings' – a reference to Livingstone's successor as London mayor.

Boyle's vision did not win universal accolades. Too political, thought some, in its choices of emphasis, in its eschewing of the Great and Good (though Churchill's statue, in a CGI moment, got to wave) and its shortage of conventional patriotism. On the evening of the ceremony itself, Conservative MP Aidan Burley blew up a Twitterstorm when he tapped out: 'Thank God the athletes have arrived! Now we can move on from leftie multicultural crap.' Firmly in the bah-humbug camp was *Daily Mail* columnist Peter Hitchens who, reviewing the closing ceremony on *Today* two weeks later, nevertheless managed to 'laugh quite a lot' because 'it was even more of a moronic inferno than the opening ceremony'. 'Even if I'd been interested,' he mused, 'I'd have been bored.'

That Hitchens was happy to laugh was presumably something of a relief to him, for – as quoted by *Today*'s James Naughtie – he had written that the whole atmosphere surrounding the 2012 games smacked of 'New Labour Totalitarianism', in the spirit of which 'he expected to be arrested for not smiling'. (The fact that David Cameron was now prime minister was a mere technicality, for he was heir of Blair.) In Hitchens's eyes, 'We forget the old monarchist Christian country that we used to be and we become funky, drug-taking New Britain.' The ceremonies 'told us that we aren't anybody any more.'

Tony Blair himself had stood down as prime minister five years before the games were held, but he challenged the Hitchens view in an interview with James Naughtie on *Today* the day after the closing ceremony:

> Naughtie: Let me ask you this: as you watched, let's say last night or the opening ceremony or parts of the games, what did you see about this country that you think has genuinely changed, let's say in the last 15/20 years?

> Blair: Well, I think, you see, the country actually expressed its values in a fantastic way throughout the whole of the Olympics. We were warm, generous-minded, [with a] sense of fair play, great British humour. We did deliver – I mean the prime minister's right about that. We actually put it on and we delivered, but right from the time we won the bid, we were anxious to portray London and Britain as it is today, and it is a place of many different cultures and faiths, which is not to say we aren't proud of our Christian heritage, but I'm also proud when I see people who come from abroad, like Mo Farah who, you know, win two Olympic golds and serve as a great example to our country.

Team GB scooped a record number of medals in 2012 (including actually topping the medals table in the Paralympic Games), and the entire country appeared to be swept up in a mood of confidence, happy to wrap itself in a flag symbolising something that was more diverse, more variegated than ever before.

In her *New York Times* review of Boyle's opening ceremony, columnist Sarah Lyall remembered back to when the New Labour government had striven to produce a British 'statement of values', prompting the London *Times* to mount a motto competition. The favourite to emerge was 'No Motto Please: We're British'.

Perhaps it could have served as Boyle's motto too.

Thought for the day : Professor Mona Siddiqui

16 January 2015

What does insulting Islam mean today – seemingly everything from provocative cartoons to having a website championing free speech. The Saudi writer Raif Badawi has been sentenced to ten years in prison and 1,000 lashes, 50 per week, for setting up a website calling for a more liberal and free society in Saudi Arabia; he was arrested in 2012 and his blog shut down.

Today he will receive the second round of lashes after Friday prayers, despite international condemnation of torture and human rights violations. As so often the cry of 'God is great' will be followed by an act of violence. The world will watch as we become increasingly desensitised to the levels of brutality perpetrated by Islamists and states of all creeds and colours. Saudi Arabia isn't the only country to violate international laws but it does so often with an air of chilling certainty that its punishments reflect piety.

If globalisation has made the world a smaller place, never before have cultural values seemed so far apart. I believe we should speak up not out of any moral high ground but rather if we stand for any kind of universal human dignity, we can't remain silent. After all, it's the appeal of a certain puritanical and violent Islam that is being played out on the streets of Europe; and what happens in distant lands affects us over here. It's one thing for leaders to march together defending free speech, and however welcome that is – it's quite another to stand up for it in the face of autocratic states.

And yet this is the real challenge because one country isn't supposed to dictate to another how it should manage its laws; political realities make it very difficult to intervene in the culture of another country. Over the last few years, writers and artists have spoken out against the destruction of all that Saudi Arabia considers an insult to its ideas of true Islam; and yet in the end we have been helpless to do anything. Today we can plead that Raif Badawi's crime is pardoned. If we remain silent in the assurance that forgiveness will just happen, it won't.

'God is great' is heard all the time but it seems to me that the words 'God is merciful' are gradually disappearing from the streets and in the pulpits. A merciful God is of no value to those for whom mercy means weakness. 'Je suis Raif' is springing up over social media but we don't need another hashtag to appreciate that the demand for a more open society can only ever be a good thing wherever we live. In Raif's own words, 'His government's hold over people's minds and society shall vanish like dust carried off in the wind,' but if this does happen, it may already be too late for Raif.

CHAPTER 5

SOCIAL

CHANGE

Gay rights in Britain: from decriminalisation to marriage

'Their love is worth the same as anyone else's love'
DAVID CAMERON, 22 MAY 2013

'Although the bill gives immunity to discreet homosexuals who live out their unfortunate condition in private, it, in fact in some cases, makes the penalties harsher if they behave flagrantly, or certainly if they deflect their homosexual impulses towards young people who are in their formative years.'

With these words, Leo Abse, a Labour MP, responded to questioning on *Today* on 20 December 1966. He was discussing the bill he was introducing to decriminalise homosexual acts in private between men aged 21 or over, and while the tone of his remarks jars horribly today, the proposal was, at the time, regarded as radical.

Leo Abse was taking up the recommendations of the ground-breaking Wolfenden Report on homosexuality, produced nearly a decade earlier, in 1957. His bill led to the 1967 Sexual Offences Act, which decriminalised sex between adult men (there was no law against lesbianism), but applied only in England and Wales; homosexual sex remained subject to the criminal law in Scotland until 1981 and in Northern Ireland until 1982. The pace of change since Abse's bill may have been slow, but the journey from that landmark legislation to equal marriage almost half a century later represents perhaps the biggest revolution in social attitudes during the lifetime of *Today*.

Even during the so-called 'Swinging Sixties', homosexuals still attracted severe censure, and there was a widespread belief that homosexuality was socially corrosive. Abse was interviewed by Patricia Brent, one of *Today*'s senior producers:

> Brent: Mr Abse, I'm sure [there are] a great many people this morning who feel that you and the government, if they eventually pass this bill, will be condoning something that is absolutely wrong and immoral.

> Abse: It is not a criminal offence to commit adultery. It is not a criminal offence to fornicate. These are not criminal offences according to our law. But the fact that the House of Commons does not make these criminal offences does not mean we approve of them. We do not condone homosexuality. What the House of Commons has decided is that the homosexual has enough troubles without,

in addition, having the fear, the insecurity and the blackmail that arises from the existing law.

Brent: A lot of people have felt that the merchant navy should have been excluded from this release from punishment. You, of course, don't agree with this. Can you explain why?

Abse: I wouldn't say I don't agree. I think that the belated representations that have been made by the shipping interests have riveted attention now to this problem, and in the House this view is expressed, and I have given undertakings very willingly that in the committee stage we will not resist, those of us who are sponsoring this bill, an amendment which will place the merchant navy in the same position as we have placed the navy.

Brent: The navy and indeed the other services are at the moment excluded from the bill, aren't they?

Abse: To the extent that it is possible for those services to commence disciplinary proceedings against the men who commit homosexual acts while they're within the service's jurisdiction. This is a disciplinary matter which arises because it is felt, I think generally, that where there are people who are in subordinate positions one to the other, that it may be a necessary matter to maintain the cohesion and discipline within the forces.

Brent: It seems to me that once you start making this sort of exception you could go on and make many more.

Abse: I think that the bill deals with the generality of matters, deals with people living under normal lives in no extraordinary circumstances. I think that one has to concede that there may be special cases when men are herded together in a hermetically male world, which could not survive without discipline, and I think a case can be argued for differentiating between that type of case and the case of those who live out their lives under normal civilian conditions.

The ban on homosexual acts within the armed forces remained in place until the end of the century. And in the immediate aftermath of the Sexual Offences Act being passed the number of arrests for 'gross indecency' by homosexuals actually increased.

The law was one area of contention. Language – and the prejudices and value-judgements it carries – was another battlefield. The terms used to describe male homosexuals – 'poof', 'queer', 'gay' among them – were themselves highly charged. On 5 September 1973 *Today* interviewed George Vickers, a pub landlord who had been granted the first ever licence in England to run an exclusively gay bar (in Nottingham).

It was still commonplace to talk about 'gay people' as distinct from 'normal people', and when Vickers was asked how he perceived the problem of discrimination against homosexuals, he replied:

> It's very, very difficult, because a normal person – I say a normal person, we think we're normal as such – but a man and a woman, they can go to a club and watch a cabaret and they can dance after. We can go to a club, we can go to a cabaret, but when it comes to the dancing and enjoying ourselves after, this is when it comes to a full stop.

The main Christian churches continued to campaign against homosexuality becoming more openly and widely accepted. At the end of December 1975 Pope Paul VI published *Persona Humana* [The Human Person]: Declaration on Certain Questions concerning Sexual Ethics, which restated the Church's traditional teaching that: 'Sexual matters can result in mortal sin... Premarital sex is contrary to the Church's doctrine. Experience teaches that love must be protected by the stability of marriage.' The document declared, 'In the present period, the corruption of morals has increased, and one of the most serious indications of this corruption is the unbridled exaltation of sex.' But it also addressed the dilemma of those gay people who practised 'homosexual relations within a sincere communion of life and love analogous to marriage'. They should, it concluded, 'certainly be treated with understanding and sustained in the hope of overcoming their personal difficulties and their inability to fit into society. Their culpability will be judged with prudence.'

However, as the BBC's correspondent Paul Tilsley pointed out on *Today* on 15 January 1976, 'The report also describes homosexuality as being intrinsically disordered and they [homosexual acts] can in no case be approved of.' It was pointed out, though, that masturbation too was deemed 'intrinsically disordered'.

Alan Clark, secretary for the Campaign for Homosexual Reform, responded on *Today*: 'The attitude of the Catholic Church has become increasingly militant in all matters sexual. Their attitude to birth control, abortion, all of the non-procreational parts of people's lives are being stamped on with increasing savagery.' Asked if he felt the recent Catholic Church report would be upsetting to homosexuals who were also practising Catholics, he continued, 'I think it will. There are many of them. They are being made to lie in the one place of course where they shouldn't have to – their church.' And what of the reaction of the homosexual community as a whole? Clark was asked. 'They are used to the attitude of the Catholic Church,' he replied, adding, 'They have always considered that the Catholic Church has been the major exponent of anti-homosexual philosophy in general.' Did he think the Vatican's latest statement would make any difference at all to homosexuals? 'I think it will harden the attitude of an awful lot of them. I think that the Catholic homosexuals may start coming out in the churches now and fighting this attitude.'

In certain British newspapers throughout the 1970s and 1980s, the abuse and shaming of gay people was considered quite acceptable. Some victims were outed in the most prurient tabloid articles and made to pay the social price. The feeling of stigma was not helped by the fact that the HIV/AIDS epidemic, emerging in its full terrifying force in the early 1980s, affected the homosexual community disproportionately badly, and was even branded 'the gay plague' for a time. On top of that, in 1988 Margaret Thatcher's Conservative government introduced 'Clause 28', a new legal amendment which had the stated aim of banning the 'intentional promoting' (but often in practice, discussion) of homosexuality in schools.

And while the use of racist language had been made a criminal offence, derogatory words continued to be used about homosexuals in many tabloids. In May 1990, the Press Council upheld a complaint against the *Sun* for using the word 'poof' in an insulting manner when describing homosexuals. Terry Sanderson, a *Gay Times* journalist, confronted the *Sun*'s Garry Bushell on the *Today* broadcast of 14 May 1990, after Bushell had repeatedly used the word in his column:

> **Sanderson: I was concerned about the abusive way in which tabloids were treating gay issues.**
>
> **Bushell: I would argue that the word is valid and it isn't even derogatory... I think this is a ridiculous decision, and the Press Council has been duped by a very militant and unrepresentative homosexual lobby.**
>
> Sanderson: This doesn't seem to tally with what I know about gay people, which is slightly more than Mr Bushell does. There have been previous complaints to the Press Council by other homosexual people and groups... this is the first time that they've upheld the principle.
>
> **Bushell: I think the militant homosexuals fuel intolerance themselves with their demands.**
>
> Sanderson: It's all very well blaming the victim for the crime, but we're not the perpetrators of this aggression in the newspapers. The newspapers themselves originate these stories...

Presenter Sue MacGregor asked Sanderson, 'Do you notice a greater aggression in the streets against gay men?' A truly tragic tale ensued: 'Absolutely. In my own area of London, only last week, a gay man was kicked to death by a gang of yobs who no doubt felt it was "just a poofter", so it didn't matter.'

A spate of killings of gay men in West London in 1989 and 1990 eventually led to the formation of OutRage, a gay group calling for the police to protect gay men rather than prosecute them. As a sign of changing times, by September 1990 a Lesbian and Gay Police Association was formed to encourage understanding of homosexual matters in policing, and to reflect its members' concerns.

As regards the law and its enactment, following the 1967 act a further goal of campaigners was to lower the homosexual age of consent from 21, which was significantly higher than the long-established heterosexual age of 16. This proved tough. In 1994, that age was reduced to 18. However, it was not until 2000 that consensual equality for homosexuals was finally achieved during New Labour's third year in power. It was under the same government that a gay identity would, for the first time in British public life, no longer discriminate anyone from achieving high political office. Chris Smith, who in 1984 had been the first MP to 'come out', was made minister for Culture, Media and Sport by Tony Blair, while other gay MPs were also given prominent government roles.

As the millennium came to a close, the gay rights debate was progressing significantly, shifting from the relationship of homosexuals to society, to the ways in which committed homosexuals might wish their relationships to be recognised. In 2002, same-sex couples as well as single people gained the right to adopt children. There was debate, as there always is for the passing of such legislation, which incrementally placed gay rights on a par with heterosexual ones and was far from a foregone conclusion.

Ian Burford, an actor in a 40-year relationship with his partner, put the case for legal equality during the *Today* broadcast of 6 December 2002. Burford had just signed a partnership register in London – an initiative organised by Mayor Ken Livingstone, but with no legal force – and wanted to highlight for listeners the ineffectiveness of that situation: that without legal recognition of long-term gay relationships, homosexuals were made vulnerable, and were denied the legal protections that committed heterosexuals enjoyed, for example, when one partner died:

> There exist serious inequalities over things like death duties, inheritance tax, joint property, next of kin, hospital visits… Somebody like ourselves, [who have] had a partnership of 40-years length now, would be at a great disadvantage if one of us were to die quickly. It wouldn't apply at all if we were considered husband and wife. Also, at a time of death, which preoccupies us as we get older, families have a great deal more say in the [current] law than someone who spent their life with that person.

But as John Humphrys explained, Tony Blair's government was considering a significant step forward: 'For years, many homosexual men and women have been saying that they should be entitled to get married or at least have the same legal rights as married couples and be able to register their relationships. For years, governments have said no. Well, it seems that has changed.' Barbara Roche, Labour minister for Social Exclusion and Equality, appeared on *Today* that morning after Ian Burford, saying, somewhat tentatively:

> I do think society has moved on. And I think we recognise that there are very many people in gay relationships and lesbian relationships who are in very loving relationships, and they may have been in very long, enduring, loving relationships, but their partnership has no recognition in law. What I'm seeking to do is to say that I think that there is a strong case for considering a civil partnership registration scheme.

Humphrys asked, 'Is it your intention, then, to put a gay relationship on the same level, to all intents and purposes, as a married relationship?' Roche replied, 'Well, we're not talking about marriage here.'

The first civil partnership was registered in December 2005. 'Now, these aren't officially recognised gay marriages,' affirmed *Today*'s James Naughtie on 19 December, 'but legal arrangements that give couples the same rights as those who are married.' It was already too much for some. Protester Reverend David McIlveen of the Free Presbyterian Church in Belfast spoke to Naughtie:

> As far as we're concerned, it is a marriage in all but name… We look to the Bible for our guidance and instruction on marriage. It is described in the Bible as a relationship between male and female for the bringing up of children in the fear and the love and the admonition of the Lord. It is revealed as being an honourable relationship, whereas the Bible speaks of same-sex relationships as being an abomination… and therefore from a biblical perspective, we're very much opposed to what is called a civil partnership.

The interview was cut unexpectedly short when the line went down, and Naughtie remarked, 'Oh, I think there's some kind of divine intervention or something there.'

When the general election in 2010 produced the Conservative and Liberal Democrat coalition government, gay marriage had not appeared in the Tory manifesto. Despite opposition from many MPs on his own side who knew it was not a popular issue among traditionalist Tory voters, Prime Minister David Cameron pushed ahead to get gay marriage approved by Parliament. During the *Today* broadcast of 22 May 2013 – the day after the House of Commons had voted its approval – Cameron spoke with feeling about his stance:

> I think it's important that we have this degree of equality and I say this as someone who's a massive supporter of marriage. I think marriage is a wonderful

institution. It helps people commit to each other. I think it's such a good institution that it should be available to gay people as well as to heterosexuals... And I think we should think about it like this, that there will be young boys in schools today who are gay, who are worried about being bullied, who are worried what society thinks of them, who can see that the highest Parliament in the land has said that their love is worth the same as anyone else's love and that we believe in equality.

More broadly, Cameron suggested that gay rights were now a pressing global issue, too: 'I think the same-sex marriage issue, I think it's important: every country across the world is having to address this. In New Zealand, the centre-right government has just legalised gay marriage; 11 states, I think 12, states in the US have now done the same thing.'

In the UK recent surveys have found around three-quarters of people now support same-sex marriage. But in Northern Ireland at the time of writing, gay people, though allowed civil partnerships, remain excluded from entering into David Cameron's 'wonderful institution' of marriage.

Today's first openly gay presenter, Evan Davis, was appointed in 2008, and worked on the programme until he left for *Newsnight* in 2014.

From Windrush to the Windrush scandal: race relations, racial tensions

'I cannot get a flat because of the colour of my face'
WILLIAM ATTA, 21 APRIL 1958

The arrival of a few hundred Caribbean men aboard the ship *Empire Windrush* at the port of Tilbury on the river Thames on 22 June 1948 has long been regarded as a pivotal moment in the forming of a multiracial Britain; it marked the beginning of mass immigration from Britain's numerous colonies and former colonies. Their ship gave its name to the early post-war immigrants from the Caribbean; the 'Windrush generation' often met a frosty reception, as did many of the immigrants from India, Pakistan and Bangladesh who followed them.

One key problem they faced was finding a home. *Today* – in its infancy in 1958 – wanted to interview a Cambridge-educated Ghanaian, William Atta, who was in London reading for the bar. The programme's producers, though, had encountered significant trouble in getting hold of this former member of the Ghana Assembly. As Atta explained when *Today* tracked him down (for the broadcast of 21 April 1958), 'I have no telephone number because I cannot get a flat because of the colour of my face.' He continued, 'I could perhaps get rooms in a house devoted entirely to coloured people, but this sort of segregation is not the way I want to lead my life when I am in London.' Atta, who came from a family of Ghanaian chiefs and aristocrats and went on to serve as his country's minister of foreign affairs, told his story to *Today*'s first presenter, Alan Skempton:

> Sometimes when I speak on the phone it seems, at first, quite hopeful – then landlords are not quite sure of my nationality and they invite me to come up and see the flat. But when I say I'm coloured, that's the end... Some people try to be nice about it, but this doesn't really make things any better. Last week I went to see a flat which had been advertised and which I liked very much. The landlady was very nice about it, but she said she had already had another application and the flat was no longer available. I had a feeling that this was just another excuse, so I got a white friend to ring up for me and ask about the flat. The landlady said

it was still available, and 'would he like to come up and see it?' – in fact, it was just as I had thought.

Ghana had become independent the previous year – the first British colony in sub-Saharan Africa to do so – and Atta warned his British audience, 'You know, you should really do something about this. If you allow it to go on, you'll be letting a few landlords and landladies do incalculable harm to relations between our countries.'

August 1958 saw racial unrest in Nottingham, followed a week later by race riots and serious violence against the black community in Notting Hill, London. Such incidents created mistrust of the police in many immigrant communities, as they felt their complaints were not being taken seriously. One positive development in reaction to that London riot was the creation, on 30 January 1959, of a Caribbean carnival in St Pancras Town Hall, televised by the BBC. It was a seed for the now internationally celebrated Notting Hill Carnival.

As the numbers of new arrivals burgeoned, so too did the forces of reaction. White nationalist organisations began forming political wings, largely motivated by opposition to black, Asian and Muslim immigration. Some such groups, like the British National Party (or BNP, founded 1960), called for voluntary repatriation; others, such as the National Front (or NF, founded in part out of the BNP in 1967), demanded compulsory repatriation. In 1962, a BNP rally in Trafalgar Square led to a race riot. Beyond the vile name-calling and abuse that many black and Asian people faced, one recurring slogan that right-wing nationalists threw at these 'wogs' was 'Go home!' – implying that Britain could never be their proper home.

In 1965 Britain's first Race Relations Act was introduced; though limited in its measures to combat discrimination, it did at least create the offence of 'incitement to racial hatred'. Additionally, the Race Relations Board was established to assess individual cases of racial discrimination and to mediate. A more comprehensive act was passed in 1968, the reasons for it highlighted in a *Today* interview on 18 April 1967, with the authors of a report that year by Political and Economic Planning (an influential think tank which had been founded in the 1930s and developed a reputation for research into social issues): 'The main point arising is that we've found substantial discrimination against coloured immigrants in employment, housing and in a number of services.'

The authors reported that employers were unembarrassed to reveal how the old colonial hierarchy applied: 'Many of the employers said that they would not promote a coloured worker so as to have authority over white British staff, because of the resistance they expected from the British staff.' There was even a kind of apartheid in certain companies: 'We also found a number of employers who installed separate canteens and toilets for the coloured workers.'

We interviewed the employers in 60 retail shops and we found that 20 of them would discriminate against immigrants, particularly by not having them [serving] on the counter, or indeed on special counters – some of them mentioned, for example, fresh foods and corsetry.

If certain immigrant populations seemed reluctant to mix with white British people, 'many of the immigrants,' the report's authors asserted, 'do go out and try to lead a British life and this was particularly true of the West Indians... These immigrants do realise that they are being discriminated against and they find it the most disappointing feature of their life.'

Mainstream political opposition to immigration was finding a home on the Conservative Party's right wing, in particular among the members of the traditionalist Monday Club, founded in 1961. The most infamously incendiary speech on race relations of the post-war period was given by the Tory shadow defence secretary, Enoch Powell, on 20 April 1968, three days before the second reading of Labour's Race Relations Bill. Powell quoted a white working-class constituent: 'In this country in 15 or 20 years' time, the black man will have the whip hand over the white man.' In Powell's eyes, hundreds of thousands of 'native' Britons felt similarly, 'in the areas that are already undergoing the total transformation to which there is no parallel in a thousand years of English history'. He described British immigration policies as 'mad', adding, for drama, 'It is like watching a nation busily engaged in heaping up its own funeral pyre.'

For the broadcast of 25 April 1968, *Today* asked some black Britons for their reactions following Powell's speech. One of them was simply resigned: 'The British have always felt this way and I think it's time it came out in the open.' But another told *Today*'s reporter, Vibart Wills, 'I work in an office where the people are mostly white English people and I've made very many friends among the English people. They come to my home, I go to theirs. We have meals together and all that – we get on very well together.' The vox pops ended with this exchange:

Wills: Excuse me. I've been talking to a number of people from overseas, a number of coloured people, and all seem to see Mr Powell as being the villain of the piece.

Man: Yes. Yes! Look, it seems to me Mr Powell used to be a teacher of Greek. It seems to me he's still living in the ancient days.

Powell was sacked from the Shadow Cabinet by the Conservative leader Edward Heath immediately after the speech. But on the political right, politicians continued over the years to question immigrant communities' loyalty towards Britain. The former Conservative minister Norman Tebbit stirred controversy in 1990 with his 'cricket test' – 'Which side do they [immigrants] cheer for?' he asked, 'It's an interesting test. Are you still harking back to where you came from or where you are?'

Tensions between segments of black and Asian urban communities and the police bubbled away throughout, surfacing alarmingly at times. One of the most violent series of riots took place across several major cities in spring and summer 1981, beginning in Brixton, South London. Ralph Smith, BBC Radio's North of England correspondent, described one day's clashes in Toxteth, Liverpool, vividly on *Today* on 7 June:

> **In broad daylight, youths broke into a dairy and hijacked half a dozen milk floats, which they used as weapons against the police, aiming them at a line of officers across the road... As night fell, the scene was illuminated by buildings burning out of control, while ranks of police fought a pitch battle with youths – some of them looked as young as 13 or 14... Patients in an old people's hospital were threatened by flames from a neighbouring building. They were rescued by a fleet of Liverpool taxi drivers who pleaded with the rioters to be allowed in to help...**

The chief constable of Merseyside, Ken Oxford, laid the blame on 'a criminal element of black youths'. The reaction to his analysis revealed the strength of feeling among many in the British black community at what they saw as the continuing racial bias of policing. Responding to the *Today* reporter Ralph Smith at a meeting with police on 3 August, one Toxteth community representative listed the recurrent general complaints about 'harassment, police attitude, lack of training, lack of police officers of ethnic minority in the police force'. Police stop-and-search policies, largely targeting black and Asian youths, would remain a bone of contention for decades.

Fear of discrimination in communities was exacerbated by sometimes violent racial attacks. The most high-profile racial murder in the 1990s was the brutal stabbing to death of 18-year-old Stephen Lawrence by a gang of white youths in London on 22 April 1993. The British-born son of Doreen and Neville Lawrence – who had come to Britain from Jamaica in the 1960s – was a promising student. Five suspects were identified early on, but police investigations were considered inept and potentially racially biased. A police attempt at prosecution failed. Stephen's parents' private prosecution failed too, in 1996; however, frustrated by the Metropolitan Police's conduct, they fought on for many years afterwards for justice.

In 1997, Labour Home Secretary Jack Straw ordered an inquiry, led by Sir William Macpherson, into both Stephen Lawrence's murder and the subsequent police investigation. Macpherson's far-reaching report of 1999 described the Metropolitan Police as 'institutionally racist' and recommended major reforms, largely carried out. It called for the strengthening of the Race Relations Act to fight racial discrimination.

When Edward Stourton spoke to Doreen Lawrence on 23 December 1999, it was in the week when Mario Pereira had been jailed for life for the torture and murder of another black man, Michael Menson, in 1997. In that case the police had initially concluded that Menson had set fire to himself as a result of depression. It was only after an inquest returned a verdict of unlawful killing that the case was reopened.

> **Stourton: Two events this week to remind us of what's been a disturbing theme throughout the year: the troubled state of race relations and the police. The Menson case raised more disturbing questions about the way investigations are conducted when the victim is black, and the family of Stephen Lawrence named 42 officers they are pursuing in a civil action. We're talking to the home secretary in a moment, but Doreen Lawrence is on the line now...**

Asked whether this year has taught us anything, Mrs Lawrence replied, 'I don't feel the police have learned anything because, yet again, it's the family who had to pursue and chase the police in order for them to do and act in the way in which they should. If the family has to take up the reins in the fight for justice it's not what the police are doing.'

> **Stourton: Well, we're talking to the home secretary in just a moment. Is there anything, or any way, you feel that the government has let you down in the way it's responded to the inquiry, into the recommendations of the inquiry into your son's death?**

> **Lawrence: I won't say that the government has let us down because I mean to say it's through them why we had the inquiry. But what I would say is that though the Race Relation[s Acts] were to bring the police in line with all other public services, I believe that they haven't gone far enough and it's just sort of skimmed the surface because I think the Race Relations [Acts], in order to bring the police in line, should have gone much further.**

The home secretary, Jack Straw, was interviewed live immediately afterwards, and defended the government's actions:

> **Straw: I know exactly the point that Doreen is making because I've talked to her about this privately. She's not suggesting for a second that we've not accepted the full force of the Macpherson recommendations, because indeed we have done. Sir William Macpherson said that we should extend the Race Relations Acts to cover the police, and we've in fact gone further than that, and we're going to cover the whole of the public service. The issue that Doreen is raising is whether the Race Relations Acts generally should prohibit what is called indirect discrimination as well as direct discrimination. There's no argument that there**

shouldn't be indirect discrimination, but it's a highly technical sort of quasi-legal issue, which is how you achieve that without throwing the baby out with the bathwater. How, for example, you end up with a situation where you can ensure that there is no indirect discrimination that you don't want, but there's all sorts of indirect discrimination that you may want – for example in favour of the elderly, in favour of the Asian elderly and so on, so it's a complicated area.

Stourton: But it's a very important question, isn't it, because in this indirect discrimination is the kind of thing that does form, what one might call, a culture of racism or institutional racism, to use that the phrase that the Lawrence inquiry report used.

Straw: Yes, it does, there's no question it's....

Stourton: And therefore, it is at the root of what does seem to be a perennial problem.

Straw: There's no question it's the issue of tackling indirect discrimination as well as direct discrimination is of huge importance and we are tackling it. We're not going down the route of legislating for indirect discrimination specifically – in the way, not that Macpherson suggested, they didn't raise this, but others have.

Stourton: So how are you going to deal with it?

Straw: ... may I just... What we're intending to do, and this has already been made clear, is to place a positive duty on all public authorities to promote equality. But in addition to that if you're talking about the police service I am systematically working through the recommendations of Macpherson, which were 70, to change the culture of the police service both in London and outside, and in that I have had the full support of the present commissioner of police Sir Paul Condon, and the new commissioner who'll take over at the end of January, John Stevens, and I accept and the police service do, that there have been very, very significant failings in two regards. One is in terms of indirect discrimination, but the other, which was as much behind the failure of the police to properly investigate the murder of Stephen Lawrence and some other murders, has been a degree of degrading of the serious investigation capacity of the police and that is also being tackled.

In addition, Sir William Macpherson's report suggested that the law of double jeopardy – where a person could not be tried twice for the same offence – be changed for cases of murder in which there was new and compelling evidence. That proved a controversial idea, even for those involved in the case. John Humphrys discussed it with Imran

Khan, who had been the Lawrence family's lawyer at the inquiry, and John Wadham, the director of the campaign group Liberty (originally the National Council for Civil Liberties) on 25 February 1999:

> Humphrys: And this other question of double jeopardy – another look being taken at the whole question of whether somebody could be tried for a crime of which he'd already been acquitted.

> Khan: Well, certainly for the Lawrences, it wouldn't apply in their case, it's not retrospective. And if you ask the Lawrences they would welcome that if there was an opportunity to get the killers of Stephen Lawrence back into court and convicted. But... as a defence lawyer, from that perspective, I wouldn't agree with the double jeopardy proposition. I think there needs to be a finality to criminal proceedings. One of those reasons is precisely what happened in this case: that you would have shoddy and incompetent police forces allowing things to go, with the prospect that, okay, if people got away with it they could come back, new evidence could come to light and they could continue. You need police officers to concentrate their mind in the investigation and ensure that people are not pursued endlessly through the criminal courts.

> Humphrys: Fair enough, Mr Wadham?

> Wadham: Well, I agree with all of that. The human rights legislation, particularly the United Nations International Covenant on Civil and Political Rights, says it's outlawed, and the reason that they outlaw it is precisely as Imran has already said. This case is actually about the incompetence and the racism of the police force. Actually, tinkering with the law, taking away the rights of defendants, wouldn't have helped. And, of course, we know from the racism within the criminal justice system generally that these kind of provisions, having a go twice at somebody who has been acquitted, will be used more often against black people than against white.

In fact, the double jeopardy law was changed – in 2005. Thanks to that, and to advances in DNA identification, in 2012 two of Stephen Lawrence's killers were eventually found guilty of murder.

With a new millennium, a new dimension was added to the problems within British race relations. Opposition to Caribbean immigration had never dwelt on religion – after all, many Caribbean families were God-fearing Christians; and Hindus, Sikhs and Muslims had developed their own places and practices of worship, co-existing peacefully alongside Britain's denominations and its secular institutions. But the aftermath of

9/11 saw the growth of a small and radicalised Islamist minority, who violently rejected everything about British life and democracy.

There was a widespread recognition that even such devastating terrorist attacks as those which occurred in London on 7 July 2005 represented the work of small numbers of radicalised individuals; but that did not stop a rise in insecurity among the larger community of British Muslims, who now experienced a climate of suspicion, and sometimes a backlash of hate crime too.

On 16 July 2005, in the aftermath of the 7/7 attacks, Edward Stourton reported on *Today* that 'This morning's tough condemnation of the London bombings from a group of senior British Muslim leaders follows the striking suggestion from the Metropolitan Police commissioner, Sir Ian Blair, on this programme that the Muslim community is close to denial about what's been happening within it.' Humera Khan, the co-founder of Al Nisa, a national women's Muslim organisation, and Dr Ghayasuddin Siddiqui, the leader of the Muslim Parliament of Great Britain, an organisation established in the 1990s to represent Muslim opinion in Britain, were in the studio to debate that accusation:

> **Siddiqui: We have everything to do. I accept it and we must accept our role in not recognising this problem. We must. And I think also one other thing that is very important is that we must recognise the failure of our mosques not to deal with these young people. In fact, what they did was to deny their entry to mosque. Instead they should have improved the quality of mosque management, appointed people who could deal with them in English language. There was no interaction. What they did by banning them [was] they allowed them to push them to outside mosque structure, where they became in control of these demagogues.**

But Humera Khan challenged the idea that the actions of the 7/7 bombers reflected badly on the Muslim community as a whole:

> **Khan: Well, I'd just like to respond firstly to this idea of somebody committing cold-blooded murder in this way. I can't understand how somebody, for example, would kill a ten-year-old girl, or the Dunblane murders. There's a mentality of a person or people who can do such a thing which is beyond comprehension and why they do it, it's also beyond comprehension. Of course, nobody will deny that the community is responsible. But I think we also have to step back from that a little bit. I feel really concerned that... all the emphasis has been on the community without looking at the responsibility of government. And, of course, Muslims tend to focus on the failure of foreign policy. But, I would focus more on the failure of home policy where the legislation has not been there adequately**

enough to look at the factors which are of concern to the Muslim community at home.

Stourton: Like what?

Khan: As far as Islamophobia is concerned, for example, people are focused on media and politics, but the way institutional Islamophobia actually works is in the system, and service delivery, where Muslims on the ground are feeling not engaged with society as a whole. I was part of the...

Stourton: But lots of people feel not engaged with society as a whole, but don't go and blow themselves up and go and kill other people.

Khan: And a lot of people who are not engaged with society do a lot of crazy things and we have to acknowledge that we're living in a world where people wrongly feel justified to do lots of crazy things. So therefore, you know, we have to contextualise the debate.

In another of the new millennium's developments, concern about immigration was pushed up the political agenda by the significant increase in European immigration, after ten new countries, mostly in Central and Eastern Europe, acceded to the European Union in 2004. Two more, Romania and Bulgaria, joined in 2007. British far-right groups were soon on the rise, too. In the 2006 local elections, the BNP registered the best results of any far-right party in British history, winning 33 seats. In the 2008 local elections, it won 100 council seats, plus one on the Greater London Assembly. In the 2009 European Parliament elections, it won two seats, in the Yorkshire and Humber region and the North West.

Appearing on *Today* the following day, the BNP's leader, Nick Griffin, told John Humphrys that their success was due to white people feeling ignored:

Griffin: It's about one group being second-class citizens and the other group being on top. And in this country which is where we are today, it's the indigenous majority who are the second-class citizens in every possible sphere, not as a consequence of the immigrants themselves, but because our ruling elite has made us second-class citizens. And that's one reason why we've got such a huge vote in the North of England.

Humphrys: So, we are second-class citizens in this country, notwithstanding the fact that the Houses of Parliament – both Houses of Parliament – are overwhelmingly white, notwithstanding the fact that Cabinet is overwhelmingly white, and so on. We are second-class citizens in our own country, are we?

> Griffin: I don't feel that the liberal elite running the BBC are second-class citizens.
>
> Humphrys: Are you obsessed with the BBC just a little bit?
>
> Griffin: No, I'm being interviewed by the BBC, and as always, asked the same damn fool questions, so I get a bit sick of the BBC. I haven't slept all night, but if you come to places like Bradford, places like Oldham, and talk to ordinary people – they're actually not just white people, also say Sikhs and Hindus – you will find that they have very serious problems living in this multiracial multicultural society, where the ruling establishment, the media, the politicians and the police force do not take anti-white racism seriously.

Griffin claimed that the mainstream political parties, 'by leaving the door to Britain open' had 'forced people to turn to a party which speaks openly about the problem of immigration, and says that while there might be a few good things about it there's also a lot of bad things'. Humphrys put that to the Labour deputy leader, Harriet Harman:

> Harman: Well, I think that people will be absolutely dismayed, and I think that it's horrific to think that we've got representing Britain in the European Parliament people who think that black people, people of Asian origin, have no place in this country. And it's not that they want them to be treated as second-class citizens – they don't want them to be citizens here at all. And I think that… what they've done is they've played on people's fears, the BNP, but they've also tried to pretend that they are less racist than they are.

At the 2010 general election the BNP fielded 323 candidates and secured 1.9 per cent of the vote. It failed to win any seats and its popularity subsequently declined.

However, the euro-sceptic UK Independence Party, or UKIP, became an increasingly significant force on the political landscape, especially after the election of Nigel Farage as leader in 2006. Farage sought to broaden the party's appeal, capitalising on concerns over immigration, and UKIP emerged as a serious threat to the Conservatives.

They responded with a 2010 manifesto pledge to restrict the level of immigration to the 'tens of thousands', and the following year the Conservative prime minister, David Cameron, pledged, 'With us, our borders will be under control and immigration will be at levels our country can manage. No ifs. No buts. That's a promise we made to the British people. And it's a promise we are keeping.' In 2012 his home secretary, Theresa May, declared, 'The aim is to create, here in Britain, a really hostile environment for illegal immigrants.' And in July 2013 her department sent advertising vans onto the streets of ethnically diverse parts of East and West London bearing the message: 'In the UK illegally? Go home or face arrest.'

But as the 2015 general election drew closer ministers were forced to admit that the government would miss its 'tens of thousands' target. In a live *Today* interview on 10 November 2014, Sarah Montague pressed the home secretary, Theresa May, on the failure to make good on its promise, and raised the issue of free movement within the European Union:

> Montague: You came to power with a promise from the Conservatives that they would get immigration down to tens of thousands. Now you're clearly, four years on, just ahead of a general election, not going to have anywhere near met that. We have of course the rise of UKIP. Do you think that what is happening with the European Union, what I suppose has always happened, makes it impossible for the Conservatives to honour that promise? Do you blame the European Union for that?

> May: Well, when we made that comment, when we said, when he said our aim was...

> Montague: You didn't want to use the word 'promise', there; wasn't it a promise?

> May: We said we would be aiming to bring the net migration down to tens of thousands, and we wanted to do that within this parliament. Yes, we were very clear that was what we wanted to do. And the reason we said that, was because we felt that the levels of the tens of thousands, which was the level of net migration we'd seen in the 1990s, was more sustainable than the levels that we'd seen previously.

> Montague: So, it's unsustainable now, and is the European Union to blame for that?

> May: I'm going to come on to the European Union point because what we have seen is that from outside the EU we've changed all the ways – the routes of immigration into the UK. And we have seen levels of net migration from outside the EU coming down to the 1990s. So where are we...

> Montague: I'm sorry, I'm just trying to focus you on the question... With regard to the European Union do you blame the EU for the fact that you haven't met your target?

> May: And I was going to come on to that because I think it's important to look at the whole context of what has happened. So... where it's outside the EU we've brought it down to the levels of the 1990s that we said we wanted to bring overall net migration down to. The issue is free movement within the European Union.

> **But we've been very clear that this is an issue that we wish to deal with. We think there should be changes in relation to the way that free movement operates. David Cameron's been very clear about that.**

Cameron's efforts to renegotiate the way freedom of movement works in the EU failed to convince the government's critics, and the issue of mass immigration played a significant part in the Brexit referendum debate in 2016. John Humphrys marked it out as one of the campaign's two main issues, along with the economy, in his special report broadcast on *Today* on 16 June:

> **Five days to go and it's still the economy and immigration dominating the referendum campaign. If immigration is indeed at the top of our list of concerns, what is it that worries us about it? Migrants taking our jobs, driving down wages, competing for houses and health services and school places? Or is it the fear of being overwhelmed in some ill-defined way?**

Humphrys focused on three places particularly affected – Keighley in West Yorkshire, Shirebrook in Derbyshire, and East London – asking how they had been changed by immigration since 1945. While the big multicultural capital was able to absorb large numbers of immigrants, in the smaller towns assimilation had proved much more problematic. Post-Brexit, a wider British Social Attitudes study in 2017 analysed the most significant issues propelling the decisions of those who voted to leave the European Union: it noted how '73 per cent of those who are worried about immigration voted Leave'. In London, however, there was a sign of something else. Here, where every creed and colour jostled, Sadiq Khan, son of Muslim immigrants, was elected mayor in 2016: the first Muslim mayor of a major Western city.

In late 2017, with Theresa May now prime minister, the *Guardian* reported on an emerging scandal. Certain elderly long-term UK residents who had, perfectly legally, immigrated from the Caribbean as children many decades before and lived normally in Britain ever since, now found themselves being deprived of NHS medical cover, losing their jobs and even, in some cases, being deported. Some may have ended up in prison, the media suggested. The problem was their paperwork, or lack of it. In the eyes of the Home Office, these people did not possess adequate official documentation to prove their Britishness – documentation never supplied to them at the point of immigration.

It turned out that no one had thought to cross-check with, for example, tax records; and that their landing cards had been destroyed by officials – for reasons of 'data protection', it was claimed. In 2018, this Windrush scandal roared to the top of the news agenda, including on *Today*. On 17 April Nick Robinson summarised proceedings from the previous day in Parliament before introducing a victim of the policy, Anthony Brian:

Robinson: 'A day of national shame' is how the MP David Lammy described it; 'wrong and appalling' was the verdict of the home secretary as she and her ministers were forced to admit that British people had faced deportation to the Caribbean simply because they couldn't produce documents to prove that this was their home country. People like Anthony Brian who says he was detained and then booked onto a flight to Jamaica, a country he left in 1965.

Brian: It's been kinda rough because since the immigration locked me up in the van – that was the first time they locked me up – it's been very stressful. They had a ticket for me, I had a plane ticket, I had to cancel it. At first I didn't want to believe it. They were telling me that they had a ticket for me and they were going to remove me on the Wednesday, so I had to get on the phone and phone my missus so that she could get to the solicitor and tell them what I knew. I got my school record, when I went to primary school here and my secondary school record, and I had my National Insurance number, what I'd had from 16, because you can't forge that. It was a nightmare, to be honest.

On the same programme BBC diplomatic correspondent James Robbins explained how the issue had 'exploded' embarrassingly for the prime minister, just at the time she was hosting a Commonwealth Heads of Government meeting:

There is a sense, I think, amongst many Caribbean governments, that their citizens, or former citizens, people who can trace their roots back to the Caribbean, have been shockingly stigmatised during this whole crisis.

The same day, Catherine Ross of Nottingham's National Caribbean Heritage Museum was interviewed on *Today*, and she offered something of a panorama of the last 70 years, recounting her experiences as a black child coming to Britain from the Caribbean island of St Kitts in the late 1950s, and the mystification that her skin colour induced: 'I still remember being called "wogs" and stuff like that – it was a horrible time... In primary school, kids used to spit on their finger and grab my arm and rub, in the hope that it would come off.' Nevertheless, she – and Britain – had evolved, adapted:

We coped last time, in the Fifties and the Sixties, and we're going to be able to do it again. But we must use the support systems within our community and within general society... This year we're celebrating 70 years of the Windrush arrival, 70 years of us giving to the community, helping to develop the UK. We've done that in terms of music, in terms of fashion, sport and so on. We've proved our right to be here... That should be celebrated.

In the midst of the Windrush scandal, on 23 April 2018, Stephen Lawrence's mother Doreen, now Baroness Lawrence, and his father Neville, along with the prime minister Theresa May, Prince Harry, the leader of the opposition and the Metropolitan Police commissioner, attended a memorial service for Stephen 25 years almost to the day after his murder. That same day, it was announced that henceforth 22 April, the date of his murder, would be commemorated annually as Stephen Lawrence Day.

In the fallout from the Windrush scandal Amber Rudd, who had been appointed home secretary when Theresa May became prime minister in 2016, resigned, saying she had 'inadvertently misled' MPs when she stated that the Home Office did not have targets for removing illegal immigrants. Chris Grayling, the transport secretary, appeared on *Today* the following morning, and Nick Robinson challenged him with the charge that the prime minister would herself have known that Amber Rudd's statement was wrong.

> Robinson: ... what politicians tend to do when anybody resigns is say it's all deeply regrettable and they've apologised and they've got to move on. There are lots of people who think you shouldn't move on, because the moment that Amber Rudd opened her mouth to say she didn't know there were targets in the Home Office, isn't it likely that the previous home secretary, one Theresa May, would have known that what had been said to MPs was not true?
>
> Grayling: Well, the reality is that we have for many years said that people who are here illegally should leave the country, people who've been found by the courts to be not here legally.
>
> Robinson: What's the answer to my question?
>
> Grayling: So, there's no question, I mean you will have seen from what Amber said over the weekend that she believed we should crack down on illegal migration.
>
> Robinson: What's the answer to my question Mr Grayling?
>
> Grayling: The current prime minister has not been home secretary for an extensive period, she will not know exactly what is happening in the home office today.

At the end of the interview Nick Robinson suggested Mr Grayling might himself be asked to step into Amber Rudd's shoes, but the transport secretary said he had no idea who the next home secretary would be. Later that day it was announced that Sajid Javid – the son of a British Pakistani Muslim family – had been appointed to the job.

The ordination of women in the Church of England

'There are oppressed people in the Church who are rejected and left out'

LIZ WELLER, 31 OCTOBER 1988

On the penultimate day of October 1988, a Sunday, a persistent American revolutionary prepared to minister to the spiritual welfare of a group of subversives in the heart of London. The location was a car park, just outside St Benet's Church, the chapel for London University's Queen Mary College. The weapons of this revolutionary act were bread, wine and candles – and, of course, words:

> **The intention for the Eucharist this evening is in thanksgiving for the staff and students of the chaplaincy for the Queen Mary College, and for all that this place has meant to the St Hilda Community, and also for all people who suffer oppression because of their gender, sexuality, religious or political views.**

'It was,' noted the BBC religious affairs correspondent Ted Harrison, 'an unorthodox service, with God being referred to as "She" and "Her" and the communion being distributed by worshippers to each other and not by the celebrant.'

It was also an act of defiance in a country where the Church of England's canon laws did not permit women to be ordained as priests. The Bishop of London, the Right Reverend Graham Leonard, had already conveyed his displeasure – and Church lawyers had gone so far as to prohibit the men and women of the St Hilda Community, an ecumenical group, from continuing to invite the Reverend Suzanne Fageol to lead worship inside St Benet's. Hence the car park. And their communion service, therefore, was a valedictory one: a farewell to the place where they had enacted their quiet rebellion for well over a year already.

'I noticed,' said Harrison to Fageol, 'that you lit a candle and made special mention of Graham Leonard. Why was that?' Fageol put it this way: 'Because in all Christian charity I really wanted to pray for the bishops of the Anglican Communion and in particular for the Bishop of London, as he and I are both in this together.' Her appeal to God was to 'Bless us and drive us out with power to fill the world with Her justice.' From among the worshippers, Deacon Liz Weller explained for *Today* listeners:

> This community isn't just about needing to have a woman presiding at the Eucharist – indeed, that hasn't happened every time – but it's a community that recognises that there are oppressed people in the Church who are rejected and left out by gender, sexuality, whatever.

In 1988, the Church of England – mother church to the worldwide Anglican churches – was lagging behind some of her offspring. In the US Episcopalian Church, women such as Suzanne Fageol had been formally allowed to enter the priesthood from 1978. In Canada, women achieved that right two years earlier.

By 1985, the Church of England's General Synod, its parliament, had voted to allow women to take a role in ministry and church services by becoming deacons, but the reform fell short of priestly ordination, much to the disappointment of the campaigners of the Movement for the Ordination of Women, who had been active since 1979. Reformers pressed on, encountering a groundswell of support but also considerable and concerted opposition. A final decision hung in the balance. And Suzanne Fageol's intervention on that Sunday in October 1988 was controversial not only to her opponents, but to some supporters too. As Ted Harrison explained on *Today*, there were 'warnings on Saturday from the Archbishop of York [John Hapgood] that she could greatly reduce the chances of women being ordained eventually in England if she "consecrated the bread and wine as a priest"'.

Four years after Reverend Fageol's controversial car-park service, on 11 November 1992, the General Synod finally voted to approve women priests. The debate lasted five-and-a-half hours, and in the House of Laity the measure secured the necessary two-thirds majority by just two votes. As part of a compromise to make the change acceptable, individual parishes were to be allowed to choose whether to have a man or woman to minister to them.

Inevitably, too, there were some who could not be reconciled to the change, including a prominent Conservative government minister. As *Today*'s Brian Redhead told listeners on 21 April 1993, 'The social security minister Ann Widdecombe has been at a ceremony at Westminster Cathedral this morning and become a Roman Catholic. And she's in our radio car outside the cathedral now, I hope.'

Indeed, she was. 'Very straightforwardly,' she said, explaining why she had taken the step, 'after the decision on November the 11th to ordain women as priests, I could not regard the Church of England as any longer part of the Catholic and Apostolic Church. As of course I say in the Creed every week, I believe in one Catholic and Apostolic Church. That meant I had to leave the Church of England.'

Ironing out some doctrinal issues had, in Widdecombe's case, delayed her conversion for a few months, but Redhead was more concerned about her future and whether such a move could provide anything more than a temporary refuge:

Redhead: But which church will you join when the Roman Catholics ordain women?

Widdecombe: The Roman Catholics are not going to ordain women, so I don't have that problem.

Redhead: Oh, they will. No, they will, you see, and all the interesting women in the Roman Catholic Church at the moment now feel that your move, in a sense, has hastened what will happen.

For Widdecombe, the fact that the heart of the Catholic Church lay in the Vatican provided a bulwark against unwelcome progressives at home: 'A few people in one country believing one thing is not likely to have the effect on Rome that it does on Canterbury.' She was to be proved right; two years later Pope (now Saint) John Paul II issued an Apostolic Letter declaring that 'The Church has no authority whatsoever to confer priestly ordination on women and that this judgement is to be definitively held by all the Church's faithful.'

Later, on the day of her reception into the Catholic Church, Widdecombe was to head to Parliament to hear mass, which would be, as she described it, the 'second part of my redemption' into the Catholic Church. Redhead wondered cheekily whether there was subtext in the timing: 'You've chosen the Queen's birthday, the Supreme Head of the Church. Is this the right moment to do it?' The timing was, Widdecombe assured him, entirely coincidental.

Among the clergy, around one in 20 left the Church of England over the decision to ordain women. They included the former Bishop of London, who also converted to Rome. In the words of the *Daily Telegraph*'s obituary, Graham Leonard was, 'The most senior Anglican churchman to convert to the Roman Catholic Church since the Reformation'.

In the Church of England, the first women – 32 in number – to finish their training were ordained on 12 March 1994. Women priests very quickly became a familiar and widely accepted part of the Church's life. The development even inspired a hugely popular TV comedy series, 'The Vicar of Dibley'; its affectionate portrayal of a bewildered village community trying to get used to its novel female vicar reached an audience well beyond regular churchgoers.

But far from settling the debate about the role of women in the Church, the ordination of women priests inevitably led to another battle over women bishops. Were women priests to be denied advancement? Once women entered the priesthood, should they not enjoy the wider rights of equality that operated, by law, in so much of the rest of society?

By 2000, the House of Bishops in the Synod had agreed at least to explore the idea of women bishops; in the same year, a woman became a dean for the first time, at Leicester Cathedral. But it took another five years for the General Synod, in 2005, even to begin a process to overcome the possible impediments – at the same time as the Church tried to devise means of mollifying opponents, just as it had done over women priests.

There followed what the BBC described as 'seven years of motions, reports, draft legislation and further debate' until an important General Synod in 2012, which, it appeared, just might pave the way forward. By this time, in the 18 years since women priests had first been ordained, the proportion of women priests had risen to one-third of all clergy. The problem regarding the episcopacy was, as John Humphrys announced on *Today* on 6 July 2012, that now 'the latest proposals contain so many safeguards for traditionalists [that] they could be defeated by the very people who've campaigned so hard for women bishops.'

Today listeners heard both sides of the debate in a report from the religious affairs correspondent, Robert Pigott. He introduced Father David Holding, who:

> **... presides amid a cloud of incense over communion at All Hallow's Gospel Oak in London. He's among High Church traditionalists who argue that Jesus' choice only of men to be his apostles means that only men should lead the church now. Put bluntly, he doubts whether women can be priests of any kind and carry out critical functions such as blessing the bread and wine of communion.**

As Pigott elaborated, 'Low Church evangelicals also have theological beliefs that cause them to reject the oversight of a woman bishop.' From this quarter, Reverend Rod Thomas, head of 'the conservative evangelical group, Reform', offered his view that 'Whilst men and women are exactly equal in the eyes of God, they have different roles to play within the Church. It urges men to show leadership. The first apostles were men and the Bible teaches quite clearly that those to be appointed as teachers should be men.'

'These arguments,' Pigott continued, 'represent only a small minority of the Church's parishes, but they could easily derail a decade of work towards women bishops. Last-minute changes were made to the legislation, giving traditionalist parishes the right to opt out of the care of a woman bishop and demand a male alternative sharing their beliefs about women clergy.'

For Canon Rosie Harper, vicar of Great Missenden, Buckinghamshire, these compromises created a serious dilemma, even though the principle, she felt, was 'a no-brainer' in the eyes of the wider population, especially the younger generation:

> **The ethics of their life is that you treat people equally. Within the Church, we don't, and therefore people are taking us less and less seriously. They're thinking the Church is out of touch, it's got lower moral standards than we have ourselves.**

If you can't get that right, why should we listen to you when you start moralising about other issues?

'I'm going to have to vote,' she continued, 'and part of me says I want to stand on my principle: all people in the Church, male or female, should have exactly the same rights and be treated in the same way. So I could stand on my principle or I could say, "I'll hold my nose and I'll vote for it."'

While Canon Harper, on balance, was inclined to accept the objectionable opt-out amendment added to the motion by the House of Bishops, because it at least would raise some women to the episcopacy, others on her side of the argument were less persuaded. For Reverend Rose Hudson-Wilkin, a Jamaican-born priest who was chaplain to both the Queen and the speaker of the House of Commons, the compromise involved a lack of equality she found unacceptable. On the same *Today* broadcast she told Justin Webb that it would mean women becoming second-class bishops and, 'We cannot allow this sort of thing to be enshrined in law, and so we would prefer for the Synod to adjourn this debate.' In the end, the motion failed to gain the two-thirds majority it needed.

Wales, Ireland and Scotland moved ahead in the meantime, sanctioning women bishops in their own churches. Two more years passed – and, this time, when the issue came up for vote again, it did so with the urgency of unfinished business. By this time, too, there had been political pressure from outside the Church, as MPs eyed an institution that was notably not in accord with secular equality legislation. Come 3 May 2014, Canon Philippa Boardman, of St Paul's Cathedral, was in the *Today* studio being interviewed by John Humphrys. She was cautiously optimistic about an imminent new dawn for women bishops:

> **Well, you know, we're hopeful the new Archbishop of Canterbury Justin Welby has come in with a real focus and a real energy to take this issue forward and they've been, you know, different waves of meetings. We've met in small groups. We've met in the largest Synod and now the debate is being taken out to the 44 dioceses. Everyone has to have a vote in their dioceses. Twenty-seven dioceses have now voted and all of them have voted in favour by over 90 per cent, so the feeling coming back from the dioceses is a very positive one... there's encouraging signs.**

This time, the surge was unstoppable. In July 2014, the Church of England General Synod, meeting in York, gathered a two-thirds majority for a further reformed plan for women bishops, with more general, nuanced provisions for listening to minority views; safeguards for those opposed to women bishops – the right to ask for a male bishop and an independent arbitrator to resolve disputes – would be guaranteed in a statement of principles by the House of Bishops. Parliamentary legislation, royal assent and a final box-tick by the General Synod completed the task by November that year. And so, Canon 33 of Church law acquired a new and highly significant sentence: 'A man or woman may be consecrated to the office of bishop.'

The year 2014 was significant for other reasons too, as John Humphrys told *Today* listeners on 3 May:

> There will be a march, a great march, on Westminster Abbey today: a march of women, of priests. They reckon a thousand of them. Not so much a protest march as a celebration of the fact that it is 20 years since the first woman was ordained as a priest in the Church of England.

Canon Boardman reminisced about those early days:

> It was a combination of being something that was very ordinary and straightforward – you know, we were using the same form of service that's always been used... wearing the same clothing, and so on. But there was also something very extraordinary, because people were hearing a woman's voice saying those words, people were seeing a woman's face behind the altar, and, at the end of the service, I said the final 'Amen', and a woman stood up and began to applaud...

'And person after person,' she added, 'stood up until the whole church was standing up and applauding.'

'Oh, wonderful!' exclaimed an enthused John Humphrys. He asked, just to be sure, 'So you didn't get any silly old fools – sorry, I withdraw that remark – you didn't get anybody chucking rotten fruit at you or anything like that?' No, was the answer, though she did recall an ordination elsewhere that was interrupted.

'The vast majority of people,' she remembered, 'were massively in favour of this development.'

'In a way,' observed Humphrys, 'it's quite remarkable how smooth it all was, isn't it, now one thinks about it 20 years on?'

On 26 January 2015 the first woman suffragan, or auxiliary, bishop was consecrated: Libby Lane became Bishop of Stockport. The first female diocesan bishop followed in 2017, with the appointment of Rachel Treweek as Bishop of Gloucester. Caroline Wyatt, the BBC's religious affairs correspondent, previewed her consecration in a report on *Today* on 22 July 2017:

> Wyatt: As Rachel Treweek looks ahead to her consecration later today, she admits she's both nervous and excited about what lies ahead. So, could that even include a bit of rebellion?

Treweek: I think women priests have had to be rebels in many ways throughout our ministry. Am I a rebel in that I deliberately want to be difficult and oppose things all the time? No. Am I a rebel in that I want to look at things from different perspectives and speak out? Then, yes; and I hope that you'll hear me speaking out on many things in years to come.

Figures published two months later showed that more women than men were entering training for ordination.

A hundred years of female emancipation

'We were prepared to die, really'

JANE WYATT, I FEBRUARY 1968

On the morning of 6 February 2018, *Today* relocated its operations to the Palace of Westminster: the programme was broadcast from St Stephen's Hall, an elegant rectangular room graced on either side by the statues of eminent past parliamentarians, which was once the House of Commons chamber. That day's presenters, Sarah Montague and Mishal Husain, explained why they were there: 'We're broadcasting from the House of Commons this morning to mark the centenary of women first getting the vote.' February 6th was the day the 1918 Representation of the People Act, giving the vote to women over 30 who fulfilled a property qualification, received royal assent.

St Stephen's Hall itself had been the scene of a dramatic act of protest in the course of the long battle to secure women's suffrage. In 1909, as Melanie Unwin, co-curator of the Voice and Vote exhibition, which was to open in Westminster later in the summer, explained for listeners, 'Five women came in. Underneath their clothing they had chains hidden and they sat down next to these four statues and, when the policemen weren't looking, they leapt up and they pulled out their chains and they chained themselves around statues.' For added authenticity, the curator wielded before Mishal Husain the actual 'porter's bolt clippers' used to unfetter the protesters. The programme also included an archive recording of a suffragette who had taken part in another protest at the palace, Muriel Matters-Porte, who recalled:

> I had already won my spurs by chaining myself to the grille of the ladies' gallery in the House of Commons. As a result of this, I was entrusted with the aerial demonstration on the day of the opening of Parliament. It was quite a little airship, 18 feet long, and written in large letters on the gas bag were three words: 'Votes for Women'.

The Representation of the People Act was passed in the last months of the First World War, which had interrupted the long campaign to win women the franchise. The delay came as a relief to some, for in the immediate years before the war the campaign had become bitter and violent – on both sides. Mishal Husain reminded listeners of the difference between the two principal campaigning groups:

> **'Suffragette' or 'suffragist'? That was the different ways in which women campaigners for the vote were described in the years before the 1918 act. Millicent Fawcett's suffragists, the original group, favoured staying within the law. Emmeline Pankhurst and her suffragettes were prepared to break it.**

It was the suffragettes' activism that stole the headlines, and it involved demonstrations and stunts such as the St Stephen's Hall occupation, as well as acts of arson, sabotage and even bombings. But these militants also suffered arrest, humiliating and sometimes brutal police treatment, imprisonments, hunger strikes and forced feeding, and – in the case of Emily Wilding Davison, who was knocked down by the King's horse when she threw herself onto the course at the Epsom Derby – even death.

The suffragettes embodied the drama of the battle for the vote, while the suffragists worked for their cause rather more out of the spotlight. 'Should we,' asked Mishal Husain, 'think of it as a divide between the two?' The historian Amanda Foreman responded, 'No, I think it's much more of a kind of a grid, that on one side you need protest and you need energy, and on the other side you need organisation and legislation, and the four together is what really produced the women's vote.'

The suffragettes' lawless campaign is often credited with bludgeoning Parliament's men into surrender, but another historian, Professor Krista Cowman, provided listeners with a corrective: 'I think you have to remember that before the suffragettes there was 50 years of constitutional campaigning and women doing things within the law.' Amanda Foreman agreed it was 'all too easy' to overlook Fawcett's movement, adding:

> **There were a number of incremental changes to the law, very important ones – the suffragists were very concerned in getting women involved in local politics first, getting on to Poor Law, school boards, Guardians of the Poor Law, and it was these incremental changes outside of London which actually led the pressure to make the final change at the end.**

Contrary to the view that the suffragettes alone 'won' women the vote, an alternative view advanced by other historians is that prior to 1914, the suffragettes actually impeded progress towards their goal by alienating sections of the population with their more extreme actions. But when Husain asked on 6 February 2018, 'Would it have happened without the suffragettes?' Krista Cowman thought, 'Probably not.' Certainly, as Husain described, they kept the cause visible, for 'in protest after protest, the suffragettes looked for new ways to capture people's attention'.

Professor Krista Cowman reminded listeners that, to an extent, the tactics of subversion were also inevitable because before 1918 women were denied the very choice that mattered: 'They had no other way of changing things, because they had no vote… They had to actually push to get the vote before they could do anything around legislative change.'

The changing social conditions brought about by the exigencies of the 'Total War' which began in 1914 in fact proved the making of the women's movement. The war projected women into the male world as never before, into factories at home and onto the frontline in field hospitals. Suffragettes and suffragists alike abandoned their campaigns on the outbreak of war, and the way women devoted themselves to the war effort made it even more difficult to deny their demands for a vote. Young men who had risked their lives in the services were similarly rewarded; the act abolished property qualifications for men altogether, and extended voting rights to all men aged 21 or over.

It would be another ten years before truly universal enfranchisement arrived, in 1928, when all British men and women were placed on an equal footing. And if the December 1918 general election was called the 'Khaki Election' because of all the men in uniform, the 1929 one became the 'Flapper Election', on account of its newly enfranchised young women.

The most illustrious name in suffragette circles, Pankhurst, was represented on that morning's *Today* by a descendant, Dr Helen Pankhurst. 'I guess,' Sarah Montague ventured, 'you obviously have no choice but to follow in their footsteps by being a women's rights activist?'

'Well,' Dr Pankhurst replied, 'how could you ignore such a heritage?'

Asked whether she was perturbed that 'it is a suffragist, Millicent Fawcett, rather than the suffragettes, who is going to be honoured with a statue', Dr Pankhurst stressed the collectivism of what the women had been fighting for:

> I think it's important to honour the whole movement, everybody involved in their different ways, and actually just narrowing it to suffragist/suffragette ignores the complexity of many other organisations that were involved; and yes, we should definitely honour Millicent because she is slightly forgotten, and it's important to look at the constitutional element of this fight, but people's heart is also in the militants, the women who stood up and said, 'Look, enough, just enough.'

As the *Today* news bulletins that morning reiterated, there was now, in February 2018, a call to pardon officially the hundreds of suffragettes who had been arrested, charged and imprisoned during their campaign. The home secretary, Amber Rudd, was interviewed, in part to respond to that suggestion. It seemed that her heart said 'yes' but her head said 'tricky':

> Well, I've seen this campaign, and I can completely understand where it's coming from – the extraordinary pain, campaign violence that these women went through in order to deliver the vote, which has been of such benefit to us for generations – so I will take a look at it. But I must be frank, it is complicated, because if you're going to give a legal pardon for things like arson and violence, it's not as straightforward as people think it might be; but I'll certainly look at proposals.

The year 1918 delivered not only women's franchise, but, in further legislation, its natural counterpart – the right of women to stand for Parliament. Women would be able to vote for women. The first to be elected, Constance Markievicz, was a Sinn Féin campaigner for Irish independence, who, as Mishal Husain put it, 'didn't take up her seat': like Bobby Sands more than 60 years later she was in prison at the time of her election. The first sitting female MP therefore would be Nancy Astor, who was elected in 1919 in a by-election. Zoom forwards a century, following the election of 2017, and, as Husain noted, 'As of the last election, a third of MPs are women, which is a record high.'

One of Nancy Astor's illustrious successors, Shirley Williams, spoke that morning in 2018 of her own experiences on entering Parliament in 1964. She reminded listeners what a long haul it had been to increase women's representation:

> Well, first of all, there were very few of us. And what's very striking, you're quite right, is that Lady Astor... was of course by herself for a very long time. Almost 20 years. There were almost no other women MPs at all, and then, by the beginning of the Thirties, you began to see a slow increase; but, really, there was no further breakthrough until the Attlee government after the war.

As for her own experiences on first becoming an MP and entering Westminster, she remembered 'a great deal of patronage; or patronising, more precisely'. In addition:

> One of the first things I did when I got into this remarkable palace was to push open every door that said on it 'Members Only'. It turned out almost all of them should have said 'Male Members Only'. The assumption was that women were not quite human, but they were quite pleasant to have around.

More positively, she discovered 'quite a strong sense of solidarity among women, across party in many cases'; anyway, when the men became too ill-trained or boorish, 'The most effective thing you can possibly do is try to slap or stamp.' 'We were,' she concluded, 'quite tough.' Her own view on posthumous pardons for the suffragettes? 'I don't think pardon's the right word. They don't deserve to be pardoned. They deserve to be celebrated. A different thing. Pardoned already means you've done something wrong. They haven't done anything wrong.'

A vast current of change was unleashed for women in the decades after 1918, and the next hundred years witnessed a rolling back of patriarchy, dramatically reconfiguring the kinds of lives that 21st-century women could live. Equal pay acts, sex discrimination acts, abortion reform, the contraceptive pill, the removal of bars to careers hitherto fenced off, maternity rights, the recognition of rape (and later rape in marriage) as serious offences – these were just a few of the most important legislative reforms.

On *Today* on 6 February 2018, many of the guests alluded to the great strides made and the battles fought, such as the famous Dagenham Ford sewing-machinists' strike in 1968 which spurred Barbara Castle – then in government – to back an Equal Pay Act. A trawl through the *Today* archives reveals a whole host of 'firsts': the first woman member of Lloyd's of London, in 1969; the first woman (Louise Peachey) admitted on the London Stock Exchange, in 1973; the first woman jockey (Charlotte Brew) at Aintree in 1976; the first men's working club to admit women as equal members – at Newcastle, in 1981.

In 1972, now in opposition in Parliament and with space in her diary for lighter things, Barbara Castle had achieved another modest first. As she told *Today*, she had wrenched the witty but old-fashioned – and very male – *Punch* magazine away from its editor for an all-women edition, corralling agony aunt Irma Kurtz and others to contribute. More significantly, the publishing company Virago Press was founded by Carmen Callil and her collaborators the following year with the aim of publishing books by women. The publisher was dedicated to women's writing and documenting women's lives, and it reissued neglected works by past women writers as well as publishing new ones. During her interview on 6 February 2018 Baroness Williams commented, 'One of the great things of the last hundred years is the gradual emergence of women as human beings, and it's a funny way to put it, but you know what I mean.'

Alongside acknowledging these genuine achievements, however, the guests on *Today* on 6 February 2018 almost unanimously rejected any idea that women now lived in a best of all possible worlds. The women's movement still had lots of work to do. Laura Bates, founder of the Everyday Sexism Project, couldn't help but notice that 'Here we sit in St Stephen's Hall surrounded by 12 statues, none of them women.' Gender pay gaps and glass ceilings were about to be revealed everywhere, including within the BBC, as larger companies began submitting wage figures for men and women under a new official requirement, which was also discussed during the programme.

Professor Alison Wolf spoke of the 'return of the servant classes, and the servant classes are overwhelmingly women'. 'Now we have,' she proposed, 'a class of wealthy people which is both male and female, but those people depend utterly on the cheap labour of huge numbers of people', many of them poorly paid women. In her view, this was a challenge for feminism, for these new class divisions were ungendered, and they could equally be women exploiting women.

In other reminders of continuing challenges, *Today* correspondent Sangita Myska revealed how, in parts of multicultural Britain, language problems and cultural taboos prevented women exercising their vote. She described also the case of 'Catherine', a disenfranchised victim of domestic abuse, who, 'divorced, and with her baby, tried to set up home in another area; but when she went to register on the electoral roll, she was told, as a victim of domestic abuse, she could only apply for anonymity for one year. Fearful her ex-husband would continue to stalk her, she chose not to register.' Catherine was now campaigning for the government to introduce lifelong anonymity for people in her position. More widely, and very soberingly, Dr Helen Pankhurst highlighted that:

The one area that stands out as the place where there's been the least change is that of violence against women. There you have legislative change, but social norms and the idea that women can be frightened and can experience so much violence – that continues to be a reality for far too many women today.

It was a perception echoed by others that morning, including Laura Bates, who contributed an ugly statistic: 'Two women a week [are] being killed by a current or former partner.' And MP Rosena Allin-Khan brought up a modern scourge which had parallels to the suffragettes:

If you look at the very women who chained themselves to the statues, where we are today, one hundred years ago, they met with an incredible backlash. That backlash exists today on the internet in the form of social media.

But the prevailing mood of *Today* on that morning of 6 February was to celebrate a profound moment of reform and the century of women's achievement which followed. As the programme neared its end, the winner of the *Today* listeners' vote for the 'most influential British woman of the last hundred years' was announced. It was not Barbara Castle (Shirley Williams's preference), nor Margaret Thatcher, nor any contemporary feminist, campaigner or high-flyer, nor even Emmeline Pankhurst or one of her radical daughters. In the end, the honour went to Millicent Garrett Fawcett, whose behind-the-scenes persistence proved crucial in winning women the vote. 'It feels like the right result,' reflected Mishal Husain.

To mark a much earlier anniversary *Today* had, in February 1968, broadcast an interview with a former suffragette. The 88-year-old Jane Wyatt was interviewed by

Bob Cunningham. She revealed just how far she had been prepared to go for female suffrage in her youth:

> Wyatt: I went down to a friend's golf course at two o'clock in the morning and cut 'Votes for Women' all over the place with vitriol. I also poured ink, in a vial, down a pillar box; and also heckled all sorts of people, prime ministers and MPs.

> Cunningham: You never chained yourself to the railings?

> Wyatt: No, no, I never had that opportunity.

> Cunningham: It sounds as if you enjoyed it. Was it fun?

> Wyatt: Well, not all the time. Sometimes we went at the risk of our lives and we were prepared to die, really, if necessary; but at the same time one always smiled through.

The spirit of her era was evoked on the February 2018 broadcast in a quotation from an Emmeline Pankhurst speech to American crowds in 1913. The suffragette leader's resounding words were read by the actor Joanna Lumley:

> Women are very slow to rouse, but once they are aroused, once they are determined, nothing on earth and nothing in heaven will make women give way. It is impossible.

Reproductive rights in modern Britain

'Someone needs to help these girls'
CAROLINE WOODROFFE, 15 MAY 1974

Today's first six decades coincided with a period of huge strides in the field of women's reproductive rights. The 1960s especially were a decade of milestones: in 1967 the Liberal MP (and future party leader) David Steel launched a private member's bill to regulate abortion. The bill had government support and passed into law as the Abortion Act on 27 October, making abortion widely available in Britain for the first time. Under the new law, abortions could be carried out by a patient's doctor, if supported by two other doctors, when the pregnancy was judged to be harmful to the mother or child's physical or mental health. The foetus had to be less than 28 weeks old.

One of the act's prominent supporters was the Labour MP and social reformer Leo Abse, who was also associated with liberalising the law on divorce and homosexuality. But on *Today* four years later, on 29 April 1971, Abse was airing concerns about the 'too reckless a pace' of the abortion legislation and its impact. 'Perhaps,' Abse told *Today* listeners, 'the terms under which anyone can obtain an abortion are too widely drawn and the result is, one suspects, that a very many people are getting abortions which should be avoidable.'

Abse's comments reflected public disquiet about the increase in abortions which followed the act; Britain's abortion rate had risen around fourfold between 1967 and 1971. The figures could be taken as a sign that the legislation had indeed been a necessary step, to give choice and protection to women who would have otherwise suffered. But concern about the rapid uptake prompted an inquiry into the operation of the Abortion Act led by Dame Elizabeth Lane, the first ever female High Court judge. Abse was interviewed about the inquiry by the *Today* presenter Malcolm Billings.

Abse was particularly worried about 'the large number of unmarried mothers' who were having abortions. He even wondered whether their own mothers and grandmothers were pressuring them into choosing abortions. In a comment that said much about Britain in 1971, Abse observed:

We're living in a world where there is a great demand, fortunately, a healthy demand for children, where adopters are waiting. We are living in a world, too, where in other countries, most unmarried mothers, in countries like Denmark, are able to bring up their own children. I think we are in danger of becoming anti-life and using abortion as too easy a method of dealing with a grave social problem.

The enemies, in Abse's view, were 'now these doctors who have disgraced the profession by setting up as professional abortionists'. He advocated 'more psychiatric support given to those who come asking for abortions'. 'I am fully satisfied,' he said, 'that if that was given, and aid was given, to get many women over the hump, that we'd have less abortions and we'd have more satisfied mothers.' The idea that counselling was the solution for women considering an abortion became a familiar theme of pro-life movements across the world.

Finally in this *Today* interview, Malcolm Billings tackled Abse head-on about the passing of the Abortion Act four years earlier: 'Having been a supporter, having helped the act through Parliament yourself, do you now regret the introduction of this act? Was it perhaps a wrong move after all?' Abse did not exactly say 'yes', but his explanation was full of regret that he had not been able to persuade his parliamentary colleagues to 'move a little slower'.

Contrary to most expectations, Mrs Justice Lane's inquiry endorsed the 1967 act. But that did not settle the abortion argument. In 1974, another private member's bill, introduced by the Labour MP James White, sought, among other amendments, a limit of 20 weeks' maximum 'gestation'. As White told Parliament, he wanted to end 'the situation in which it is possible for unborn children to be slain even though they have reached a stage at which modern techniques might enable them to survive'. Scientific and medical advances, which have enabled premature babies to survive at ever-younger ages, have inevitably played a prominent part in keeping the debate live and the law under scrutiny.

Unusually, though, in terms of procedure, the House of Commons agreed to put the Abortion (Amendment) Bill before a specially convened select committee. But before the committee even got to its discussions, there was more controversy. Who would be on the committee? The motion proposing the members was blocked by a vocal minority of mainly women MPs from all parties, who were angry that just four of the 15 proposed members would be women. In turn, Conservative MP Teddy Taylor, objecting to the 'frivolous' countermove, told the House:

Although it is distinctly unwise these days for any Conservative to minimise the contribution that ladies can make to the political progress of Britain, I cannot believe that the House would consider it appropriate that a bill of this

kind should be considered by a select committee consisting entirely of women Members [of Parliament] and effectively packed with opponents of the bill.

The Labour MP Lena Jeger responded that 'There is nothing less frivolous than abortion to the women members of this House, to the women of this country, to the men who care for those women, and to their families.'

One of the four women already selected, veteran Labour MP Joyce Butler, was on *Today* that morning, 26 February 1975, expressing every sympathy with the rebels:

It is a matter of appreciating that for more than one-half of the population, which women are, there are very special problems… They [men] can't get inside the problem of women in the same way that women can; and I mean I think that this move which women MPs have made on abortion is part of a general realisation of women throughout the country – because it isn't just in Parliament – that we do need more women to express the woman's point of view on a whole range of issues.

She concluded that she would be happy with 'a majority of women on the committee'. However, the make-up of the committee, which included David Steel, Leo Abse and the bill's proponent James White, did not change. Eventually, its report accepted some recommendations. The government agreed to hospital safeguards in the event of the need to resuscitate children aborted after 20 weeks who showed signs of life.

The Abortion Act survived this challenge, but the perceived threat to it spurred the creation of a National Abortion Campaign in March 1975, which was able to muster 20,000 for a pro-choice demonstration. The wider women's movement was making its voice heard. By that year, too, another statistic was coming to the aid of those who believed in choice: there were no recorded deaths of mothers from illegal abortions.

In its main provisions, the Abortion Act endures today – its most significant qualification since 1967 being a reduction in the standard limit for termination to 24 weeks in 1991, in accordance with prevailing medical recommendations. To date, Northern Ireland, exempted from the original Abortion Act, remains beyond its provisions. However, this situation was thrown starkly into relief by the 2018 referendum decision in the Irish Republic to legalise abortion there.

There was another reform in reproductive rights in that landmark year of 1967: legal moves to make the relatively novel contraceptive pill, introduced in 1961, available to unmarried women for the first time. The take-up was significant; by the end of the 1960s, it is estimated that around one million British women were using 'the pill'.

The social effects have been profound. Women acquired choices: if and when to have children; to enjoy the same sexual freedoms traditionally associated with men; to pursue, if they wish, a career without the interruption of motherhood, or at least to choose when to take that career break. The pill offered protection, not only from unwanted pregnancy, but from a potentially unwanted future life of undesired motherhood, or undesired marriage (to avoid the social stigma of being an unmarried mother).

In 1973, Parliament took another step, deciding that contraception should be made available via the National Health Service, and the following year controversy erupted about giving contraceptive advice to girls under 16, so below the age of consent. In May 1974, a Department of Health and Social Security (DHSS) circular advised doctors that, while they should ask girls who came to them to speak to their parents, the lack of parental consent was no impediment to giving contraceptive advice.

Caroline Woodroffe, head of the Brook Advisory Centres for family planning at the time, was invited onto *Today* on 15 May 1974 to debate the issue with Dr Margaret White, a GP and Justice of the Peace, as well as an anti-abortion campaigner. Woodroffe was asked why this circular was necessary, and replied:

> **Because in 1972, 4,300 girls under 16 had either babies or abortions; obviously more than that were risking pregnancy. Someone needs to help these girls. It's not a question of whether or not they should be having sex; they're having it already. We've got to find a way of helping them not to get pregnant. They may fear that if they go to the doctor, the doctor has got to tell their parents.**

Dr White could not have disagreed more:

> **Well, first of all, I'd like to say that this circular makes me hang my head in shame for Britain. Not only is the child not going to be protected by the government against lecherous louts, it's now not going to be allowed to be protected by its parents against lecherous louts. This in fact will increase – and I am willing to bet on this quite a lot – this will increase, not decrease, the number of illegitimate pregnancies.**

It would also, Dr White claimed, increase the incidence of venereal disease, which she put down to the availability of the pill: assertions which Woodroffe disputed.

The 1974 DHSS circular was reissued in 1980, which provoked a fierce reaction from the dogged campaigner Victoria Gillick. Mrs Gillick, a Roman Catholic with ten children, challenged it in the courts after failing to gain reassurance from her local health authority that her own daughters could not be given independent contraceptive advice. Gillick wanted a ban on that option for teenage girls nationwide; she argued that prescribing contraception to a girl under 16 was an offence since the doctor concerned would have been encouraging sex with a minor.

Having failed to persuade the High Court in 1983 that the 1980 circular was unlawful, she succeeded in overturning that original ruling in the Appeal Court in 1984, which meant that doctors who refused to involve parents in contraceptive discussions with girls were now potentially open to legal action. But on 17 October 1985 five Law Lords narrowly reversed (3–2) the Appeal Court's ruling after the government appealed. The guidelines would remain. The case gave rise to the legal concept known as 'Gillick competence', still used in medical law to decide whether a child (under 16 years of age) is able to consent to his or her own medical treatment, without the need for parental permission or knowledge.

In the course of this long legal battle the vocal Mrs Gillick, became a hugely controversial figure, admired in some quarters, vilified in others. On the day the news of the Law Lords' decision came through, she found herself confronting the prominent feminist author and broadcaster Germaine Greer; as *Today* explained on 18 October 1985, the two were debating the motion 'the permissive society has enslaved women rather than liberated them' at the Oxford Union. Tempers flared even before a single word had been uttered, as the *Today* reporter Jonathan Charles explained:

> As Mrs Gillick stepped into the debating chamber she was greeted with enthusiastic applause. That was because most of the 200 demonstrators had been kept out in the cold. Mrs Gillick had faced them as she arrived at the union, and there were a number of scuffles. Inside the building, there were more protesters blocking her path. Mrs Gillick and her husband then appeared to lose their tempers and while she kicked the demonstrators, her husband hit several around the head. Oxford police say a number of complaints have been received and they're investigating the incident. Mrs Gillick said, 'I haven't got as far as the House of Lords to be intimidated by a bunch of kids.'

In the chamber, she apologised:

> Before I go any further, I would like to apologise for having trodden on anybody. Can they please bear it with good grace and take it on behalf of the suffering that my children have stood, have withstood from other young men and women who have abused them? I did it on their behalf.

Then, as Jonathan Charles reported:

> Charles: She went on to talk about the House of Lords ruling and said she regarded it as an appalling defeat. Parents would now have no means of being told if their daughters were on the pill and no means of stopping it. The permissive society had won a dangerous victory and she told the audience that the ruling would have serious repercussions.

Gillick: There's not going to be a reduction in deaths from cervical cancer, sterility from venereal diseases, illegitimate babies, backstreet abortions or suicides – I think there's going to be an increase. I think that what it will mean is that school sex education, instead of treating women as precious, instead of treating the girls as in some way part of the ecology of this world to be treated with respect, they will simply keep on with the old mechanics of contraception and the mechanics of sexual intercourse.

Germaine Greer did not leap to any instinctive defence of the 'permissive society', but rather drew distinctions between what the state permitted, what it mandated and individual decision-making. 'In the end,' as *Today* related it, 'Mrs Gillick was to suffer her second reverse of the day. The motion... was defeated by 170 votes. The audience seemed as unconvinced by Mrs Gillick's argument as the Law Lords had been earlier in the day.'

Over the 1980s and 1990s, teenage pregnancies (under 18 years of age) continued to rise, but by 2015 the rate had dropped dramatically – the lowest, the *Guardian* claimed, 'since records began in the late 1960s'. It appeared that a concerted government campaign launched in 1999 had achieved its desired result, and that programmes of sex education in schools, more teenagers staying in education and a range of other factors were driving the downward trend. The abortion rate for under-18s was falling too.

Those statistics reflect another trend – in the United Kingdom, as elsewhere in the Western world, women are having their children much later in life than they used to, just as they are marrying later, if at all. That can be seen as a reflection of the whole range of transformations in women's lives and choices, and of changes in social attitudes – the stigmas attached to cohabitation, single parenthood and, more recently, gay parenthood have all diminished.

Delaying conception has created its own challenges, and the reproductive revolution has seen dramatic breakthroughs in enabling conception as well as preventing it.

In 1977, Britain's first 'test-tube' baby, Louise Brown, was born, conceived in a lab through the innovative process of IVF (in-vitro fertilisation). Since then, science has developed a range of methods to help those with fertility problems to become parents. And the new technologies have generated new controversies. On 3 February 2015, *Today*'s Sarah Montague described just the latest of these dilemmas:

For the first time ever, fertility doctors want to use a technique that will introduce a tiny amount of DNA from a third person into the creation of a new life. The DNA would come not from the nucleus of that person's cells, which is what determines our appearance and characteristics, but from their mitochondria, which provides energy to the cell and has its own DNA. It's a small amount,

NOTABLE GUESTS & GUEST EDITORS

Salvador Dali recording an interview for the *Today* programme, 1959.

HRH the Prince of Wales delivers Thought for the Day on New Year's Day, 2000.

Today guest editor – and former Labour minister – David Blunkett turns the tables
by interviewing John Humphrys in 2005.

The Dalai Lama being interviewed by Evan Davis, 2008.

John Humphrys interviews physicist Professor Stephen Hawking to mark
his 70th birthday, 2012. With them are the *Today* science correspondent
Tom Feilden and locations engineer Lee Chaundy.

HM Queen Elizabeth II visits the *Today* studio during the official opening of New Broadcasting House,
the BBC's new headquarters, 2013. Also pictured are presenter James Naughtie and the
BBC director general Lord (Tony) Hall.

Cyclist and *Today* guest editor Sir Bradley Wiggins with Justin Webb and Nick Robinson, 2015.

Andrew Parker, director general of MI5, in the *Today* studio
with Mishal Husain for his first live broadcast interview, 2015.

Former US president Jimmy Carter, pictured with John Humphrys in 2016

The author John le Carré being interviewed by James Naughtie for the *Today* programme, 2017.

HRH Prince Harry joins his guests on air in the studio as *Today* guest editor, 2017.

Former US president Barack Obama being interviewed by HRH Prince Harry,
as part of Prince Harry's guest editorship, 2017.

The artist Damien Hirst being interviewed for the programme about his exhibition at Houghton Hall in Norfolk, 2018.

On the 70th anniversary of the NHS, 2018, the chief executive of NHS England, Simon Stevens, holds one of the original leaflets used to announce its foundation.

PRESENTERS

Jack de Manio, 1959.

Pat Simmons, the voice of the speaking clock, tells the time on the *Today* programme, presented by Jack de Manio (left) and John Timpson, 1971.

Robert Robinson pours a drink for co-presenter John Timpson
at a farewell breakfast on the day Robinson left the programme, 1974.
Des Lynam, occasional co-presenter of the programme, looks on.

Libby Purves, who reported for and
presented the *Today* programme, 1979.

Brian Redhead, presenter from 1975 to 1994.

Peter Hobday and Brian Redhead in the *Today* studio, 1988.

Anna Ford and John Humphrys in the *Today* studio, 1993.

Today presenters photographed together to mark the programme's
30th anniversary, 1987. Back row: Brian Redhead and John Humphrys.
Front row: Peter Hobday and Sue MacGregor.

Presenters Jenni Murray, John Humphrys and Brian Redhead pictured in 1986.

Today presenters 1994. Left to right: James Naughtie, Sue MacGregor, Peter Hobday, Anna Ford and John Humphrys,.

Sue MacGregor and John Humphrys in the *Today* studio, 1997.

Today presenters celebrate the programme's 50th anniversary, 2007.
Left to right: Carolyn Quinn, Edward Stourton, John Humphrys, Sarah Montague and James Naughtie.

Presenter Evan Davis in the *Today* studio in BBC Television Centre, 2008.

Justin Webb prepares to interview Charles Hay, British ambassador to Seoul, for a special edition of the *Today* programme broadcast live from South Korea, 2017.

Mishal Husain presents her first edition of the *Today* programme, October 2013.

As guest editor, Lenny Henry explored diversity and representation, and his 2014 programme featured a presentation team from BAME backgrounds. Left to right: Linda Yueh, Reeta Chakrabarti, Jay Wynne, Nkem Ifejika, Lenny Henry, Mishal Husain and Karthi Gnanasegaram.

Nick Robinson in the studio at New Broadcasting House on his first day as a presenter of the *Today* programme, November 2015.

James Naughtie's last programme as presenter, 2015.
Behind him left to right: John Humphrys, Justin Webb, Nick Robinson,
Sarah Montague, Evan Davis, Garry Richardson and Mishal Husain.

Current and former *Today* presenters gather at Wigmore Hall in London for a special
60th-anniversary edition. Back row left to right: Edward Stourton, Nick Robinson, Justin Webb
and Sarah Montague; middle row left to right: Mishal Husain, John Humphrys, James Naughtie and
Carolyn Quinn; front row left to right: Libby Purves, Sue MacGregor and Garry Richardson.

and may be limited to a small part of the cell, but it would result in a permanent change to the genetic code that is passed on to future generations. And, of course, that has never happened before.

Later that day MPs were due to vote on whether to allow the new technique. In the *Today* studio Montague spoke to Vicky Holliday, who had brought her 13-month old daughter Jessica in with her. Jessica was suffering from the life-limiting mitochondrial disease, and her mother spoke with passion about the new technique, which would enable her to undergo IVF in the knowledge that her future children would not inherit the disease:

> Holliday: Mitochondrial disease is just horrific, the way that it affects children and it shortens lives, and the suffering children and adults have to go through with this disease. If there's a technique out there which means we can eradicate mitochondrial disease to stop it being passed down to future generations, then we really need to urge MPs to vote today for this.

The Conservative MP Jacob Rees-Mogg came onto the programme to represent the ethical concerns about the technique expressed by, among others, the Church of England and the Catholic Church.

> Rees-Mogg: I think the difficulty with it is that it starts a process which is very hard for us to see where it stops. Once the germline [genetic inheritance] is changed, at what point do you decide that that isn't allowable in other cases? At the moment there is a very clear boundary that babies cannot be genetically altered ... Once that you've decided that they can, even for a small number of genes, you have done something very profound, and then it's merely a matter of degree as to what you do next.

Vicky Holliday stood her ground:

> Holliday: I think what the MP there was referring to was the idea that it's a slippery slope. Today MPs are going to vote on mitochondrial DNA, we're not talking about nucleal DNA, or what else might happen in future germline diseases, we're talking about mitochondrial disease and people need to think about that in the moment and make a decision based on that.

> Montague: And your argument would be if you could eradicate mitochondrial disease that would be a good thing?

> Holliday: Why wouldn't it be?

Grammar schools
– a tale of love and hate

'Selection is not about choice'
MISHAL HUSAIN, 9 SEPTEMBER 2016

'Let's get onto grammar schools,' said *Today*'s Justin Webb breezily as, on 11 May 2018, he introduced an item on the announcement that £50 million would be allocated to selective schools which offered improved access to disadvantaged children. 'The fundamental point about giving this money to grammar schools', he continued, 'is that you could have spent it – it's a relatively modest sum – but you could have spent it on all children and you have chosen to spend it on a few.'

The education secretary, Damian Hinds, who had been appointed to the job only four months earlier, explained:

> **Well, there've been about 800,000 new school places created since 2010 and part of that has come from free schools, part of it has come from schools expanding – and schools continue to be able to expand, and we continue to have capital funding available to all types of school to expand. It's just that, you know, grammar schools, selective schools, haven't been able to expand in that same sort of way. And... as the population grows, as it moves, we do have a need for new school places. And what this means is just that... selective schools will also be able to expand in the same way, in the same way as other schools. They wouldn't be attracting more money than those other schools as a result, because...the money follows the expansion. It should just be possible in all places, and we just want more good school places, more choice for parents, reflecting the existing diversity we have in the system.**

The item – and the defensive tone of the education secretary's comments – reflected the way a controversy which had dominated education in the 1960s and '70s had, quite unexpectedly, returned to mainstream politics towards the end of the second decade of the new millennium.

In the mid-1960s the state-funded secondary schools comprised mainly 'secondary moderns' (and some technical schools) with an emphasis on vocational and practical education, along with a top layer of academic and selective grammar schools. Some of the grammar schools were centuries old and still maintained links with their founding trade guilds and other benefactors; others were of much more recent creation, following Rab Butler's 1944 Education Act, which laid the foundations for post-war secondary education. The 11-plus examination decided which children went where: secondary moderns absorbed most pupils – those who did less well in the exam – while the best-performing could enter the grammar schools.

The champions of grammar schools saw them as meritocratic institutions which encouraged social mobility, offering an answer to the entrenched social dominance of the privately funded public schools. For critics, most of the problems lay in the collateral damage from creaming off the top academic layer of an age group. Pupils at secondary moderns, it was argued, arrived already marked by failure, were therefore not expected to achieve academically and were given few tools to do so. Relatively few went on to university. And for all the bright working-class kids who passed the 11-plus, the grammar schools' intake remained overwhelmingly middle class.

Harold Wilson's first Labour government decided to end that division – to replace grammar schools and secondary moderns with new comprehensive schools which would cater to all ability levels. In 1965 Anthony Crosland, the education secretary, sent out what was known as 'Circular 10/65', ordering local education authorities to begin converting their schools to the comprehensive system. When Margaret Thatcher became education secretary in Edward Heath's Conservative government of 1970 she withdrew Circular 10/65 and gave local education authorities more freedom to make their own choices. But Mrs Thatcher did not attempt a wholesale reversal of the comprehensive system, and in the 1970s, history seemed to be moving in only one direction. Increasingly, schools were under pressure either to submit themselves to comprehensive status, or to preserve selection but leave the state system altogether, ultimately turning themselves into private schools.

Manchester Grammar School (founded 1515), perhaps the most famous grammar in the country, chose the latter course. Some pockets of local authority-funded grammars remained, notably in areas of solid Conservative local government, such as Buckinghamshire and Kent, and elsewhere other individual schools clung on to their former status. In Wolverhampton, the Boys' Grammar School (founded 1512) went independent, while the Girls' High School (founded 1911) battled on, maintaining selection within the state system. In the mid-1960s, about one in four state schools were grammars; by 2015, the proportion would be just one in 20.

The Conservative governments of 1979 to 1997 did not try to roll back the tide that had swept over grammar schools, but in 1980 the government controversially introduced an 'assisted places' scheme, using public money to fund a proportion of pupils in the independent-schools sector – a sector that had grown as the number of grammars had shrunk, and to which increasing numbers of parents, fearful of their local comprehensive, were taking recourse. Tony Blair's landslide Labour victory in 1997 put an end to that.

Under Labour, devolution would mean that Westminster could determine education for England alone. The Blair government also imposed a ban on the creation of new grammar schools, though there was no government pressure on remaining grammar schools to change their status – unless parents chose to do so by 'ballot'. On *Today* 10 May 2000, John Humphrys introduced a report by the BBC's education correspondent, Mike Baker, on the first vote to take place under the new legislation:

> **Humphrys:** The result of the first grammar school ballot to take place under the government's new rules will be announced today. Parents in Ripon, North Yorkshire, have been voting on whether or not to end selective admission at one of England's oldest grammar schools, Ripon Grammar. The ballot closes today after what's been a somewhat bitter campaign. The result will be a test case for the other 163 grammar schools in Britain that still survive...

Mike Baker reported that 'the rules forbid the active involvement of local councils', so the campaign for change had been 'left to enthusiastic volunteer parents':

> **Baker:** Parents in five other areas of the country are currently trying to collect petitions to trigger further ballots. None are yet close, and all are finding the regulations are making it hard to contact those parents eligible to vote ... Independent experts like David Crook of the Institute of Education believe Labour's long and troubled history over the grammar schools, and its determination to focus on other areas of education, have encouraged ministers to stay on the sidelines.

> **Crook:** Well, I think the government is saying that it wants to concentrate on the bigger picture. It wants to focus on raising standards in all our schools and all our secondary schools, the grammar schools to an extent seem to be a distraction. They don't want to get drawn in too much to the question of what happens to 164 grammar schools.

The outcome of the Ripon ballot was a 2:1 victory for keeping the selective school.

The years of New Labour rule saw many changes in education, not least the introduction of 'academies' and 'specialist school' status (the latter even including an element of quasi-selection according to 'aptitude') as ways to turn around failing schools and move away from what Alastair Campbell, Tony Blair's communications director, famously called the 'bog-standard comprehensive'. The period also saw, ironically, an increase in grammar school pupils' numbers, as existing grammars expanded. Under

Michael Howard's leadership the Conservative opposition re-embraced the ideal of the grammar school (in the Commons in 2003 Howard taunted Tony Blair with the sally 'Let me make it clear: this grammar-school boy will take no lessons from that public-school boy on the importance of children from less privileged backgrounds gaining access to university'), but the Old Etonian David Cameron reversed that after becoming leader in 2005. On the morning of 22 May 2007, he declared on *Today*, 'I lead. I don't follow my party; I lead them.' He dismissed the champions of grammar schools as a minority who were 'splashing around in the shallow end of the educational debate'. Parents, he asserted, 'don't want children divided into successes and failures at 11'.

From 2010 onwards, therefore, despite shake-ups in the curriculum and exam structures, the coalition and then Conservative governments under Cameron made no moves to breathe new life into the idea of grammar schools. There was even a brief furore in Kent in 2015, where one grammar school audaciously decided to expand on a new site ten miles away, prompting the question: 'What's an expansion, and what's a new school?'

Then came the referendum on Britain's membership of the European Union; grammar-school educated Theresa May became prime minister following David Cameron's resignation and on 9 September 2016 she announced – and Sarah Montague paraphrased on *Today* – that 'Every school in England will be able to select its students by their academic achievement if they want, but if they do, they must have quotas for children from low-income homes.' As Montague explained, Mrs May had come to believe that 'Children's potential is being sacrificed because of dogma and ideology – that's what the prime minister will say today when she uses her first major speech on domestic policy to end the ban on grammar schools.'

The low-income criterion was widely interpreted as an attempt to fend off the inevitable criticism, a good dose of which came immediately on that morning's *Today* from Michael Wilshaw, chief inspector of schools. 'Tosh and nonsense,' he said, a 'retrograde step':

> **If grammar schools were the answer to social mobility, why aren't there more in London, which is the standout performer, you know, in our nation? Poor children in London, who go mainly to comprehensive school, mostly to comprehensive all-ability schools, are doing phenomenally well, getting good GCSE and A-level results and going off to university.**

Wilshaw also highlighted the way the world had changed since the heyday of the grammar schools. In an earlier era, when British employment was dominated by heavy manufacturing and unskilled or semi-skilled labour, the country had no need for large numbers of educated citizens. But Wilshaw stressed that had changed:

We will fail as a nation – and this is really important to say – we will fail as a nation if we only get the top 15–20 per cent of our children achieving well. We've got to, if we're going to compete with the best in the world, get many more children to achieve well in our schools.

He also emphasised that the 'top 10–20 per cent of youngsters, they affect the whole culture of the school', to which Sarah Montague asked the question that parents of bright children often ask: 'But are you saying that the most able children really need to almost pay the price for everybody?' Rejecting notions that able children suffer in good all-ability schools, Wilshaw returned several times to the perennial argument against grammars: 'If you take away those bright children from the comprehensive system, the comprehensive system would become secondary moderns.'

Appearing on that same morning's *Today* in September 2016 was comprehensive-educated education secretary Justine Greening. 'What,' asked Mishal Husain, 'is the evidence base on which you're making the argument for new selective schools?'

Greening's responses alluded to the twin ideas that adding more grammars to the overall school mix would add to parental choice, and 'we absolutely need those places there for disadvantaged children and children from low-income backgrounds' because 'we also know that children on free school meals who get into grammars do twice as well, actually, as other children who are in grammars, so it really does turbo-charge their education and their prospects.'

But, Husain observed, 'If you look at the evidence from Kent, which is a county with many grammar schools, you can see that the children from the poorest neighbourhoods in Kent have a much smaller chance of getting into the county's grammar schools than those from the richest neighbourhoods.' This was, Greening responded, exactly why 'part of the proposals... are around how we can make sure that if grammars are able to expand or be set up, that they take a greater proportion of pupils from those lower-income households.' In short, as she put it, the whole proposal was 'to free up the system more, but also with conditions'.

The discussion came back to the question of choice:

Husain: Right, you're talking about choice and that's for obvious reasons – it's a very popular word for politicians. Selection is not about choice. It's about putting your children through a system which then chooses them on the basis of whatever testing regime is in place at the time; and the children who don't get through that would end up, in effect, going to what would be like the secondary-modern schools of old, because from the children who would go to a comprehensive school, you would cream off the very best, send them to another school – and everyone else gets left behind.

Greening: Well, I don't agree with that at all. This is about saying that at the moment, parents don't get choice. There are many parents who would like to be able to send their child to a local grammar school, but there isn't one there, so it's about doing a better job of more diversity in the system and creating more choice for parents…

'What we can't do,' Greening added, 'is allow a politically dogmatic-driven debate about the education system, as it was in the 1960s and the 1970s, to get in the way of looking at practical steps of what's going to be necessary to make sure that Britain is a country where everyone can do well.'

Whether grammar schools were socially divisive or not, the new initiative was causing ripples, even within the broader Conservative church. By 7 March 2017, *Today*'s John Humphrys was telling listeners: 'The chancellor will say in his budget tomorrow that there will be more money for new school places in England – and this is the controversial bit – some of them will be grammar schools.' On hand to discuss was Nick Hillman, director of the Higher Education Policy Institute and a one-time special adviser to former minister for universities David Willetts. Humphrys put forward the popular appeal of grammar schools among parents, but Hillman challenged the evidence:

Certainly, some parents will say that, although it does matter how you ask the question. If you say to parents, 'Do you want more grammar schools?' they say, 'Absolutely, yes we do.' If you say to parents, 'Do you want more secondary-modern schools?' they're not so keen.

Hillman also brought up an urban/rural divide with regard to accessibility: in the countryside, he said, 'You often only have one school in commutable distance, so you just need a good school in the area.' It was difficult to see exactly how a selective school could serve such a location, which raised a further question: were grammar schools to cater only to urban-dwellers?

Humphrys and Hillman then touched on a fundamental dilemma: how to balance the general good and the individual good. Hillman felt:

The debate goes to the heart of politics in my opinion. If people who support grammar schools are more concerned by the individual, some individuals do better in grammar schools… If you think of the community as made up of lots of individuals, and you worry about the overall average achievement within a society, then there is evidence that… the overall achievement can be a bit worse…

'We're all concerned,' Humphrys suggested, 'only with the individual: that individual being our child or children.' Perhaps that is why the grammar-school debate has proved so difficult to bury completely. As *Today*'s Mishal Husain summed it up on 9 September 2016: 'Divisive, regressive, cruel to children who lose out; or a reward for merit and an engine of social mobility? The grammar-school debate is fierce.'

Mrs May's attempt to give new life to grammar schools was, however, to fall victim to the political turmoil which marked her time in office. She was forced to abandon her plan to lift the ban on new grammar schools after losing her majority in the 2017 general election. The comprehensive-educated Justine Greening left the government in January 2018, and it was left to Damian Hinds, an alumnus of a Roman Catholic grammar school in Manchester, to carry forward the more modest proposals for increasing the size of existing selective schools.

The fox-hunting furore
– cruel sport or class war?

'Colourful scenes of olde England'
ANN WIDDECOMBE MP, HOUSE OF COMMONS, 28 DECEMBER 1997

In the late 1990s and early 2000s, the fox entered the heart of political debate. It brought hundreds of thousands of protesters onto the streets, provoked bitterness and violence, caused a security scare at Westminster, fuelled controversies over parliamentary reform, and even dominated a whole *Today* programme. How so?

Fox-hunting first arrived in Britain in the latter decades of the 17th century, one of several French customs imported after Charles II's return from Continental exile. Packs of foxhounds were reared for the purpose, though at that time, and into the 18th century, any self-respecting nobleman with the wherewithal to do it would have much preferred to hunt stags. But fox-hunting proliferated as stag-hunting declined, evolving its own rural infrastructure and subculture, securing its own place in the rhythms and rituals of country life.

But as a way of keeping down a countryside pest, a hunt, with all its paraphernalia and ostentation, seemed an extravagant palaver. Which raised the question why? Many decided that it was the thrill of the chase, and herein lay the objection in the 20th century, as animals acquired new levels of respect and were understood as sentient beings capable of suffering. From this viewpoint, to despatch a fox instantly with the flash of a rifle or shotgun was one thing; to have it run for its life until the hounds got to it was quite another. As early as 1949, MPs were discussing legislation to ban fox-hunting.

By 1982, some Kent county councillors were denying in official minutes that 'the pursuit of animals is either a sport or an efficient means of population control' and raised a motion to ban 'fox-hunting, otter-hunting, stag-hunting, beagling [using dogs to hunt on foot] and coursing [hunting rabbits or hares with dogs] from property owned by this council'. On 24 February 1982 *Today* heard from some indignant locals, including Elizabeth Jackson, the master of the East Sussex and Romney Hunt. She was interviewed by the programme's reporter Hugh Sykes, who put to her the argument that fox-hunting was uncivilised:

> Jackson: Fox-hunting, I don't think fox-hunting is uncivilized, no, I don't. I've been brought up with it all my life, I've always been used it.

Sykes: Is that justified? Are you justifying it by saying, 'It's there'?

Jackson: I'm not justifying it, I don't feel I have to justify it. It's part of everyday life as far as I'm concerned, and many, many more people think the same way too.

'Does this boil down to a fundamental clash of cultures: town versus country?' wondered Hugh Sykes. Undoubtedly, there was a political dimension that was distinct from that of animal rights. In the early 1990s, it was Labour MPs at the forefront of private members' bills to try and ban fox-hunting; Labour has traditionally performed well in inner cities and industrial areas, so for them there was no real political cost attached to banning what, to many of their voters, was toffs' nonsense. For Conservatives representing rural areas, the very opposite applied – vocal groups among their constituents felt their way of life was under attack. Debating in Parliament, Michael Heseltine, who represented the Oxfordshire seat of Henley for more than a quarter of a century, spoke for many anti-ban MPs when he said, on 28 November 1997, 'Labour members largely represent urban constituencies. Let them take care as they see their communities dissipated by the pressures of modern life, before they destroy the cohesion of the rural countryside.'

In 1997 Labour was elected on a manifesto which included the promise to hold a free vote in Parliament on banning hunting. A private member's bill put forward by the Labour MP Michael Foster reached a second reading, and some of the most memorable anti-hunting oratory was supplied by the former Conservative minister Ann Widdecombe, who declared in her Commons speech of 28 November 1997: 'Yes, the scenes of a hunt are splendid, so splendid that they are all over my dining-room curtains, but they are colourful scenes of olde England, and in olde England, not in modern Britain, they belong.' An estimated quarter of a million people turned out in support of hunting for a march organised by the Countryside Alliance on 1 March 1998, and the bill was drowned under a sea of amendments, running out of time to be debated.

Then, on 8 July 1999, in John Humphrys' words the next morning, Tony Blair 'delighted half the country... and appalled the other half' by announcing his intention to ban hunting with dogs 'as soon as we possibly can'. *Today* exposed Labour divisions on the issue by inviting the anti-hunt Michael Foster and, from the House of Lords, the pro-hunt Baroness Mallalieu to battle it out. The peer quickly adopted the argument that foxes were a pretext for 'an attack on people':

It's a terrible misconception that the people who enjoy hunting, for whom it is a way of life and a culture, are rich nobs. It's not. Down here, where I am at the moment on Exmoor, it is everybody. It's the whole community, and the economy would be devastated, the social life would be devastated, the people would be devastated. They're good people; they don't deserve to be persecuted.

Foster resisted this familiar theme of the pro-hunt lobby: 'This is not an attack on people; it's not an outbreak of class war. This is a cross-party political push to end what is an unacceptable form of cruelty and barbarism all conducted in the name of sport.'

Baroness Mallalieu invoked democracy too: 'It's about the rights of minorities, who may be misunderstood, may not be generally popular with urban dwellers, choosing to live in a way that they have done for generations and which has worked. I've hunted for 30 years,' added the baroness, before drawing a fine distinction: 'I have never seen anybody take pleasure in the death of an animal. I think there's a great pleasure in the efficient dispatch, a job that has to be well done.' She added, 'I love fox hunting. I love it because I love the people, I love being out with nature' – at which point John Humphrys rather cheekily suggested, 'Well, go for a walk with them.'

'Who is going to compensate the people down here where I am now, which is a fragile hill-farming community clinging to the edge of solvency?' Baroness Mallalieu asked during that interview. The question of the economics of hunting seemed to be answered in June 2000, when the Home Office-sponsored Burns Inquiry came up with a figure of around 7,000 hunting-related jobs. Five years later, Evan Davis, at that time the BBC's economics editor, noted during the *Today* broadcast of 19 February 2005 that such figures paled beside annual variations among those employed in farming ('last year the workforce in agriculture grew by 16,000'), which themselves paled by contrast with those employed in rural service industries, such as tourism.

In February 2001, a 179-member majority of MPs backed a complete ban on fox-hunting, but the House of Lords still massively voted against it, despite the fact that by now all but 92 hereditary peers had been removed by Tony Blair's reform of the Upper House. So the first Blair government ended with no hunting ban in place. In the second New Labour term in office, from May 2001, the government sought a 'third way', such as selective, licensed hunts (while outlawing stag-hunting and hare-coursing), but most MPs still wanted a complete ban. Meanwhile, politicians in the devolved Scottish Parliament stole a march on their Westminster counterparts, banning hunting in 2002.

On 15 September 2004 around 20,000 anti-ban campaigners squared up against riot police on the streets of Westminster. A handful of protestors even managed, with suspected inside help from a pass-holder, to reach the floor of the House of Commons itself – a major publicity coup, which dominated the subsequent headlines.

On *Today* the next morning, Janet George, director of the Countryside Action Network, deplored the police's 'excessive use of batons and force' on the streets, but was quietly proud that a group that some people had regarded as 'a bunch of country bumpkins... managed to get past all the government security and right on to the floor of the House of Commons, with nothing but peaceful intentions'. For Labour, Sir Stuart Bell MP was generally appalled at the intrusion of 'young men who were quite big and quite tall and quite aggressive' and he foresaw a revolution in Westminster security as a result: 'There will be a barrage; there will be a pedestrianisation before the House; there will be armed guards around the chamber...' Bell's tone was sometimes apocalyptic: 'These images yesterday have been shown throughout the world and on television screens. And other democracies will suffer. The whole concept of democracy has suffered yesterday...'

Finally, in November 2004, after seven years of parliamentary battles, the speaker of the House of Commons invoked the Parliament Act, which allows the Commons to override opposition to a bill from the Lords. A ban on hunting with dogs came into law on 18 February 2005. The following morning's *Today* was devoted in large part to the first day's 'hunting' after the ban, with Edward Stourton co-presenting the programme from the ancient Beaufort Hunt at Badminton, Gloucestershire. Would anyone take any notice of the law? Environment correspondent Richard Black explained to listeners the lingering tussle:

> You've got Rural Affairs Minister Alun Michael, who said yesterday the law is absolutely clear, and that's the view which is echoed by the anti-hunt groups as well; but the hunts themselves and the Countryside Alliance say there are lots and lots of loopholes in the law which can be exploited. Now, one of them is you go out to 'drag hunt', so the hounds are chasing the scent of a dead fox which has been laid down on the ground, but if they happen to come across the scent of a live fox then they're going to chase it and there's nothing that the huntsmen could do about it. Now, whether that actually is legal or not, I guess in the long term will be up for the courts to decide.

This was not the only ambiguity.

> You've also got this issue that they're allowed to flush [foxes] out from hiding using pairs of dogs, but some people in the Countryside Alliance have been saying, 'Well, what happens if you have lots and lots and lots of pairs of dogs?'

The usual disruptors of hunts – hunt saboteurs – were still in evidence, and so too were monitors from organisations such as the League Against Cruel Sports. They did not worry Beaufort's hunt secretary, who, according to *Today*'s reporter Nicola Stanbridge, 'said to me he'd be prepared to break the ban. He said that bad laws shouldn't be observed – he likened it to the poll tax – and there's bound to be foxes accidentally killed, he said, while the hounds are chasing a scent.' Stanbridge had been present just a few days earlier at the Beaufort's last legal hunt of the old kind, an experience she found 'astonishing': 'It culminated, actually, in the evening with an anti-hunt MP and his member of staff being attacked in Badminton.'

One of those young men who had invaded the Commons in 2004, David Redvers, was on hand to pooh-pooh the new laws on the basis that you can't teach an old dog new tricks:

> **You can't just suddenly turn them from being fox-killing machines to being aniseed-chasing lapdogs – it just doesn't happen. The fact of the matter is, obviously, while this law is in place, hunts will do their very best to stay within the law, but I can guarantee you: every day that there's hunting, there will be a fox killed.**

The philosopher Roger Scruton, kitted out for the hunt, laid out his own anti-ban credentials, advocating hunting as 'woven into the fabric of the society', including its many ancillary activities. But the owner of an Oxfordshire wildlife sanctuary articulated her counter-balancing perspective, lest anyone regard countryside-dwellers as monocultural:

> **I was brought up in Quorn Hunt country in Leicestershire in a village, and the hunt then, as they are now, [was] a tiny clique entirely separate from the rest of us, disapproved of roundly by virtually everybody… Most people in the countryside come across the hunt when they're blocking the roads, when their hounds are rampaging through their gardens, on occasions when they're killing their pets…**

In David Redvers's view, the pro-hunting lobby would keep going 'until this government is removed'. And when the prospect of a general election loomed towards the end of the decade, David Cameron's Conservatives were advertising a free vote on repealing the ban, should they win. On 19 October 2009, *Today*'s James Naughtie spoke to Shadow Environment Secretary Nick Herbert, putting it to him that:

> **Presumably what you want to avoid is the farcical situation that we got during the passage of the law, which was done through private members' means, and which took a huge amount of time. It's often said that more time was taken up in the Commons discussing the fox-hunting ban than discussing the Iraq War.**

'That's exactly right. Seven hundred hours of parliamentary time,' Herbert reminded listeners, and now he wanted to remove 'a law that is widely seen, frankly, to be completely unworkable'. In the end, the voters did not give him a chance, delivering a hung Parliament and then the compromise of a coalition government.

Nearly a decade later, in January 2018, an electorally bruised Prime Minister Theresa May was back on the subject – but the trail had gone cold. May told the BBC's Andrew Marr that on the doorsteps, voters had delivered 'a clear message' about repealing the ban, and 'That's why I say there won't be a vote on fox-hunting during this Parliament.'

On that last day of legal fox-hunting, back in 2005, *Today*'s Nicola Stanbridge paused to reflect on what she was witnessing:

> Like a small army crossing farms and fields, it seems like a sledgehammer to crack a nut. The hounds are picking up a scent, but the foxes are getting away. Land Rovers and cars are clogging the country lanes and, traipsing through fields after the rain, everyone is muddied up to their eyeballs.

'The day draws to a close,' she concluded, 'and our fox gets to live another day.'

House of Lords reform and the dilution of aristocratic power

'A long chapter of history is being closed tonight'
LORD STRATHCLYDE, HOUSE OF LORDS, 27 JUNE 1999

'A cancer has permeated every function of the body,' proclaimed the 4th Baron Wedgwood, 'and we must purge it!' The consequence of not doing so, Lord Wedgwood declared, would be 'eternal shame'. His target was Tony Blair's 1999 bill to reform the House of Lords, depriving hundreds of the UK's hereditary peers of their historic role in influencing the laws of the land, a privilege held through the accident of birth (Wedgwood was descended from the potter Josiah Wedgwood). The reform threatened to change the balance of power within Parliament as a whole, to the detriment of the Conservative Party, which could generally count the 'hereditaries' as natural supporters.

House of Lords reform was being debated as far back as the 1880s, and in 1908 a select committee under Lord Rosebery, a former prime minister, proposed a limit on the size of the House and elections to decide which peers should be allowed to sit. The following year saw a constitutional crisis, when the Upper House tried to vote down the so-called 'People's Budget' proposed by the Liberal chancellor David Lloyd George. Just over a century later, on 27 June 2012, introducing an item on the latest attempt to reform the Lords, *Today*'s Justin Webb reminded listeners of the rebuke Lloyd George delivered to the noble lords:

> **The question will be whether 500 men, ordinary men, chosen accidentally from among the unemployed, override the judgement of millions of people who are engaged in the industry which makes the wealth of the country?**

The People's Budget crisis resulted in the 1911 Parliament Act, which stripped away the Lords' ability to veto or block laws, especially regarding money matters, instead reducing its powers to delaying new legislation. It was a major shift of power to the Lower House in Parliament. In 1949, the Lords' powers of delay were themselves reduced, from two years to one. And the character of the Lords was soon to change anyway. The 1958 Life Peerages Act sanctioned the regular granting of life peerages, and the new barons and, for the first time, baronesses (whose titles would die with them) took their seats alongside the hereditaries, Lords Spiritual (bishops) and senior judges.

The right to recommend the appointment of peers gives prime ministers great powers of patronage, and has sometimes been a source of scandal. Lloyd George himself (who was made a hereditary earl before he died) was famously accused of selling honours in return for donations to his Liberal Party. In the era of life peerages, the most notorious resignation honours list was that drawn up by Harold Wilson in 1976. His former press secretary Joe Haines immortalised it as the 'Lavender List', after the tint of paper on which it was supposedly recorded by Wilson's long-serving and indomitable private secretary Marcia Williams, who had herself been ennobled as Baroness Falkender two years earlier. Among the honours were nine new peerages, and the new lords including show-business executives Sir Lew Grade and Sir Bernard Delfont, and the colourful chairman of the textile company that manufactured Wilson's trademark 'Gannex' raincoats, Sir Joseph Kagan.

On *Today* on the morning of 4 November 1976, the venerable Labour peer Lord Shinwell joined the chorus of criticism the list had provoked. 'Manny' Shinwell, as he was known during his long career as a Labour MP, was first elected to the Commons in 1922, refused office during Churchill's wartime coalition and presided over the nationalisation of the coal industry under Clement Atlee's 1945 Labour government. He was already in his 90s at the time of his interview with the *Today* reporter David Mellor:

Shinwell: I am interested in the fact that these people have been sent to the House of Lords without having any political qualifications or knowledge either of procedure or political matters – why are they there at all? Why have they accepted appointments to the House of Lords? There's no reason why they should. If they accepted the appointment what was it for? Only to have the honour of being a member of the House of Lords, but they have no intention of attending? I'm not angry about it, I'm a bit amused by the whole idea, and I'm surprised that those who sent them haven't got the common sense to refrain from sending them.

Mellor: Doesn't it make people like you, though, who even at your advanced years may I say, attend regularly when Lady Falkender and the showbusiness peers like Lord Grade and Lord Delfont don't show up? I mean, doesn't this make you feel defeated in a way?

Shinwell: There was no valid reason for their appointment at all, none whatsoever. If they had any qualifications it would be different, but what qualifications have they got? I can understand businessmen or those associated with industry, or science or with medicine, experts in particular subjects being sent to the House of Lords, even if they've got no political associations or political knowledge, because it's useful to have a forum of that kind to enable experts to express an opinion, it's very desirable.

'Do you think,' Mellor asked Lord Shinwell, 'that Mr Wilson in some cases may have made a tactical error in selecting some of the people he did to be elevated to peerage?' The peer was unambiguous: 'I don't think the term "tactical" is appropriate; I think it was a stupid error, quite frankly.'

Joe Haines, the chief critic of the list from among Wilson's erstwhile inner circle, told the BBC he had particularly warned Wilson about Kagan's murky tax affairs. Three years later, Kagan was under arrest and would go to prison for tax evasion: his knighthood was withdrawn, but he still held onto his seat in the House of Lords.

When Tony Blair won his 1997 landslide he included House of Lords reform in his first Queen's Speech; his proposed measure was billed as a 'first stage' of reform – the removal of hereditary peers' right to a House of Lords seat. For Conservative MPs, drastically reduced in number in the 1997 general election, the potential loss of decades of inbuilt Conservative domination in the Lords was an alarming prospect.

On *Today* on 3 December 1998 the veteran Conservative MP Alan Clark – himself the son of a peer, the art historian Lord (Kenneth) Clark – opposed any thought of a compromise:

I think... the implications are horrendous. It means that the Conservative Party... is reducing itself to a kind of minority that is shutting itself off even from its ancient traditions and its ancient linkages in the constitution and so on.

But any hopes that the Conservative Party leader William Hague might have had of resisting the change had been undermined by the revelation that the Conservative leader in the House of Lords, Robert Cranborne, had been pursuing his own channel of diplomacy with the Labour government. Cranborne was what we might call today the 'poster child' of the hereditary system. He was descended from two of Queen Elizabeth I's close counsellors (William Cecil, the 1st Baron Burghley, and his son Robert Cecil, the 1st Earl of Salisbury), he was the great-great grandson of the 3rd Marquess of Salisbury, who served three terms as a Tory prime minister, and when he was elected to the Commons in 1976 he was the seventh consecutive generation of his family to secure a seat. John Major elevated him to the Lords by an archaic process (used less than a hundred times in the previous 400 years) known as a 'writ of acceleration', which allowed the eldest sons of peers to take a seat in the Lords by adopting one of their father's minor titles (in this case Baron Cecil of Essendon).

Cranborne had not cleared the deal he had been discussing with Labour with his party leader and William Hague sacked him (Cranborne later confessed to behaving like an 'ill-trained spaniel'), but his deal had some support among his colleagues. At a meeting on 2 December 1998 Tory peers defied their leader and supported the Cranborne deal. The following morning *Today* broadcast an interview with another hereditary peer, the Earl of Onslow. Speaking to the BBC political correspondent Gary O'Donoghue, Onlsow weighed in behind Cranborne and criticised his sacking:

> Onslow: I think it's a great pity. I think he [William Hague] was... unjustified in not backing Robert's judgement. I've admired Robert enormously and on this occasion I admired him even more so.

> O'Donoghue: What consequences would this have for Mr Hague's authority?

> Onslow: Well, he talked about imposing discipline on the party; well, the whip has always lain extremely lightly upon my shoulders, and I ceased to be a guardsman nearly 40 years ago. And Mr Hague can talk about discipline, as far as I'm concerned, as long as he likes.

> O'Donoghue: To what extent do you think the deal is supported – as cut by Robert Cranborne? To what extent is it supported on the Tory benches in the Upper House?

> Onslow: Well, judging by the meeting I should think probably a hundred per cent.

> O'Donoghue: And overall, how do you think William Hague has handled the business?

> Onslow: Pass.

> O'Donoghue: Not very well, in other words?

> Onslow: Pass.

William Hague himself was also interviewed on the programme that morning by James Naughtie – and was unapologetic:

> Hague: I have appointed Lord Strathclyde [also a hereditary peer] as the new leader in the House of Lords. I'll be making further appointments in the House of Lords today. I didn't choose to be talking about this subject yesterday, but I've faced a situation in which the party and the country were being bounced into something which was wrong, which was against everything that we had said about how we would approach Lords reform. Now I want people to be able to respect my party for standing up for what it believes. When I say something I mean what I say, and I will stand by it.

> Naughtie: How little did you know about this deal?

Hague: Oh, I have known that such things were under discussion for some time, but we had also decided not to proceed with it for the reasons that I've explained: that our main objections to House of Lords reform remain, and so it was absolutely wrong of Robert Cranbourne to try to proceed with it against the wishes of the majority of the party. He knows that it was absolutely wrong. He's accepted that I was right to sack him and in his own words he behaved outrageously. The parliamentary party are, I think, unanimous in the opinion that I have done the right thing and I will have discipline in my party.

As things turned out, Hague took Cranborne's deal in the end. Labour's House of Lords Bill allowed 92 hereditary peers to remain in situ – in theory on a temporary basis.

'Last night,' announced *Today*'s James Naughtie on 27 October 1999, 'the House of Lords voted to remove the parliamentary rights of hereditary peers. It was a debate in which the opponents of the government's plans expressed sadness, despair and ultimately resignation.' David Wilby, a correspondent on the BBC's parliamentary team, continued, 'Their number includes the descendants of medieval barons, former prime ministers, even the illegitimate sons of the monarchy, but a vote late last night swept away centuries of tradition.'

The third reading of the House of Lords Bill on 26 June 1999 had passed the Lords by 221 votes to 80, with the majority of Conservatives following their party's instruction to abstain. It was not an evening without drama, as David Wilby described in *Today*'s Yesterday in Parliament slot:

Onto the Woolsack to condemn the Lords reform as a plot hatched in Brussels leapt the bearded Earl of Burford, the heir to the Duke of St Albans. Balanced precariously on the wool-stuffed traditional seat of the Lord Chancellor and waving his arms wildly, Lord Burford called on peers to stand up for Queen and country and reject the bill. Then, this descendant of Charles II's mistress Nell Gwynn was escorted out of the Palace [of Westminster] by the House authorities.

Lord Cranborne, more soberly, was – in Wilby's words – urging peers 'not to rock the boat' and jeopardise his deal, though he was still able to find words of contempt: 'As a government, not as individuals, I don't trust them much further than I can spit, which is not very far with a dry mouth.'

His successor as Conservative leader in the Lords, Lord Strathclyde, was by turns lurid and fatalistic:

The prime minister has taken a knife and scored a giant gash across the face of history... A long chapter of history is being closed tonight. But, my lords, the tale

is now told. The past is done. The glass is shattered, and it cannot be remade...
The point is the future, the future of this House, the future of our Parliament.

Another Conservative, Lord Ferrers, knew that to exercise the party's majority in the Lords and vote down the bill would reap the whirlwind: 'My lords, I believe that if we were to vote against this in any great measure, it would meet with the most appalling disapproval of Another Place [the Commons], of people in the country, of the government as a whole.'

Baroness Jay, the Labour leader in the Lords (and the daughter of the former Labour prime minister Jim Callaghan) spoke for the government and, in Wilby's words, 'reminded peers what the legislation was all about':

It is the start of a process to reform the second chamber of Parliament. To make it fit to serve the whole country in the 21st century. We believe a necessary first step is to remove the profoundly undemocratic element that the hereditary peers represent. We believe it is a change that is long overdue.

She had a succinct valediction for her noble friends: 'The time has come to wish them well and to say thank you and goodbye.'

In November 1999, just in time for the end of the 20th century, the new law came into effect, and more than 600 peers of the realm – or at least those of them who had been in the habit of attending Parliament – lost their right to sit on the red leather benches of the Upper House.

Their departure was intended, as Baroness Jay had asserted, to be a beginning; but the next stage in Lords reform proved an elusive goal. In 2007, a white paper proposing a half-elected, half-appointed House of Lords met with resounding defeat: a majority in the Commons wanted a wholly elected chamber, while the Lords preferred appointment-only. However, in 2010 a new bill appeared as a consequence of the internal trade-offs between the two parties of the new coalition government. As Ben Wright, chief political correspondent for Radio 4, told *Today* listeners on 27 June 2012:

It was a Liberal Democrat condition for joining the coalition: a completion of Lords reform that started a century ago. All party leaderships have pledged to support the bill, and the Cabinet backs it, but this could still be one of the most controversial and hard-fought pieces of legislation in years.

This new reform bill envisaged a House of Lords numbering 450, populated largely by elected members (80 per cent), with the rest appointed. 'The issue,' as it was put in the news bulletin read by Neil Sleat, 'is hugely important for the Liberal Democrats, but there's deep unhappiness among many Conservative MPs.' Moreover, it was not just the plan itself that stirred up complaints; it was the coalition government's intention to shortcut the debate by the procedure of 'guillotining' discussion. This latter decision in particular stoked resentment and opposition.

On 27 June 2012, *Today* broadcast a debate between two supporters of the coalition government with different views – the senior Liberal Democrat MP Jo Swinson and a Conservative member of a committee on Lords reform (and later deputy speaker of the Commons), Eleanor Laing.

Swinson emphasised that the role of a new Upper House would still remain to scrutinise and improve legislation. But Justin Webb challenged her, citing the frequently voiced suggestion that elected members of a new chamber would, by virtue of their 'mandate', get ideas above their station. As Ben Wright had put it, 'Some believe it could lead to constitutional chaos... challenging the primacy of the Commons.' Swinson was sure that candidates and electors alike would know the difference, but Eleanor Laing pounced on this argument and ran with it, asserting that 'If you have two elected chambers which challenge each other, you reduce democracy.'

'Do you?' asked a sceptical Justin Webb. Having been the BBC's man in the United States prior to presenting *Today*, he had experience of a not unsuccessful country that seemed to get by with two elected chambers. Laing, though, was unconvinced by examples from countries with federal systems, and ultimately she thought that 'If you elect people, they will behave as elected people.' Swinson was equally unconvinced by Laing: 'I just find it ridiculous that Eleanor is seriously, with a straight face, saying that you will reduce democracy by having elections for the second chamber.'

Webb then brought up the matter of democratic debate, reminding listeners that not only were MPs complaining of lack of discussion, but there was no plan to offer the people a referendum on this constitutional change. Swinson took the long view: 'This "not enough time" suggestion is just laughable. You know, we've been discussing this for more than a hundred years.' She added that all parties had promised reform in their manifestos. Laing, though, went on to the offensive:

> There's a far bigger issue here: why are the Liberal Democrats so keen on doing this when nobody out there in the country cares about it? And the answer is quite simple. What this is really about is giving the Liberal Democrats a permanent balance of power in the second chamber, by a system of proportional representation, which the country rejected a year ago.

Liberal Democrats were indeed still recovering from the defeat of their proposal for a version of proportional representation in a referendum the previous year.

'I believe,' continued Laing, 'that David Cameron has a duty to the coalition': that and that alone, she concluded, had to be Cameron's reason for backing reform now in the face of his party's grumblings.

When the BBC's political editor Nick Robinson analysed the exchange between the two politicians, he first offered a lesson from history:

> Everyone knows in Westminster – in a sense you've got a glimpse of it there – that every previous attempt to reform the House of Lords – and, boy, are we talking quite a few attempts over a very long time – has failed, thanks to an alliance of people in favour of reform voting with people who are against reform. The famous example, Michael Foot, who went on to be leader of the Labour Party, wanted to abolish the House of Lords altogether, and Enoch Powell, who wanted no change to it, they came together in the 1960s and stopped reform.

The predictable came to pass. By September 2102, the bill was withdrawn.

Debate about House of Lords reform has rumbled on, but the Brexit referendum threw up more immediately pressing constitutional questions. At the time of writing the Upper House still includes 92 hereditary peers, though they have introduced their own version of democracy. When one of their number dies or retires, other hereditary peers in the Lords conduct a ballot on a replacement. The *Independent* newspaper has called it 'Britain's tiniest, poshest by-election'.

The drugs dilemma: to liberalise or not to liberalise?

'I thought it was cool'

RECOVERING DRUG ADDICT 'SUZANNE', 31 MARCH 1985

'There was a UN convention in 1961 on narcotic drugs; its aim was to create a drug-free world. Well, that didn't go too well. Not only is the world, 50 years later, awash with drugs, but the money that drug barons make funds all manner of awful society-sapping activities.' With these words, *Today*'s Justin Webb, on 17 November 2011, offered a pithy summary of the illegal drugs trade over the previous half-century.

The 1961 convention to which he referred was an update of a 1931 treaty. It aimed to prohibit the production and supply of illegal drugs from source, as well as similar synthetic drugs invented in the previous 30 years and – with an eye to the future – drugs yet to be created. Bona fide drugs were identified as those manufactured under licence for medical and research purposes. Nearly all countries signed up to the stated aims of the convention; however, each country was then left to apply its own laws as it saw fit. The response in the United Kingdom eventually was the Misuse of Drugs Act 1971, which introduced the hierarchical classification of controlled drugs, from the most dangerous Class A ones down to Class C. The legislation made the home secretary a key player in what developed into periodic, much-disputed reviews of these classifications.

Today has frequently reflected on the way drug use remains so widespread despite the law. On 5 March 1979 the *Today* reporter David Mellor interviewed John McVicar, an ex-con and former armed robber turned writer, about drugs in prisons:

McVicar: The big ones are the things that take you out of the prison really, obviously cannabis and LSD. There was a bit of a shortage of LSD in the latter period that I was in prison. Obviously, there is some smuggling by prisoners, but that tends to be an unreliable source. The main sort of regular sources are, of course, crooked warders, who bring it in for a fee. I mean a lot of people would say, well, that's just what he would say! I think there's some objective evidence to support what I say. If the prisoners were smuggling it in, they'd also be smuggling in other things such as explosives and perhaps firearms to facilitate an escape. The fact is there are no firearms or explosives turning up in prison, so that rather tends to support the view that it is the warders controlling the supply lines.

Mellor: What sort of a business is this in hard cash terms?

McVicar: Usually the deals are £1 deals. The example I gave of a guy in Long Lartin [a Category A, or high security, prison in Worcestershire], for instance, who could turn over three hundred £1 deals. He'd perhaps pay about £80 for the drug, £40 to the warder and he'd have a runner who perhaps he'd give £10 to, so the economics are quite lucrative – he'd probably be earning £150–170 a week.

Mellor: This was one case – I mean, was this just an isolated case did you find?

McVicar: What, in Long Lartin? Oh no, I think you'll find in all maximum-security long-term prisons there is a pretty thriving trade in cannabis and LSD.

Mellor: There was a case in Birmingham the other day where a man was found guilty of smuggling drugs into a prison in the centre – in the hole – of a packet of Polo mints! I mean it really sounds so bizarre, is this the sort of thing that goes on?

McVicar: Yes, I mean, as I say, there is various attempts by prisoners – you know, it's an unregular supply, what prisoners get in. But one of the reasons... [behind] where the regular supply comes from, is that POA – the Prison Officers' Association – is very touchy about its members being searched or questioned, and they have a very strong stranglehold over prisons, and the police rarely get called in. I mean it's really the police policing themselves again, except this time it's the prison warders...

Six years later, on 31 March 1985, *Today* focused on another face of the continuing drugs problem, broadcasting interviews with recovering addicts of the Narcotics Anonymous group conducted by the investigative reporter Peter Marshall.

'Suzanne' had started young, at 12 or 13, with cough medicine, thinking optimistically that drugs would broaden life's horizons:

I know that I was always very attracted to that kind of lifestyle. I thought the people who took drugs were widening their minds. I thought that if you wanted to really have a full life you had to try everything that came along. I thought it was cool.

Another interviewee, 'Richard', had never held down a job and had depended on crime to fund his drug habit. But his drugs of choice were, in his head, linked with becoming a different person:

Depending on what drugs I was using at the time, I tended to fit into a role. When I was using a lot of cannabis I was like a hippie, you know. When I used a lot of magic mushrooms, I was like a space cadet, or whatever. When I was using a lot of speed, I was more like a punk. When I was using cocaine, I was like a jet-setter. And when I was using heroin, I was like a sleazy junkie in the end.

Today has covered the drugs debate from many angles, and one of the most enduring and heated controversies has been whether liberalising the laws regarding drug use would reduce or exacerbate the harms experienced. Those who are for liberalisation typically argue, for example, that legalisation through regulated outlets would do three key things: recognise the reality of the extremely widespread nature of drug-taking; drastically reduce the quantity of drugs coming to market and control drug strength; and halt the massive black market, which has consumed so many police resources, fuelled vicious gang culture and clogged prisons. Those against liberalisation, however, have typically feared that leniency would lead to an increase, possibly a sharp increase, in the use of drugs overall.

In 2000, at the Conservative Party Conference, Shadow Home Secretary Ann Widdecombe called for a zero-tolerance approach to cannabis, which, if ever implemented, could have led to large numbers of pot-smokers acquiring a criminal record – including, it turned out, several of her Shadow Cabinet colleagues, who admitted to youthful indiscretions. There were off-the-record briefings from sources close to the party leader, William Hague, suggesting that he did not support the initiative. The job of defending the policy on *Today* fell to the party chairman, Michael Ancram; he was interviewed on 5 October by the *Today* presenter Sue MacGregor, who was co-presenting the programme from the conference in Bournemouth:

> Ancram: I mean, I think what is useful in this is what Ann Widdecombe was saying yesterday – and we are all saying as a party – that if you are going to be taken seriously in terms of law and order, unlike this government, you have to show you mean [what you say] when you say you're going to be tough on the causes of crime. And we know that a lot of crime is now drugs related. You can't have a policy where you're saying we're going to be tough on those causes, and then allow the police to turn a blind eye when they see it happening.
>
> MacGregor: Was it discussed by the Shadow Cabinet?
>
> Ancram: It was developed in the way that policies are developed. We have a clearing process for all policies and it went through that.
>
> MacGregor: Did the Shadow Cabinet discuss it?
>
> Ancram: Shadow Cabinet doesn't discuss all policies and it would be impossible for the Shadow Cabinet discuss all policies in detail.
>
> MacGregor: I'll take that as a no.

Labour also discovered that the politics of drugs could be toxic. In 2004, the Labour government downgraded cannabis to Class C status. However, a further review in 2009 reversed the decision, also keeping ecstasy as a Class A drug, despite calls to downgrade that. Professor David Nutt, then chair of the government's Advisory Council on the Misuse of Drugs, called the Labour administration's decisions politically motivated; he was forced to resign. Nutt immediately led a new, independent committee to try and take what he described as a more scientifically balanced look at the evidence for the level of harm of different drugs, and on 1 November 2010 he appeared on *Today* to fight his corner. Presenter Justin Webb introduced the issue:

> **We're being told today that alcohol is a more dangerous drug than heroin or crack cocaine. Not, of course, to an individual user, but to society generally. The message comes from Professor David Nutt... who with colleagues on the Independent Scientific Committee on Drugs has produced a very serious, scientifically argued attack on current drugs legislation.**

Nutt summarised his study:

> **We have taken the government's recently published 16 parameters of harms – all the harms a drug can do: nine to the individual; seven to society. We've rated 20 drugs across those and it turns out that alcohol is the most harmful drug to society, whereas crack, heroin, crystal meth and then alcohol are the most harmful drugs to the individual.**

For the counterview, *Today* turned to Peter Hitchens, the Conservative *Mail on Sunday* columnist (and later author of *The War We Never Fought: the British Establishment's Surrender to Drugs*): 'First of all,' he declared, 'the report is barely written in recognisable English and seems to me to be a heap of pseudo-science.' Webb interjected: 'It's peer-reviewed in *The Lancet*', a qualification that Hitchens dismissed. In his view, 'Of course alcohol does more damage in our society – because it's legal.' He then brought up his suspicions of an agenda behind such reports:

> **There is a very powerful, very well-financed campaign at the moment to undermine the laws restricting the sale of many dangerous drugs. If heroin, if particularly cannabis – a specially nasty and dangerous drug because of the unpredictable way in which it can inflict permanent mental illness on some of its users – if these were legalised, or, as these people now euphemistically say, 'decriminalised' or regulated, then their harms would be far, far greater than those of alcohol... If we had legal heroin, legal cannabis, legal crack cocaine, we would have colossal social and health damage.**

In response, Professor Nutt rejected the view that he was advocating legalising the hardest drugs and defended his committee's methodology. He disagreed with Hitchens's analysis of the harms of cannabis, too, and pointed out that, for a young person, receiving a criminal record could prove more dangerous to them and their lives than smoking cannabis itself.

What actions, Justin Webb wondered, did Nutt want the government to take? In Nutt's view:

> They need to accept the fact that the Misuse of Drugs Act is really past its sell-by date. We need to completely review the way in which we deal with all drugs, not just illegal drugs, because that's an arbitrary and non-scientific description. We need to review the whole way in which society regulates, controls, reduces the harms of drugs.

It was a view supported on the programme a year later by Molly Meacher, a crossbench peer and former social worker who chaired the All-Party Parliamentary Group for Drug Policy Reform, which championed the decriminalisation of drugs. Lady Meacher was in discussion with Christian Guy, the policy director of the Centre for Social Justice think tank:

> Meacher: If you leave it in the hands of the criminals, you get skunk and it can be harmful to, admittedly, a limited number of people – but it can be harmful. If you regulate it, and we've got an excellent piece of very rigorous cost-benefit analysis coming out today at our conference, which shows that if you control the composition of cannabis, as you were indicating, Justin, then you, of course, make it very much safer. You also then provide it through outlets quite separate from the criminal gangs, so young people who might go and get a very safe form of cannabis...

> Webb: Does the government want to be in the cannabis business? What sort of signal does that send out?

> Meacher: We don't want the government to be in the cannabis business, but what we do want to do is reduce the dangers of cannabis. We want to pull cannabis away from the hard drugs that really are dangerous to people, and then by pulling the cannabis away you reduce hard-drug use and then you reduce crime, and that's what the British public want – a reduction in crime and drug-related crime. Sixty per cent of our people are in prison because of this...

> Guy: The British public want a clear signal on what is right and wrong. They see the dangers of cannabis, there is good evidence now that it is linked to psychotic

illness, it's a gateway drug to other drugs, and if you look at countries such as Holland where they have legalised, they're backtracking fast because they've seen a failure on this.

In 2017, *Today* returned to similar territory in a discussion of the evidence thrown up by an experiment in Portugal. The country had historically suffered from a bad drugs problem, but in 2001 it had declassified usage and possession on a small scale as a criminal offence, instead turning it into an 'administrative' offence. On 14 July 2017, Ron Hogg, the Durham police, crime and victims' commissioner, was in interview with *Today*'s Sarah Montague, and he spoke up for the Portuguese model. 'To shy away from the decriminalisation' that had produced 'clear evidence it will help to reduce harm' was, he thought, 'shameful':

> What we've seen in Portugal, where they decriminalised drugs over 12 years ago, drugs use – let's be quite clear, they're still tackling organised crime groups, and that's what we want to do here – it has shown that actually the level of drug use in Portugal has decreased, the number of deaths has decreased, the number of people injecting has decreased and the numbers in treatment, successful treatment, is increasing. And organised crime is suffering. There's a clear message from there.

Hogg expressed disappointment at the British government's latest treatment strategy for the drug-dependent, which was just then being unveiled. Although this promised a lot more tailoring of treatment to individual needs, plus joined-up local provisions for them, it offered no more money for the local health authorities charged with administering such treatment programmes. In Hogg's view, it was simply not enough.

Montague then introduced what seemed like a positive note for the United Kingdom: 'The statistics do, though, show that fewer people are taking drugs.' But Hogg explained:

> Fewer people are taking drugs, but let's be quite clear about what the statistics also show: across Europe, we have the highest usage of heroin, ecstasy and amphetamine; we have a drug-induced death rate at 60.3 per million, which is three times higher than Europe. So the harm that is being caused is exponentially increasing year-upon-year and we must tackle this and we must tackle it vigorously.

The perception that the proliferation of drugs was mainly a problem for inner cities and hotspots such as certain coastal towns has been dealt a blow by recent trends, as Nick Robinson told listeners during a *Today* report on 16 May 2018. 'Drug dealing in small towns across the country is increasingly controlled by the powerful and aggressive gangs based in the big cities, who enforce their control by exploiting children and using extreme violence. It's thought to be one of the causes of a dramatic rise in knife crime,' he announced, dispiritingly.

BBC news correspondent Wyre Davies filled out the details of this trend towards 'county lines', as the practice of using young people to traffic drugs into rural areas became known:

> This is how it works: drugs-runners arriving in provincial towns hand out a mobile-phone number to their customers, and this is the county-line number. The key thing is that this virtually untraceable number is held by the anonymous dealer back in the city. They have no obvious contact with the drugs, but have total control over what drugs are sold and when... The National Crime Agency says there are now more than a thousand county lines across the UK, a four-fold increase in just four years.

'Some youth workers and academics,' Davies continued, 'have accused swingeing government cuts to youth services for the dramatic rise in young people being drawn towards county lines. Home Office minister Victoria Atkins points to a new £40 million initiative to combat violent crime, but she admits money alone isn't enough.'

In the same broadcast, Mike Barton, chief constable of Durham and head of crime operations for the National Police Chiefs' Council, highlighted the scale of the problem and hit out at cuts in police spending – and indeed at the whole idea of enforcement as the answer:

> One of the issues – and the government minister [Victoria Atkins] pointed this out – is we can't arrest our way out. We won't ever, nor ever have, solved a societal issue by arresting our way out of it. And just because the law prohibits something, it doesn't make it go away. And that's certainly what we're finding with drugs... and if the government do say that their policies are working, well, sadly, they're not, because there are recent warning signs: an 18 per cent increase in opiate and crack use in [the] East of England; and a 21 per cent increase in crack in the South-East.

On 4 January 2019 Mishal Husain began the *Today* headlines with 'Police are warning that criminals are getting jobs in prisons so they can smuggle drugs to inmates'. She trailed a report from inside a prison, then later in the programme the Conservative prisons minister, Rory Stewart, told John Humphrys about his plans for piloting new body-scanners at prison entrances:

> As we've tightened down on other ways of getting drugs in – so as we've put up better fencing, better meshing, and as we've got better at analysing mail –

people are bringing in drugs more inside their bodies than they were in the past. I need to re-emphasise, of course, that the vast majority of our prison officers are incredibly dedicated public servants, but you will always have people who are tempted to do this.

Forty years after John McVicar's interview about 'crooked warders', the problem remained as intractable as ever.

Thought for the day : Canon Angela Tilby

8 March 2018

Good morning. Today is International Women's Day and I am thinking of a well-brought-up young woman who was thrown into prison with four companions for breaking the rules of patriarchy: disobeying her father, her husband, and the state. She was nursing an infant son at the time and one of her companions was heavily pregnant. After a brief show trial they were all sentenced to death and duly executed.

This could be the sad story of any number of young women who face punishment today for refusing to obey husbands, fathers and a male-run state in which women have no rights and no voice.

But this particular story is nearly 2,000 years old. It comes from Roman North Africa. The young woman's name was Vibia Perpetua and her crime was to have chosen to be a Christian. This involved not only breaking the law – Christian men were persecuted too – but a scandalous disregard of accepted ideas of femininity. Yesterday Perpetua was remembered in the calendar of saints.

In the days before her execution Perpetua kept a diary in which she recorded a sequence of symbolic dreams. In the first dream she was trying to climb a ladder which was hung with instruments of torture. There was a dragon at the ladder's foot – she jumped on it and climbed up. She came to a garden where an elderly shepherd welcomed her and gave her a cup of milk. She then dreamt of her little brother who had died of cancer in infancy and was lonely and thirsty in a hot dingy place. Then she saw him healed, drinking freely from a golden bowl. In her final dream she was being oiled all over in preparation for a fight to the death with a huge ugly man. She pummelled her opponent to the ground and stepped on his head. The next day she and her companions were executed.

Anyone who thinks women have only recently fought to be regarded as equal, or only recently begun to question male authority, or only recently been regarded as spiritual leaders should consider the story of Perpetua. She was such a new Christian that her dreams contain imagery from both her new faith and from her pagan past. To fight her opponent in the ring she was prepared with oil, the oil of Christian anointing, but also the oil of any male wrestler fighting for glory. For her, death was a triumph, but she also kept her sense of propriety. An account of her end describes how she was brought before the crowds in the amphitheatre where she was thrown to the ground and gored by a wild heifer. At which point she re-arranged her tunic and asked for a pin to fasten her hair. That's not only dying with dignity. It's dying with style. I find that last gesture of defiance in the face of brutality extraordinarily powerful.

Women down the centuries have only asked to be human as they have aspired to change the world.

CHAPTER 6

THE NATURAL WORLD, SCIENCE AND TECHNOLOGY

Beagle 2 and British space endeavour

'We have to go back to Mars'
COLIN PILLINGER, 24 MAY 2004

Christmas 2003, and many in Britain were awaiting the most amazing of gifts from outer space – a message from Mars. On 25 December, the British-built lander, Beagle 2, was meant to touch down on the Red Planet and start transmitting back to Earth. The following day, *Today* presenter Edward Stourton introduced developments in the space story that had gripped so many listeners:

> **The phrase of the day was supposed to be 'The Beagle has landed!' Instead, this morning's headlines offer a more mournful plea: 'Beagle, phone home!' Efforts to detect a signal from the elusive British spacecraft have met with nothing more than the silence of space.**

It was a bitterly disappointing turn of events. The charismatic British leader of the project, Colin Pillinger, professor at the Open University, previously of NASA, had fired the public imagination with his passion for the project – and his distinctive West Country accent helped to brand Beagle as an authentically British enterprise in a field where Britain had not often made the running.

The BBC's first aerospace correspondent, Reginald Turnill, was appointed in 1958, the year after *Today* first went on the air. For much of the decade that followed space was the preserve of the superpowers, as the Soviets and the Americans raced one another to new frontiers (although France launched the first cat into space in 1963). The Soviets put the first human into space in 1961, and at the end of the 1960s the American Apollo 11 mission landed the first humans on the moon. A week after the Apollo landings there was a 'fly-by' of Mars by the unmanned Mariner 6 and 7 crafts, and 1 August 1969 *Today* broadcast Turnill going through some of the Mars pictures sent back by Mariner 6 with the rocket scientist William Pickering:

> **Pickering: The photographs which we've seen tonight – and they've turned out to be very good, particularly for the first run-through of the data – they're really remarkable pictures.**

Turnill: Well, I confess that although I was overwhelmed by the clarity of the pictures, I was terribly disappointed that it looks so much like the moon. How did you feel about that?

Pickering: I'm afraid the Lunar 4 photographs had already told us to expect to find craters on the planet. This confirms it, and in fact shows we have craters over a large area of the planet, presumably over most of the planet. However, there are still features about Mars which are different from the moon; for example, the atmosphere, we know that Mars has an atmosphere, thin, indeed, but nevertheless there. We know that the appearance of Mars changes with the seasons. These are things that obviously distinguish it from the moon, and obviously have to be examined and explored and hopefully these photographs will give us a clue. I don't think these photographs either prove or disprove the possibility of life.

Turnill: No water and, alas, no canals.

Pickering: (laughs) We didn't see any.

Robots became the new explorers, pushing the boundaries further. In 1976 NASA even managed the first successful landing on the Red Planet. Nearer to Earth, the Americans and the Soviets developed space stations and space shuttles, working with both robots and astronauts.

The British space programme did not consider manned missions worth the trouble, and in the 1970s and 1980s, successive British governments wavered over funding space research. By 1971, as the Prospero satellite – the only British satellite launched into space using purely British technology – shot off from Australia, the government had already cut funding to the project. When the European Space Agency (ESA) was established in 1975, however, the British authorities were happy to back the joint venture to some degree, with British scientists providing much of the initial expertise.

During the 1980s, under Margaret Thatcher's Conservative government, the future of public-backed space exploration seemed uncertain. The British government sold its 51.7 per cent shareholding in British Aerospace in 1981. But in 1985 the British National Space Centre (BNSC) was founded as a voluntary partnership between various government departments. The now-privatised British Aerospace continued to contribute to major ESA projects, for instance building the Giotto spacecraft which launched in 1985 and became the first-ever spacecraft to study a comet close up – Halley's Comet, no less. British Aerospace would also go on to construct Eurostar satellites for Hertfordshire-based telecommunications specialist Inmarsat, making Britain a world leader in satellites.

Meanwhile, the first French and German astronauts were heading into space, on Soviet and American missions. And in 1991 the first British astronaut joined the Russian-operated Mir space station, which had been orbiting the Earth since 1986. Helen Sharman, a trained chemist, beat over 13,000 applicants for the opportunity. She reflected on her experience in an interview with *Today*'s James Naughtie much later – during a broadcast on 18 March 2015 to mark the 50th anniversary of the first human walk in space by Alexey Leonov, who had helped to train her. Naughtie asked her for her enduring memory of her trip to space:

> I think the memories that last the longest are the emotional ones, they're the ones about the people up there. We had a problem docking on the space station. With the three of us launching into space on a Soyuz spacecraft, after two days we docked on to the space station, but it was a manual docking – you're never quite sure if it's going to work. We've done it in the training, but you've never done it for real, and you trust those people with your life and they trust you with theirs. And then we did reach the space station in one piece, opened the hatch and greeted the two people who'd been up there for six months. And can you imagine, they haven't seen anybody else for six months, so of course they were delighted to see us in one piece, because if we hadn't then they wouldn't have had any more compatriots, for a bit longer anyway. And that feeling of elation, the camaraderie, that togetherness, and that's what really does last with me. It still lasts now.

Colin Pillinger proved very adept at capitalising on the glamour of space when he launched his Beagle project. He even galvanised pop stars such as Blur's Alex James into becoming huge fans. Blur composed a track to be launched into space with Beagle 2, and Pillinger told *Today* on 30 January 2002 about the significance of the band's participation:

> We have to announce our arrival and normally we send back some piece of computer gobbledygook and [we] wanted to have something that was instantly recognisable... When we started this project we really needed to demonstrate credibility... and we also need[ed] to raise a lot of cash... hence the link up with Blur, because they could provide both media appeal and they could provide this signal for us.

Another enthusiast was Young British Artist Damien Hirst, who painted the 'test card' for Beagle 2, which was intended to help calibrate its cameras and spectrometers after landing.

Beagle 2 itself was a small but exceptionally sophisticated robot, conceived by a group of British scientists to search for signs of life on Mars. Funding was a struggle, but various scientific organisations contributed, the aerospace manufacturing group EADS-Atrium came in as an industrial partner, and the Department of Trade and Industry dipped into its pocket too. But the, at times desperate, efforts involved reflected the problems of getting British government backing for significant space endeavours. And Beagle 2 was merely hitch-hiking on a much larger expedition organised by ESA.

So on that Christmas Day 2003, Professor Pillinger was 'on the verge of realising his dream' as Beagle 2 prepared to land on Mars. But triumph was replaced by confusion, as *Today* revealed the following day. During the anxious wait for news on the programme, musician Alex James commented, 'It's Schrodinger's cat in a box, innit? It has landed and it hasn't landed. We don't know. There's two parallel universes.' BBC science correspondent Pallab Ghosh, reporting for *Today*, was with those waiting for news:

> **Then came the moment we'd all been waiting for, the call from NASA... but it was not the news we'd been hoping for. No sign of Beagle... The magic of Christmas had suddenly evaporated.**

The astronomer royal, Sir Martin Rees, reminded *Today*'s listeners of the odds against Beagle's success:

> **It was a very high-risk project because, of the attempts to land on Mars in the past, only a third have succeeded. And this was a specially cut-price, specially ingenious one, so clearly the odds were stacked against it from the start. But I admire immensely the enthusiasm of the Open University team and the many small high-tech companies who have devised this very ingenious project.**

Rees made a telling comparison: 'Let me give an analogy, to put this all in perspective. The cost of the entire UK space-science programme is about the cost of sponsoring one Formula 1 racing team.' Pleas from various British scientists for more government support of space programmes would follow on *Today* down the years.

The subsequent inquiry on Beagle 2 cited inadequate funding as one of the reasons for failure, along with the breakneck speed at which the project had to be put together, and the fact that Colin Pillinger had to steer it *and* market it *and* fundraise for it. The day the inquiry report was due to be published, 24 May 2004, *Today*'s Sarah Montague interviewed Pillinger, who dismissed suggestions that the money spent on the expedition had been wasted:

> **Let me tell you that the science that we were going to do with Beagle 2 was world-class. It's still world-class. No agency is doing it. No agency is capable of doing it. If we don't go back with a repeat of Beagle 2 or something very much like it, we**

will actually be throwing the baby out with the bathwater. So, yes, we have to go back to Mars and we have to do this science to see whether Mars has life on it or did have life on it. Indeed, are we alone in the universe? There's much to be done.

And he expressed pride in another achievement:

One of the things that we also did in this mission was to inspire the country... We convinced the government that the country wanted to do space research and we must expect that if we want to convince young people to go into science and engineering, you mustn't tell them that they have to become actuaries; in other words, take no risks at all.

On the Continent, ESA was forging ahead, for example by sending the Herschel and Planck observatories into space. 'It's Europe's biggest space project to date,' explained *Today* presenter Evan Davis on 14 May 2009:

The Herschel telescope... will study the birth and evolution of stars and galaxies; the smaller Planck observatory focuses on the radiation from the Big Bang itself. At nearly €2 billion, the overall cost of the project puts the European Space Agency firmly in the astronomical Premier League alongside NASA.

Individual British scientists were deeply involved, including ESA's director of science, Professor David Southwood, who proudly trumpeted his organisation's achievement that morning:

I don't like to use the word 'ground-breaking' for a space mission, but this is pioneering stuff. We are, if you like, putting our marker in the ground to say: 'Hey, we're back and we're ahead of you!' And that will be taken, I'm sure, in good spirit by our American colleagues.

True, the British government avoided participating in many ESA programmes, notably any manned missions. However, on 23 March 2010 *Today*'s Justin Webb announced a shift: 'There is to be a new executive agency for space travel... The intention is that the UK gets a bigger share of the global space industry.' Webb interviewed a British major, a trainee astronaut with ESA, one Tim Peake, about the creation of this British executive agency. In Peake's words:

It's not a case of forging our way on our own, really. Every country that contributes to the European Space Agency also has their own national directives and their own national policy. And what that enables us to do is to work together as a team and to get involved in programmes that no one single nation could possibly afford to get involved in. And without this kind of cooperation and partnership, we would not be able to launch many of the space-based scientific missions that we're doing at the moment.

Webb, referring back to the money sunk into the disappointing Beagle 2 mission, asked, 'And, long term, this is an area where we as a nation will make money, rather than just sending it all off into space, never seeing it again?' Peake was feeling positive: 'Absolutely... even during the economic downturn, the space sector has been one of the few industries that's shown steady growth. And for a relatively small input, we're getting very good economic returns from this part of the industry.' He spelt out benefits in detail:

> The UK space industry is a real hidden success story: over 68,000 people in the UK working for the UK space sector, contributing £6.5 billion to the economy. So that's really where we focus the UK space industry's efforts: in coordinating both national programmes and working alongside ESA to contribute to European programmes as well.

While lagging far behind the French and Germans – each now boasting over ten astronauts – the British government funded Peake's astronautical ambitions to the tune of £60 million. On 20 May 2013, Professor Colin Pillinger was back on *Today* to champion the value of his mission. There was debate about whether in future space exploration robots would, in most cases, ultimately replace humans. Not completely, in Pillinger's view: 'You can get excited about robots. Robots can do things that are too dangerous for astronauts. But there are many things that robots can't do.'

Tim Peake eventually flew off into space on 15 December 2015. He was, as *Today*'s John Humphrys described him that same morning, 'The first *official* British astronaut – there have been other British people in space, of course, but not paid for by the British taxpayer, not wearing our flag on their sleeve.' Listeners heard from the popular broadcaster Professor Brian Cox, who made a passionate plea for greater British government funding:

> Our societies can afford these endeavours, all of the endeavours, both robotic exploration and manned space flight, if they want to. I mean, just one figure, is that [for] the ISS [International Space Station], the number is something like $150 billion, spread over many decades actually... which is less than 0.2 per cent of the world GDP in a single year that's been spent.

Cox was asked about his hopes for the future: 'I'd like to see humans on Mars in my lifetime. But the next big mission is a robotic mission for the UK, which is the ExoMars mission, which could – *could* – find evidence that there was or still is life on Mars, and that's extremely exciting.'

Colin Pillinger did not live to witness Peake's triumph. He had died in 2014. The following year there was a postscript to his great adventure: a NASA Mars spacecraft took images of Beagle 2 on the Red Planet's surface. The pictures showed that two of the robot's four solar panels had failed to activate, blocking its communications antenna.

The challenge of Mars remains irresistible, and was taken up by others. On 5 May 2018, NASA launched its InSight Mars lander; and that morning's *Today* interviewed two British scientists working on the project. Professor Tom Pike explained this expedition: 'It's really to get below the surface of Mars, of another planet... All of the missions up to this point have been literally scratching the surface, not looking deep down inside another planet.' Dr Rain Irshad of the British government's Rutherford Appleton Laboratory, which was involved in making sensors for the mission, considered spin-off discoveries:

> We know that the conditions on Mars may well at some point have been sufficient to sustain life. So we know that it had rivers. We know that it had these active volcanoes. And at one point it would have had a magnetic field. So it will tell us an awful lot about what happened perhaps to that life, about the fundamental fact, the origin of life, why it flourished on Earth; and potentially [we may] learn how life on Earth could be impacted in the future by some of the things that did happen to Mars.

Dr Irshad provided insight into the long-term planning for such space programmes:

> There is a next step... NASA is already working on Mars 2020, which is a mission that's going to send out a rover to collect samples from the surface of Mars... And then in Mars 2027, we're going to send out a sample-fetch rover which will collect all of those samples, bring them to a Mars ascent vehicle, launch them up to an orbiter, which will then bring them back to Earth, probably for around 2029.

An enthusiastic Justin Webb was keen to put something in the diary for *Today*: 'We'll keep in touch with you and be interested... in what's about to happen – but also do come back in 2029. It's a date.'

The ozone crisis – an environmental lesson

'So, not to be too melodramatic about it, how long do we have?'

JOHN HUMPHRYS, 12 NOVEMBER 1988

We're well versed in the Doomsday scenarios associated with global warming: areas devastated by drought; rising sea levels; ice caps melting; crops failing; and so on. But while the world frets, indeed argues, about what to do, scientists are waking up to the importance of another related problem – the threat posed by the oceans becoming more acid. In the 250 years since the start of the industrial revolution, the acidity of the seas has increased by 30 per cent. And all the signs are that that's beginning to have an impact on the fundamental biology of marine ecosystems.

John Humphrys painted that bleak picture for his *Today* listeners on 26 January 2010, as he introduced a new front in the battle over climate change – this time in the seas. Humankind's impact on the environment has been an increasingly salient feature of *Today*'s 21st-century agenda. The programme's archive also contains an illuminating narrative about an often forgotten environmental crisis which *did* prompt decisive intergovernmental action.

From 1973, the American chemists Sherwood Rowland and Mario Molina studied the impact that chlorofluorocarbons (or CFCs) were having on the Earth's stratosphere. CFCs were widely used in coolants and aerosols; the two chemists discovered that CFC molecules were releasing chlorine high up, and that that chlorine was in turn breaking down the ozone layer, the region of the stratosphere which protects the Earth by absorbing most of the sun's ultraviolet radiation. Some critics at the time dismissed their work as 'science fiction', but in 1995 they shared a Nobel Prize for it, along with Dutch scientist Paul J. Crutzen, who had looked at the thinning ozone layer at the poles.

The polar dimension of the problem caught the popular imagination, especially after the British Antarctic Survey produced compelling evidence that the ozone layer was under imminent threat in the mid-1980s: the survey team spotted a 'hole' in the ozone layer close to the South Pole. The ozone issue acquired a new urgency, and that lent weight to the argument that because the environment and climate do not stop at national borders, measures to protect them required international coordination.

The United Nations Environment Programme played a leading role, initiating a World Plan of Action. In 1985, the UN's Vienna Convention for the Protection of the Ozone Layer was held; this led, two years later, to the signing of the so-called Montreal Protocol, a treaty designed to ensure the phasing out of CFCs. At this stage, however, there were some significant omissions from the list of nations signing up with a promise to take action.

On the *Today* broadcast of 28 November 1988, John Humphrys interviewed Dr Robin Russell-Jones, the organiser of an upcoming meeting of the world's leading experts on the ozone layer, which was due to take place in London. The exchange provided an update on the many developments since the mid-1980s. First, what about that notorious hole? 'As far as the hole over Antarctica is concerned, it's actually slightly smaller this year than it was last year, but that is not any cause for complacency,' Russell-Jones replied. He elaborated:

> The scenarios still predict that, as chlorine and bromine build up in the stratosphere, there will be a gradual thinning of the stratospheric ozone over the entire globe and that we will begin to see effects from that fairly early on in the next century... The effects of that on human health will be a significant rise in the incidence of melanoma and non-melanoma skin cancer and a rise in the prevalence of cataracts.

Human health consequences aside, he was 'bound to say, though, that there are other effects on ecosystems which will be equally important'.

'So we've heard of various measures taken to stop the production of chloro-fluorocarbons, CFCs,' noted Humphrys. 'Is that going to be enough?' Russell-Jones explained:

> [The Montreal Protocol] commits signatory nations to a 50 per cent cut in consumption by the end of the century. All the scientists involved in this debate agree that that is not going to be anything like enough. Even if the Montreal Protocol was fully implemented, you would still see a doubling of the amount of chlorine in the atmosphere within the next 50 years.

'And the fact is,' added Humphrys, 'that the Montreal Convention is not going to be fully implemented, as you put it, because two of the biggest nations in the world are not even signatories to it.' Russell-Jones agreed:

> Yes, one of the major problems is that China and India have refused to sign the Montreal Protocol. In fact, they haven't even signed the Vienna Convention

for the Protection of the Ozone Layer, so they don't even accept a problem exists. Now both China and India have very considerable CFC-manufacturing capacity. And if they fulfil their pledge to provide a fridge for every household in the country by the end of the century – fridges use CFCs as the coolant – then they would wipe out everything that the developed nations were trying to achieve.

Sobering news indeed. 'So, not to be too melodramatic about it, how long do we have?' asked the presenter:

Russell-Jones: Well, I think decisions need to be taken very soon in order to correct what is building up into a very serious environmental crisis.

Humphrys: But we can't take decisions on behalf of India and China…

Russell-Jones: No, what is quite clear, where you're dealing with issues of global environmental problems, is that no one country can actually do very much on its own. It requires international agreements and it requires major international initiatives. And I'm delighted on that score that the prime minister [Margaret Thatcher] last week announced that she's going to be calling and hosting an ozone conference in March of next year for this very purpose, to try and get on board the non-signatory nations.

At the time of that London conference, experts from developing countries took the opportunity to point out what they felt was the hypocrisy of the West. And on the *Today* broadcast of 1 March 1989, Professor Rashmi Mayur, director of urban development at the Institute of Bombay, defended the governments of big developing countries:

India, along with China and Brazil, has not signed the Montreal Protocol because these three countries, and particularly India, feels that this is not their problem, in the sense that they have not created this problem. As you well know that 95 per cent of the CFC used and released in the atmosphere is by all these developed countries. Only 5 per cent is contributed by developing countries. And so India feels that we really are not responsible for this, and our signing and asking us to sign this treaty, by which we reduce our low consumption of the CFC by 50 per cent by 1998, is asking too much of us, because, as it is, we are consuming so little.

Later on the same programme, however, Margaret Thatcher's environment secretary, Nicholas Ridley, told Sue MacGregor that to be effective, any action needed to be global.

... CFCs are the most imminent and dangerous of all the problems and we've taken an initiative, in that we have a major international conference starting next Sunday, where I hope over a hundred nations will be represented – the main nations who are discharging and using these substances. And we might come out of that conference with the world agreement that we really must hasten forward the phasing out of CFCs throughout the whole world. That is what matters – it's the whole world in this which is vital.

For Peter Usher, the head of the UN Atmospheric Research Centre in Nairobi, the answer had to lie in technology and innovation, as he told *Today* that morning:

The problem that we do have is how to treat the developing world that might well require refrigeration, air-conditioning, building materials: all currently using CFCs in their manufacture. The new substitutes, the new technology, must be made available to them at the earliest possible juncture.

Britain faced a broader challenge to its record on the environment. On 29 April 1990, Lord Melchett from Greenpeace was on *Today* to lambast Mrs Thatcher's environment minister, Chris Patten, with Greenpeace's report 'Why Britain Remains the Dirty Man of Europe'. Lord Melchett identified a range of failures, from maintaining emissions of the greenhouse gas carbon dioxide (CO_2) while Europe was pressing on with reductions, to being the 'second-largest importer of hazardous waste in Europe'. The focus for his attack was acid rain, the environmental cause of the moment; Britain was the biggest emitter of sulphur dioxide in Europe – which was killing trees and polluting lakes in Norway and Northern Europe.

John Humphrys pressed Chris Patten on the point about CO_2 emissions:

Humphrys: ...the 25 per cent reduction in carbon dioxide that Germany is planning: we are not doing the same, we're proposing no cut. Why not?

Patten: No, it's not actually true. Germany are talking about feasibility studies to see whether a 25 per cent reduction is possible. We're committing ourselves to stabilisation at present levels by the year 2005, we are proposing a 20 per cent cut in all greenhouse-gas emissions by that time, and we are putting forward not just an aspiration, but we'll be putting forward tomorrow a programme for actually achieving that. But if I can just deal with the general point about who's the 'dirty man of Europe' and who isn't. It really is a preposterous point. I'm afraid it's a bit typical of Greenpeace, who don't have a monopoly of concern for the environment. The European Commission produced a league table earlier this year. We were placed in the better half of it. I want to see us doing even better. There have been 90 cases taken to the European Court of Justice about breaches of environmental directives since 1981. Only two of them affecting the United Kingdom. So let's put all that nonsense about the 'dirty man of Europe' on one side, and talk about policy in a sensible way.

He went on:

Patten: We are committed to a massive programme – about six billion pounds of expenditure – to clean up our power stations and to reduce acid rain. We have commitments which we have entered into, binding commitments which we intend to keep. We've reduced emissions by about 40 per cent since 1970, by nearly 25 per cent since 1980, which was when Lord Melchett ceased to be a rather blushing member of a Labour government which had a terrible environmental record.

Humphrys: But we still export more sulphur pollution than any other Western European.

Patten: And West Germany, which Lord Melchett was talking about, has about 34 per cent of its electricity from nuclear power. Now, if Lord Melchett's argument is that he wants us to increase massively our nuclear contribution, then it would be an interesting change in line for Greenpeace to make. But there are obviously greater difficulties when you start with more fossil fuel-based power than some other countries.

Two days later, the programme's focus was back on the ozone layer. On 1 May 1990, Brian Redhead chaired what resembled a quasi-trial on air, as Tracy Heslop of Greenpeace accused the chemicals giant ICI of gross inaction. By then, everyone knew the words 'ozone layer'. Heslop laid out the charge sheet:

ICI stand in the dock accused of destroying the ozone layer and for very good reasons. They're actually one of the largest producers of CFCs in Western Europe as well as the biggest exporter from the UK. They're the UK's sole manufacturer of the powerful ozone destroyer methyl chloroform, and also produce large quantities of destructive halons and carbon tetrachloride, which are also known to damage the ozone layer. All in all, they're still making 200,000 tonnes a year of ozone destroyers and plan to produce them for at least another ten years.

'Chris Tane: guilty or not guilty?' Brian Redhead asked ICI's spokesman, who pleaded:

We've never made any secret of the fact that we are a large producer of CFCs. That's because society needs CFCs to have things like refrigerators. We are, however, totally committed to phasing out CFCs as soon as alternatives are available... We're spending over £100 million in doing that. We're leading the world, in fact, in developing the new chemistry to do that. And in the meantime, we have the world's most comprehensive recovery and recycling service for CFCs.

Heslop was adamant that ICI should stop producing CFCs straight away. Redhead asked Tane about the consequences of such a radical move and received a list of the drawbacks:

> There would certainly be a lot of people out of work. It's not only that. If we stop making CFCs now there would be no refrigerators for our homes; there'd be no frozen food; no hospital blood banks; no air-conditioning of hospital theatres; no drugs refrigeration; and so on.

Eventually, China, India and Brazil *did* sign the Montreal Protocol, as did virtually every other nation on Earth: a remarkable achievement. Combined with technical innovation, it led to the stabilising of the ozone layer, and has come to be regarded as one of the most successful treaties of all time – even if full recovery of the ozone layer is forecast to take another half-century or so.

There have, however, been plenty of global environmental challenges since then, and as one major international conference on the environment has followed another, there has been a recurring pattern of similar acrimonious debate between the developed and developing world. Leading nations have been accused of dragging their heels: on cutting CO_2 emissions, for example, and on committing money to help developing nations combat global warming. The issue was raised in the British government-commissioned Stern Review of 2006, which concluded that climate change could hugely damage the global economy if left unchecked.

Nicholas Stern (now Lord Stern), a distinguished economist, was interviewed on *Today* on 30 October 2006, the day his report was published, by Edward Stourton:

> Stourton: You put the cost of fixing it [climate change] at one per cent of the world's GDP. How would that money be spent and how can you be so certain that that is an accurate and realistic figure?

> Stern: ... if you're talking about a transition to a low-carbon economy you can't be absolutely precise in these numbers. What you can do is make a judgement to look at the technologies that could come forward, ask how much they might cost, how much with wise R and D [research and development] we might bring those costs down. And that leads you to that sort of estimate, and it is a set of expenditures [which] would come about because people would be paying through tax or carbon trading, or implicitly via regulation they would be paying more for goods that are carbon intensive. And, of course, the relative price of

goods that are less carbon intensive would come down. But you're right, this has to be international, unless this is international we will not make the reductions on the scale which is required.

Stourton: And who will be paying that one per cent?

Stern: Ultimately it will be consumers with higher prices.

Stourton: I mean, will it be different between different parts of the world? Will a country in Africa, for example, be expected to pay one per cent of its GDP, or should we be paying a bit more than that?

Stern: We should be paying a little more than that. If you think of the equity of all this, the poor countries will be hit earliest and hardest and the responsibility for the greenhouse gases currently in the atmosphere is largely the rich countries. They're responsible for 70–75 per cent of the greenhouse gases in the atmosphere. So, from the point of view of ability to cope with the implications of climate change and past responsibility, I think it's only right that the rich countries should pay a little more. If the rich countries pay for it all you're talking about 1.3 per cent or something like that. So the increase in the cost to the rich countries for taking on bigger responsibilities would be very manageable.

In 2009, the much-publicised Copenhagen Climate Summit proved shambolic. It was preceded in Britain by a hacker's leak of private emails between science academics in the UK and USA, purportedly showing collusion in covering up evidence counter to their theories of man-made global warming. Although inquiries later concluded that had not been the case, the episode encouraged climate-change deniers.

At the summit itself, President Obama brokered an agreement with a limited group of countries to keep temperature rises to less than two degrees Celsius; it also proposed annual payments, rising to $100 billion by 2020, to help developing countries make the transition to cleaner economies. But the plan ran into trouble, and as the talks ground on, Britain's representative, the Labour secretary of state for energy and climate change, Ed Miliband, left the plenary session to talk to John Humphrys:

Miliband: I'd rather hoped it would have been done some hours ago, but we've faced a number of twists and turns. I'm still hoping it's going to happen because there is a rather broad consensus for this, but unfortunately we have a few countries which are still uncertain about whether they want to go forward. And when you're looking for essentially unanimity and that makes life quite difficult.

Humphrys: And even if you do get consensus on it, it's not a good agreement, is it? It's pretty woolly – nobody knows where that 100 billion is going to come from, if it's going to come from anywhere?

Miliband: I think we would have wanted a more comprehensive agreement, a legally binding one. I think it's good that we've made a start. We've made a start in terms of the emissions cuts that countries are going to do and, crucially, in terms of finance as you just mentioned, but that does rely on getting the agreement. And in a sense some people might have wanted a stronger agreement. I wanted a stronger agreement. Today's events showed the difficulty we face, which is we are dealing with incredibly complex issues, and trying to get 192 countries signed up in anyone's book – that's not an easy task.

The Paris Climate Accord of 2015 seemed to offer more hope. It paved the way to a future of much more balanced international environmental cooperation, with the big polluters committing far more. But that agreement was made before Donald Trump became president of the United States. In June 2017, just months after taking office, he announced his intention to withdraw his country from the Paris agreement as soon as possible, on the basis of defending US economic interests.

There remains a vocal minority adamant that climate change has no man-made contribution, that any changes identifiable are part of natural cycles over time. However, whether on land or in the rivers, in the skies or in the seas, *most* of the relevant expert scientists see ticking time bombs in the global environment caused by human activity. And the story of the ozone layer underlines that, as Robin Russell-Jones told *Today* listeners on 2 November 1988, 'No one country can actually do very much on its own.'

The BSE/CJD crisis – food flaws, scientific uncertainties and political blandishments

'The politicians and the civil servants who got it so badly wrong'

JOHN HUMPHRYS, 27 OCTOBER 2000

'BSE, the disease which sends cows mad – it rots their brains.' *Today* presenter Brian Redhead didn't beat about the bush when describing bovine spongiform encephalopathy (BSE), commonly known as mad cow disease, on 10 January 1990.

Brain-rotting spongiform encephalopathies of the kind that BSE represented were not new; a version in sheep, scrapie, had been identified by the 18th century. There was also a known human spongiform encephalopathy, Creutzfeldt-Jakob disease (CJD) identified in the 1920s, though the two were unconnected. But BSE was first diagnosed in Britain in November 1986, and not until mid-1987 were ministers informed of the disease – a delay, later criticised. In April 1988, the government established a committee, chaired by Sir Richard Southwood, professor of zoology at Oxford University, to consider all the risks the BSE crisis posed. A further investigative body, the Tyrrell Committee, began work the same year.

The leading hypothesis for the BSE outbreak was that scrapie had jumped species, transforming from scrapie in sheep to BSE in cattle. This evolution occurred because of the way abattoirs made meat-and-bone meal from dead, naturally herbivore, sheep and cattle – which was then fed back to the next generation of those herbivores. A question now preying on the public's mind was, if the disease could jump one species, could it jump another? In other words, was it possible for humans to develop CJD from eating BSE-infected cows?

Almost a year after his committee convened, Southwood published the results of its research. In a broadcast of 28 February 1989, Alex Kirby, the BBC's agriculture and environment correspondent, presented the key findings of the Southwood Report, working back through the chain of concerns:

> There've been worries that human health could be at risk after people have eaten meat from a diseased animal. The report says the risk appears remote. It believes

that cattle have caught BSE after being fed meat-and-bone meal made from sheep infected with a similar disease, scrapie, but that scrapie itself poses no human threat and that therefore we should probably not worry about BSE either.

Ministers, although basing their decisions on expert advice from independent scientists, seemed to fall between stools, wishing both to follow the precautionary principle, in order to avoid the very slight risk to humans that scientists signalled might be possible, and to protect the interests of the massive farming and food sectors. That same morning, Alex Kirby asked agriculture minister John MacGregor whether people should be reassured by the Southwood Report:

The public should, because we asked Sir Richard and his team to look at *all* the risks in every direction. And as you will have seen from the report, in some cases he's recommending action which he acknowledges deals with an extreme theoretical risk – very, very unlikely to happen – but nevertheless we've taken his advice and taken the action to deal with that... And Sir Richard himself is saying that there is no risk to humans from eating meat.

Kirby related a question and answer regarding the report: 'So did its authors entertain the possibility that BSE could threaten humans? "Yes," says Sir Richard.'

Southwood himself then spoke directly, with more nuance than John MacGregor: 'Of course, one must entertain any low possibility. There's a possibility that you and I could be struck by lightning tomorrow and therefore one takes certain precautions, but it's a very unlikely possibility.' Kirby wondered, 'Is the risk of contaminating [*sic*] brain disease through eating beef as remote as the chance of being struck by lightning, do you think?' 'More remote' was Southwood's view.

Dr Jim Hope of Edinburgh's Neuropathogenesis Unit made important distinctions:

I personally think it is unlikely that BSE in beef, for instance, will prove to be a danger to man. I'm a little more concerned about the use of BSE-affected brain material and offal for human consumption. Simply from our knowledge of scrapie we know that these tissues harbour the greatest quantities of virus and obviously the higher the amount of virus there is, the greater the threat would be.

Alex Kirby pressed him further: 'Have we reached the stage, do you think, where all food that is fed to animals reared for food, animals and birds, should exclude any material of animal origin?' To which the expert responded, 'I personally would subscribe to that now.'

Bit by bit, the British government did ban certain practices. In February 1989, it forbade the use of beef offal in baby food. Who even knew that it had featured in such products? Then, in July 1989, the European Commission halted exports of British cattle born before July 1988. In November 1989, the British agriculture minister placed a ban on the use of any cow brains and spinal cord for human consumption; it was perhaps the most important decision of all, in hindsight.

But public and press anxiety was growing. On 10 January 1990, *Today*'s Brian Redhead announced that 'The government is to spend an extra £6 million on BSE.' He asked food minister David Maclean, 'Now, are you worried because in fact there is a danger that human beings are at risk from this beef?' Maclean aimed for balance:

> **No, we're not worried, but we set up an expert committee under Dr Tyrrell and I think if you do have an expert committee which recommends long-term research over the next six, seven years, then I think you're under an obligation to carry out what they suggest. And, of course, this is all as ultra-precautionary measures.**

However, Redhead pointed out how more and more cattle were being affected by BSE: 'A large number of cases, many more than people were first speculating, are being reported every month – 9,000 new ones, did I read?' 'Yes,' Maclean retorted, 'but that's the level we expected in a disease which had been caused through feed fed to ruminants, and there is no suggestion that the actual level is increasing or it's passed on from mother to daughter.'

Redhead brought up reactions abroad: 'Israel, Australia, Germany, America... they won't allow our beef in now.' This rejection of British beef in certain European Community countries was a topic that particularly exercised David Maclean:

> **Well, Germany has tried to stop our beef coming in, quite contrary to EC rules, and the EC Commission has come very firmly down on Britain's side and the EC Standing Veterinary Committee has very firmly agreed with Britain that there is no danger to human health through BSE.**

In fact, the damage to British beef sales was disastrous; and it would take many years until confidence returned on the foreign markets.

Redhead focused on the economic plight of farmers who were seeing their herds destroyed, but Maclean thought that 'The 50 per cent compensation we pay to farmers who have diseased animals which cannot be used for human food, we think that's generous in the circumstances.' Redhead questioned safety: 'You say "cannot be used for human consumption". There's no danger of them going on selling meat from the infected cow?' Maclean was confident:

> **No, well, we've got a belt and two pairs of braces here. The belt is that we catch 99 per cent [of infected cows] on the farms and they're sent for destruction. Any which go to market... all the offals are removed and destroyed, that's the next pair of braces... and finally, of course, we have our excellent vets from the state**

veterinary service prowling round the markets, and so on, doing spot-checks. So there's lots of safeguards.

Continuing the metaphor, Redhead offered 'a cummerbund as well. Why not buy up all the calves born of the infected animals and you just clear the whole thing up once and for all?'

More bullish still was the new agriculture minister, John Gummer. At a Suffolk boat show on 16 May 1990, he memorably tried to get his young daughter to take a bite from a beefburger, in order to demonstrate that families and children in particular should not fear eating British beef. He railed against French authorities for banning its sale. However, by then many Britons were avoiding British beef too, and a number of local authorities had taken it off school menus. But Gummer was backed by the country's chief medical officer, Donald Acheson, who affirmed that 'Beef can be eaten safely by everyone, both adults and children, including patients in hospital.'

Others, though, had grounds for gravely troubling concerns about a human illness associated with BSE. Appearing on the *Today* broadcast of 15 May 1990, a Mrs Newman gave a harrowing description of her mother's tragic decline:

> **She started being unsteady on her feet. She started seeing things that weren't there. Laughing at nothing. And she had aged about 20 years in that two weeks. My mother cooked all her life. Every day she prepared meat, often licking her finger, and we are convinced that she contracted the disease [CJD] via an infection through the chopping and cutting of meat.**

Dr Wendy Grant was then introduced. Grant was a recently retired chief specialist in brain disease; Jeremy Vine, then a *Today* reporter (later better known as the host of his own Radio 2 programme), explained that she 'has since attracted much attention by saying she's very worried about British beef passing on BSE to humans. But she still questions Mrs Newman's certainty.' Dr Grant explained her thinking:

> **If her mother had dealings with cattle brains – supposing that she made meat pies – and if she occasionally had a cut finger, it is theoretically possible that she could have got the BSE infection, but it's equally possible that she's one of the so-called spontaneous cases [of CJD], of which there are something like between 25 and 30 every year in the United Kingdom.**

That said, Dr Grant was one of the earliest scientific campaigners to argue, for example, for more rigorous practices in abattoirs to avoid contamination of cow meat with infected cows' brains.

That same morning on *Today*, Jeremy Vine launched into a gruesome comparison of brains attacked by scrapie, BSE and CJD respectively, before asking, 'So the key point is this: can a human being contract Creutzfeldt-Jakob disease after eating meat infected by BSE?' For the answer, he introduced the professor emeritus of neurology at Oxford University, Bryan Matthews, who replied straightforwardly: 'I think it's certainly possible, yes.' 'Why's that?' Vine responded. '[Because] transmission has been effected in animals by feeding infected brain to animals. The animals developed the spongiform encephalopathy later on. It showed that these diseases can be transmitted by eating.'

Another deeply distressing case of CJD was described on the *Today* broadcast of 16 November 1991. One expert was clear that a Mrs Walkden had contracted the illness from diseased cow parts:

> **For Professor Richard Lacey, a food specialist at Leeds University, this is what happened, for Mrs Walkden had never undergone the brain surgery or hormone injections which are known risks of CJD. There's no other explanation here, there's no evidence of implants and so on and I think we have to look at the meat source because these infectious agents are only found in mammals which means meat, the most obvious source is a cow product because we eat cows.**

Colin Maclean, technical director at the British Meat and Livestock Association, dismissed that notion:

> **We can assure you that there is no relationship between the level of the animal encephalopathies in any country and the level of the human encephalopathies. So, for example, they have CJD in Australia and they do not have BSE and they do not have the sheep disease scrapie. And yet they have CJD at exactly the same level as we do in England. So all the evidence is that there's no relationship between these conditions whatsoever.**

Professor Lacey, who would go on to call for the extreme step of culling the entire British cattle herd to halt BSE, was one of the experts calling for far greater caution who found themselves vilified in certain quarters. Commercial pressures were still high.

Through the early 1990s, the death toll among cattle continued to rise. On 25 June 1992, Brian Redhead posed the question on *Today*: 'Is BSE... the worst crisis for British farming this century? The latest figures show that more than a thousand cases of BSE are being confirmed every month and it's the highest monthly figure since the epidemic began.' However, as epidemiologists had predicted, following the safety measures put in place, the epidemic was finally reaching its peak.

From 1990, the government had established a CJD national surveillance unit to monitor cases in humans and to investigate links with BSE. Between 1993 and 1995, four farmers with BSE-infected herds contracted CJD, but it was a 19-year-old student, Stephen Churchill, who became the first actual fatality, in 1995. The surveillance unit recognised these cases were of a new variant CJD (vCJD), most likely associated with the BSE epidemic.

On 20 March 1996, health minister Stephen Dorrell was forced to make a public announcement that scientists had established a link between BSE and vCJD. Ten cases had been discovered. The assertive reassurance from government and industry, and from the chief veterinary officer and chief medical officer, over the years had proved misplaced. Just four months previously, Dorrell himself had, embarrassingly, said there was no conceivable risk from beef.

Gradually, the BSE epidemic diminished. Eventually, the international ban on British beef would be lifted, but the reputational damage to the British food and farming sectors was great. The agony of families seeing loved ones waste away from vCJD continued. By the year 2000, some 85 Britons had died of the dreadful disease.

Once in power, New Labour ordered an inquiry into the BSE crisis, chaired by Lord Phillips. On 27 October 2000, John Humphrys announced on *Today*:

> **The report into the BSE disaster said anyone who hoped to find villains and scapegoats in it should go away disappointed. But in a sense they have found them; not villains or scapegoats perhaps... but a long list of the politicians and the civil servants who got it so badly wrong for one reason or another, that the public was, in the words of many newspapers this morning, 'betrayed'.**

Virtually all the ministers named in the report refused to be interviewed. But Stephen Dorrell did apologise, though not without mentioning that, 'The scientists ought, if they are engaged in this type of situation, to be pushed to refine their position.' Yet, looking back at the opinions expressed by the expert scientists on *Today*, such as Hope, Grant, Lacey, Matthews and others, they had all quite clearly indicated that there was a very small risk of BSE being passed on to humans. Interviewed by Humphrys that same morning, Lord Phillips, emphasised that scientists could only present ministers with a range of options of actions to take in the case of a crisis; he added, 'At the end of the day, the politicians decide which of those options to adopt and it involves a balancing exercise.'

Had there been any government cover-up? Humphrys pressed Lord Phillips:

> **What your report did was uncover a degree of secrecy in the ministry [of agriculture] that clearly should not have existed. Civil servants, for reasons best known to themselves, didn't want us to trouble our pretty little heads with all of this worrying stuff; didn't even want ministers to know what was going on.**

Lord Phillips objected, 'No, that's putting it much too high.'

'Is it?' Humphrys replied. 'We had a scientist who worked at the ministry on this programme yesterday saying he was directed away from doing research that he thought as a scientist he should have been doing.'

Lord Phillips stood firm:

An enormous amount of research was put in hand into BSE. There was no deliberate attempt to avoid looking at the particular issues. In the first six months we found that there was an embargo on information about the disease, until it was clear what its nature was. After that, there was not concealment of fact from the public. We *have* found, however, that there was what we've called a campaign of reassurance, entirely bona fide, directed to the rather narrow question, 'Is it safe to eat beef?', not always making it plain that when the answer was given – 'Yes, it is safe to eat beef' – that was because the potentially dangerous bits of the cow had been or should have been removed in the slaughterhouse.

Humphrys's final question was: 'And in future, should all such decisions be removed from the Ministry of Agriculture, because they exist, many people believe, to serve the producers' interests?' Lord Phillips's answer was understated yet revealing: 'Steps have already been taken to divorce the interests of the consumer from the interests of the agricultural community. I think those steps are beneficial.'

In terms of vCJD victims, some 176 fatalities were registered in Britain up to 2012; 50 in the rest of the world. It may appear that contracting vCJD was pretty much as unlikely as being struck by lightning. The destruction of infected animals and prevention of offal from infected animals entering the food chain helped stop a greater spread of the disease. But during the BSE inquiry, Dr David Tyrrell, the man who had chaired the investigative committee set up in 1988, complained that his committee had been put under pressure and falsely reassured by the then government that effective controls were in place in slaughterhouses to stop contaminating practices. In 1990, therefore, the committee had said that the risks from eating beef were no higher than the risks of everyday life. In fact, there had been not nearly enough inspectors, and that lack of checks had probably contributed to the prolonging of the BSE outbreak.

And in a reminder of the long-term trading damage caused by the BSE crisis, it took China until 2018 to accept imports of British beef once more.

Nuclear power and its hazards

*'We thought that we had identified all
the main risks and hazards'*

SIR KELVIN SPENCER, 8 APRIL 1983

Sir Kelvin Spencer was the chief scientist at the Ministry of Fuel and Power in the 1950s, and played a central role the development of Britain's civil nuclear power programme. That background gave great weight to his warning on *Today* on 8 April 1983:

> I left the nuclear scene in an official capacity at the end of the 1950s, and we then thought that we had – by 'we', I mean not only the scientists in government service, but those outside as well – we thought that we had identified all the main risks and hazards in connection with using nuclear energy for electrical power stations. Since then, in the 1960s and 1970s, this has shown how wrong we've been.

Sir Kelvin's nuclear career began in the shadow of the nuclear bombs dropped on Hiroshima and Nagasaki in 1945. For him the idea that the same technology could be used for civil purposes was, in the words of an obituary (contributed to the *Independent* by the senior Labour figure Tony Benn) 'a classic case of the conversion of "swords into ploughshares"', which offered the hope of 'endless supplies of energy that would be cheap, safe and peaceful'.

The first of Britain's nuclear reactors was, however, still military in purpose. Work to construct the reactors at Windscale, where uranium was to be converted into weapons-grade plutonium, began in 1947. They were built close to the resort of Seascale on the Irish Sea, just west of the beautiful, dramatic and immensely popular tourist area of the Lake District. Subsequently, in 1956, Queen Elizabeth II opened the Calder Hall nuclear power plant, located next to Windscale, which was hailed as the first industrial-scale nuclear power station in the world. Windscale and Calder Hall were later incorporated into the greater Sellafield nuclear reprocessing site – a considerable concentration of nuclear facilities in one location.

Expectations were high amid claims that Calder Hall would produce electricity that was, in the words of an American champion of nuclear energy, 'too cheap to meter'. Rather, it transpired that it was primarily producing plutonium for Britain's nuclear weapons and generating little power for the grid. It was an example of the kind of misleading information which fed a profound and persistent suspicion among critics and the general public about the nuclear industry. Sir Kelvin spoke on *Today* with the authority of a former insider. Reflecting on previous decades, he acknowledged the vulnerabilities inherent to nuclear technology, and expanded on the risks:

There's terrorism; there is a vulnerability of nuclear stations in a non-nuclear war; there's decommissioning time [of] expired stations; and there's a problem of the safe, long-term disposal of long-life radioactive waste.

Graham Leach, a BBC correspondent who also did presenting shifts on *Today,* pressed him over whether 'scientists have been able to identify the hazards and been able to control them' since Sir Kelvin left the nuclear industry.

'The answer,' Spencer responded disconcertingly, 'is no.'

They've identified quite a lot that had not been identified in the 1950s and the work that they've done in such things as the safe disposal of long-life radioactive waste, far from having solved that – although they say they have – they have found that it is far more difficult (in fact, it is impossible) to do it at all.

Sir Kelvin's time at the Ministry of Power and Fuel had included the worst-ever nuclear incident on British soil, the fire which broke out at the Windscale Pile-1 nuclear reactor on 10 October 1957. The fire burned for 16 hours, and there were fears that it might cause a nuclear explosion. Fortunately, water tamed the conflagration, but not before there was radioactive leakage. The drinking of milk from cows grazing within a wide radius was temporarily forbidden.

Despite that ban, it later became apparent that the true extent of the dangers stemming from the fire had been kept from the public at the time. Cabinet papers released on 1 January 1988, under the 30-year rule which regulates the release of confidential government documents, showed that the full findings of the report into the inquiry had been suppressed 'because', as *Today*'s Peter Hobday put it that morning, 'Mr [Harold] Macmillan, the then prime minister, didn't want to jeopardise Anglo-American relations, especially on the nuclear front and the sharing of nuclear secrets.'

'But,' Hobday asked, 'should Whitehall be so economical with nuclear truths?' He added, 'Indeed, intriguingly it seems only now that the clean-up is being completed at Windscale 30 years on, the announcement being made only weeks before the Cabinet papers became available. Or am I being too suspicious?'

Hobday interviewed Dr John Gittus, a director of the UK Atomic Energy Agency, who strongly defended the openness of the British nuclear specialists, saying that reports published in 1957 and 1958 had explained the nature of the accident and made recommendations for significant changes. Dr Gittus pointed out that, in general,

'Information concerned with defence matters was withheld from the public and was never publicised.' And he criticised the way journalists had treated the released Cabinet papers on Windscale: 'I think a danger does arise because of the way in which this particular information is being handled: the Cabinet papers are released; people rush to read them; and then you get a rather poorly digested account of what people think they've seen.'

Dr Gittus also argued that '...If we do have nuclear incidents today, even the very smallest event that happens in one of our nuclear installations is public knowledge within hours, that is evidence of the great openness of the industry today.' When Peter Hobday asked him, 'So would you say that at the present moment you are open and indeed the industry is never economical with the truth?', Gittus replied that he thought the industry 'very open'. His evidence was tourism:

> I mean, you've seen many demonstrations of that. I believe, for example, that the Sellafield plant today, which is now operated by British Nuclear Fuels Limited, is one of the major tourist attractions in Cumbria, and indeed one of the major tourist attractions in this country. And that is an illustration, one of many, of just how open the industry is today.

The Windscale fire occurred at a time of burgeoning anti-nuclear protest. The Campaign for Nuclear Disarmament (CND), which began with the famed Aldermaston marches, pitted itself primarily against Britain's nuclear weapons programme, but also fought the building of nuclear power stations. Other campaigning groups, such as Greenpeace and Friends of the Earth, joined the anti-nuclear chorus. And throughout the 1980s, Sellafield was repeatedly in the news for safety breaches. On 24 July 1985, *Today*'s John Timpson announced:

> British Nuclear Fuels, which is a state-owned company, has been fined £10,000, with £60,000 costs, on three charges relating to the pollution of Cumbrian beaches with radioactive waste in 1983. It was found guilty at Carlisle Crown Court of failing to keep radiation levels as low as possible, failing to warn people that they risked being exposed to radioactive material on the beaches and failing to keep proper records at its reprocessing plant at Sellafield.

BBC science correspondent Clive Cookson underlined the debt owed to those who had revealed the issue:

> Of course, the outcome of the trial delighted the anti-nuclear group Greenpeace, whose divers were the first to discover that highly radioactive material had been discharged from Sellafield. According to Greenpeace campaigner George

Pritchard, local businesses whose trade suffered after the accident will benefit most from the guilty verdicts.

An earlier *Today* report of 24 August 1984 had described Seascale as 'a ghost resort' following the November 1983 leak: 'Normally, the newsagent sells 2,000 buckets and spades. This year, she's sold less than 50.'

Clive Cookson's report on 24 July 1985 highlighted the symbolic importance of the case: 'These are the first criminal convictions in the history of the British nuclear industry. And they're bound to inflict new damage on the reputation of British Nuclear Fuels.' He summarised what had happened like this:

> **Both sides agreed during the trial that the incident started from a misunderstanding between two shift managers. As a result, highly radioactive waste was accidentally discharged into the Irish Sea from a storage tank. The company admitted that it did not have an adequate system for recording what was in the tank.**

'The defence,' Cookson explained, 'argued that it was not criminally liable because the company had taken all reasonable precautions to protect the public from radiation.' However, the 11 people who mattered came to a different view: 'The jury disagreed and by a ten-to-one majority convicted British Nuclear Fuels on three charges.'

By early the following year British Nuclear Fuels was again under pressure. On 19 February 1986 *Today* broadcast an interview with the company's Harold Bolter about four recent leaks. The interview was conducted by one of the programme's reporters, Olenka Frenkiel, and was perhaps not as reassuring as Mr Bolter intended:

> **Bolter: You talk about the four accidents in recent weeks. I think the first thing we have to say is, those accidents have not led to the death of anyone.**
>
> **Frenkiel: We don't know that yet, do we?**
>
> **Bolter: We do. Those people are still alive who were involved in that incident.**
>
> **Frenkiel: But it takes more than a month to kill somebody from radiation poisoning.**
>
> **Bolter: Not necessarily. If somebody had a blast of radiation they would die immediately. What I am saying is that that incident did not lead to the immediate death of anyone. We have accidents in other industries which lead to that. What you're suggesting is, perhaps, some time in the future, whatever happened to them might lead to a cancer which might lead to a death. I'm telling you that at these radiation levels, no, it will not.**

Frenkiel: You're dealing with one of the most deadly substances known to human beings. It affects not only the immediate human being touched by it, but can affect future generations. Are you suggesting that you can safely have four more leaks next month and four more leaks the month afterwards and you would still feel that it was an adequate safety record?

Bolter: As far as I'm concerned, any leak should not happen. Any leak at that place and our intention obviously is to prevent such leaks by regular maintenance, by checks. What I'm saying of these four leaks, they were minor. Yes, it concerns me that they happened. Obviously, I would be even more concerned if they involve pipelines for example carrying more radioactive materials. But I think what worries me is that an interview like this is talking about the minor leaks when we haven't had the major ones for you to worry about. Goodness knows what fun you would have if anything mildly serious were to happen.

The world's worst nuclear accident to date occurred at Chernobyl in Ukraine when, on 26 April 1986, one of the power station's four reactors exploded. The Soviet state instinctively sought to conceal what had happened, but to no avail. This was a nuclear-power disaster on a frightening scale, by far the largest to date, spreading radiation across Europe.

A week later, on 2 May, *Today*'s Sue MacGregor explored the ramifications of Chernobyl for Britain's nuclear industry with Jonathon Porritt, who was at that time director of Friends of the Earth. 'It's not really possible, though,' MacGregor observed, 'to compare the reactor that blew up in the Soviet Union with the sort of reactors you're worried about in this country. They're completely different designs.' Porritt replied:

It's true that the Russian reactor is a completely different design, unique to the Russian nuclear programme, but it's not true to say that there aren't important comparisons between reactor design there and reactors here. The kind of accident involving a loss of coolant, for instance, is something that could affect all of our reactors.

...

I suppose the thing that we feel is most in common between the two nuclear industries is this obsessive attempt to cover up information and to be secret[ive] about things and not to tell people the truth. That's not a technical similarity. That is, if you like, a political similarity.

'Is it,' MacGregor wondered, 'complacent to point out that our safety record is really pretty good with that one exception [Windscale] and, you know, that was a long, long time ago?' Porritt drew relatively little comfort from that:

> No, it's right that people should point out the safety record here is what they call good. Let's just get that in perspective, though, as we've suddenly seen with that one accident. You only need one accident to make those safety records look pretty thin. And, again, people said that this kind of accident would take place once in a million years. Well, the fact of the matter is, we've now seen Three Mile Island [the accident at an American nuclear plant in Harrisburg, Pennsylvania, in March 1979], we've had the accident at Windscale, we've now had Chernobyl. Everybody knows that these accidents *will* take place. The question is, how often?

The club of nuclear nations has now expanded. Some nuclear powers, such as France, have demonstrated their confidence in a nuclear solution to energy needs by pressing ahead with a major campaign of nuclear power-plant construction. British policy has been less certain. In keeping with the privatisation strategy of the Thatcher and Major years, the Conservatives sold off Britain's eight most modern nuclear power stations as 'British Energy' in 1996, while the older reactors, unattractive commercially, remained in public ownership.

In March 2011, the world was given a stark reminder of the vulnerabilities of the nuclear industry when a tsunami badly damaged Japan's Fukushima nuclear facility. James Naughtie covered the story for *Today* from Japan, and three days after the disaster, on 15 March, he interviewed Noriyuki Shikata from the Japanese prime minister's office.

> Naughtie: Isn't this bound to suggest to people who've been very worried about the nuclear programme, given the earthquake history of the country, that they were right all along, that this kind of thing was going to happen and that it will cause injury and some deaths which could have been avoided?

> Shikata: Well, Japan imports, for example, 99 per cent of oil from overseas and we import about 90 per cent of oil from the Middle East, and it is a very important energy security policy to have a nuclear power plants programme. At the same time... Japan is an earthquake-prone country, and I'm sure we will have a more intensive debate on the location of new nuclear power plants.

The Fukushima disaster was enough to shock a few Western European countries, such as Germany and Italy, into stepping back from nuclear power altogether,

In Britain, the last Labour government, the coalition of 2010–2015 and the Conservative governments elected in 2015 and 2017 all saw a need for new nuclear capacity. And the debate about whether renewable resources can adequately replace fossil fuels remains as live now as it was when Sir Kelvin Spencer was interviewed on *Today* in 1983. When Graham Leach challenged him that, 'At the end of the day, nuclear power may be all we have to fall back on when the natural sources of energy run out', Sir Kelvin replied, 'Well, the natural resources of energy – that is, the wind, the waves and the tides, and so on – will never run out so long as Planet Earth is in existence.'

HIV/AIDS –
the alleged 'gay plague'

'Some theatre cleaners are worried they
may catch it from gay actors'
JOHN TIMPSON, 19 FEBRUARY 1985

The disease AIDS continues to cause disquiet among various groups of workers who fear that they're in danger of contracting it during the course of their duties: prison officers, firemen, ambulance men... the latest are some theatre cleaners in Swansea who are worried they may catch it from some gay actors who are performing there, although the director has told the cleaners that it's only caught through sexual contact... But it's reached the stage now where the government's chief medical officer has intervened.

So reported John Timpson for *Today* on the morning of 19 February 1985. His words reflected the near-hysteria over the epidemic comprising the HIV virus, and the associated diseases labelled AIDS (Acquired Immune Deficiency Syndrome) that had spread to all parts of Britain. The association between the condition and homosexuality had, at one stage, even led to the acronym GRID, for 'Gay Related Immune Deficiency'.

It soon became apparent that the field of sufferers was larger and much more varied: intravenous drug users who shared HIV-infected needles fell victim, as did female prostitutes, and haemophiliacs were also becoming infected via blood transfusions. One reason the epidemic became, in the first instance, so closely associated with gay men in the West was that the United States and Western Europe were at the forefront of medical research, and the first clusters of the epidemic in those places were spotted among gay men.

In 1981, US clinicians had noticed how groups of previously healthy gay men in liberal Los Angeles, San Francisco and New York were contracting unusual, virulent diseases. The world-leading epidemic-investigating American Centers for Disease Control (CDC) coined the term 'Acquired Immune Deficiency Syndrome' (AIDS) in September 1982 to encompass these. But at the same time, there were cases identified elsewhere, for example in the heterosexual Haitian community in America, and in Africa among heterosexual Ugandans.

Researchers were able to identify that the virus was transmitted through bodily fluids, notably blood, but also semen or breast milk – though not saliva. It took scientists time to backtrack and understand the origins of the HIV/AIDS epidemic. They did appreciate that the worst human epidemics generally occur when a powerful virus jumps from one species to another – and in this case they concluded that simian immunodeficiency virus (SIV) had transferred from primates to people in Central Africa earlier in the 20th century; hence, since the mid-1980s, its labelling as 'human immunodeficiency virus' (HIV). We now know that by 1980 HIV was already present in a small number of people on five continents.

The way HIV/AIDS spread and was treated in the developed and developing worlds was very different, but stigma was a factor everywhere. In developed countries, where individuals in the public eye helped agencies push for understanding and fundraised for research on treatments, HIV/AIDS began to be held at bay; in the developing world, the lack of affordable drugs, the refusal of political leaders to confront the situation honestly, plus all manner of problems with social conditions and local beliefs meant that HIV/AIDS stayed far more destructive for longer.

On 24 April 1984, Bill Turnbull, a freelance reporter working in the United States (he later joined the BBC as a *Today* reporter and was the main presenter of 'BBC Breakfast' from 2001 to 2016) announced on *Today* that, 'It's the top priority of the United States Health Department – an epidemic that's caused public panic and private agony. More than 4,000 people have become its victims; 1,800 of them have died.' But this was a particularly important moment, for, as he continued:

> AIDS has triggered one of the most intensive investigations of medical research ever seen, and although last week French scientists announced that *they* had discovered a virus that may be the cause of the disease, yesterday US Health Secretary Margaret Heckler was eager to draw the spotlight to Washington.

Listeners heard Heckler declare, 'The probable cause of AIDS has been found.' It was, she described:

> A variant of a known human cancer virus called HTLV-III. Second, not only has the agent been identified, but a new process has been developed to mass-produce this virus. We now have a blood test for AIDS which we hope can be widely available within about six months. With a blood test we can identify AIDS victims with essentially 100 per cent certainty. Thus we should be able to ensure that blood for transfusions is free from AIDS. We'll also be able to promptly and easily diagnose people infected by the virus and perhaps develop ways to prevent the full syndrome from occurring. Finally, we also believe that

the new process will enable us to develop a vaccine to prevent AIDS in the future. We hope to have such a vaccine ready for testing in approximately two years.

These were huge developments. But there was a tussle over where the credit belonged. A team at Paris's Pasteur Institute seemed to have identified the responsible virus – or, more precisely, *retrovirus* – already. A feud developed between Luc Montagnier's research group in Paris and Robert Gallo's in America. They had, in fact, both published a paper in the same edition of the journal *Science* in 1983, outlining their findings.

It was not just scientific pride that was at stake, because a US government patent for an AIDS test had been filed on the back of Gallo's work. In 1986, it was determined that the patent would be shared. A detailed scientific investigation followed: Montagnier's group was credited with first discovering the AIDS-causing retrovirus; Gallo's team with proving the link between the two. (Montagnier and his colleague Françoise Barré-Sinoussi would be awarded the Nobel Prize for their work in 2008.)

In 1984, though, Margaret Heckler was jumping too far ahead regarding a vaccine. In Bill Turnbull's report on 24 April he spoke to the director of a US Gay Men's Health Crisis Center, Rodger McFarlane, who was rightly sceptical: 'I find that extremely optimistic, possibly very misleading. We still haven't managed to vaccinate herpes. And only recently hepatitis.' Antiretroviral drugs would eventually prove to be the way to block the advance of the disease for many in the West, but AIDS would remain a devastating disease, especially as the costs of the drugs rose. In the rest of the world, supply and affordability of drug treatments became huge stumbling blocks.

In Britain, the Terrence Higgins Trust was created very early (1982) to campaign for understanding of HIV/AIDS and sufferers. Tony Whitehead, its chairman, joined a *Today* discussion on 19 February 1985, about the way fear of the disease had even driven some to suicide. He also presented an eloquent summary of the facts about the way the disease is transmitted:

> **It is not a sexuality which puts people at risk, it is behaviour. It is a sexually transmitted disease and, although more prevalent among gay men, could be transmitted to *anyone* who is having a sexual relationship with other people, and therefore it is important to make sure that people realise that although particular groups have a very high risk, comparatively, everybody who is sexually active outside of a long-standing monogamous relationship may be at some risk.**

England's chief medical officer, Dr Donald Acheson, was invited onto the same programme. 'Doctor,' asked John Timpson, 'how great are the hazards of giving the kiss of life to people who may have AIDS?' Acheson replied:

> I think the first thing to say is that we're dealing with a very rare disease. There have only been 120 cases in round figures in the United Kingdom, where we have 60 million people living, so that from the point of view of a person who needs resuscitation, I think they should always get it. The chance of an ambulance driver or fireman meeting somebody with AIDS who requires resuscitation is really very remote, and they really must get this into proportion.

'There is no evidence,' he continued, 'from the very substantial American experience of this disease that it is transmitted through saliva on cups and saucers, on crockery, glasses and things of that sort.'

> We know of no circumstances where a person who is positive to the virus cannot continue to work in a particular place. He is not a risk to anybody, or she is not a risk to anyone, by social contact. And that sort of problem, which has led to ostracism and stigmatisation of people, has complicated their problems. Some of them have lost their houses which the council or something like that feels that they shouldn't continue to live in. And these things are quite inappropriate reactions to this problem, tend to make it go underground and make the public health hazard greater.

Acheson was 'pretty sure that it isn't going to go away. And we've all got to learn to live with it and be sensible.' He targeted his advice:

> The things that are going to make a difference are, first of all, the homosexual community altering its behaviour – this has already happened in the United States. They have to move to the position where they take many fewer partners.

On a possible cure, Acheson was cautious:

> It would be quite wrong of me to suggest that over the next year or two we can look forward with certainty to a vaccine. I think it will be some time before we have either the treatment or the prevention.

To try and change behaviour, the British health secretary of the time, the Conservative Norman Fowler, backed a hard-hitting advertising campaign with the slogan 'AIDS, Don't Die of Ignorance'. It would be the country's biggest-ever health campaign, and Fowler became something of an apostle for the use of condoms.

But a 'Play Safe' AIDS campaign aired on BBC Radio 1 drew fire from the Catholic Church. The general secretary of the Catholic Bishops' Conference of England and Wales, Fr Vincent Nichols (later Cardinal Nichols, Archbishop of Westminster) appeared on *Today* on 11 December 1986:

It's important that people face the fundamental questions that are raised by the spread of this AIDS virus and not avoid them. It seems to them [the bishops] that the Radio 1 approach is particularly mistaken in this because it is failing in its simple message of 'play safe'; it's failing to raise any of these real moral questions. At best, it is avoiding them. And, at worst, I think it can be seen as condoning or encouraging casual sex and promiscuity. 'Play safe', when applied to sexual activity, I think, is selling young people short, who actually are capable of higher moral standards than that message suggests.

One advantage the Western world had in the campaign against HIV/AIDS was that many prominent celebrities raised awareness of the dangers, fundraised for research, and donated generously. There were casualties among their own number. Hollywood screen idol Rock Hudson was one of the earliest celebrities to succumb to AIDS. The BBC North America correspondent James Cox (later the presenter of Radio 4's *The World This Weekend*), reporting for *Today* on 3 October 1985, the morning after Hudson's death, pointed to the actor's courage in coming out publicly about his illness; the broadcast also outlined the celebrity support Hudson had received:

Hudson's friends and co-stars like Elizabeth Taylor and Linda Evans rallied round to try to dispel the cloud of suspicion and fear surrounding AIDS victims and to raise money to find a cure. At one such benefit concert last month, actor Burt Lancaster read out a personal message from the then dying Hudson: 'I can at least know that my own misfortune has had some positive work.'

Hudson left a quarter of a million dollars to AIDS research.

In the UK, Diana, Princess of Wales, helped to break down stigmatising myths; she was famously photographed on 19 April 1987 shaking the hand of an AIDS patient at the first London hospital unit dedicated to the disease. The likes of Elton John were prominent, too, in campaigning for the cause.

But the global rock star Freddie Mercury of the band Queen, so flamboyant on stage, felt that he could not declare publicly that he had AIDS until on his deathbed. The following morning, 25 November 1991, the DJ and presenter Paul Gambaccini paid tribute on *Today*:

Of course, it is the last great gift he's given us really, because it's a sad fact that it has taken, and will take, the deaths of more loved public personalities to change the way that many people feel about this disease.

Even Chris Smith, who had become Britain's first openly gay MP in 1984, took 17 years before he revealed his HIV status, in 2005; the first MP to do so, he decided to reveal his 1987 diagnosis after Nelson Mandela announced that his son had died of AIDS.

As late as August 1991, *Today* was also reporting on issues of official misinformation and discrimination. It was revealed that disturbing, often highly inaccurate details regarding people supposed to have HIV/AIDS were being stored on the Police National Computer (PNC). One woman, Leslie Coulson, told *Today* she had discovered a photograph of herself displayed on the wall of her local police station under the headline 'AIDS'. By the time she'd had a test to prove she was HIV negative, the rumours had already spread:

> Coulson: I can't go into bars anymore. I've got no friends. My family was really shocked and wondering what was up with me, and I had to like, to talk to my Mam and say I haven't got AIDS – I don't know why it's been put up there. I can't get nowhere to live. I couldn't take a flat in Church Street because there were people in there skitting me, saying I'd got AIDS and this, that and the other. I've lost all my friends.

But John Burrow, chief constable of Essex, in the same report, defended the practice, saying:

> Police officers are frequently called upon to deal with incidents where blood and other body fluids are there, and I think whilst the general rule is that you treat everybody with the care that you would expect, if the person was suffering from HIV or was HIV positive, then I think the additional safeguard of saying to the officer, 'We understand that this person may be HIV positive' would give him that additional safeguard. And I think as senior officers we owe it to our policemen on the streets doing their day-to-day duty to warn them of such dangers.

However, Madeleine Colvin from the civil liberties group Liberty warned that the system was chaotic and open to abuse, saying:

> The information recorded under the warning signals on for example the PNC is usually highly speculative, often inaccurate, and can lead to the kind of scandalous abuse which happened in Cleveland. Unfortunately, the state of the criminal records system in this country, particularly the intelligence information held by the police, is completely out of control. We have a number of instances where information is being wrongly disclosed.

UNAIDS, the United Nations programme on HIV/AIDS, has estimated that between the early 1980s and 2017 more than 70 million people were diagnosed as having HIV worldwide, roughly half of them dying from AIDS-related diseases. In the UK, as *Today* discussed on 9 April 2018, one-third of those with HIV/AIDS were women.

As for treatment, concerted efforts by the likes of the United Nations, the World Health Organisation, the US government and charitable organisations such as the Gates Foundation have greatly helped overcome the obstacle of providing affordable antiretroviral drugs in Africa. The number of AIDS-related deaths has been reduced by 51 per cent since 2004.

To date, a vaccine to prevent HIV remains elusive. However, a *cure* could be in sight. Presenter Justin Webb announced on *Today* on 1 April 2016:

> **There's some very good news about the fight against HIV today. Not news that is going to have an immediate impact, but encouraging nonetheless. Researchers have managed to use gene-editing technology to take the virus out of infected cells.**

In the words of science commentator Professor Matthew Cobb in that same broadcast: 'I think there is definitely a glimmer of light on the horizon.'

Stephen Hawking and Peter Higgs: masters of the universe

'He changed the way we thought about the universe'
JOHN HUMPHRYS, 14 MARCH 2018

Some of the most exciting leaps of the imagination in science since the Second World War have been achieved by British physicists. Two stand out, and both Stephen Hawking and Peter Higgs have often been celebrated on *Today*.

Hawking 'changed the way we thought about the universe', announced John Humphrys on *Today* on 14 March 2018, the day after the scientist's death. 'For a man who could not utter a syllable, he was a brilliant communicator.' In that automaton's voice – through which he was forced to speak because of his motor neurone disease (MND) – he sounded like something of an oracle... one who spoke not in riddles, but in the clearest, purest sentences. He encouraged us to grapple with his explanations of black holes (collapsed stars); of how our universe came about from one singularity, the Big Bang; and of a possible unified theory of the universe.

People also hugely admired his life of triumph over adversity. When, as a student at Cambridge in 1963, Hawking was diagnosed with MND, it had looked as though his extremely promising career in research would be cut tragically short; he was given only two years to live. However, overcoming his disability, he went on to become one of the most inspiring scientists in the world, living on a good half-century longer than his doctors had first predicted, proving able to popularise science like few others, and turning his crippling disability to advantage.

In contrast, Peter Higgs has been more discreet. His work has been based on his imagining of a key new particle, the Higgs boson. He believed that the discovery of this subatomic particle would solve the puzzle of the inconsistencies in the otherwise beautiful 'Standard Model' – a model, built up by leading physicists in the 20th century, which seemingly offered a near-complete, but not perfect, explanation of how the whole subatomic universe operates.

Both Hawking and Higgs have proved feisty atheists, believing the laws of physics explain the birth and existence of our universe, without a need for any creator God. They have both shared opinions beyond physics, too – for example being extremely critical of Conservative Party policies on education. However, the two clashed over the Higgs boson, Hawking once betting it could not be found, Higgs retorting (according to the *Guardian* of 3 September 2002) that Hawking's 'celebrity status gives him credibility that others do not have'. When the Higgs boson was discovered in 2012, Hawking graciously conceded defeat, saying Higgs should be awarded a Nobel Prize – which he was, in 2013.

Hawking had several interactions with *Today* over the years. On 1 February 1988, he was interviewed following the announcement that he was the co-winner of the prestigious Wolf Prize in Physics, along with Professor Roger Penrose – who himself had been an early inspiration to Hawking, furthering understanding of Einstein's gravitational relativity, the Big Bang theory and black holes. With typical good humour, Hawking explained, 'My disability has not been a serious handicap. Theoretical physics is a good field for disabled people, because it is all in the mind.' Asked whether he felt the prize would make any difference to his work, he responded:

People in science don't make discoveries in the hope of getting prizes, but for the excitement of finding something new about the universe. Someone once said scientists and prostitutes get paid for doing what they enjoy.

Hawking was asked: 'How much do your discoveries affect ordinary people?' His reply was disarming, for, to him, human curiosity was as fundamental as the basics of life:

My work on the origin of the universe will not help to feed people. It will not even help them to wash their clothes. But there is more to life than just eating and doing your laundry. We all want to know where we come from and why we are here.

His book, *A Brief History of Time*, was published that year and became a surprise bestseller, often jokingly described as the least-read, most-bought book ever.

In 2003 Hawking was among those invited to guest-edit the programme, and later, to celebrate his upcoming 70th birthday, *Today*'s science correspondent Tom Feilden headed to Hawking's study in Cambridge to ask him selected questions posed by listeners; his answers were broadcast on the programme on 6 January 2012. By then, Hawking had retired as Lucasian Professor – the post once held by that greatest British genius of physics, Sir Isaac Newton – but remained deeply involved in theoretical physics and its teaching. Hawking never displayed any of Newton's religious anxieties. In response to the simple starter question 'Was there a time when there was nothing?' Hawking reiterated some of his oft-repeated basic views:

The origin of the universe can be explained by the laws of physics, without any need for miracles or divine intervention. These laws predict that the universe was spontaneously created out of nothing in a rapidly expanding state. This is called inflation, because it is like the way prices in the shops go up at an ever-increasing rate. Time is defined only with the universe, so it makes no sense to talk about time before the universe began. It would be like asking for a point south of the South Pole.

Hawking moved on to discuss the question 'Is there a conceivable way we could ever detect and study other universes if they exist?' The theoretical physicist stepped up several gears, but his track remained clear:

Our best bet for a theory of everything is M-theory. One prediction of M-theory is that there are many different universes with different values for the physical constants. This might explain why the physical constants we measure seem fine-tuned to the values required for life to exist. It is no surprise that we observe the physical constants to be finely tuned; if they weren't, we wouldn't be here to observe them. One way of testing this would be to look for features in the cosmic microwave background radiation which would indicate the collision of another universe with ours in the distant past.

Lastly in this *Today* birthday special, Hawking moved to the possibilities of human exploration. Feilden had pointed out earlier how Hawking had even played a cameo part in *Star Trek*; he now sounded like a character from that immensely popular television series made flesh, as he answered the question 'Do you think the human race will survive all potential disasters and eventually colonise the stars?' Hawking responded:

It is possible that the human race could become extinct, but it is not inevitable. I think it is almost certain that a disaster such as nuclear war or global warming will befall the Earth within a thousand years. It is essential that we colonise space. I believe that we will eventually establish self-sustaining colonies on Mars and other bodies in the solar system, although probably not within the next hundred years. I am optimistic that progress in science and technology will eventually enable humans to spread beyond the solar system and out into the far reaches of the universe.

On 14 March 2018, the morning after Stephen Hawking's death, *Today* invited leading cosmologist Carlos Frenk, professor at Durham University, and media-friendly Brian Cox, professor of physics at Manchester University, to explain his greatest concepts. Cox focused on Hawking's ground-breaking work on black holes. 'The picture of a black hole, a completely collapsed star' used to be regarded as 'something from which nothing can escape'. But, as Cox described it, what Hawking had shown was that:

> They have a temperature, so they radiate away into space and ultimately would evaporate away into the universe again – and that's called Hawking Radiation. And that idea, that if things fall into a black hole, they're not gone forever – the black hole gives its contents back to the universe eventually – is absolutely fundamental... That will be a result that is remembered forever... It's often described as being one of the first windows onto a theory beyond Einstein's theory of gravity.

Frenk contributed in turn:

> The idea that Stephen and others had, was that all structures in the universe, galaxies and so on, began life from tiny fluctuations of subatomic origin, what we call quantum fluctuations. So he actually worked out how these very tiny irregularities in the early universe would seed the universe with these small perturbations that over billions of years would grow into the galaxies that we see today. He was a pioneer, not just in the story and understanding of black holes, but also in an understanding of the complexity and beauty of the universe. So he's one of the founders, really, of modern cosmology in this respect.

The two scientists described how Hawking's special physical condition, combined with his lust for life, had galvanised him to the very end. Frenk commented on how, because his body had restricted what he could do physically,

> ... he had to abstract. He had to be able to synthesise and express very concisely... The book where I learnt relativity [*The Large-Scale Structure of Space-Time*], in fact that he wrote with George Ellis, is a masterpiece, is a jewel, is unlike any other book, purely because of the way in which the concepts are expressed. And I remember, in those days, long equations were the norm in physics. His book has not a single long equation, but he has the most profound thoughts. It's just pure sheer beauty and logic.

Cox explained how

> The last time I saw him, at his 75th birthday party, he was talking about the new gravitational wave experiments where we've seen the collisions of black holes, and speculating that those results might be able to prove some of his theorems once and for all.

Among many awards Hawking won was the Fundamental Physics Prize, in 2012. It is now the most lucrative science prize in the world, worth some $3 million, and was set up by Russian internet tycoon Yuri Milner, who was himself a former theoretical physicist. Despite Hawking's many accolades, however, one in particular persistently eluded him. Frenk, on *Today*, considered why Hawking perhaps didn't receive the ultimate science prize for his enormous contributions to theoretical physics:

> It's interesting: he never got the Nobel Prize; and he said, well, he would have got the Nobel Prize had anybody seen one of these black holes that Brian was talking about evaporating... We haven't seen them evaporate, possibly because you have to wait a very, very long time before this process occurs, and we didn't have enough time.

Hawking always wanted to inspire new generations of scientists, and *Today's* tribute included an extract from his 2016 Reith lectures: 'Despite recent triumphs, there are many new and deep mysteries that remain for you to solve, and keep a sense of wonder about our vast and complex universe and what makes it exist.' A sentence from Tom Feilden summed up Hawking's exceptional scientific life: 'Not bad for a man who was told he had just months to live when he was diagnosed with motor neurone disease in 1963.'

In contrast to Hawking's fame and widespread acclaim, physicist Peter Higgs was not high-profile: he published little, and he didn't fit in with the expectations of modern university life at Edinburgh. He even confessed candidly that at times he struggled to keep up with developments on research into particle physics. But Evan Davis, presenting *Today* on 4 August 2008, delivered a fine introduction to the scientist:

> Professor Higgs is the theoretical physicist who first suggested there must be another elemental particle we haven't seen yet, that gives mass to all the others. It was such a good idea, his colleagues named it the Higgs boson.

Tom Feilden explained the importance of the concept, as Peter Higgs 'came up with an explanation for some of the basic inconsistencies in what's come to be known as the Standard Model of particle physics.' Higgs himself went into some elementary detail with Feilden about how his seminal idea had germinated:

> I'd long been puzzled about the way people use symmetries in particle physics. If you imagine the crudest form of symmetry, which is mirror image, it's as if the image in the mirror, it's not quite the same as the object that's being reflected, so the symmetries are broken; and it was in 1964 that I realised that there was a way out... The first paper that I wrote was very short, less than two sides of A4, simply stating what the way was of avoiding this difficulty. Then I realised that

what I had to do was actually to produce a simple example of how this would work in particle physics. So I then listed a few sort of consequences in terms of what would be an experimental signature and one of those was the first reference to what's called the Higgs boson.

Higgs's great idea was not immediately accepted, but in the following decades many became convinced of his brilliant prediction and worked on his theory, including Belgians François Englert and Robert Brout. Jim Al-Khalili, professor of physics at Surrey University, explained further the importance of the conjectured particle on the same 2008 edition of *Today*:

> The Higgs boson plays this fundamental role in particle physics. It's actually been dubbed by some people as the 'god particle', which basically implies that it's somehow so important that it explains how and why all the other particles exist and so, if the Higgs boson exists, it then provides that deeper explanation.

Important it may have been, but it irritated Higgs when certain religious figures distorted the casually given nickname, suggesting that it implied the particle would demonstrate the existence of a divinity.

The reason for the attention drawn to the particle on *Today* on that particular summer's morning in 2008 was that it was the day the Large Hadron Collider (LHC) was going to be switched on. The LHC was the world's most powerful particle accelerator: a huge underground tunnel in which two streams of hadrons (particles) could be made to collide; it was nicknamed the 'atom-smasher' because of the consequences of that collision. It was located at the ground-breaking underground physics research centre of CERN (the Conseil Européen pour la Recherche Nucléaire), based on the Swiss-French border. Founded in 1954 as a major European science centre to rival the American ones, CERN had since attracted many leading European physicists through its doors. In 2008, scientists at CERN had already been working on the particle project for some 16 years. As Tom Feilden put it, 'The search for the Higgs boson has now developed into the biggest and most expensive scientific experiment ever undertaken.'

Peter Higgs stood humbly to the side of the experiment:

> I'm always a bit embarrassed when my name is used as if the discovery of this particle is really the only thing that the machine is supposed to do. Because that's not true. There's a lot more to the LHC programme than just finding the Higgs boson. To me, the Higgs boson is just a matter of unfinished business.

Tom Feilden began describing the awesome experiment due to take place in the LHC: '[In] a 27-kilometre-long tunnel... beams of protons cooled to minus-270 degrees will be hurled at velocities approaching the speed of light, before being smashed into each other.' Jim Al-Khalili explained, 'When these two beams of protons cross, they collide with such incredible energy that out of that energy will be produced these elementary building blocks, these different kinds of particles.'

Even though the LHC proved fiendishly difficult to control, eventually a Higgs boson was identified by two CERN detector teams, with the news announced on 4 July 2012. This boson was calculated to have a mass 130 times greater than a proton. There remained much work to do in order to decipher exactly what type of boson had been seen, and whether there might be more than one kind – opening up new realms of possibilities in physics. In the meantime, Higgs was awarded the Nobel Prize in 2013, along with François Englert (Brout had died), for his pioneering thoughts and work on the particle named after him.

Stephen Hawking, in another extract from his Reith lectures, replayed on *Today* after his death, provided an eloquent justification for the airtime the programme has devoted to these two physicists and their achievements:

> **You also must remember that science and technology are changing our world dramatically, so it's important to ensure that these changes are heading in the right directions. In a democratic society, this means that everyone needs to have a basic understanding of science to make informed decisions about the future.**

Concorde – the superstar of supersonic travel

'And in future, Mr Minister, let us always drink to the Entente Concordiale!'

TONY BENN, 11 DECEMBER 1967

With a combination of humour, bilateral friendship and boundless optimism for a shining future, a British government minister, in the French city of Toulouse, celebrated a new age of supersonic travel on 11 December 1967:

> Only one disagreement has marred the cooperation between Britain and France in this project, and this was a disagreement about how to spell the aircraft. With a typical British common sense, we have spelt it 'Concord' with a 'd', which is how you pronounce it... In Britain, we have noted the French generosity – indeed extravagance – in adding an 'e' to the end of 'Concorde', and no amount of official discussion or ministerial meetings have been able so far to resolve this difference. And I have now decided, Mr Minister, to resolve it myself! In future, in Britain, we shall add an 'e' to 'Concorde' too. We shall add it for 'excellence'; we shall add it for 'England'; we shall add it for 'Europe' towards which we are moving; we shall add it for 'entry'; we shall add it for the *'entente'*. And in future, Mr Minister, let us always drink to the *Entente Concordiale*!

When *Today* listeners heard this speech, the first Concorde prototype '001' had been rolled out in Toulouse. The words were delivered by Anthony Wedgwood Benn MP, Labour's technology minister, better known in later years as Tony Benn. The tone is all the more striking in the light of his fierce opposition to Britain's membership of the European Union in the 1970s.

Benn might have had his constituents at least partially in mind: he served as an MP for Bristol, Britain's aviation equivalent of Toulouse, where the first British Concorde was being built – and where all subsequent ones would be constructed. Whatever his motivations, he would remain one of Concorde's greatest advocates throughout its history and its ups and downs. Even at the time of that lavish speech, there had already been more significant disputes within the British government over the new wonder plane than the mere spelling of its name.

The roots of the Concorde project in Britain lay in a 1950s research programme called 'British Supersonic Transport'. At the Royal Aircraft Establishment, a Welsh whizz-kid, Morien Morgan, had begun looking at the possibility of a supersonic passenger plane, which led to the development of the so-called 'slender delta' concept, adapting military technology. To some, Morgan would become known as 'the father of Concorde'. By 1960, the British government was officially backing the building of a commercial supersonic jet and had corralled the aviation industry into forming a consortium, the British Aircraft Corporation (BAC; later British Aerospace), to develop the planes. Meanwhile, separately, the French government had called for bids to develop its own supersonic plane in the late 1950s, with Sud-Aviation (later Aérospatiale) winning the contract.

After consulting each other, the British and French governments realised they were working on very similar projects – there was even talk of some industrial espionage – and that the costs each country would incur were enormous. It made practical sense to swallow a little national pride and collaborate. The two nations signed an agreement in 1962 to develop jointly a supersonic model.

On that day in Toulouse in 1967, many marvelled at Concorde's first public display. Both the plane's broad triangular wings and bird-like head, with its drooping beak, would make Concorde immediately recognisable in the skies. The design was memorable, but more impressive by far was the engineering that created the first supersonic commercial jet in the Western world, able to cruise at Mach 2.02 (equivalent to a ground speed of 1,334 mph), more than twice the speed of sound. It was, in short, an amazing technological feat.

One of the speakers at Toulouse was BAC's managing director, Sir George Edwards. Reginald Turnill, the BBC's aerospace correspondent, explained to his listeners how Edwards 'said firmly in front of the many American visitors that "Concorde would fly many years before America's rival plane could do so... We are out in front, so we must not feel lonely, nor must we lose our nerve."'

Listeners also heard that:

Monsieur Jean Chamant, France's transport minister, gracefully emphasised that though the first prototype was coming out of a French hangar, the result was as much British as French. And he said that Concorde would make it possible to go to New York and back again in a day, with a day's work done in between.

There was just one problem. In late 1967, Concorde had yet to fly. Even getting to prototype stage had come at a hefty price. While the Concorde project was prestigious, it was by no means certain that it could ever become a commercial success, although the

British and French governments were banking on that in the 1960s. It was a gamble that both administrations kept making, despite the odd moment of wavering.

There would be stumbles before Concorde's maiden flight, and obstacles to overcome before it could fly to New York. And there was competition, surprisingly not so much from the Americans, but from the Soviet Union, which was well advanced on its own supersonic airliner. After much wrangling, the USA would eventually give up on its own costly supersonic aircraft programme in 1971, despite interventions from President Richard Nixon to try and save it. By contrast, the Soviets, with their Tupolev Tu-144, were able to claim the prize for the world's first supersonic aircraft flight, a year after Toulouse, on 31 December 1968; the aircraft broke the sound barrier six months later on 5 June 1969. At least, by that time, Concorde's first prototype had made its maiden flight circling above Toulouse on 2 March 1969, breaking the sound barrier on 1 October of that year.

Then, at the Paris Air Show of 1973, a Tupolev Tu-144 had a devastating accident. The exact reason for the crash, which killed 12 people, has been much disputed. It was discovered that a French Mirage jet had flown up unexpectedly, perhaps to take a closer look at the rival technology, and had possibly, accidentally, distracted the Soviet pilot. Another theory was that the Soviet pilot, having seen the Concorde display before his own flight, was attempting, riskily, to outshine his French counterpart. Whatever the cause, the result was a slowdown in the Tupolev's commercial development.

There were still battles ahead for Concorde, both to make it a successful plane commercially, and to make it an acceptable plane environmentally. On 15 February 1973, Tony Benn, now in opposition, was questioned by *Today* presenter Malcolm Billings regarding concerns that the Concorde project might be cancelled. Thus far, only the British and French national airlines had placed firm orders for any of the supersonic planes. Benn, though, remained bullish and upbeat:

> **Let's look at it as a real aircraft: it is technically perfect; I think there's no question about that. It's met all its requirements. It's been ordered by BOAC and Air France. The supersonic world is here anyway because the Russians have built one and intend to put it into service. And whereas we had hoped to get a lot more orders at this stage, it's now obvious I think that we shall have to wait until entry into service before the orders really come in.**

'The difficulty for the government and everybody,' he acknowledged, 'lies in this next two-year period.' But Billings remained to be convinced: 'If the American airlines aren't going to buy it, who is?'

As far as Benn was concerned, this was jumping the gun:

> Well, I don't think one can say, you see, yet, that the American airlines are not going to buy it, because I don't think anybody has any doubts that when it flies the Atlantic under BOAC and Air France colours – and the only way you can fly a supersonic is by Concorde on European airlines – that the American airlines will buy it…

Benn was keen to discourage talk of 'cancellation', asserting: 'I don't believe that is on the cards, myself, at this moment.' But, being in opposition, he could not be *sure*, adding, 'Subject to correction.'

Malcolm Billings, challenging Benn further, summarised the anti-Concorde case: 'Critics of Concorde, of course, have said that it should never have been built; that it's too expensive – too expensive to buy, too expensive to run; and that the airlines don't want it. What's your comment on that?' Benn replied:

> Well, that's an argument appropriate to 1962. But when all this effort has gone into it, and you have produced something which really is a very superb aircraft and where there is undoubtedly a demand, particularly, I think, on the long oceanic flights, it would be really crazy to cancel it now.

Despite Benn's confidence, by the end of 1973 virtually all of the other companies that had put in speculative orders for Concordes had withdrawn them. The steep rise in the price of petrol that accompanied the 1973 oil crisis and further commercial strains on airlines played their part. However, the British and French governments and their national carriers remained committed.

Only 20 Concordes were ever built in the end, of which 14 flew commercially. As costs had skyrocketed, the British and French governments had to provide colossal financial support to get them off the ground. Concorde's first commercial flights began in January 1976, but to surprising destinations: British flights served Bahrain; French flights Rio de Janeiro. On 3 March 1976, reporting for *Today* aboard a flight to Bahrain, correspondent John Sergeant (later the BBC's chief political correspondent) mulled over the expense of the whole project:

> One thought that's going through my mind is that the British taxpayer paid more than £500 million to develop this aircraft – that's more than £10 for every man, woman and child in the country; so I see this as my attempt to get the ten quid back.

American airlines would *never* buy Concordes; there was some debate as to whether nationalistic sour grapes at the Franco-British technological triumph played a part. More immediately, in the mid-1970s environmental battles beckoned, as Concorde could not yet land in US cities. Sleek and aquiline, even beautiful, the aircraft might be; quiet it was not. As *Today* listeners heard on 6 January 1976, one British prelate, the outspoken Hugh Montefiore, Bishop of Kingston (later Bishop of Birmingham), was even crossing the Atlantic to encourage American resistance to this devil in the sky at a hearing in Washington D.C. The BBC science correspondent James Wilkinson gave a flavour of the bishop's colourful presentation:

> 'The noise,' he said, 'is not hell, for hell goes on forever. It is more like a secular form of purgatory. I can best compare it,' he said, 'to an inflamed gallbladder – intermittent, but the spasms can leave you speechless.'

Wilkinson asked Montefiore why his words had made such an impact:

> Well, it's difficult to know. I think it's perhaps due to the fact that so many speeches before mine were all about sticks for measuring noise in decibels and so on, and I'm concerned about the impact of noise on people, the effect it has on people. And I think, probably, it was that human factor which aroused some interest.

'I've come over here,' Montefiore explained, 'as president of the Heathrow Association for Control of Aircraft Noise, and we are concerned about the noise of take-off and landing at Heathrow only.' However, the bishop had his personal objections too:

> If I was coming out here under my own hat as well, I would add other factors. One of those would be the fact that Concorde will only benefit the very rich – 20-per-cent-plus first-class fares – and only small numbers – only 100 to 108 in each flight) – and I wish that all that vast amount of money was spent on other transportation systems which help those who don't own private transport.

Wilkinson wondered, 'What about the aspect that this does represent a vast investment by Britain and France and there's a certain amount of national pride attached to it as well?' Montefiore seemed sure of his figures:

> Well, yes, it is a vast investment, but, so far as I understand it – I'm not an economist – but I understand it can't actually break even unless we build the 131st plane which, obviously, we shall never do, as there are no plans to build more than 16, so financially speaking it's going to operate at a loss and therefore it would be cheaper to cut it out. As for prestige, well, yes, that is true, and it is a wonderful piece of technology. There will be people who feel that. But I do think you must remember that the only poll taken in Britain shows that the majority of people who held an opinion – 57 per cent – were against it.

'I think,' Montefiore added, 'most people are on my side.'

Returning to the matter of the debate in Washington, Wilkinson asked the bishop, 'What are the chances, do you think, of you winning the day and Concorde not being allowed to land in America?' Montefiore had reasons for confidence, though he was worried about the influence of the transatlantic 'special relationship':

Well, I've been very impressed by the openness of these proceedings. I think everybody here has been. I only wish to goodness we had this sort of open government, instead of decisions made behind closed doors and rules being bent. I think that reason will prevail, which means that the side I'm on will win. If it doesn't win, it will be for what people think are political reasons of the great alliance.

Eventually, flights to Washington began in May 1976, although court actions delayed flights to New York until November 1977. For the environmental opponents, the fact that Concorde did not fly at supersonic speed over land was small comfort; its turbo-jet engines, produced by Rolls-Royce and French partner SNECMA, were essentially of a type developed for high-performance military jets, and therefore always extremely noisy. The amount of fuel the planes guzzled was huge and expensive, too. Those drawbacks were the price to pay for an airliner that could slash flying times in half. Concorde's wealthy customers flying from London to New York arrived an hour earlier (local time) than they had departed, hence the Concorde motto, 'Arrive before you leave.'

The Soviet supersonic project was not yet quite out of the game. A first commercial Tupolev Tu-144 line started between Moscow and Kazakhstan in November 1977. But in May 1978, another accident meant the planes were withdrawn from passenger service, thereafter being used for a few years mainly for freight transport. Concorde continued to be a record-breaking airliner, and not just because of the steepness of the prices for its seats. In February 1996, it achieved its ultimate transatlantic flight record, in 2 hours 52 minutes.

It was also, until very near the end, extremely safe. Concorde boasted an impeccable flight safety record through to the start of the new millennium. However, real cracks eventually began to show on some of British Airways' Concordes – a development noted just days before the catastrophic crash of Air France Flight 4590 on 25 July 2000, outside Paris Charles de Gaulle Airport. The accident left 113 people dead, destroyed the aircraft – and shattered confidence.

The morning after the disaster, *Today*'s James Naughtie, presenting *Today* from close to the crash site near Paris, spoke of how 'a triumph of technology has been indelibly sullied'. He interviewed Tony Benn, who by now was a respected, if disillusioned, elder statesman sitting on the backbenches of Tony Blair's New Labour government. He would stand down from Parliament the following year. But intact was his idealism over what the Concorde project, so much associated with him, had represented.

> **Naughtie:** The point about Concorde... is that it has had such a huge impact on people in Britain and in France, where, uniquely, I suppose, it became a national symbol of sorts for both countries.

> **Benn:** Oh yes. I think there's no doubt about it: here was an example of very high technology and high skill coming to fruition successfully. And at the time it was being built, it was bitterly criticised by all sorts of people who didn't like it, but what they forgot was it was a symbol of peace, it was a symbol of the movement of people across the world; it was something that really had a lot going for it. And I'm very, very proud to have been involved and to have played some part in preventing successive British governments from cancelling it.

After the accident, the whole Concorde fleet was suspended for a time, as investigators tried to work out what had happened. The French air-accident investigation team identified that a titanium part which had fallen from another plane was the root cause of the tragedy, but the Concorde involved had also proved devastatingly vulnerable. 'I think,' Tony Benn told James Naughtie on 26 July 2000, 'people will see this in perspective as the time goes by and I hope to see Concorde fly again.' For a time, his wish was granted. Concordes flew commercially from late 2001 until 2003, but it proved a messy coda. Increasingly, aircraft parts showed signs of weakness, but Europe's Airbus company was reluctant to make replacements. Meanwhile, financial losses rose – the commercial side of operations was under as great a strain as ever. Finally, the show was over.

Concorde is gone, but not forgotten. It provided a unique service, and its design has made it the most distinctive and striking commercial airliner of all time. While most of the Concordes ever built now stand quietly in museums, they remain star attractions. As one passenger put it to reporter John Sergeant during their exclusive flight, described on 3 March 1976:

> I think that you can't actually put it in terms of money. The excitement of being on the Concorde was sufficient, surely, and if there's anything to be proud of, it's got to be that particular plane.

The triumphs and travails of the Channel Tunnel

'From today, Britain is no longer an island'
SUE MACGREGOR, 6 MAY 1994

The Queen, with John Major, will leave Waterloo station in just under three hours' time, using what's perhaps the greatest engineering project of this century, the longest undersea tunnel in the world, linking two countries which have stared suspiciously across the waters at each other for centuries.

With these words, on 6 May 1994, *Today*'s Sue MacGregor, co-presenting the programme from Folkestone, announced the inauguration of the Channel Tunnel. This world-class piece of engineering seemed to look to a dynamic, interconnected future – as MacGregor suggested several times that morning, it also challenged Britain's historic sense of itself as an island nation.

As *Today* had tracked the evolving project over the years, there had been an inevitable focus on practical matters – the engineering, the costs, the possibilities. Would its colossal budget, for example, ever allow it to become a viable business? MacGregor drew attention to the delays and eye-popping expense: 'It's a year late in starting and it's cost £10 billion – that's over twice as much as the original estimate. Can it recoup that investment; and who's going to have to be persuaded to use it?' There were other costs too: it is sobering to remember that ten workers died during the building of the Channel Tunnel.

Sue MacGregor told listeners that 'Yesterday, the Consumer Association brought out the results of a survey which shows that nearly half of the people they talked to are worried about using it.' Concerns ranged from anxieties about all that water over one's head to fear of invasion, whether by human aggressors or by rabid continental rats. There were nightmare scenarios of accidents and fires in a tunnel measuring 31 miles (50 kilometres) in total, of which 23 miles (37 kilometres) would be under the sea.

Nothing, however, could dent the staggering technological achievement that was being celebrated. There were three tunnels in all: two main rail tunnels, plus a service tunnel. The Seikan undersea tunnel in Japan might have been longer and deeper, but its undersea portion was not as extensive as the Channel Tunnel's. Mainland Britain, separated from the Continent some 8,000 years earlier at the end of the last ice age, now boasted a land link back to Europe. In MacGregor's simple encapsulation: 'From today, Britain is no longer an island.'

Given the achievement, there was some perhaps inevitable competition for credit. 'Now this side of the Channel,' noted MacGregor, 'we tend to think of the whole thing as a British project.' She asked BBC Paris correspondent Stephen Jessel whether the French thought of the completed tunnel as their own. It seemed, from Jessel's reply, that the French were a little less inclined to jingoism:

> No, I don't think they do. But they certainly don't think of it as a British project. After all, the tunnel was built by a consortium of five French and five British companies. The French banks are very heavily involved in the financing; too heavily, some of them might think. I believe most of the shareholders are French. This is seen as a Franco-British operation.

Perhaps, though, the French had some rights to conceptual ownership. MacGregor looked back to what, from a 19th-century British perspective, would have been an alarming prospect: 'After all, Napoleon thought it up, didn't he, in 1802 or something?'

It is true that the creation of a Channel tunnel had been a long time coming, its advent postponed by British fears more than once. There is a traceable history of more than two centuries of ideas about linking Britain and France before the final realisation of the project. Wildly enthusiastic and imaginative French and British engineers proposed ingenious concepts, from tunnels to jetties to bridges; some of the suggestions even involving the creation of artificial islands as stopping points along the way.

Napoleon had indeed gathered French troops at Boulogne, within sight of the English coast, and contemplated how a tunnel might work to his advantage – or, as MacGregor put it, he 'wanted an engineer to dig a hole'. The Frenchman Albert Mathieu-Favier came up with the idea, around 1801, of two levels of undersea tunnels: the upper one for horse-and-coach transport; the lower one to evacuate any water infiltrations.

By the middle of the 19th century, Franco-British relations were much warmer. France remained a hugely important trading partner, as well as Britain's closest continental neighbour. As the tourism industry began to develop, there were even more reasons for more people to think about travelling to the other shore and beyond. Ambitious ideas for a tunnel began finding new favour.

In 1875 both the British and French parliaments actually approved proceeding with a Channel tunnel project, and early in the 1880s tunnelling even commenced. But certain British politicians and newspapers whipped up national security concerns. The British government got cold feet and halted the whole project. Decades passed, and two world wars intervened.

But finally, on 6 February 1964, the French and British governments agreed to proceed together… when the time was right. They felt confident they would be able to raise the capital without private investors.

Time passed. No tunnelling began. On *Today* on 13 September 1973, Barney Bamford, a freelance reporter who frequently worked for BBC radio outlets, interviewed the chairman of the Channel Tunnel Company, one Leo d'Erlanger – a grandson of one of the tunnel pioneers of the 1880s project, and, despite the French-sounding name, a prominent figure in Britain, where the family had settled in the late 19th century – about the slow progress. 'Why do you think it has been delayed so long?' Bamford asked. 'Do you think it was political? Do you think it was financial, or because of technical reasons?'

D'Erlanger blamed the politicians: 'Oh, certainly not technical reasons, because it's a piece of cake, technically. It's entirely political.' Blame, too, was attached to 'public opinion in this country', which, in his eyes, 'moves rather slowly and takes to anything fresh with difficulty – that's a national characteristic. And furthermore, of course, there are interested parties who are against it. You can't expect a very, very momentous question of this magnitude not creating enemies.'

'Do you think,' Bamford wondered, 'the tunnel will benefit industry and commerce of this country?' On this point, d'Erlanger was unequivocal:

> Oh, very much so… The facility afforded to manufacturers and merchants by virtue of the tunnel, their being able to reach their markets abroad with great facility, with no transhipment, no weather hazards, nothing – this is an immense asset. The Channel Tunnel is an absolute must. We're not competitive in the great markets of Europe unless we have a free approach to them. But quite apart from the fact that all the figures, independently [support it]… all the research which has gone into it from independent parties and very highly qualified people shows that it's going to be a tremendous success financially for this country.

'Quite apart from that,' he added, 'it's symbolic – now Europe is Europe and we're in Europe.' Britain was turning its focus away from its far-flung colonies to Europe on its doorstep; it had just joined the EEC.

However, the British economy was in the doldrums, and the Channel Tunnel faced the usual challenges of all high-spending capital projects in hard economic times. The Labour government, back in power, rapidly withdrew from the project at the start of 1975. The Conservative victory in 1979 placed a prime minister in 10 Downing Street who liked the Channel Tunnel as a concept, but Margaret Thatcher was adamant that no British public money would be sunk into it. Socialist French president François Mitterrand, who came to power in 1981, accepted that, but the French won a different argument. Thatcher's vision was car-centric, of a cross-Channel motorway. However, this vision presented costly technical difficulties, for instance in dealing with ventilation to remove dangerous car fumes. The French government preferred a car- and lorry-carrying rail service, supporting cheaper, safer collective transport.

In June 1986, a Franco-British consortium called the Channel Tunnel Company/France-Manche rail project won the bid and was awarded the contract. It evolved into Eurotunnel, the company that would oversee both the making of the tunnel and its running for decades to come. The construction funds would be raised from shareholders and from enormous loans.

Eurotunnel appointed tough co-chairmen, André Bénard and Alastair Morton. There were delays and the costs spiralled; at times it seemed the project might collapse completely. Sir Alastair (as he became in 1992) repeatedly had to duck and dive when interviewed on *Today* about Eurotunnel's sluggish progress. On 8 April 1993, he sounded like a man stalling for time, saying, 'What needs to be comprehended for both British Rail/SNCF's intercity trains, the Eurostar, and the Eurotunnel's shuttles... is that you begin and you build up... So the tunnel is open from April, but you will be in first gear, as it were, with services.' He was being interviewed by Anna Ford, who was a member of the *Today* presenting team for six years from 1993. 'So when,' she asked, 'are the first passenger services going to be available?' Morton imagined 'some time in June' and claimed, 'The problem is the commissioning of the rolling stock.'

Ford, picking up the driving metaphor, observed, 'You just seem to be in neutral at the moment.' Morton admitted there were a few more hurdles, but added, 'What journalists keep saying is we don't start until the late summer. That's not correct.' In fact, the first operations only began a *year* later, in 1994. At the same time, Eurotunnel's vast debt mountain was growing.

To be successful, the Channel Tunnel would have to attract a large number of passengers away from the ferries in particular. However, on that inauguration day of 6 May 1994 Sue MacGregor questioned a few British ferry passengers – and most said they would stick with what they knew.

Eurotunnel also had to capture a large slice of the road-haulage market to be successful. But the lorry drivers MacGregor quizzed were mostly ambivalent. The first liked his routine: 'I'd think I'd have to give it a whirl... but I don't think I'd use it all the time. I think I like the boats too much. I like my hour break.' The second was fearful: 'I wouldn't use it if you paid me. I feel safer on the boat because at least if the boat goes down I can swim for it. No, it's too claustrophobic.' A third lorry driver needed a commercial incentive: 'It all depends on the price. I mean, I'm an owner-driver...' Eurotunnel's projected passenger figures looked very ambitious.

MacGregor observed on that day: 'This time next year, we'll know if the optimists are right.' And Alastair Morton was back on *Today* on 14 September 1995 to face a grilling from John Humphrys, who began:

> Well, next time you cast a worried eye over your mortgage repayment and wince, imagine a debt of £8 billion. That works out at £2 million a day, give or take the odd shilling. And that is the scale of the problem facing Eurotunnel. They built the tunnel, it works – a great engineering feat – but paying for it is another matter. That's why they've just announced that they are suspending those interest payments.

Then, he turned to Morton:

> Humphrys: So, you're broke?
>
> Morton: I wouldn't say that, no.
>
> Humphrys: Sounds like it.
>
> Morton: We are uncoupling the financing, financial engineering, of the tunnel from the project engineering, which has been a great success, as you say, and this has no effect on services.

Morton explained the technical details of the credit agreement, which he said allowed for the rescheduling of interest payments, before accepting that 'what has to happen is a sharing of pain'. The reason for the lower-than-anticipated revenues was, in his view, intense loss-leading competition from the traditional cross-Channel carriers:

> Morton: Ferries have cut their fares. Revenues go down with that. Until the ferries either kill each other or commit joint suicide, the revenues are likely to be lower than expected. We have arrived at number one in a few months across the Dover–Calais straits, so we're building up quite nicely, but the revenues aren't: that's the point.
>
> Humphrys: But the ferries may not kill each other; they may kill you.
>
> Morton: That is unlikely. The tunnel will not go away... And you can ask Jeffrey Sterling, the chairman of P&O [Ferries], to be a witness on that. He has always said this. We have to face the fact that once the tunnel is open, he said, it will stay, it will be open, it will go on, for the 50 years and more that it's intended.

'Isn't there another option,' Humphrys mused, 'and that is that Eurotunnel goes bankrupt?' Morton rejected the prospect: 'It's a very unlikely option indeed.' For good measure, he added, 'You can't sell a hole in the ground for much if you've closed it.'

In 1996 a fire in the tunnel, caused by a lorry, injured two people, and undermined public confidence. The damage to infrastructure slowed services for months. In the aftermath of the fire, John Humphrys interviewed the assistant secretary general of the Fire Brigades Union, Mike Fordham, who five years previously had said that open carriages to carry lorries should not be allowed. He reiterated this view on that morning's programme, and also said that passengers should be separated from their cars on the Eurotunnel to allow the carriages to be sprayed with the gas necessary to extinguish any future fire.

Humphrys put those points to the new chairman of Eurotunnel, Robert Malpas, who responded:

> There are several points of view about safety in the tunnel. If you talk to the Swiss authorities you find that lorries go on to flat cars, with no sides, no tops, drivers stay in their cabs and they go through the tunnel and they consider that highly safe, indeed they have a wonderful safety record.

A couple of later fires were better controlled.

Although the French had completed their side of the high-speed rail link, from Paris to the tunnel, by the time the tunnel opened, the British only really caught up 13 years later, and at a cost of £5.8 billion. In November 2007, the revamped St Pancras station, now St Pancras International, which became the London Eurostar terminal, opened for business.

Into the new millennium, the Eurotunnel company staggered on, restructuring debt, and seeing and surviving boardroom coups. Some of the numbers began to go in the right direction. Passenger and lorry volumes on the Eurostar and Eurotunnel 'Le Shuttle' services were becoming significant, including – each year after 2013 – some 20-million-plus passengers using the two services.

The day after the inauguration of the Channel Tunnel, on 7 May 1994, the controversial *Sun* columnist Garry Bushell was invited to give vent to his views on *Today*. He invoked Shakespeare's patriotic poetry of 'this sceptred isle... this fortress built by Nature for herself / Against infection and the hand of war', as well as the spirit of 'the great Englishman Enoch Powell'. 'Now,' Bushell asserted, 'this England's independence and our natural defences have been breached by the Channel Tunnel, as the British Isles are reunited with mainland Europe for the first time since the Atlantic flood ten thousand years ago.'

Bushell conceded that the tunnel itself was 'at least a magnificent feat of engineering' but added:

> Less praiseworthy is the softly-softly political process that seeks to strip us of other symbols of national identity. Even the teaching of our history is under

question. Inch by inch the very essence of Britishness is being eaten away... And we have traded our democracy for provincial status in a corporate Eurostate.

More than 20 years later views like that would be heard again during the 2016 Brexit referendum campaign. But Britain's island status may have been changed for good: 'The tunnel will not go away,' said the once-beleaguered Alastair Morton, under pressure on *Today*, and it hasn't.

From gene science to new frontiers in medicine

'Here you are, you're playing God'

JAMES NAUGHTIE, 27 MAY 1999

In 2016, a big brash building, the Francis Crick Institute, opened beside the St Pancras International railway station in London. This major new biomedical research centre was named after the British member of the very famous Nobel Prize-winning group of scientists who, in 1953, identified the double-helix structure of DNA – aka the deoxyribonucleic acid molecules concealed inside the body's cells. For their discovery, Francis Crick, American James Watson and New Zealand-born Maurice Wilkins won a joint Nobel Prize in 1962 – though not Rosalind Franklin, who died in 1958 but whose contribution has since received much attention.

At the time of that monumental discovery, Crick had exclaimed (according to Watson) that they had 'found the secret of life'. Now, 60 years later, the institute named after him drew on those secrets to commence its cutting-edge research at the highest level. Thanks to the study of the genes discovered within DNA, the field of biomedicine had exploded in importance in the decades since.

On 26 June 2000, *Today*'s James Naughtie had an opportunity to talk to James Watson, 'one of the founding fathers' of DNA research. Since the scientists' breakthrough in 1953, the understanding of DNA had grown enormously and, on this day in 2000, another major milestone for the human race was about to be reached. Naughtie did not hold back:

> The announcement that the genetic code has been cracked is being made today and you can choose almost any superlative to describe it. Some say it's much more important that the splitting of the atom, makes getting to the moon seem a bit of a game. A bishop is quoted this morning as saying the biotech revolution will make the industrial revolution seem a minor blip on the chart of human history.

Watson, in more measured mood, explained a gradual advance in DNA research from the 1950s onwards in slow, modest tones:

> Well, back in 1953, when we saw the DNA molecule, we just wanted to basically know how the information was in it: the general principles by which you encoded

information by sequences of DNA. And the first breakthroughs took eight years, before we really saw the thing. And then we didn't have any means by which human beings could ever read the messages within the ordinary DNA molecules. So a few people thought about it, but most of us didn't think about it until 1975, when [Frederick] Sanger and [Walter] Gilbert came up with their extraordinarily powerful methods for sequencing – that is, reading DNA messages.

'And now,' Naughtie offered, 'within a couple of years, this mystery that you glimpsed in 1953 is going to be solved.'

'Well,' Watson replied, 'we'll have the human... books of instruction. I say books, because if you put it in book form, it would be 500 large telephone books, so there is a lot of information.'

The science of genes is bursting with large numbers. DNA molecules – consisting of extremely long strands of molecular subunits called nucleotides – make up chromosomes, 23 pairs of which exist within the nucleus of each cell in the human body. But each DNA molecule contains billions of the four nucleotide letters (paired A and T, or C and G), certain sections of which form the genes. Sometimes compared to written-down recipes, genes not only contain the hereditary information passed down from generation to generation, but also transmit that information within the body, enabling the growth, development and functioning of tissues and organs. DNA confers uniqueness on an individual.

No wonder it had been a gigantic challenge to go through a single DNA molecule, noting down, in order, all the information contained within. Such sequencing as was achieved in June 2000 has been hailed as a huge breakthrough in science because, once you can read the DNA and gene structures, that opens up the possibility of altering or editing them – for example, to halt hereditary diseases of all kinds. And it is these possibilities that lie at the root of the new biomedical research.

As Watson suggested with his reference with Sanger and Gilbert, when it came to gene sequencing there were two earlier inspirational scientists to whom a great debt was owed. On 21 November 2013, Sir Paul Nurse, the first director of the Crick Institute, and himself Nobel Prize-winning British geneticist, appeared on *Today* to pay homage to one of them. Presenter Sarah Montague opened with a typically understated quote from Fred Sanger himself: 'I'm just a chap who messed about in a lab.' Well, Montague continued, 'Messing about in his lab led to him winning the Nobel Prize for chemistry *twice*; the only Briton to win two Nobel Prizes.' Sir Paul Nurse sang his praises:

Fred Sanger was a giant among scientists, one of the greatest scientists of the 20th century. And all his work was done in Britain... He did two great discoveries, for which he got the two Nobel Prizes. The first was to determine the amino acid

sequence of the protein insulin… But not content with that, he then went on to determine a way of sequencing DNA, I mean our hereditary material. And he worked out a method that was actually ultimately used for the sequencing of the human genome; he used it to sequence the first genomes back in the 1980s.

He concluded, 'These are major, major milestones in the history of science.'

'And on which so much medicine, and I suppose all science, depends now?' Montague added. To which Nurse simply responded, 'Absolutely correct.'

Sanger already had his own eponymous building, now the Wellcome-Sanger Institute, located near Cambridge. It was here that some of the vital research was carried out through the 1990s, and whose results were revealed on that day in 2000. The aim of the Human Genome Project (HGP) was not just to map, but to understand all the genes in human beings. It is perhaps one of the greatest pieces of international public science ever devised.

Yet another world-class British geneticist would work at the Sanger Centre (as the building was previously known): Professor John Sulston. He and colleagues had earlier sequenced the genome of a nematode worm, to prove that sequencing the DNA of a whole animal was actually feasible. This work not only earned him his place on the HGP, but led to his own Nobel Prize in 2002.

The publicly funded HGP, a massive scientific enterprise, was initiated in the USA, where James Watson became its American director from the outset, from 1988 to 1992. But it was a multinational venture, in which Watson persuaded exceptional cooperation between various governments and top scientists, and which would take years to complete. In addition, it found itself facing a controversial private competitor.

As this dogged work got underway, a fortuitous discovery had already led to an important early application of DNA-related technology. On 10 September 2009, *Today* presenter James Naughtie harked back to that bit of luck in an English laboratory in 1984:

> **It's exactly 25 years since Sir Alec Jeffreys, a young research scientist in those days at the University of Leicester, discovered genetic fingerprinting: the unique barcode of the DNA inside every individual. It can be used to distinguish between close relatives, for example, sorting out paternity questions; and, of course, as we've discovered, [is] helpful in tracking down and convicting criminals.**

DNA fingerprinting led to DNA profiling in crime investigations. *Today's* science correspondent Tom Feilden reminded listeners how 'Its potential to trap serious criminals was soon realised when in 1988 the rapist and murderer Colin Pitchfork was the first to be convicted using DNA evidence.' Thereafter, DNA analysis became increasingly refined; minute traces on clothes, for instance, finally led to the conviction of some of the murderers of the teenager Stephen Lawrence, years after he was stabbed to death in London.

However, the science and applications of DNA research have also prompted ethical, social and political controversies. Even within the area of crime, the subsequent building up of a massive police DNA database, which stored thousands upon thousands of samples from criminals and non-criminals alike, earned many critics – including Jeffreys himself, 'the father of DNA profiling'. As Jeffreys explained on that *Today* broadcast of 10 September 2009:

> We now have a database which is populated with... the order of 800,000 entirely innocent people... So this does raise very serious issues of discrimination and breach of genetic privacy, stigmatisation... My view is very simply that they should not be on that database at all.

Back in the 1980s, early attempts were already being made at gene therapy for certain human diseases. *Today* reported, on 22 November 1984, on an attempt by a London-based team to extract an infection-free blood-clotting protein, factor VIII, to help haemophiliacs. The programme interviewed Dr Frances Rotblat. He described how 'it's made by what we call genetic engineering':

> Scientists working with me at the [London] Royal Free Hospital have isolated this protein from human blood so that we can characterise what it is. And over in the United States, they used this protein to analyse it and to find the gene and therefore that's what we would call cloning it. And then this cloned gene has been inserted into hamster kidney cells and those cells are now being grown up in huge vats and those cells are secreting factor VIII into the vats and you can extract it out.

It was progress but, in fact, it took until 2017 before a breakthrough in treating haemophilia through genetic engineering was actually achieved, in a London trial on a small number of patients.

These evolving uses of DNA promised exciting advances; they also inevitably brought up major ethical questions about how far it is acceptable to manipulate the building blocks of human life. (Similar questions have proved controversial enough in the genetic modification of crops.) Prominent among the issues has been cloning, or copying, at the DNA molecular level, because once gene-cloning became possible, the cloning of an entire animal was on the cards. Enter Dolly the sheep, 'born' in 1996.

Three years after her artificial creation at the Roslin Institute for animal science research at Edinburgh University, the leader of the team, Professor Ian Wilmut, was interviewed on *Today* on 27 May 1999 about signs of her 'accelerated genetic ageing'. Wilmut recalled the original process, saying, 'You may remember that she was produced from a cell taken from a six-year-old ewe. She herself is now nearly three years. And so the question we've asked is: is this mechanism set for a three-year-old ewe or a nine-year-old?'

'And what's the answer?' wondered James Naughtie. It was nine years, 'but that particular clock has not been reset during the process of cloning... and it's obvious that we need to do a lot more research to understand.'

'Well, of course you realise,' Naughtie continued, 'the people who are against the whole business, and worry about where it will end, seize on this and say, "Here you are, you're playing God, you're getting into worlds that you don't understand. This is just a glimpse of, you know, a Frankenstein future." That's what they'd say, wouldn't they?'

Wilmut agreed that 'we would share some of those concerns because we would only use the technology as it is believed to be safe' – but he also felt that should not prevent the achievement of great prizes:

> **What we have to understand at the same time as being aware of this concern is that this is a technology which shortly will be producing proteins like clotting factors that are needed to treat human diseases. It has the potential, within five or ten years, to provide organs like kidneys or hearts, which are desperately needed by some human patients who will die otherwise.**

Professor Wilmut appeared again on *Today* a decade later, on 2 March 2009, to announce a major development by his team, with much potential: the creation of highly adaptable stem cells for improved biomedicine. These stem cells avoided the controversial use of human embryos, which had got many critics extremely exercised. Human embryo cells had been used, to date, because in their infancy they are not specialised, making them much more versatile. But in 2009 Wilmut announced:

> **What my colleagues have done is to develop a method of taking cells from a person and being able to obtain from them cells which are equivalent to those taken from an embryo, so that they will multiply many times, which is very important if you want to study them or use them. They will form all of the different tissues and that means that, in principle, at some time in the future, we will be able to use these as a source of cells for therapy to replace those that have either died or become abnormal inside a patient.**

John Humphrys asked Wilmut, 'Would it, in theory, be possible one day to grow a new heart or a new liver, or something?'

The professor downplayed such possibilities:

> Those organs are incredibly complex, so I think that's actually very unlikely. It's much more likely that people will produce a mixture of the type of cells that are needed and put them into the right sort of place and encourage the heart then to repair, or the liver, to repair itself.

He also contemplated how this stem-cell treatment could, in the long run, help sufferers of debilitating, progressive diseases like Parkinson's or motor neurone disease. However, tests on animals and safety trials still needed to be undertaken.

The new technologies of course had huge commercial potential, and that led to a controversy of a different kind in the late 1990s. The pace of research had sped up when American Dr Craig Venter led a private challenge to the public Human Genome Project venture. His aim was to sequence the genome first, using a different method, and, most significantly, then to patent the genes themselves, raising the prospect of private enterprise owning the intellectual property rights for future biomedical developments.

James Naughtie discussed the controversy with James Watson during their *Today* conversation on 26 June 2000, as the entire sequencing drama was reaching its conclusion, stating, 'It does seem as if we may be about to get a joint announcement from the commercial project and the publicly funded one.' He asked Watson, 'Now, if that's the case, is it desirable, in your view, after all the arguments about an agreement, to do this jointly?' Watson replied generously, with good grace:

> Well, you know, there's one general sequence and all our data is put, basically, in the public domain within 24 hours. So the commercial enterprise means there's even more data, and so to the extent that they release their data and make it easily available, you know, [then] our sequences, our books, will be better.

'Are you worried,' Naughtie asked, 'about the business of patenting particular genes?' Watson drew distinctions:

> I think I'm much more for patenting *uses* of genes rather than genes themselves. But I'm not a lawyer and no matter what I *want*, I'm afraid the judges and lawyers are the ones who are going to tell us what can be patented and not patented.

Professor John Sulston was much more combative in his view that individual genes should not be patented by private companies. This was recalled by *Today* presenter Sarah Montague, interviewing Sulston on 25 May 2010 about another case involving Dr Venter's enterprise, this time concerning efforts to patent artificially created life forms. 'You effectively clashed with Dr Venter ten years ago when you were sequencing the genome and he came alongside in the private sector,' she said. 'And it was actually the race between you that led you to win – you might object to that word – but do you think you can win again?'

Sulston clarified the point regarding the HPG conflict with Venter: 'We clashed precisely over the issue of data release. It was not a race for the genome; it was about releasing data.' Regarding the new conflict, he said of Venter's team:

> They are using this really rather pretty little experiment, but not one of major importance in itself, to claim an *enormous* range of possibilities which really would give them control of *all* bioengineering into the future. And it seems to me that this is exactly the sort of thing we *don't* want the patent system to do.

'But wouldn't the patent system then look at that and say, "Look, if that is their experiment... then they cannot claim these patents"?' asked Montague. 'That's what one would hope,' said Sulston, 'but the trouble is that we know that in the past, people have put through exactly such broad claims.' And he had an example:

> The company Myriad Genetics, that I've been part of a challenge to in the courts in New York recently, has got control of a couple of genes such that any woman who wants testing for familial breast cancer has to pay $3,000 if she's in America, which is beyond the means of many uninsured people... I think the answer is... to have the bar much higher, but it requires the intellectual patent [IP] offices and the patent attorneys in particular, who do drive this system rather heavily, to agree that it's far too easy to get patents and far too difficult to revoke them.

In his view, 'The IP system is something that's fine in its way if it's kept as a tool, but it's been raised into an ideology of the way we run the world's economy.' (In 2013, the US Supreme Court made a ruling that distinguished between unmodified genes as unpatentable products of nature, but left matters more open when there was scientific invention involved.)

Progress in tailored, individual genetic medicine generally has proved slower than first expected. When the exciting scientific discoveries about the genome were initially made, an imminent bioengineered future seemed closely within reach. Yet on 19 April 2001, Alan Milburn, Britain's health secretary, told *Today*, 'There's going to be no Big Bang in the National Health Service or anywhere else when it comes to advances in genetics. It's more likely, so the experts and scientists tell us, that we will see a slow burn.'

Sixteen years later, on 4 July 2017, England's chief medical officer, Dame Sally Davies, appeared on *Today* to bring listeners up to date. She was particularly enthused about recent advances via the ambitious English 100,000 Genome Project, which aimed to sequence this number of genomes from 70,000 NHS patients with cancer and rare diseases:

> What that has shown us is we can do this for patients with rare diseases... But it's also the project that's shown us we can do cancer, [if] not easily... so the NHS

is undergoing a *massive* transformation to make sure that we *can* collect the right samples... We now know that over two-thirds of patients who have their scans of their tumours have what we call an actionable gene – we find something which means either they don't need a certain treatment, or it will have horrid side effects, or a particular treatment will work.

Describing itself as the 'largest national sequencing project of its kind in the world', its website sums up the project's aims as being to 'create an ethical and transparent programme based on consent; to bring benefit to patients and set up a genomic medicine service for the NHS; to enable new scientific discovery and medical insights; and to kick start the development of a UK genomics industry'.

As Dame Sally Davies put it, 'We've got a cottage industry in genomics; we need to make it a big, proper service for patients that's delivered close to them.'

The Information Age

'Yes! I really want to get my brain linked to
a computer as soon as possible!'
KEVIN WARWICK, 30 DECEMBER 1999

At an apposite moment – close to the end of a millennium, on 30 December 1999 – *Today*'s Sue MacGregor cast a retrospective eye on the story so far, saying, 'Now, looking back on this century... perhaps the most remarkable area of progress has been how we communicate with each other electronically: the wind-up telephones of Edwardian times have progressed to a tiny handheld phone which will link you to the World Wide Web...'

She hosted a conversation between professor John Bray, a former head of BT's research establishment, and Kevin Warwick, Professor of cybernetics at Reading University. Bray underlined the huge shift that had occurred, and gave listeners a sense of perspective:

> It's difficult to realise that up to 1950 there were just ten voice telephone channels between the United Kingdom [and] the United States, and between the UK and Australia. It wasn't until the 1950s when the first telephone cable was laid across the Atlantic – providing a mere 24 channels – that the real expansion of worldwide telephone communication began.

It was the US military that was, to begin with, particularly attracted to the idea of linking computers to form formidable networks. But then the interconnected technology broke out into the wider world. Highly inventive engineers and visionaries, many of them working in what became known as Silicon Valley in California, developed the crucial technology required, all powered by silicon semiconductor chips. While the early internet and electronic mail of the 1970s were still reserved for the privileged few, personal computers – as opposed to giant office machines – were slowly becoming available, and the phenomenon really took off in the 1980s.

Truly high-performance, internet-linked computers and telephones only became common in the West in the 1990s, just as the World Wide Web was being developed by an inspired, generous-minded Briton. In 1989, Tim Berners-Lee first set out the principles of the Web. This was, in essence, the idea of linking documents via computers using a common hypertext. Initially, the brainwave was Berners-Lee's way of helping colleagues communicate; he was then working for CERN, the European particle physics research centre. But then his creation's horizons expanded. By the early 1990s, the Web had gone worldwide. And although some US institutions sought patent rights for their own version of a Web, Berners-Lee and CERN were determined that theirs should be available to all, free of royalties or restrictions.

Berners-Lee served as a guest editor on *Today* on 26 December 2013. As fizzing with enthusiasm as ever, he was asked by presenter Mishal Husain about the early days of the Web: 'Could you ever have imagined at that stage what it would end up as?'

'No' was the simple answer, though he elaborated:

> I couldn't imagine it, because so much of what's been put on the Web is the result of [the] creativity of individuals. It's sort of innovation of people – out there. And bang! The human mind, when given a blank sheet of paper – or, for that matter, a blank webpage – can always come up with incredible new things.

Characteristically, he accentuated the positive, focusing on the creativity unleashed by the Web. But Mishal Husain asked him about his fears, too, for his creation. Prominent among them was that we take its very existence for granted:

> What we're now seeing is, because the thing has become so ubiquitous, because it's so much a part of people's lives, then there is a huge amount of temptation, from either governments or corporations – or sometimes, when you look at them, you can't tell which is which in some countries – to be able to control it. And it's not like the air that we breathe. We kind of assume it's going to be there in the morning. [But] somebody could turn it off overnight.

Certainly, authoritarian regimes have frequently demonstrated that the internet is by no means every individual's plaything, as libertarian idealists once dreamt. In China, for example, unless you are ingenious, you cannot google, tweet, use your gmail or watch YouTube.

With the growth of the big players in the new markets created by the technology, product launches became occasions of fanfare and international news, even back in the mid-1990s. Microsoft's Bill Gates came on *Today* on 25 August 1995 to vaunt the merits of both the internet and his company's new Windows 95 operating system, although he gave away the fact that the latter would be redundant in three years' time because of planned updates. Barry Fox, a computer consultant to the *New Scientist* magazine, was less than complimentary, detecting the eternal upgrade loop that consumers would soon become trapped in:

> It will generate a lot of lovely money for the poor starving Bill Gates and it will cause a great deal of misery to people who believe that this is some kind of

panacea... And that is, in many people, going to cause terrible problems, because they will try and upgrade existing equipment where actually it would be far easier to throw it out and buy something new, which is of course exactly why the rest of the computer industry is so thrilled by this. It's going to give them the chance to sell a whole lot of new computers to people who've already got perfectly good ones.

In those early days, access to the internet, and indeed the need for it, were still open to question. A *Today* broadcast of 24 February 1995 featured Marlene Sticher, who ran a council initiative in Amsterdam which provided computer terminals in public places for anyone to use, for free. It was a way, in her words, 'to avoid the problem of the information-rich and the information-poor'. But, she acknowledged, providing terminals was 'Only one part of it. I think people really have to know why they should use this kind of information technologies and to feel comfortable with it.' This was when it was still possible for people to wonder whether they wanted, or needed, an Information Age.

With all the uses of the new technology there came the abuses, too. Security has been a major issue, for states and corporations as well as individuals. From the early days, there was plenty of evidence of information superhighway robbery. And on 24 November 1994, *Today* listeners heard from journalist Steve Fleming, who described an alarming amount of secret information he had sourced from BT's databases, and to which he had gained access simply via the internet:

> The depth, scope and range of this information... has allowed the journalists at the *Independent* and myself to construct a detailed picture of the government's defence communication network, its underground bunkers, the telephone installations at GCHQ, MI5, MI6, Downing Street, Buckingham Palace – it's really the most serious security breach I can ever remember.

Since the new millennium, social-media platforms, notably Facebook and Twitter and now Instagram, have attracted vast numbers of subscribers and created great new possibilities. With their growth and reach, they have also been placed under an intensifying spotlight. Concerns have grown over the exploitation of such platforms to influence their users' opinions, during recent democratic votes in the UK, France and the USA; suspicion has focused on political groups, foreign governments and vested interests. In turn, such activities have prompted postmortems, investigations and a furore over the spread of 'fake news'.

And as the world's population emits more and more personal and financial information over the internet, the issue of privacy has become paramount. When British political consultancy firm Cambridge Analytica was investigated for its exploitation of data mined from Facebook users – by the millions, and without their consent in most cases – the issue went all the way up to Congressional hearings in the USA. During these, the usually reticent Facebook founder Mark Zuckerberg faced his inquisitors. (It turned out that his own private information had been breached too.)

Today secured an interview, on 21 March 2018, with university academic Aleksandr Kogan who had acquired the personal data of so many Facebook users and passed it on to Cambridge Analytica. Mishal Husain was interviewing:

> Husain: You say you don't know how your data was used... If it turns out it (data set) was used in the American presidential campaign, how will that make you feel?
>
> Kogan: Absolutely horrible. Mr Trump is not somebody whose values align well with mine. At the time, though, I know that it probably wasn't helpful, but the accuracy of this data has been extremely exaggerated. In practice my best guess is that we were six times more likely to get everything wrong about a person as we were to get everything right about a person. I personally don't think micro-targeting is an effective way to use such data sets.
>
> Husain: You don't think it could sway an election?
>
> Kogan: I personally don't think so, I think it could have only hurt the campaign.
>
> Husain: The Trump campaign?
>
> Kogan: Yes, any campaign.

Later in the programme she talked to BBC technology correspondent Rory Cellan-Jones, who neatly encapsulated the tacit contract established between platform providers and their users, saying, 'The bargain is: we give you all of these services for free; in return you give us your data and we can use it to micro-target adverts at you.' 'But,' Mishal Husain continued, 'the realm we're in now is one where the questions are about political messaging and political campaigning; not just the adverts that you see.' In response, Cellan-Jones reminded listeners: 'This is not new.' He continued:

> Those in that industry will point to the 2012 Obama campaign, for example, as having been brilliant and innovative in using data, perhaps with much more clarity and transparency, but still it was hailed as a great innovation then and it's now being seen as something far more dangerous, far more powerful, far more done in the shadows. And I think regulators in particular have failed to catch up with that.

Mishal Husain visited Twitter's UK headquarters for *Today* on 9 May 2017 and discussed Twitter's role in political discourse in the lead-up to the snap British general election of that year. The platform's spokesman, David Wilding, was at pains to draw attention to the exceptional openness of Twitter, whereby everyone was allowed 'to respond instantly to any views with which they disagreed'. But Husain pointed to worrying gaps in safety on a platform that was, ultimately, largely unregulated:

> **What you're putting forward is essentially a very hands-off attitude to the content on your platform. And I understand why there's an argument about censorship. But it's also true that if you look at the experience of many women politicians in particular, the amount of abuse they get – this is one example, Jess Phillips, the Labour MP, receiving more than 600 messages in one night about raping her – now, do you not have any responsibility to put that to a stop?**

Wilding, although unable to point to anyone at the Twitter UK headquarters dedicated to controlling such matters, did say that Twitter counted safety as its number-one priority.

On 13 September 2017, *Today* presenter Nick Robinson was in Silicon Valley for an interview with Evan Williams, one of Twitter's founders. Williams described his optimistic naivety at the outset, when 'we all had very little idea, but we had these, sort of, utopian visions'. Robinson reminded Williams, 'You once said that you wanted the internet to make us all smarter. Is that still your goal?' Williams's reply was thoughtful:

> **I think one of my big learnings over the last couple of decades is that access to information alone doesn't make us smarter. And the fake news thing that people then have been talking about the last few months, I think is one small part of it. Another even bigger part, I think, is the quality and the depth of the information. Is it actually building our understanding or deepening our understanding of the world? Or is it just noise?**

On Donald Trump's unprecedented use of Twitter through the 2016 US presidential campaign and beyond, Williams reflected:

> **The much bigger issue, it's not Donald Trump using Twitter, period, that got him elected, even if he says so. It's the quality of the information we consume that is reinforcing dangerous beliefs and isolating people and limiting people's open-mindedness and respect for truth and there's a media ecosystem that is supported and thrives on attention, period. And that is what's making us all dumber and not smarter, and Donald Trump is a symptom of that.**

Robinson asked, 'Do all these warnings about fake news, about abuse online, about commercialism, make you lose that optimism?' Williams replied, 'Well, the people of Silicon Valley, in general, are extremely well intentioned.' He added:

> Yes, they want to make money and they want to have power and they want fame and they have egos, but, I think, as an industry, the people really, really want to make good things happen and they know how to... It is just really, really early. And there are bugs, if you will, in any system when you develop it. And then you make it better. That's what we do here. We make it better...

When Tim Berners-Lee guest-edited *Today* on 26 December 2013, he looked to an internet encouraging diversity, difference and open-minded tolerance: 'A whole lot more people will come online, a whole lot more languages. There will be more and more Arabic, more Chinese, more and more, I *hope*, dialects, all kinds of interesting cultures being represented... I hope we'll use it more and more for understanding people.' But he, too, has voiced increasing concern, in recent articles, about major forces interfering more and more with net neutrality.

In 1999, one man – Professor Kevin Warwick of the University of Reading – wanted to be immersed in the new era more than most, as he explained to Sue MacGregor on the *Today* broadcast of 30 December.

> **MacGregor:** I think you want it to be so user-friendly that you've put an implant in your arm, so that your arm will know what it wants the computer to do, is that right?
>
> **Warwick:** Yes. I think we're going to see the electronic signals that are in the human brain and the electronic signals that are in the computer on the net – I think we'll see those much more closely connected than the present. I really want to get my brain linked to a computer as soon as possible!
>
> **MacGregor:** And you're going to be one of the guinea pigs?
>
> **Warwick:** I would love to be. Yes. I really want to get my brain linked to a computer as soon as possible.
>
> **MacGregor:** Through your arm?
>
> **Warwick:** Through my arm, in the first instance. I think it's just stepping into the future in a small way. That's putting the toe in the water. But in the long term, I think people will be transmitting thoughts, signals, as was said, telepath[icall]y.'

At this juncture, an enthusiastic Professor John Bray joined in the excitement: 'At my age – I'm an octogenarian – what I'm really looking for is a new brain!'

The knowns and unknowns of artificial intelligence

'Should we be scared?'

PRINCE HARRY, 27 DECEMBER 2017

On 30 December John Humphrys interviewed Murray Shanahan, professor of robotics at Imperial College, London, about Go, a game of circular black and white 'stones', which are placed on a board containing 19 x 19 spaces. 'Notoriously,' the professor explained, '[Go is] much more complex than chess... the number of possibilities is just vastly greater.' They were discussing a March 2016 match played in Seoul, South Korea, between Lee Sedol, one of the most renowned masters of this fiendishly difficult game (with 18 world titles to his name) and a computer program called AlphaGo, developed by the London-based company DeepMind.

The software had already established its credentials the previous year, by defeating the (human) European Go champion resoundingly, 5–0. But in Seoul in 2016, during the second game, it appeared to be having a nervous breakdown. Its move 37 was so bizarre, so contrary to all the conventional thinking about the game – thinking that had been developed over hundreds of years – that it had to be an error. Or did it?

'If I recall,' Professor Shanahan remembered, '[Mr Sedol] had to stand up and go and have a cigarette.' He seemed unnerved, and he was right to be. AlphaGo's apparent clanger proved to be a masterstroke, paving the way to victory in that game, and in the series, which it won 4–1. As Professor Shanahan put it, AlphaGo 'combined this ability to spot patterns – and it learned to spot patterns – with the ability to search through hundreds of thousands of possible futures and possible games'. What could a mere human do against *that*? Given the odds, perhaps the other truly remarkable number from that event is the one game that Lee Sedol managed to salvage.

Humphrys had been to Google's London headquarters to record the interview; as he told the listeners, Professor Shanahan 'spends most of his time now working for DeepMind', which had been bought by the internet giant three years after being founded. Despite the company's Go triumph, Professor Shanahan was anxious to put its achievements in the field of Artificial Intelligence (AI) into perspective:

> We're nowhere near the capability of making judgements about the ordinary everyday world that humans and children and even perhaps clever animals can

make; but nevertheless, computers can arrive at very, very difficult, complicated decisions based on huge amounts of data, and do very, very impressive things – and we're just at the beginning, I think, of being able to endow them with increasing cognitive sophistication.

He was 'pretty surprised by the AlphaGo achievements', but to reassure any listeners concerned that they might become obsolete he described:

… Moravec's paradox, which is named after a roboticist called Hans Moravec, where he pointed out that many of the things that we humans find very difficult to do are quite easy for computers, like multiplying enormous numbers together or calculating all the digits of pi or indeed even playing chess, which turns out to be easier for a computer than you might think. Now, conversely, some things that we find absolutely trivial are very, very hard to get a computer to do.

In other words, impressive though AlphaGo's feat was, it was to a large extent still an act of number-crunching. Elsewhere on that morning's *Today*, another professor, Tony Prescott, explained that 'Right now, all AIs, even the ones created by big companies like Google DeepMind, just do one thing. They're narrow experts, not general-purpose intelligence.' So far, it seems, AI has been turning out idiots savants, although, as Professor Shanahan put it, 'If you have enough mere calculation, it starts to look extraordinary and magical.'

Today presenter John Humphrys remained sceptical about the aspirations for AI. The lesson of human endeavour was, for him, 'That if we can do something, we do it; we want to do it. We didn't want or need the atom bomb, but we did it because we could do it.' He asked Professor Shanahan, 'Do you want one day to be able to endow a machine with human emotions or human judgements?' At this, Shanahan drew the line, less because of what he called a 'Hollywood idea of a sort of, you know, angry artificial intelligence that's kind of greedy and wants to supplant humans', and more because, 'If we reached a point where we knew how to build such machines, then we'd be facing a huge ethical dilemma. Then suddenly you're potentially in a position to make something that's capable of suffering and, you know, do you really want to do that?'

That edition of *Today* was guest-edited by an 'AI Robot', and AI was a theme of that year's guest-edited programmes. Three days earlier, on 27 December 2017, Prince Harry, during his edition of the programme, conducted an in-depth interview with the enthused and loquacious co-founder and CEO of DeepMind, Demis Hassabis. The organisation had nothing if not ambition. 'So, DeepMind's mission, if I'm right,' announced the prince, 'is to solve intelligence; and then use intelligence to solve everything else. This is a pretty bold statement.'

Hassabis acknowledged it was 'a very ambitious mission statement', but filled out the detail. 'Solving intelligence' meant, in effect, going beyond AlphaGo and the already proliferating range of single-purpose AI technologies to 'create general-purpose learning machines'. He went on to explain:

The algorithms that we build are neuroscience-inspired, and we're trying to sort of mimic some of the ways that the brain solves these complex problems; and what we hope is if we – if we solve intelligence and artificial intelligence in this kind of very general way, we'll be able to apply this technology to a really wide range of domains.

'Should we be scared?' wondered the prince. Hassabis was emphatic:

No. Of course, I spent my whole career working on AI because I think it will be one of the most beneficial technologies ever for humanity, especially in the ways that we'll be able to leverage it to, you know, make these advances in science and medicine that we, I think, we desperately need.

Yet he acknowledged that 'As with any powerful technology, it's going to cause a lot of disruption and change, and change can be scary. So I think we have to make sure that we think ahead of time, you know, how to deploy these technologies in an ethical, responsible way that benefits everyone.'

To reassure listeners – although his words might have had the opposite effect for some – Hassabis outlined the ways in which AI was already penetrating everyday lives, 'integrated into all sorts of things we use'. These included image recognition, voice recognition, customised Netflix recommendations... right up to DeepMind's pilot medical projects – diagnosing diabetes from retinal scans and trying to detect breast cancer using machine learning – and optimising energy use on Google's premises.

Prince Harry reminded Hassabis, 'One of the things you said to me the last time we met was the path of AI is inevitable.' Inevitable, perhaps, in that it was not going to stop, but that only meant that choice – the question of ethics – became paramount, as evident in Hassabis's reply. 'We can deploy it for real good in areas like science or medicine, or people could do bad things with it, and I think it's down to us as a society to decide how we want to deploy and use these things.' Hassabis's own organisation boasted an 'Ethics and Society' division, which was dedicated to looking at 'the big economic questions and ethical questions and policy questions around... how *should* these kinds of technologies be used responsibly?' 'We hope,' Hassabis added, to 'act as a kind of thought leaders' in the field as a whole.

Hassabis readily acknowledged the need for regulation and controls but divided that issue in two. In realms of life that already encompassed regulations, such as roads, the addition of driverless cars – another example of AI happening before our eyes – was a matter of building on what existed already. More problematic was identifying the purposes and needs of regulation elsewhere, for, as Hassabis put it, 'The technology's too nascent still for us to have a good answer to that question.' However, that answer, when it came, had to be global: 'Because this is, you know, innovation happening... around the world, so the world sort of needs to agree, or the UN or something needs to agree, what they want to do.'

Hassabis described himself as a 'huge believer in the powerful good of science and technology'. He nevertheless stressed the imaginative reach needed to consider the unintended consequences that people feared. 'You need to think harder about that at the beginning as you're making a technology – not wait until the problems appear and then try and run and catch up.' His London-based company had mushroomed to 700+ employees – 'over 60 nationalities, more than 400 PhDs, so it's really the biggest collection of brainpower anywhere in the world on this topic' – and it sounded as if they had plenty to do and to think about.

On 30 December 2017 a robotic voice told *Today* listeners, 'For weeks, a team of researchers at the University of Sheffield has been working to create me, a synthetic Mishal, to discover if the *Today* programme has any need for human presenters.' This electronic Mishal Husain, the 'Mishal-bot', had been force-fed with data in the form of the presenter's past interviews, in an attempt to produce a conversationally similar version, drawing on her typical vocabulary and speech patterns. In other respects, admittedly, the Mishal-bot was rather un-Husain like, as the real presenter revealed, 'It looks a bit like an oversized baby, large, bald yellowish head, sensors along its body. It doesn't have any legs...'

Professor Tony Prescott, one of the Mishal-bot's creators (its usual name, by the way, was the i-Cub), described how, 'For the past seven years, we've been developing AI for this robot, trying to understand and reverse-engineer human intelligence.' Listeners were then treated to a semi-scripted conversation between the professor and his electronic baby, which had a few good jokes: 'This job of radio presenter isn't so hard. Perhaps they don't have general intelligence either.' Then Prescott described the processes that were going on, and their limitations. Among the latter, 'AIs will take things very literally, so they will not get metaphor'; and when the Mishal-bot interrupted him to say he'd been talking too long, it was not a judgement of the relevance (or otherwise) of what he was saying, rather a response to a 'register that she has' – again, the data.

The real proof of the pudding followed – an entirely unscripted conversation with the human presenter: Mishal versus Mishal-bot. They tried to tackle current affairs. For any Luddites listening, the results were reassuringly surreal:

Husain: Yes, your way of talking is quite familiar to me. Do you really think the job of a radio presenter is an easy one?

Mishal-bot: Great. What do you mean? Can you give an example?

Husain: I think you're avoiding the question. It was what you said earlier, about the job of the radio presenter being an easy one.

Mishal-bot: I'm just wondering where you're minded to go with this.

Husain: OK, let's talk about Jeremy Corbyn.

Mishal-bot: We can create a new kind of politics.

Husain: And Boris Johnson.

Mishal-bot: Good morning, Mishal. Tell me: how was I created?

'So that was quite a good illustration, Tony,' concluded the real Mishal, 'of the limitations of all of this.' The professor agreed. People should not yet mistake anything a robot currently says as *understanding*, much less as self-awareness:

> You can build chatbots that have an extensive range of knowledge and question-answering ability and you can have devices, like Amazon Alexa and IBM Watson, that can go [and] collect information from the internet to answer questions, but although these systems are very powerful, very useful, they have this general failing that they don't understand what they're telling you.

Invoking the early approach to theoretical AI of mathematician and pioneer Alan Turing, Professor Prescott described the effort to move from narrow AI to general AI as an effort 'to take a machine and give it a bunch of sensors and raise that as you would a child':

> Children and adults are good at everything: a whole range of different skills that we have to acquire in order to survive. So, if we can bring up a robot, if you like, in the same way, if we can allow it to learn about its world, then it could acquire general artificial intelligence.

At least, that was the aspiration and the focus of the research at the University of Sheffield, to use 'the raw sensory streams, sort of vision and hearing, and getting the robot to make sense of those for itself'.

Mishal Husain introduced the Mishal-bot by telling listeners, 'One recent study suggested that four-million jobs in this country will go in the next decade as businesses turn to robots rather than human beings, including in accounting, finance, advertising, marketing and media.' The Mishal-bot experiment suggested that for now, at least, the role of *Today* presenter is safe.

Thought for the day: Reverend Dr Colin Morris

9 April 2007

A few days ago I heard a television reporter in the Sudan say, 'Life around here is cheap.' We knew exactly what he meant as we observed the prone and emaciated bodies lying around him. But it's not true. Life is incredibly expensive. Do something very simple. Toss a coin in the air and catch it. What precisely did you do? Well, someone who knows about such things explained to me that you sensed the energy of the toss and triangulated the position of the coin throughout its flight with your binocular vision. You shut out distractions from your other senses that might have diverted your attention, then you brought into action an extraordinary signal mechanism which triggered off one set of muscles after another in a sequence of ground-to-air control processes so effective that you caught the coin without consciously thinking about it.

Now ask an expert in micro-electronics what it would cost to put together a device which can do that and miniaturise it so that it will operate for three score years and ten in an ultra-microscopic part of you. I guess you wouldn't have much change out of the cost of the new Wembley stadium.

Then there's the hand that caught the coin. I love watching the complicated manoeuvres those very costly modern robots can perform, but the most advanced of them is crude compared to the flexibility, strength and sensitivity of the human hand. How much would the technology cost to create a human hand that can play Mozart or paint the Mona Lisa. And the hand is just one component of the incredibly complex system that makes up the human organism. Life cheap?

We've only got to look in a mirror and realise we are staring at a fantastic investment of billions of years of evolutionary pain, in which countless species went to the wall, to make us who and what we are. You would regard it as lunacy to put your foot through the radio which is transmitting my voice because you disagree with me (after all, you've only got to put up with it for two and a half minutes), yet that radio is a stone-age implement compared to the walking miracles we are busy maiming and killing in half a dozen parts of the world because they think and behave differently from us.

Our society is rapidly losing our sense of self-esteem. I suppose the point at which we start combating this disease is in having an active sense of our own self-worth. Long before there was any argument between the evolutionists and the creationists, the Psalmist wrote that we human beings are just a little lower than God – I love the gentle irony of that phrase – 'just a little lower than God'. If you're not disposed to be religious, then just toss a coin and catch it. And that's nothing compared to your capability to do a thousand things more important such as giving and receiving love.

ENDNOTES

A large general debt is owed to the extensive and varied content of the BBC's online materials, which have been a treasure trove. An essential reference resource for facts and figures in the later 20th century has been Chris Cook and John Stevenson's *Longman Companion to Britain since 1945*, 2nd edition, 2000.

The following additional sources (including for any non-BBC quotations) have proved of particular help:

Chapter 1

SEGREGATION AND CIVIL RIGHTS IN THE AMERICAN SOUTH

Joan K Harris, 'Vivian Malone Jones: Black student whose enrolment marked the beginning of the end of segregation in the US south', 18 October 2005 (obituary)

John F Kennedy, 'Executive Order 11111 – Providing Assistance for the Removal of Obstructions of Combinations Within the State of Alabama', 11 June 1963

Douglas Martin, 'Vivian Malone Jones, 63, Dies; First black graduate of University of Alabama' 14 October 2005 (obituary)

'Voting Rights Act (1965)', from the general records of the United States Government Record Group 11, US National Archives, www.ourdocuments.gov

DIPLOMACY IN TATTERS DURING THE IRANIAN REVOLUTION

David Barrett and Jacqui Goddard, 'Ben Affleck's new film *Argo* upsets British diplomats who helped Americans in Iran', 20 October 2012 (online; this, and several other sources, quote Arthur Wyatt's concluding words)

Hansard, HC (Deb 6 November 1979) vol. 973 cc225–8 (Douglas Hurd)

'The Iranian Hostage Crisis', Office of the Historian, Bureau of Public Affairs, United States Department of State (online)

APARTHEID AND ITS INTERNATIONAL OPPONENTS

Anti-Apartheid Movement Archives, www.aamarchives.org

'Anti-Apartheid Movement: A 40-Year Perspective' (transcript), event at South Africa House, 25–26 June 1999 (online)

Peter Hain, 'The Long Battle Behind South Africa's Moment of Glory', *Guardian*, 11 July 2010 (online)

'June 26th in London', *Transvaal Indian Congress Bulletin*, July 1959 (online)

Tony Leon, 'When Crooked Politicians Were Not Tolerated', *Business Day*, 20 August 2013 (online)

THE MINERS' STRIKE, 1984–5

Different sources have different figures for the numbers of working miners and pits open at the beginning of the miners' strike in 1984. The numbers given here are drawn from the BBC and what used to be the Coal Authority.

R W Apple, Jr, 'Macmillan, at 90, rouses the Lords', *New York Times*, 14 November 1984 (online)

John Gapper, 'Orgreave revisited', *Financial Times*, 17 June 2016 (online)

Nick Higham, 'Cabinet Papers Reveal "Secret Coal Pits Closure Plan"', BBC News, 3 January 2014 (online)

Donald Macintyre, 'How the Miner's Strike of 1984–85 Changed Britain For Ever', *New Statesman*, 16 June 2014

Norman Tebbit, 'Battle for Britain', *Daily Mail*, 13 March 2008 (online)

THE WOMEN'S PEACE CAMP AT GREENHAM COMMON

Lord Beloff, 'The Anti-CND Campaign' memo, Thatcher MSS (Churchill Archive Centre) THCR 1/4/2 part 3 f9; available on Margaret Thatcher Foundation website www.margaretthatcher.org

'Greenham Common: A Chronology', *Guardian*, 5 September 2006 (online)

'Greenham Common Women's Peace Camp', www.greenhamwpc.org.uk

'Greenham: A common inheritance', www.greenham-common.org.uk

Hansard, HC (Deb 1 November 1983) vol. 47 cc723-6

Historic England, 'Cruise Missile Shelter Complex, Greenham Common Airbase', Ancient Monuments list entry 1021040

John Nott, Defence minute to Margaret Thatcher (20 October 1982), TNA PREM19/979 f349 (declassified 2013); also available on Margaret Thatcher Foundation website

'Records of Greenham Common Women's Peace Camp (Yellow Gate), TNA summary (5GCW) of materials compiled by Sarah Hipperson, held at London School of Economics

Jean Stead, 'The Greenham Common Peace Camp and Its Legacy', *Guardian*, 5 September 2006 (online)

THE FALL OF THE BERLIN WALL

'Egon Bahr, *Ostpolitik* proponent', *Daily Telegraph*, 21 September 2015 (obituary)

'Gorbachev's Speech to the UN, December 7 1988', CNN Cold War, as hosted by Temple University (online)

'Soviet Record of Conversation between M S Gorbachev and the General Secretary of the Central Committee of the Socialist Unity Party of Germany (SED), Egon Krenz, 1 November 1989', translated by Svetlana Savranska for National Security Archive, *Cold War International History Project Bulletin*, 12–13, pp. 18–19

CHINA'S BRIEF EXPERIMENT WITH DEMOCRATIC PROTEST

'China's Future: Enter the Dragon', the *Economist*, 9 July 2009 (review of *When China Rules the World* by Martin Jaques)

Dennis Kavanagh and Christopher Riches (eds), *A Dictionary of Political Biography*, Oxford University Press, 2009

'Memory of Tiananmen – the Tank Man', www.pbs.org (includes selected extracts from *The Tiananmen Papers*)

James Miles, 'Tiananmen Killings: Were the media right?', BBC, 2 June 2009 (online)

David Pilling, '*When China Rules the World*: Review', *Financial Times*, 13 June 2009

CIVIL DISOBEDIENCE AND THE POLL TAX

Hansard, HL (Deb 28 January 1986) vol. 470 cc557–68

Nick Higham, 'National Archives: Thatcher's Poll Tax miscalculation', BBC News, 30 December 2016 (on release of Cabinet papers for 1989 and 1990)

Tom Peck, 'Margaret Thatcher was Furious at John Major's Decision to Scrap the Poll Tax, Official Documents Reveal', *Independent*, 29 December 2017

Chris Wheal, 'Poll Tax is History', *Guardian*, 14 April 1999

REVOLTING STUDENTS AND THE STUDENT FEES IMBROGLIO

Richard Adams and Sonia Sodha, 'Tuition Fees Should Be Scrapped, says "Architet" of fees Andrew Adonis', *Guardian*, 7 July 2017

Robert Anderson, 'University Fees in historical perspective', 8 February 2016, policy paper for www.historyandpolicy.org

Guardian datablog, 9 December 2019 (which has the breakdown)

Paul Lewis, Jeevan Vasagar, Rachel Williams, Matthew Taylor, 'Student Protest over Fees Turns Violent', *Guardian*, 10 November 2010

Jeevan Vasagar, Paul Lewis, Matthew Taylor and Adam Gabbatt, 'Students Take to Streets for Protest Against Tuition Fees', *Guardian*, 10 November 2010

Securing a Sustainable Future for Higher Eduction (the Browne Report), 12 October 2010

EGYPT'S EIGHTEEN DAYS AND THE ARAB SPRING

Lydia Smith, 'Arab Spring 5 Years On: Timeline of the Major Events and Uprisings in the Middle East', *International Business Times*, 25 January 2016

THE BRITISH RIOTS OF 2011

After the Riots: The Final Report of the Riots Communities and Victims Panel, 28 March 2012

Gavin Berman, 'The August 2011 Riots: A statistical summary', House of Lords briefing paper SN06099, October 2011

Michael Biggs and Arne L. Kalleberg, 'The Causes and Consequences of the 2011 London Riots', Oxford University Press blog

Danny Dorling, 'Mapping the August 2011 Riots', *New Statesman*, 5 August 2014

'Mark Duggan's Death and the London Riots', ITV News, 8 January 2014 (online)

Simon Hollingsworth, 'What the 2011 Summer Riots Were Really About', VICE, 6 August 2016 (online)

'Sociological Perspectives on the London Riots', 27 June 2017, revisesociology.com (useful resource summarising statistics, with links to related sources on the sociology of the riots)

Chapter 2

THE ELECTORAL UPSET OF 1970

Ian Aitken, 'Enoch Powell Dismissed for "Racialist" Speech', *Guardian*, 22 April 1968

Tim Bale, 'General Election: The Parallels With 1970's Shock Result', *Financial Times*, 17 April 2015 (online)

Neil Clark, 'Labour's Great Upset', *New Statesman*, 5 May 2010 (online)

Stuart Jeffries, 'Britain's Most Racist Election: The story of Smethwick, 50 years on', *Guardian*, 15 October 2014 (online)

BRITAIN JOINS THE COMMON MARKET, 1 JANUARY 1973

Linda Colley, *Acts of Union and Disunion*, London: Profile Books, 2014

WINTER OF DISCONTENT

Andrew Marr, *A History of Modern Britain*, London: Pan Books, 2008 (paperback edition; p. 368 for Healey and the IMF)

Tara Martin López, *The Winter of Discontent: Myth, memory, and history*, Liverpool: Liverpool University Press, 2014 (pp. 94–5 for Hull and secondary picketing)

THE RISE AND FALL OF MARGARET THATCHER

Andrew Marr, *A History of Modern Britain*, London: Pan Books, 2008 (paperback edition)

'Margaret Thatcher: Brief Chronology 1925–90' and 'Biography', Margaret Thatcher Foundation website

Margaret Thatcher, *The Downing Street Years*, London: HarperCollins, 1993 (pp. 379–83 on Brighton bomb; reproduced by Margaret Thatcher Foundation)

Peter Wilby, 'Margaret Thatcher's Education Legacy is Still With Us – Driven on by Gove', *Guardian*, 15 April 2013 (online)

NEW LABOUR'S ROAD TO POWER

'New Labour', Wikipedia, https://en.wikipedia.org (for New Labour definition cited)

Aisha Gani, 'Clause IV: A brief history', *Guardian*, 9 August 2015 (online)

Michael White, 'Blair Defines the New Labour', *Guardian*, 5 October 1994 (online)

Tony Blair, Labour Leader's Conference speeches, 1994 and 1995, available via BBC, British Political Speech website www.britishpoliticalspeech.org, and other sources

THE PARLIAMENTARY EXPENSES SCANDAL, 2009

David Barrett and Andy Bloxham, 'MPs' Expenses: The timeline', *Daily Telegraph*, 3 October 2010 (online)

David Hencke, 'Details of MPs' Expenses Could Still Be Exempted from FoI Act', *Guardian*, 22 January 2009 (online)

John Harris, '"It Will Take Years for My Reputation to Recover"', *Guardian*, 21 May 2009 (online; on Hazel Blears)

THE SCOTTISH REFERENDUM, 2014

Linda Colley, *Acts of Union and Disunion*, London: Profile Books, 2014

Chapter 3

For this chapter in general, a debt of thanks is owed to the academic staff of King's College London's MA programme War Studies Online, for the insights gained over a decade and more of collaboration with them.

SANDS, HUNGER STRIKES AND NORTHERN IRELAND'S TROUBLES

Roy Greenslade, 'The IRA Hunger Strike and Fleet Street's Graveyard of Truth', *Guardian*, 17 June 2011 (online)

Ian Miller, 'Why H-Block Hunger Strikers Were Not Force-Fed', *Irish Times*, 5 July 2016 (online)

Ministry of Defence, 'UK Armed Forces Deaths: Operational deaths post World War II, 3 September 1945 to 17 February 2016', MoD, 31 March 2016

WAR REPORTING AND THE FALKLANDS CONFLICT, 1982

Julian Barnes, 'The Worst Reported War Since the Crimean', *Guardian*, 25 February 2002 (online)

Michael Frenchman, 'Britain Puts Forward Four Options on Falklands', *The Times*, 28 November 1980; also reproduced by Margaret Thatcher Foundation

Hansard HC (Deb 2 December 1980) vol. 995 cc128–34

Richard Norton-Taylor and Rob Evans, 'UK Led Secret Talks to Cede Sovereignty', *Guardian*, 28 June 2005 (online)

Hugh Noyes, 'Commons is United by Suspicion of Ridley Intentions on Falklands', *The Times*, 3 December 1980; also reproduced by Margaret Thatcher Foundation

Tom Rowley, 'Margaret Thatcher Papers: BBC "assisted the enemy during the Falklands War"', *Daily Telegraph*, 18 June 2015

Sarah Tudor, 'Falklands War: 35 Years Anniversary', House of Lords, Library in Focus, 2017

The Times, 'An Option for the Falklands', Comment, 28 November 1980; also reproduced by Margaret Thatcher Foundation

Caroline Wyatt, 'The Falklands for Journalists: The Ultimate Embed Experience' (2012), BBC blog, 1 April 2012 (for Brian Hanrahan's recollections and comparisons with Crimean War)

SADDAM'S 'GUESTS' AND THE GULF WAR

'Context of August 8, 1990: Iraqis Use Americans as Human Shields', History Commons, www.historycommons.org (includes diary extracts of US Deputy Chief of Mission Joseph Wilson)

Hansard, HC (Deb 11 December 1990) vol. 182 cc822–911

Stewart Payne and Davie Rennie, '1990 Human Shields Scorn Volunteers', *Daily Telegraph*, 25 February 2003 (for recollections of Wendy Major)

Joseph B. Treaster, 'Confrontation in the Gulf: 700 Women and Children Freed; Thousands of Westerners Remain', *New York Times*, 2 September 1990

NATO'S FIRST WAR – KOSOVO, 1999

NATO, 'Kosovo Air Campaign', 7 April 2016, www.nato.int

NATO, 'NATO's Role in Relation to the Conflict in Kosovo', 15 July 1999, www.nato.int

9/11 AND THE ADVENT OF THE NEW TERRORISM

Andy Coghlan, 'Deaths From 9/11-related Illness Are Set to Exceed Initial Toll', *New Scientist*, 12 September 2016 (online)

'Pentagon Memorial Timeline', *Washington Post* (online; for figures of Pentagon dead)

FROM RECONSTRUCTION TO COUNTER-INSURGENCY IN AFGHANISTAN

Channel 4 News, 'Factcheck: A shot in Afghanistan?', 14 July 2009 (online)

Hansard, HC (Deb 27 March 2006), col. 538

Hansard, HC (Deb 13 July 2009), col. 3

William Maley, 'Provincial Reconstruction Teams in Afghanistan: How they arrived and where they are going', *NATO Review*, Issue 3, 2007 (online)

Ministry of Defence, 'Half-a-Decade in Helmand', MoD, 3 June 2011 (for blotting paper quotation)

National Army Museum, 'War in Afghanistan', www.nam.ac.uk

Francis Elliott, Marie Woolf and Raymond Whitaker, 'Betrayed: How we have failed our troops in Afghanistan', *Independent*, 30 September 2006 (online)

John Reid, 'Full Text of John Reid's Speech', *Guardian*, 20 February 2016 (online; text of speech given at King's College London about challenges of modern theatres of war)

World Health Organization, 'Afghanistan', www.who.int (includes latest life expectancy statistics)

THE IRAQ WAR AND THE CITY OF SINBAD

David Blair, 'Iraq: Is life better in Basra?', *Daily Telegraph*, 30 April 2009 (online)

'Britain Suffered Defeat in Iraq, Says US General', BBC News, 29 September 2010 (online; for quotations from General Jonathan Shaw)

Stephen Fidler, 'How the British Lost Basra', *Financial Times*, 20 August 2007 (online)

THE HUBRIS OF ISLAMIC STATE

Jane Martinson, 'BBC to Review Use of "Islamic State" After MPs Protest Against Term', *Guardian*, 29 June 2015 (online)

Chapter 4

THE OPENING CEREMONY OF THE LONDON 2012 OLYMPICS

'2012 Things to Remember the London Olympics by: Part 1', *Independent*, 14 August 2012 (online; item 343 was Aidan Burley's tweet)

Lauren Collins, 'Danny Boyle Wins the Gold,' the *New Yorker*, 27 July 2012

Sarah Lyall, 'A Five-Ring Opening Circus, Weirdly and Unabashedly British', *New York Times*, 27 July 2012

THE INTERVIEWER, THE ARTIST, AND THE UNMADE BED

Maev Kennedy, 'Tracey Emin Sends a Message of Love to Rest of Europe via St Pancras', *Guardian*, 10 April 2018 (online)

James Edgar, 'John Humphrys Questions Whether Damien Hirst Will Be Remembered in 50 Years', *Daily Telegraph*, 19 January 2014 (online; for Humphrys' artistic bone quotation)

'Tracey Emin RA', Royal Academy of Arts profile, www.royalacademy.org.uk

'Tracey Emin', Saatchi Gallery Artist's profile, www.saatchigallery.com

THE RUSHDIE AFFAIR, 1988–98

Alison Flood, 'Salman Rushdie Reveals Details of Fatwa Memoir', 12 April 2012 (online)

Kenan Malik, 'Shadow of the Fatwa', *Index on Censorship*, Issue 37, 2008

'The Satanic Verses: A Chronology [1989]', reprinted in *Index on Censorship*, Issue 37, 2008

Sanjay Subrahmanyam, 'The Angel and the Toady', *Guardian*, 14 February 2009 (online)

'William Tyndale's New Testament', British Library (online; history and images of British Library edition)

Steven R. Weisman, 'Japanese Translator of Rushdie Book Found Slain', *New York Times*, 13 July 1991 (online)

THE PRESS, THE POLITICIANS AND THE AUSTRALIAN ENTREPRENEUR

Harold Evans, 'How Thatcher and Murdoch Made Their Secret Deal', *Guardian*, 28 April 2015 (online; includes Evans's quotation about 'greatest extension of monopoly power')

Jon Henley, 'Rupert Murdoch and the Battle of Wapping: 25 years on', *Guardian*, 27 July 2011

Donald Macintyre, 'Wapping Dispute 30 Years On: How Rupert Murdoch changed labour relations – and newspapers – forever', *Independent*, 21 January 2016 (online)

Andrew Neil, 'Wapping: Legacy of Rupert's revolution', *Guardian*, 15 January 2006

Lisa O'Carroll, 'Phone-hacking scandal: timeline', *Guardian*, 24 June 2014 (online)

'Rupert Murdoch Says His Newspapers Are Struggling in Digital Age', agency report, *Guardian*, 16 November 2017 (online)

Chris Tryhorn, 'Rupert Murdoch: A lifetime of deals', *Guardian*, 18 July 2007 (online)

ACTORS' LIVES AND THE ART OF ACTING

Eric Shorter, 'Phyllis Calvert: Bourgeois beauty of the British stage and screen', *Guardian* (online; obituary)

Marvine Howe, 'Dame Flora Robson is Dead: A leading actress in Britain', *New York Times*, 8 July 1984 (online)

ENGLISH WRITERS, EXPLORING ENGLISHNESS

Gillian Darley, 'Greeneland in Sweden: When Graham Greene Let Himself Go', *Guardian*, 29 August 2015 (online)

Chapter 5

THE ORDINATION OF WOMEN IN THE CHURCH OF ENGLAND

Fabiana Barticioti, 'Archive of the Movement for the Ordination of Women', London School of Economics Library, blog, 1 December 2016 (online)

John Bingham, 'Women Bishops: What are the issues?', *Daily Telegraph*, 14 July 2014 (online)

Church of Scotland, 'Church Celebrates 50 Years Since First Women Ordained as Elders', 25 May 2016 (online)

Catherine Nancekievill, 'Growing Vocations', Church of England Ministry Division, 2017 (online; including statistics for women training for ordination)

'The Rt Rev Mgr Graham Leonard', *Daily Telegraph*, 6 January 2010 (online; obituary)

Hattie Williams, 'More Women Than Men Enter Clergy Training', *Church Times*, 27 September 2017 (online)

A HUNDRED YEARS OF FEMALE EMANCIPATION

Ian Beckett, *Home Front 1914–1918: How Britain Survived the Great War*, Kew: The National Archives, 2006

British Library 'Sisterhood and After', www.bl.uk

Fawcett Society, 'Equality: It's about time: 150 years of progress on women's rights and gender equality 1866–2016', www.fawcettsociety.org

UK Parliament, 'St Stephen's Hall', www.parliament.uk

REPRODUCTIVE RIGHTS IN MODERN BRITAIN

'Dr Margaret White', *Daily Telegraph*, 2 May 2013 (online; obituary)

Clare Dyer, 'The Gillick Judgment', *British Medical Journal*, vol. 291, 26 October 1985

FPS sexual health charity, 'Under-16s: Consent and confidentiality in sexual health services', April 2016, www.fpa.org.uk

Hansard, HC (Deb 7 February 1975) vol. 885 cc1757–868

William Robert Johnston, 'Historical Abortion Statistics, United Kingdom', Johnston's Archive (online)

Liz Lightfoot, 'What the Gillick Ruling Means', *Daily Telegraph*, 30 January 2006 (online)

Amelia Hill, 'How the UK Halved Its Teenage Pregnancy Rate', *Guardian*, 18 July 2016 (online)

National Health Service, 'The Contraceptive Pill, 1961', in the NHS 'History – Through the Years' (online)

Wendy Savage, 'Fifty Years on, the Abortion Act Should Be Celebrated – and Updated', *Guardian*, 27 October 2017 Timeline of abortion in English law, www.abortionrights.org

Sally Wheale, 'I Will Not Let It Go', *Guardian*, 21 November 2000 (online; on Victoria Gillick)

Ashley Wivel, 'Abortion Policy and Politics on the Lane Committee of Enquiry, 1971–74', summary, *Social History of Medicine*, vol. 11, issue 1, 1998

GRAMMAR SCHOOLS – A TALE OF LOVE AND HATE

Hansard, HC (Deb 3 Dec 2003), col. 498

Liz Lightfoot, 'Rise of Grammar Schools Defies Labour', *Daily Telegraph*, 27 March 2004 (online)

THE FOX-HUNTING FURORE – CRUEL SPORT OR CLASS WAR?

Hansard, HC (Deb 28 Nov 1997), col. 1251

Christopher Hope, 'Ann Widdecombe Says Her Peerage Was Blocked by David Cameron Because of Her Opposition to Fox-Hunting', *Daily Telegraph*, 26 May 2013 (online)

Kent County Council, Minutes of Meeting of Kent County Council Held at County Hall, Maidstone, 22 July 1982

HOUSE OF LORDS REFORM AND THE DILUTION OF ARISTOCRATIC POWER

Chris Clarke and Matthew Purvis, 'House of Lords Reform Since 1997: A chronology', House of Lords Library note, 31 July 1999

Ian Cruse, 'Public Attitudes Towards the House of Lords and House of Lords Reform', House of Lords Library note (summary), 28 May 2012

Guardian staff and agencies, 'Cash-for-Honours' Timeline, 11 October 2007 (online)

Maev Kennedy, 'From Lloyd George to the Lavender List: The history of honours scandals', *Guardian*, 1 August 2016

Karl McDonald, 'Britain's Tiniest, Poshest By-election Is Underway – Among Hereditary Peers', *The I*, 6 July 2017 (online)

Matthew Purvis, 'Resignation Honours: Peerage creations since 1958', House of Lords Library briefing, 12 July 2016

UK Parliament, 'House of Lords Reform' (timeline), www.parliament.uk

UK Parliament, 'History of the House of Lords', www.parliament.uk

Chapter 6

THE KNOWNS AND UNKNOWNS OF ARTIFICIAL INTELLIGENCE

Lee Bell, 'AI Versus Machine Learning: What's the difference?', *Wired*, 1 December 2016 (online)

DeepMind, 'AlphaGo / DeepMind', https://deepmind.com/research/alphago/

Nick Heath, 'Why AI Could Destroy More Jobs Than It Creates, and How to Save Them', TechRepublic, no date, www.techrepublic.com

Jane Wakefield, 'Are You Scared Yet? Meet Norman, the Psycopathic AI', BBC Technology, 2 June 2018 (online)

INDEX

ACKNOWLEDGEMENTS

This was a big project, and it would not have been remotely possible without the efforts of a large team. The *Today* programme long pre-dates the age of digital storage, and mining this treasure trove required hard work and imaginative research. Two producers with longstanding *Today* links, Laura Cooper and John Neal, and Sarah Harrison, a former producer in BBC current affairs, pulled off some miracles and somehow managed to remain good humoured throughout. By the time I became involved in the project Mark Hawkins-Dady and Philippe Barbour had already given the book its shape and done a huge amount of work to provide the necessary context for the material from the programme's archives.

At Octopus Denise Bates, the Group Publishing Director, and Romilly Morgan, our editor, were unfailingly supportive and positive throughout what was, inevitably with a project such as this, a long gestation period. Sybella Stephens, Senior Managing Editor, has overseen the production of a truly handsome volume.

At the BBC I am especially grateful to Malcolm Balen, who read everything and provided unfailingly acute advice. Christine Morgan, Head of Radio, Religion and Ethics, kindly supplied Thought for the Day. I would also like to thank *Today*'s editor Sarah Sands and my colleagues Martha Kearney and Nick Robinson for their contributions. Gary Richardson advised on the sport essay (not my forte) and almost all the past and current *Today* presenters I asked for suggestions responded generously. I would also like to acknowledge the help and support of Ben Batson, Senior Manager, Commercial Business Development, and Ellie Caddell, Commerical Rights and Business Affairs Manager. Finally, my thanks go to my ever efficient and supportive agent, Gordon Wise at Curtis Brown.

Edward Stourton

Thank you to Denise Bates and Romilly Morgan, who commissioned the book; my ever-stalwart co-author Philippe Barbour (who sends heartfelt thanks to Claire, Tata and Tim; and John Lotherington); Sybella Stephens, an impeccable managing editor; Laura Cooper, John Neal, Edward Stourton and team at the BBC, for disinterring audio recordings and more; Kate Moore and Caroline Taggart, respectively, for copy editing and proofreading; Richard, for his advice; Daniel, in memory of yesterdays; and finally to Martha and Jamie, my best of todays.

Mark Hawkins-Dady

The Publishers would like to thank Nick Alway, Dr Martin Farr, Nick Gallop, Dr Matthew Jones, Dr Lina Khatib, Professor Mike Lynch, Professor Helen Parr, Dr Gareth Price and Dr Cerwyn Moore.

PICTURE CREDITS